A HISTORY OF IRELAND IN 250 EPISODES

to Patricia & Tom with best wishes

JONATHAN BARDON ～

Jonathan Bardon

Gill & Macmillan

Gill & Macmillan Ltd
Hume Avenue, Park West, Dublin 12
with associated companies throughout the world
www.gillmacmillan.ie

© Jonathan Bardon 2008
978 07171 4453 2

Index compiled by Kate Murphy
Typography design by Make Communication
Print origination by Carole Lynch
Printed and bound in Great Britain by MPG Books Ltd,
Bodmin, Cornwall

This book is typeset in Linotype Minion and
Neue Helvetica.

The paper used in this book comes from the wood pulp
of managed forests. For every tree felled, at least one
tree is planted, thereby renewing natural resources.

A CIP catalogue record for this book is available
from the British Library.

5 4 3 2 1

CONTENTS

PREFACE

In 2005 I was asked by BBC Radio Ulster to write 240 five-minute programmes to cover the history of Ireland from earliest times to 1939. These episodes were broadcast every weekday for a year in 2006–7. This book is largely based on the scripts for those programmes, together with an additional ten episodes and an epilogue to bring the history up to date. The aim of each broadcast was to tell a story from Irish history which was sufficiently self-contained for those listeners who had not heard the previous broadcast. In the same way the reader should be able to open this book at random to enjoy a fully understandable snippet of Irish history. The episodes, read in sequence, provide a narrative history of Ireland. Only after the last episode of the BBC series had been broadcast did I discover that the whole idea of relating the history of the island in numerous short episodes was that of Alison Finch, who subsequently produced all the programmes.

Trawling through the archives is a core activity for the professional historian. Historians also must consult and build on the scholarly work of their predecessors and contemporaries. In a book of this scope, spanning all of the time that humans have been in Ireland, the author is especially reliant on the published findings of specialists. I hope that these writers will consider acknowledgment of their work in the references and bibliography in part an expression of my gratitude. It has been a real privilege to be reminded of the vigorous good health of historical research in Ireland. Encountering gems, sometimes by accident, which have informed some of the episodes, has been a delight. For example, had I not been a member of the Clogher Historical Society, almost certainly I would not have come across the account by Ramon de Perellós, translated by Dorothy M. Carpenter, of his pilgrimage from Catalonia to Lough Derg in 1397 which I used in episodes 42 and 43.

I urge young historians not to cast the works of Victorian historians too hastily aside. After all, some, such as Sir John Gilbert, had the opportunity to consult records subsequently destroyed in the Four Courts in 1922. Also nineteenth-century historians liked to quote contemporary documents at length—particularly useful for this book where I want the reader to have access to voices from the past. Thomas Wright, for example, in his *History of Ireland* published in 1870, includes long extracts from speeches and correspondence of leading figures in Irish political life in the eighteenth century not easily accessible elsewhere. And material useful to the historian can be found beyond libraries and record offices. Here are some examples.

'I got the essay done!' And a good essay it was too. A police officer in the Royal Ulster Constabulary, he explained with a broad smile that he had written it in the back of a Land Rover before going in, truncheon in hand, to deal with rioters in north Belfast. It was April 1969 and I was teaching adult students about the First World War in the Jaffe Centre, a former Jewish primary school on Belfast's Cliftonville Road—a building subsequently reduced to ashes during convulsions accompanying the Drumcree crisis in July 1996. At the end of the class another student, Kathleen Page, came up to me with a single sheet of paper: this was a letter written by Herbert Beattie in July 1916 which vividly described the horrors of the first day of the Battle of the Somme. An extract from the letter can be read in Episode 220—no doubt the seventeen-year-old's idiosyncratic spelling enabled the letter to escape his officer's censoring pencil.

I spent much of my spare time in my teens in the 1950s at the end of the west pier in Dún Laoghaire. Here I fished with former employees of the gas-works, who had been presented with orange-painted bicycles on retirement. In the winter dark, while rats formed a great semicircle round us (waiting for us to throw them an undersized whiting or two), one man gave me a vivid account of the great Dublin lock-out of 1913 and how members of the Dublin Metropolitan Police batoned people all round him when listening to Jim Larkin in O'Connell Street.

Shortly after being asked to write articles for a Sunday newspaper to com-memorate the fiftieth anniversary of the Battle of the Somme in 1966, I was rushed to hospital to have my appendix removed. After the operation I found six veterans of the battle in my ward, and one of them also had fought in the Boer War. Naturally, I recorded as many of their memories as I could. One of them recalled little: he was a Catholic who had enlisted in what had been a temperance battalion of the Ulster Volunteer Force, and he drank the tots of rum his comrades refused before going over the top. The former water keeper of the Argideen river in west Cork, Johnny Murphy, recounted in detail for me how in his youth a neighbouring family had resisted eviction by boiling up a cauldron of porridge and hurling spoonfuls of it at the bailiffs.

Every home, I say to students, has material of historical interest within it. Included in my own are: photographs of Edward VII's visit to Dublin in 1907, with the GPO in O'Connell Street draped in Union Flags, taken by my maternal grandfather, Donald Whiteside; a photograph I took at the request of a farmer in Co. Wicklow at the age of twelve, showing a steam threshing machine in action; a copy of the *Baghdad Times* in 1922 which contained a detailed account of the bombardment of the Four Courts written by an eyewitness, my father, then aged sixteen; and a fragile typescript entitled 'An Irishman in Iraq: Ten Years in Mesopotamia', written on the banks of the River Tigris in 1930 by my grandfather, Captain James Bardon—no doubt little remains today of the many bridges he built there in the 1920s. Memories and memorabilia do much to enliven the past and—if treated with suitable caution—add to our understanding of it.

I was less than half-way through writing the BBC series when the first episodes were being broadcast. The skill, versatility and enthusiasm of the actors, particularly in their interpretation of extracts from annals, letters and other documents from the past, constantly inspired me to greater efforts. I am very grateful to them. They were: Frances Tomelty, James Greene, Patrick FitzSymons, Seán Crummey and Richard Dormer. Many years earlier, being unable to read music, I asked Nonie Murray to sing for me eighteenth-century songs and ballads, many of them long forgotten and not then available on records. These songs are very different from, for example, the more popular ballads on the 1798 rebellion, composed long after the event. I was delighted that she sang some of these for the programmes, and I consider her interpretation of 'Harry Flood's Election Song' to be the finest available. My thanks, too, to Dee McDowell for singing twentieth-century ballads, and to Lucy Donnelly and Ellen Colton for their spirited renditions of skipping rhymes and recruiting posters.

I am particularly grateful to Alison Finch, who by a constant stream of queries worked unceasingly to ensure that listeners—and subsequently readers—who had no previous knowledge of Irish history would not encounter obscurities and unexplained terminology. My thanks, too, to Susan Lovell and Peter Johnston for backing one of the most ambitious projects ever undertaken by BBC Radio Ulster, and to Bert Tosh and the late Kieran Hegarty for their helpful scrutiny of the scripts before broadcast. The radio series is published as a download by BBC Audiobooks and is available at www. audible.co.uk.

In the 1970s I wrote several documentary entertainments, not for publication but to be performed in a variety of venues by a cast of students and colleagues. They will recognise the reappearance of some of the material I compiled then in this book, and their enthusiasm did much to spur me on to further efforts. They include Pat Brown, Norman Wylie, Henry Bell, Dorothy Wiley, Michael Collins, Oliver Boylan, Jim McConville, Cathy Clugston and the late Bridgheen McWade. Teaching students—particularly adult students returning to study asking searching questions—has constantly helped to shape the way I write. In my last formal year of teaching I am grateful for the lively, intelligent participation of students in the School of History in Queen's University, Belfast, especially Briege Rice and Ruth Patterson Taylor, and in the University of Babeş-Bolyai in Cluj-Napoca, Romania, particularly Narcisa Braşoveanu, Ioana Rosa, Lucia Ponoran and Georgian Sas.

Most sincere thanks are due to the following for many kindnesses, particularly for drawing my attention to useful sources, for reading some of the scripts, or giving me helpful comments as the episodes were broadcast: Liam Kennedy and Fearghal McGarry; Kevin Lagan; Ian Green, Sean Connolly and David Hayton; Trevor Parkhill; Bill (W. H.) Crawford; Liviu Cotrau and Adrian Radu; Brendan McAllister; Douglas Carson; Patrick Speight; Barbara and Kieran Fagan; Carol and Richard Hawkins; Barbara Carnaghan and Carol Tweedale; Norbert and Margaret Bannon; Máire and Dermot Neary; Rosemary McCreery and Martin Godfrey; Babs and Tom McDade; Jane Conroy and John Waddell; Dorothy Barry; Frank Murray; Brian M. Walker; John Hunter; Cecilia Linehan, Margaret Kennedy, Thelma Sheil and Bill Brown; Colm Cavanagh; Michael Maultsaid; Patrick Maume; and Brian Lambkin and Kay Muhr. I am also grateful for the assistance of the staffs of the Public Record Office of Northern Ireland, the State Paper Office, Belfast Central Library, the National Library and the Linen Hall Library.

Colm Croker edited the text for this book with painstaking care and sensitivity, displaying in the process an encyclopaedic knowledge of the full course of Irish history.

THE IRISH LANDSCAPE: THE LAST ICE AGE AND AFTER

It is an arresting thought that human beings had been living in Australia for 40,000 years before the very first people came to live in Ireland. Indeed, Ireland became inhabited very late in all the time that *homo sapiens* has roamed the Earth. The explanation for this is the last Ice Age.

Today Ireland is a detached fragment of the Eurasian landmass, from which it is separated by shallow seas. It was not always so, and if the ocean was to drop a mere hundred metres, the country would be joined again, not only with Britain but also to the European mainland. Around two million years ago severe cold conditions set in over north-western Europe. The Ice Age had begun. Then the ice relented to give way over the last 750,000 years to alternating cycles of warmth and cold.

The Munsterian Ice Age, lasting between 300,000 and 130,000 years ago, covered the entire country with two great elongated domes of ice, in places a mile thick. After a warm spell of some fifteen thousand years during which the woolly mammoth and musk ox roamed over chilly grasslands, the last Ice Age, known as the Midlandian, spread over the northern half of the country, with additional ice caps in the Wicklow and the Cork and Kerry mountains. The ice sheets began to dissolve about 15,000 BC, and two thousand years later they had all but disappeared. They left behind a landscape which had been scoured and smoothed by flowing ice. Retreating glaciers carved out U-shaped valleys and steep-sided corries. Soil and rocks had been shifted enormous distances and dumped as rubble in huge mounds of boulder clay, known as drumlins, in their tens of thousands, particularly around Clew Bay and stretching across southern Ulster from Strangford Lough to Donegal Bay. Meltwater flowing under the ice left behind sinuous ridges of gravels, known as eskers; often several miles long and up to twenty metres in height, these provided invaluable routeways later on across the boggy midlands.

The bare earth was first colonised by grasses, sorrels and dwarf willow. Half a millennium later juniper and birch flourished. Reindeer and the giant Irish deer grazed over this tundra. Then these pioneering species were all but killed off by a six-hundred-year cold snap known after a Co. Wicklow lough as the Nahanagan stadial. Around 8000 BC the process of colonisation had to begin again. As the permafrost melted the tundra, grasslands attracted willow, juniper, birch and hazel, and the larger trees soon followed.

It was now a race against time for plants and animals to reach Ireland. At first so much water was still locked up in ice further north that land bridges with the European mainland remained open. Then sea levels, which had been about sixteen metres lower than they are today, began to rise. Oak, wych-elm, holly, yew, ash, hawthorn, blackthorn and alder made it in time, but the last land bridges across the Irish Sea were almost certainly swept away by 8000 BC. Trees such as beech and sycamore remained on the British shore until brought over by man in the Middle Ages. Curiously, the strawberry tree seems to have come directly from north-western Spain to Ireland without ever having reached Britain. Animals including brown bears, wild boar, wolves, otters, badgers, red deer, stoats, pine martens, red squirrels, mountain hares, wild cats, pigmy shrews and woodmice arrived in time to make their home in Ireland. Fallow and roe deer, beavers, weasels, harvest mice, voles and polecats were left behind. The range of freshwater fish was also limited to little more than salmon, trout, arctic char, shad, lampreys and eels. Perch, pike and other coarse fish had to await later introduction by monks.

Were the first people to arrive in Ireland able to travel across land bridges running across the Irish Sea? It seems unlikely that they could walk further than the Isle of Man without getting their feet wet. The climate which greeted the first humans was much like our own, but the landscape was dramatically different.

A dense forest canopy covered the island so completely that a red squirrel could travel from Ireland's most northerly point, Malin Head, to Mizen Head in Co. Cork without ever having to touch the ground. Sessile oaks and wych-elms dominated the wild wood, particularly on the rich glacial soils; ash was locally prominent on light limestone ground, especially in Co. Fermanagh; hazel woods flourished on thinner soils and, in season, provided rich feeding for wild boar; alder preferred the wetter lough margins; and the Scots pine, once Ireland's most dominant tree, was confined to hill slopes and the western seaboard. Only the highest peaks, the loughs, the rivers and peat bogs, beginning to form as the rains became more persistent, were bereft of trees.

Episode 2 ∾

MESOLITHIC IRELAND

Just south of Coleraine a great ridge of basalt lies in the path of the Bann, and, after a serene passage from Lough Beg, the river is funnelled between bluffs to cascade in rapids and through weirs and sluices into a long estuary leading north-west to the Atlantic. Here in 1973, where waters draining off nearly half the surface of Ulster meet the tide, archaeologists began to unearth evidence of the very first human presence in Ireland.

Worked flints had been brought to the surface the year before close to Mount Sandel Fort near Coleraine when land was being prepared for a new housing estate. In 1973 Peter Woodman and his team of archaeologists began what seemed a routine investigation only to discover—after the carbon dating of charred hazelnut shells—that human beings had dwelt here between 7000 and 6500 BC. The generally accepted date of the arrival of people in Ireland had been put back by more than a thousand years. Over five seasons the site was meticulously excavated and its contents sieved, sifted and chemically analysed by specialists. Their findings cast a unique shaft of light back over nine millennia to focus on life in a Mesolithic encampment in Ireland.

In an artificially enlarged hollow the remains of four large huts were found. The slope of the post-holes showed that large saplings had been driven into the ground in a rough circle and bent over to form a domed roof by being lashed together. Lighter branches may have been interwoven to add strength and rigidity. Then each hut was covered with bark or deer hide and reinforced against the north wind with grass turfs lifted from inside. Around six metres wide, each hut gave shelter to perhaps a dozen people gathered a round a bowl-shaped hearth in the centre.

The last ice sheets had retreated only about three thousand years earlier, and the sea level was around five metres lower than it is today. The falls and rapids by Mount Sandel must then have made a majestic sight; below them, in early summer, salmon waited in thousands for a flood to take them upstream to spawn, and sea bass foraged at high tide in pursuit of crabs, flounder and smolts. Scale-shaped flints found in abundance almost certainly had been set in poles to harpoon these fish, together with myriads of eels moving down from Lough Neagh in autumn. Autumn too was the season for gathering hazelnuts: these were supplemented by crab-apple, goosegrass, vetches and the seeds of water lilies—these last resemble popcorn when dropped into hot fat. In midwinter wild pigs, fattened on the abundant hazel nuts, began their rutting, and male yearlings, driven out by mature boars, were vulnerable then to hunting parties armed with flint-tipped spears and arrows. This too was the time for trapping birds in the forest and overwintering wildfowl.

Flint had to be carried from as far away as the beaches of Portrush in Co. Antrim and Downhill in Co. Londonderry, and was utilised to give service for as long as possible. At a tool-working area to the west of the hollow, flint cores were roughed out and fashioned into picks and axes, while the smaller blades struck from them were shaped into knives, arrowheads, hide-scrapers, awls and harpoon flakes. One axe had traces of red ochre on its surface, which gives a hint that these people painted themselves on ceremonial occasions.

Clearly these people of the Middle Stone Age moved about in bands from place to place. The coastline has yielded up the most numerous sites, concentrated around Strangford Lough, along the Antrim coast, around Dublin and Wicklow, as far south as the Dingle peninsula and as far west as Galway Bay. Here shellfish, limpets in particular, formed a central part of the diet.

The Antrim coast was particularly attractive because here in the chalk layers is the largest area of exposed flint on the island. Elsewhere in Ireland these early inhabitants used chert, like flint formed of silicon dioxide but found embedded in carboniferous limestone. Certainly this was the case at Lough Boora, a major Middle Stone Age site in Co. Offaly, where chert was fashioned into implements very similar to those found at Mount Sandel.

For at least three thousand years these hunter-gatherers lived undisturbed in Ireland. Over the whole island these Stone Age people may not have numbered more than a couple of thousand. Certainly they made little impression on the landscape. During those three thousand years the rains became more persistent, cold winters and hot summers became less frequent, and oak, alder and elm began to tower over the hazel. Pine and birch woods covered the hills and mountains. The only technological advance that these early inhabitants made in these millennia was an increase in the size of the stone implements they made.

Episode 3 ∿

NEOLITHIC IRELAND: THE FIRST FARMERS

From around 4000 BC a dramatic transformation of the Irish economy began. Until then a small scattered population had lived exclusively by foraging, trapping and hunting. Now they began to clear the land of trees to create pastures for domestic stock and cultivation ridges for growing cereals.

Intrepid family groups began to venture across the Irish Sea and the North Channel in dug-out canoes and skin-covered boats. The perils of crossing the sea in frail craft with frightened and thirsty horned beasts can be imagined. Some of these people were newcomers, but it may be that some of the original inhabitants had learned of these farming techniques—first developed in the Middle East—and crossed over to obtain grain, cattle, sheep and pigs from Britain.

On landing, the first task was to find a stand of elm, a reliable guide to fertile and easily worked soil. Perhaps because conditions were generally too wet in Britain and Ireland for burning the forests, farmers there preferred to spread out through the wood girdling the trees with their stone axes, causing them to die back and open up the canopy. Meanwhile the women and children put up shelters and gathered leaves, twigs and other fodder to carry the cattle and sheep through their first critical winter. When the clearings lost their fertility, the farmers simply moved on to create new pastures.

In the fourth millennium BC farming was helped by a significant improvement in the climate, with average temperatures one or two degrees centigrade higher than present temperatures. The tree line was around three hundred metres higher than today, and this allowed these people to till the soil and graze their stock on high ground. The main crops were barley and emmer wheat, and, when cut with stone edged sickles, the cereals were ground with rubbing-stones on saddle querns and eaten as gruel or bread and perhaps converted into fermented drinks.

The flaked flint axe-heads of Mesolithic settlers could not easily cope with the task of ring-barking and tree-felling. Heavier polished axe-heads replaced them, and it has recently been demonstrated that one person using one of these axes can cut down a young birch tree in fifteen minutes. In a bog at Roosky, Co. Longford, one axe-head was found still in its haft of alder. Archaeologists have recorded no fewer than 18,000 axes in Ireland fashioned from a wide variety of rock types including mudstone, shale, schist and sandstone. The most highly prized stone was porcellanite, formed sixty million years earlier when hot Antrim lavas poured over clays to compress them into this hard china-like stone. Specialist factories emerged at Tievebulliagh, Co. Antrim, and on Rathlin Island; from here polished porcellanite axe-heads were traded as far away as Dorset and the Shetlands.

As techniques improved and the population rose communities became more settled. Substantial houses began to replace simple huts and shelters. At Ballynagilly, near Cookstown in Co. Tyrone, the oldest Neolithic house in either Britain or Ireland was found in 1969. This rectangular dwelling, six metres by six and a half metres, was partly made of wattle-and-daub walls, the remainder consisting of radially split oak placed upright in trench foundations. Substantial posts evidently marked the position of thatched roof supports. During construction work on a natural gas pipeline at Tankardstown in Co. Limerick in 1988 a similar house was unearthed, except that it was built entirely of oak planking with corner posts and external roof supports. Even more sophisticated dwellings were excavated at Lough Gur in Co. Limerick. The largest possessed a stone-lined damp-proof course and cavity walls insulated with brushwood and rushes.

These early Neolithic farmers generally moved on when the fields they created had lost their fertility, but not always. One of the most remarkable discoveries in recent times is a complex settlement in north Mayo known as the Céide Fields. Here a series of rectangular fields had been created by a series of low stone walls, some as long as two kilometres. An enormous amount of labour and co-operative effort must have been required over several centuries. Cultivating cereals in the smaller fields and keeping cattle in the large ones, this area was intensively farmed between 3700 and 3200 BC.

On nearly all excavated Neolithic sites fragments of pottery were found. Even the earliest pots, known as Carinated Bowls, were carefully fashioned from well-kneaded clay from which air bubbles and grit had been removed; the finished vessels were then meticulously polished before firing. Distinctive styles emerged, named by archaeologists as Lyles Hill ware, Goodland pottery, Carrowkeel ware, Grooved Ware and the like, with lugs, incised ornament and cord-impressed decoration. Many pots have been located at ritual sites, demonstrating that belief in the afterlife was powerful in Neolithic Ireland.

Episode 4 ~

NEOLITHIC MEGALITHS

Just west of Sligo town on the top of Knocknarea mountain glistens a massive cairn visible from many miles around. Known as Queen Maeve's tomb, this is just about the largest Stone Age monument to be seen anywhere in Europe. Clearly, over many years, a well-organised community struggled uphill with tens of thousands of great rocks to create this artificial mound as a monument to their dead. What is more, this enormous monument erected in the fourth millennium BC is no mere heap of stones: almost certainly it contains a carefully constructed passage grave which has yet to be excavated.

As Neolithic farmers removed much of Ireland's forest canopy, cleared the scrub, worked the ground with stone-shod adzes and wooden ploughs for crops of corn, and tended their herds, they created settled communities which grew in numbers and wealth. Firmly believing in an afterlife and laying claim to the lands they occupied, they venerated the bones of their ancestors. Archaeologists call these monuments megaliths, after the Greek words for large stones. More than 1,200 megalithic monuments have been identified in Ireland.

The Carrowmore complex, on flat land looking up at Knocknarea, is the largest megalithic cemetery in the whole of Europe. To view the array of around eighty-five portal tombs, passage graves and chambered burial mounds is an awesome experience.

Court cairns, the earliest megalithic monuments, were probably temples of a kind, where farming communities paid respect to departed ancestors and invoked magical help to ensure good harvests. One of the most impressive court tombs is at Creevykeel in Co. Sligo; it has a characteristic semicircular forecourt constructed with massive stones and paved with cobbles, leading to a wedge-shaped mound seventy metres long with chambers for the dead roofed with large flat slabs.

Portal tombs, or dolmens, are the most splendid and striking reminders of Ireland's Stone Age farmers, particularly when seen against the skyline. Built of three or more great upright stones, carrying a massive capstone sloping downwards towards the back, these above-ground graves were described incorrectly in the nineteenth century as 'druids' altars'. Capstones of enormous size, sometimes brought from a considerable distance, had to be placed on the stone uprights, presumably hauled up earthen or stone ramps by men using oxen, ropes, timber sledges and rollers, and then lifted in stages by means of levers and platforms raised gradually to the required height. The capstone at Brownshill, Co. Carlow, is estimated to weigh a hundred tons.

The most awe-inspiring creations of Neolithic farmers in Ireland are the passage tombs, regarded as the first great achievements of monumental architecture in prehistoric Europe. The most magnificent are to be found in the huge necropolis in the Boyne Valley, Co. Meath. This includes Dowth and Knowth, the latter being a great tomb of carefully layered sods, shale, clay and stones, surrounded by eighteen smaller graves. Here in the large mound two long passages were carefully given an equinoctial orientation: one to receive the sun when it rose on 20–21 March, the spring equinox marking the start of the sowing season; and the other on the 22–23 September equinox, to celebrate the harvest. A flint macehead, exquisitely carved with sunken lozenge-shaped facets and spirals, was found at the entrance, where stones richly decorated with spirals, circles, boxed rectangles and arcs were placed.

On top of a small hillock overlooking the Boyne is the finest passage grave of them all—Newgrange. Towards the end of the fourth millennium BC a great mound, just over 103 metres in diameter, was raised using some 200,000 tons of material from the Boyne a kilometre away, faced all over with slabs of sparkling white quartz and surrounded by ninety-seven kerbstones, many of them elaborately carved. The twenty-four-metre passage rises gently to a burial chamber with three niches, each containing shallow stone basins. Archaeologists were astonished at the dryness of the passage and the chamber: the slabs forming the roof slope slightly downwards from the centre to prevent damp percolating down, and they had not only been caulked with sea sand and burnt soil but also etched with grooves to drain off rain water.

It was at the winter solstice in 1968 that Professor Michael O'Kelly discovered the most renowned feature of Newgrange. He noticed that the sun, as it rose above the horizon to the south-east at 8.58 a.m., cast a pencil-thin beam of light into the centre of the burial chamber, striking the triple-spiral motif carved in the deepest recess of the tomb. Seventeen minutes later it was gone. The ray of sunlight reaches here only on the day of the winter solstice. Only a highly organised and sophisticated society, equipped as it was with little more than stone, could have created such a powerfully moving way of delivering the message that the dead could look forward to a new life beyond, just as nature began a fresh period of growth after the depths of midwinter.

Episode 5 ⁓

COPPER, BRONZE AND GOLD: 2000–1000 BC

In 1962 the geologist John Jackson began to explore one of the very few prehistoric copper mines to survive in Europe, Mount Gabriel in west Cork. The miners had cut a total of twenty-five mineshafts into the hill, then lit fires as far along the shafts as they would stay alight, and finally thrown water on to the hot rock to shatter it. With the use of large cobbles collected from the sea shore, grooved to give anchorage to ropes, the broken rock was scooped out, smashed and made ready for the furnace. First the ore had to be roasted gently to burn out the sulphur, and then more fiercely fired with charcoal fanned with bellows. The total weight of copper and bronze objects found and dated to the early Bronze Age is around 750 kilograms—impressive enough in itself—but this is only a tiny proportion of what was produced: Jackson estimated that the prehistoric mines in this south-western corner of Ireland produced no fewer than 370 tonnes of finished copper. Copper is made stronger and more malleable and turned into bronze when it is mixed with other metals. At this early stage it seems that arsenic, available close by, was the main additive.

Most evocative of a bygone culture shining across the centuries are the astonishingly rich finds of gold made in Ireland. Gold almost certainly was panned in the beds of streams flowing off ancient igneous rocks, particularly in Co. Wicklow. As the last millennium BC progressed, so the quantity and quality of gold objects in Ireland increased remarkably. The finds from this period are among the most elaborately decorated to be found anywhere in Europe.

The largest gold hoard to be found anywhere outside the eastern Mediterranean was unearthed close to the hillfort of Mooghaun in the 1850s. Known as the 'Great Clare Find', the 146 ornaments included a great number of pennanular bracelets with expanded terminals and dress fastenings so heavy that they must have been a burden to wear.

Another hoard discovered at Gorteenreagh, also in Co. Clare, included a gold lock-ring hair fastener so perfectly and intricately fashioned that modern jewellers are convinced it would be almost impossible to copy. It consists of two conical shapes and a tube with a neat slit into which locks of hair were enclosed. Only after microscopic examination was it discovered that the tiny concentric lines on the cones were made up of perfectly laid wires a mere third of a millimetre wide.

The quality of the gold-working was matched by that of the bronze-smiths. The craft of the bronze worker was well illustrated by the discovery in the 1820s of a hoard of over two hundred objects in a bog at Dowris in Co. Offaly. Dating from around 700 BC, it included twenty-six beautifully crafted bronze horns which can be blown either at the side or at the end to produce a powerful sound similar to that of an Australian didjeridoo. These seem to have been modelled on cattle horns and may have been connected with the widespread fertility cult centred on the bull. This is probably the explanation for round bronze objects thought to represent a bull's scrotum.

The Dowris hoard also contained fine swords, socketed axes, razors and a set of tools for a carpenter, including gouges, chisels and knives. Expertly crafted from riveted sheets of bronze is a great cauldron with two large rings so that it could be suspended over a fire and then carried to a feast, fully laden and suspended from a pole on the shoulders of two strong men. A beautiful flesh-hook, decorated with birds, found at Dunaverney, Co. Antrim, was no doubt for guests to fish out pieces of stewed meat from such cauldrons.

The archaeological finds from the last millennium BC are dominated by bronze weapons, including a fearsome eighty-centimetre-long rapier from Lissane in Co. Down. Copper was now mixed with lead and with tin, most of it thought to have been found in the beds of Co. Wicklow streams, but the rest undoubtedly imported from Cornwall. New methods of core casting, using twin-valved moulds, made it possible to construct spear-heads with hollow sockets for secure fastening on shafts, and axe-heads with raised flanges for hammering onto handles. Numerous shields date from this period, many made of leather stretched while wet on wooden moulds and then hammered on—experiments have shown that these shields provided a more effective defence than bronze.

A new and deadlier slashing sword also makes its appearance. Clearly this was a time of more intensive warfare. And why have so many valuable objects been found secreted in the ground? There is mounting evidence that this was a period of growing social turmoil, and that precious gold and bronze pieces were left as votive offerings to appease the deities in times of trouble.

Episode 6 ~

BEFORE THE CELTS

What caused peoples in Ireland to place so many precious objects, including heavy gold ornaments, deep in the soil? The answer seems to be that rapid change dislocated communities, bringing about circumstances they could not explain, so that they felt the need to appease the gods by ever more generous offerings.

Climatic change certainly created problems. The winds came more regularly from the Atlantic, bringing persistent rains. Cultivated soils became leached of their fertility, and slowly peat bogs extended, driving communities downhill where the stiff clays were more difficult to work. At the same time the population of Ireland was rising, and disputes over the possession of land almost certainly intensified.

An elaborate complex of paired stone circles and alignments at Beaghmore, on the southern slopes of the Sperrin Mountains, seems to have been a ceremonial site where the aid of the gods was invoked to maintain fertility. Here the soil was becoming exhausted from overgrazing around 1500 BC.

Stone circles from the Bronze Age are found all over Ireland, particularly in Ulster and the south-west. Some have stones of modest size, as at Drumskinny in Co. Fermanagh, while others, such as the Ballynoe stone circle in Co. Down, are constructed from boulders weighing many tons. Some stones are taller than the rest and are set with flat stones to point to particular features aligned with the rising and setting of the sun on days of special significance such as the solstice and equinox. Standing stones are sometimes associated with these circles, but others, including the seven-metre stone at Punchestown in Co. Kildare, mysteriously stand alone.

The Giant's Ring, by the Lagan river outside Belfast, was clearly a place of ritual importance. Here a great bank four metres high encircles a flat area two hundred metres across, with a portal tomb in the middle. We can only speculate about the ancient rituals performed in such places. There are some five hundred wedge-shaped tombs in Ireland, and here and elsewhere the broken remains of flat-bottomed beakers have been found in such quantity that archaeologists for long referred to the Bronze Age inhabitants of Ireland as 'Beaker People'.

Careful examination of pollen shows that cereal crops became more wide-spread and that the land was more intensively cultivated. The great forest canopy was much reduced, and there is evidence that some woodland was carefully managed. Trees, such as hazel and ash, were not uprooted but coppiced close to ground level so that, after three or four years, tall, straight branches grew up to be harvested for fencing, posts, axe handles, spear shafts and firewood.

The fine beaker ware, carefully decorated, was favoured for votive offerings, but these people also mixed grit into the clay before it was coiled and smoothed into everyday pots capable of withstanding heat during cooking. A speciality of Bronze Age Ireland was the *fulacht fiadh*, a cooking place con-structed close to a stream. A rectangular trough was dug into the ground and lined with oak planks. This was first filled with water, and stones heated in a fire close by were then thrown into the water and replenished with further hot stones until it boiled. An experiment carried out by Professor Michael O'Kelly, at a site at Ballyvourney, Co. Cork, demonstrated that water could be brought to the boil in half an hour and that hot stones added every few minutes kept the water simmering merrily. Following the modern recipe of twenty minutes to the pound and twenty minutes over, he cooked a straw-wrapped ten-pound leg of mutton to perfection.

Metal-working had begun in Ireland around 2000 BC, at a time when Egypt's second golden age of the Middle Kingdom flourished, the Hittites were invading Anatolia, the Mycenaeans were advancing into Greece, and the Minoan sea empire centred on Knossos was approaching its zenith. By the middle of the last millennium BC Hittite power was but a memory, Knossos was in ruins, and the Mycenaeans, once conquerors, were now the vanquished. Barbarians from the north and east, advancing on horseback and with superior metallurgical skills, were transforming the ancient cradles of civilisation.

These convulsions sent shock waves westwards to the Atlantic seaboard. Pushed from behind and seeking fresh lands by the sword, fresh arrivals in Ireland brought with them new cultures and more sophisticated weaponry. Perhaps it was they who led bands of warriors to construct imposing stone forts with elaborate *chevaux-de-frise* defences at places such as Dún Aengus on a high cliff edge on Inishmore in the Aran Islands, off the coast of Co. Galway.

One of the most exquisite votive offerings of gold to be found in Ireland was the Broighter hoard, secreted in a bog in Co. Londonderry. It includes a charming model boat with oars, a cup, necklaces, and a torc with intricate, swirling patterns; this latter object, with its distinctive style and mode of execution, demonstrates indisputably that the Celts had arrived in Ireland.

Episode 7 ∾

THE COMING OF THE CELTS

The Celts were the first people north of the Alps to emerge into recorded history. Their distinctive culture evolved during the second millennium BC between the east bank of the Rhine and Bohemia. Then it spread southeast into the Balkans, north towards Denmark, and west to France, northern Spain, Portugal, the Netherlands and Britain. By around 500 BC the Celts dominated much of the northern half of Europe. They sacked Rome in 390 BC and looted the temple of the oracle at Delphi in 278 BC, crossing the Hellespont to conquer a province of Anatolia thereafter.

The Greeks called them Celts, the Romans named them Gauls, and they left their mark in placenames across Europe and beyond. Examples include Galicia, the north-western province of Spain, and Galati in Romania, and later St Paul was to write epistles to the Galatians in what is now the state of Turkey. They named the Rhine, the Danube and many of the great rivers of the continent. The cult of Lug spread across Europe, and places as far apart as Louth, León, London, Leiden, Lyon and Legnica preserve the memory of devotion to this Celtic sun god.

When did the Celts come to Ireland? A clear answer cannot be given because they do not seem to have formed a distinct race. Celtic civilisation may have been created by a people in central Europe, but it was primarily a culture—a language and a way of life—spread from one people to another. Archaeologists have searched in vain for evidence of dramatic invasions of Ireland, and they now prefer to think of a steady infiltration from Britain and the European mainland over the centuries. The first Celtic-speakers may have come to Ireland as early as 1000 BC. They were arriving in greater numbers from about 500 BC; equipped with iron weapons, led by nobles on horseback or in chariots, and commanding the countryside from their hillforts, they brought the native peoples of Ireland under subjection.

The most successful piece of propaganda ever produced in Ireland was *Lebor Gabála Érenn* ('The Book of the Taking of Ireland'), compiled in the eleventh century, but drawing on traditions going back several centuries earlier. This was an elaborate attempt to reconcile ideas the Irish had of their remote origins with the Bible, in particular the Book of Genesis. According to this account, Ireland was successively inhabited by five blood-related invading groups.

The first to come was Cessair, granddaughter of Noah, who arrived with three men and fifty maidens. Of that party only Fintan survived the Flood. Then after a gap of three hundred years another group led by Partholón landed in Ireland, but all except one died of plague. The third invasion was led by Nemed, a ruler of the Scythians in Greece. In Ireland they were oppressed by evil monster spirits, the Fomoirí, better known as the Formorians. They were forced back to Greece, where they made boats out of their bags, and calling themselves the Fir Bolg (literally, the 'bag men'), they made a successful return. Their five leaders became kings of the five provinces of Ireland.

The fourth invasion was by the Tuatha Dé Danann, who had learned the arts of magic in the northern world. They defeated the Fir Bolg at the Battle of Moytura, and, in a second battle in the same place, they routed the Formorians. The Dé Danann hero Lug the Long-Handed slew the Formorian Balar of the Baleful Eye at Moytura and was rewarded by becoming the King of Ireland for forty years.

The last conquest recorded in the *Lebor Gabála* was achieved by the Gaels. Fénius, a descendent of Japheth son of Noah, was at the Tower of Babel, where he selected the best elements of all the languages there to create the Irish language. His descendent, Goídil, who gave his name to the Gaels, had Pharaoh's daughter Scotta as his mother. His grandson, Éber Scott, after wandering the world, conquered Spain. One winter evening, from a tall tower, Ireland was seen on the horizon. Soon afterwards the sons of Míl, the ruler of Spain, led a successful invasion, and their descendents, the Gaels, ruled Ireland since that time.

All of this is, of course, nonsense. The word 'Gael' was originally a Welsh word for the Irish. The term 'Scot' had nothing to do with Pharaoh's daughter, but was the Roman word for an Irishman. The Fir Bolg were probably Belgae, a group of tribes conquered by Julius Caesar. What is remarkable is that much of this confabulated pseudo-history was believed for centuries to come. Right up to the nineteenth century both scholars and politicians referred to the early Irish as Milesians (after Míl), and it was only later that the terms 'Celts' and 'Celtic' were preferred. However, the *Lebor Gabála*, in its account of the Tuatha Dé Danann, does provide a very comprehensive description of the gods of the Irish before the coming of Christianity.

Episode 8 ∾

PREPARING FOR THE OTHER-WORLD IN PRE-CHRISTIAN CELTIC IRELAND

The Tuatha Dé Danann, in effect, were the gods of the pre-Christian Celts in Ireland. These were to become the *sídhe* who, when conquered, became invisible and lived in fairy mounds. Lir was one of their kings and the story of his children—changed into swans by his third wife Aoife—is one of the most poignant in western literature. Lir's son, Manannán mac Lir, was god of the sea. The greatest of the gods was the Dagda, who had beaten off the monster Formorians when they attacked in a magical mist. The best-loved was Lug the Long-Handed, the god of sun and fertility. Maeve—who appears as Queen Mab in Shakespeare's plays—was the goddess of drunkenness. Which god is represented by the so-called Tandragee Idol from Co. Armagh is not known; certainly he looks ferocious with a horned helmet and a threatening right arm.

In Ireland the Celtic year began with *Samhain*, now Hallowe'en, when cattle had been brought in from their summer grazing; this was a time when spirits flew free between the real world and the other world. *Imbolg*, the first day of February, marked the start of the lambing season; and the feast of *Bealtine*, at the start of May, was for the purification of cattle driven ceremoniously between two fires. *Lughnasa*, the first day of August, celebrated the harvest and paid homage to Lug the sun god.

It is now becoming clear that the ancient capitals of Ireland were ritual rather than political sites. These include: Emain Macha (or Navan Fort) near Armagh, the capital of Ulster; Cruachain (or Rathcroghan) in Co. Roscommon, the capital of Connacht; Dún Ailinne near Kilcullen, Co. Kildare, the capital of Leinster; and Tara in Co. Meath, long regarded as the capital of Ireland. It is clear that they were not constructed for military purposes as the ditch in each of the locations was placed *inside* rather than outside the great circular earthen enclosures. If defence was needed, it was against hostile spirits from the Otherworld.

At Emain Macha archaeologists found evidence that a great circular temple, forty-three metres in diameter, had been built, probably by a whole community acting together. Held up by concentric rows of posts thicker than telegraph poles and steadied by horizontal planks, the roof had been covered with a cairn of stones enveloped with sods. Then the whole structure had been deliberately set on fire. No one knows why. Had this been a ritual to invoke the aid of the gods while the kingdom was under attack? Remains of a similar structure were found at Dún Ailinne, and it may have provided tiered seating for large numbers of devotees until it too was purposely destroyed.

No king of importance could hope to rule with authority unless fully initiated at one of these ancient sites. Lia Fáil, the Stone of Destiny, can still be seen at Tara—it was said to cry out in approval when the rightful king was inaugurated. Whether the Turoe Stone from Co. Galway was an oracle, a totem or a phallic symbol is impossible to say: a glacial erratic granite boulder, it is covered in swirling Celtic art motifs similar to those etched on metal objects. As in other parts of Celtic Europe, Ireland has produced two- and three-headed figures. The finest was found at Corleck in Co. Cavan, a block of local sandstone carved with three faces, each one different but all wide-eyed and thin-lipped.

Like their continental counterparts, the Celts in Ireland assuaged the anger of the gods by casting their valuables into sacred pools. Had they not done so, the archaeological record would be very much the poorer. One of these pools, close to Emain Macha, yielded up four large bronze horns magnificently decorated in the Celtic style known as La Tène after a site in Switzerland. First developed in central Europe, this imaginative art, in contrast with the realism and natural beauty preferred by Greek and Roman artists, delighted in restless symbols and intricate curvilinear patterns. The earliest examples of this art can be seen on bronze scabbards from Lisnacrogher, Co. Antrim. Iron, of course, tended to rust away completely, and fewer than two dozen swords have survived from this period. Irish craftsmen added their own stamp to this style, most notably by using the compass to create arc patterns. This artistry is well displayed in the trumpet curves and tiny bird's heads on the Bann Disc (now the symbol of the Ulster Museum) and portions of the so-called Petrie Crown, found in Co. Cork, which include a solar symbol, the sun represented by a wheel, and a stylised depiction of the boat of the sun drawn across the heavens by birds.

In hoards deliberately placed in rivers, lakes and pools after around 300 BC, bronze horse-bits are the commonest surviving metal artefacts. It demonstrates the crucial role of the horse in helping to keep the ruling caste in power.

Episode 9 ⌁

KINGS AND CHAMPIONS

At the dawn of the Christian era Ireland was firmly under the domination of Celtic-speaking military rulers. They enforced their rule from well-defended forts where high-born men served as a warrior elite riding on horseback, equipped with lances, throwing-spears and short iron swords held in richly decorated bronze scabbards, and defended with large round shields. They were eager for fame, to beat their opponents in single combat and return to the banqueting hall to claim the 'champion's portion' at the ensuing feast.

The oldest vernacular epic in western European literature is the *Táin Bó Cuailgne*, 'The Cattle Raid of Cooley': it tells how Queen Maeve of Connacht made war on King Conor Mac Nessa of Ulster to win possession of the Brown Bull of Cuailgne, and how, during a long campaign, the champion Cúchulainn single-handedly held back the men of Connacht by Ferdia's Ford. The earliest versions of the *Táin* are believed to have been written down in monasteries in the eighth century, and some verse sections are thought to date from two centuries earlier. It probably had a long oral existence before being committed to vellum. Fedelm, a girl who declared herself to be the woman poet of Connacht, drew up to Queen Maeve in her chariot and told her of her vision of Cúchulainn and of his prowess:

> I see a battle; a blond man
> with much blood about his belt
> and a hero-halo round his head.
> His brow is full of victories.
>
> A noble countenance I see,
> Working effect on womenfolk;
> a young man of sweet colouring;
> a form dragonish in fray.
>
> His great valour brings to mind
> Cúchulainn of Muirthemne,
> The hound of Culann, full of fame.
> Who he is I cannot tell
> But I see, now, the whole host
> Coloured crimson by his hand.

> Whole hosts he will destroy,
> making dense massacre.
> In thousands you will yield your heads.
> I am Fedelm. I hide nothing.

The *Táin* and other tales in the Ulster Cycle at their best possess arresting power, vividly graphic yet stylised, in which stark reality and magic intertwine and the principal characters are ordinary mortals able on occasion to act like gods. From these epic tales the historian gets a vivid picture of an aristocratic Iron Age society remarkably similar in many respects to Celtic Gaul as described by Roman writers. To what extent these stories are based on actual events is difficult to say.

There are remains of at least eighty hillforts dating from this period. Constructed usually of unmortared stone and with one, two or three defensive ramparts, commanding a clear view of the surrounding countryside, many remain imposing structures to this day. Some of the most notable examples include a remarkable cluster around Baltinglass in Co. Wicklow, the massive circular defences of Staigue Fort in Co. Kerry, and the Grianán of Aileach, on high ground at the base of the Inishowen peninsula, built massively of stone with inset stairways, wall passages and triple earthen bank defences. A remarkable series of earthworks runs across southern Ulster, beginning as the so-called Dane's Cast near Scarva, Co. Down, continuing (double-banked and double-ditched, eight metres high) as the Dorsey in south Armagh, reappearing in Co. Monaghan as the Worm Ditch and intermittently as the Black Pig's Dyke to Donegal Bay. Tree-ring analysis shows that timber for the Dorsey had been felled in 95 BC. Almost certainly these defences were designed to close off routeways to the north and to impede the driving of stolen cattle southwards.

The High-Kings of Tara never ruled the whole island; indeed, until the eleventh century the title was little more than an honorary one. Ireland then was a land of many kingdoms, all with constantly shifting frontiers. Early kingdoms were given tribal names. Examples include: the *Ciarraige*, the 'black-haired people', who named Kerry; the *Dartraige*, the 'calf people', who named both a barony in Monaghan and the Dartry Mountains in Co. Leitrim; and the *Conn Maicne Mara*, the 'sons of the wolves of the sea', from whom the Connemara region derives its name. Later peoples called themselves after gods, and their tribal names have the suffix *–achta*, meaning 'followers of' as in the *Connachta*, 'the followers of Conn', who gave their name to the western province of Ireland.

Meanwhile the Celtic domination of Europe north of the Alps was collapsing before the might of Rome. By 133 BC the Roman conquest of Spain was complete, and in 59 BC Julius Caesar began his conquest of Gaul. In 56 BC the Veneti were overwhelmed in Armorica and the Belgae were in retreat. Caesar invaded Britain in 55 BC, and three years later, in his account of the Gallic wars, he was the first to apply the word 'Hibernia' to Ireland.

By AD 43 the Emperor Claudius had conquered Britain. Roman legions penetrated Caledonia as far as the Highland Line. Just across the sea to the west lay Hibernia—would this island be a worthy addition to the Empire?

Episode 10 ∿

AGRICOLA PLANS TO CONQUER IRELAND

In AD 82 Gnaeus Julius Agricola, governor of Britain, summoned his fleet into the Solway Firth to take aboard his waiting cohorts. Ireland was directly across the sea, and this land he meant to conquer—a climax to a dazzling career the Empire would not forget. Posted to Britain as military tribune twenty-one years before, Agricola had been in the thick of the fighting with the Iceni and Brigantes during Boudicca's uprising. Placed in command of the xxth Legion, he directed the Irish Sea flotilla for a time; perhaps it had been then that the notion that Ireland was worthy of conquest had formed in his mind. Now, having returned after distinguished service as a governor in Gaul and a consul in Rome, Agricola swept all before him: in the fastness of Snowdonia he reduced the Ordovices to abject submission, and then, pressing relentlessly northwards into Caledonia, he reached the base of the Highlands, harried the Inner Isles with his fleet, and ordered the erection of a network of castella.

The Roman Empire knew little enough about this island of Hibernia on the north-west edge of its world. Sailing directions, written by a sea captain of the Greek colony of Massilia about 525 BC, referred to Ireland as the 'Sacred Isle' two days' voyage from Armorica and significantly larger than Britain. However, Himilco, the Carthaginian, journeying to the 'Tin Isles of Scilly' around 480 BC, warned of dense seaweed entanglements and threatening sea monsters beyond. It was the epic voyage of Pytheas, another Greek from Massilia, who visited Norway and circumnavigated Britain about 300 BC, which gave Mediterranean traders Ireland's correct position; this explorer's account does not survive, but it seems to have formed the basis of Ptolemy's map of Ireland, prepared in the second century AD. Known only from a fifteenth-century copy, this map includes some identifiable names, such as

Buvinda (the River Boyne), *Senos* (the River Shannon), *Logia* (the Lagan or Belfast Lough), *Isamnion* (Navan Fort) and *Volunti* (the Ulaid, the people of Ulster). Even after Julius Caesar invaded Britain in 55 BC, the Greek geographer and historian Strabo was asserting that the Irish 'think it decent to eat up their dead parents', but fifty years later Pomponius Mela was better informed about Ireland:

Its climate is unfavourable for the maturing of crops, but there is such a profuse growth of grass, and this is as sweet as it is rich, that the cattle can sate themselves in a short part of the day.

The historian Tacitus was a more acute observer, and his descriptions of the Britons and continental Celts in the first century AD dovetail remarkably well with the picture presented in the early Irish law tracts and heroic tales. For information about the Celts of the British Isles, Tacitus relied on his father-in-law, Agricola:

Ireland is small in comparison with Britain, but larger than the islands of the Mediterranean. In soil and climate, and in the character and civilisation of its inhabitants, it is much like Britain; and its approaches and harbours have now become better known from merchants who trade there.

And it is from Tacitus that we learn that the invasion of Ireland was planned with a king in exile:

Agricola received in friendly fashion an Irish petty king who had been driven out in a civil war, and kept him for use when opportunity offered. I have often heard him say that Ireland could be conquered and held by one legion and a modest force of auxiliary troops; and that it would be advantageous in dealing with Britain too if Roman forces were on all sides and the spectacle of freedom were, so to say, banished out of sight.

Was this Irish king, Tuathail Techtmar, forced to seek aid in Britain to recover his throne? We cannot be certain. However, Agricola's invasion was not to be: a legion of Germans stationed in Galloway mutinied, and there was disturbing news of Pictish rebellion. The Emperor Domitian ordered his governor north, and later, after Agricola's recall, the Romans retired behind Hadrian's Wall. Ireland would not become part of the Roman Empire after all.

Yet there are tantalising indications that the influence of Rome on Ireland was greater than previously thought. It seems likely that bands of soldiers who had served in the legions sailed to Ireland to conquer lands for themselves there. In 1842 the stamp, or trademark, of an oculist—an eye specialist who

travelled with Roman legions—was found by the River Suir in Co. Tipperary.
Simple everyday Roman items—such as ladles, nail-cleaners, brooches, a lead
seal and an iron barrel padlock—have been found in places as far apart as
Bantry in Co. Cork and Clogher in Co. Tyrone. Several Roman burial sites
have been unearthed, including one at Stoneyford in Co. Kilkenny containing
the cremated ashes of a woman in a glass urn, together with her bronze
mirror and cosmetics phial.

Episode 11 ~

PATRICK THE BRITON

There is good reason to believe that some of the most powerful kingdoms
in Ireland at the beginning of the Christian era were carved out by
warrior tribes driven west from Gaul and Britain by Roman expansion.

By the beginning of the fifth century the situation had changed dramatically. The Roman Empire was reeling under the attack of German-speaking
peoples from central and northern Europe seeking new corn lands and
pastures. Legion after legion was withdrawn from the outposts to defend
Rome, itself weakened by civil dissensions. In Britain the towns and villas fell
into decay, bath-houses were abandoned, the great sewers of York became
blocked with excrement, and the once-thriving town of Winchester became
completely deserted.

From the north came the Picts, from the east the Angles and Saxons and
from the west the Irish. Irish raiders found rich pickings. In 1854 a hoard of
Roman loot was found at Ballinrees, just west of Coleraine, including 1,500
silver coins, silver ingots and silver bars weighing five kilograms. Five hundred
silver coins were unearthed near the Giant's Causeway, three hundred more
nearby at Bushmills, and in 1940 pieces of cut silver plate and four silver
ingots were discovered at Balline in Co. Limerick. Coins dated these raids to
the early fifth century.

Roman Britain in its death throes had become Christian. From there and
from Gaul Christianity had been brought by traders and others to the south
of Ireland. We know this because in 431 Pope Celestine sent a churchman
from Auxerre, Palladius Patricius, as a bishop to 'the Irish believing in Christ'.
Of the first missionaries we know very little except that Iserninus founded a
church at Kilashee near Naas in Co. Kildare and that others were established
at Aghade in Co. Carlow and Kilcullen in Co. Kildare by another evangelist

named Auxilius. Unquestionably, however, the main credit for bringing Christianity to Ireland must go to the man we now know as St Patrick, the author of the very first document in Irish history, his own autobiographical *Confessio*.

Patrick was not yet sixteen when he was seized by Irish pirates from Bannaventum Taburniae, a Romanised town somewhere in western Britain. Once in Ireland, he was sold as a slave and taken 200,000 paces—that is, 200 miles—westwards, probably to Tirawley in north Co. Mayo. There he herded sheep and cattle for six years. In his extreme loneliness he turned to God for comfort:

> The love of God and the fear of Him came to me more and more, and my faith increased, and my spirit was stirred, so that in one day I used to say up to a hundred prayers and at night as many, and I stayed in the forests and on the mountains, and before daylight I used to be roused to prayer in snow and frost and rain.

One night, Patrick tells us, he heard a voice bidding him to return to his fatherland. A ship was waiting for him, he was told. Not doubting that this was God speaking to him, Patrick obeyed and fled his master. For two hundred miles he trudged alone along the cattle tracks until he came to the Irish Sea, where, indeed, a ship was making ready to sail. After much persuasion, the captain agreed to take him. Once across the sea, Patrick walked with the ship's crew through dense, uninhabited forests. Angry and disappointed at not finding anyone to trade with or to rob, the captain turned to Patrick:

> You say your God is great and all powerful, so why can't you pray for us, for we are in danger from hunger, so that it is going to be hard for us to see any other man again.

Patrick replied:

> Turn from your own faith with your whole heart to my Lord God, for nothing is impossible to him, so that today he will send you food on your journey until you are satisfied.

Shortly afterwards a herd of wild pigs appeared and some were killed by the sailors—just in time for many of them had collapsed from hunger.

Somehow Patrick found his home again. His parents joyfully embraced their long-lost son and pleaded with him not to leave them again. But Patrick could not forget the land which had enslaved him. One night in a dream Patrick tells us that he saw a man coming from Ireland with many letters. One he handed to Patrick entitled *Vox Hiberniae*, the Voice of the Irish. As he began to read he seemed to hear the people he had known in Ireland calling with one voice: 'We beg you, holy boy, to come and walk among us once again.' Many years later Patrick could still recall: 'It completely broke my heart, and I could read no more and woke up.' Patrick had no doubt now what he should do: he must return to Ireland and preach the Gospel there.

Episode 12 ❧

THE EARLY IRISH CHURCH

Assailed though they were by heathens from all sides, the Romanised Britons managed for long to maintain a vigorously evangelical church. And it was this church that clearly gave Patrick full support for his determination to bring Christianity to the Irish. He returned to his studies, somewhat embarrassed at the poor quality of his Latin as he sat as a mature student in classes with much younger boys—'I have not studied like the others,' he wrote, admitting that his Latin was always simple and cumbersome. He took holy orders, was appointed Bishop of the Irish by the British church, and returned to Ireland.

Patrick's very humility frustrates the inquiry of historians: his writings give no clues about the location of his British home, or when he came back to Ireland, or where he preached. It is quite clear that he preached to Irish people who knew nothing of Christianity. It is likely that he carried out his work mainly in the northern half of Ireland, for it is there that places traditionally associated with him are located, including Armagh, Templepatrick, Saul, Downpatrick, Lough Derg and Croagh Patrick. The new religion was particularly successful among the ruling class, and early churches tended to be located close to royal sites—Armagh, for example, was within sight of the capital of the kingdom of Ulster, Emain Macha. Of course, conversion was not instantaneous, and old beliefs and traditions survived for centuries after Patrick's time. Patrick expressed delight at the success of his mission: 'I cannot be silent about the great benefits and the great grace which the Lord has deigned to bestow upon me in the land of captivity.'

Though there were later stories told about Patrick's contests with druids, there is no record of anyone being martyred for acceptance of Christianity, except when a British prince made an assault on an Irish Christian community. In his 'Letter against Coroticus' Patrick expressed his anger and grief that British Christians could slay his Irish converts. They were newly baptised, in their white clothing—the oil still shining on their heads—cruelly butchered and slaughtered by the sword.... Greedy wolves, they have glutted themselves with the congregation of the Lord, which indeed was increasing splendidly in Ireland, with the closest care, and made up of the sons of Irish raiders and the daughters of kings who had become monks and virgins of Christ—I cannot say how many! So may the wrong done not please you! And even into Hell may it give you no pleasure!

Early native tradition firmly establishes Patrick as Ireland's apostle. The Annals of Ulster state that Patrick died on 17 March 492 in the 120th year of his age. This need not be taken seriously, and, indeed, his mission cannot be confidently dated: it was probably some time in the middle or late fifth century.

Patrick seems to have established a church along the lines of that which prevailed in the western Roman Empire in his final years. In other words, there were churches with parishes grouped together in dioceses ruled by bishops and with boundaries similar to those of Irish kingdoms of the time. Ireland, however, had no towns to form the centre of parishes and no cities capable of being capitals of dioceses. Fairly soon after Patrick's death monasteries became the favoured type of Christian community in Ireland. Much of the inspiration came from the flourishing Coptic Christian monasteries which flourished in north Africa. Here men like St Anthony cut themselves off from the temptations of the cities and settled in desert valleys and barren mountains.

The earliest monastic foundations in Ireland were established by Finian at Clonard and Ciarán at Clonmacnoise in the early sixth century, though most members of both these communities were wiped out by plague in 548 and 549. Local kings vied with one another to be patrons of monasteries, and their founders became revered for centuries to come. Their forebears had cast precious objects into sacred pools; now they made grants of land to monasteries. Some monasteries soon became the nearest equivalent Ireland had to towns, with substantial populations, thriving markets, schools and even prisons. The management of them usually passed to hereditary lay abbots, and some became so worldly that they even went to war with one another—two hundred were killed in 760 in a battle between the monasteries of Birr and Clonmacnoise.

The best-known Irish monasteries, however, became celebrated for their strict discipline and asceticism. These included those set up by the Céli Dé (the 'Vassals of God'), who strictly observed canonical hours, with two monks remaining in church all night between the offices keeping up a round of prayer. They were advised to 'bestow no friendship or confidence on womankind', and no travel, work or food preparation was permitted on the Sabbath.

Whether they were worldly or ascetic, Irish monasteries became famous centres of scholarship. Even though Ireland had never been a Roman province and Latin was for everyone there a foreign language, Irish monasteries played a pivotal role in preserving and celebrating the civilisation of the classical world now overwhelmed by Germanic conquerors from the north.

Episode 13 ～

A LAND OF MANY KINGS

Many Irish people claim to be descended from kings. It is not altogether preposterous. From the beginning of the Christian era to the coming of the Normans in the twelfth century there were probably no fewer than 150 kings in Ireland at any given date—a remarkably high number when the population was probably no more than half a million.

Each king ruled over a tribal kingdom, a population group which formed a distinct political entity known as a *tuath*, which literally means a people. According to the law tracts, there were three grades of kings: *rí tuaithe*, king of a *tuath*; *ruirí*, king over several petty kingdoms; and *rí ruirech*, king of a province.

Irish people were intensely conscious of status, and family trees were carefully memorised and recorded. The family group containing those who were *rígdamnaí*, literally 'king-material', was limited to the *derbfine*, which means 'certain family'; even so, this was a very large group which included first cousins and extended over four generations. Succession was further complicated by the fact that Irish kings usually had more than one wife, and right into the late sixteenth century they often practised what could be described as serial monogamy—sending one wife back to her father after a few years and taking on another. The last High-King of Ireland, Rory O'Connor, had six wives, and Hugh O'Neill, the last Earl of Tyrone, had five. Even with high levels of infant mortality, this meant that, on the death of a king, fierce succession disputes could ensue. As a result, many ruling families attempted to reduce the possibility of such disputes by appointing a *tánaiste*, a word meaning 'second' or 'expected heir'. An eighth-century tract asks: '*Tánaiste* of a king, why is he so called? Because the whole *tuath* looks to him for kingship without strife.'

The reality was that in any kingdom a man might make himself king so long as he was popular enough and powerful enough to do so. Certainly dynasties were constantly rising and falling. Ruling families usually named themselves after an ancestor, real or imagined. In Connacht, for example, in the eighth century the dominant rulers were the Uí Fiachrach, 'descendants of Fiacra'. Over time this family split into two groups fighting each other for supremacy, one based around the River Moy and the other in the south of the province. Then they were challenged by another dynasty, the Uí Briúin of Roscommon. After triumphing, the Uí Briúin split into several branches: the ancestors of the O'Flahertys of Lough Corrib and Connemara, the O'Rourkes of Bréifne in Leitrim and Cavan, and the O'Connors of Roscommon who by the twelfth century were rulers of Connacht and supplied the last high-king.

Once a king was chosen by the high-born, he was not crowned but inaugurated in a ceremony usually held on an ancient Neolithic or Bronze Age site, such as Tara in Meath or Carnfree in Roscommon. The site had to include a special slab or flagstone (such as the Scottish Stone of Scone) and a sacred tree or *doire*, a grove of oak trees, which appears in many place-names—for example, Derrygonnelly in Co. Fermanagh, means the 'oak grove of the O'Connollys' and was an inauguration site. In pre-Christian times the king was the priest of his people, and the inauguration was a kind of marriage between him and the kingdom, which was considered female. Indeed, the word *feis*, which now means a feast or festival, used to mean a marriage. In the twelfth century Gerald of Wales enjoyed horrifying his readers with descriptions of the barbarities of the Irish. In his *Topography* he gives an account of an inauguration ceremony of the O'Donnell kings in Donegal:

> A white mare is brought forward into the middle of the assembly. He who is to be inaugurated embraces the animal before all, professing himself to be a beast also. The mare is then killed immediately, cut up in pieces, and boiled in water. A bath is prepared for the man afterwards in the same water. He sits in the bath surrounded by all his people and quaffs and drinks of the water in which he is bathed dipping his mouth into it. When this unrighteous rite has been carried out, his kingship has been conferred.

This may not have been pure invention: similar rites are recorded in other parts of the Indo-European world, and bathing in broth with miraculous results is described in 'The Cattle-Raid of Cooley'. Other descriptions of inauguration ceremonies involve the handing of a hazel wand to the king by a leading chieftain, often from an ousted dynasty, the procession of clergy and nobles carrying holy relics round the king in circular motion, and the ceremonial fitting of a shoe. The climax was the recitation of a poem in praise of the new monarch composed by a revered member of society, the *file*, or poet.

Episode 14 ～

POETS, JUDGES, NOBLES, THE FREE AND THE UNFREE

Equal in status to the warrior nobility were the *filí*, the poets. These in pagan times had been druids, and, even long after the introduction of Christianity, they were credited with supernatural powers of divination. The honour of a king or nobleman could be destroyed by the satire of a poet, and this was much feared. Failure to pay him properly for a poem might produce a satire in response, and in the old Irish tales such a satire could bring the victim's face up in blisters. The poet had to master the craft of poetry, praise his patron and be learned in history and literature. He was honoured and feared like the *brahmin* at the other end of the Indo-European world.

Poets were members of a highly privileged caste known as the *áes dána*, the 'men of art', which also included judges, jurists, bards, metalworkers and genealogists. They preserved the vernacular lore and, with the introduction of writing, were able to enrich it with the new Latin learning. They surrendered their most obvious pagan functions with the arrival of Christianity, but survived remarkably well until the overthrow of the Gaelic order in the seventeenth century.

Much of what we know about early Christian Irish society is derived from the Brehon Laws, a name derived from the *brithemain*, a word meaning 'judges'. Most of them are contained in a lawbook called *Senchas Már*, loosely translated as 'the great collection of ancient tradition'. Compiled in the seventh century, these laws show that the Irish were obsessed by status. Everyone had their *enech*, or 'honour-price', which, since the Irish had no currency, was calculated in cattle. The lowest was a *sét*, equal to a heifer; a *cumal* equalled seven milch cows; and the honour-price of a king of a *tuath* was seven cumals—the price that would have to be paid to the family of a king if he was gravely wronged. Failure to abide by a legal judgment, for example if a debt had not been paid, could be advertised by the victim going on hunger-strike outside the wrongdoer's door, and this disgrace might lead to the loss of an honour-price. It was laid down:

He who does not give a pledge to fasting is an evader of all. He who disregards all things is paid neither by God nor man.

The status of noblemen depended on the number of clients they could maintain, in addition to lands and property. They formed the warrior class, travelling to the battlefield on horseback or by chariot. Conflicts in early Christian Ireland were numerous, but most of the lower classes were exempt from them, though they might face ruin and death following cattle-raids.

It was the custom of kings and nobles to send their children to be fostered by others, partly to promote good relations with neighbours. Girls were sent away between the ages of seven and fourteen, and boys between seven and seventeen. They called their foster-parents *aite* and *muime*, which can be exactly translated as 'daddy' and 'mammy' and which illustrates the powerful bond that existed between foster-parents and their charges.

The advent of Christianity notwithstanding, the Brehon Laws fully recognised relationships which were strongly disapproved of by the church. Divorce could be obtained with relative ease, and elaborate laws were set out on how the property of the divorced should be divided. It was much more difficult for women to cast aside their husbands, and if they left without good cause, they lost all rights in society. It was much easier for men: the laws not only permitted regular marriage but also less formal unions and the use of concubines. Boys born of concubines made no demands on property and could become loyal servants and fighting-men. Using the Old Testament as justification, more than one wife was permitted. Wives could be passed on from one husband to the next. The famous Gormlaith was first the wife of Olaf, King of Dublin, then of Malachy, King of Meath, then of Brian Boru, and was later offered to Sigurd the Fat of the Orkneys.

Below the *nemed*, the 'sacred' classes of kings, men of the arts and the nobility, were the *sóer*, the 'free' who were high-ranking commoners, and the *dóer*, the unfree, who were utterly dependent on those above them for access to land. Manual labour was despised by the aristocracy—a king could lose his honour-price if seen with an axe or a spade—and so the functioning of the economy depended heavily on farmers with many obligations.

Episode 15 ～

HOMESTEADS AND CRANNOGS

In modern Irish *baile* means a town, but in earlier times this word, which has left its mark on so many of our placenames, and is anglicised as 'bally', simply meant a settlement. In fact, until the coming of the Vikings, there were no towns in Ireland at all. The settlement pattern was entirely dispersed and rural, and the economy depended almost entirely on farming.

Around 45,000 remains of ringforts have been identified in Ireland. Strictly speaking, these were not forts but circular enclosed homesteads of varying size. In rocky or mountainous areas, where the fort was known as a *caiseal* or *cathair*, the wall was made of unmortared stone without a surrounding ditch. The word *ráth* referred to a ringfort with an earthen bank—and occasionally two or three—surrounded by a ditch, and the term *lios* was applied to the enclosed space inside. These elements appear in placenames in their tens of thousands:

Cahersiveen: 'little Saibh's fort'; *Caherdaniel*: 'Donal's fort'; *Cahermore*: 'big fort'; and there are places called *Caher* or *Cahir* in the counties of Tipperary, Clare and Cork.

Cashelreagh: 'grey fort'; *Moygashel*: 'fort of the plain'; *Cashelbane*: 'white fort'; *Cashleen*: 'little fort'; and there dozens of places simply called *Cashel*, in, for example, the counties of Donegal, Tipperary, Londonderry, Down, Carlow and Laois.

Rathdrum: 'hill fort'; *Rathfriland*: 'Fraoile's fort'; *Rathglass*: 'green fort'; *Rathcoole*: 'Cumhal's fort'; *Rathlin O'Birne*: 'O'Byrne's little fort'; and *Rathmore*, meaning 'large fort', is found in several counties including Antrim, Meath, Tyrone, Limerick, Kerry and Kildare.

Lisnaskea: 'fort of the hawthorns'; *Lissycasey*: 'O'Casey's fort'; *Lisduff*: 'black fort'; *Lislea*: 'grey fort'; *Lismore*: 'big fort'; *Lisnamuck*: 'fort of the pig'; *Listowel*: 'Tuathal's fort'; *Lisheen*: 'little fort'.

The earthen and stone circular banks and walls would have kept out wolves and would-be cattle-thieves and marauders, but not a determined attack. These were simply the homes of extended families, and the enclosure served as a farmyard for chickens and pigs and for activities such as butter-churning. Inside the enclosure there was room for around six houses; generally these were round, though some, for example at Carraig Aille in Co. Limerick and Leacanabuile in Co. Kerry, were rectangular. Excavations in 1984 at the Deer Park Farms near Glenarm in Co. Antrim found that people had lived there continuously between the sixth and tenth centuries. The houses here had been constructed of two concentric rings of hazel wattles, strengthened with thick upright posts, to create a kind of cavity wall filled with straw, grass, moss and heather for insulation—and one house had a thatch of reeds woven into the circular outer wall for added comfort. The wattle walls were designed to slope inwards to form a roof which was then covered with reeds or straw. The people who lived in these houses liked to see the sun rise in the morning, and nearly all ringforts have entrances facing east.

A feature of later ringforts which for long intrigued archaeologists was what they termed a 'souterrain'. A souterrain was an underground passage leading to a chamber, carefully drained, lined with stone flags, provided with ventilation shafts, and roofed with stone lintels covered over with grass sods. It now seems certain that these were temporary hiding-places for use if the homestead was attacked, and that valuables—such as an imported glass vessel found in one at Mullaroe, Co. Sligo—and precious seedcorn and food, which needed to be kept cool in summer, were stored here. The poor may not have been able to afford to maintain ringforts, and archaeologists are increasingly coming across more modest dwellings without any embankments, for example at Ballynavenooragh on the slopes of Mount Brandon on the Dingle peninsula.

The remains of some two thousand lake dwellings have been identified in Ireland. Known as 'crannogs', these were wholly or partly artificial made of split timber (sometimes fitted together with pegs) and layers of soil, brushwood, peat and stones retained by a timber palisade. Many were found with remains of landing-stages, jetties and dugout boats. Since considerable resources of labour were needed to build them, these were dwelling-places for the better-off and were designed for defence. Lagore crannog in Co. Meath, for example, was the residence of the Kings of South Brega between the seventh and tenth centuries. Here there had evidently been a massacre, as broken skulls and a great many weapons were found. Some crannogs may have served as the equivalent of holiday homes for the wealthy where recreations such as fishing, wildfowling and hunting could be carried on. Possibly because they were making so many valuable and portable objects, metalworkers seem to have found crannogs secure places for practising their crafts. Many luxury decorated bronze and silver pieces have been found on crannogs, and one at Bofeenaun in Co. Mayo was entirely devoted to iron forging and smithing. The main activity of the vast majority living in the Irish countryside was, of course, the production of food.

Episode 16 ⌒

LIVING OFF THE LAND

Ringforts have generally been found in clusters of two or three, hinting that they were the homesteads of a *derbfine*, a four-generation lineage group—in other words, a large extended family. These farming communities gave every indication of being complex family co-operatives. Visiting Ireland in the twelfth century, Gerald of Wales had a poor opinion of Irish farming practices:

They use fields generally as a pasture.... Little is cultivated, and even less sown. The fields cultivated are so few because of the neglect of those who cultivate them.... For given only to leisure, and devoted only to laziness, they think that the greatest pleasure is not to work.... This people is, then, a barbarous people ...

Archaeologists, using aerial photography, pollen analysis, dendrochronology and other sophisticated techniques, have proved Gerald wrong. In plots close to the ringfort, onions, carrots, parsnips, cabbages, chives, leeks and beans were grown. In rectangular fields, carefully fenced against domestic animals, red deer and wild boar, the ground was turned over to cultivate corn. The poor used no more than a spade, a simple wooden implement with an iron sheath. Most extended families, however, could put together a team of four oxen yoked abreast to draw a plough, which from the tenth century onwards was fitted with a heavy share to cut the furrow and a coulter for turning the sod. Harrowing to break up the clods was done with a horse, since oxen were too slow for this task. Whole families turned out for harvesting in September to cut the corn close to the ear with iron-socketed or tanged reaping-hooks. After being stacked in a rick in the ringfort enclosure, the corn was threshed with flails. Ireland's wet climate meant that in most years the corn had to be dried in kilns before being winnowed to remove the chaff.

For most people corn meant two- or six-eared barley, though in the wetter north-west oats were preferred. In Ireland's uncertain climate wheat was a luxury grain, grown mostly in the south-east, to be eaten by kings and nobles. A miracle attributed to several Irish saints was that they turned fields of barley into wheat. The laborious task of grinding corn was assigned to women using the rotary quern which, in early Christian times, replaced the saddle quern. Many families, however, were prepared to pay for the use of a corn mill. Probably the most sophisticated engines available in Ireland at the time, these mills were two-storey structures built over a stream: water, released by sluice-gates down a millrace, poured onto the dished paddles of a horizontal wheel to turn the millstone above. Recent examples from Strangford Lough show that the wheels there were rotated by the power of the ebbing tide.

Cattle formed the mainstay of the mixed Irish farming economy. White animals with red ears were especially prized, but most were small and black like the modern Kerry breed. Male calves were slaughtered for meat and to supply the monasteries with vellum, except for those kept for breeding and to draw ploughs. Milch cows were worth twice as much as heifers and were slaughtered only when they were past their best. Cattle were driven out onto common pastures, herded and protected by dogs, and cows were milked for butter- and cheese-making. There was no-hay making; instead, in the autumn the cattle were put into fields that had been fenced off over the summer, where they were able to graze the long stubble left after the harvest. Animals which could not be kept fed over the winter were slaughtered then to provide not only meat for salting but also leather, sinew, tallow, bone and horn. Sheep were less important and were kept for their dark wool more than for their meat. Pigs, long-legged and shaggy, driven out into the woods to fatten up on acorns, were highly prized.

A curious feature of early Christian Ireland is the almost total absence of pottery. Instead bowls and platters were made from turned wood; baskets were much used; and barrels and butter-churns were constructed from staved wood. The Irish ate barley in the form of gruel and bread, oatcakes and porridge, butter—fresh when in season, heavily salted during the winter—buttermilk curds, meat when they could get it, vegetables from the gardens, and cultivated apples from fenced-off orchards. Fresh milk was a luxury, and generally food was washed down with home-made ale and buttermilk. The woods provided wild garlic, raspberries, blackberries and hazelnuts. Though the wild boar was hunted to extinction by the twelfth century, much game—especially red deer, hares and wildfowl—was consumed. Salmon, trout and eels also found favour, but it took the Vikings to teach the Irish how to enjoy sea fish. Shellfish were despised as food fit only for the destitute. Famine and disease were never too far away, and when they struck they triggered dislocating movements of population. The plague of 1084, which the annals stated killed one in four, was seen to be the work of

demons which came from the northern isles of the world, three battalions of them, and there were three thousand in each battalion.... This is the way they were seen by Mac Gilla Lugáin: wherever their heat and fury reached, there their poison was taken, for there was a sword of fire in each of them, and each of them was as high as the clouds of the sky.

These words were written in a monastery, an establishment which by this time was developing into the nearest equivalent Ireland had to a town.

Episode 17 ∾

SAINTS AND SCHOLARS

Eight miles out beyond the rugged Iveragh peninsula in south-west Kerry the lonely island of Skellig Michael, a pyramid of bare rock, rises to a peak seven hundred feet above the Atlantic Ocean. In winter, gales howl round its crags and gigantic waves thunder at the base of is cliffs. Even in summer the sea is rarely calm, and it is not easy to make a landing. Only sea-pinks and a few other hardy plants can survive in its thin soil. This is, perhaps, the most desolate place in Ireland, fit only for fish-hunting gannets and puffins. Yet nearly one and a half thousand years ago Skellig rock was chosen by Irish monks as a site for their monastery, where they would leave behind the world of violence and the temptation of ambition and riches.

Lacking both timber and mortar, they used only the rock around them. On the brow of a five-hundred-foot precipice the monks placed pieces of hewn rock on the ground to form flat terraces which they surrounded with great drystone walls. Then on the highest terrace they erected six beehive-shaped cells nestling against the rock. So perfectly were these stones fitted together that even today the driving rain cannot penetrate the uncemented walls and corbelled roofs.

Inside the cells, where the monks studied and slept, the walls are carefully smoothed, with built-in stone cupboards and stone hooks for book satchels, and the floors are paved and drained. Two oratories, looking like upturned boats, built in much the same way as the cells and decorated with simple crosses, served as places of worship. In summer, when great shoals of mackerel broke the surface of the ocean in pursuit of sprats, and when sea-birds nested on the rock, the monks could survive on gulls' eggs, fish and herbs grown in the scanty soil of the monastery garden. During winter gales they must have hungered, and no doubt some of the monks buried in the tiny graveyard died of starvation.

The greatest Irish monasteries, such as Monasterboice in Co. Louth and Clonmacnoise in Co. Offaly, were placed on fertile lands, where, patronised by kings, they became centres of wealth and population as well as of craftsmanship and scholarship. However, many Irish were determined to remove themselves from worldly temptation: they joined communities on remote mountainsides and on lake and sea islands, though none were perhaps as desolate as Skellig.

These ascetic monks and nuns ate only one meal a day, and only on very special occasions were they allowed to eat meat. The 'Good Rule of Bangor', written by Columbanus, detailed the regime for the ascetic religious life:

Let the monks' food be poor and taken in the evening, and their drink such as to avoid drunkenness, so that it may both maintain life and not harm their souls: vegetables, beans, flour mixed with water, together with a small loaf of bread, lest the stomach be burdened and the mind confused. We must fast daily, just as we must feed daily.

Stiff penalties were laid down for those who dared to break the demanding rules:

Him who has not waited for grace at table and has not responded Amen, it is ordained to correct with six blows. Likewise him who has spoken while eating it is ordained to correct with six blows. Let him who has cut the table with a knife be corrected with ten blows. He who with unclean hands receives the blessed bread, with twelve blows.

The main purpose of the monastic life was worship by constant prayer, psalms and songs of praise:

Those who have gone before us have appointed three Psalms at each of the day-time hours. But at night-fall twelve Psalms are chanted, and at midnight likewise; but towards morning twenty-four are appointed.

Part of each day was spent in private study and in the scriptorium—the thirst for scholarship seems to have been as strong as that for the simple life. Many of the monks composed religious poems and hymns:

> Raise your voice in praise, O people!
> Praise the Lord God everywhere
> Since the little birds must praise Him—
> They who have no soul but air.

Manuscripts from early Christian Ireland are frequently embellished with little poems in praise of nature, often written in the margins, such as this one:

> A hedge of trees is all around;
> The blackbird's praise I shall not hide;
> Above my book so smoothly lined
> The birds are singing far and wide.
>
> In a green cloak of bushy boughs
> The cuckoo pipes his melodies—
> Be good to me, God, on Judgment Day!—
> How well I write beneath the trees!

Irish monks were particularly fond of writing invocations—perhaps in the style formerly composed by pagan druids. This one, rewritten by Mrs Alexander in Victorian times, has become a favourite hymn:

> Be thou my vision, O Lord of my heart,
> Naught be all else to me, save that thou art;
> Thou my best thought in the day and the night,
> Waking or sleeping, thy presence my light ...

Episode 18 ～

'NOT THE WORK OF MEN BUT OF ANGELS'

From the Roman Empire which they helped to destroy the Irish obtained Christianity and, with it, the art of writing. The earliest known form of the Irish language is carved in Ogam, a primitive script made up of groupings of notches on the angular corner of stones. Irish monks soon learned the Latin script and began to write it in a distinct native style.

The Romans wrote on Egyptian papyrus, but this material made from Nile reeds disintegrated quickly in the damp Irish climate. While other parts of Europe were moving over to parchment, made from sheepskin, the Irish preferred the more expensive skins of new-born calves which, after being tanned and carefully scraped free of hair, were turned into smooth and almost luminous vellum.

The earliest surviving Irish manuscript is a copy of the Psalms, known as the *Cathach* (the 'Battler'), because it was later carried into battle as a talisman by the O'Donnells. An ancient tradition, which may well be true, attributes the writing of the *Cathach* to Colmcille himself. And most of the great illuminated Irish manuscripts were written and decorated in monasteries founded by him.

Monks cut their own goose quills and prepared inks from carefully collected pigments. The Irish developed their own unique insular half-uncial, majuscule and miniscule script and specialised in enlarged capital letters at the beginning of paragraphs. In time these capital letters increased in size and elaboration. Scribes often tried to relieve this arduous work by scribbling in the margins, for example:

Let no reader blame this writing for my arm is cramped from too much work.

Another wrote:

Alas! My hand! O my breast, Holy Virgin! This page is difficult.

—but he seems to have recovered a few pages later when he tells us:

The third hour. Time for dinner!

Another exclaims:

> I am sad without food today! A blessing on the soul of Fergus! Amen. I am
> very cold! ... Love lasts while the money lasts.

Another cut himself, probably sharpening his quill, and drew a black circle
round the blot of blood on the page with this note:

> Blood from the finger of Melaghlin.

'Goodbye, little book,' a scribe had written when he finished his creation, and
another concludes with these words:

> This is sad! O little book!—A day will come in truth, when someone over
> thy page will say, 'The hand that wrote it is no more'.

Other scribes wrote verse:

> My hand is weary with writing,
> My sharp quill is not steady,
> My slender-beaked pen juts forth
> A black draught of dark-blue ink.
>
> A stream of the wisdom of blessed God
> Springs from my fair-brown shapely hand:
> On the page it squirts its draught
> Of ink of the green-skinned holly.
>
> My little dripping pen travels
> Across the plain of shining books,
> Without ceasing for the wealth of the great—
> Whence my hand is weary with writing.

The greatest achievements of early Christian Ireland are the magnificent
illuminated Gospels and other sacred texts. The Book of Durrow, completed
around 670, was the first to include a so-called carpet page, an abstract design
based on intricate Celtic interlacing. The high point of manuscript illumination was reached in the Book of Kells, which combines strong sweeping
compositions with astonishingly detailed, almost microscopic, ornament. The
most admired page combines the sacred *chi-rho* monogram with images of
Christ, the Resurrection and the Eucharist; and the stately rounded script is
punctuated with scenes such as cats pursuing mice, an otter seizing a fish, a

cock with hens, and a greyhound hunting. It has a good claim to be the most beautiful book executed during the first millennium. Overseas, Gospels and commentaries almost as accomplished can be found in greatest number in the monastery founded by St Gall in Switzerland, carried there by Irish pilgrims or written there by Irish scribes. After examining the Book of Kildare, now lost, Gerald of Wales came to the conclusion that it was 'not the work of men but of angels'.

The greatest Irish monasteries developed into sophisticated communities served by, among others, specialist craftsmen. These men produced superlative metalwork of extraordinary refinement and delicacy. These were liturgical vessels and reliquaries, that is, containers for holy bells, bishops' staffs and a wide range of saints' relics. These include the Ardagh Chalice, the Cross of Cong and, found as recently as 1980, the altar service found at Derrynaflan in Co. Tipperary, including an outstandingly beautiful chalice.

The most distinctive reminders of early Christian Ireland are the high crosses characterised by a ring of stone that connects the arms to the upright. Erected in the precincts of monasteries, they depicted not only the crucifixion but also a wide range of scenes illustrating episodes from the Old and New Testaments. The one at Kells, Co. Meath, may have been put up to give thanks for the safe transfer to that site of the monastic community of Iona, which had fallen prey to Viking attack.

Episode 19 ⌒

ST COLUMBA, ST COLUMBANUS AND THE WANDERING IRISH

It was from the little kingdom of Dál Riata in the extreme north-east of Ireland that the Gaelic colonisation of Scotland began towards the end of the fifth century. Argyll means 'eastern province of the Gael', and it was here that the first settlements were made. For more than a century territory on both sides of the Straits of Moyle—the North Channel—formed one kingdom ruled by a dynasty tracing ancestry from Fergus Mór mac Erc. By the middle of the sixth century Bruide, King of the Picts, threatened to overwhelm the Irish interlopers, and so Dál Riata turned for help to the Northern Uí Néill, the most powerful dynastic group in northern Ireland. The necessary pact was sealed at Druim Ceit at Mullagh near Derry in 575.

The man who negotiated this alliance was an Uí Néill prince and a renowned churchman, Columcille, St Columba. Born at Gartan in Donegal, Columba studied under Finnian at Moville in Co. Down and at Clonard on the Boyne and returned to build his own monastery at Derry in 546. The high-born Columba could draw on impressive resources. In addition, the Dál Riata king, Aedán mac Gabráin, granted Columba the island of Iona off the west of Scotland for a new foundation. For the next two centuries and longer Iona was to be the most famous centre of Christian learning in the Celtic world. A poem attributed to Columba illustrates his devotion to scholarship:

> I send my little pen dripping unceasingly
> Over an assemblage of books of great beauty,
> To enrich the possessions of men of art—
> Whence my hand is weary with writing.

It was in Iona that King Oswald, the Anglo-Saxon King of Northumbria, took refuge during a challenge to his power. Travelling from the island by currach and by foot, St Aidan converted the king, began the evangelisation of his people, and established a celebrated monastery on Lindisfarne.

Some Irish monks simply put out to sea and let the wind take them away. This is how the Irish came to be the very first humans to set foot in Iceland. One monk there, describing the midnight sun, reported that it was so bright he could see the lice on his hair-shirt.

As a centre of learning and Christian zeal, Bangor in north Down rivalled Iona. Its founder Comgall seems to have worked with Columba. The 'Good Rule of Bangor' included these words:

> Blessed family of Bangor, founded on unerring faith, adorned with salvation's hope, perfect in charity. Ship never distressed though beaten by waves; fully prepared for nuptials, spouse for the sovereign Lord. House full of delicious things and built on a rock; and no less the true vine brought out of Egypt's land.

The text of the 'Good Rule' is not to be found in Ireland, but in Milan— evidence that the great Irish mission to the European mainland had begun.

Towards the end of the sixth century, by the ruined Roman fort of Annegray in the Vosges mountains, Irish pilgrims halted after travelling more than nine hundred miles from Bangor. Here, under the direction of their leader, Columbanus, they built three monasteries

In his forthright condemnation of the worldliness of the Frankish church, Columbanus aroused the hostility of Theoderic, King of Burgundy. Forced to move on, the Irish monks struck overland to the Rhine, where they made their way upstream. This inspired Columbanus to write his 'boat song':

Lo, little bark on twin-horned Rhine
From forests hewn to skim the brine.
Heave, lads, and let the echoes ring.

The tempests howl, the storms dismay,
But manly strength can win the day
Heave, lads, and let the echoes ring.

The king of virtues vowed a prize
For him who wins, for him who tries.
Think, lads, of Christ and echo him.

When they reached Lake Constance, they preached to Germans, who had not heard the Gospel before, and founded a monastery at Bregenz. The restless Columbanus was eager to travel on, but Gall, one of the Bangor monks, stayed to become the local patron saint—a church, a town and a canton in Switzerland are called St Gallen to this day. Columbanus pressed on to northern Italy to found another monastery at Bobbio, where his tomb can still be seen. He inspired a great flood of Irish pilgrims and scholars to make their way to the European mainland in the decades to come.

Episode 20 ～

THE COMING OF THE VIKINGS

For almost a thousand years, unlike almost every other part of Europe, Ireland was free from large-scale invasion. Then, in the year 795, Rathlin Island was attacked. Within the next few years a succession of undefended monasteries along the coast fell victim to Viking raids.

There was an astonishing and awfully great oppression over all Erinn, throughout its breadth, by powerful azure Norsemen, and by fierce hardhearted Danes, during a lengthened period, and for a long time, for the space of eight score and ten years, or, according to some authorities, two hundred years.

So wrote the author of *Cogadh Gaedhel re Gallaibh* ('Wars of the Irish with the Foreigners') at the beginning of his long history of the impact of the Viking raids on his country. So frequent and devastating were the assaults that one monk wrote in the margin of his manuscript a poem in thanks for the storm raging outside:

> Fierce and wild is the wind tonight,
> It tosses the tresses of the sea to white;
> On such a night I take my ease;
> Fierce Northmen only course the quiet seas.

Once the Frankish emperor Charlemagne had broken up the fleets of Frisian pirates in the North Sea, nothing formidable stood in the way of the Vikings, leaving them masters of the north Atlantic. Their longships, some over seventy feet long, were well designed to cope with the hazards of the ocean: built of seasoned overlapping oak planks, riveted with iron, and bound to the ribs with tough pine roots, their hulls could not only flex to the swell but also, with their shallow draught, negotiate treacherous mud banks at the mouths of rivers. Churches and monasteries suffered most in the early attacks, the raiders being attracted to them not only by precious liturgical vessels and reliquaries but also by their rich stores of butter and corn. Since the records were written by monks, the Northmen were viewed as black-hearted barbarians by the chroniclers:

In a word, although there were an hundred hard-steeled iron heads on one neck, and an hundred sharp, ready, cool, never-rusting, brazen tongues on each head, and an hundred garrulous, loud, unceasing voices from each tongue, they could not recount, or narrate, or enumerate, or tell, what all the Gaedhil suffered in common, both men and women, laity and clergy, old and young, noble and ignoble, of hardship and of injury, and of oppression, in every house, from these valiant, wrathful, foreign, purely pagan people.

Ruled by a disorganised multiplicity of kings frequently in conflict with one another, the Irish were unable to put up a united resistance to the Vikings. In addition, these raiders—most of them Norse rather than Danes—were more formidably armed than the Irish, their helmets being fitted with protective nose pieces, their torsos covered in flexible coats of mail, and their weaponry comprising fearsome battle-axes and long slashing swords edged with superbly welded hard steel. Shallows and waterfalls proved no protection—the invaders simply carried their longships past such obstructions to navigable water upstream.

The Northmen were not always victorious. For the year 811 the Annals of Ulster have this terse entry:

A slaughter of the heathens by the Ulaid.

This must have been a significant achievement, because the same victory was recorded in the court of Charlemagne. A major fresh assault was launched in 821, when great numbers of women were seized at Howth and even the seemingly impregnable Skellig rock was attacked. In 837 two formidable fleets, each made up of sixty ships, penetrated the Liffey and Boyne rivers. The Book of Leinster recorded this campaigning and, in particular, the exploits of one Viking leader, Turgeis:

> There came a great royal fleet into the north of Ireland with Turgeis. This Turgeis assumed the sovereignty of the foreigners of Ireland. A fleet of them took possession of Lough Neagh. Another fleet took possession of Louth. Another on Lough Ree.
>
>   Moreover, Armagh was plundered by them three times in the same month, and Turgeis himself took he abbacy of Armagh; and Forannan, Abbot of Armagh, was driven away and went to Munster, and the Shrine of Patrick with him.... After this came Turgeis upon Lough Ree, and from thence were plundered Meath and Connacht; and Clonmacnoise and Clonfert, and the churches of Lough Derg in like manner. Clonmacnoise was taken by his wife. It was on the altar of the great church she used to make prophecies.... There came great sea-belched shoals of foreigners into Munster, so that there was not a point thereof without a fleet. A fleet carried off Forannan and they broke the shrine of Patrick.

Longford is in the very heart of Ireland, yet it is named after a defended stockade for longships brought far up the River Shannon. It seemed that no part of Ireland was safe from the Vikings. Some of these Northmen, indeed, had decided to stay and make Ireland their home.

Episode 21 ⌣

THE WARS OF THE GAEL AND THE GALL

In the year 837 a fleet of over sixty longships from the Orkneys and the Western Isles passed the headland of Howth and steered into the shelter of Dublin Bay. The striped woollen sails were reefed down, the helmsmen raised their deep steering oars, warriors slung out their shields over the gunwales, and, seated on heavy carved chests, they sculled in unison towards the mouth of the Liffey river.

As the men invoked the aid of Odin and Thor, and shook great iron rattles to ward off evil spirits, the grim dragon carvings adorning the high prows struck terror into the settlements on the south bank of the estuary. For the churches clustered round the Poddle, a stream flowing into the Liffey from the south-west, there could be but poor defence against these Norse in their iron mail-shirts, wielding their battle-axes. No doubt these churches yielded a rich booty of precious vestments, reliquaries and book covers to be taken back to the lands of the far north.

Four years later these Vikings returned; but this time they had come not to raid but to stay. By the black pool—in Irish *Dubh Linn*—formed where the Poddle met the Liffey, they pulled their longships ashore onto a dry bank, covered them, lashed them down, and erected a stockade around their vessels for protection. Here a ridge of well-drained ground provided an obvious place for the Norse to overwinter and build a stronghold. This is where Dublin Castle now stands. With the coming of every summer, more bands of Northmen arrived and settled there, making it the principal colony of the Vikings in Ireland.

Just upstream from this stronghold, the Irish had made a crossing-place: hurdles of interwoven saplings, sunk with great boulders, gave a firm footing for people and cattle wading across the Liffey at low tide. This was *Áth Cliath*, the 'ford of hurdles'. *Áth Cliath* and *Dubh Linn* together held a key position, for it was there that the principal routeways from Munster, Leinster, Connacht and Ulster converged. For the Norse, their stronghold was a base from which attacks could be directed not only deep into the fertile plains of Kildare but also against the neighbouring island of Britain.

In 857 Olaf the White, the first recorded ruler of Viking Dublin, joined forces with Ivar the Boneless, son of the Danish warrior-king, Ragnar Hairy-Britches; together they harried Scotland and Northumbria. When Olaf was slain in a skirmish, Ivar won the leadership of all the Norse in Ireland and the Danes in York. Too great an interest in Britain, however, held dangers for the foreigners of Dublin. Irish kings sank their differences and threw themselves with great force upon Dublin:

902: The expulsion of the Unbelievers from Ireland, i.e. from their ship-fortress at Dublin, by Maelfindia son of Flannacán with the men of Brega, and Cerball son of Muirecán with his Leinstermen. They left a great part of their fleet, and escaped half dead, wounded and broken.

Dublin, however, was too valuable a base to abandon altogether. The grandsons of Ivar the Boneless, Ragnall and Sitric the Squinty, in 914 launched the most terrifying Viking invasion Ireland had yet seen:

The whole of Munster became filled with immense floods and countless sea-vomiting of ships, boats and fleets.... There was no place in Erinn without numerous fleets of Danes and pirates; so that they made spoil-land, and sword-land, and conquered land of her.

After three years Sitric the Squinty, advancing north from Waterford up the Barrow river, recovered Dublin for the Vikings after fierce conflicts:

Though numerous were the oft-victorious clans of the many-familied Erinn, yet not one of them was able to give relief, alleviation, or deliverance from that oppression, and tyranny, from the numbers and multitudes, and the cruelty and the wrath of the brutal, ferocious, untamed, implacable hordes, by whom that oppression was inflicted, because of the excellence of their polished, ample, treble, heavy, trusty, glittering corselets; and their hardy, strong valiant swords; and their well-riveted long spears; and their ready, brilliant arms of valour besides.

Niall Glúndubh, of the Uí Néill dynasty, put together a formidable coalition, and with a great host he advanced on Dublin. There, outside the city walls in 919, he was utterly routed by the Northmen and slain, along with twelve other Irish kings. The Annals of Ulster lamented:

Mournful today is virginal Ireland
Without a mighty king in command of hostages;
It is to view the heaven and not to see the sun
To behold Niall's plain without Niall.

These Vikings had come to stay. They made Dublin into a great trading city, a central port of call on a great semicircular trade route extending from the Mediterranean to Norway and Iceland and beyond. In one of the Icelandic sagas this advice was given:

Fare thou south to Dublin,
That track is most renowned.

Episode 22 ~

VIKING TOWNS AND CITIES

It was not only in Dublin that the Vikings made permanent settlements in Ireland. All along the southern and eastern coasts they converted their temporary ship-fortresses into the island's first towns. The ferocity of resistance from the Uí Néill and the Ulaid—who on more than one occasion actually defeated the Northmen on their own element, the sea—probably explains why they managed only to establish toe-holds in Ulster, at Larne, Ballyholme, Strangford and Carlingford. Limerick, on the Shannon estuary, and Waterford, where the Suir, Barrow and Nore rivers meet to join the sea, became great cities. Many coastal place names are of Old Norse origin and indicate where the Vikings built their towns:

> *Wexford*: 'fjord of Veig'; *Wicklow*: 'Viking meadow'; *Arklow*: 'Arnkell's meadow'; *Carlingford*: 'the hag's fjord'; *Helvick*: 'safe inlet'; *Saltee*: 'salt island'; *Strangford*: 'rough fjord'; *Waterford*: 'windy fjord'; *Dursey*: 'deer island'; *Smerwick*: 'butter bay'.

Dublin, however, was always pre-eminent; here the Vikings not only built a city but also settled the country around it. The Irish called it *Fine Gall*, 'foreign people', and Ireland's most recently created county council has been named Fingal after it. Here there are numerous placenames of Viking origin:

> *Howth*: 'rocky headland'; *Oxmantown*: 'the town of the men from the east'; *Skerries*: 'rocks'; *Dalkey*: 'dagger island'; *Lambay*: 'lamb's island'; *Ireland's Eye*: 'Ireland's island'; *Leixlip*: 'salmon leap'.

Indeed, *Ireland* is the name the Vikings gave to the land of Erinn. In addition, a great many Norse words were adopted by the Irish and incorporated into Gaelic, including the words for market, anchor, helmet, boat, button, garden, banner, rudder and penny—the Vikings of Dublin were the first to mint coins in Ireland.

There had been high-kings in Ireland since the beginning of the island's recorded history, but none had ever governed the whole country. When the Vikings had begun their attacks at the end of the eighth century, they faced not one strong ruler but many kings. The men from the north never conquered all of Ireland—indeed, their invasions seem to have encouraged several more powerful rulers to make the high-kingship a reality.

Limerick, on the estuary of the River Shannon, the Vikings made into one of their great cities. It was in the course of seemingly endless wars that the men of a small neighbouring kingdom, Dál Cais, sacked Limerick in the year 967. The annalistic composition entitled *The Wars of the Gael with the Gall* proudly recorded this Irish triumph:

> They carried off their jewels and their best property, and their saddles beautiful and foreign; their gold and their silver; their beautifully woven cloth of all colours; and their satins and silken cloth. They carried away their soft, youthful, bright, matchless girls; their blooming silk-clad young women; and their active, large and well-formed boys. The fort and the good town they reduced to a cloud of smoke and to red fire afterwards.

Helped by this booty, the men of Dál Cais extended their power. Under the command of their leader, Brian, they seized control of the whole of Munster. After many campaigns and battles, the other kingdoms of Ireland, one by one, yielded. Everywhere the advancing warlord was known as Brian Boru, 'Brian of the Tributes'. In the year 999 Brian overwhelmed a combined army of Dublin Vikings and Leinstermen. When Máel Mórda, King of Leinster, and Sitric Silkenbeard, King of Dublin, submitted, Brian Boru was acknowledged as High-King of Ireland—the first high-king ever to win the support of every part of the island. For the first time for many generations Ireland was at peace. Brian Boru made a circuit of the whole country in 1005, and, according to the annals, he sent out fleets from Dublin and Waterford to levy tribute from the Welsh, the Saxons and the Scots. He gave generous gifts to the church, to the needy and to scholars. For almost fifteen years Brian Boru ruled as the unchallenged High-King of Ireland. But Brian had made enemies. He had won his crown not by birth, but by the sword.

Episode 23 ∾

BRIAN BORU AND THE BATTLE OF CLONTARF

Nothing irked Máel Mórda, King of Leinster, more than a journey to pay homage to Brian at his palace at Kincora. Brian had made his sister Gormflaith his queen, only to cast her aside for another. Finally, insulted by Brian's arrogant son Murchad during a game of chess, the King of Leinster could stand it no longer. He rode off without so much as bidding farewell to the high-king, back to his fort at Naas. And when Brian sent a messenger after him to call him back, Máel Mórda lashed at the fellow with his yew horse-switch, smashing his skull to pieces.

There was no turning back now. Brian had sworn revenge; and Máel Mórda would no longer submit Leinster to Brian's authority. Sitric Silkenbeard too resented the many humiliating defeats he had suffered at Brian's hands and the loss of his city's independence. Dublin was the mightiest Viking city in Ireland. It had become a Viking kingdom even before Denmark, Norway and Sweden had kings. To throw off Brian's yoke would be a real prize.

That very year, 1013, had not King Sven of Denmark conquered all of England? Might not the Northmen win a kingdom to match it in Ireland? The King of Dublin and the King of Leinster knew they could not win without help. Longships—one of them with Sitric aboard—left Dublin to sail across the Irish Sea and to the Hebrides and beyond. After many months they returned with firm offers of support.

Good Friday, 23 April 1014: this day the fate not only of Dublin but of all Ireland would be decided, and, whatever the outcome, this conflict would be long remembered in the island's annals and in the sagas of the Northmen. Looking east towards Howth from the fortified earthen wall along the southern Liffey shore, Sitric Silkenbeard could see silhouetted against the rising sun the massed prows of longships stretching round into the bay. His heart leaped to see these Vikings he had summoned fall in behind their captains on the foreshore. There were, it is said, fighting men from as far away as Norway and France; King Brodar of the Isle of Man, with his long black hair tucked into his belt; and Earl Sigurd the Fat of the Orkneys.

Now on the one side of that battle [wrote the Irish annalist] were the shouting, hateful, powerful, wrestling, murderous, hostile Northmen. These had for the purposes of combat, sharp, swift, fatal arrows, which had been anointed and browned in the blood of dragons and toads, and the water snakes of hell. They had with them hideous, barbarous quivers; and polished yellow-shining bows; and strong, broad, green, sharp, rough, dark spears, in the stout, bold, hard hands of pirates. They had also with them polished, pliable, triple-plated, heavy, stout corselets of double-refined iron, and heroic, heavy, hard-striking, strong, powerful, stout swords.

This day, along with King Máel Mórda and all his men of Leinster, these Northmen would do battle not only with Irishmen from a host of kingdoms but also with Brian's Viking subjects from Limerick and Waterford. This would not be a simple battle between Irishmen and Northmen: Irish would fight Irish, and Vikings would fight Vikings.

As Sitric's warriors set out for Dubhghall's Bridge, built to span the deepest channel of the Liffey at *Áth Cliath*, the 'ford of hurdles', the King of Dublin remained behind to command the city's defence. Brian too would not be a combatant, for he was now over seventy years old; as he prayed in his tent for victory his son Murchad led out a mighty host—the men of Munster, the Norse of Limerick and Waterford, Ospak of Man, and Connacht allies. The Dublin army, advancing north-east, crossed the Tolka stream and drew up in formation at Clontarf with their backs to the sea to stand beside their allies from overseas.

Challenges by champions to engage in single combat began the battle; then, to the sound of horrible war-cries, the two sides closed in:

> And there was fought between them a battle furious, bloody, repulsive, crimson, gory, boisterous, manly, rough, fierce, unmerciful, hostile, on both sides; and they began to hew and cleave, and stab, and cut, to slaughter, to mutilate each other ...

Never before had so great a battle been fought on Irish soil. Never before had so many men of noble birth lost their lives in one engagement in Ireland: among them were Murchad, Earl Sigurd, the Mormaer of Mar, Máel Mórda, and the two kings leading the Connacht forces. Late in the afternoon the Leinster-Norse army began to fall back to Dubhghall's Bridge and into the advancing tide, and here there was a fearful slaughter:

> They retreated therefore to the sea, like a herd of cows in heat, from sun, and from gadflies and from insects; and they were pursued closely, rapidly and lightly; and the foreigners were drowned in great numbers in the sea, and they lay in heaps and hundreds ...

Brodar of Man escaped the massacre on the shore and hacked his way through the lines to reach Brian's tent; there he swept aside the bodyguard and, with one blow of his battle-axe, cleft the head of the old king in two. The enraged Munster warriors pursued Brodar, formed a ring around him with branches, cut open his belly, tied his entrails to a tree, and led him round it till he died.

Long after, tales of the battle were recited by northern firesides; Valkyries were seen weaving a web of battle with swords on a loom of death; and in the Icelandic *Njal's Saga* Earl Gilli spoke of his vision before the battle:

> I have been where warriors wrestled,
> High in Erin sang the sword,
> Boss to boss met many bucklers;
> Steel rang sharp on rattling helm;
> I can tell of all their struggle;

Sigurd fell in flight of spears;
Brian fell, but kept his kingdom
Ere he lost one drop of blood.

Episode 24 ∽

'A TREMBLING SOD'

The assassination of Brian Boru at the moment of victory made certain that, for a long time to come, all Ireland would not be ruled by one man. Brian had made the high-kingship a reality, and now the provincial kings were locked in a violent and inconclusive contest to become the ruler of the whole island. Brian's death also ensured that the Vikings would stay. Indeed, their towns and cities continued to grow, and the Northmen did much to promote the modernisation of Ireland by drawing the country more closely into European trade networks. The Norse settlements became like other Irish kingdoms, and they were perpetually involved in interprovincial power struggles. No contender for the high-kingship had any hope of succeeding without the support of Dublin, which in the eleventh century became perhaps the most prosperous and populous city in the Viking world.

Historians began to understand the real importance of Viking Dublin in the 1970s. At that time wholesale clearance to build new civic offices at Wood Quay presented archaeologists with an unrivalled opportunity. The finds were dramatic enough in themselves, but what gave the excavations international importance was the extraordinary level of preservation: wood, sally rods, leather cloth and other fragile organic substances had survived to such a degree that the structure of dwellings, pathways and workshops could be plainly seen. Olivia O'Leary of the *Irish Times* reported on the work in progress:

Down on the site, workers pace their little sections like children on a beach tip-toe around the ankle-high walls of their sand castles. The whole outlines of wooden houses are there. The post and wattle walls come to a foot and more above the ground; the posts are sturdy, about the thickness of your fist, and the wattle twigs wind around them like basket-work cemented with mud ... there are mounds of mussel and cockle shells there. The workers say there was a distinct odour from the cesspits when they were first opened and human turds are carefully removed to the finds tray along with bronze cloakpins and bone combs.

The meticulous removal of centuries-old detritus revealed the extent to which Viking Dublin had become a city of specialised craftsworkers. Tools, generally of iron, were numerous: hammers, a woodworker's plane with its iron blade, axes, drawknives, chisels, punches, awls, boring-bits, tongs, shears, with hones and rotating grindstones for giving a sharp edge to them. Glass linen-smoothers, wooden beetles, weighted spindles, wooden reels, sewing-needles of bronze, bone and iron, and hundreds of fragments of fine woven cloth revealed a sophisticated level of textile-making. The finding of board games, model wooden longships and bone whistles for children captured the public imagin-ation, and the unearthing of a hitherto unknown section of Viking city wall— with remains of severed heads, a babe in arms, and a tenth-century pet terrier on the old shoreline—kept the excavations in the headlines.

Sitric Silkenbeard's father, King Olaf Cuarán, had been baptised in 979 and his people soon after. Sitric himself built Dublin's first cathedral, Christ Church, in 1038—it was probably constructed in wood. It dominated the high ground above the Liffey, overlooking a crowded and thriving community. Some had houses made of wooden planking thrust into the soil, but most were content with thatched dwellings of post and wattle, daubed with mud and manure to keep out the wind and the rain. Here, in good times, rich stews simmered on central hearths. In fair weather, away from the acrid smoke of their cramped dwellings, women, with their hair tied back in fine nets, spun yarn deftly with spindle and whorl, and craftsmen plied their trades: carpen-ters with their chisels; turners with lathes; leatherworkers with punch and awl; tanners curing hides with oak bark in deep wicker-lined pits; cutlers sharp-ening blades on revolving hones; bronze-workers etching intricate designs on bone trial pieces; and comb-makers shaping slivers of antler cast by red deer in the neighbouring woods. Here merchants sold earthenware jars of wine, and bought slaves, hides, and exquisitely worked Irish silver and bronze. The city must also have been a shipbuilding centre, for the remains of the largest Viking ship ever found was discovered to have been made of oak from Dublin.

Dublin was such a prize that the King of Norway, Magnus Barelegs (so called because he gave up trews to wear an Irish tunic), seized the city in 1102 and declared: 'Why should I return home since my heart is in Dublin? There is an Irish girl whom I love better than myself.' However, Magnus was killed in the following year in a skirmish near Downpatrick. Henceforth, the struggle to rule the whole island would be left to Irish kings. So fierce was their war-ring that one annalist declared they were making Ireland 'a trembling sod'.

Episode 25 ᔍ

THE RAPE OF DERVORGILLA

For a century and a half after the Battle of Clontarf the provincial kings of Ireland vied with one another and fought one another to become the High-King of Ireland. The descendants of Brian Boru, the O'Briens, quickly lost power to Dermot mac Máel na mBó, King of Leinster. Dermot seized Dublin in 1052 and in time forced most of the kings of Ireland to acknowledge him as high-king. In addition, he used Dublin's formidable fleet of longships to dominate the Irish Sea and become ruler of the Isle of Man and the Western Isles. Harold Godwinson spent the winter of 1051–2 in Ireland under Dermot's protection, and after Harold had been defeated and killed at the Battle of Hastings in 1066 his sons found refuge with this powerful Irish high-king.

When Dermot was killed in battle in 1072, he was described by an annalist as the 'King of Ireland with opposition'. All succeeding high-kings, winning control of most but never all of Ireland, could be described as 'kings with opposition'. Dermot's replacement was a grandson of Brian Boru, Turlough O'Brien. His son Murtagh O'Brien succeeded him in 1086 and came very close to being the ruler of all Ireland. The most tenacious opposition always seemed to come from Ulster, and for a time an Uí Néill ruler, Donal MacLochlainn, became high-king.

Not only did Irish kings wage war against one another in contest for the high-kingship, but, within each dynasty, there were constant succession disputes—this was almost inevitable when, by Irish law, all sons and grandsons had a claim on the throne when a king died. In these ruthless struggles, defeated claimants were frequently ritually blinded or otherwise maimed.

In 1151 the annals record a great battle at Móin Mór in north Cork and claimed that 7,000 Munstermen were killed. This marked the rise of Turlough O'Connor, King of Connacht, who defeated the O'Briens and divided Munster in two, into Thomond (north Munster) and Desmond (south Munster).

It might be possible to pass over this dreary, seemingly interminable warfare but for the fact that it was to lead to the coming of the Normans to Ireland. That story begins with a deadly conflict between Tiernan O'Rourke, the one-eyed King of Bréifne, and Dermot MacMurrough, King of Leinster. Their quarrel was principally over the rich pastures of the kingdom of Meath, but it was further embittered by the love between Dermot and Tiernan's wife, Dervorgilla. One night in 1152 hooves thundered away from the Bréifne capital of Dromahair as Dermot carried off Dervorgilla together with a great prey of cattle. This humiliation burned in Tiernan's memory and filled his

heart with vengeful hatred to his dying day. The events were recorded by
Gerald of Wales a few years later:

> On an occasion when O'Rourke had gone off on an expedition to far distant
> parts, his wife, whom he had left on an island, was abducted by the aforesaid
> Dermot, who had long been burning with love for her and took advantage
> of her husband's absence. No doubt she was abducted because she wanted
> to be and, since 'woman is always a fickle and inconstant creature', she her-
> self arranged that she should become the kidnapper's prize.
>
> Almost all the world's most notable catastrophes have been caused by
> women, witness Mark Antony and Troy. King O'Rourke was stirred to
> extreme anger on two counts, of which however the disgrace, rather than
> the loss of his wife, grieved him more deeply, and he vented all the venom
> of his fury with a view to revenge.

O'Rourke had to wait fourteen years for his revenge, for Dermot had
hitched his fortunes to the rising star of Murtagh MacLochlainn. In 1166
Murtagh captured and blinded the Ulaid king, Eochaid MacDonleavy, in defiance of solemn guarantees given by the Archbishop of Armagh. The revulsion
following this act of treachery caused Murtagh's support to drop away, and
shortly afterwards this high-king was killed in a skirmish. The Norman-
French poem *The Song of Dermot and the Earl* continues the story:

> O'Rourke, much grieving,
> To Connacht went in all haste.
> To the king of Connacht he relates all;
> Very earnestly he besought him
> To make ready for him
> Some of his household and of his men
> So that he could avenge his shame.

Rory O'Connor of Connacht, now rapidly establishing his claim to the high-
kingship, gave his blessing to Tiernan's punitive expedition. The men of
Bréifne, supported by the Dublin Norse and the King of Meath, swept into
Leinster and devastated MacMurrough's kingdom. Dermot had no choice but
to flee from Ireland. Rory O'Connor then made a circuit of Ireland and won
the submission of all the kings of the island. At last it seemed that one man
had become the High-King of Ireland without opposition.

Rory O'Connor, however, had reckoned without Dermot and his new-
found friends.

Episode 26 ⌇

'AT BAGINBUN, IRELAND WAS LOST AND WON'

Early in the tenth century Charles the Simple, King of France, desperate to end the ravaging of his dominions by the Northmen, made an agreement to give Rolf the Ganger a province of northern France in return for peace. These Vikings settled contentedly, married French girls and learned to speak their language. Soon this province of Normandy became a powerful state, and in 1066, led by their Duke William, the Normans defeated Harold of England at Hastings. The conquest of England was ruthlessly completed within a few years, and Norman barons were beginning to penetrate into south Wales and southern Scotland. Other Normans carved out a kingdom for themselves in southern Italy and Sicily, while the descendants of William the Conqueror extended their dominions in other parts of France. The genius of the Normans for organisation and effective government, together with their skill in warfare, made them feared and respected far and wide.

> O king of heaven, awful is the deed done in Ireland today, the kalends of August, that is, the expulsion overseas, by the men of Ireland, of Dermot son of Donnchad MacMurrough, King of Leinster and the Northmen. Alas, alas, what shall I do?

So exclaimed the scribe of the Book of Leinster when Dermot, his wife and daughter and a small group of followers fled to England on 1 August 1166. Dermot, however, had plans to recover his kingdom. He called on his friend Robert fitz Harding, the reeve of Bristol. Fitz Harding advised him to seek out his king, Henry II, by now the most powerful monarch in western Europe. Dermot travelled to Aquitaine and, according to *The Song of Dermot and the Earl,* addressed Henry as follows:

> Hear, noble king, whence I was born, of what country.
> Of Ireland I was born a lord, in Ireland acknowledged king;
> But wrongfully my own people have cast me out of my kingdom.
> To you I come to make plaint, good sire,
> In the presence of the barons of your empire.
> Your liege-man I shall become henceforth all the days of my life,
> On condition that you be my helper so that I do not lose at all ...

Henry listened sympathetically, for Dermot had championed his claim to the English throne in the past, and, according to Gerald of Wales, he granted him letters patent in the following terms:

> Henry, King of England, Duke of Normandy and Aquitaine, and Count of Anjou, gives his greetings to all his faithful subjects.... When you receive this present letter, be advised that we have admitted to our most intimate grace and favour Dermot, Prince of Leinster. Wherefore, if any person from within our wide dominions wishes to help in restoring him, as having done us fealty and homage, let him know that he has our goodwill and permission to do this.

On a clear day Norman barons in south-west Wales could see the mountains of Wexford and Wicklow across the sea, seeming to beckon them on to further conquest. Now they could go by invitation, and eagerly they pledged their support to Dermot in return for promises of land. To the greatest of them, Richard fitz Gilbert de Clare, Lord of Striguil, better known as 'Strongbow', MacMurrough pledged the hand of his daughter Aoife in marriage, and the kingdom of Leinster when Dermot himself died.

In August 1167 Dermot slipped back to Leinster with a small force of Flemings under Richard fitz Godebert of Rhos. Naturally the high-king, Rory O'Connor, and Tiernan O'Rourke of Bréifne made an appearance, but they allowed themselves to bought off: Dermot paid Tiernan a hundred ounces of gold as the honour-price for the abduction of Dervorgilla fifteen years before, and to Rory he gave seven hostages.

Dermot passed an anxious year in 1168 without any sign of Norman help. Not until May 1169 did a substantial contingent arrive: some three hundred fighting-men, packed into three ships setting out from Milford Haven and led by Robert fitz Stephen, Hervey de Montmorency and Maurice de Prendergast. Landing at Bannow Bay they advanced on the Viking town of Wexford and forced its submission. Such a modest force was not enough to enable Dermot to recover his kingdom. Dermot had to contend with an attack from the neighbouring kingdom of Ossory, and when the high-king and the King of Bréifne returned, Dermot had no choice but to hand over his son Conor as a hostage.

At last, early in May 1170, reinforcements commanded by Raymond 'le Gros' fitz Gerald arrived in a creek eight miles to the east of Waterford city. This place is known as Baginbun, named after the two ships which carried over the invaders, *La Bague* and *La Bonne*, and immortalised in the rhyme:

> At the creek of Baginbun
> Ireland was lost and won.

A momentous new era in the history of the island had begun.

Episode 27 ∿

WATERFORD AND DUBLIN:
A TALE OF TWO SIEGES

The foreigners who came to help Dermot MacMurrough recover his kingdom of Leinster were as much Welsh as they were Norman and Flemish. At the core was a tightly-knit family group, all descended from a remarkable Welsh princess, Nesta, daughter of Rhys ap Tewdwr, who had children by Stephen, Constable of Cardigan (father of Robert fitz Stephen), King Henry I of England (grandfather of Meiler fitz Henry), Gerald of Windsor, to whom she was married—and she had children by at least one other man. Even if Gerald was not actually their father or grandfather, most were happy to be named fitz Gerald and to be described as the 'Geraldines'.

Raymond le Gros and his men ensconced themselves in the old rath at Baginbun and soon found themselves besieged by a mixed force of Norse from Waterford and Irish from the kingdom of Decies. Outnumbered ten to one, their situation was desperate, as Gerald of Wales—himself also a Geraldine—informs us:

> Raymond with his men—conspicuous for their gallantry, though few in number—went out to meet them and engaged them in a most unequal contest. But because such a small force, though an excellent one, could not withstand such large numbers on level ground, they turned back to their camp. In their haste to enter it, they allowed the enemy, who were pursuing them from behind, inside the doors.... When Raymond saw that his men were in the direst straits, he turned bravely to face the enemy, and in the very doorway transfixed with his sword the first to enter.

The defenders then drove out from the fort a herd of cattle, and in the ensuing stampede the attackers were scattered and suffered fearful slaughter. Soon after, according to *The Song of Dermot and the Earl*, followed an atrocity:

> Of the Irish there were taken
> Quite as many as seventy.
> But the noble knights
> Had them beheaded.
> To a wench they gave
> An axe of tempered steel,
> And she beheaded them all

And threw their bodies over the cliff,
Because she had that day
Lost her lover in the combat.
Alice of Abergavenny was her name
Who served the Irish thus.

Meanwhile Strongbow was on his way. Gerald of Wales continues:

Having made the necessary preparations for such an important venture,
Earl Richard [Strongbow] passed through the coastal regions of south
Wales on his way to St David's, and collected together the pick of the fighting men in those parts. When everything needful for a naval expedition on
such a scale had been procured and made ready, he embarked at Milford
Haven, a following wind filled his sails, and he put in at Waterford with two
hundred knights and about a thousand others on St Bartholomew's Eve....

On the following day, when rumour had spread of this event, Raymond
went to meet the earl with forty knights.... They joined forces to carry forward to the assault of the city those battle standards which were already
menacing its walls. They were twice vigorously repulsed by the citizens.
Then Raymond noticed a small building which hung down from the town
wall on the outside by a beam. He quickly sent in armed men to cut down
the aforesaid beam. The building immediately collapsed, and with it a considerable part of the wall. The invaders eagerly effected an entry, rushed
into the city and won a most bloody victory, large numbers of the citizens
being slaughtered in the streets.

At the moment of victory Dermot MacMurrough arrived, and, after the
rulers of Waterford, both called Sitric, were executed in Reginald's Tower, his
daughter Aoife was married to Strongbow amidst the ruins of the city. The
next objective was Dublin. Here the high-king, Rory O'Connor, had assembled a formidable army outside the walls at the urgent request of Earl Hasculf,
the city's ruler. Hasculf guarded the approaches along the coast at Bray and
the Scalp, while from the plain of Clondalkin Rory kept watch over Slí
Cualann, the road on the western side of the Wicklow Mountains. Dermot
knew his own kingdom, however, and brought his allies across the thickly
wooded plateau from Glenmacnaas to Sally Gap, and from there over the
flank of Kippure Mountain to Rathfarnham.

Seeing the impressive array of mailed horsemen and archers emerge from
the woods, Hasculf sent out Laurence O'Toole, the Archbishop of Dublin, to
seek terms. The Norman adventurers had come too far to parley now. With
Milo de Cogan and Raymond le Gros in the van, Strongbow's men made a
furious assault on the walls, overran the city and butchered many citizens.

Hasculf was fortunate to make his escape by ship. So swift had been the Norman triumph that Rory could do nothing for Dublin; the high-king's sole response was to put three hostages to death, one of them a son of Dermot MacMurrough. Strongbow was near to his objective of creating a dominion for himself in Ireland—and this was a matter of growing concern for his liege lord, Henry II.

Episode 28 ⌒

HENRY II COMES TO IRELAND

Strongbow had seized Waterford and Dublin, and Dermot MacMurrough had been restored to his kingdom of Leinster; but neither Hasculf, Earl of Dublin, nor Rory O'Connor, High-King of Ireland, were prepared to accept this new state of affairs. During the winter of 1170–71 the newcomers repaired Dublin city's defences and built a motte castle surrounded by a deep ditch. Then, in the spring of 1171, the whole Norman enterprise was threatened with disaster. Hearing that Dermot was dying in Ferns, Strongbow sped southwards to claim the kingdom pledged to him, only to find that the Leinstermen, rallying to Murtagh MacMurrough, had risen in revolt against their new overlords.

Earl Hasculf now returned with sixty longships filled with warriors from the Northern Isles, led by John the Wode, a famous berserker fighter. At the mouth of the Liffey the Northmen leaped from their vessels to advance in phalanx on the city walls. They were, in the words of Gerald of Wales,

> warlike figures, clad in mail in every part of their body after the Danish manner. Some wore long coats of mail, others iron plates skilfully knitted together, and they had round, red shields protected by iron round the edge. These men, whose iron will matched their armour, drew up their ranks and made an attack on the walls at the eastern gate.

At the first onset a knight's hip-bone, protected though it was by an iron cuirass, was cut away with one blow of a Viking battle-axe. Milo de Cogan, appointed governor of Dublin by Strongbow, was forced to retreat behind the wall; his brother Richard and his men, however, made an unobserved sortie through the southern gate and rounded on the attackers' rear.

The Northmen now faced a new enemy. Mounted knights—protected by chain-mail from head to toe, carrying kite-shaped leather shields, secure on high-fronted saddles and with their feet firmly placed in stirrups—were able to charge the foe directly with long lances. In support were Welsh longbow-men, and Flemish foot-soldiers with crossbows shooting mail-piercing arrows. The Norse were put to flight; John the Wode was slain by Walter de Ridelsford; and Hasculf was dragged back from the shore.

His life was spared [recorded Gerald of Wales] with a view to ransom, and he was in the court, in Milo's presence, when in everyone's hearing he made the following angry assertion: 'This is only our first attempt. But if only I am spared, this will be followed by other expeditions on a far larger scale, and having a different outcome from this one.' When they heard him say this he was immediately beheaded on Milo's orders, and these arrogant words cost him that life which he had been mercifully granted only a short while before.

Next the Normans had to face a great Gaelic host led by Rory O'Connor with his own men of Connacht, O'Rourke of Bréifne, O'Carroll from Ulster, and Murtagh MacMurrough with his Leinster kinsmen. With no knowledge of siege-engines, the high-king counted on starvation to bring the invaders to sub-mission, and with the help of thirty longships from Man and the Isles, he very nearly succeeded. A daring stroke was needed to extricate the garrison from its desperate position. Shortly after noon, on an early September day in 1171, picked fighting-men burst out of Dublin, the van of twenty knights led by Raymond le Gros, followed by Milo de Cogan's company of thirty knights, with Strongbow in the rear commanding forty knights. Crossing Dubhgall's Bridge and taking a circular route over the Tolka, they fell on the Irish camp so suddenly that Rory, bathing in the river at Castleknock, barely escaped with his life. Hundreds of the Irish were slain, and the foreigners now had secure possession of Dublin.

Henry II, the most powerful monarch in western Europe, ruler of England, Normandy, Brittany, Anjou, Aquitaine, and much of Wales, viewed Strongbow's victories with deep misgiving. The defeat of the high-king pre-sented him with a spectre—an independent Norman state which could threaten his empire from the west. Henry prepared a great expedition for Ireland, though the cares of his vast dominions lay heavy on his shoulders. There was another reason for removing himself from his usual sphere of activity: he was deeply implicated in the murder of Thomas Becket, Archbishop of Canterbury, and cardinal legates had arrived in Normandy to put embarrassing questions to the king concerning the atrocity.

On St Luke's Day, 18 October 1171, four hundred ships entered Waterford haven, and King Henry's progress from there to Dublin was one of the finest triumphs of his long reign. So great was the royal retinue and baggage that camp had to be made outside the city walls at the Thingmote, a forty-foot-high man-made hill where the Vikings held their assemblies. On this spot a great hall was built of stripped willow rods. Here Henry held court and received the submission of a queue of Irish kings, acknowledging his new title as Lord of Ireland.

Episode 29 ∽

THE LORDSHIP OF IRELAND

As the solemn festival of our Lord's birth drew near, the princes of that land came to Dublin in great number to view the king's court. There they greatly admired the sumptuous and plentiful fare of the English table and the most elegant service of the royal domestics. Throughout the great hall, in obedience to the king's wishes they began to eat the flesh of the heron, which they had hitherto loathed.

Henry II was a noted practical joker, and the rank, fishy flesh of the heron was loathed not only by the Irish but by everyone. Courtesy and respect prevailed, nevertheless. The Irish had never seen an army of such size in their country before and were certainly not about to put its strength to the test. From the moment he had landed in Waterford, Irish kings had lined up to make their submission to this alien ruler and to acknowledge him as Lord of Ireland. Of course, they may have had little understanding of feudal terminology and of the obligations involved in giving fealty to a liege lord. At the same time, Henry did not attempt to detach Irish princes from their duty to their high-king, and when Rory O'Connor made his submission, there was no suggestion that he should cease to be high-king.

Henry II possessed a great asset: back in 1155 John of Salisbury, adviser to the Archbishop of Canterbury, had prevailed on Pope Adrian IV to grant Ireland to Henry. It just so happened that Adrian, born Nicholas Breakspear, was the only Englishman ever to have been elected pope. John of Salisbury explained later:

In response to my petition the pope granted and donated Ireland to the illustrious King of England, Henry, to be held by him and his successors.... He did this in virtue of the long-established right, reputed to derive from the donation of Constantine, whereby all islands are considered to belong to the Roman Church.

This was the notorious bull *Laudabiliter.*

At the time of its original issue Henry II's mother, the Empress Matilda, discouraged him from attempting to act on this papal grant. Now the bull *Laudabiliter* suited him well: it gave him the opportunity to make amends with the church in the wake of the murder in Canterbury Cathedral of Thomas Becket. Furthermore, English and Irish bishops alike keenly supported a campaign to reform the church in Ireland. Gerald of Wales, a cleric himself, was in no doubt that such reform was overdue:

> This is a filthy people, wallowing in vice. Of all peoples it is the least instructed in the rudiments of the Faith. They do not yet pay tithes or first fruits or contract marriages. They do not avoid incest. They do not attend God's church with true reverence. Moreover, men in many places in Ireland, I shall not say marry, but rather debauch, the wives of their dead brothers.

This condemnation, as with many other observations made by Gerald on the Irish, was completely unfair. It was true that the Celtic Church still deviated somewhat from accepted practice in the Roman Church—in particular by allowing many clergy to marry—but even before the arrival of the Normans synods had been held to promote standardisation. In any case, Henry II won credit not only from the papacy but also from the higher clergy in Ireland for sponsoring a synod at Cashel to promote reform.

Perhaps Henry's main purpose in coming to Ireland was to clip Strongbow's wings, though his fear that the earl intended to set up a separate Norman state in Ireland was probably unfounded. The city of Dublin, for which Strongbow's men fought so hard, the king gave to the men of Bristol who had fitted out his great expedition to Ireland. He put a strict limit on the borders of Strongbow's possession of Leinster by granting the fertile land of Meath—for so long disputed between Dermot and Tiernan—to Hugh de Lacy, provided he could conquer it. For himself Henry took the title of 'Lord of Ireland'—with the unwritten assumption that the lordship covered only the territory possessed by the Norman newcomers. During the winter of 1171–2 Henry became anxious to return to the heart of his dominions:

> Then Aeolus burst asunder the bars of his prison and the heaving billows of the sea were churned up. The storms raged so unceasingly and with such persistence that throughout that whole winter scarcely a single ship had succeeded in making a crossing to the island, and no one could get any news whatsoever from other lands.... Meanwhile the king stayed at Wexford, being extremely anxious to hear any rumours from across the sea ... but after mid-Lent the winds at long last went into the east, and ships

arrived both from England and Aquitaine, bringing news of a grave development and of evil deeds.

Henry returned to a sea of troubles, but his lordship of Ireland was now firmly established, and it was destined to grow.

Episode 30 ∾

CONQUESTS AND A FAILED TREATY

In May 1172 Henry II faced the papal legates at Savigny in western France, and his argument that he had gone to Ireland to reform the church there served him well. The king then had to contend with the rebellion of his three older sons, Henry, Geoffrey and Richard. When the French king, Louis VII, attacked his possessions, Henry had to call on the assistance of his Irish vassals. Strongbow and de Lacy brought over strong contingents which helped Henry to reassert his authority in his dominions.

While Henry II and leading Normans were absent from Ireland, Irish kings quickly forgot the submissions they had made in 1171. Though the high-king himself took up arms, there was no concerted Gaelic resistance to the Norman newcomers. Dermot MacCarthy, King of Desmond, and Donal O'Brien, King of Thomond, were such inveterate enemies that they were both prepared, when it suited them, to fight alongside Norman adventurers. The inevitable consequence was that Norman barons were able to win new territories for themselves.

Hugh de Lacy made a successful advance into Meath, where he was challenged by Tiernan O'Rourke. A parley was arranged, Gerald of Wales informs us:

The one-eyed king [O'Rourke], nursing villainous treachery in his heart, pretended to go a little to the side to make water, and signalled to his men to come up at once with the utmost speed. Returning with axe raised, the traitor cut off the arm of the interpreter, Hugh de Lacy twice fell backwards, and the knight Griffin with his lance transfixed O'Rourke. His head was cut off and afterwards sent to the English king. All were routed and scattered across the plains, and the slaughter continued on a massive scale right up to the edge of the distant forests.

So died the King of Bréifne, described in the Annals of Tigernach as 'deedful leopard of the Gael, Leth Cuinn's man of battle and lasting defence, Erin's raider and invader, surpasser of the Gael in might and abundance'.

Both Rory O'Connor and Henry II were anxious to restore some stability to the country. Their representatives met at Windsor in 1175, and Henry agreed to forbid further Norman conquests provided the high-king would keep Irish rulers at peace. This treaty was a complete failure. Henry was too busy dealing with his rebellious sons, while Rory faced rebellion from his own sons and grandchildren. Milo de Cogan made a successful raid into Connacht in 1177 at the invitation of one of Rory's sons, Murchad—when Milo left, the high-king had Murchad blinded to punish him for his perfidy.

The Normans thrust into the south-west and conquered most of Desmond with the help of Donal O'Brien of Thomond. The year 1177 also witnessed the invasion of Ulster.

Early in February John de Courcy, a knight from Cumbria, took twenty-two mailed horsemen and around three hundred foot-soldiers out of Dublin northwards over the Moyry Pass and then eastwards to Downpatrick, the capital of the ancient kingdom of the Dál Fiatach. So unexpected was this Norman incursion that the local king, Rory MacDonleavy, fled with all his people. Invoking his authority as over-king of the Ulaid, MacDonleavy returned with a great host. Defensive earthworks, hastily thrown up by de Courcy's men, were too incomplete, and so it was by the banks of the River Quoile, Gerald of Wales informs us, that the battle was fought:

> To begin with they showered down a hail of arrows and spears at long range. Then they came to close quarters, lance encountered lance, sword met sword.... After an intense and for a long time indecisive struggle between these unevenly matched forces, John's courage at last won him the victory, and a great number of the enemy were killed along the sea shore where they had taken refuge.... Blood pouring from their wounds remained on the surface of the slippery ground and easily came up to the knees and legs of their pursuers.

An even greater coalition, including the leading prelates of the province, joined Rory in a great assault on Downpatrick in June, but to no avail. The Annals of Inisfallen record:

> The Archbishop of Armagh, the Bishop of Down, and all the clergy were taken prisoners; and the English got possession of the croziers of St Comgall and St Dachiarog, the Book of Armagh, besides a bell called Ceolan an Tighearna. They afterwards, however, set the bishops at liberty and restored the Book of Armagh and the bell, but they killed all the inferior clergy and kept the other noble relics.

Over the next few years John de Courcy fought many campaigns and seized control of the coastlands. The sea was his essential lifeline, made more secure when he married Affreca, daughter of Godred, King of Man, which gave him the use of a formidable fleet. For quarter of a century he ruled his Ulster lands with as much independence as a warlord. And like all the Norman adventurers, he kept his conquests secure by building castles.

Episode 31 ᠕

JOHN, LORD OF IRELAND

Even though they were already going out of fashion in England, motte castles were erected in every part of Ireland occupied by the first Norman invaders. A motte was a fortification erected on top of an artificial mound; the steeply sided, roughly circular mound was partly constructed with soil from its surrounding ditch but raised higher by soil brought in from further afield, carefully sloped inwards to provide stability. A few had an additional base court, or 'bailey', such as Dromore in Co. Down, particularly if they were intended to house permanent garrisons. The knight in command of a motte lived in a fortified hall built on the mound's flat top; the hall was generally made of timber, but later might be replaced by a stone tower, as at Clough in Co. Down. In Co. Wexford especially, heavily fortified moated houses were favoured.

Once a territory had been pacified, it was secured by stone castles. The site had to be chosen carefully, with solid rock as a stable base for preference. The largest of all was Trim Castle, built by Hugh de Lacy, extending over three acres, though it may not have been complete before this Lord of Meath was murdered in 1186 by an Irishman known as 'the Fox'. At its centre was a massive 'donjon', square in shape, to which was added a square tower at each of the four corners. The main defences were curtain walls which formed a D-shape along the banks of the River Boyne, from which water was diverted to make a water-filled ditch around the walls. The largest keep in Ireland was erected at Carrickfergus on a tongue of rock jutting into Belfast Lough. Behind a curtain wall, masons built this massive rectangular tower with walls nine feet thick from local basalt, red sandstone from Whiteabbey, and cream Cultra limestone shipped across the lough, to rise ninety feet above the rock. Some of the most formidable castles were built for the crown, most notably by King John.

When he was parcelling out responsibilities to his untrustworthy sons in 1177, Henry II decided to make his youngest, John, Lord of Ireland. Since John was then only ten, the lordship had to be administered by a royal governor—as it was ever after. In 1185 John was sent to visit his lordship, and with him travelled his tutor, Gerald of Wales:

As soon as the king's son arrived in Ireland, there came to meet him at Waterford the Irish of those parts, men of some note, who had hitherto been loyal to the English and peacefully disposed. They greeted him as their lord and received him with the kiss of peace. But our newly arrived Normans treated them with contempt and derision, and showing them scant respect, pulled some of them about by their beards, which were large and flowing according to the native custom. For their part they removed themselves and all their belongings to a safe distance, and made for the court of the king of Limerick.... So with one accord they plotted to resist.

Henry II died in 1189; his son Henry was already dead; Geoffrey had been fatally wounded during a tournament in Paris; and Richard the Lionheart succeeded his father. After a colourful career on crusade and in foreign captivity Richard died in 1199, and John was now not only Lord of Ireland but King of England. John proved to be a vengeful and capricious monarch who trusted no one. When John de Courcy spoke out of turn about the succession, John authorised the son of Hugh de Lacy, also called Hugh, to drive him out of his conquests in Antrim and Down. King John ignominiously lost possession of Normandy, and this made him all the more determined to tighten his control in Ireland. Norman barons in Ireland had become rich and powerful at the expense of the Gaelic Irish. They included William the Marshal, who had married Strongbow's daughter and inherited Leinster to add to his estates in Wales and Normandy; Theobald Walter, ancestor of the Butlers, who conquered much of the counties of Kilkenny and Tipperary; and William de Braose, Lord of Limerick. King John was deeply jealous of their power.

William de Braose became John's sworn enemy. Not only had he fallen behind in payments to the crown, but, worse still, his wife Matilda de Saint-Valéry had denied the king her son as hostage, saying to the royal messenger: 'I will not deliver up my son to your lord, King John, for he basely murdered his nephew Arthur, when he should have kept him in honourable custody.' As John prepared a great expedition to break the power of his overmighty subject, de Braose took refuge in Ulster with his kinsman Hugh de Lacy. On 20 June 1210 the king was in Waterford with 7,000 knights, archers and foot-soldiers. It was the mightiest army yet seen in Ireland. Who on the island could resist his power now?

Episode 32 ~

'DREADING THE FURY OF THE KING'

Apart from some terse entries in the annals and parchment rolls recording royal expenditure, there is no detailed account of King John's momentous expedition to Ireland in the year 1210. We do know that nine days after disembarking at Waterford on 20 June he was in Dublin, his force increased by feudal levies from Munster and Leinster. Unavailingly did barons from the north plead for mercy towards their lord, Hugh de Lacy. John advanced and was joined in Meath by Cathal Crobhderg O'Connor, who had succeeded his brother Rory as King of Connacht. The Annals of Inisfallen record:

> When Hugh de Lacy had discovered that the king was going to the north, he burned his own castles and he himself fled to Carrickfergus, leaving the chiefs of his people burning, levelling and destroying the castles of the country and dreading the fury of the king....When the king saw this disrespect offered him, he marched from Drogheda to Carlingford.

To avoid a likely ambush in the Moyry Pass, the king transported his army over Carlingford Lough with a bridge made with boats and hundreds of pontoons brought from Dorset, Somerset and York. Then, while his men marched by the coast by Kilkeel and Annalong, the king himself sailed to Ardglass in Lecale and rested there in Jordan de Saukeville's castle. Dundrum Castle looked impregnable with its great round keep recently constructed by de Lacy. John, however, had brought with him an intimidating array of siege-engines; there must have been a fight here, for workmen were paid on 14 July to make repairs to the castle:

> To Nicholas Carpenter, ten shillings; Ralph de Presbury, fifteen shillings; Master Osbert Quarrier and Alberic Ditcher, seven shillings and sixpence; Master Pinell and Ernulf, miners, one mark.

Two days later John was in Downpatrick, where he paid £40 to his soldiers and lost five shillings in a board game with Warin fitz Gerald. Soon afterwards siege was laid to Carrickfergus by land and by sea, and in a short time the castle surrendered. King John stayed at Carrickfergus for ten days making many payments, including £532 to Henry de Ver as wages for bailiffs, knights and sailors; 1,004 marks to English noblemen; and £2 12s 6d for repairs to the castle. He ordered the Bishop of Norwich to have galleys built at Antrim to patrol Lough Neagh; received homage from the King of Tír Eóghain; paid sixty shillings to mariners from Bayonne; lost another ten shillings to Warin fitz Gerald at Downpatrick early in August; and then left for England.

And what happened to William de Braose and Hugh de Lacy? They both escaped to France, but Matilda de Braose and her son William were captured at sea and brought to King John. Matilda and her infant son were cast into prison and there, by the king's orders, starved to death. Hugh de Lacy survived to be given back his earldom of Ulster in the reign of Henry III.

On his departure, King John had the satisfaction of knowing that not a baron, king or chieftain would defy his authority. The king had seven cantreds or baronies in his possession in Connacht, and the ruler of the remainder of that province, Cathal Crobhderg, paid fealty as his liege subject. The castles of Carrickfergus, Dundrum, Athlone, Trim and several other great Irish fortresses were under direct royal control. In 1204 John had ordered the building of Dublin Castle:

> We command you to construct a strong castle there with good ditches and strong walls in a suitable place for the governance and, if need be, the defence of the town; for this at present you are to take 300 marks which Geoffrey fitz Robert owes us.

Dublin Castle swiftly became the administrative heart of the lordship. Here taxes, rents from royal demesne lands, fines and other profits of justice were accounted for at the exchequer—which an illustration of the time shows was, indeed, a chequer-board—staffed by a treasurer, the chancellor and barons of the exchequer. Here too was the letter-writing office directed by the chancellor where official rolls and correspondence were stored. The chancellor also had charge of the great seal and had to travel about with the royal governor to ensure that documents were authenticated. The royal governor acted as the viceroy, chaired meetings of the council, and called up leading barons to provide military support when required. The common law of England became the law of the lordship of Ireland, and it was administered by the royal governor, travelling justices and by sheriffs. The process of creating counties had begun; the county was the equivalent of a shire in England, and here the sheriff had responsibility, with the power to call out a posse of local men if needed.

The number of counties increased steadily in the thirteenth century, a time when the frontiers of the English lordship of Ireland were being extended deep into Gaelic territory.

Episode 33 ∿

THE ENGLISH COLONY

When Strongbow died in 1176, the only heir to his possessions in Leinster was his daughter Isabella. On coming of age in 1189, she wed William the Marshal, one of the most powerful barons in the land and owner of vast estates in Normandy, England, Wales and—now, thanks to his marriage—Ireland. When King John died in 1216, Marshal (who had adopted his title as his surname) was chosen to be regent until Henry iii came of age. All this time he worked hard and often ruthlessly to promote the economic development of his Leinster lands.

Three large rivers—the Barrow, the Nore and the Suir—ran through the heartland of Marshal's estates. As they were navigable far upstream and accessible to foreign trade, Marshal cleared the Irish from their fertile valleys (including the MacGillapatricks, the rulers of Ossory), introduced tenants from England and Wales, and ordered the building of towns along their banks. He made Kilkenny the capital of his lordship of Leinster, and large towns grew up around his castles of Carlow and Ferns. His prize project was New Ross, a deep-water port he developed just below where the Barrow joins the Nore. New Ross soon became a great trading centre, outstripping Wexford and Waterford and rivalling Dublin. Between 1275 and 1279 £2,079 was raised in wool custom dues from New Ross, £658 more than from Waterford, its nearest competitor in Ireland's wool trade. During the same years New Ross exported no fewer than 1,871,207 fleeces and 623,402 hides. When after William Marshal died New Ross was threatened by a baronial quarrel, the citizens decided to work with one accord to protect the town, an event celebrated in the Norman-French poem, *The Walling of New Ross*:

> I have a desire to versify in French
> If you will be pleased to listen,
> For words that are not heard
> Are not worth a clove of garlic ...
> I shall tell you the name of the town:
> 'Ros' you are to call it,
> It is the new bridge of Ros.
> What they feared was that they had no town walls ...
> They made a resolution thus; that a wall of stone and mortar
> They would build round the town.

The hundreds of labourers they hired made little progress, so the citizens agreed to do the work themselves, beginning on Mondays with the vintners, mercers, merchants and drapers:

A thousand and more I tell you truly,
Go to work there every Monday
With fine banners and insignia
And flutes and tabors.
And as soon as it strikes three
The citizens return home
And their banners go ahead of them.
The young folk singing loudly,
Carolling up and down the town,
Joyfully go to labour.
And the priests, when they have sung mass,
Go to work at the fosse,
And apply themselves energetically;
More so than other people ...
The seamen, when they are at home,
In fine manner go to the fosse;
Their banner goes before them, a ship painted in the middle ...
On Tuesday then following
Go tailors and robe trimmers ...
On Wednesday then following
Goes another group of people; leather workers, tanners, butchers ...
Their banners are painted as befits their trade.

The bakers and small traders worked on Thursdays, the porters on Fridays, and finally 350 carpenters on Saturdays—all worked with a will until the wall was finished; and indeed, the ramparts of New Ross are still impressive today.

Other successful Norman ports included Drogheda, founded by Hugh de Lacy in the 1180s; Dundalk, laid out by the de Verdons; and Carrickfergus, begun by John de Courcy and then developed as a royal town thereafter. The Vikings had built Ireland's first towns, but it was left to the Normans to develop inland towns. Those who accompanied the first Norman invaders were for the most part English, Welsh and Flemish, hoping to advance their fortunes in Ireland. Settling in hostile territory, they tended to cluster round mottes, stone castles and defended manor houses to form the nucleus of the majority of the island's inland towns, with the exception of Ulster. Kings and barons alike were eager to promote urban growth, since it brought increased revenues and customs. Charters were issued giving towns certain privileges, including the right to hold annual fairs and weekly markets. The areas most heavily colonised included the countryside north of Dublin, much of Meath, Wexford county and the valleys of the rivers flowing into Waterford harbour. Concentrations of placenames ending with *ton* or *town* indicate where settlement of these newcomers was most successful. Examples include: Trimleston, Julianstown, Gormanstown and Bellewstown in Co. Meath; Damastown, Milltown, Booterstown and Williamstown in Co. Dublin; Piercetown, Horetown, Bastardstown and Heavenstown in Co. Wexford; and Thomastown, Rochestown and Nicholastown in Co. Kilkenny. Inhabitants included craftsmen and merchants, but the great majority of colonists had come over to farm the land.

Episode 34 ∽

FEUDAL IRELAND

By the late thirteenth century around two-thirds of Ireland had been conquered by the Normans. The newcomers had taken the most fertile land, and the reason why wild, mountainous country was left to the Gaelic Irish was partly because the land was so unyielding that it was hardly worth the bother of seizing it.

The 'lordship of Ireland' was, in practice, the conquered land ruled by the King of England who from the time of King John was also the Lord of Ireland. Over this lordship French feudal law, modified somewhat by English custom, prevailed. Elaborate rules regulated the services to be rendered to a lord, and the duties of a lord to protect those who gave service. At the top were the great lords who gave military service to the crown in return for their estates. For example, Hugh de Lacy, Lord of Meath, had to provide fifty knights to Henry II. These barons sublet much of their land to 'free tenants' who had to provide military service as rent. These men in turn would sublet to humbler individuals who paid money or labour service for their farms. In the most densely settled manors the native Irish were forced out. Generally, however, Irish farmers were allowed to stay on, provided they accepted a reduced status in society—indeed, Hugh de Lacy offered free cows to Irish farmers to come back to the lands he had conquered in Meath. These Irish, equivalent to villeins and serfs in England, were known as 'betaghs' from the Irish word for a food-rendering client, *biatach*.

A manor was the lord's estate. A 1304 survey of the manor of Cloncurry, Co. Kildare, showed that there were: 43 free tenants; 112 burgesses holding two ploughlands—that is, about 600 acres—for 112 shillings a year; 40 farmers renting anything from twenty acres to half an acre; 63 betaghs holding thirty-four and a half acres between them; and 24 cottars paying between 2d and 4d a year for their little plots. Some lesser tenants paid rent in the form of free labour, but at Cloncurry the manor depended on paid service:

> The weeding of an acre costs one penny and the cost of mowing, tying and stooking in the field of an acre of wheat is 10 pence, and of an acre of oats is 8 pence, and the cost of carting and stacking in the haggard and the thatching of the stack is 3 pence per acre. And the cost of threshing a crannock of oats is 2 pence. And 5 crannocks of wheat and of oats can be winnowed for one penny.... And each driver and carter gets for his wages 6 shillings and the sower gets the same as the bird-scarer.

Fragments from manorial account books for Grangegorman and Old Ross include incidental expenses such as 15d for a vet—described as 'a certain medical man'; 3½d for sulphur and 21d for butter to heal the sore necks of oxen; and 1½d a day to a man to make holes in four thousand shingles destined for the granary roof.

The inclusion in placenames of the element 'grange' provides a clue that the newcomers placed a greater emphasis than before on the cultivation of corn. Certainly the Irish grew a great deal of corn, but the Normans wanted to increase output for export—they knew that there was a good market for it particularly in the cloth-making areas of Flanders. In this they were helped by a distinct improvement in the weather in the twelfth and thirteenth centuries. Wheat became a more popular crop. On the larger manors there were now eight oxen in a plough team, which was reckoned to be able to plough twenty-five acres in a season.

The lord's personal farm, which supplied his household, retainers and visitors, was a compact estate known as the demesne. All the rest of the manor was cultivated in large, open fields, where tenants held strips in each to take their share of good and bad soil. One man in Rathcoole, Co. Dublin, had twenty-six acres of arable land widely scattered about in no fewer than twenty strips. The open fields, by agreement, followed a three-course rotation of crops: winter corn, spring corn, and fallow—in other words, a third of the land was left uncultivated in rotation to allow it to recover fertility. The main income of manors still depended on domestic stock, however. The most significant change was the growing emphasis on sheep to provide wool for sale to the Frescobaldi, the Bardi and the Ricardi, great Italian wool merchants from Lucca and Florence.

In the lordship of Ireland the growth in profits and population had been spectacular during the thirteenth century. There was little indication that the ensuing century would be marked by a succession of disasters which came close to destroying it.

Episode 35 ∽

'A GREAT AFFLICTION BEFELL THE COUNTRY'

The first entry in the Annals of Connacht is for the year 1224:

> A heavy and terrible shower fell in part of Connacht this year which brought about disease and very great sickness among the cows and beasts of those regions.... Nor was it strange that these portentous things should happen in Connacht at that time, for a great affliction befell the country then, the loss of Cathal Crobhderg son of Turlough O'Connor, King of Connacht; the king most feared and dreaded on every hand in Ireland; the king who carried out most plunderings against the Foreigners and Gaels who opposed him; the king who was the fiercest and harshest towards his enemies that ever lived; the king who most blinded, killed and mutilated rebellious and disaffected subjects ...

... and so on and so on. What the annalist did not know was that Cathal Crobhderg was the last great Gaelic king ever to rule in Ireland. Cathal had survived because he was careful to make arrangements with the English kings and royal governors, pay annual rent to the crown, and obtain papal approval for his authority. Hugh, his heir by feudal law, lacked his father's wisdom, and soon he was in conflict with relatives and neighbouring barons alike. The full-scale Norman conquest of Connacht ensued.

In 1235 a great invasion force was put together by a Co. Tipperary baron, Richard de Burgo. The war was taken to the Atlantic Ocean, and naval engagements involving O'Flahertys and O'Malleys were at their fiercest around the numerous islands of Clew Bay. After ravaging Murrisk and Achill Island in north Mayo, the invaders advanced northwards and inland to make an assault on the island fortress of the Rock on Lough Key in Roscommon, as the Annals of Connacht relate:

> Then a fleet of ships with galleries and siege-engines came to the lake, and they mounted a catapult on a small platform and many stones were hurled

by it into the Rock. And since they could not take it by this means they made numerous vessels out of the houses of Ardcarne, collected all the fuel of the district and putting it on board these rafts set it alight. They bound empty barrels about these rafts to keep them afloat, and sent one of their larger ships, protected by a roof of planking, to tow the rafts to the Rock and so set it afire.

But the people in the fortress were seized with fear and came out, and the Royal Governor put in a garrison of armed and armoured Foreigners, well furnished with food and drink. They left the people of Connacht without food or clothing or cattle.

Though the O'Connors and their allies were able to recover the Rock for a time, their power was broken. The five cantreds or baronies nearest Athlone were reserved for King Henry III, but Richard de Burgo became the Lord of Connacht and the possessor of twenty-five cantreds. He built a great castle at Loughrea in east Galway and made it his principal manor. His allies included members of the FitzGerald and de Lacy families who acquired much of the land of Co. Sligo. Even the remote Erris peninsula fell to the Barrett family. Maurice FitzGerald founded Sligo town; and, around another de Burgo castle, the town of Galway began to grow, attracting Anglo-Norman merchant families, the fourteen most prominent becoming known as the 'Tribes of Galway'.

In a desperate attempt to halt the Norman expansion, a famous agreement was made at Caoluisce, that is Belleek in Co. Fermanagh, in 1258. There Hugh O'Connor of Connacht and Tadhg O'Brien of Thomond 'gave the kingship of the Gaels of Ireland to Brian O'Neill'. Brian was a descendant of what had been the most powerful dynasty in Ireland at the time of St Patrick, the Uí Néill, the descendants of Niall of the Nine Hostages. At one time the Uí Néill had ruled Meath and all of Ulster west of the River Bann. Now Brian, as King of Tír Eóghain, made a determined bid to revive the old glory days. In 1260, with a great Gaelic coalition behind him, Brian advanced into the earldom of Ulster to do battle with the foreigners:

Hugh O'Connor went to join Brian O'Neill in the North, taking many of the chief men of Connacht with him. O'Neill and the chief men of Cenél Eóghain went, together with Hugh O'Connor, to Downpatrick to attack the Foreigners, and the Foreigners of that place defeated them both. Brian O'Neill, king of the Gaels of Ireland, was killed.

The death of Brian at the Battle of Downpatrick, along with dozens of highborn Gaelic commanders, seemed to end all hope of halting further conquest, but already some Gaelic rulers were beginning to recover lost territory—a process rapidly hastened by the invasion of Edward Bruce and the Scots.

Episode 36 ∿

EDWARD BRUCE 'CAUSED THE WHOLE OF IRELAND TO TREMBLE'

One reason why the lordship of Ireland was gravely weakened in the final decades of the thirteenth century was that Edward I waged endless wars. While he campaigned in Gascony, fought the Scots and conquered north Wales, encircling it with great castles, the king had constantly called his Irish vassals to his side, imposed heavy emergency war taxes on them, seized grain without paying for it, and even had sections of his Welsh castles prefabricated in Dublin and shipped across the Irish Sea to Anglesey.

His son, Edward II, was then ignominiously routed by the Scots at Bannockburn in 1314. Robert Bruce, the victor, knew that the English king had drawn heavily on his Irish lordship to prosecute the war, and was determined to destroy it. King Robert knew Ireland well: he had taken refuge on Rathlin in 1294 and 1306, and in 1302 he had married Elizabeth, daughter of Richard de Burgo, the 'Red Earl' of Ulster and Lord of Connacht.

It was to his brother Edward that Robert Bruce entrusted the invasion of Ireland. A formidable Scots expeditionary force disembarked at Larne on 26 May 1315:

> Edward came to Ireland, landing on the coast of north Ulster with the men of three hundred ships, and his warlike slaughtering army caused the whole of Ireland to tremble, both Gael and Foreigner. He began by harrying the choicest part of Ulster, burning Rathmore in Moylinny, and Dundalk, and killing their inhabitants. He then burned Ardee and took the hostages and lordship of the whole province without opposition, and all the Gaels of Ireland called him King of Ireland.

When news of the landing of the Scots arrived, the royal governor, Edmund Butler, was in Munster and the Red Earl was in Connacht attending to his vast estates there. Butler advanced northwards to defend Dublin, while de Burgo made his way to meet the Scots head on:

> He brought together a great army from all sides to Roscommon at first, marching thence to Athlone and obliquely through Meath, their numbers being about twenty battalions; and this time the Foreigners spared not saint or shrine, however sacred, nor churchmen or laymen or sanctuary,

but went wasting and ravaging across Ireland from the Shannon in the south to Coleraine and Inishowen in the north.... Now Edward and his army threw down the bridge of Coleraine to hinder the earl; and he followed them up and encamped opposite Edward; and between them they left neither wood nor lea nor corn nor crop nor stead nor barn, but fired and burnt them all.

The two armies finally met in battle by the Kellswater at Connor. There on 10 September the Scots spearmen completely overwhelmed the earl's feudal host.

Close to Connor, the royal castle of Carrickfergus held out. The garrison was reduced to eating hides as the Scots attempted to starve the castle into submission. A parley was arranged in June 1316; the defenders then treacherously seized the Scots negotiators, and later eight of these men were killed and eaten by the garrison. After a siege lasting more than a year Carrickfergus surrendered to Bruce in September 1316.

Meanwhile Edward Bruce was sweeping all before him: he defeated de Lacys in Meath in December 1315, before crushing the royal governor's army at Ardscull, Co. Kildare, in January. On 1 May 1316 Edward had himself crowned King of Ireland at Dundalk, and his brother, King Robert, joined him in December. After inflicting another defeat on the Red Earl, the two brothers advanced on Dublin. The frantic citizens demolished St Saviour's Priory and brought its stone across the River Liffey to build a wall along the quays. Further supplies of stone were obtained from St Mary's Abbey, where the citizens had locked up the Red Earl after he had taken refuge in the city, just in case he would be tempted to join King Robert, his daughter's husband. The bridge of Dublin was torn down, and, by direction of the mayor, dwellings outside the walls were set on fire. Lacking siege-engines and seeing the desperate measures taken, the Scots turned back.

The Bruce invasion was beginning to fail. Above all, the Scots were being weakened by hunger as a terrible famine took hold in the country. The Bruce brothers rampaged across the country, plundering as far south as Limerick. There was little left to seize during a winter that was even harsher than the one before it. The Laud Annals assert that

[The Scots] were so destroyed with hunger that they raised the bodies of the dead from the cemeteries ... and their women devoured their own children from hunger.... They were reduced to eating each one another, so that out of 10,000 there remained only about 300 who escaped the vengeance of God.

Hunger was to stalk the land many times in the decades that followed the failure of this great Scottish enterprise.

Episode 37 ∿

'FAMINE FILLED THE COUNTRY'

In July 1318 John of Athy, admiral of Edward II's fleet, captured Thomas Dun, who had organised transportation for the Scots across the North Channel. His supply lines cut, Edward Bruce, who had invaded Ireland three years before, was now on the defensive. His brother, King Robert of Scotland, left Ireland shortly after a newly appointed royal governor, Roger Mortimer, arrived with a substantial force from England. Edward marched south from Ulster, only to meet a formidable army under the command of John de Bermingham at the hill of Faughart near Dundalk. There Edward Bruce, who had crowned himself King of Ireland only a few miles away two years before, was defeated and killed. Not only the English rejoiced at his death: the Annals of Connacht contain this arresting entry for the year 1318:

> Edward Bruce, he who was the common ruin of the Gaels and Foreigners of Ireland, was by the Foreigners of Ireland killed at Dundalk by dint of fierce fighting.... And never was there a better deed done for the Irish than this, since the beginning of the world and the banishing of the Formorians from Ireland. For in this Bruce's time, for three years and a half, falsehood and famine and homicide filled the country, and undoubtedly men ate each other in Ireland.

The Bruce invasion had led to the devastation of much of the island, but it was the English colony there that had suffered most. In more senses than one, the climate of the times was to accelerate the contraction of the lordship of Ireland in the fourteenth century. A steady deterioration of the weather across the northern hemisphere brought in its wake a succession of poor harvests and outbreaks of disease among grazing animals. Norse settlers, for example, were forced by starvation to abandon Greenland to the Inuit. Reports of cannibalism in Europe were made with greater regularity. Was this global cooling the result of volcanic eruptions in Iceland? We cannot be certain. Dendrochronological data—that is, the interpretation of oak-tree growth-rings—demonstrate a general lowering of summer temperatures. What is evident is the proliferation of reports, from a wide variety of sources, telling of hunger and disease. These sources include the Annals of Connacht:

1317:   Great famine this year throughout Ireland.
1318:   Snow the like of which had not been seen for many a long year.
1322:   Great cattle-plague throughout Ireland, the like of which had never been known before.

1324: The same cattle-plague was in all Ireland this year. It was called the Mael Domnaig.

1325: The cattle-plague throughout Ireland still.

1327: A great and widespread visitation of the smallpox throughout Ireland this year, which carried off both lowly and great.

1328: Much thunder and lightning this year, whereby much of the fruit and produce of all Ireland was ruined, and the corn grew up white and blind.... A great and intolerable wind this summer, with scarcity of food and clothing.... A general visitation of the sickness called *slaedan* [influenza] throughout Ireland. It lasted three or four days with each person whom it attacked, and it was next to death for him.

1335: Heavy snow in the spring, which killed most of the small birds of all Ireland.

1338: Nearly all the sheep in Ireland died this year.

1339: The cattle and winter grass of Ireland suffered much from frost and snow.

1358: A heavy shower fell in Carbury in the summer, each hail-stone thereof fully as big as a crab-apple.

1363: A great wind this year, which wrecked churches and houses and sank many ships and boats.

The thirteenth century had been a time of population growth and rising prosperity. Prospects seemed good for the many English attracted over by the opportunity to get land in Ireland, celebrated in an anonymous poem of the time;

> I am of Ireland
> And of the holy land
> Of Ireland.
> Good sir, pray I thee
> For of saint charité
> **Come dance with me**
> **In Ireland.**

The ensuing century was, in contrast, a very different one for inhabitants of the Irish lordship.

By the beginning of the fourteenth century only mountainous, boggy and generally infertile areas had not been colonised. These included: the Dublin/Wicklow Mountains; the Slieve Bloom Mountains and the Bog of Allen in the midlands; wilder parts of west Cork and Kerry; and Connemara in Co. Galway. Though Hugh de Lacy and Richard de Burgo had extended their earldom along the north coast to Inishowen, by far the most extensive region remaining under Gaelic rule was central and western Ulster; officials in Dublin referred to this part of the north outside their control as the 'Great Irishry'.

Acute food shortages made it very tempting for the Gaelic Irish to burst out of their impoverished lands to plunder and seek to recover the fertile plains their forebears had lost to the Normans. Their attacks became ever more successful after the colony had been ravaged by the Black Death.

Episode 38 ～

THE BLACK DEATH

The Black Death arrived in western Europe in the year 1347. This fearful bacillus appeared in three main forms of plague—bubonic, pneumonic and septicaemic. Some forms were transmitted by fleas carried principally by black rats, and, when the rats were killed by this disease, the fleas sought other hosts including human beings. People infected by the commonest form suffered painful swellings or buboes in the groin, armpits and the neck. Symptoms included sudden chills, hallucination and delirium. Between fifty and eighty per cent of victims died within a week.

The Black Death made its first appearance in Ireland in the prosperous Co. Dublin port of Howth in late July 1348. Soon the Black Death was raging in Dublin, Drogheda and Dundalk, and during the autumn it spread inland to the manors of Louth, Meath and Co. Dublin. Waterford was hit next, and traders took the disease up the River Nore to Kilkenny. Here Friar Clyn was keeping a chronicle, and he recorded the arrival of the plague:

> More people in the world have died in such a short time of plague than has been heard of since the beginning of time.... The pestilence was so contagious that whosoever touched the sick and the dead was immediately infected and died, so that penitent and confessor were carried to the grave.... That pestilence deprived of human inhabitants villages and cities, so that there was scarcely found a man to dwell therein.

Friar Clyn tells us that the arrival of the Black Death prompted a pilgrimage to *Teach Moling*, the house of St Moling, on the River Barrow in Co. Carlow:

> 1348: In this year particularly in the months of September and October there came together from diverse parts of Ireland, bishops and prelates,

churchmen and religious, lords and others to the pilgrimage at *Teach Moling,* in troops and multitudes....

Some came from feelings of devotion, but others, and they the majority, from dread of the plague, which then grew very rife.

By Christmas Day 1348 fifty per cent of all the Franciscan friars of Drogheda had died of the plague. In the following months the Black Death reaped a terrible harvest in Kilkenny. Friar Clyn continued:

Many died of boils and abscesses and pustules which erupted on their shins or under their armpits; others died frantic with pain in their head and others spitting blood.... This plague was at its height in Kilkenny during Lent; for on the sixth day of March eight of the Friars Preachers died. There was hardly a house in which only one had died, but as a rule man and wife with their children and all the family went the common way of death.

The striking feature of the Black Death in Ireland is that it raged principally in the ports and towns. In short, the English colony was much more severely affected than the Gaelic Irish living in the countryside. The Irish annals, never slow to mention disasters, made only very brief references to the Black Death. The Annals of Ulster has only one reference, specifically mentioning one area in Roscommon:

1349: The great plague of the general disease that was throughout Ireland prevailed in Moylurg this year so that great destruction of people was inflicted therein. Matthew, son of Cathal O'Rourke, died thereof.

Meanwhile Friar Clyn knew his end was near:

I, Brother Clyn of the Friars Minor of Kilkenny, have written in this book the notable events which befell in my time.... So that notable deeds shall not be lost from the memory of future generations, I, seeing many ills, waiting for death till it come, have committed to writing what I have truly heard; and lest the writing perish with the writer, I leave parchment for continuing the work, if haply any man of the race of Adam escape this pestilence and continue the work which I have begun.

Then, beneath a blot of ink, is written in another hand:

Here, it seems, the author died.

On Christmas Eve 1350 one young man wrote this prayer:

The second year after the coming of the plague into Ireland. And I am Hugh, son of Conor Mac Aodhagáin; under the safeguard of the King of Heaven and earth who is here tonight I place myself and may He put this great Plague past me and past my friends and may we be once more in joy and happiness. Amen. Pater Noster.

He survived, but on most of the manors of the lordship of Ireland many did not. We do not know how many victims there were, except for Colemanstown in the royal manor of Newcastle Lyons, Co. Dublin, where 84 per cent of the tenants were, it was reported, 'cut off by the late pestilence'. Certainly there were many manors with vacant farms. This weakened colony in Ireland was therefore less able to defend itself against the native Irish, now employing mercenaries from the Western Isles of Scotland.

Episode 39 ~

GALLOWGLASSES

The most prominent feature in the pretty town of Ballyshannon in south Donegal is a tall, ornate Victorian building which for very many decades has had the name of the proprietor prominently displayed across its frontage: Gallogley. It is an unusual surname, but it is a vivid reminder of the crucial role played by a fresh group of newcomers to Ireland in the late Middle Ages.

The ability of Gaelic lords to win back lost territory is in part explained by their employment of *gallóglaigh*, which literally means 'young foreign warriors'. Confusingly, the annalists referred both to the Vikings and the English as the *Gall*, the foreigners. The word *gallóglaigh* was anglicised by the colonists in Ireland as 'gallowglasses'. Gallowglasses were of mixed Viking-Gaelic blood, who after the King of Scotland had broken any remaining power the King of Norway had in his land at the Battle of Largs in 1263, sought employment for their arms in Ireland. When Robert Bruce, King of Scotland, brought over reinforcements to help his brother Edward in 1316, the annals noted that he had with him a great force of gallowglasses. Thereafter more and more of these fighting-men came south to Ireland from the Western Isles.

A high proportion of the gallowglasses were descendants of a Viking Lord of the Isles named Somerled, which means 'summer wanderer'. These men broke up into warring clans, and it was often those who were defeated in these petty conflicts that came to Ireland to seek their fortunes. In spring they would plough their small fields, plant their seed oats, and then gather their weapons and armour to row and sail across the North Channel to Ulster, there to offer their services to the highest bidder. Previously driven into the more remote regions of the island, Gaelic lords were taking advantage of the growing weakness of the lordship of Ireland by campaigning to recover the lands lost by their ancestors. Many were eager to employ these warriors from the Isles. The O'Donnells, the ruling family of the lordship of Tír Conaill in what is now Co. Donegal, were among the first to engage gallowglasses; but instead of fighting the English, they used them to drive the O'Neills out of the fertile country around the Foyle. Their leading gallowglass clan, the MacSweeneys, at first were paid in kind:

> This is how the levy was made; two gallowglasses for each quarter of land, and two cows for each gallowlass deficient, that is, one cow for the man himself and one for his equipment. And Clan Sweeney say they are responsible for these as follows, that for each man equipped with a coat of mail and a breastplate, another should have a jack and a helmet: that there should be no forfeit for a helmet deficient except the gallowglass's brain (dashed out for want of it).

Each gallowglass had a manservant to carry his coat of mail and a boy who looked after the food and did the cooking. He fought in traditional Viking style, wielding an axe or a spar, 'much like the axe of the Tower' as one viceroy, Sir Anthony St Leger, described it. St Leger who faced gallowglasses in battle on many an occasion, believed that 'These sort of men be those that do not lightly abandon the field, but bide the brunt to the death.' Gallowglass fighting-men stiffened the ranks of native Irish foot-soldiers, or kerne, who, according to St Leger,

> fight bare naked, saving their shirts to hide their privates; and those have darts and short bows: which sort of people be both hardy and deliver to search woods and marshes, in which they be hard to be beaten.

When the summer season of fighting was over, these Scottish warriors—provided they had survived—received their pay, mostly in the form of butter and beef, and sailed back to the Isles in time to reap, thrash and winnow their harvests. In time gallowglasses acquired land as a more secure source of income. The MacSweeneys got territory in Donegal and divided into three clans: MacSweeney na Doe (na Doe comes from *na dTuath*, meaning 'of the Tribes') in the Rosses and around Creeslough; MacSweeney Fanad on the peninsula named after them just west of Lough Swilly; and MacSweeney Banagh in the vicinity of Slieve League. A branch of the MacDonnells, settled in the lands about Ballygawley in Co. Tyrone, became a powerful arm of the O'Neills of Tír Eóghain in their struggle to become the leading Gaelic rulers of Ireland. Another cohort of MacDonnells, the lords of Kintyre and Islay, made their home in the Glens of Antrim.

During the fourteenth century bands of gallowglasses spread out all over Gaelic Ireland to seek employment for their arms. These men from *Innse Gall*—the Irish name for the Hebrides—bore surnames now familiar all over the country, including MacCabe, MacRory, MacDougall, MacDowell and MacSheehy. They were to help Gaelic lords bring the English lordship of Ireland to its knees.

Episode 40 ∿

'MORE IRISH THAN THE IRISH THEMSELVES'

Gerald of Wales and other English commentators frequently criticised the disorder which often followed after the death of an Irish king or chieftain. Gaelic succession disputes could certainly be bloody and dislocating, but the feudal law of primogeniture also had its problems. The male line ran out in several leading Norman settler families, including the de Lacys in Meath in 1243, and not one of the sons of William Marshal, Lord of Leinster, produced a male heir. Then, in 1333, William de Burgo, the young Earl of Ulster and Lord of Connacht—one of the greatest landholders in western Europe—was murdered by some of his tenants near Shankill church outside Belfast in 1333. Known as the Brown Earl, William had only a two-year-old baby girl, Elizabeth, as his heir. The de Burgo lordship rapidly disintegrated thereafter.

One of the additional reasons for the collapse of the vast de Burgo lordship was that descendants of the first Norman conquerors were going native or were becoming, in the often-quoted phrase, 'more Irish than the Irish themselves'. Increasingly isolated from the heart of the English lordship in Dublin Castle, these families adopted the Irish language and dress, married into native Gaelic ruling families, engaged Irish harpers and poets, and gained the confidence to throw off their feudal allegiance to the English crown.

Junior branches of the de Burgo family changed their name to *Burcach*, which later became familiar in its anglicised form, 'Burke'. They usurped the lands of the rightful Lord of Connacht, Lionel of Clarence, and when he died in 1368 an inquisition recorded that manors which used to be worth £200 a year were now worth nothing 'because they are occupied by Edmund de Burgo knight and other rebels of the king, both English and Irish, nor has any minister of the king dared go thither to execute his office'.

Two major branches of gaelicised de Burgos adopted the surname 'MacWilliam'. An army had to be sent in 1320 to Munster against 'rebels John fitz Maurice and David de Barry and their followers, namely of the name of Burke and Barry'. Members of the de la Rochefort family simply adopted the name Roche, and a branch of the once powerful de Berminghams became known as Mac Pheorais, 'son of Piers', after one of their number. The family of le Sauvage (which is Norman-French for 'countryman') in the Ards peninsula simply became 'Savage'. Those described by the Dublin government as 'degenerate English' were in effect becoming independent warlords with their own private armies, known as 'routs', and waged war on each other, often in alliance with the Gaelic Irish, in defiance of central government.

Many of the descendants of Norman barons who remained loyal to the crown increasingly spent their time out of Ireland. In 1297 the Irish parliament attempted to do something about this by passing the following decree:

Magnates and others who remain outside this land, and who cause the profit of their land to be sent to them from this land, sending nothing here to protect their tenants, shall henceforth allow a sufficient portion at least to remain in the hands of bailiffs, by which their own lands may be sufficiently protected and defended, if it should happen that war or disturbance of peace is stirred up there by anyone.

There is little evidence that this parliamentary order was obeyed.

The Irish parliament was an institution almost as ancient as the English one. The first recorded parliament was in 1264, and thereafter, at irregular intervals, the 'justiciar' or royal governor would call leading peers, knights and burgesses to meet in Dublin, Drogheda, Kilkenny or other convenient places in the lordship. These were representatives of the English colony, and it was only later that Gaelic lords, in favour with the crown, were invited to attend. Both Lords and Commons took the opportunity during parliamentary sessions to petition the crown. They sought help to enable them to combat both the Irish and the rebel gaelicised Norman barons. A parliament meeting at Kilkenny in 1341 complained to Edward III about men 'who are sent out of England to govern them, who themselves have little knowledge of your land of Ireland'—a complaint to be repeated by generations of loyalists in ensuing centuries about badly briefed ministers being sent over by London governments to take charge of the administration of Ireland. The petition continued:

Likewise, sire, although there is in every march of your land of Ireland enough and more of the Irish enemies to trouble your English people who have no power to stop them, save the grace of God which maintains them, sire, still more do the extortions and oppressions of your ministers trouble them than does war with the Irish.

Twenty years were to pass before the king felt able to respond to this appeal by sending over his son Lionel with a large English army.

Episode 41 ᕰ

THE STATUTE OF KILKENNY

The wasting Hundred Years' War in France hastened the steady erosion of the lordship of Ireland to the benefit of both Gaelic lords and independent gaelicised warlords. English monarchs simply lacked the funds to respond to the frantic appeals for help. Then a brief respite in the French wars gave Edward III the opportunity to do something. A great council of his liege subjects had met in Kilkenny in 1360 and made a report on

the mischiefs, perils and estate of your land of Ireland, which is on the point of being lost.... The Irish, your enemies, of one assent and covenant, commence to levy war throughout all your land, burning, destroying and preying daily on your lieges of those parts.... As a work of charity, [send] a good sufficient chieftain, stocked and strengthened with men and treasure ... as a noble and gracious prince is bound to do for his lieges.

The king was moved to respond with this message:

Because Ireland is now subject to such devastation and destruction ... that it will be soon plunged into total ruin, we have for the salvation of the said land ordained that our dear son Lionel shall proceed thither with all dispatch and with a great army.

Lionel, whom the king now appointed his 'lieutenant', or governor of Ireland, and who was soon to be created Duke of Clarence, was Edward's second son, and because he had married the daughter of the murdered William de Burgo, he was also nominally Earl of Ulster. The great lords who held estates in

Ireland but lived in England, numbering sixty-four in all, were summoned to join him or face the confiscation of their Irish lands. A great expedition was organised and equipped in 1361. Lionel personally supervised the fitting out of his flagship, with a blue carpet for his cabin, coloured worsteds as hangings, four sconces, ten round lanterns, and an image of St Christopher to ensure a safe voyage. Nine hundred men at arms and mounted archers under the command of the veteran Earl of Stafford accompanied him.

Were there enough troops to enable the new lieutenant to do what was expected of him? Clearly Stafford did not think so because he immediately set about hiring from the O'Kennedy chief mounted warriors, known as 'hobelars', at 4d a day and foot-soldiers at 1½d each a day. This led to dissension when Lionel issued a proclamation stipulating that no person born in Ireland should come near his camp—an order which was followed by the murder of about a hundred of his men.

Lionel settled himself in Dublin Castle, where he set up a splendid court, improved the garden to please his wife, and held tournaments. Meanwhile the Earl of Stafford campaigned vigorously round the country. Art MacMurrough, King of Leinster, was taken prisoner; the O'Connors were punished for making a raid on Meath; much of Co. Cork was recovered; and the O'Mores of Leix were attacked. Several leading Gaelic lords made their submission, including O'Neill of Tír Eóghain and O'Brien of Thomond. By 1364 the clerk of the wages had paid out the immense sum of £22,000, but more was needed. Lionel returned briefly to England to raise another great force, only to be told by his father that, according to his information, Ireland was 'sunk in the greatest wretchedness'.

Against all advice, Clarence moved the king's exchequer to the royal castle of Carlow, the treasurer complaining that 'Carlow is on the frontier of the Irish rebels; there is no safe access to it by the king's lieges.'

Then in 1366, rather suddenly, Lionel summoned a parliament at Kilkenny. In this parliament was enacted the notorious statute which would be forever linked with the name of Clarence. Its main purpose was to bring a halt to 'degeneracy', that is, to the adoption by the English of Irish ways:

It is ordained and established that no alliance by marriage, fostering of children, concubinage or sexual liaison or in any other manner be made henceforth between English and Irish on one side or the other....

Also, it is ordained and established that every Englishman use the English language, and be called by an English name, abandoning completely the Irish method of naming, and that every Englishman use English style in appearance, riding and dress....

No Englishman worth one hundred shillings a year in land, holdings or rent shall ride otherwise than on the saddle in the English style....

Also it is agreed and established that no house of religion which is situated among the English shall in the future receive any Irishman to their profession....

The English in Ireland were forbidden to play hurling, but were to practise archery instead. In all, there were thirty-six articles in the Statute of Kilkenny, all of them laying down severe penalties if the ordinances were flouted or broken.

It is one thing to legislate, quite another to enforce. The statute proved to be a dead letter, as a Catalan pilgrim was to discover some years later.

Episode 42 ∾

'INTO THE LAND OF THE SAVAGE IRISH WHERE KING O'NEILL REIGNED SUPREME'

In 1386 Prince John of Aragon wrote to his friend, Ramon, Viscount of Perellós and of Roda in Catalonia:

We beg you to send us, in writing, the whole story of that knight who you said went into St Patrick's Purgatory, and what he saw and what happened to him in that Purgatory; for we earnestly wish to know of it.

In the course of time the prince became King John I of Aragon and chose Ramon as his chamberlain, sending him on several foreign missions. Then, on 19 May 1396, disaster struck. The king died suddenly, frightened to death, it was said, by the sight of an enormous she-wolf when he was out hunting alone. The grief-stricken Ramon immediately feared that his royal master's soul would be in torment in Hell, for King John had died without confession or the rites of the church. The viscount declared his intention of journeying to Lough Derg in the remote fastness of the north-west of Ireland, concerning which the late king had earlier expressed such a keen interest. Here, he had read, a soul would be spared the pains of Hell if the pilgrim could survive the dangers of St Patrick's Purgatory, located on a small island in the lake. An audience in Avignon with Pope Benedict XIII was not encouraging:

He strongly advised me against it and he frightened me greatly, warning me that I should not do it for any reason whatsoever. Besides what he himself said to me, he had some of the cardinals closest to him speak to me.... They restrained me with such force that I was barely able to get away from them.

Ramon received a papal blessing, nevertheless, and on his way called in at Paris to get letters of recommendation from King Charles VI of France. King Richard II of England received him well, and after spending ten days with him, the viscount chartered a ship at Chester and crossed the Irish Sea:

Then I reached Ireland and a few days later I landed in Dublin which is quite a big city. There I met the Earl of March, who received me very well because of the letters of recommendation from the king, for the government of that island was in his charge. I told him of the journey I intended to make. This lord advised me strongly against it.... I would have to travel a great distance and go through lands of savage, ungoverned people whom no man should trust. The other reason was that the Purgatory was a very dangerous thing and many a good knight had been lost there, never to return. When he saw that I was still that way inclined, he gave me horses and jewels and also two squires.

The earl's men would take the Catalan visitor no further than Dundalk, where they handed him over to John Colton, the Archbishop of Armagh. The archbishop said earnestly:

Unless I deliberately wished to lose my life, I should on no account attempt to go there. He then had me go into the sacristy of the church where he admonished me very strongly. He begged me not to enter the Purgatory and he told me of the many perils and horrible things which had befallen several other men who were lost there.... When he saw he could not change my mind, he heard my confession and in great secrecy I received Our Lord from his hand.... He sent a message to King O'Neill, who was in the city of Armagh.

John Colton was the only English-born Archbishop of Armagh to be brave enough to visit the Gaelic parts of his ecclesiastical province for almost two centuries. He certainly had met Niall Mór O'Neill, the ruler of Tír Eóghain, but he took no chances: he gave Ramon an escort of a hundred men:

I went into the land of the savage Irish where King O'Neill reigned supreme. When I had ridden some five leagues, the hundred armed men did not dare to proceed any further. So they remained on a hill and I took my leave of them and continued on myself.

O'Neill gave him a warm welcome and his first taste of Ulster oatcakes. Then Ramon went on to Termon Magrath, the ecclesiastical lands which included Lough Derg. The ground was so soft that he had to go on foot by Lower Lough Erne and on to Lough Derg:

> There is so much water everywhere that a man can barely cross over even the highest mountains without sinking to his waist.... I went across the lake in a boat made of hollowed-out wood, for there were no other boats.... Then they urged me strongly not to go into the Purgatory.... When they saw how very determined I was, the prior and all the clerks sang Requiem Mass early in the morning.... They all did this for me because they did not wish to leave anything undone.

There in the pit Ramon entered the Purgatory in search of the soul of his dead master King John.

Episode 43 ~

A CATALAN PILGRIM AMONG THE UNCONQUERED IRISH

In 1397, as we have seen, Ramon, Viscount of Perellós, travelled from Catalonia almost to the edge of the known world, to Lough Derg in the north-west of Ireland. There, after many adventures, he visited St Patrick's Purgatory to save the soul of his dead king by his pilgrimage. There, he tells us,

> I was sweating and overcome.... There were many grave and pitiful types of torture and countless numbers of people ... and there I saw the king, Don John of Aragon, who by God's grace, was on the road to salvation.

Ramon's description of the Purgatory can be read with a sceptical eye, but what makes him different from other foreign pilgrims to Lough Derg—and some came in these years from as far away as Hungary, Switzerland and Italy—is that he alone left us descriptions of the Gaelic Irish.

After leaving Lough Derg, Ramon was received by the ruler of Tír Eóghain, Niall Mór O'Neill:

We were very well received, with great joy and delight, and I spent the feast of Christmas with him. He held a great court in their fashion which to us seems very strange for someone of his status.... His table was of rushes spread out on the ground, while nearby they placed delicate grass for him to wipe his mouth. They used to carry the meat to him on poles.

Ramon tells us that when he first arrived in O'Neill's territory,

The king sent me an ox and his cook to prepare it. In all his court there was no milk to drink, nor bread, nor wine, but as a great gift he sent me two cakes as thin as wafers and as pliable as raw dough. They were made of oats and of earth and they were as black as coal, but very tasty.

They are among the most beautiful men and women that I have seen anywhere in the world. They do not sow corn, nor have they any wine. Their only meat is ox-meat. The great lords drink milk and others meat-broth, and the common people drink water. But they have plenty of butter, for oxen and cows provide all their meat.

Ramon was mistaken in his belief that the Gaelic people here did not grow corn—at this time of the year the stubble fields would have been turned over to cattle. Concerning their living conditions and semi-nomadic lifestyle, he commented:

Their dwellings are communal and most of them are set up near the oxen, and they move on through the pastures, like the swarms of Barbary in the land of the Sultan.

He described the dress of the Irish he met as follows:

The great lords wear tunics without a lining, reaching to the knee, cut very low at the neck, almost in the style of women, and they wear great hoods which hang down to the waist, the point of which is narrow as a finger. They wear neither hose nor shoes, nor do they wear breeches, and they wear their spurs on their bare heels. The king was dressed like that on Christmas Day, and so were all the clerks and knights and even the bishops and abbots and the great lords.

The poor wear cloaks, good or bad. The queen was barefoot, and her handmaidens, twenty in number, were dressed with their shameful parts showing. And you should know that all those people were no more ashamed of this than showing their faces.

The Catalan nobleman was told to expect 'savage, ungoverned people', but he was pleasantly surprised to find that he could discuss international affairs with O'Neill and his courtiers in Latin:

> The king spoke to me at length, asking me about the Christian kings, especially the kings of France, Aragon and Castile, and about the customs and the way they lived.... They consider their own customs to be more advantageous than any others in the whole world.

Ramon was impressed by the numbers of fine horses and by the warriors who formed O'Neill's retinue:

> They ride without a saddle on a cushion, and each one wears a cloak according to his rank. They are armed with coats of mail and round iron helmets like the Moors and Saracens. They have swords and very long knives and long lances, two fathoms in length. Their swords are like those of the Saracens.... The knives are long, narrow and thin as one's little finger, and they are very sharp.... Some use bows which are not very long—only half the size of English bows, but their range is just as good. Their way of fighting is like that of the Saracens, who shout in the same manner. They are very courageous. They are still at war with the English and have been for a long time.

The prize of bringing that war to an end was one that was to elude the English king, Richard II.

Episode 44 ～

RICHARD II'S GREAT EXPEDITION TO IRELAND

In 1385 the Irish great council sent a report to the king concerning

> the mischiefs and very great evils in the land of Ireland, the seignory of the king.... At this next season, as is likely, there will be made a conquest of the greater part of the land of Ireland ... Because of the weakness and poverty of the English lieges, they are not able or know how to find or think of other remedy except the coming of our king, our lord, in his own person.

The greatest single threat was the rise of Art MacMurrough Kavanagh, who had won recognition from his people as King of Leinster. From the forests of the Blackstairs Mountains he overran the neighbouring fertile lowlands, forcing the authorities to pay him an annual fee to keep the road clear from Carlow to Kilkenny. And on his behalf the O'Byrnes and the O'Tooles came down from the mountains overlooking Dublin to exact a 'black rent' from the citizens as a price for ending their destructive raids.

It became obvious to Richard II that the entire lordship of Ireland would be lost if he did not take decisive action. In 1394 the king announced that he was going to Ireland in person. All those holders of land in Ireland who had removed themselves to England were ordered to join the king on pain of forfeiture—a threat strictly enforced. John Orewell, the king's serjeant, was ordered to

> search and inform himself from Thames mouth and thence as far as Exeter ... how many and what sort of ships with their equipment may be had there for the passage of the king and his army to Ireland; to enjoin on the owners and masters that they have them prepared and arrayed with all speed under penalty of forfeiture.

Nearly two hundred ships were seized. They had to be fitted with castles fore and aft for archers and provided with special gangways, stalls and enclosures for war-horses. The army gathering at Milford Haven was by far the largest yet prepared for Ireland. Altogether King Richard had nearly 10,000 men at his disposal.

Landing at Waterford on 2 October, Richard wrote in French to Thomas, Archbishop of York, Chancellor of England:

> We were only a day and a night at sea in our crossing; and so we arrived at our city of Waterford, in Ireland, where we were by our citizens there received with great joy, and where from one day to another our loyal lieges come to offer us their services against every design of the others who have been rebels in our absence.

Richard ringed the Wicklow and Blackstairs Mountains with heavily armed positions, ravaged the foothills to deny MacMurrough supplies, and completed his ring of steel by closely patrolling the coastline with his castellated ships. Then, when the trees shed their leaves, making refuge in the woods difficult, he sent in raiding parties of mounted longbow archers. The king sent a stream of letters to Archbishop Thomas to report one success after another:

> The Marshal had several fine engagements, in one of which he slew many people of the said MacMurrough, and burned nine villages and preyed of

his cattle up to the number of 8,000.... If he had not been foreseen, he would have found the said MacMurrough and his wife in their beds.

The French chronicler Froissart recorded the successful outcome:

The great power that the king had over with him abashed the Irish; also the sea was closed from them on all parts ... when the Irishmen saw the great number of men at war that King Richard had in Ireland, the Irishmen advised themselves and came to obeisance.

On 7 January 1395 King Art MacMurrough and his vassals submitted at Tullow in Carlow and swore to be faithful subjects on the *Bacall Íosa*, the relic of the staff of Christ seized at Downpatrick by John de Courcy in 1177. Art agreed to quit Leinster with all his people and serve the king with his men as paid warriors. King Richard wrote to his chancellor:

In all ways let the Author of all be praised. It seems to us that all of the Land of Leinster is conquered, and apparently truly at peace—by reason of the Divine providence and the good government which we intend to apply thereto.

From all over Ireland warlords came to submit in person to Richard. Each man removed his hat, girdle and weapons and, on his knees, put his hands, palms joined, between those of the king. The oath was then taken in Irish and then translated for the benefit of the royal entourage into English. Among the eighty chieftains who made submission was Niall Mór O'Neill of Tír Eóghain.

After nine months in Ireland Richard II returned triumphantly to England, convinced that he had saved the Irish lordship from destruction.

Episode 45 ∾

THE PALE

In June 1398 Roger Mortimer, Earl of March, Lord of Trim, Earl of Ulster and Lord of Connacht, was killed in a skirmish against the Gaelic Irish near Carlow. For Richard II this was a disaster that set him on the road to ruin and death. Mortimer had been the king's appointed lieutenant and chief governor of Ireland and, by English law, owner of almost half the land of Ireland. In practice, Mortimer had real possession of only a fraction of this inheritance. And since the king's departure from Ireland in 1395 one by one the Irish lords had thrown aside the oaths of loyalty they had made to Richard in person.

The great expedition the king had led to Ireland at such immense cost had been for nothing. Once the garrisons ringing the mountains had been withdrawn, Art MacMurrough once again assumed the title 'King of Leinster'. Not only Gaelic chieftains but also Anglo-Irish lords went into rebellion.

In despair, Richard decided to come to Ireland again in 1399. After landing in Ireland, he wrote to his uncle, Edmund, Duke of York:

> Dear and well-beloved, we greet you with whole heart, making you to know that by the grace of God we have arrived in our city of Waterford the first day of this present month of June.... Since our arrival we thank God both for a prey of a great number of beasts made by our nephew the Duke of Surrey, as well as for a 'journey' made upon MacMurrough, O'Byrne and the rest, to the discomfiture of the enemy. We have had a very good beginning, trusting in the Almighty that He will lead us, and that shortly, to a good conclusion of our undertaking.

Shortly afterwards, however, the expedition began to fail. Richard recklessly forged into the dense woods of the mountains, where his army was worn down by repeated ambushes. In addition, the royal coffers were fast emptying. So unpopular was this expedition in England that the Duke of Lancaster raised a successful rebellion there. Richard had to hasten back, only to be made prisoner and be thrown into the Tower of London, from whence he was eventually taken away and murdered.

Almost a century of internecine warfare followed in England as the Houses of Lancaster and York contested for the crown in what became known as the Wars of the Roses. Inevitably the lordship of Ireland was once more in peril. Most of the descendants of the original Norman colonists had either 'gone native' and become rebels or had returned to live more safely in England. A great many ordinary colonists, believing their prospects to be bleak in Ireland, also left the island, as a petition to Henry v from the Irish parliament of 1421 made clear:

> Day to day we are burdened with divers intolerable charges and wars, so that humble tenants, the artificers and labourers of the said land daily depart in great numbers from your said land to your kingdom of England and remain there, whereby the husbandry of your said land is greatly injured and disused and your said lieges greatly weakened in their power of resisting the malice of your said enemies.

Henry, preoccupied with French campaigns, offered no help. The author of *The Little Book on English Policy* gave this warning in 1427:

> To kepen Yreland that it be not loste,
> For it is a boterasse and a poste,
> Undre England and Wales is another.
> God forbede but eche were othere brothere,
> Of one ligeaunce dewe unto the kynge.

But most in Ireland felt no allegiance to the English crown, and the author pointed out that 'the wylde Yrishe' had regained so much of the lordship of Ireland that

> Our grounde there is a little cornere
> To all Yrelande in treue comparisone.

This was a correct assessment. At the same time the Irish Council reported in desperation to Henry VI that 'his land of Ireland is well-nigh destroyed, and inhabited with his enemies and rebels', with the consequence that the royal writ only ran in an area around Dublin 'scarcely thirty miles in length and twenty miles in breadth'.

The council was referring to the 'Pale'. The Dublin government had erected paling, put up fortifications, dug trenches, given grants towards the building of castles, appointed guards to hold the bridges, and assigned watchmen— paid by a tax called 'smokesilver'—to light warning beacons when danger threatened. The Pale ran from Dundalk in the north, inland to Naas in Co. Kildare, and then back to the coast just eight miles south of Dublin at Bray. Other coastal towns such as Waterford, Cork and Galway also attempted to remain loyal to the English crown. They included Carrickfergus, described in 1468 as 'a garrison of war ... surrounded by Irish and Scots, without succour of the English for sixty miles'. And on the main gate of Galway was inscribed:

From the fury of the O'Flahertys, good Lord deliver us.

The truth was, most of Ireland was beyond the Pale.

Episode 46 ~

BEYOND THE PALE

Just south-west of Newtownstewart, adjacent to the Mourne river in Co. Tyrone, stand the ruins of what is known locally as Harry Avery's Castle. Built by Énrí Aimhréidh O'Neill, this castle with its polygonal curtain wall and high D-shaped towers is evidence that the Gaelic Irish had learned much from the English. Soon after it was built, however, large castles were going out of fashion, being too expensive to garrison, maintain and repair.

With as much enthusiasm as the remaining Anglo-Irish barons, Gaelic lords began to build tower-houses. These were intended as residences, but at the same time they were constructed for defence—often at the expense of comfort. A typical tower-house was a single rectangular tall keep, at least twelve metres high and slightly tapered, with two towers flanking the main entrance. The dimly lit ground floor was the store-room, with a semicircular barrel-vault roof, temporarily supported by woven wicker mats until the mortar had set—it was important that the first-floor roof was not made of wood in case of an attack by fire. The upper storeys were reached by a narrow winding staircase up one of the towers, lit by arrow slits; this was always cunningly designed to allow the defender, coming down the stairs, and not the attacker coming up, to use his sword with his right arm. Food was cooked in braziers on the first floor and taken to the banqueting hall above. The lord slept on the uppermost storey under a gable roof shingled with oak. Tower-houses had cells, built-in latrines, window seats and secret chambers in hollows within the haunches of stone vaults. Some had as many as six storeys. A notable feature was a bold arch connecting the two flanking towers; here was a 'murder hole' for shooting down at, or dropping heavy stones on, or pouring boiling water over, assailants attempting to ram the door below. (Contrary to popular belief, boiling oil was not poured on attackers: it was much too expensive.)

The ruins of tower-houses are present in every county, with the greatest concentration in Limerick and Down. Those in the counties of Dublin, Kildare, Meath and Louth were known as 'ten-pound' houses because they attracted government grants in an attempt to strengthen the defences of the Pale. Some, including the tower-house in Belfast by the River Farset in what is now Castle Junction, have long since been removed. Those at Blarney, Co. Cork, and Bunratty, Co. Clare, have become famous tourist attractions. Others, such as that in Donegal town built by the O'Donnells, became incorporated into larger castles at a later date. Anyone standing at Portaferry quay in Co. Down can see a remarkable number of tower-houses in all directions, including those at Strangford, Audleystown, Kilclief and Jordan's Castle in Ardglass.

The recovery of so much land by Gaelic lords ensured the spread of the old Gaelic way of life. Though still proudly regarding themselves as 'English', very many descendants of the first Norman conquerors had become completely gaelicised and virtually indistinguishable from their native neighbours. By the beginning of the fifteenth century it is likely than Irish was the language of at least ninety per cent of the population. Though Gaelic Ireland was fractured politically into innumerable lordships, it maintained a remarkable cultural unity. Indeed, it could be said that from the Outer Hebrides to the Dingle and Iveragh peninsulas in the far south-west of Ireland the Gaelic world knew a cultural unity not yet achieved in the English-speaking regions of the British Isles—the professional learned classes ensured that there was no difference between Gaelic in Scotland and Ireland until the seventeenth century. The North Channel formed a line of communication, not a barrier; the real cultural frontiers were the Highland Line, south of which lived Scots speaking English, and the boundary of the Pale, the anglicised region around Dublin, known by crown officials as the 'land of peace' and the rest of Ireland, which they named the 'land of war'.

As in the days before the coming of the Normans, Gaelic lords made sure the learned classes were well supported. Certain families, often guardians of church lands, became specialists: for example, the McGraths and O'Husseys were poets and historians; the O'Breslins were lawyers; the O'Duignans and MacCarrolls were musicians; and the O'Hickeys and O'Cassidys were physicians. Tadhg Dall Ó hUiginn was one of many who celebrated this way of life. This is an extract from his poem 'Fermanagh is the Paradise of Ireland':

> None interfereth with any other in this earthly paradise;
> There is none bent on spoil, nor any man suffering injustice.
> There is no reaver's track in the grass ...
> No misfortune threatening her cattle, no spoiler plundering her ...
> Fermanagh of the fortunate ramparts is the Adam's paradise of Inisfail.

That paradise would be shattered in the course of the sixteenth century.

Episode 47 ～

GARRET MÓR FITZGERALD, THE GREAT EARL OF KILDARE

As long as England was dislocated by the Wars of the Roses both the Gaelic lords and the warlords of Norman origin in Ireland were secure in their virtual independence. They only had each other to fear. English monarchs had almost no money to spare for Ireland. A stop-gap solution was to turn to a great lord in Ireland to shoulder the burden of government.

The three most powerful Anglo-Irish lords were the Earls of Desmond, Ormond and Kildare. The problem with the FitzGeralds of Munster, Earls of Desmond, was that they had become too gaelicised and frequently rebelled. The Butlers, the Earls of Ormond, tended to back losers in the Wars of the Roses, and their lands were under constant attack from the Irish. The most suitable candidates for the post of royal governor were the FitzGeralds of Leinster, the Earls of Kildare, who possessed great estates adjoining the Pale.

Then, in 1485, a new era began with the victory of the Lancastrian, Henry Tudor, at the Battle of Bosworth. The Wars of the Roses were over. How would the new Tudor monarch, Henry vii, govern Ireland?

The royal governor since 1478 had been Garret Mór FitzGerald, the eighth Earl of Kildare. Henry vii was inclined to keep the Earl of Kildare in his post, but his trust was severely tested in 1487. An Oxford priest arrived in Dublin with a young boy, Lambert Simnel, who claimed to be the Earl of Warwick, the Yorkist candidate for the throne. The Earl of Kildare and many other lords gave him an enthusiastic welcome, proclaimed him king, and on 24 May solemnly crowned him in Christ Church Cathedral. Worse still, Kildare provided Simnel with an army which invaded England, only be routed at Stoke in June. Then embarrassing details emerged: the real Earl of Warwick was a prisoner in the Tower of London, and Lambert Simnel was proved to be an impostor.

Henry vii magnanimously pardoned the earl. For his part, Kildare buried the hatchet with his deadly enemy the Earl of Ormond, for long the king's ally. At a tense meeting between the two sides in St Patrick's Cathedral Ormond's representative, his bastard son Sir James of Ormond, fearing that his life was in danger, fled into the chapter house and bolted the door. At length tempers cooled, and a tentative reconciliation was arranged. A hole was cut in the door of the chapter house, and Sir James put his hand through the hole to shake hands with Garret Mór. This is the origin of the well-known Irish phrase 'chancing your arm'.

For a brief period Kildare was replaced as governor by the experienced English soldier Sir Edward Poynings. Poynings quarrelled with Kildare, charged him with treason, and sent the earl as a prisoner to England in the spring of 1495. Garret Mór, however, was able to disprove the charge of treason in the presence of the king. The earl's swaggering before Henry so infuriated the Bishop of Meath that he shouted out: 'You see the sort of man he is; all Ireland cannot rule him.' 'No?', replied King Henry. 'Then he must be the man to rule all Ireland.' In 1496 the Earl of Kildare returned in triumph to Ireland as the king' governor, newly married to Henry vii's first cousin, Elizabeth St John. An agent of the king reported that Kildare's return was widely welcomed:

> Now thanked be God the king hath peace in all the land without any great charge or cost to him. His grace could have put no man in authority here that in so short a space and with so little cost could have set this land in so good order as it is now but this man only.

The Earl of Kildare covered all his own expenses to such an extent that Henry was able to withdraw his army from Ireland altogether. Others, of course, had to pay for the administration and for Kildare's private army, known as the Guild of St George. Great sums of protection money were extracted from lesser lords; the Irish parliament was cajoled into allowing the earl to annex lands abandoned by Englishmen in the country; and—like many other powerful men—Kildare imposed what was known as 'coyne and livery', that is, the seizure of food and the quartering of troops on other people's lands.

The high point of the Great Earl's long rule was a successful expedition against Ulick Burke, Lord of Clanricarde, and his Irish allies in Connacht, in 1504. At Knockdoe, 'the Hill of the Axes', Burke's forces were shattered in the greatest battle fought in late medieval Ireland. The Annals of Ulster recorded that of nine battalions in Burke's army 'there escaped not alive of them but one thin battalion alone ... so that the field became uneven from those heaps of slaughter'. It had been a very long time since English royal power had been felt west of the River Shannon.

When the Great Earl of Kildare died in 1513 of a gunshot wound while fighting the O'Mores, he was virtually the ruler of Ireland. The king had no hesitation in appointing his son, the ninth earl, known to the Irish as Garret Óg, as his governor. But Garret Óg was not the man his father had been, and the days of the Kildare hegemony were now numbered.

Episode 48 ⌣

THE DECLINE OF THE HOUSE
OF KILDARE

When Garret Óg FitzGerald succeeded his father as the ninth Earl of Kildare in 1513, he was, without doubt, the most powerful lord in the land of Ireland. The county of Kildare was entirely in his possession, and he controlled further large tracts of land within an area comprising nine modern counties. He had been recently granted the valuable salmon fisheries of the River Bann and the customs of the Ulster ports of Ardglass and Strangford. He possessed countless head of cattle and over a thousand horses, the right to hold his own courts in Kildare, his own standing army which included gallowglass mercenaries from the Hebrides, and an impressive collection of castles. His income was further increased by various dues and charges imposed on his tenants. Every farmer on his estates of Carlow, for example, had to render to him one sheep out of every flock, a hen at Christmas, a dish of butter in May and another in autumn, and each dealer in beer paid four gallons for every brewing. Great numbers of lesser lords, including far-distant Gaelic chiefs, paid him protection money and regularly gave him the free use of their soldiers. In addition, the earl held the supremely powerful post of governor of Ireland.

Henry VIII toyed with the idea of attempting to govern his Irish lordship without this man. In 1520 he summoned Kildare to England, where he kept him a virtual prisoner, and sent over Thomas Howard, Earl of Surrey, as his governor. Surrey did his best, but after two years he had expended nearly £20,000 with very little to show for it. Henry had expensive military commitments in France, and, after giving the job to the Earl of Ormond for a time, set Kildare free and reappointed him as governor. The great attraction of employing Garret Óg was that—by fair means and foul—he raised all his own revenue, thereby ensuring that Ireland was not a burden on the London exchequer.

Garret Óg, however, proved an overmighty subject: for example, he quarrelled unendingly and ferociously with the Butlers of Ormond—for long the king's faithful supporters—and led an expedition into Ulster without royal permission. In addition, the earl used the Gaelic custom, known as *cuid oíche*, which forced landholders to entertain him and his attendants for days on end without payment, insisting that his hounds be given the same rations as a man. The king also received numerous complaints of his imposition of coyne and livery, the enforced billeting and maintenance of the earl's soldiers by local communities:

After their harvests are ended there, the kernes, the gallowglass and other breachlesse soldiers with horses and horsegrooms, enter into the villages with much cruelty and fierceness, they continue there with great rapine and spoil, and they leave nothing else behind for payment but lice, lechery and intolerable penury for all the year after.

King Henry once more summoned Garret Óg to London. After prolonged procrastination the earl did eventually consent to travel, but not before he had appointed his son Thomas as deputy governor in his place and removed the king's cannon from Dublin Castle, storing the guns in his own castle of Maynooth. Actually by the time he reached London, Garret Óg was dying— just like his father before him—mortally wounded by a gunshot wound he had received fighting the Irish in Leinster. The Spanish ambassador wrote to Emperor Charles v:

The Earl of Kildare is here sick both in body and brain by the shot of an arquebus.... There is no hope of his recovery, so that he must not be counted among those who will serve your Majesty.

Thomas FitzGerald, Lord Offaly, the earl's eldest son, was so well known for his love of finery that he was called 'Silken Thomas'. Later the Dublin attorney Richard Stanihurst described him as follows:

He was of stature tall and personable, in countenance amiable, a white face and withal somewhat ruddy, delicately in each limb featured, a rolling tongue, a rich utterance, of nature flexible and kind, very soon carried where he fancied, easily with stubbornness appeased.

Believing a report that his father had been executed, Silken Thomas melodramatically entered Dublin with a thousand men on 11 June 1534. Then with a bodyguard of 140 horsemen, clothed in coats of mail, he rode to St Mary's Abbey, where the council was in session. There Silken Thomas surrendered the sword of state, resigned his office, and renounced his allegiance to the king before a terrified council.

Episode 49 ∿

THE REBELLION OF SILKEN THOMAS

The Earl of Kildare, Chief Governor of Ireland [Garret Óg], the most illustrious of the English and Irish of Ireland in his time, died in captivity in London. After which, his son Thomas proceeded to avenge his father upon the English, and all who had been instrumental in removing him from Ireland. He resigned the king's sword, and did many injuries to the English.

In these words the Annals of the Four Masters chronicled the death in the Tower of London of Garret Óg FitzGerald, ninth Earl of Kildare, and the outbreak of the great rebellion of his son Silken Thomas against Henry VIII in 1534. The account continues:

The Archbishop of Dublin came by his death through him, for he had been opposed to his father; many others were slain along with him. He took Dublin from Newgate outwards, and pledges and hostages were given by the rest of the town through fear of him. The son of the earl on this occasion totally plundered and devastated Fingall from Three Rock Mountain to Drogheda, and made all Meath tremble beneath his feet.

Silken Thomas forged an alliance with Conor O'Brien, the Lord of Thomond, who in turn was seeking Spanish aid. Thomas was also sure of the support of his father's cousin, Conn Bacach O'Neill of Tír Eóghain. Then he issued an ultimatum that all those of English birth should immediately leave the country or face the consequences. There was no turning back now.

If Silken Thomas was to succeed, he had to take the capital. He laid siege to Dublin Castle, but the fortress was too strong, and it was well equipped to withstand a long siege. The garrison was even able to sally out, capture artillery pieces, and kill over a hundred of Thomas's gallowglasses. Narrowly avoiding capture, Silken Thomas made the fatal error of agreeing to a six-week truce. The immediate reason for this decision was that Piers Butler, Earl of Ormond, had remained loyal to King Henry and was ravaging the Kildare lands. When Conn Bacach arrived with his O'Neills from Tír Eóghain, he was sent, not to take Dublin but to take on Ormond in south Leinster.

Lord Thomas, now the tenth Earl of Kildare, hoped that the Emperor Charles V would send him aid, but all he got was some gunpowder and ammunition from a Spanish vessel putting in at Dingle in Kerry. Sir William

Skeffington landed in Dublin on 24 October. Though he brought with him the largest English army Ireland had seen in over a century, it took Skeffington months of bloody campaigning before he closed in on Maynooth Castle in Co. Kildare, Thomas's main stronghold. For six days in March 1535 Skeffington's cannon battered the castle. In the end Maynooth was taken, not solely by cannon fire, as Thomas's foster-brother informs us:

> Christopher Paris, to whose care the guard of the castle was principally committed, being blinded by avarice, privately agreed with Skeffington, for a certain sum of money to deliver up the castle.... The appointed night being come, he made the guard drunk, who being then buried in wine and sleep, the castle was easily won a little before day, the scaling ladders being applied to it.

Silken Thomas managed to escape, but one by one his allies made their peace with Skeffington. Finally on 24 August 1535 he surrendered to the newly appointed marshal of the English army, who was also his uncle-in-law, Lord Leonard Grey. Richard Stanihurst tells us that Lord Thomas,

> being in conference with Lord Grey ... was persuaded to submit himself to the king's mercy, with the governor's faithful and undoubted promise that he should be pardoned on his repair to England. And to the end that no treachery might have been misdeemed on either side, they both received the sacrament openly in the camp, as an infallible seal of the covenants and conditions of either part agreed.

It would have been better for Silken Thomas if he had held out in the Bog of Allen like his Gaelic Irish allies. On his arrival in London, the English Lord Chancellor expressed his amazement that

> so arrant and cankered a traitor should come into the king's sight, free and out of ward. If this be intended, that he should have mercy, I marvel much, that divers of the king's council in Ireland have told the king, afore this time, that there should never be good peace and order in Ireland, till the blood of the Geraldines were wholly extinct.

Henry VIII was a suspicious and ruthless monarch who would brook no opposition from over-powerful subjects. Now, early in 1537, he had no hesitation: Silken Thomas, along with five of his uncles, was condemned to a traitor's death. The Grey Friars in London recorded their end:

> The 3rd day of February the Lord Fytzgaarad with hys five unkelles of Ireland ... were draune from the Tower in to Tyborne, and there alle hongyd

and hedded and quartered, save the Lord Thomas for he was but hongyd and heeded and his body buryd at the Crost Freeres in the qwrere, and the quarters with their heddes set up about the cittie.

Just before the execution Lord Leonard Grey and Lord Chancellor Thomas Cromwell appropriated Silken Thomas's jewellery. For entirely unconnected and separate reasons, both men were to be beheaded on the orders of Henry VIII during the next four years.

Episode 50 ～

THE CHURCH IN TURMOIL

Throughout the Middle Ages all the people who lived in Ireland, natives and colonists alike, were Christians, and all, of course, were Catholics. There were some differences, however. In the English-controlled lordship the church was organised in much the same way as in France and England. In the areas beyond the reach of the English—more than half the island—the church was still run in the old Irish way. Above all, in Gaelic areas the rule of celibacy was everywhere ignored.

John Colton was the only Archbishop of Armagh who in several centuries had the courage to visit his flock in both the English and Gaelic parts of Ireland. This Englishman had taken a considerable risk in visiting Derry in the heart of Gaelic Ulster in 1397. He was kindly received, however, and was lodged there in the Black Abbey of the Augustinian canons. There he confirmed the election of Hugh Gillibride O'Doherty as abbot, but at the same time he issued this clergyman with a strict instruction to

dismiss and expel from your dwelling, cohabitation and care that Catherine whom it is said you have lately taken into concubinage and shall never afterwards take up with her again ... and that you should make no promise concerning any other concubine whom, heaven forbid, you should take to yourself in future.

But Archbishop Colton was wasting his breath: his attempt to make clergy in Gaelic areas remain celibate was a complete failure. For example, Cathal MacManus, Archdeacon of Clogher, proudly recorded in the Annals of Ulster the names of over a dozen children he had fathered—yet his obituary declared him to be 'a gem of purity and a turtle-dove of chastity'.

There is no doubt that the church throughout Ireland enjoyed strong and warm support. Gaelic lords, particularly in Ulster, went out of their way to fund the building of friaries. The friars, especially the Franciscans, were extremely popular because they were dedicated to a simple communal life, open-air preaching and pastoral work among the people. Donegal friary was founded in 1474 by Finola O'Connor, wife of the Lord of Tír Conaill; Bonamargy friary was built in 1500 by Rory MacQuillan, Lord of the Route; and others sprang up at Larne, Massereene, Lambeg, Sligo, and all over what the English described as the 'land of war'.

This friary building boom was in full swing in the 1530s when Henry VIII dissolved the monasteries in England. Soon afterwards he decided to get rid of the monasteries in Ireland as well.

When the papacy refused to allow Henry VIII to divorce Catherine of Aragon in order to marry Anne Boleyn, the king severed the English church from Rome and declared himself to be the head of that church. In May 1536 a parliament in Dublin agreed to accept Henry VIII as the supreme head of the Irish church:

> Forasmuch as this land of Ireland is depending and belonging justly and rightfully to the imperial crown of England, for increase in virtue in Christ's religion within the said land of Ireland, and to repress and extirpate all errors, heresies and other enormities and abuses, heretofore used in the same: be it enacted by authority of this present parliament that the king our sovereign lord, his heirs and successors ... shall be accepted, taken, and reputed the only supreme head in earth of the whole church of Ireland.

There is no doubt that Irish nobles, knights and burgesses attending this parliament were deeply unhappy about this break with the Roman church. But too many of them feared for their lives, having been involved so recently, however indirectly, in the rebellion of Silken Thomas FitzGerald: they therefore passed the legislation as the king wished. The task of enforcing the act was given to Archbishop Browne of Dublin, who sent out this instruction to the clergy:

> I exhort you all, that ye deface the said Bishop of Rome in all your books, where he is named pope, and that ye shall have from henceforth no trust in him, nor in his bulls or pardons, which, beforetime, with his juggling, casts of binding and loosing, he sold you for your money ... and also that ye fear not his great thunder claps of excommunication, for they cannot hurt you.

The Irish clergy, including those most loyal to the crown, were aghast. They were even more shaken when a royal commission recommended the shutting down of Irish monasteries, stating its reasons for doing so in the bluntest terms:

> It being manifestly apparent that the monks and nuns dwelling there being so addicted, partly to their own superstitious ceremonies, partly to the pernicious worship of idols, and to the pestiferous doctrines of the Roman pontiff, that the whole Irish people may be speedily infected, to their total destruction, by the example of these persons ...

Ireland was experiencing the first impact of a profound upheaval in western Christianity—the Reformation.

Episode 51 ∽

'SOBER WAYS, POLITIC DRIFTS, AND AMIABLE PERSUASIONS'

During the reign of the Tudor monarchs in the sixteenth century England grew more prosperous and powerful. The population was rising and ambitious younger sons, inheriting nothing at home, sought their fortunes elsewhere. Ireland, with a sparse population, attracted the English, just as the Spaniards were drawn across the Atlantic to Mexico and Peru.

Henry VIII was determined to recover all the lands in Ireland his predecessors had lost. But how was Ireland to be reconquered? One of the king's correspondents, signing himself 'Pandor', gave the following advice:

> Yf the king were as wise as Salamon the Sage, he shalle never subdue the wylde Iryshe to his obeysaunce, without dreadde of the swerde, and of the myght and streyngthe of his power, and of his Englyshe subgettes, orderyd as aforesayd; for aslong as they may resyste and save their lyffes, they will never obey the kyng.

Certainly Lord Leonard Grey put his faith in brute military force when he was appointed chief governor in 1536. With great energy and skill, Grey transported cannon on carts across rough country. He drove the O'Byrnes into their fastness of Glenmalure, recovered Athlone Castle for the crown, besieged Dungannon, and, after a fierce artillery battle, smashed down the bridge over the Shannon at Limerick in the face of the O'Briens.

King Henry was informed that 'Irishmen were never in such fear as they be at this instant time'. So alarmed were the Gaelic lords of Ulster by this vigorous campaigning that they sank their differences to unite in a great attack on the Pale in 1539, as the annals record:

> O'Neill and O'Donnell, by mutual permission and encouragement, made a hosting into Meath, devastating and burning the country as far as Tara; and never in later times had the Gaels assembled against the Foreigners an army which destroyed more of the wealth of Meath than this army. Immense were the booties of gold, silver, copper, iron and valuables of all kinds.

The governor, however, brought in men by sea to cut them off in Co. Monaghan:

> And as they were returning from this expedition loaded with pride and haughtiness and spoil, Lord Leonard followed after them together with a full muster and men from a large fleet in Carlingford harbour.... The army of the Gaels was overtaken at Bellahoe, to wit, and they were not able to array themselves in order but fled leaving much of their spoils.

But Lord Leonard Grey had his enemies, and he fell foul of his capricious monarch. His ally at court, Thomas Cromwell, was executed on Tower Hill in June 1540, and, despite all his military triumphs in Ireland, Lord Leonard followed him to the same scaffold exactly a year later.

Henry VIII found Grey's aggressive campaigning far too great a burden on his treasury. Could the Irish not be cajoled into loyalty rather than battered by cannon into submission? In an attempt to stop more and more of the English in Ireland going native, the king persuaded the Irish parliament to make the adoption of Irish dress, customs and language illegal in the Pale:

> Be it enacted ... that no person or persons, the king's subjects within this land ... shall be shorn, or shaven above the ears, or have any hair growing upon their upper lips ... or wear any shirt, smock, kerchief or linen cap, coloured or dyed with saffron ... and that no person or persons shall wear any mantles, coat or hood made after the Irish fashion ...
>
>   Every person shall use and speak commonly the English language ... and keep their house and households, as near as ever they can, according to the English order, condition and manner.

That statute proved as difficult to enforce as previous ones. More effective measures were needed. In a long letter the king set out his thoughts: to 'bring Irish captains to further obedience' and to recover royal lands, he suggested 'circumspect and politic ways', which thing must as yet rather be practised by sober ways, politic drifts, and amiable persuasions, founded in law and reason, than by rigorous dealing, or any other enforcement by strength and violence. And, to be plain unto you, to spend so much money for the reduction of that land, to bring the Irishry in appearance only of obedience ... it were a thing of little policy, less advantage, and least effect.

Sir Anthony St Leger, appointed chief governor in 1540, was a firm believer in 'amiable persuasions'. His scheme, known as 'surrender and regrant', was to erase the partition of Ireland between the English Pale and the Great Irishry. Henceforth Gaelic lords were to be invited to hold their lands by English feudal law from the king; the recommended procedure was that they would drop their traditional Irish titles and give up their lands to the king, receiving them back immediately with English titles. It was a scheme which was to enjoy a remarkable amount of initial success.

Episode 52 ～

CONN BACACH O'NEILL VISITS LONDON

Forasmuch as the king our most gracious dread sovereign lord, and his Grace's most noble progenitors, Kings of England, have been Lords of this land of Ireland ... be it enacted, ordained and established by authority of this present parliament, that the King's highness, his heirs and successors, Kings of England, be always Kings of this land of Ireland, and that his Majesty, his heirs and successors, have the name, style, title, and honour of King of this land of Ireland, with all manner prerogatives, dignities and other things whatsoever they be to the majesty of a king imperial belonging ...

And so the Irish parliament in 1541 gave Henry VIII the title 'King of Ireland'. No great protest followed. It was one thing, however, to assume a new title—it was another to make it a reality over large tracts of Ireland entirely beyond English control.

For most of the sixteenth century the viceroy, the royal governor, was given the title 'Lord Deputy'. Lord Deputy St Leger's scheme to get Irish lords to make their peace and adopt English titles seemed to be working well.

Turlough O'Toole, lord of the mountains overlooking Dublin, was the first to surrender his lands to the king and then have them regranted with a knighthood. He also agreed to stop exacting a 'black rent' from Dubliners, to use the English habit and manner, to teach his children to speak English, and to support the Lord Deputy with his fighting-men when required.

One by one nearly all the lords submitted and received English titles. Murrough O'Brien became Earl of Thomond; Ulick MacWilliam Burke of Connacht became Earl of Clanricarde; Dermot MacCarthy, Lord of Muskerry, got a knighthood; and so on. The greatest coup was to get the most powerful Gaelic lord in Ulster—and probably in the whole of Ireland—to submit. He was 'The O'Neill', Conn Bacach O'Neill, Lord of Tír Eóghain. Admittedly, St Leger had to fight a ruthless winter campaign against him, during which twenty-one days were spent destroying butter and corn in mid-Ulster. Then this man who had fought in common cause with Silken Thomas in his rebellion, put his X mark to a formal submission, confessing 'that by my ignorance, and for lack of knowledge of my bounded duty of allegiance, I have most grievously offended your Majesty'.

On Sunday 1 October 1542 Conn Bacach was in London to receive his new title of Earl of Tyrone. Before being presented to Henry VIII, he put on his robes in the queen's closet at Greenwich, which was 'richly hanged with cloth of arras, and well strewed with rushes':

And immediately after the King's Majesty, being under the cloth of state, accompanied with all his noblemen, councillors and others, came in the earl, led between the Earl of Oxenford, and the Earl of Hertford, the Viscount Lisle bearing before him his sword, the hilt upwards, Garter before him, bearing his letters patent; and so proceeded to the King's Majesty, who received of Garter the letters patent, and took them to Mr Wriotesley, secretary, to read them openly. And when the Viscount Lisle presented unto the king the sword, and the king girt the said sword baudrickwise [on his belt], the foresaid earl kneeling, and the other lords standing that led him. And so the patent read out, the King's Highness took him his letters patent, and he gave him thanks in his language, and a priest made answer of his saying in English. And so the earls in order aforesaid took their leave of the King's Highness, and departed unto the place appointed for their dinners, the Earl of Tyrone bearing his letters patent himself, the trumpets blowing before him unto the chamber which was the king's lodging. And so they sat at dinner. At the second course Garter proclaimed the king's style, and after the said new earl's in manner following: Du très haut et puissant Seigneur Con O'Neill, Comte de Tyrone, en le Royaume d'Irelande.

Having paid £10 to the office of arms and twenty angels for the hire of the gown, the first Earl of Tyrone tipped the trumpeters forty shillings and returned in triumph to Ulster.

St Leger's policy of conciliation was producing results, but others at court sought subjugation not co-operation, and their advice gained favour. When Henry VIII died in 1547, he was succeeded by his ten-year-old son, now Edward VI. Real power was exercised by Lord Protectors. St Leger was sidelined and then recalled in 1551. The Lord Deputies who came after him were determined on conquest and on the imposition of the Protestant religion on Ireland. In November 1551 the very first book to be printed in Ireland was published. It was the Book of Common Prayer, in which was set out the form of worship now by command to be followed in all the churches of Ireland.

Episode 53 ⁓

RELIGIOUS STRIFE AND PLANTATION

A heresy and a new error sprang up in England, through pride, vainglory, avarice and lust, and through many strange sciences, so that the men of England went into opposition to the pope and to Rome. And they styled the king Chief Head of the Church of God in his own kingdom. New laws and statutes were enacted ... they destroyed the orders, namely the monks, canons, nuns and the four poor orders, i.e. the orders of the Minors, Preachers, Carmelites and Augustinians; and the livings of all these were taken up for the king. They broke down the monasteries, and sold their roofs and bells.... They afterwards burned the images, shrines and relics, of the saints of Ireland and England; they likewise burned the celebrated image of Mary at Trim, which used to heal the blind, the deaf, and the crippled; and they also burned the *Bachall Íosa*, the staff of Jesus, which was in Dublin, performing miracles from the time of St Patrick ...

This account, taken from the Annals of the Four Masters, reflects the widespread alarm created by the introduction of the Protestant Reformation into Ireland in the sixteenth century. Yet Donegal Abbey and its sister foundation at Drowes, where these annals were compiled, were safe for the moment. It was in the English Pale and other fertile plains within easy reach of Dublin that the crown's new religious policies had their most immediate impact. The Palesmen, as they often called themselves, were horrified—they, the descendants of Norman and English conquerors, were genuinely loyal to the crown, but nearly all of them remained devout Catholics, viewing Protestant doctrine as heresy. Many of them had relatives who held ecclesiastical office and were now facing dismissal for refusing to use the Book of Common Prayer in church.

In addition, rich monastic lands in eastern Ireland were either seized by the crown or granted to recently arrived royal officials, men known as the 'New English'. For example, Nicholas Bagenal, a knight from Staffordshire appointed marshal of the king's army in Ireland, was granted the confiscated lands of Newry Abbey in south Down. The Palesmen, soon to be known as the 'Old English', were having their loyalty tested to the limit.

The drive to introduce Protestantism was particularly vigorous during the reign of Edward vi. But when Edward died in 1553, his successor, Queen Mary, immediately restored the Catholic religion. The Old English citizens of Kilkenny city were overjoyed and celebrated in front of St Canice's Cathedral:

> They rang all the bells ... they flung up their caps to the battlement of the great temple, with smilings and laughings most dissolutely ... they brought forth their copes, candlesticks, holy water stock, cross, and censers, they mustered forth in general procession most gorgeously, all the town over, with *Sancta Maria, ora pro nobis* and the rest of the Latin litany.

Queen Mary, however, gave her full support to those at court who thought that tough military action was the only lesson the rebellious Gaelic Irish would understand. Her commanders launched repeated campaigns into the interior. In an attempt to extend the frontiers of the Pale westwards, two midland counties were confiscated from the Irish there and renamed: Leix became 'Queen's County' and Offaly was titled 'King's County' after Mary's husband, King Philip II of Spain—names these counties retained well into the twentieth century.

An ambitious scheme was launched to 'plant' or colonise these two counties with loyal subjects. Two forts were renamed Maryborough and Philipstown in the hope that they would become flourishing towns. Government officials contemplated driving out and even killing all the Irish inhabitants of the area, but rejected this suggestion on the grounds that it would be, as one put it, 'a marvellous sumptuous charge'. In the end it was only the Gaelic nobles who were either executed or expelled, and the native population was squeezed into one-third of the plantation area. In return for rent payable to the crown, land was allocated to 'Englishmen born in England or Ireland'—most of the colonists, in fact, were families from the Pale.

The plantation of Leix and Offaly was only a very limited success. The leading Gaelic families in the region, the O'Connors, O'Mores and O'Dempseys, rebelled at least fourteen times in the ensuing decades. The hope was that the royal government could make a profit: in practice, the cost of protecting the colonists and crushing the surviving dispossessed was ruinous. As Sir Henry Sidney reflected some twenty years later, 'The revenue of both the countries countervails not the twentieth part of the charge, so that the purchase of that plot is, and hath been, very dear.'

In 1558 Mary died and without an heir. Her successor was Elizabeth. It was during her long reign that Ireland was to be conquered from end to end by the English for the first time. To do that she had to concentrate on subjugating the most Gaelic part of Ireland, the province of Ulster.

Episode 54 ∾

SHANE THE PROUD

By the middle of the sixteenth century the Tudor monarchs had recovered control of much of Ireland, but that did not include Ulster. At one time the earldom of Ulster had stretched round from Carlingford Lough, along the coasts of Antrim and Down and over to the Inishowen peninsula. But from the early fourteenth century onwards it slowly disintegrated.

Emerging from their woody fastness of Glenconkeyne in the heart of the province, the descendants of Áedh Buidhe O'Neill—a former King of Tír Eóghain—crossed the lower Bann and carved out a new lordship for themselves from the shattered remnants of the Norman earldom. The Savage family was driven out of the Six Mile Water valley and hung on precariously at the tip of the Ards peninsula. The Magennises of Iveagh and the MacCartans of Kinelarty engulfed central and southern Co. Down, while Clann Aodha Buidhe—which means the 'family of yellow-haired Hugh'—dominated a sweep of territory extending from Larne inland to Lough Neagh at Shane's Castle and taking in also the castle of Belfast and north Down, including much of the Ards. This territory the English called 'Clandeboye' after the ruling family which had conquered it.

Driven out of Co. Down, the MacQuillans conquered the area around Coleraine which became known as 'The Route', named from their 'rout', the usual contemporary term for a private army. Close by, a branch of the Hebridean MacDonnells, the Lords of Islay and Kintyre, made a new home in the Glens of Antrim. With every reverse they suffered in Scotland, fresh waves of MacDonnells arrived. Henry VIII had received this warning:

The Scots inhabit now busily a great part of Ulster, which is the king's inheritance; and it is greatly to be feared, unless in short time they be driven from the same, that they, bringing in more number daily, will ... with the aid of the king's disobedient Irish rebels, expel the king from his whole seignory there.

By the beginning of Elizabeth's reign in 1558 that prediction had proved correct. In all of Ulster, only Carrickfergus, the port of Ardglass and Sir Nicholas Bagenal's lands in Newry lay within the area under the crown's full control.

By far the most powerful man in Ulster was Shane O'Neill of Tyrone. Brutal, vindictive and drunken, Shane had driven his aged father, Conn Bacach, into the Pale, where he died soon after. Conn, created first Earl of Tyrone in 1542, had nominated Matthew, another son, as his heir, and this had been accepted in London. The problem was that the earl had married several times and had innumerable offspring. By Gaelic law, each one of his sons could claim to compete to succeed him. In a fierce succession dispute, Shane had come out on top. He had murdered his half-brother Matthew, whom he claimed—probably correctly—to have been Conn's illegitimate son by a blacksmith's wife.

To his own people he was *Seaán an Díomais*, Shane the Proud: arrogant, ruthless and wily, he was without rival in Tyrone. He aspired to dominate the Antrim Scots, the Clandeboye O'Neills and the O'Donnells of Tír Conaill. By 1560 so many Scottish mercenaries had entered his service that the viceroy, Sir William Fitzwilliam, sent a desperate appeal to the English government: 'Send us over men that we may fight ere we die.'

Though Queen Elizabeth refused to recognise Shane as Earl of Tyrone, at first she seemed to hope the problem would somehow go away. Then Shane swept south and launched an attack on the Pale. After that, in May 1561, he moved west against Calvagh O'Donnell, Lord of Tír Conaill. Calvagh's wife, Catherine, seems to have become infatuated with Shane; certainly she led Calvagh into a trap while he was besieging a rebellious kinsman in Glenveagh. The O'Donnell chief was bound in chains, and Catherine became Shane's mistress, only to be abused cruelly and cast aside soon after.

The problem for Elizabeth was that Calvagh was at that time supposed to be an ally of the English crown. She sent over the Earl of Sussex as her viceroy. The earl forged his way into Ulster, only to find that Shane O'Neill had pulled back into the forests with his cattle. Cut off by floods and running out of supplies, Sussex had no choice but to make a humiliating retreat. In desperation the earl concocted a plan to poison Shane, with a contingency scheme— which he frankly explained to the queen—to murder the poisoner should he fail. Nothing came of this plan.

Given an additional £2,000, reinforcements from Berwick and a supporting fleet, Sussex invaded again. This time he got as far as Omagh, where he slaughtered a great herd of Shane's brood mares and cattle. However, he failed to make contact with the fleet to be revictualled and once again had to retreat ignominiously by the way he had come.

The queen felt she had no recourse but to make her peace with Shane, and to this end she invited him to London.

Episode 55 ◌

THE FALL OF SHANE O'NEILL

Unable to bring about his defeat on the battlefield, Queen Elizabeth swallowed her pride and invited Shane O'Neill, the ruler of Tyrone, to her capital. On 3 January 1562 Shane entered London, accompanied by the Earls of Kildare and Ormond, and with an escort of fifty gallowglasses. Bare-headed, with hair flowing onto their shoulders, wearing short tunics, heavy cloaks, and linen vests dyed saffron with urine, the warriors drew crowds of onlookers as large as those that had turned out to gape at native Americans and Chinese in the city a short time before. Shane would not allow Kildare, his cousin, and Ormond, kinsman of the queen, to leave his side for a moment.

Next day at Greenwich, in the presence of ambassadors and all the court, Shane threw himself to the floor before Elizabeth. Then rising to his knees, he made a passionate speech in Irish, punctuated by howls which caused great astonishment. 'For lack of education and civility I have offended ...', he began, the words of his speech being translated into English by the Earl of Kildare. Elizabeth eventually agreed to recognise Shane as 'captain' of Tyrone on condition that he kept the peace for the next six months.

Almost as soon as he was back in Ulster, Shane O'Neill was making devastating raids on his neighbours. Desperately attempting a last stand on an island on Lough Erne, Hugh Maguire, Lord of Fermanagh, penned a frantic appeal to the queen's governor:

> I cannot scape neither by land nor by water, except God and your Lordship do help me at this need; all my country are against me because of their great losses and for fear, and all my men's pleasure is that I should yield myself to Shane.

A punitive expedition to Ulster led by the Earl of Sussex in 1563 failed to bring O'Neill to heel. To complete his domination of all of Ulster, Shane then prepared to strike at the MacDonnells of Antrim.

As Shane bore down on the Glens in 1565, the Scots set their beacons ablaze on Fair Head and the high ground behind Torr Head. The men of Kintyre seized their weapons and manned their galleys, but it was already too late. Sorley Boy MacDonnell, who had been leading the defence of the Glens, fell back to join his brother James, and together they made a desperate last stand by the slopes of Knocklayd. Shane overwhelmed the Scots, as he triumphantly reported in a letter written in Latin and sent to Dublin Castle:

> God, best and greatest, and for the welfare of her Majesty the Queen, gave us the victory against them. James and his brother Sorley were taken prisoners, besides many of the Scottish nobility were captured, and great numbers of their men killed, amounting in all to six or seven hundred.

James died of his wounds, Dunseverick fell, Ballycastle was taken, and—after Shane threatened to starve Sorley Boy to death—Dunluce capitulated. O'Neill had all Ulster in thrall, as he exultantly declared in a letter to Sir Henry Sidney:

> I am in blood and power better than the best of them.... My ancestors were Kings of Ulster, Ulster was theirs, and shall be mine. And for O'Donnell, he shall never come into his country if I can keep him out of it, nor Bagenal into the Newry, nor the Earl of Kildare into Lecale. They are mine; with this sword I won them, with this sword I will keep them. This is my answer.

The queen was horrified that such slaughter had been claimed on her behalf, and she wrote to Sir Henry Sidney, her new Lord Deputy, to ask how 'such a cankred dangerous rebel' might be 'utterly extirped'.

Sidney's invasion of the north in 1566, though it was supported by a fleet in Lough Foyle, failed to crush O'Neill. In the end it was Shane's neighbours in Ulster who brought about his downfall. In 1567 as the O'Neills crossed the River Swilly at Farsetmore they met a furious onslaught of O'Donnells and MacSweeneys, as the annals record:

> They proceeded to strike, mangle, slaughter, and cut down one another for a long time, so that men were soon laid low, heroes wounded, youths slain, and robust heroes mangled in the slaughter.

Shane's warriors retreated into the advancing tide, there to be drowned or cut down. O'Neill himself fled eastward to take refuge with the MacDonnells in the Glens. It was an extraordinary decision, but perhaps Shane hoped that by openly associating with Sorley Boy he could buy protection. The MacDonnells prepared a feast at Glenshesk in an apparent mood of reconciliation. They 'fell to quaffing'—as one report put it—and a quarrel broke out, during which O'Neill was hacked to death. Shane's head was sent 'pickled in a pipkin' to Sidney, who placed it on a spike over Dublin Castle gate-arch. But many more campaigns would have to be fought before Ulster would be subdued.

Episode 56 ∿

A FAILED PLANTATION AND A BLOODY FEAST IN BELFAST

The killing of Shane O'Neill did little to increase English power in Ulster. Queen Elizabeth did not feel she had money to spare for more expensive military expeditions. Perhaps private enterprise could achieve something there? Certainly Sir William Cecil, the queen's secretary, thought so. Enterprising Englishmen could be encouraged to 'plant' or colonise parts of the province, build 'haven towns' and bring in 'good husbandmen, plough wrights, cart wrights and smiths, and serve there under such gentlemen as shall inhabit there'. The queen was convinced and approved a scheme put forward by one of her Privy Councillors, Sir Thomas Smith. He obtained letters patent entitling him and his son, also called Thomas, to the lands of eastern Ulster held by the Clandeboye O'Neills. His plan was to remove all the Irish except for poor labourers, who were to be kept on to till the soil. Here, his publicity brochure proclaimed,

> Every Irishman shall be forbidden to wear English apparel or weapon on pain of death.... No Irishman, born of Irish race and brought up Irish, shall purchase land, bear office, be chosen of any jury.

Cecil was so confident of this venture's success that he invested £333 6s 8d in it.

When he heard of it, Lord Deputy Sir William Fitzwilliam was furious. Had not Brian MacPhelim O'Neill, Lord of Clandeboye, recently been knighted for his service against Shane O'Neill of Tyrone? Actually Smith's enterprise was doomed from the outset. Only around a hundred prospective colonists disembarked at Strangford village in August 1572. Led by Sir Thomas's inexperienced son, the expedition moved north towards Newtownards, only to find that Sir Brian MacPhelim was burning any building which might give shelter to the English. Smith had to seek refuge in Ringhaddy Castle, and it was in vain that he appealed to Dublin for help. He was killed by his Irish servants in the following year, and his body was boiled and fed to dogs. By then a more ambitious enterprise was already under way.

Walter Devereux, Earl of Essex, was so certain of success that he mortgaged most of his great estates in England and Wales to raise the £10,000 he thought was needed. Elizabeth, grateful for Essex's service in foiling an escape attempt by Mary Queen of Scots, gave him title to most of Co. Antrim and money to cover half the cost of the thousand soldiers he had raised.

Setting out from Liverpool on 16 August 1573, Essex had to take shelter from a storm on the Copeland Islands before landing at Carrickfergus. Sir Brian MacPhelim thought it politic not to quarrel with such a powerful English noble; as Essex reported, 'I took him by the hand, as a sign of his restitution to her Highness's service.' Relations between the two men soon became strained, however, after Essex seized thousands of cattle. Relations between Essex and his gentlemen colonists were hardly any better. In November the earl wrote in complaint to the queen:

> The adventurers, of whom the most part, not having forgotten the delicacies of England, and wanting the resolute minds to endure a year or two in this waste country, [have] forsaken me, feigning excuses to repair home where I hear they give forth speeches in dislike of the enterprise ... [and] the common hired soldiers, both horsemen and footmen, mislike of their pay.

In the following year Essex was given the new title of 'General Captain in All Ulster', but his plantation was failing to take shape. In frustration, Essex hanged some Devon men for attempted desertion, and imprisoned Captain Piers, custodian of Carrickfergus Castle, for being too friendly to Sir Brian MacPhelim. Turlough Luineach O'Neill, the successor to Shane O'Neill in Tír Eóghain, was also offering friendship to Sir Brian, so the earl slaughtered a band of his followers taking refuge on a river island at Banbridge and invaded mid-Ulster, burning corn all down the Clogher and Blackwater valleys. Essex got as far as Derry, but the wily Turlough kept giving him the slip by disappearing into the forests and mountains.

Peace was restored with Sir Brian, but this was to occasion an act of treachery. In October 1574 Essex and his principal followers were invited to a feast in Belfast Castle, Sir Brian's tower-house which stood on ground now occupied by Castle Place in the centre of the city. The annals record:

> They passed three nights and days together pleasantly and cheerfully. At the expiration of this time, as they were agreeably drinking and making merry, Brian, his brother, and his wife, were seized upon by the earl, and all his people put unsparingly to the sword—men, women, youths, and maidens—

in Brian's own presence. Brian was afterwards sent to Dublin, together with his wife and brother, where they were cut in quarters. Such was the end of their feast.

This cruelty did nothing to advance Essex's cause. Nor did an act of equal barbarity carried out the following summer on Rathlin.

Episode 57 ~

AN ENGLISH QUEEN, A SCOTTISH LADY AND A DARK DAUGHTER

The MacDonnells, Gaelic-speaking Scots from the Western Isles, had carved out a powerful lordship for themselves in Ireland to add to their possessions in Islay and Kintyre. Centred on the Glens of Antrim, their Irish territory stretching from Larne to Coleraine, bristled with castles. Joining them were MacNeills, MacAllisters, MacKays and MacRandalbanes from Kintyre and Gigha, and, from the Rinns of Islay, the Magees after whom Islandmagee is named.

The Lord of the Glens, Sorley Boy MacDonnell, was one of the most astute leaders in the Gaelic world. In the Isles he had made his peace with the Campbells and arranged the marriage of his brother's widow, Lady Agnes (herself a Campbell) to the strongest ruler in Ulster, Turlough Luineach O'Neill of Tyrone. Finola, Lady Agnes's daughter, was married in turn to Hugh O'Donnell, Lord of Tír Conaill. Finola—known as Inghean Dubh, the 'dark daughter'—herself exercised formidable power in Donegal.

These arrangements formed the basis of a powerful coalition. Had Elizabeth been better informed, she might have made a useful ally of Sorley Boy. Instead, in 1575, the queen approved the plan of her general in Ulster, the Earl of Essex, to smash the power of the MacDonnells. A fleet was fitted out in Carrickfergus harbour, including three frigates under the command of Francis Drake, already famous for seizing a Spanish treasure convoy. Captain John Norris (after whom Mountnorris in Co. Armagh is named), the son of a Groom of the Stole executed for having an affair with Anne Boleyn, took command of the soldiers crowding on board the vessels bound for Rathlin Island.

The assault fleet reached Arkill Bay on the east side of the island on the morning of 22 July 1575. Captain Norris's men, Essex reported, 'did with valiant minds leap to land, and charged them so hotly, as they drave them to retire with speed, chasing them to a castle which they had of very great strength'. The castle, with many women and children inside, was pounded by ship's guns for four days. But without a well, and with its wooden ramparts destroyed by red-hot cannon-balls, it could hold out no longer. At dawn on 26 July the garrison surrendered on condition their lives were spared; but, it was reported,

> The soldiers, being moved and much stirred with the loss of their fellows that were slain, and desirous of revenge, made request, or rather pressed, to have the killing of them, which they did all.... There were slain that came out of the castle of all sorts 200.... They be occupied still in killing, and have slain that they have found hidden in caves and in the cliffs of the sea to the number of 300 or 400 more.

Essex passed on to the queen information he had received from a spy that Sorley Boy 'stood upon the mainland of the Glynnes and saw the taking of the island, and was like to run mad for sorrow (as the spy saith), turning and tormenting himself, and saying that he had then lost all that ever he had'.

Elizabeth did not condemn this cruelty: instead she promoted Norris and gave Drake a special audience at court. And to Essex the queen wrote in her elegant italic script:

> If lines could value life; or thanks could answer praise, I should esteem my pen's labour the best employed time that many years had lent me ... your most loving cousin and sovereign E.R.

In spite of this apparent victory, Essex was running out of men and money. He was a long way from realising his project of conquering and colonising Ulster. His optimism remained unbounded. He dreamed of making Belfast a great port: 'I resolve not to build but at one place; namely, at Belfast; and that of little charge; a small town there will keep the passage, and shall command the plains of Clandeboye.' And he added: 'For my part I will not leave the enterprise as long as I have any foot of land in England unsold.'

But even the queen knew he had failed. Essex pulled back in despair to Dublin, where in September 1576, rather suddenly, he died of dysentery. He was thirty-six years old. Just how quickly English royal power had faded in Ulster is reflected in an urgent memorandum sent from Carrickfergus less than four years later:

> Here is a great bruit of 2000 Scots landed in Clandeboye. Turlough Luineach's marriage with the Scot is the cause of all this, and if her Majesty

does not provide against her devices, this Scottish woman will make a new Scotland of Ulster. She hath already planted a good foundation; for she in Tyrone, and her daughter in Tyrconnell, do carry all the sway in the North.

Elizabeth could do nothing in response: she had a rebellion to crush in the far south of Ireland.

Episode 58 ~

'WARRING AGAINST A SHE-TYRANT': HOLY WAR IN MUNSTER

In February 1565, by the Knockmealdown Mountains in Co. Waterford, Gerald FitzGerald, the fifteenth Earl of Desmond, and Thomas Butler, the tenth Earl of Ormond, met in furious battle. These descendants of the first Norman conquerors, the two most powerful warlords in Munster, were then summoned to court: there Queen Elizabeth sternly charged them with waging a private war in her realm. They were bound over for £20,000 each to keep the peace and sent back to Ireland.

Ormond thereafter behaved himself, but Desmond did not—he could not endure the undermining of his authority by the crown officials, and, like so many of his vassals, he was appalled by the establishment of a Protestant church with the queen as its supreme governor. In 1567 the Lord Deputy had him arrested, forfeited his bond for £20,000 and dispatched the earl to spend the next five years languishing in the Tower of London. During his absence his cousin James FitzMaurice FitzGerald and his brother Sir John of Desmond managed the earl's vast properties as best they could, deeply resenting growing English interference.

In 1569 James FitzMaurice and Sir John led an angry revolt, besieging Cork and the Ormond capital, Kilkenny. The colonel commanding Elizabeth's forces, Sir Humphrey Gilbert, crushed the rebellion with a savagery unusual even for that time. In six weeks he took twenty-three castles and in each one slaughtered all those inside, men, women and children; and as every defeated rebel made abject surrender he had to walk down a grisly corridor of severed heads.

The Earl of Desmond was allowed back to Ireland in 1573. A man who by several accounts was not the full shilling, Desmond threw off his English clothes and put on Irish dress as a warning that he would not tolerate further erosion of his traditional power by Protestant heretics. His cousin James FitzMaurice, deciding to seek the aid of Catholic rulers, sailed to France with his wife and children in 1575. Eventually he managed to obtain an audience with Pope Gregory XIII in Rome, who provided him with a thousand Italian swordsmen. On their way to Ireland there was an irritating delay when King Sebastian of Portugal commandeered the force to fight in Morocco. FitzMaurice, unlike some of those who had been forced to fight the Moors, survived the experience to reassemble his Italians and to recruit some Spanish soldiers. Hearing of these preparations, the royal council in Dublin issued instructions to naval captains:

> Make sail along the west and north-west sea coasts, for the pursuit, appre-hending, and plaguing of any traitors or malefactors adherent to the pro-claimed traitors.... Search all passengers for letters, books, ciphers, or other kind of suspect matter, that may tend either to the defacing of religion or to the dishonour of the Queen's most excellent Majesty.... Make stay of any French, Spanish, Flemish, or Scottish ships and convoy them into the Shannon.

Sailing from Corunna, the force managed to evade these patrols to put in at Smerwick harbour in Co. Kerry on 18 July 1579. A spy reported:

> The traitor upon Saturday last came out of his ship. Two friars were his ancient-bearers.... A bishop, with a crozier-staff and his mitre, was next the friars. After came the traitor himself at the head of his company and went to seek for flesh and kine.

At Smerwick they built a fort which became known as *Dún an Óir*, the 'fort of gold'. With them was an English priest, the pope's emissary, who had helped FitzMaurice to compose his propaganda:

> The cause of this war is God's glory, for it is our care to restore the visible honour of the holy altar which the heretics have impiously taken away. The glory of Christ is belied by the heretics, who deny that his sacraments confer grace ... and the glory of the Catholic Church they also belie.
>
> This war is undertaken for the defence of the Catholic religion against the heretics.... We are warring against a she-tyrant who has deservedly lost her royal power by refusing to listen to Christ in the person of her vicar, and through daring to subject Christ's Church to her feminine sex on matters of faith.

Soon Sir John of Desmond joined his cousin FitzMaurice, and swordsmen and gallowglasses from lordships all over Cork, Kerry, Limerick and Tipperary thronged to join the insurrection. Shortly afterwards FitzMaurice was killed while attempting to seize some horses, and Sir John of Desmond took command. Eventually, after much hesitation, the Earl of Desmond himself joined the revolt.

For more than a year a vicious war raged across the south, neither side showing any mercy. On the English government's behalf, the Earl of Ormond laid waste extensive tracts of his rival's earldom, while the FitzGeralds sacked the town of Youghal. Then Pope Gregory sent more Italians and Spaniards, who joined their compatriots at Smerwick in September 1580. There was to be a terrible outcome.

Episode 59 ~

THE PLANTATION OF MUNSTER

For more than a year the forces of the crown had been engaged in crushing a great rebellion led by the FitzGeralds in Munster. As one by one the insurgent castles capitulated, Lord Deputy Grey closed in on the Dingle peninsula during the autumn of 1580. Here at Smerwick harbour a force of Italians and Spaniards sent to help the Irish prepared to make a desperate last stand in the fort known as *Dún an Óir*. Grey waited until Admiral Sir William Winter at last sailed in with his squadron. Then he took action:

> The sailors took some culverins quietly out of the ships at night and dragged them by the nearest way and set them in position. The soldiers meanwhile on the other side set up their great pieces for battery against the walls and both of them at once played for four whole days upon the fort.... As they saw no succour coming from Spain nor from Desmond, they raised the white flag and begged for a parley.

When the commander of the joint Spanish and Italian expeditionary force admitted that they had been sent by Pope Gregory in defence of the Catholic faith, the Lord Deputy replied to him that the pope was 'a detestable shaveling, the right Antichrist and general ambitious tyrant over all right principalities, and patron of the diabolical faith'. Nevertheless, the Italian hugged the Lord Deputy's knees, believing that he had capitulated on the promise of his men's lives. Officers came out with their banners trailing and surrendered the fort. 'And then', the Lord Deputy chillingly reported to the queen, 'put I in certain bands, who straight fell to execution. There were 600 slain.' There was no reproof from the queen: indeed, she wrote on top of Grey's despatch in her own hand:

> The mighty hand of the Almighty's power hath shewed manifest the force of his strength ... in which action I joy that you have been chosen the instrument of his glory which I mean to give you no cause to forethink.

The quelling of the rebellion took another year. Its military leader, John of Desmond, was killed at the beginning of 1582, and his head was forwarded to the Lord Deputy as a 'new year gift'. The Earl of Desmond himself was found hiding in a cabin a year later and was summarily slaughtered; his head was sent to Queen Elizabeth.

Great tracts of the south of Ireland were left in ruins and a terrible famine swept across the land. The Lord Deputy's secretary, Edmund Spenser, had witnessed the massacre at Smerwick. Now he described the suffering of the ordinary people in Munster:

> Notwithstanding that [Munster] was a most rich and plentiful country, full of corn and cattle, yet ere one year and a half they were brought to such wretchedness, as that any stony heart would have rued the same. Out of every corner of the woods and glens they came creeping forth upon their hands, for their legs would not bear them; they looked like anatomies of death, they spake like ghosts crying out of their graves; they did eat of the dead carrions, happy were they if they could find them, yea, and one another soon after.... And if they found a plot of watercresses or shamrocks, there they flocked as to a feast for the time, yet not able long to continue there withal; that in a short space there were none almost left, and a most populous and plentiful country suddenly made void of man and beast.

Walter Raleigh, a captain who had superintended the slaughter at Smerwick, was one of many who argued that now was the time to colonise the confiscated estates of the Earl of Desmond and his adherents. A hasty survey was made in 1584, and finally in 1586 the decision was taken to settle people of English birth on the confiscated lands. The lands were divided into portions of between 12,000 and 4,000 acres, each to be granted to an 'undertaker', that is, a man who undertook to bring in a specified number of families to work the land—no Gaelic Irish tenants were permitted. Demand was strong, and eventually thirty-five undertakers were successful in getting estates. It was not long, however, before the plantation of Munster began to run into trouble.

The principal drawback in implementing the scheme was that not enough ordinary English farming families came over, and those that did were fatally exposed in the turbulent conditions following the outbreak of war between England and Spain.

Throughout the spring of 1588 the supposedly invincible Armada, 130 vessels in all, massed before Lisbon, took on stores and made ready for the invasion of England. After years of vacillation Philip II of Spain, the most powerful monarch in the world, had embarked finally on war with Elizabeth. The fate of Ireland as well as of England hung in the balance.

Episode 60 ∿

THE WRECK OF THE ARMADA

From the time the Armada entered the English Channel, Philip II's dream of conquering England was turning to dust. Raked by English cannon fire and scattered by fireships, the Spanish fleet could do no other than take flight up the North Sea, around the Shetlands and westwards deep into the Atlantic. In the mountainous seas stirred up by autumn gales some Armada vessels were driven inexorably towards the western shores of Ireland. Eating only ship's biscuit riddled with weevils and parched by lack of fresh water, the crews were exhausted, ill, and many were dying. Such men posed no threat to English power in Ireland.

In Dublin Castle Sir William Fitzwilliam, Queen Elizabeth's Lord Deputy, was starved of news. Had the Spanish invaded England? When a messenger galloped into the courtyard with news of great ships seen all along the west coast, Fitzwilliam's anxiety became acute. His orders were clear: put to the sword any Spaniard who stepped ashore.

Twenty-four men survived the wreck of a frigate in Tralee Bay, only to be seized and hanged there by the orders of Lady Denny. Don Juan Martinez de Recalde, Admiral of the Biscay Squadron, Captain General of the Ocean Sea, and second-in-command of the Invincible Armada, anchored inside the Blasket Islands. Now, like so many of his crew, Recalde was dying. All that was left on board his galleon, a spy reported to Fitzwilliam, were '25 pipes of wine, and very little bread, and no water, but what they brought out of Spain, which stinketh marvellously; and their flesh meat they cannot eat, their drouth is so great'. Eight men sent ashore at Dunquin had their throats cut. After forcing the terrified islanders at gunpoint to give him water, Recalde sailed away.

Close by, the *Nuestra Señora de la Rosa* tried to anchor in Blasket Sound. Dragged by the tide and split open on a hidden reef, the galleon sank; all 700 on board drowned save for one man. Seven vessels entered the Shannon estuary, flying white flags, but the Sheriff of Clare refused gold and an offer to exchange barrels of wine for casks of water. Don Pedro de Mendoza landed at Clare Island off the Mayo coast, but he and his crew of a hundred men had their treasure seized and were butchered there by the O'Malley chief. On a neighbouring strand at Burrishoole a galleon ran aground on sand. Local people rushed upon them and killed them for their finery.

At Galway harbour Don Luis de Cordoba put men ashore, only to see them taken prisoner. Townspeople tore at them, ripping off their gold chains. The rest of the crew were taken by fishermen; some were so weak that 'they could not swallow what food they were given, but vomited it straight away'. All were then hanged or shot, with the exception of Don Luis, who was held for ransom.

On 14 September *La Trinidad Valencera* sought shelter in the lee of the Inishowen peninsula. Despite being one of the greatest ships of the Armada, the vessel was dangerously overloaded and had been shipping water in the wild south-westerly storm. Limping down the eastern shore, the ship cast anchor and the Commander of the Regiment of Naples, Don Alonso de Luzon, sent a cockboat ashore. As a survivor informed Philip II, 'They landed with rapiers in their hands whereupon they found four or five savages who bade them welcome and used them well until twenty more wild men came unto them, after which time they took away a bag of money.' The 'wild men' were O'Dohertys of Inishowen, and they did what they could for the stricken Spanish. For two days boats and curraghs plied back and forth with supplies until suddenly *La Trinidad Valencera* sank; forty men who were below decks were drowned. In the 1980s the Derry Sub-Aqua Club, diving in Kinnagoe Bay, found remains of the wreck, including a massive siege-gun embossed with the name of Philip II in Latin; it now stands at the entrance of the Tower Museum. Don Alonso made up his mind to cross the Foyle and seek the help of the MacDonnells of the Glens. With barely the strength to make the journey, this mixed band of Spaniards, Neapolitans, Greeks and Dalmatians set out with banners flying and drums beating. By nightfall they had travelled only as far as Galliagh, close to Derry, and here they were confronted by Irish soldiers in English pay. After a brisk skirmish Alonso's exhausted men surrendered on condition that they would be treated as prisoners of war. As soon as they had given up their weapons, however, they were stripped naked and at first light taken into a field. There almost two hundred of them were butchered.

This massacre notwithstanding, it was in the far north-west, remote from Dublin, that Spanish castaways were to be given vital help by the native Irish.

Episode 61 ⌁

THE LAST VOYAGE OF THE *GIRONA*

Don Alonso Martinez de Leiva de Rioja, Knight of Santiago, Commander of Alcuescar, was general-in-chief of the land forces of the Armada entrusted with the conquest of England. By September 1588 his only concern was to survive. Enduring the terror of mountainous waves round Scotland and in the North Atlantic, de Leiva's ship, *Sancta Maria Rata Encoronada*, was driven on to the Mayo coast, where it foundered in Blacksod Bay. The survivors transferred to a transport vessel; however, to reach Spain in such an overladen ship was impossible, and so de Leiva set out for neutral Scotland. A strong southwesterly pushed the ship northwards past Erris, across Donegal Bay to skirt the sea-cliffs of Slieve League, only to be driven at night into Loughros More Bay. Here, an Irishman on board recalled, 'Falling to anchor, there fell a great storm which brake in sunder all their cables and struck them upon ground.' Although his leg had been broken against the capstan, de Leiva rallied the survivors to entrench themselves on an island in Kiltooris Lough.

A week later the commander heard that three Spanish vessels had taken shelter in Killybegs harbour. Perhaps a thousand men accompanied de Leiva across the mountain pass to join their compatriots. Here only one Spanish ship remained afloat, the *Girona*, a three-masted galleas with thirty-six oars pulled by 244 rowers. De Leiva resolved to repair the ship and sail for Scotland. A spy dashed off a message to Dublin Castle:

> The Spaniards are buying workhorses and mares for food. The best of the Spaniards in MacSweeney's country are going away and will leave the rest to shift for themselves because the ship cannot receive them all.

About 1,300 Spaniards crowded aboard the *Girona* at Killybegs, as another spy reported:

> The 26th instant October the said galley departed from the said harbour with as many Spaniards as she could carry.... The Spaniards gave MacSweeney, at their departure, twelve butts of sack wine ... the MacSweeneys and their followers have gotten great store of the Spanish calivers and muskets.

The *Girona* negotiated the wild waters off Bloody Foreland and Inishowen, only to have her rudder smashed by a northerly gale which blew the vessel on to the north Antrim coast. Close to the Giant's Causeway at Lacada Point the ship struck a long basalt reef and split apart. The disaster of that terrible night was so great that the death toll was only two hundred short of the number lost in the *Titanic* in 1912. In the pitch blackness close to midnight, with a strong tide sweeping away from the reef, only nine men survived.

Three hundred and eighty years later the Belgian archaeologist Robert Sténuit discovered the wreck and brought *Girona*'s treasures to the surface. This, the most complete collection of Armada archaeological findings, is a permanent reminder of the flower of the Spanish nobility who died with Don Alonso, and the nameless sailors, conscripts and galley slaves who perished in these cold northern waters.

A survivor of the Armada, commenting on this loss of life, wrote: 'The gentlemen were so many that a list of their names would fill a quire of paper.' That survivor was Captain Francisco de Cuellar. He had been on board one of three ships—the *San Juan*, the *Lavia* and the *Santa Maria de Vision*—forced to take shelter in Sligo Bay, half a league from the shore at Streedagh. After five days at anchor, he recalled,

> There sprang up so great a storm on our beam, with a sea up to the heavens, so that the cables could not hold nor the sails serve us.... We were driven ashore, with all three ships upon a beach with very fine sand, shut in on one side and the other by great rocks. Such a thing was never seen; for within the space of an hour all three ships were broken to pieces, so that there did not escape three hundred men, and more than one thousand were drowned.

The secretary to the Irish Council reported to London: 'At my late being in Sligo I numbered in one strand of less than five miles in length above 1,100 dead corpses of men which the sea had driven upon the shore.'

Most of the survivors were put to the sword or hanged, but Captain Cuellar managed to reach some friendly Irish inland:

> The savages are well affected to us Spaniards, because they realise that we are attacking the heretics and are their great enemies. If it was not for those natives who kept us as if belonging to themselves, not one of our people would have escaped. We owe them a good turn for that, though they were the first to rob us and strip us when were cast on shore.

Protected by the MacClancys and O'Rourkes in Leitrim, Cuellar survived to describe how those Irish lived.

Episode 62 ∾

THE ADVENTURES OF CAPTAIN FRANCISCO DE CUELLAR

In the autumn of 1588 three Spanish Armada ships were smashed to pieces by a storm in Sligo Bay. When Captain Francisco de Cuellar managed to reach the shore by clinging to a door broken off a hatchway, the Irish, stripping castaways of their valuables, left him alone because his clothes were drenched in blood from all his injuries. He joined another young Spaniard. Two armed Irishmen approached them:

> They were sorry to see us [Cuellar later recalled] and cut a quantity of rushes and grass, covered us well, and then betook themselves to the shore to plunder.
>
> When fast asleep I was disturbed by a great noise of men on horseback who were going to plunder the ships. I turned to call my companion, and found he was dead, which occasioned me great affliction and grief.

Walking with difficulty, Cuellar reached a monastery:

> I found the church and the images of the saints burned and completely ruined, and twelve Spaniards hanging within the church by the act of the Lutheran English, who went about searching for us to make an end of all of us.

Limping inland, he entered a wood, when

> An old savage came out from behind the rocks, and two young men with their arms—one English—and a girl of the age of twenty years, most beautiful in the extreme.... The Englishman came up saying, 'Yield, Spanish poltroon' ... he cut the sinew of my right leg.

They stripped him and to their delight found his gold chain worth a thousand dollars. The girl, however, took pity on him:

> The girl lamented very much to see the bad treatment I received, and asked them to leave me the clothes.... Moreover, they had taken away some relics of great value. These the savage damsel took and hung round her neck, making me a sign that she was a Christian: which she was in like manner to Mahomet.

Cuellar made his way to the mountains, where he met some Irish who gave him a horse and a boy to guide him. His journey, however, was still beset by danger:

> We heard a very great noise, and the boy said to me, by signs, 'Save yourself, Spain' (for so they call us); 'many Sassana are coming this way and they will make bits of you if you do not hide yourself.' They call the English 'Sassanas'. God delivered me from them.

He did not escape another party of men, who left him completely naked. Making a covering for himself with an old mat and bracken, he struggled on. Eventually a priest took him to the chief of the MacClancys of Leitrim:

> The wife of [MacClancy] was very beautiful in the extreme, and showed me much kindness. One day we were sitting in the sun and it came to be suggested that I should examine their hands and tell their fortunes. I began to look at the hands of each, and to say to them a hundred thousand absurdities, which pleased them so much that there was no other Spaniard better than I ...

Meanwhile Queen Elizabeth's Lord Deputy, Sir William Fitzwilliam, was on the march. Could Rossclogher Castle, MacClancy's fortress standing on a crannog in Lough Melvin, hold out against the English?

> This savage [Cuellar's account continues], taking into consideration the great force that was coming against him, decided to fly to the mountains.... The chief, with dishevelled hair down to his eyes, burning with rage, said he could not remain.... We, the nine Spaniards who were there, decided to say to the savage that we wished to hold the castle and defend it to the death.... The enemy was very indignant at it, and came upon the castle with his forces ... without being able to approach close on account of the water which intervened.
>
> We had been besieged for seventeen days, when Our Lord saw fit to deliver us from that enemy by great falls of snow, to such an extent that he was compelled to depart with his force.

The grateful MacClancy chief offered his sister in marriage to Cuellar, but the Spanish captain preferred to make his way northwards into Ulster until he reached the lordship of the O'Cahans, now in the county of Londonderry:

> Some women kept me there for a month and a half in safety, and cured me. In the [village] which was composed of thatched huts, were some very beautiful girls, with whom I was very friendly.

When the English came to take him away, these girls helped him to escape to the shores of Lough Neagh. There he was introduced to a Catholic bishop who arranged a vessel to take Cuellar and some other Spaniards to Scotland and from there to Spanish Flanders. By October 1589 he had reached Antwerp, where he wrote the letter which contains the narrative of his adventures.

It is an account which tells us much about how the Irish lived in the late sixteenth century.

Episode 63 ~

'THE WILD IRISH ARE BARBAROUS AND MOST FILTHY IN THEIR DIET'

The Spanish Armada castaway, Captain Francisco de Cuellar, lived with the Irish in the far north-west of Ireland for almost a year. Though he was grateful for their kindness to him, he and other Spaniards without hesitation described the Irish as savages:

> The custom of these savages is to live as brute beasts in the mountains, which are very rugged in that part of Ireland where we lost ourselves. They are great walkers, and inured to toil. The men are all large-bodied, and of handsome features and limbs; and as active as the roe-deer. The most of the women are very beautiful, but badly got up. They do not eat oftener than once a day, and this is at night; and that which they usually eat is butter with oaten bread. They drink sour milk, for they have no other drink; they don't drink water, although it is the best in the world. On feast days they eat some flesh half-cooked without bread or salt, as that is their custom.

Edmund Campion, an English scholar subsequently executed as a Jesuit traitor, commented on what was on the menu of the Irish:

> Shamrocks, watercresses, roots and other herbs they feed upon, oatmeal and butter they cram together. They drink whey, milk and beef-broth, flesh they devour without bread, corn such as they have they keep for their horses.

There is no doubt that cattle were at the heart of the Gaelic farming economy and that dairy produce formed the most important part of the diet.

Oats had a much better chance of ripening than wheat, particularly in the wetter parts of the north and the west. On one occasion the O'Donnells fell upon Shane O'Neill's warriors while they were holding out their helmets to be served raw oatmeal with molten butter poured over it. Fresh milk was generally too precious to be drunk in any quantity, but buttermilk was widely consumed. Fynes Moryson, secretary to Lord Deputy Mountjoy, wrote that the people 'esteem for a great dainty sour curds, vulgarly called Bonaclabbe'. This was *bainne clabair*, or bonnyclabber: clotted milk. Blood was sometimes drawn from below the ears of living cattle or horses and mixed with butter to form a jelly. Moryson adds that 'No meat they fancy so much as pork, the fatter the better.'

By this time wine was imported by the Gaelic lords in exchange for hides or, for example in Tír Conaill, as payment by Spaniards for the right to fish. Malted oats and barley could not only be brewed to make ale, but was now often distilled to make *uisce beathadh*, whiskey, the 'water of life', much favoured by English commanders for medicinal purposes. Sir Josias Bodley found priests in eastern Ulster pouring 'usquebaugh down their throats by day and by night'.

As the sixteenth century drew to a close, few Englishmen travelled all parts of Ireland as much as the Lord Deputy's secretary, Fynes Moryson. It should be remembered that his uncomplimentary accounts were written about the Irish who were constantly on the move as the forces of Queen Elizabeth were closing in on them:

> The wild Irish, inhabiting many and large provinces, are barbarous and most filthy in their diet. They scum the seething pot with an handful of straw, and strain their milk taken from the cow through a like handful of straw, none of the cleanest, and so cleanse, or rather more defile the pot and milk. They devour great morsels of meat unsalted, and they eat commonly swine's flesh, seldom mutton, and all these pieces of flesh ... they seethe in a hollow tree, lapped in a raw cow's hide, and so set over the fire, and therewith swallow whole lumps of filthy butter.

Moryson, like other English observers, mentions the liking the Irish had for shamrock—almost certainly this was wood sorrel (known to some today as 'Sour Sally'), rightly regarded as a piquant enhancement to a good, fresh salad:

> They willingly eat the herb shamrock, being of a sharp taste, which as they run and are chased to and fro, they snatch like beasts out of the ditches.... They drink milk like nectar, warmed with a stone first cast into the fire, or else beef-broth mingled with milk; but when they come to any market town to sell a cow or a horse, they never return home, till they have drunk

the price in Spanish wine (which they call the King of Spain's Daughter), or in Irish 'usquebaugh' till they have out-slept two or three days' drunkenness. And not only the common sort, but even the lords and their wives, the more they want this drink at home, the more they swallow it when they come to it, till they be as drunk as beggars.

As more and more of the island fell under their control, the English found much about its people to both attract and repel them.

Episode 64 ∿

'A FIT HOUSE FOR AN OUTLAW, A MEET BED FOR A REBEL, AND AN APT CLOAK FOR A THIEF'

The Spanish Armada castaway, Captain Francisco de Cuellar, found the Irish men who protected him handsome and fine-limbed, and was constantly encountering Irish girls 'beautiful in the extreme'. He was not, however, impressed by their dress:

They clothe themselves, according to their habit, with tight trousers and short loose coats of very coarse goat's hair. They cover themselves with blankets, and wear their hair down to their eyes.

The 'goat's hair' was probably coarse sheep's wool, and 'blankets' were the mantles which were the most distinctive item of Irish dress. The mantle was an enveloping outer woollen cloak. These rectangular garments were worn by everyone in Ireland, young and old, rich and poor. The most popular mantles had a tufted or curled nap raised with the aid of a teasel seed-head. These tufts on the inside of the mantle helped with insulation and were treated with a mixture of honey and vinegar to stop them uncurling. Tightly woven mantles were remarkably waterproof; when they were issued to English soldiers in Ireland in 1600, it was argued that

Being never so wet, [the mantles] will presently with a little shaking and wringing be presently dry; for want of which the soldiers, lying abroad, marching and keeping watch and ward in cold and wet in winter time, die in the Irish ague and in flux pitifully.

Fynes Moryson, Lord Deputy Mountjoy's secretary, described the mantle as

> a fit house for an outlaw, a meet bed for a rebel, and an apt cloke for a thief.
> First the outlaw, being for his many crimes and villanies banished from the
> towns and houses of honest men and wandering in waste places, far from
> danger of law, maketh his mantle his house, and under it covereth himself
> from the wrath of heaven, from the offence of the earth, and from the fight
> of men. When it raineth, it is his pent-house, when it bloweth it is his tent,
> when it freezeth, it is his tabernacle. In summer he can wear it loose; in
> winter, he can wrap it close; at all times he can use it; never heavy, never
> cumbersome.
>
> Likewise for a rebel it is serviceable: for in his war he maketh when he
> still flieth from his foe, and lurketh in the thick woods, it is his bed, yea, and
> almost his household stuff.... Yea, and oftentimes their mantle serveth
> them, when they are near driven, being wrapped about their left arm, in
> stead of a shield; for it is hard to cut through with a sword, besides, it is
> light to bear, light to throw away, and being (as they commonly are) naked,
> it is to them all in all.

The better-off made some attempt to keep up with the latest Spanish, Flemish
and English fashions, but Edmund Campion was only one of many who
observed the love that Irish men had for voluminous shirts and hanging sleeves:

> Linen shirts the rich do wear for wantonness and bravery, with wide hang-
> ing sleeves pleated, thirty yards are little enough for one of them. They have
> now left their saffron, and learn to wash their shirts, four or five times in a
> year. Proud they are of long crisped glibs, and do nourish the same with all
> their cunning: to crop the front thereof they take it for a notable piece of
> villainy.

A 'glib' was a thick roll of hair at the forehead; a law of 1537 specifically forbade the English in Ireland to wear their hair in this fashion.

A lady's gown, dating from the late sixteenth century, was found in remarkably good condition in a bog in Co. Tipperary. Beautifully tailored, it has a
very low U-shaped neckline with an opening down to the front to a low waist
which appears to be pointed over the stomach. The extraordinarily heavy
ankle-length full skirt is made of twenty-three triangular pieces of cloth sewn
together, measuring no fewer than 22½ feet at the bottom. There are ninety-
two folds formed by welts sewn at intervals. It also has a small stand collar at
the back of the neck.

Irish women seem to have been quite happy to expose their breasts in full
in polite society. Nor were they ashamed to be naked, as a Czech nobleman

discovered in 1601. Just what Jaroslav z Donína was doing in what is now Co. Londonderry in the middle of a devastating rebellion is impossible to say. Anyway, he encountered sixteen high-born women, all naked, with 'which strange sight his eyes being dazzled, they led him into the house' to converse politely in Latin in front of the fire. Joining them, the Lord O'Cahan threw all his clothes off and was surprised that the Bohemian baron was too bashful to do likewise.

As the sixteenth century was drawing to a close, outsiders were learning a great deal more about the country which the English, for the first time, were conquering from end to end.

Episode 65 ❧

THE CAPTURE OF RED HUGH O'DONNELL

Let us have no more such rash, unadvised journeys without good ground as your last journey in the north.... Take heed ere you use us so again.

This was Queen Elizabeth's stinging reproof to her Lord Deputy, Sir John Perrot, after yet another expensive and futile expedition against the MacDonnells of the Glens. Eventually Perrot's uncontrollable rages brought about his downfall. Punching the aged marshal, Sir Nicholas Bagenal, in the face before the whole Irish Council didn't help, and soon afterwards Perrot was thrown into the Tower of London, where he died. Nevertheless, Perrot had achieved one thing in Ulster that pleased the queen—he had captured Red Hugh O'Donnell, son of one of the most powerful Gaelic chieftains in Ireland, the Lord of Tír Conaill. Red Hugh's biographer, Lughaidh O'Clery, a cousin of the best known of the Four Masters of Donegal, tells the story:

That capture took place in this way. A vessel was got ready, with black gun-wale, deceptive, precisely at Michaelmas in the year 1587, in Dublin, with a murderous, odious crew, with abundance of wine for barter to trade with, to see if they could get an opportunity for seizing on Hugh O'Donnell. By the advice of Lord Deputy Sir John Perrot and of the council too this was done secretly.... The vessel went out from the harbour of Dublin till she came to Lough Swilly.... She stopped there opposite Rathmullan out in the sea.... A part of her crew went on shore after a while in the guise of merchants.

When the fifteen-year-old Red Hugh turned up, he and his companions accepted an invitation to come aboard to taste the wine:

> They were served and feasted with a variety of food and drink till they were merry and cheerful. While they were enjoying themselves drinking, their arms were taken from them and the door of the hatch-way was shut behind them and made prisoners.

The ship had by now put out to sea, and on its arrival in Dublin Red Hugh was held captive in Dublin Castle:

> Hugh O'Donnell was in chains for the space of three years and three months. It was anguish and sickness of mind and great pain to be as he was.... He was always meditating and searching how to find a way of escape.... That castle was situated such. There was a broad deep trench full of water all round it and a solid bridge of boards over it opposite the door of the castle, and a grim-visaged party of the English outside and inside the gate to guard it.... However, there is no watch of which advantage may not be taken at last.

One of Red Hugh's kinsmen made the journey from Donegal and arranged an escape. First he jammed the drawbridge with a thick piece of wood stuck into the chain. Then, from the window of their cell Red Hugh and some of his fellow-prisoners lowered themselves by a long rope on to the drawbridge, and made their escape:

> The gates of the royal city were wide open. They leaped over fences and enclosures and walls outside the town until they stopped at the slope of the mountain opposite.... They did not delay on their way till they crossed Three Rock Mountain before that morning. As they were tired and weary, they went into a dense wood and they remained in it till early dawn.

Red Hugh was unable to continue:

> He could not go on with his companions because his white-skinned tender feet were wounded and pierced by the furze and thick briars, as his shoes had fallen off his feet owing to the loosening of the seams and ties from the wet. It was a great sorrow and affliction to his companions, and as they could do nothing for him, they took leave of him.

Unfortunately for Red Hugh, the Irish who lived here, the O'Tooles, fearful that the crown would wreak vengeance on them for giving refuge to such a distinguished fugitive, took him back in bonds to Dublin Castle:

> Iron manacles were put on him as tight as could be, and they put him in the same prison, and they watched and guarded him the best way they could.
>
> His escape in this way was heard of universally throughout the land of Erin, and his recapture. There came a great gloom over the Irish, and the courage of their soldiers, and the minds of their champions, and the hearts of their heroes were confounded at hearing that news. There were many princesses and noble white-breasted maidens sorrowing and lamenting on his account. There were many high-born nobles weeping in secret for him.... And with good reason, for the multitude expected through him relief would come to them from the dreadful slavery and bondage in which the English held them.

One Gaelic lord in particular was determined that Red Hugh O'Donnell should not remain in chains. He was Hugh O'Neill, Earl of Tyrone.

Episode 66 ∽

THE ESCAPE OF RED HUGH O'DONNELL

In the sixteenth century Tír Eóghain was by far the most powerful Gaelic lordship in Ireland. The O'Neills had chosen as their chief Turlough Luineach O'Neill. This wily lord took care to keep on good terms with his neighbours, and, protected by a large force of Scots mercenaries known as Redshanks, he commanded respect. Though the English refused to recognise Turlough's authority, they had failed completely to dislodge him. In despair, the Lord Deputy in Dublin Castle hoped he would drink himself to death: 'Sir Turlough is very old and what with decay of nature through his age and over-run with drink which daily he is in, he is utterly past government.' After heavy drinking sessions Turlough would lie unconscious for more than two days at a time. But this O'Neill had a tough constitution and was to live until 1595.

By English law, the rightful Earl of Tyrone was Hugh O'Neill, son of the murdered Matthew and brother of the murdered Brian, and whose close relative Shane had also been murdered. To be sure that he in turn would not be murdered, the infant Hugh had been taken to the Pale close to Dublin and there given a good English education. In 1585 Hugh O'Neill was formally granted the title of Earl of Tyrone and sent back to Ulster to restore obedience to the English crown. Settling himself in Dungannon, the earl steadily increased his power in Tyrone, slowly undermining the authority of the now ailing Turlough Luineach, who was based in Strabane. By 1590 it was the independent power of the Earl of Tyrone, not that of Turlough Luineach, which was causing alarm in Dublin Castle.

Tír Conaill, together with the neighbouring regions under the control of the O'Donnell chieftain, certainly constituted the second most powerful Gaelic lordship of Ireland. There Finola, wife of Sir Hugh O'Donnell and known as Inghean Dubh, the 'dark daughter', had worked hard to ensure that her son, Red Hugh, would succeed to the lordship. But in 1587 Red Hugh had been captured and incarcerated in Dublin Castle. An escape attempt in 1591 had failed. Now the Earl of Tyrone plotted to defy the English crown and arrange the escape of Red Hugh. If he succeeded, the earl would bind together the two greatest lordships of Ireland in friendship and end centuries of debilitating rivalry between them.

The Earl of Tyrone had many friends in and about Dublin. Using bribes on a spectacular scale, the earl ensured Red Hugh's escape from Dublin Castle. On Christmas Eve 1592 a guard smuggled Red Hugh and his companions out through a privy, and they swiftly escaped to the mountains. Lughaidh O'Clery's biography of Red Hugh describes what then ensued:

> The hostages who escaped with Hugh were Henry and Art [O'Neill], the two sons of Shane. They came to the slopes of Three Rock Mountain, where Hugh had come the first time he escaped. The night came on with a violent downpour and slippery slime of snow, so that it was not easy for the high-born nobles to walk on account of the want of clothing. This hurried journey was more severe on Art than on Hugh, and his gait was feeble and slow, for he was corpulent and thick-thighed. It was not so with Hugh, for he had not passed the period of boyhood, and he was active and light.

Forced to halt under a cliff, they sent a servant on to get help from Fiach MacHugh O'Byrne of Glenmalure, who had often routed English forces sent against him. When O'Byrne's men found the Ulstermen, they were a sorry sight:

> Alas! Truly the state of these nobles was not happy to the heroes who had come to seek for them. They had neither cloaks nor clothing for protection, so that they seemed like sods of earth covered up by the snow. Art died at

last and was buried in the place. Hugh's strength was on the increase after drinking, except his two feet were like dead members, owing to the swelling and blistering from frost and snow.

Hugh was carried to shelter on a litter and was then, in a journey lasting many weeks, taken to Dungannon to meet the man who had arranged and financed his escape, the Earl of Tyrone. When they heard that Red Hugh had returned to Tír Conaill, the crown forces swiftly evacuated the region:

> When the English learned that Red Hugh who had escaped was come to the country, a quaking fear and a great terror seized upon them, and they resolved to leave the country....
>
> As for Hugh O'Donnell, he returned to Ballyshannon. He called in physicians to examine his feet, but they could not cure him until his two great toes were cut off in the end.

The bond between Red Hugh and Hugh O'Neill would never thereafter be broken. Close co-operation was vital: the power of the English crown was extending, and nowhere more rapidly than in the province of Connacht.

Episode 67 ꙫ

GRANUAILE: THE PIRATE QUEEN OF CONNACHT

During the fourteenth and fifteenth centuries nearly all of the province of Connacht had fallen out of the control of the English crown. Descendants of the Norman conquerors of earlier times had gone native, married local girls, and had adopted Gaelic customs and Gaelic surnames. For example, the de Burgos had become MacWilliam Burkes, the Barretts became MacPaddens, the Stauntons became MacEvillys, the Dexters became MacJordans, the Nagles became MacCostellos, and the Prendergasts became MacMorrises. And the Gaelic families which had never been overcome remained strong; they included the O'Connors, the O'Dowds, the O'Garas, the O'Flahertys and the O'Malleys.

The tide turned in the sixteenth century. Some lords were prepared to accept knighthoods and other English titles; for example, the lord who bore the gaelicised title of Upper MacWilliam Burke in Co. Galway was ennobled as the Earl of Clanricarde. Others were alarmed as growing English power eroded their independence. One of these was Granuaile, Gráinne O'Malley. The O'Malleys dominated the entire coastlands and islands of Mayo and maintained a formidable fleet of galleys. In 1546, at the age of sixteen, Gráinne was married to Donal O'Flaherty, head of another strong seafaring family based in Connemara.

Though she bore three children in rapid succession, Gráinne—often called Grace or Grany O'Malley by the English—soon acquired a reputation as a pirate queen and a military commander of some renown. Because of his aggressive behaviour, her husband Donal got the nickname 'the Cock', and she was in turn was called 'the Hen'. When Donal was murdered by the Joyces of eastern Connemara, she fought back with fury. The castle on an island in Lough Corrib she defended with such determination became known as 'Hen's Castle', the name it still bears today.

From then on Gráinne's main opponents were the English. She led another defence of Hen's Castle and forced the crown forces to retire only after she ordered the lead from the roof to be torn off, melted down and then poured onto the heads of her assailants. In 1566 she married Risdeárd-in-Iarainn, a Lower MacWilliam Burke, or, as the English called him, 'Richard-in-Iron'. This marriage alliance created an alarming challenge to royal authority throughout the province of Connacht.

In an attempt to strengthen government control in the province, Sir Edward Fitton was appointed the first Lord President of Connacht in 1569. Fitton made many enemies by smashing holy images in churches, or 'idols' as he called them, and his cruelties attracted criticism even from his own colleagues in Dublin and London. Inevitably, he felt he had to curb the power of Richard-in-Iron and his wife. In 1574 Fitton advanced on their main fortress, Rockfleet Castle at the head of an inlet in Clew Bay. Here Gráinne had a long chain from her favourite ship tied to her bedpost every night in case anyone would be tempted to steal the vessel.

After a three-week siege, the English were forced to withdraw with heavy losses. Three years later, without being summoned, Gráinne travelled to Galway to talk terms with Lord Deputy Sidney, as he recalled:

There came to me also a famous feminine sea captain called Grany Imallye, and offered her services to me, wheresoever I would command her, with three galleys and 200 fighting men, either in Scotland or Ireland; she brought with her her husband for she was as well by sea as by land well more than Mrs Mate with him; he was of the Nether Burkes and called by nickname Richard-in-Iron. This is a notorious woman in all the coasts of Ireland.

Then in 1577, Gráinne O'Malley overreached herself by plundering the lands further south in the province of Munster. She was arrested, as the Lord President of Munster informed the Lord Deputy:

> Grany O'Malley, a woman that hath impudently passed the part of womanhood and been a great spoiler, and chief commander and director of thieves and murderers at sea to spoil this province, having been apprehended by the Earl of Desmond this last year, his Lordship hath now sent her to Limerick where she remains in safe keeping.

She was sent as a captive to the capital and held in Dublin Castle. After a time she was released on condition of good behaviour. Her husband, Richard-in-Iron, was recognised by the queen as the head of the Lower MacWilliam Burkes in Mayo and was knighted in 1581. The Lord President of Connacht observed that 'Grany O'Malley thinketh herself no small lady'.

Gráinne O'Malley was a survivor, and for the next twenty years she struggled hard to keep her independence as Queen Elizabeth's rule spread to every corner of Connacht.

Episode 68 ⌒

GRANUAILE AND THE COMPOSITION OF CONNACHT

Commanding a large fleet of galleys and ruling the western coastlands and islands from Inishbofin to Achill, Gráinne O'Malley had married for a second time in 1566 and become the wife of 'Richard-in-Iron' Burke, the greatest lord in all of Mayo. Their combined territories formed one of the most extensive lordships in Connacht.

Gráinne's reign as the most powerful woman in the west did not end when her husband died in 1582. She certainly needed her wits about her, however, if she was to survive the inexorable extension of English royal power in the province. In 1584 Sir Richard Bingham became Lord President of Connacht. A merciless soldier and an able governor, Bingham crushed all opposition, and, one by one, the great lords of the province submitted.

In 1585 the Lord President unveiled his ambitious scheme to impose an ordered regime upon the province he governed. This he called the 'Composition of Connacht'. The lords of the province were no longer to live by billeting their warriors on the lands of their tenants and by the seizing of butter, corn and cattle as tribute. Henceforth the employment of mercenary soldiers was forbidden. Tenant farmers would hereafter pay money rents to these lords, who in turn would pay taxes to the English crown and abide by English laws. In short, these great landowners were no longer allowed to be independent warlords.

The Composition of Connacht worked quite well in southern Connacht, but it was a different matter in the northern part of the province. Here Gráinne O'Malley was among those who refused to be reconciled to the new regime. Bingham decided he had no choice but to deal in person with this proud woman. After hanging in public seventy men from leading Connacht families for failure to pay rent, Bingham advanced northwards from Galway in February 1586. But with the help of her son-in-law, Richard Burke of Achill, known as the 'Devil's Hook', Gráinne successfully defended her fortress on an island on Lough Mask, called Hag's Castle. White-capped waves stirred up by a storm foiled Bingham's attack by boats.

Eventually she was brought to heel and she travelled to Dublin in 1588 to seek and obtain a pardon from the Lord Deputy. But this restless woman could not be long at peace. Her name persistently crops up in reports sent by Bingham to London. In April 1590, for example,

> Grana O'Malley, with two or three baggage boats full of knaves committed some spoil in the Island of Arran.... Richard Burk, the Devil's Hook, hath Grana O'Malley in hand till she restore the spoils and repair the harms.

In other words, the Devil's Hook acted as a guarantor of Gráinne's future good behaviour. Foolish man. Her continued piracy caused Bingham to write to the queen's secretary 'to gyve your honour Knowledge of her naughty disposicion towards the state'. In another letter Bingham condemned her as 'a notable trai- toress and nurse to all the rebellions in the Province for forty years'.

In 1593 Gráinne decided to counter Bingham's criticisms and appeal to Elizabeth herself. She wrote to the queen in the third person, humbly beseeching

> Her Majesty of your princely bounty and liberality to grant her some maintenance for the little time she has to live ... and to grant unto your said subject under your most gracious hand of signet, free liberty during her life to invade with sword and fire all your highness' enemies.

The queen summoned her to London, and, despite her age, Gráinne cap- tained one of her galleys and sailed to meet her. These O'Malley vessels were the most substantial ever to have been built by the native Irish: each one was capable of taking up to 300 crew and was propelled by sails and thirty oars, each oar being manned by more than one rower. Gráinne steered out of Clew Bay, dotted with islands, with her castles of Westport, Rockfleet, Burrishoole, Murrisk and Clare Island in view, out into the Atlantic, past Inishturk, Inishark and Inishbofin—where she had another castle—south beyond Connemara and the Aran Islands, and on round the Blaskets and the wild headlands of Kerry. Then she directed her ship beyond Cape Clear and across St George's Channel eastwards to England, past the Scilly Isles and Penzance, down the English Channel and into the Thames estuary.

There is no detailed record of the meeting at Greenwich between the pirate queen and Queen Elizabeth. Clearly she got much of what she wanted, for afterwards Elizabeth informed Bingham:

Grany ne Maly hath made humble suit to us.... We are content, so as the old woman may understand we yield thereof so she is hereof informed and departeth with great thankfulness.... And further, for the pity to be had of this aged woman ... we require [you] to deal with her sons in our name to yield to her some maintenance for her living the rest of her old years.... And this we do write in her favour as she showeth herself dutiful, although she hath in former times lived out of order.... She hath confessed the same with assured promises by oath ... that she will fight in our quarrel with all the world.

Bingham, for his part, very much doubted that Gráinne would behave herself in future, and he was right. She was to join forces with the Gaelic lords of Ulster and made her fleet of galleys available to them in the Nine Years War, a great rebellion which was to convulse Ireland from end to end. That rebellion, which was to last until 1603, the year when both Gráinne and Elizabeth died, began as the island castle of Enniskillen in Co. Fermanagh came under siege during the winter of 1593–4.

Episode 69 ∿

THE NINE YEARS WAR BEGINS

When Hugh Roe MacMahon, the principal Gaelic lord of Monaghan, made war on rival members of his family and raided cattle in the barony of Farney, the property of the Earl of Essex, Lord Deputy Sir William

Fitzwilliam decided to teach him a lesson. In 1590 he led an expedition north from Dublin, captured Hugh Roe and hanged him. This severe punishment was followed by a partition of the extensive MacMahon lands. These estates were apportioned to five leading MacMahons and to the heads of some other prominent families in the area.

The English officials in Dublin Castle were delighted with the results of this experiment. Not one of the new owners of these modest Co. Monaghan estates would be strong enough to threaten rebellion—indeed, each was happy to pay taxes to the crown in return for a secure title to farms which they could pass on by English law to an eldest son. The Master of the Ordnance concluded that this sort of division was 'the soundest and surest way to bring Ireland to due obedience'.

Described as a 'native plantation', this exercise in social engineering, this application of the principle of 'divide and rule', was surely more effective than repeated expensive military expeditions. A similar scheme was drawn up for the neighbouring O'Reilly lordship of East Bréifne, now renamed as Co. Cavan. West Bréifne, which became Co. Leitrim, was another plum ripe for the picking—particularly after its lord, Sir Brian O'Rourke, had been hanged, drawn and quartered as a traitor at Tyburn. One official described the planned 'native plantation' of Leitrim as 'indeed pleasing to God, highly profitable to the queen, and the precedent of it a light and candle to their neighbours of the north to find out speedily the way to wealth, civility and obedience'. Sir Henry Bagenal, the queen's marshal, who had extensive estates around Newry, agreed with this view. Now he sought the break-up of the great Gaelic lordships of Ulster: 'The chiefest, or rather the only means to reduce these barbarous people to obedience is to disunite them as all may be enforced to depend on the queen'.

Not surprisingly, Hugh O'Neill, the Earl of Tyrone, viewed these developments with mounting alarm. Given a good English education in the Pale near Dublin, he had been expected to promote the interests of the crown in the heart of Ulster. The earl, however, proved rather more independent and wilful than expected. For example, he took the law into his own hands by crushing the forces of the seven sons of the legendary Shane O'Neill, and in 1590 he executed one of them—Hugh Gavelach MacShane—pulling on the hangman's rope himself. To fend off criticism and to delay plans to subdivide Tyrone, the earl paid regular bribes to Lord Deputy Fitzwilliam, who was rumoured 'to fill his own bags daily and hourly' with the sixteenth-century equivalent of brown-paper envelopes.

Then the government decided to break up the lands of the Maguires in Co. Fermanagh. When a sheriff arrived, accompanied by troops, this was too much for the Lord of Fermanagh, Hugh Maguire, who rose in rebellion. As one of the principal nobles of Ireland, the Earl of Tyrone was expected to campaign with the queen's marshal when he was in Ulster. O'Neill had a good record in this respect, and now in 1593 he rode alongside Marshal Bagenal. When they reached Fermanagh, they faced not only the Maguires but also the newly elected Lord of Tír Conaill, Red Hugh O'Donnell. Yet only the year before Hugh O'Neill had organised the dramatic escape of Red Hugh from imprisonment in Dublin Castle. To which side did the earl really belong?

Hugh Maguire made a desperate last stand in his island castle of Enniskillen. As the crown forces pounded the walls with cannon Captain Dowdall launched a large boat on the lough, put a hundred men into it, using hides stretched over curved branches to protect them from missiles hurled on to the deck by hides. The helmsman steered the boat under the castle's barbican, and the attackers made a breech with pickaxes. The Maguires quickly surrendered. Now it was the English who occupied the castle.

Soon, however, it would be the English garrison which would be in danger. This was because Hugh O'Neill, the Earl of Tyrone, had joined Red Hugh O'Donnell and Hugh Maguire in rebellion against the queen. On 7 August 1594 a relief force bringing food supplies and munitions to Enniskillen was ambushed fording the River Arney—as the Annals of the Four Masters record, 'The name of the ford at which this great victory was gained was changed to the Ford of the Biscuits, from the number of biscuits and small cakes left there to the victors on that day.'

The great rebellion, led by the Gaelic lords of Ulster and known later as the Nine Years War, had begun. In February 1595 O'Neill joined O'Donnell and Maguire to destroy Blackwater Fort near Benburb. Then, on 13 June, Marshal Bagenal, after bringing supplies to Monaghan Fort, was overwhelmed at Clontibret. Sir Edward York, in command of the cavalry, ruefully observed that the Earl of Tyrone commanded a highly professional force, admitting 'that in no place whatsoever he had served in all his life he never saw more readier or perfecter shot'. Clontibret demonstrated that English garrisons placed in hostile territory were highly vulnerable; yet Elizabeth's government could see no other way of taming the Ulster lords than by maintaining fortified posts in their territories. Using such tactics and facing such adversaries, the English were to endure many more humiliating reverses before this spreading rebellion could be quelled.

Episode 70 ∿

'FREEING THE COUNTRY FROM THE ROD OF TYRANNICAL EVIL'

By 1595 it was estimated that Hugh O'Neill, Earl of Tyrone, commanded no fewer than one thousand horsemen, one thousand pikemen and four thousand foot-soldiers shouldering modern firearms. He had brought together the squabbling ruling families of Gaelic Ulster under his command, had proved himself a skilled tactician in battle, and was now leading his people in the most dangerous Irish rebellion Queen Elizabeth had ever faced in the course of her long reign.

Elizabeth's forces lost control of nearly all of Ulster. Now Red Hugh O'Donnell of Tír Conaill, the earl's most loyal ally, carried the revolt successfully into Connacht. The English lost Sligo Castle, and Sir Richard Bingham, the Lord President of Connacht, failed in his attempt to retake it in July 1595. Tearing down lattice work from the neighbouring abbey, Bingham made a great siege-engine equipped with wheels and covered in hides. But as his men hiding under it tried to undermine the castle stonework, the Irish defenders smashed it with rocks, causing the attackers to flee.

Meanwhile the Lord Deputy formally proclaimed O'Neill a traitor in Newry. When his army approached Dungannon, O'Neill, realising his castle could not withstand the heavy cannon his spies had seen, demolished it 'in so great haste [that one night it was] stately and high in the sight of all our army, the next day by noon it was so low that it could scarcely be discerned.'

Having suffered so many reverses, the English had no choice but to agree to a truce. Immediately after the death of Mabel Bagenal—the earl's third wife and sister of the queen's marshal—Hugh O'Neill had married Catherine Magennis, daughter of the Lord of Iveagh. He spent a pleasant honeymoon with the young lady, who was less than half his age, fishing together for salmon on the River Bann at Castleroe. Then a messenger arrived. A Spanish ship had put in at Killybegs with munitions from King Philip II and relics from the pope. Its captain, Don Alonso Cobos, refused to speak to anyone but O'Neill and O'Donnell. He walked forty miles to meet these Irish lords secretly at Lifford in north Donegal. There, in spite of the truce, O'Neill and O'Donnell signed and sealed a letter to the Prince of the Asturias, son of the King of Spain, appealing for his help:

We have already written, most Serene Prince, to the Great King your father, what we thought most necessary for our country. We implore that Your

Highness will aid in his clemency this most excellent and just cause, that of asserting Catholic liberty and of freeing the country from the rod of tyrannical evil, and that, with the help of the Divine Majesty, he may win for Christ an infinite number of souls, snatching them from the jaws of hell, and may wholly destroy the ministers of satanic fury.

At Lifford, May 16th, 1596.

This letter, impressed by Hugh O'Neill with his seal of the Red Hand of Ulster, was an indication that the rebellion of the Gaelic lords of the north was no longer just an irritating distraction for the government of Queen Elizabeth. Ireland was being drawn into the titanic and deadly struggle between the Protestant and Catholic powers of Europe. Philip II, the ruler of the greatest empire in the world and the principal champion of the Catholic cause, was eager to help O'Neill and O'Donnell fight the English heretics. His officers advised him on suitable places to bring a Spanish army ashore, including Limerick, Sligo, Carlingford, Teelin and Killybegs. Again and again, however, things went wrong for King Philip.

In June 1596 the English and Dutch fleets joined together to wreak havoc on Spain's most important naval port, Cadiz. They burned the city and captured or destroyed fifty-seven ships. It was not until October that eighty-one vessels left Lisbon bound for Donegal. Here Red Hugh O'Donnell stockpiled oats and butter to feed the Spanish when they landed. Nineteen more galleons from Seville joined this fleet, and more vessels from El Ferrol were sailing to meet this great invasion armada when it was overwhelmed by a terrible storm. More than two thousand men perished in the ocean, and at least thirty-two ships were lost.

In the following year, 1597, Philip tried again to send help to the Irish. Another armada sailed out, made up of no fewer than 136 vessels carrying nearly 13,000 men. Once again the invasion fleet was scattered and overwhelmed by Atlantic gales. Now almost bankrupt, the King of Spain could not summon enough strength for a third attempt. Philip was so depressed that he shut himself away in his remote palace and refused to speak to anyone.

Yet now was the very time to aid the Gaelic lords. Reports from Ireland in 1598 brought news of a dazzling victory in Ulster—the Battle of the Yellow Ford.

Episode 71 ⌒

'THE SCURVY FORT OF BLACKWATER'

In 1597 the newly appointed Lord Deputy of Ireland, Thomas Lord Burgh, wrote to Queen Elizabeth to assure her that he would not spare himself to bring about the defeat of Hugh O'Neill, Earl of Tyrone:

> I will encamp by him, force him, follow; omit no opportunity by night or day.... I will, God willing, stick to him and if need be lie on the ground and drink water ten weeks.

He launched a two-pronged attack on Ulster. From the west the governor of Connacht marched his troops as far as Belleek, only to be driven back over the River Erne at Ballyshannon, many of his men being swept to their deaths over falls where the hydroelectric dam now stands. The governor's force was saved from annihilation by the Irish only by a heavy downpour which extinguished the slow-burning matches or fuses used in those days to fire handguns.

Meanwhile the Lord Deputy blundered deep into Tyrone, where he built a new Blackwater Fort near Benburb to replace the one the Irish had destroyed a couple of years before. He was delighted with his work: 'It is my first child ... an eyesore in the heart of O'Neill's country.' Then, while on campaign in Ulster, the Lord Deputy fell victim to fever; he was carried on a litter to Newry, where he died in October 1597. Burgh's 'eyesore in O'Neill's country' soon became a serious headache for the English—how could the Blackwater garrison in the middle of hostile Tyrone be supplied? The plan was to take food and munitions from Belfast Lough to Antrim and from there across Lough Neagh to the River Blackwater. Shane MacBrian, a lord of Clandeboye, interfered with that scheme somewhat by hanging and disembowelling the members of the English garrison placed in Belfast Castle. Then the governor of Carrickfergus Castle, Sir John Chichester, foolishly fell out with the MacDonnells of the Glens. During a parley outside the castle he ordered an attack and was shot through the head, 180 of his men being killed with him. At a single stroke all English gains in eastern Ulster were lost. The previously neutral MacDonnells now became formidable allies of Hugh O'Neill—and the isolation of Blackwater Fort was complete.

The queen's experienced commander-in-chief firmly believed that Blackwater Fort should be pulled down and its garrison brought back to safety. He wrote to the queen's secretary:

I protest to God the scurvy fort of Blackwater which cannot long be held, doth more touch my heart than all the spoils that ever were made by traitors on mine own lands. The fort was always falling, and never victualled but once (by myself) without an army.

His advice was ignored. The position of the garrison of 150 men in the heart of Ulster was becoming intolerable: desperate sallies had to be made from the walls to bring in wood and water; and the soldiers were reduced to eating grass on the ramparts.

Fresh English troops arrived in Dublin in July 1598. The queen's marshal, Sir Henry Bagenal, agreed to use these soldiers to bring food and ammunition to Blackwater Fort. He led northwards three hundred cavalry and four thousand foot-soldiers—the largest armies to have entered Ulster for many years. Hugh O'Neill had long prepared for this opportunity. For months his men had been engaged in digging a deep trench a mile long between two treacherous bogs. His plan was to draw the crown forces towards this trench into a carefully laid ambush. He himself was in command on the left, Red Hugh O'Donnell on the right, Randal MacDonnell was close by, and Sir Hugh Maguire led the Irish horsemen.

As Bagenal thrust across country his army was assailed by caliver and musket shot fired from the woods, where the Irish were safe from the English cavalry. Pack-horses and four cannon dragged by bullocks held up regiments marching behind, widely separating English troops at the front who were advancing into O'Neill's trap. Then a heavy cannon stuck fast in the bed of a stream oozing from a bog—the yellow ford which gave the battle its name. Bagenal rode back to help pull the gun out, but when he raised the visor of his helmet he was shot in the face and fell, mortally wounded. The Irish closed in as the English threw down their weapons and fled back wildly to the mêlée at the ford. This defeat became a disaster when a soldier, refilling his powder horn, exploded two barrels of gunpowder with his slow-burning match. Finally, it was reported, the Irish 'came on amain with a full cry after their manner'.

It was the greatest victory the Gaelic lords of Ulster had ever achieved over the crown. The northern rebellion spread southwards, and English rule in Ireland was shaken to its foundations.

Episode 72 ❧

'A QUICK END MADE OF A SLOW PROCEEDING': THE EARL OF ESSEX'S FAILURE

The Battle of the Yellow Ford, fought in the heart of Tyrone during the summer of 1598, was almost certainly the most disastrous defeat the English ever suffered at the hands of the Irish. News of the victory won by the Gaelic lords of the north spread rapidly southwards. In Connacht Red Hugh O'Donnell of Tír Conaill won almost total control. In the midlands the O'Mores and the O'Connors slaughtered families which had been settled by the English crown on their lands. In the far south the Munster plantation— that is, the colony of English promoted by Queen Elizabeth in that province— completely collapsed. Some settlers had their tongues cut out and their noses cut off by the rebellious Irish. One survivor told of

> infants taken from the nurse's breast and the brains dashed against the walls; the heart plucked out of the body in the view of the wife, who was forced to yield the use of her apron to wipe the blood off the murderer's fingers.

Castles fell to the Irish one after another. In Co. Cork alone it was reported that fifty-four villages had been burnt. Even Dublin was under threat from the O'Byrnes and their allies in the mountains overlooking the city. When the queen heard that her Irish Council had been trying to negotiate a truce with the leader of the rebellion, Hugh O'Neill, the Earl of Tyrone, she was furious:

> We may not pass over this foul error to our dishonour, when you of our council framed such a letter to the traitor, after the defeat, as never was read the like for baseness ... if you shall peruse it again, when you are yourselves, that you will be ashamed of your own absurdities and grieved that any fear or rashness should ever make you authors of an action so much to your sovereign's dishonour and to the increasing of the traitor's insolency.

Elizabeth had no longer any wish to talk. The Battle of the Yellow Ford convinced her that she must empty her coffers, if need be, to defeat this rebellion. Over the winter of 1598–9 troops were levied on an unprecedented scale across England. As these regiments raised in the shires landed at Kinsale, Cork and Waterford shortly before Christmas, 2,000 seasoned troops were transferred from the war in the Netherlands to Ireland. By early 1599 there were at least 17,000 English troops in Ireland. Rich contracts for food, munitions, camp equipment and medical supplies—including liquorice and aniseed—were made with London merchants. For the first time a regular postal service was set up between London, the port of Holyhead in Wales and Dublin—it cost £634 18s 4d a year.

The Earl of Essex was chosen to command this army the like of which had never been seen in Ireland before. This was a mistake. The old queen allowed her heart to rule her head. She had owed a lot to his father, who had lost everything he had in Ireland more than twenty years before. Elizabeth had a misplaced affection for this dashing but unstable young man.

As Essex was sailing towards Ireland in April 1599 a vessel put out from Dublin to greet him. It was swamped in a rough sea and took down with it the Earl of Kildare and eighteen other Leinster lords. That was an ill-omened start. 'By God I will beat Tyrone in the field,' Essex had declared. But instead of directly confronting the Gaelic lords of the north, he campaigned against their allies in the south to no great effect. In Queen's County—now Co. Laois—the Irish made a successful ambush in a narrow defile, called the 'Pass of the Plumes' because so many decorated helmets were left behind. Much time was wasted in besieging Cahir Castle on the River Suir, and by the time Essex had reached Limerick he was losing an alarming number of men from sickness. Then news arrived that the governor of Connacht, Sir Conyers Clifford, had been piked to death in a disastrous engagement with the O'Rourkes in Roscommon.

Back in London Elizabeth fretted that the Earl of Essex was costing her a thousand pounds a day. As reports of aimless expeditions were brought to her, one courtier observed: 'She walks much in her privy chamber, and stamps with her feet at ill news, and thrusts her rusty sword at times into the arras in great rage.'

Worse news was to follow. When Essex finally marched northwards, he made a truce with Hugh O'Neill. When she heard of it, Elizabeth was outraged. Describing the truce as 'a quick end made of a slow proceeding', she observed: 'To trust this traitor upon oath is to trust a devil upon his religion.'

In the following year she chose a new commander, capable of turning the tide of this great Irish rebellion—Lord Mountjoy.

Episode 73 ⌣

MOUNTJOY AND DOCWRA

Charles Blount, Lord Mountjoy, though only thirty-six years old when he was appointed Lord Deputy of Ireland in January 1600, believed himself to be in constant bad health. He took an afternoon nap in his tent when on campaign, and, his secretary Fynes Moryson informs us,

> He wore jerkins and round hose and cloaks lined with velvet, and white beaver hats, and besides his ordinary stockings of silk, he wore under boots another pair of woollen, with a pair of high linen boot-hose, yea three waistcoats in cold weather, and a thick ruff, besides a russet scarf about his neck thrice folded under it. I never observed any of his age and strength to keep his body so warm.... He took tobacco abundantly, which I think preserved him from sickness, especially in Ireland, where the foggy air of the bogs do most prejudice the health.

He nevertheless inspired his men with greater success than any English commander before him, and he appeared to be fearless in battle—at different times his horse was shot under him, his greyhound running beside him was shot dead, and his chaplain, one of his secretaries and a gentleman of his chamber were killed close by him.

Since 1594 the Gaelic lords of Ulster had won so many victories that Queen Elizabeth had come close to losing Ireland altogether. Now Mountjoy planned to break this rebellion by starving the people. He preferred to fight in winter when it was more difficult for the Irish to hide in the leafless woods, and when their stores of corn and butter could be burnt, and their cattle down from their summer pastures could be more easily slaughtered.

Mountjoy began by sending an expedition to Lough Foyle to drive a wedge between the territories of the two principal rebel leaders, Hugh O'Neill, Earl of Tyrone, and Red Hugh O'Donnell, Lord of Tír Conaill. On 7 May 1600 an impressive fleet sailed out of Carrickfergus harbour with some 4,000 soldiers and 200 cavalry on board under the command of Sir Henry Docwra. After becoming grounded on sandbanks in the lough for two days, the ships advanced up the Foyle, where, as he tells us, Docwra laid the foundations of the modern city of Derry:

> On the 22nd of May we put the army in order to march and went to the Derry, a place in manner of an island wherein were the ruins of an old abbey, of a bishop's house, of two churches and at one end of it an old

castle, the river called Lough Foyle encompassing it all on one side, and a bog most commonly wet dividing it from the main land.

This piece of ground we possessed ourselves without resistance, and judging it a fit place to make our main plantation in, at that end where the castle stood, being closer to the waterside, I presently resolved to raise a fort to keep our store of munition and victuals in.

Using rubble from old buildings bound by mortar made from cockle-shells collected from the mud, Docwra's men completed the fortifications before the end of the summer. Red Hugh was close by, and any time the English ventured out the Irish fiercely attacked them. The O'Donnells seized two hundred of their horses, and in one skirmish Docwra was severely wounded in the head by a spear and had to spend three weeks recovering in his tent.

Then his luck changed. Ships came in with fresh supplies and horses, and some Irish leaders, who knew the countryside well, came over to the English side. Docwra began to fight his way upstream. Meanwhile the Lord Deputy approached the Moyry Pass, the gateway to Ulster running between Dundalk and Newry. Red Hugh could only hope to evict Docwra with O'Neill's help, and that he could not do until the Earl of Tyrone had driven back Mountjoy.

On seeing Tyrone's elaborate defences, Mountjoy observed: 'These barbarous people had far exceeded our custom and our expectation.' In a report to London he described the pass:

Being naturally one of the most difficult passages in Ireland, fortified with good art, and with admirable industry, the enemy having raised from mountain to mountain, from wood to wood, and from bog to bog, long traverses, with huge and high flankers of great stones, mingled with turf and staked in both sides with pallisadoes wattled and possessed of one of the greatest armies that ever they were able to make. But that which was our main impediment, was the extremity of the weather, and the great rain, which made the rivers impassable.

On the afternoon of Thursday 2 October 1600 the Irish advanced with pike and handgun in formidable array. Mountjoy threw five regiments against them, but after three hours of close fighting the English fell back in confusion.

Nevertheless, the tide was beginning to turn against the Gaelic lords of Ulster.

Episode 74 ⤳

'WE SPARE NONE OF WHAT QUALITY OR SEX SOEVER'

In the autumn of 1600 English armies, having recovered control of most of the rest of the island, were closing in on Ulster. From his base at the head of Lough Foyle at Derry, Sir Henry Docwra was advancing up the River Mourne and driving a wedge between the two great lordships of Tyrone and Tír Conaill. North of Dundalk, Lord Deputy Mountjoy was battling hard to break through the elaborately constructed defences the Irish had built across the Moyry Pass.

Then, quite suddenly, the leader of the rebellion, Hugh O'Neill, the Earl of Tyrone, withdrew his forces from the Moyry Pass. No one knows why he did this. Was it to help his ally Red Hugh O'Donnell against Docwra? Did O'Neill hope to negotiate a truce? Mountjoy wanted no truce. When he reached Newry, his secretary informs us,

> His Lordship putting all the army in arms, with all the drums and trumpets, and a great volley of shot, proclaimed Tyrone's head, with a promise of £2,000 to him that brought him alive, and £1,000 to him that brought him dead.

Captain Edward Blayney and Captain Josias Bodley were sent into Tyrone to take O'Neill's greatest stronghold, an island fortress on Lough Lurcan:

> They both went together to discover the island, which done Captain Bodley made ready thirty arrows of wildfire, and close to the water the shot playing incessantly on the island, while the other delivered their arrows, suddenly the houses fired, and burnt so vehemently, as the rebels lodging there, forsook the island and swam to the further shore.... Great store of butter, corn, meal, and powder, was spoiled in the island, which all the rebels of that country made their magazine.

The English commanders set about starving and terrorising the population into submission. When the lord of the MacSweenys of Fanad refused to surrender, Docwra took swift and ruthless action:

> In revenge whereof I presently hung up his hostages, and I made another journey upon him, burnt and destroyed his houses and corn, whereupon winter approaching ensued the death of most of his people.

Sir Arthur Chichester, using Carrickfergus as his base, crossed Lough Neagh to create havoc on the western shores. In May 1601 he reported to Mountjoy:

> We have killed, burnt, and spoiled all along the lough within four miles of Dungannon, from whence we returned hither yesterday; in which journeys we have killed above one hundred people of all sorts, besides such as were burnt, how many I know not. We spare none of what quality or sex soever, and it hath bred much terror in the people ... and Tyrone himself lay within a mile of this place, but kept himself safe.

Mountjoy urged his commanders:

> Burn all the dwellings and destroy the corn in the ground, which might be done by encamping upon, and cutting it down with swords.

He himself, his secretary records,

> destroyed the rebels' corn about Armagh (whereof he found great abundance) and would destroy the rest, this course causing famine, being the only way to reduce or root out the rebels.

Meanwhile Queen Elizabeth was given this assurance: 'When the plough and breeding of cattle shall cease, then will the rebellion end.'

Indeed, there was every reason to believe that starvation and rebellion was bringing the rebellion to a close when Mountjoy received an urgent despatch telling him that the Spaniards had arrived.

When King Philip III of Spain was told by his advisers that he was all but bankrupt and that he could not afford to send help to Ireland, he replied: 'The expedition must go this year; to that end the council will put all in order with the utmost speed. I myself will see that the money is provided.' Philip appointed Don Diego de Brochero y Añaya as admiral and Don Juan del Águila as the military commander; the latter was a curious choice, since to take the post he had to be released from jail where he had been placed on a charge of mistreating his troops. After sailing out from Lisbon with half a million ducats and 4,500 men, the fleet halted thirty leagues from the Irish coast. A fierce argument followed on board the flagship *San Andrés*: Águila wanted to comply with O'Neill's request that they disembark at Killybegs in Tír Conaill, but Brochero insisted on landing at Kinsale in Co. Cork.

Brochero won the argument, and on 21 September 1601 the Spanish sailed up the estuary of the River Bandon and seized control of the walled town of Kinsale. Another argument followed: Brochero, declaring that his sailors were on the point of mutiny, refused to keep his ships in Ireland. After unloading supplies carelessly on mudbanks, spoiling much of the food with salt water, Brochero sailed away. Finding himself surrounded by the English, Águila dashed off a frantic appeal to O'Neill and O'Donnell, calling on them to march south to join him.

Episode 75 ~

THE BATTLE OF CHRISTMAS EVE

In September 1601, from Kinsale, a walled town on the Bandon river estuary in west Cork, Don Juan del Águila sent a messenger northwards with this message for the Gaelic lords of Ulster:

> I was confident your Excellencies would have come. I beseech you so to do, with as much speed, and as well furnished as you possibly may.... I will give the enemy their hands full from the town, and their first fury resisted, all is ended.

Fewer than 4,000 in number, the Spaniards could do little more than sit tight and wait for Hugh O'Neill, Red Hugh O'Donnell and their allies to march south. Lord Deputy Mountjoy was soon in control: his army completely surrounded Kinsale, digging trenches as deep as a lance-length, and built platforms from which cannon pounded the town continuously. Queen Elizabeth's vessels captured forts in the estuary downstream as reinforcements raised in the English shires came ashore nearby at Oysterhaven.

O'Neill was reluctant to leave the fastness of Ulster, but O'Donnell insisted that they had no choice but to march south. The Annals of the Four Masters record:

> The resolution they came to, with one mind and one intention was that each lord should proceed without dallying or delaying, to aid and assist the Spaniards.... O'Donnell was the first prepared to go on this expedition.... As for O'Neill, he left a week after All Hallowtide.

Sir George Carew, the Lord President of Munster, advanced north to block Red Hugh's approach in Co. Tipperary. But O'Donnell gave him the slip by taking his men over a treacherous bog which had frozen hard overnight in the Slievephelim Mountains. O'Neill took an easterly route and ravaged the counties around Dublin to weaken the Lord Deputy's supply lines.

The Irish from the north and the west had covered over three hundred miles in the depths of a bitterly cold winter, wading river after river, often up to the chest, and drew up to Kinsale in good order, camping to the north of the English entrenchments. Another small Spanish force, led by Don Pedro de Zubiaur, had driven back a squadron of English naval vessels and landed further south at Castlehaven. These Spaniards joined the Ulstermen at Kinsale with O'Sullivans, O'Driscolls and MacCarthys.

The Spanish in Kinsale, the English besieging them, and the Irish surrounding the English, all suffered terrible losses from hunger, disease and the wet and the cold. Men on watch dropped dead during the night. The Lord Deputy's secretary wrote:

And it was most true, that our men daily died by dozens, so as the sick and runaways considered, we were grown as weak as at our first setting down.

It was admitted that the English lost some 6,000 men in this way during the siege. The Spanish made a fierce sally from the town and spiked two of the English heavy guns. But the cost in lives was high, and the men were weak from lack of food. The English too made an assault, but failed to breach Kinsale's walls. Del Águila's desperate appeal to the Irish to attack without delay was foiled when his message was intercepted by the English. On 23 December O'Neill finally agreed to Red Hugh's pleadings that the Irish, numbering around 6,000, should launch a full-scale attack on the English lines at dawn on Christmas Eve. The Lord Deputy' secretary recalled:

All the night was clear with lightning (as in the former nights were great lightnings with thunder) to the astonishment of many.... This night our horsemen set to watch, to their seeming did see lamps burn at the points of their spears in the midst of these lightning flashes.... Suddenly one of the Lord President's horsemen called the Lord Deputy at his door, and told him, that Tyrone's army was come up very near to our camp.

The horseman had seen the slow-burning fuses of the Irish handguns glowing in the dark. Red Hugh's army lost its way in the half-light, and Hugh O'Neill, against the advice of the Spanish officers, halted behind boggy ground. Vital time was lost as the three massive Irish armies finally made a co-ordinated advance. Dawn had come when Mountjoy ordered his captains to charge the Irish with their cavalry. O'Neill saw his great army scattered and slaughtered. Mountjoy's secretary's account concludes:

The Irish not used to fight in plain ground, and something amazed with the blowing up of a gunpowder bag (they having upon the like fright defeated the English at Blackwater), but most discouraged to see their horse fly, being all chiefs and gentlemen, were suddenly routed, and our men followed the execution.

It was all over before the Spanish realised what had happened, and their sally from the town came too late.

This was the most terrible defeat the Gaelic Irish had ever suffered in the entire history of their conflict with the English. In less than two years all of Ireland from end to end would be conquered by the English crown for the very first time.

Episode 76 ~

THE TREATY OF MELLIFONT

The Annals of the Four Masters recognised that the victory of Lord Deputy Mountjoy over Hugh O'Neill, Red Hugh O'Donnell and the Spanish at Kinsale on Christmas Eve 1601 was a catastrophe from which Gaelic Ireland would never recover:

> Manifest was the displeasure of God, and misfortune to the Irish of fine Fodhla.... Immense and countless was the loss in that place; for the prowess and valour, prosperity and affluence, nobleness and chivalry, dignity and renown, bravery and protection, devotion and pure religion, of the island, were lost in this engagement.

Red Hugh sailed for Spain; twice he was given an audience with Philip iii, but the king was unwilling to provide further aid to the Irish. The Tír Conaill chief died at Simancas in August 1602, poisoned, it was said, by an English spy. Hugh O'Neill, the Earl of Tyrone, tried to negotiate a compromise peace, but Queen Elizabeth would not hear of it. She instructed her Lord Deputy:

> We do now require you very earnestly to be very wary in taking the submissions of these rebels.... Next we do require you, even whilst the iron is hot, so to strike, as this may not only prove a good summer's journey, but may deserve the title of that action which is the war's conclusion. For furtherance whereof we have spared no charge.

The concluding months of this great rebellion of the northern Gaelic lords were among the most terrible. Docwra, busy rounding up rebels around Ballyshannon, reported that those who

> came into my hands alive ... I caused the soldiers to hew in pieces with their swords.... The axe is now at the root of the tree, and I may well say, the neck of the rebellion as good as utterly broken.

The Lord Deputy was in the heart of Tyrone, where he took the opportunity to smash the ancient inauguration chair of the O'Neills as well as to destroy the harvest. A terrible man-made famine now began to sweep across Ulster, as Mountjoy's secretary, Fynes Moryson, recorded:

> Now because I have often made mention formerly of our destroying the rebels' corn, and using all means to famish them, let me by two or three examples show the miserable estate to which the rebels were thereby brought. Sir Arthur Chichester and the other commanders saw a most horrible spectacle of three children (whereof the eldest was not above ten years old), all eating and gnawing with their teeth the entrails of their mother, upon whose flesh they had fed twenty days past, and having eaten all from the feet upward to the bare bones, roasting it continually by a slow fire, were now coming to the eating of her said entrails in like sort roasted, yet not divided from the body, being as yet raw....
>
> No spectacle was more frequent in the ditches of towns, and especially in wasted countries, than to see multitudes of these poor people dead with their mouths all coloured green by eating nettles, docks, and all things they could rend above ground.

Queen Elizabeth at last relented and instructed her Lord Deputy to offer a pardon. The Earl of Tyrone, who had been desperately fighting a rearguard action in the forests of Glenconkeyne, eagerly accepted the offer of a safe-conduct. This was brought to him by his old friend Sir Garret Moore, who took him to his estate of Mellifont Abbey in March 1603 to meet Lord Mountjoy face to face. O'Neill was astonished at the lenient terms offered to him. What was the explanation? The answer was that Mountjoy knew what the earl did not know: that the old queen had died just a few days previously. James vi of Scotland was now James i of England, Scotland, Wales and Ireland. No one, particularly Mountjoy, knew what his policy would be.

Provided he renounced the title of The O'Neill and handed the church lands of Ulster to the crown, the earl was allowed to retain his lordship over most of his traditional territory. On 2 June 1603 Hugh O'Neill and the newly elected Lord of Tír Conaill, Rory O'Donnell, left Ireland in the company of

Lord Deputy Mountjoy. After narrowly avoiding shipwreck, they arrived in England, where the Gaelic lords were pelted with stones and mud by women who had lost their menfolk in the Irish wars. They were well received by King James I, and O'Donnell was created the Earl of Tyrconnell. This generous pardon infuriated those English officers who had risked their lives campaigning in Ireland. One of them wrote angrily:

> I have lived ... to see that damnable rebel Tyrone brought to England, honoured and well liked.... How I did labour after that knave's destruction! I adventured perils by sea and land, was near starving, ate horse flesh in Munster, and all to quell that man, who now smileth in peace at those who did hazard their lives to destroy him: and now doth dare us old commanders with his presence and protection.

However, he and other men who had served the crown were soon to have the satisfaction of seeing these proud Gaelic lords lose all that they had.

Episode 77 ～

'REMEMBER, REMEMBER, THE FIFTH OF NOVEMBER'

We must now turn our attention to the 'Old English'. Who were they? These were descendants of Norman colonists, and of the people they brought over the Irish Sea with them. They lived mostly in Dublin and the area surrounding it known as 'the Pale', in towns, and in the fertile plains of Leinster. Though nearly all of them were able to speak Irish fluently, at the beginning of the seventeenth century they were proud to call themselves English—specifically 'Old' English to distinguish themselves from the 'New' English who had arrived in the sixteenth century. The Old English were loyal to the crown, and many of them had fought in the Lord Deputy's armies. But they were also Catholics and were loyal to the pope.

The Old English had high hopes that the new king, James I, would grant them toleration. Queen Elizabeth had stipulated that all inhabitants of Ireland should attend Protestant churches and recognise her as the supreme governor of the church. In fact her government in Ireland had been far too busy crushing the rebellion led by the Earl of Tyrone to enforce these laws.

What would King James do, now that peace had returned to Ireland? To their horror, the Old English found that the king was determined to make them Protestants. Sir Arthur Chichester, appointed Lord Deputy in 1605, launched a programme of religious persecution on a scale never before witnessed in Ireland. One official informed the king that the country swarmed with

> priests, Jesuits, seminaries, friars, and Romish bishops; if there be not speedy means to free this kingdom of this wicked rabble, much mischief will burst forth in a very short time.... It is high time they were banished.

King James issued a proclamation on 4 July 1605, declaring that he would fight to his knees in blood rather than grant toleration. He would never

> give liberty of conscience ... to his subjects in that kingdom ... [or] confirm the hopes of any creature that they should ever have from him any toleration to exercise any other religion than that which is agreeable to God's Word.

Now rigidly enforced was an earlier law which fined ordinary Catholics a shilling for every Sunday they failed to attend a Protestant church. (A working man's wage in those days was five shillings a week.) Letters were delivered to sixteen leading Catholic gentlemen in Dublin fining them £100 each. Catholic clergy were ordered out of the country:

> All priests whatsoever made and ordained by any authority derived or pretended to be derived from the see of Rome shall, before the tenth day of December, depart out of the kingdom of Ireland.

It proved difficult to enforce these laws in the more remote and more Gaelic parts of the island. And so it was the Old English, especially in Dublin, who suffered most. The leading Catholic noblemen and gentry of the Pale sent a petition to Lord Deputy Chichester to protest against this persecution. But in that very month, on 5 November 1605, the Gunpowder Plot to blow up the Houses of Parliament had been discovered. This was no time for Catholics in either England or Ireland to be demanding the redress of grievances.

The petitioners were put under house arrest. Sir Patrick Barnewall and other Catholic leaders were cast into the dungeons of Dublin Castle. Chichester personally led the campaign to force Catholics to attend Protestant services. One Catholic gentleman went as far as the church door and then would go no further, whereupon, according to Henry Fitzsimon, Chichester

> told him savagely to go in, and seeing he could not prevail on him, struck him a cruel blow on the head with his stick. Then the mace-bearer attacked

him so savagely that he fell to the ground like a dead man, and the Lord Deputy had him dragged into church, where he lay insensible and gasping all the time of the sermon, and no one dared to approach him. Some of his friends afterwards took him home, where he gave his blessed soul to God in two hours.

Unpaid fines were forcibly collected:

No doors, no enclosures, no wall can stop them in their course; they are unmoved by the shrieks of the females and by the weeping of the children. Everything is torn open, and whatever is of any value is set aside to be taken away, whatever is worthless is thrown in the streets, and devoted to the flames ...

Meanwhile a similar reign of terror raged in Galway and in the towns of Munster, as a priest reported:

They rush in crowds into the houses of these servants of God, break open doors, tear off locks, ransack shops, leave no corner unsearched, and carry off everything they can lay their hands on, besides taking the owners prisoners.

Hearing that their leader, Sir Patrick Barnewall, had been incarcerated in the Tower of London, some Catholic Old English began to plan an uprising. The man who was doing most to encourage them was none other than the Earl of Tyrone. His plotting was to lead directly to what has been long remembered as the 'Flight of the Earls'.

Episode 78 ∿

'I KNOW THAT THEY WISH TO KILL HIM BY POISON OR BY ANY POSSIBLE MEANS'

After nine years of revolt against the English crown the Gaelic lords could count themselves lucky to have survived. They still had their titles and their lands.

All was not well, however. English officers who had done so much to conquer the whole island of Ireland were infuriated by these generous pardons.

They felt they should have been rewarded with lands confiscated from traitors. Officials appointed to serve in Ireland by King James set out to undermine the Earl of Tyrone and the other Gaelic lords. One of these was Sir
Arthur Chichester, the former governor of Carrickfergus who had been
appointed the king's Lord Deputy in Ireland in 1605. A former Lord Deputy
had noticed what he described as Chichester's 'greedy gathering' of lands and
property. Another official was Sir John Davies, appointed Solicitor-General
for Ireland in 1603. He wanted to impose English law on

> the Irishry in the province of Ulster ... the most rude and unreformed part
> of Ireland, and the seat and nest of the last great rebellion, [so] that the next
> generation will in tongue and heart and every way else become English; so
> as there will be no difference or distinction, but the Irish Sea betwixt us.

Together Chichester and Davies whittled away at O'Neill's authority, so that,
Chichester reported, 'now the law of England, and the Ministers thereof, were
shackles and handlocks unto him, and the garrisons planted in his country
were as pricks in his side'.

Meanwhile the Earl of Tyrconnell's position was becoming desperate. A
commission appointed in 1605 'for division and bounding of the lords' and
gentlemen's livings' had ruled that the O'Boyles, MacSweeneys and others did
not have to pay rent to the earl. Other fertile lands had been occupied by the
newly appointed bishop of the three dioceses of Derry, Raphoe and Clogher,
George Montgomery. His wife Susan wrote to her brother in May 1605:

> My Lord Bishop will be at home before Wednesday night. The king hath
> bestowed on him three Irish bishoprics; the names of them I cannot
> remember, they are so strange, except one, which is Derry: I pray God it
> will make us all merry.

A year later she wrote:

> We are settled in the Derry, in a very pretty little house builded after the
> English fashion.... I think that Mr Montgomery hath many thousand acres
> of as good land as any in England; if it were peopled, it were worth many
> hundreds of pounds by the years.

Much of this land had been the Earl of Tyrconnell's; now he was left only with
poor mountainous land, and it was noticed that he was 'very meanly followed'.

The same Bishop Montgomery also laid claim to large parts of the Earl
of Tyrone's territory. This led the earl to write in complaint to the king in May
1607:

Whereas it pleased Your Highness of your great bounty to restore me to
such lands as I and my ancestors had and enjoyed ... but now, most gracious
Sovereign, there are so many that seek to despoil me of the greatest part of
the residue which Your Majesty was pleased I should hold ... for the Lord
Bishop of Derry, not contented with the great living Your Majesty has been
pleased to bestow on him, seeketh to have a great part of my lands, where-
unto none of his predecessors ever made claim.

Bishop Montgomery also encouraged Donal O'Cahan, whose lordship
extended over lands which now make up much of Co. Londonderry, to set
aside his wife, who was O'Neill's daughter, and also to deny the Earl of
Tyrone's traditional overlordship in his territory and to refuse to pay him any
rent. The dispute became so bitter that King James summoned them both to
London.

It is quite clear that, once in London, Tyrone became convinced that his life
was in danger. Certainly the Spanish ambassador at King James's court
thought so too, stating that 'I know that they wish to kill him by poison or by
any possible means ... their fear of him gnaws at their entrails.'

In the early summer of 1607 the government in London was told by Sir
Christopher St Lawrence (subsequently Lord Howth) that a plot was being
prepared in Ireland by a league of gentlemen opposed to the crown. There
was, he reported,

a general revolt intended by many of the nobility and principal persons of
this land, together with the cities and towns of the greatest strength; and
that they will shake off the yoke of the English government, as they term it,
and adhere to the Spaniard.

We now know that the leader of this conspiracy was none other than Hugh
O'Neill, Earl of Tyrone. Did King James know that Tyrone was in this plot?
Actually the king did not know, but O'Neill could not be sure.

News that the plot had been uncovered settled the matter for the two earls:
they would take flight from Ireland and make for Spain. Indeed, the ship to
take them there was already on the high seas.

Episode 79 ∾

THE FLIGHT OF THE EARLS

Cúchonnacht Maguire, Lord of Fermanagh, had had enough humiliation at the hands of the English. A royal commission appointed in 1605 had taken away half of his ancestral lands. He was certain he and other Gaelic lords would be beggared by the crown. The only answer was to get the help of the King of Spain to drive the English out and restore the Catholic religion.

Even though he had made peace with England in 1604, King Philip III of Spain was only too eager to help. He sent money to Rory O'Donnell, Earl of Tyrconnell, and Hugh O'Neill, Earl of Tyrone, and together they hatched an elaborate plot to escape from Ireland and return soon after with a great army.

Cúchonnacht Maguire planned the enterprise for more than a year. Described by the Annals of the Four Masters as a 'rapid-marching adventurous man, endowed with wisdom and beauty of person', he was such a master of disguise that it was said his nearest friends would have found it hard to identify him. Provided with silver and gold by Philip III, Maguire set sail in great secret from the French port of Nantes and made for Ulster. Near to its destination the ship was arrested by a Scottish warship and held for two days. Fortunately Maguire had put nets and salt aboard and was able to convince his captors that he had come to Ulster only to fish.

On 25 August 1607 the vessel sailed into Lough Swilly and anchored off Rathmullan. At nightfall a man came ashore with Spanish ducats and set out to bring news to the Earl of Tyrconnell of the ship's arrival. Two days later a messenger reached the Earl of Tyrone, who was staying with his friend Sir Garret Moore at Mellifont, Co. Louth. Sir Arthur Chichester, the Lord Deputy, was in the area and found Tyrone's departure a little strange:

> The manner of his departure, carrying his little son with him who was brought up in Sir Garret's house, made me suspect he had mischief in his head; harm I knew he could do none, if they were upon their keeping, for he was altogether without arms and munition; and his flight beyond the seas I should never have suspected ...

Making his way from Mellifont to Dundalk, and from there to Armagh and Dungannon, he stopped only when he reached 'the Craobh', a house on a lough in the wilds of Tyrone. Here his family and servants were waiting for him. Then on Wednesday 2 September they set off across the Sperrin Mountains for Lough Swilly. According to the Attorney-General,

He travelled all night with his impediments, that is, his women and children; and it is likewise reported that the countess, his wife, being exceedingly weary, slipped down from her horse, and weeping, said she could go no farther; whereupon the earl drew his sword, and swore a great oath that he would kill her in the place, if she would not pass on with him, and put on a more cheerful countenance withal.

When they reached Rathmullan, a child with six toes on one foot, which was considered very lucky, was sent for; it is said that they 'took the infant violently ... which terrified the foster-father'. They crowded aboard the vessel, the cream of Ulster's Gaelic aristocracy; but in the haste of leaving, many, including the Earl of Tyrone's son Conn, were left behind. Then, as the earls themselves later reported to King Philip, at noon on Friday 4 September,

> leaving their horses on the shore with no one to hold their bridles, they went aboard a ship to the number of about one hundred persons, including soldiers, women and principal gentlemen.

Tadhg Ó Cianáin, who sailed with the earls, tells us that they planned to sail straight for Spain:

> They were on the sea for thirteen days with excessive storm and dangerous bad weather. A cross of gold which O'Neill had, and which contained a portion of the Cross of the Crucifixion and many other relics, being put by them into the sea trailing after the ship, gave them great relief. At the end of that time, much to their surprise, they met in the middle of the sea two small hawks, merlins, which alighted on the ship. The hawks were caught and were fed afterwards.

Fierce contrary winds forced them to change course for France. They made landfall at the mouth of the River Seine. Here the local governor treated them well, and in return the earls presented him with the hawks they had captured at sea. Only when he obtained permission from the King of France, however, would the governor let them go on to Spanish Flanders. They did not then know that they would never return to their native Ulster.

Episode 80 〜

'WE WOULD RATHER HAVE CHOSEN TO DIE IN OUR OWN COUNTRY'

On 4 September 1607 the Earls of Tyrone and Tyrconnell and their families and followers sailed away from Ireland, never to return. For Franciscan friars writing their annals in Donegal this was an unparalleled disaster:

> Woe to the heart that meditated, woe to the mind that conceived, woe to the council that decided on, the project of their setting out on this voyage, without knowing whether they should ever return to their native principalities or patrimonies to the end of the world.

Forced by storms to land in France, the earls found that they were famous throughout Catholic Europe. They were champions of the faith against the heretics. Their long war against Queen Elizabeth had seemed like the struggle of David against Goliath. King Henry iv of France described Hugh O'Neill, Earl of Tyrone, as being the third greatest general in Europe. When the earls arrived in Spanish Flanders—now the state of Belgium—the Archduke Albert and his wife, the Infanta Isabel, gave them luxurious apartments in their palace. Two days later they were given a military escort to Brussels, where the Marqués of Spínola invited them to a splendid banquet. Tadhg Ó Cianáin was there:

> When greetings had been exchanged in abundance, they entered the hall of the marquis.... He himself arranged each one in his place, seating O'Neill in his own place at the head of the table, the papal nuncio to his right, the Earl of Tyrconnell to his left, O'Neill's children and Maguire next the earl and the Spanish ambassador and the Duke of Aumale on the other side.... The rest of the illustrious, respected nobles at table, the marquis himself, and the Duke of Osuna were at the end of the table opposite O'Neill. The excellent dinner which they partook of was grand and costly enough for a king, and nothing inferior was the banquet. Gold and silver plate was displayed inside that no king or prince in Christendom might be ashamed to have.

Back in Ireland the Attorney-General, Sir John Davies, was convinced that

O'Neill and his train of barbarous men, women and children ... will be taken for a company of gypsies and be exceedingly scorned.... The formal Spanish courtier will hardly believe he is the same O'Neill which maintained so long a war against the crown of England.

Davies was quite wrong. The exiled Irish made a very favourable impression and were treated with great respect. The governor of Tournai had cannons fired in salute as they entered his town. But what was to be done with the Irish lords and their families?

The Spanish government of Flanders had just signed a truce with Holland, a close ally of England. O'Neill and O'Donnell could not remain in Flanders. More important, Philip III of Spain had decided to remain at peace with James I. To leave the Irish in Flanders or bring them to Spain would almost be an act of war. And so it was decided to transfer the Irish exiles to Italy under the protection of the pope.

The pope agreed to pay the Irish nobles large pensions, and on behalf of the Spanish king the Marqués of Spínola gave the earls 12,000 crowns in silver. But the earls had left their native land with the purpose of putting themselves at the head of a Spanish army in order to invade Ireland and drive out the English. Now this grand design was being set aside. The Spanish ambassador in Brussels wrote to his king in December 1607 telling him how disappointed he was that the earls were being sent out of his dominions to Italy:

His Highness gave his word to the ambassador of England that within very few days they would leave [Flanders] ....

I do not know how the earls will take this and I confess to Your Majesty that it seems to me His Highness has taken a harsh decision on this matter with regard to people who have given such service to God and Your Majesty.

So it was that the Flight of the Earls from Ulster had been for nothing. It was in vain that O'Neill and O'Donnell sent an appeal to King Philip on 17 December 1607:

Señor

His Serene Highness orders that we leave his states so that he may keep a promise he made to the King of England.... This has caused us much sorrow and astonishment.... As God is our witness, we would rather have chosen to die in our own country than to see ourselves treated in this manner by a prince in whom we placed our greatest trust.... Our concern is the pleasure and satisfaction it will give the heretics to see us thus treated.

Indeed, King James was delighted to hear the news. It gave him the opportunity to put into effect one of the grandest projects of his reign—the plantation of Ulster.

Episode 81 ～

'BRING IN COLONIES OF CIVIL PEOPLE OF ENGLAND AND SCOTLAND'

The Earls of Tyrconnell and Tyrone, along with some of the noblest Gaelic families in Ulster, had sailed away from Ireland in 1607. Their intention was to return with a great Spanish army to drive the English back across the Irish Sea. But King Philip III, in spite of all the gold of Mexico and the silver of Peru, was almost bankrupt. He could not afford to keep his promises to the Catholics of Ireland. The Gaelic lords were sent out of his dominions to Italy. One disaster followed another.

On their way from Flanders to Rome they lost most of the money given to them by the Spanish. Tadhg Ó Cianáin was with them and described how this occurred:

Saint Patrick's day precisely, the seventeenth of March ... they advanced through the Alps. Now the mountains were laden and filled with snow and ice, and the roads and paths were narrow and rugged. They reached a high bridge in a very deep glen called the Devil's Bridge. One of O'Neill's horses, which was carrying some of his money, about £120, fell down the face of the high, frozen, snowy cliff.... Great labour was experienced in bringing up the horse alone, but the money decided to remain blocking the violent, deep, destructive torrent which flows under the bridge through the middle of the glen.

When they eventually arrived in Rome, they were well received by the pope and cardinals and given a house. Soon, however, they were running out of money, as the Spanish ambassador in Rome reported to Philip III:

I beg Your Majesty to give them some extra financial aid. Their grant is barely sufficient for their food and in other respects they suffer great want.

They are so poor that one must have compassion for them. The pope gives them a house but not one stick of furniture and they have neither beds nor chairs. The unfortunates have not money to buy such bare necessities.

Nor did the climate of Italy suit these northerners. The Earl of Tyrconnell died of fever in Rome in July 1608. Six months later the same disease carried off Séamus, a lord of the MacMahons, and also Cúchonnacht Maguire, Lord of Fermanagh—the man who had done most to organise the flight of the earls and their companions from Ulster. The Earl of Tyrone's son Hugh—the Baron of Dungannon—died of fever in 1609. And, finally, Hugh O'Neill, the Earl of Tyrone, breathed his last in Rome on 10 July 1616. With him died the last hope that the Gaelic lords of Ulster would return to Ireland with a Spanish army.

Meanwhile, back in Ireland, a Dublin Castle official wrote to King James I: 'The undutiful departure of the Earls of Tyrone, Tyrconnell and Maguire offers good occasion for a plantation.' It certainly did. The king's Lord Deputy, Sir Arthur Chichester, also thought that the Flight of the Earls offered an unrivalled opportunity. He could not understand why O'Neill had so suddenly left Ulster: 'It were strange that he should quit an earldom, and so large and beneficial a territory for smoke and castles in the air.' Chichester urged King James to seize the moment, condemn the exiles as traitors, confiscate their lands and colonise Ulster with loyal subjects:

If His Majesty will, during their absence, assume the countries into his possession, divide the lands amongst the inhabitants ... and will bestow the rest upon servitors and men of worth here, and withal bring in colonies of civil people of England and Scotland ... the country will ever after be happily settled.

The king hesitated—could he really confiscate all those lands in Ulster simply because their owners had left the country? Yes he could, the Attorney-General assured him and convened a grand jury. The earls were condemned as outlaws on the rather flimsy charge that when they had assembled at Rathmullan in September 1607 they were, in effect, levying war against the king. Finally, in December 1607, the lands of the departed Gaelic lords were confiscated and put in the possession of the king.

King James now threw himself with enormous enthusiasm into this grand project which he named the 'plantation of Ulster'. It would give him a unique opportunity to reward at little cost the many who had claims on his purse. The conquest of Ireland had cost Queen Elizabeth at least two million pounds. King James was left with a huge debt; many merchants and suppliers might be delighted to be paid with landed estates. Certainly his 'servitors', that is, the army commanders and civil servants, looked forward to generous grants of lands in Ulster.

Above all, the successful plantation of much of Antrim and Down—which had begun at the start of his reign in 1603—gave every indication that the colonisation of the rest of Ulster could be a triumphant success.

Episode 82 ∿

A LUCKY ESCAPE, SCOTTISH LAIRDS AND THE DIVISION OF CLANDEBOYE

At the close of the Nine Years War in 1603 Conn MacNeill O'Neill, Lord of Upper Clandeboye and the Great Ards, held a party in his castle of Castlereagh. On the third day he ran out of wine and sent a number of his armed retainers into the village of Belfast to get more. These men became involved in some sort of altercation with English troops stationed there, as a result of which Conn himself was placed under arrest and flung into a dungeon in Carrickfergus Castle.

Not long afterwards Sir Hugh Montgomery, sixth Laird of Braidstane in Scotland, came to his aid. First he sent over an agent to win the heart of the jailer's daughter. This man 'ply'd his oar so well that in a few nights he had certain proofs of the bride's cordial love'. Lady O'Neill also played her part by smuggling in rope to her husband Conn in two big cheeses, 'the meat being neatly taken out, and filled with cords, well packed in, and the holes handsomely made up again'. Then the jailer's daughter opened the dungeon cell and Conn O'Neill lowered himself down the rope to a waiting boat to be taken across the sea to Largs and freedom.

Sir Hugh Montgomery had served King James I for many years as a secret agent. Without too much difficulty the king was persuaded to give Conn a pardon on condition that he gave one-third of his lordship to Sir Hugh Montgomery and another third to Sir James Hamilton, also a secret agent of the king.

In this bizarre way began the most successful scheme of 'plantation', that is, colonisation, of any part of Ireland in the seventeenth century. The triple division was agreed in April 1605. Conn O'Neill was probably fortunate to emerge from these tortuous dealings with sixty townlands, centred on Castlereagh and comprising half of Upper Clandeboye. Hamilton's estates were partly in north Down around Bangor and Holywood and partly on the western shores of Strangford Lough around Killyleagh. Montgomery got much of the Ards peninsula and made Newtownards his base.

Following the victory of crown forces in Ireland, local Gaelic lords of Antrim and Down had to be careful to keep out of trouble. Many of them had joined the Earl of Tyrone in his rebellion against Queen Elizabeth. Now they eagerly gave up part of their estates in return for a secure title to the lands they kept for themselves. For example, Phelim MacCartan was confirmed in his possession of Kinelarty in south-east Down provided he gave a third of his estates to Sir Edward Cromwell, a soldier from County Rutland.

At the close of the rebellion Co. Down in particular had suffered severe loss of life during a terrible famine caused by troops slaughtering cattle and destroying crops. Inviting Scots and English to settle on their lands would not only please the king but also ensure that the land would be farmed again. Sir Randal MacDonnell of the Glens of Antrim had fought at Kinsale against the crown in 1601. Now he carefully cultivated his friendship with King James, who in turn welcomed MacDonnell's support on the other side of the North Channel against the Campbell clan in Argyll. Catholic though he was, Sir Randal invited many Presbyterian Scots to cross over and become tenants on his estates. King James was so pleased that he raised Sir Randal to the peerage as the Earl of Antrim in 1620.

Many of the officers who had commanded crown forces against the Irish in rebellion were younger sons of gentlemen who, under English and Scottish law, did not inherit estates at home. Victory against the Irish gave them the opportunity to set themselves up as independent landed gentlemen. They included Captain Hugh Clotworthy at Massereene, Captain Roger Langford at Muckamore, Sir Fulke Conway at Killultagh, Sir Edward Trevor in south Down, Ensign John Dalway in east Antrim, Sir Faithful Fortescue in north Antrim, Sir Thomas Phillips at Toome, and Sir Moses Hill and Sir Arthur Chichester in the Lagan valley.

Sir Arthur Chichester, the former governor of Carrickfergus, was appointed Lord Deputy in 1605. He had been granted lands in Carrickfergus, Belfast and the lower Lagan valley. Once he was the king's chief governor, he felt he must make every effort to develop his grant. He ordered the firing of more than a million bricks to turn Belfast into a town. Commissioners appointed by King James were impressed:

> The town of Belfast is plotted out in a good form, wherein are many families of English, Scottish and some Manxmen already inhabiting, of which some are artificers who have built good timber houses with chimneys after the manner of the English Pale, and one inn with very good lodgings which is a great comfort to travellers in those parts.

The British colonisation of Ulster was well under way.

Episode 83 ~

PLANTING DOWN AND ANTRIM

Very soon after the beginning of James I's reign in 1603 hundreds of English and Scots began to cross the Irish Sea to start a new life in eastern Ulster. Much of this countryside had been devastated in the recent rebellion. In 1606 Sir Hugh Montgomery returned from raising what he called 'recruits of money' in Scotland to arrive in his new estate in Co. Down. He found

> those parishes more wasted than America (when the Spaniards landed there).... Thirty cabins could not be found, nor any stone walls, but ruined roofless churches, and a few vaults at Grey Abbey, and a stump of an old castle in Newtown....
>
> But Sir Hugh in the said spring brought over with him divers artificers, as smiths, masons, carpenters, etc.... They soon made cottages and booths for themselves, because sods and saplings of ashes, alders, and birch trees with rushes for thatch, and bushes for wattles, were at hand. And also they made a shelter of the said stump of the castle for Sir Hugh, whose residence was mostly there.

Irish labourers felled timber in the forest of Slut Neal by the River Lagan. Floated downstream to Belfast, the logs were taken from there by sea to Donaghadee and Newtownards. The harbour built by Sir Hugh at Donaghadee became very busy; here arrived 'a constant flux of passengers daily coming over [ignoring] evil report of wolves and woodkerns'.

With proper ploughing, and fertilised with seaweed gathered from the shore, the soil gave bountiful harvests in 1606 and 1607. Every parish had a watermill provided by Lady Montgomery to grind corn. According to records preserved by the Montgomery family, the Co. Down colony was flourishing:

> Now every body minded their trades, and the plough, and the spade, building and setting of fruit trees, etc., in orchards and gardens, and by ditching in their grounds. The old women spun, and the young women plied their nimble fingers at knitting—and every body was innocently busy. Now the golden peaceable age renewed, no strife, contention, querulous lawyers, or Scottish or Irish feuds, between clans and families, and surnames, disturbing the tranquillity of those times; and the towns and temples were erected, with other great works done (even in troublesome years).

Of course, this is a rosy, romantic picture. But there is no denying the success of the Scottish settlement in north and east Down. The king's commissioners reported in 1611:

> Sir Hugh Montgomery knight hath repaired part of the Abbey of Newtown for his own dwelling, and made a good town of a hundred houses or thereabouts all peopled with Scots.

In addition, a school was built and the master paid £20 a year 'to teach Latin, Greek and Logics, allowing the scholars a green for recreation at golf, football, and archery'.

The commissioners also liked what was happening along the north Down coast:

> Sir James Hamilton knight hath builded a fair stone house at the town of Bangor in the Upper Clandeboye.... The town consists of 80 new houses all inhabited with Scottishmen and Englishmen. And hath brought out of England 20 artificers, who are making materials of timber, brick and stone for another house there.
>
> The said Sir James Hamilton is preparing to build another house in Holywood three miles from Bangor and two hundred thousand of bricks with other materials ready at the place, where there are some 20 houses inhabited with English and Scots.

In the Lagan valley the Lord Deputy, Sir Arthur Chichester, had rented out land to his provost-marshal, Sir Moses Hill. Hill built a house at Stranmillis, and, where Shaw's Bridge stands today, he had erected 'a strong fort built upon a passage on the plains of Malone with a strong palisado'.

In Belfast the royal commissioners found 'many masons, bricklayers and other labourers awork' putting up a fine manor house, a castle for Sir Arthur which 'will defend the passage over the ford at Belfast between Upper and Lower Clandeboye, and likewise the bridge over the river of Owenvarra between Malone and Belfast'. This castle, standing where today High Street joins Castle Junction, dominated Belfast until April 1708, when it was accidentally burnt down.

Chichester rarely had time to be in Belfast now. His duties as chief governor of Ireland required him to be based largely in Dublin Castle. It was here that, early in 1608, he was preparing the details of the 'plantation of Ulster', the king's ambitious scheme to colonise western and central Ulster with industrious and reliable English and Scottish families.

Then a messenger galloped into the castle courtyard bearing momentous news: Sir Cahir O'Doherty, Lord of Inishowen, had raised the banner of rebellion once more in the north. It was a revolt which was eventually to cause the king to scrap his original plan of colonisation—his plantation of Ulster would become an enterprise on a scale never yet seen in western Europe.

Episode 84 ∿

THE REBELLION OF SIR CAHIR O'DOHERTY

Sir Cahir O'Doherty had changed sides to join the English towards the end of the Nine Years War. When that rebellion had ended in 1603, he had been restored to his lordship of Inishowen in north Donegal. After the Earl of Tyrone and the Earl of Tyrconnell had sailed away with the noble Gaelic families of Ulster in 1607, O'Doherty had been chairman of the grand jury which had judged the earls to be guilty of treason. Then, a few months later, he was pushed too far.

The new English governor of Derry, Sir George Paulet, was contemptuous of the native Irish and in an argument punched O'Doherty in the face. The Lord of Inishowen, the Annals of the Four Masters record, 'would rather have suffered death than live to brook such insult and dishonour'.

O'Doherty began his rebellion in a rather unusual way. On 18 April 1608 he invited the governor of Culmore Fort, Captain Henry Hart, and his wife to dinner in his new castle at Burt. He enticed Hart upstairs, put a knife to his throat, and, as the captain's wife screamed for mercy, O'Doherty threatened that 'if she or he did not take some present course for the delivery of Culmore into his hands, both they and their children should die'. By this ruse, Culmore—a strategic fort which commanded the entrance to Lough Foyle— fell to O'Doherty.

The following night O'Doherty attacked Derry, took the lower fort without difficulty, shot Governor Paulet dead, and then encountered fierce resistance in the upper fort. A surviving defender recalled:

Lieutenant Gordon, hearing the shot, issued forth naked upon the rampier, with his rapier and dagger, where, with one soldier in his company, he set upon the enemy and killed two of them, using most comfortable words of courage to the soldiers to fight for their lives; but the enemy being far more in number, one struck him on the forehead with a stone, whereat, being somewhat amazed, they rushed upon him and killed him and the soldiers also.

As dawn broke the surviving townspeople barricaded themselves in the Bishop's House and adjacent dwellings. However,

> Destitute of victuals and munition, and seeing a piece brought by the enemy from Culmore, and ready mounted to batter the said houses, and wearied with the lamentable outcry of women and children, after much parley and messages to and fro, [they] yielded the said houses.

The Irish set fire to Derry and Strabane soon after, and factions of O'Cahans, O'Hanlons and MacSweeneys joined O'Doherty, threatening to spread the revolt across Ulster. The king's marshal was soon on hand, however, to recover the burnt shell of Derry. In the wild country of north Donegal O'Doherty was cornered near Kilmacrenan and killed at the Rock of Doon. Meanwhile Lord Deputy Sir Arthur Chichester crushed the O'Hanlons in Co. Armagh and moved into Tyrone, executing dozens by hanging, 'a death which they contemn more than any other nation living; they are generally so stupid by nature, or so tough or disposed by their priests, that they show no remorse of conscience, or fear of death'. Another force in north Donegal besieged Doe Castle, 'the strongest hold in all the province which endured a hundred blows of the demi-cannon before it yielded'.

The governor of Ballyshannon brought up five warships to hunt down O'Donnells who had retreated to the islands, took the castle on Tory Island and slaughtered the defenders. When the O'Gallaghers' castle of Glenveagh fell, the rebellion was over. The crown forces now had control of country which, Chichester admitted, only recently had been as inaccessible as 'the kingdom of China'. The Lord Deputy was not impressed by the scenery we appreciate so much today, describing it as 'one of the most barren, uncouth, and desolate countries that could be seen, fit only to confine rebels and ill spirits into'.

From Coleraine the Attorney-General wrote to King James I assuring him that he had six counties 'now in demesne and actual possession in this province; which is a greater extent of land than any prince in Europe has to dispose of'. This was an accurate assessment. The crushing of O'Doherty's rebellion had resulted in the seizing of extensive lands to add to the vast territories confiscated from the earls who had fled from Lough Swilly the year before. The scale of the 'plantation of Ulster', the king's ambitious scheme to colonise the province with loyal British subjects, was now greatly magnified. This was the era of colonial expansion when England sought to catch up with Spain, Portugal and Holland. Only a year before the first successful band of English settlers had crossed the Atlantic for Virginia. As for Chichester, he declared he would 'rather labour with my hands in the plantation of Ulster than dance or play in that of Virginia'.

Episode 85 ⟿

THE PLANTATION OF ULSTER

The summer assizes of 1608 confiscated virtually all the territory of Ulster west of the River Bann for King James I. English and Scots were already busily colonising the counties of Antrim and Down. The lands of Co. Monaghan had been redistributed in Queen Elizabeth's day. Out of the nine counties of the northern province, that left six to be included in the 'plantation of Ulster': Armagh, Tyrone, Fermanagh, Cavan and counties then named Tyrconnell and Coleraine. This colonising project, the king explained to his Lord Deputy, would be a civilising enterprise which would 'establish the true religion of Christ among men ... almost lost in superstition'. Besides, a plantation would pacify Ulster and secure the province against the risk of further native rebellion and foreign invasion.

The first thing to be done was to make a detailed survey of the vast territory to be colonised. 'To avoid His Majesty's further charge', the decision was made not to attempt to measure the land but to conduct an inquiry. The traditional Irish local land divisions caused much confusion. The basic units were the *townlands,* called *tates* in Co. Fermanagh, *polls* in Co. Cavan, and *ballyboes* elsewhere. Each townland was supposed to be enough to support one extended family—small and compact on good land, and more extensive in mountainous and boggy areas. Groups of townlands made up larger divisions known as *ballybetaghs* and *quarters*. The commissioners making the inquiry found it all very perplexing. In the end they decided to make grants based on the ancient land divisions, keeping the Irish names in an anglicised form. Tattyreagh, for example, means the 'grey townland'.

In April 1610 a detailed brochure was published in London. Readers of what became known as the 'Printed Book' could find out all the terms and conditions of the plantation. The confiscated land of each county was divided into 'precincts', often based on the existing structure of baronies, and each precinct was subdivided into large, middle and small estates, or 'proportions'. It soon became clear that separation was the essence of the scheme.

The largest group of colonists, known as 'undertakers', had to clear their estates completely of native Irish inhabitants. Undertakers had to be English or 'inland' Scots who had taken the Oath of Supremacy—that is, they had to be Protestants—and, having removed the natives, they had to 'undertake' to colonise their estates with British Protestants. Indeed, it was during the Ulster plantation that the term 'British' came into general use—officials got tired of constantly saying 'English, Scots, Welsh and Manxmen'. The undertakers paid rent of £5 6s 8d annually to the king for every thousand acres. In all, they received over a quarter of the confiscated land.

Another group of grantees were termed 'servitors'. They were councillors of state, captains and lieutenants with military commands and other servants of the crown, and, between them, they were assigned about one-fifth of the plantation lands. They did not have to remove the native Irish, but they enjoyed reduced rents if they brought in British colonists. Their estates were not merely rewards for past service to the crown: servitors were expected to play a key role in the defence of the plantation.

Between one-quarter and one-fifth of the confiscated lands were allocated to what were described as the 'deserving' native Irish. This was less generous than it seemed, because a number of these grants were for the lifetime only of those named in them.

The leading planters of all categories had to build towns, parish churches, schools and forts. The Church of Ireland received over a thousand townlands. Trinity College Dublin, founded in the reign of Elizabeth, was also given generous grants.

It was not long before noblemen, adventurers, gentlemen and courtiers began applying to the king for lands in Ulster. King James issued a special proclamation for Scotland, urging his original subjects to become planters:

Forasmeikle as the Kingis Maiestie haueing resolued to reduce and setle vndre a perfyte obedience the north pairt of the Kingdome of Ireland, which now by the providence of Almichtie God, and by the power and strength of his Maiesties royal army, is fred and disburdynit of the former rebellious and disobedient inhabitants thairof ... his Maiestie, for this effect, hes tane a verie princelie and good course, alswell for establischeing of religioun, justice, and ciuilitie within the saidis boundis, as for planting of colonies thairin, and distributeing of the same boundis to lauchfull, ansuerable, and weill affected subiectis, vpon certane easie, tolerable, and profitable conditionis, and although thair be no want of grite nomberis of the cuntrey people of England, who, with all glaidnes, wald imbrace the saidis conditionis, and transport thame selfiss, with thair families, to Yreland ... yit, his sacred Maiestie, out of his vnspeikable love and tender affectioun towards his Maiesties antient and native subiectis of this king-dome ... hes bene pleasit to mak chose of thame to be Partinairis with his saidis subiectis of England, in the distribution foirsaid ...

The great migration to Ulster had begun, drawn from every class of British society.

Episode 86 ～

'MAKE SPEED, GET THEE TO ULSTER'

Uring the summer of 1610 Thomas Blennerhasset and his brother Sir Edward travelled with their families and servants from Norfolk to Ireland. Both of these Englishmen had been granted estates by King James I in the precinct of Lurg in north Fermanagh. They were planters known as 'undertakers', that is, they undertook to clear their Ulster estates of the native Irish and to colonise them with loyal Protestants from Britain.

Thomas Blennerhasset was so delighted with his Fermanagh lands that he wrote a pamphlet urging his fellow-Englishmen to join him. His main argument was that Ulster had lost most of its population from conflict and famine during the last great rebellion. The province's fertile soil was just waiting to be properly farmed by his fellow-countrymen:

> Fayre England, thy flourishing sister, brave Hibernia; (with most respective termes) commendeth unto thy due consideration her yongest daughter, depopulated Ulster.... Dispoyled, she presents her-selfe (as it were) in a ragged sabled robe, ragged (indeed) there remayneth nothing but ruynes and desolation, with a very little showe of any humanitie: of her selfe she aboundeth with many the best blessings of God.... Fayre England, she hath more people than she can well sustaine; goodly Ulster for want of people unmanured, her pleasant fieldes and riche groundes, they remaine if not desolate, worse.... Make speede, get thee to Ulster, serve God, be sober.

It was widely believed then that England was overpopulated. And it was certainly true that many of the king's Scottish, English and Welsh subjects were eager to get a slice of the action in Ulster. Not for many centuries in western Europe had so much land been made available for colonisation. Much of it was ideal for the grazing of cattle and the cultivation of corn. Most of the rivers swarmed with salmon, and vast numbers were netted, trapped and salted by the native Irish for export to Spain and elsewhere. And a rich eel fishery flourished at Toome, where the River Bann flows out of Lough Neagh.

Ireland still possessed great forests. Some of the largest of these were in the six counties of the Ulster plantation: around Lough Erne, in south Armagh, and—the largest—in Glenconkeyne at the foot of the Sperrin Mountains. Unlike farmland, stands of oak, elm, ash, alder and willow offered a quick return on investment. Once felled and seasoned, wood fetched a good price when split, sawn and shaped into planks for rafters, ship timber and staves ready to be fashioned by coopers into barrels. Branches could be chopped up, piled high and covered with ash ready to be converted into charcoal for the smelting of iron. England and Scotland were among the first countries in Europe to have their forests seriously depleted. One Scot bemoaned the loss of trees in his native land:

> Ah! what makes now, my Countrey looke so bare?
> Thus voyd of planting, Woods and Forests fayre.

As the great migration to Ulster got under way it was clear that the colonists were drawn from every class of British society. Some were noblemen like the Earl of Abercorn and the Earl of Ochiltree from Scotland who responded to a personal appeal from King James to take estates in Co. Tyrone 'for a countenance and a strength to the rest'. Others were former army commanders who had helped to conquer this province—men like Sir Basil Brooke with the proportion of Edencarn in Donegal; Sir Richard Wingfield, who had led the victorious cavalry charge at the Battle of Kinsale, and who was granted the proportion of Benburb in Co. Tyrone; and the king's Lord Deputy, Sir Arthur Chichester, who received the proportion of Dungannon to add to his vast estates in Inishowen and Co. Antrim.

All of these planters brought over relatives, neighbours, trusted comrades-in-arms, stonemasons, carpenters, thatchers, labourers and tenant farmers. In the initial stages of the plantation the estates granted to Englishmen were occupied by colonists who were mostly English. For example, in north Armagh the Brownlow brothers from Nottinghamshire and other undertakers from Staffordshire enticed over many of their English tenants. They included families from the Vale of Evesham who carried over apple-tree saplings, ensuring that in time Armagh would be known as the 'Orchard County'. No fewer than four members of the Cunningham family from Wigtonshire got estates in Co. Donegal—virtually all of the families they persuaded to join them were from this south-western corner of Scotland. Indeed, most of the Scots—judging by their surnames—came from Ayrshire, Wigtonshire, Clydeside, Lanark, Renfrew, Sterlingshire and the Borders.

The English colonists had more capital, but the Scots were the most determined. Sir William Alexander observed: 'Scotland by reason of her populousnesse being constrained to disburden her selfe (like the painfull Bees) did every yeere send forth swarmes.'

Some parts of Ulster, however, were not attracting swarms of planters. For this reason King James now turned to the city of London.

Episode 87 ∾

THE LONDONDERRY PLANTATION

For centuries the clans living in the Southern Uplands, on the borders of Scotland and England, had been raiders living by plundering the farms on either side of the mountains. Then, in 1603, when he became ruler of both Scotland and England, King James I was determined to suppress these proud and lawless Borderers. A joint royal commission of English and Scots ruthlessly crushed the clans in the hills and enforced the king's law by the gallows. The Johnston family alone faced seventy-seven charges of slaughter in 1609.

Those who had lived by plunder now had no work. The king was assured that in every Border parish there was 'ane grit number fund of ydle people without any calling, industrie, or lauthfull means to leif by'. Royal officers often offered them a stark choice: face the dungeon or the noose, or go to Ireland. Other Borderers on the run had already made their way to Ulster as fast as they could. Perhaps that is why the Rev. Andrew Stewart of Donaghadee claimed that 'From Scotland came many, and from England not a few, yet all of them generally the scum of both nations, who, for debt or breaking and fleeing from justice, or seeking shelter, came thither.'

Most of them preferred to put a good distance between themselves and the Borders, which is why so many of them ended up in Co. Fermanagh. Their surnames—Johnston, Armstrong, Elliott and Beattie, in that order— dominated the muster rolls of colonists in that county. Indeed, it was only at the beginning of the twenty-first century that Johnston ceased to be the commonest surname in Co. Fermanagh.

The part of Ulster which proved to be least attractive to planters was what was then called the county of Coleraine. Sir Thomas Phillips, described as 'a very discreet and valiant commander at all times', had done much to develop his grant of church lands here. In April 1609 he travelled to London. There he explained to the king and his advisers that his colony was dangerously exposed to the native Irish. In the lowlands of the county the O'Cahans seethed with resentment at the loss of their ancient territory. Elsewhere

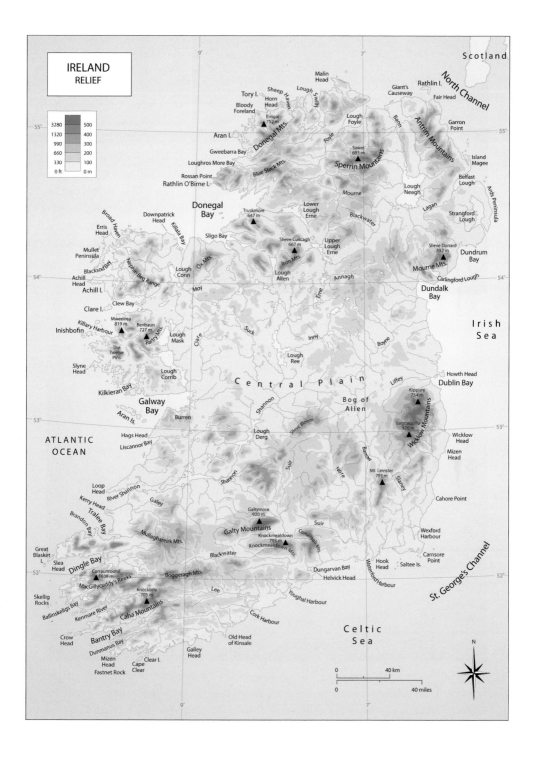

IRELAND
RELIEF

3280   500
1320   400
990   300
660   200
330   100
0 ft   0 m

Scotland

Malin
Head

Tory I.
Sheep Haven
Lough Swilly
Giant's
Causeway
Rathlin I.
North Channel
Fair Head

Bloody
Foreland
Horn
Head
Errigal
752 m
Lough
Foyle
Garron
Point

Aran I.
Donegal Mts.
Antrim Mountains

Gweebarra Bay
Sawel
683 m
Island
Magee

Loughros More Bay
Blue Stack Mts.
Sperrin Mountains
Belfast
Lough

Rossan Point
Rathlin O'Birne I.
Mourne
Lough
Neagh
Strangford
Lough
Ards Peninsula

Broad Haven
Downpatrick
Head
Killala Bay
Donegal
Bay
Truskmore
647 m
Lower
Lough
Erne
Blackwater
Lagan
Belfast
Lough

Erris
Head
Sligo Bay
Slieve Cuilcagh
667 m
Upper
Lough
Erne
Slieve Donard
852 m
Dundrum
Bay

Mullet
Peninsula
Lough
Conn
Iron Mts.
Lough
Allen
Annagh
Mourne Mts.
Carlingford Lough

Blacksod Bay
Ox Mts.
Dundalk
Bay

Achill
Head
Nephin Beg Range
Moy
Erne

Achill I.

Clare I.
Clew Bay
Suck

Inishbofin
Killary Harbour
Mweelrea
819 m
Benbaun
727 m
Partry Mts.
Lough
Mask
Clare
Inny
Boyne
Irish
Sea

The
Twelve
Pins
Lough
Ree

Slyne
Head
Lough
Corrib
Central Plain
Liffey
Howth Head
Dublin Bay

Kilkieran Bay
Kippure
754 m

Galway
Bay
Burren
Shannon
Bog of
Allen
Wicklow Mountains
Wicklow
Head

Aran Is.
Slieve Bloom
Lugnaquilla
926 m
Mizen
Head

ATLANTIC
OCEAN
Hags Head
Liscannor Bay
Lough
Derg

Loop
Head
River Shannon
Galey
Shannon
Nore
Barrow
Mt. Leinster
793 m
Slaney
Cahore Point

Kerry Head
Tralee Bay
Brandon Bay
Galtymore
920 m
Wexford
Harbour

Great
Blasket
I.
Slea
Head
Dingle Bay
Mullaghareirk Mts.
Galty Mountains
Knockmealdown
793 m
Knockmealdown Mts.
Comeragh Mts.
Suir
Carnsore
Point
Saltee Is.

Corrauntoohil
1038 m
MacGillycuddy's Reeks
Boggeragh Mts.
Blackwater
Dungarvan Bay
Helvick Head
Hook
Head
Waterford Harbour
St. George's Channel

Skellig
Rocks
Knockboy
705 m
Lee
Youghal Harbour

Ballinskelligs Bay
Kenmare River
Caha Mountains
Cork Harbour

Crow
Head
Bantry Bay
Old Head
of Kinsale
Celtic
Sea

Dunmanus Bay
Galley
Head

Mizen
Head
Cape
Clear
Clear I.

Fastnet Rock

0   40 km

0   40 miles

N

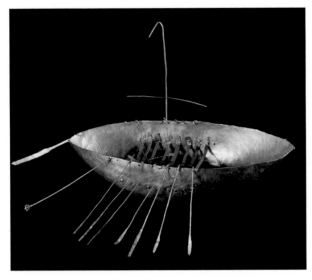

A miniature gold boat, just under 20 centimetres in length, found during ploughing in 1896 at Broighter, near Limavady, Co. Londonderry. This was part of a hoard of seven gold objects including a magnificent torc decorated in the distinctive La Tène Celtic style. This hoard was buried around the first century BC, possibly as a votive offering to the sea god, Manannán mac Lir. (*National Museum of Ireland*)

Skellig Michael, an early monastery built on a remote, precipitous rock in the Atlantic off the Kerry coast. In the foreground are 'beehive huts', painstakingly built of stone without mortar, the dwellings for monks in this ascetic community. Remote though it was, Skellig Michael was one of the first Irish monasteries to be attacked by the Vikings. (*Department of the Environment*)

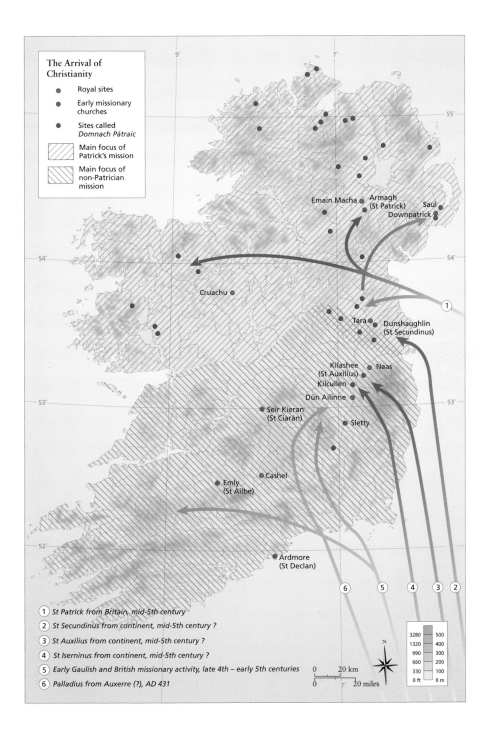

The Arrival of
Christianity

- ● Royal sites
- ● Early missionary churches
- ● Sites called *Domnach Pátraic*
- ▨ Main focus of Patrick's mission
- ▨ Main focus of non-Patrician mission

Emain Macha   Armagh
(St Patrick)   Saul
Downpatrick

Cruachu

Tara   Dunshaughlin
(St Secundinus)

Kilashee   Naas
(St Auxilius)
Kilcullen
Dún Ailinne

Seir Kieran
(St Ciarán)   Sletty

Cashel

Emly
(St Ailbe)

Ardmore
(St Declan)

① St Patrick from Britain, mid-5th century
② St Secundinus from continent, mid-5th century ?
③ St Auxilius from continent, mid-5th century ?
④ St Iserninus from continent, mid-5th century ?
⑤ Early Gaulish and British missionary activity, late 4th – early 5th centuries
⑥ Palladius from Auxerre (?), AD 431

0   20 km
0   20 miles

3280   500
1320   400
990   300
660   200
330   100
0 ft   0 m

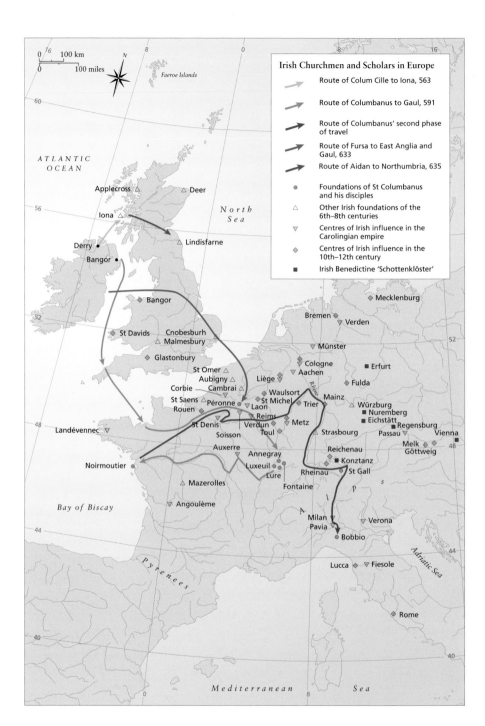

Irish Churchmen and Scholars in Europe

Route of Colum Cille to Iona, 563

Route of Columbanus to Gaul, 591

Route of Columbanus' second phase of travel

Route of Fursa to East Anglia and Gaul, 633

Route of Aidan to Northumbria, 635

- Foundations of St Columbanus and his disciples
△ Other Irish foundations of the 6th–8th centuries
▽ Centres of Irish influence in the Carolingian empire
◇ Centres of Irish influence in the 10th–12th century
■ Irish Benedictine 'Schottenklöster'

0 100 km
0 100 miles
N

Faeroe Islands

ATLANTIC OCEAN

North Sea

Applecross △
△ Deer
Iona △
Derry ●
Bangor ●

△ Lindisfarne

◇ Bangor

Mecklenburg ◇

Bremen ◇
▽ Verden

St Davids ◇
Cnobesburh
△ Malmesbury

▽ Münster

◇ Glastonbury

Cologne ◇
St Omer △
△ Aachen
Aubigny △
Liège ◇
Erfurt ■
Corbie
Cambrai △
◇ Fulda
St Saens △
Waulsort ◇
Mainz ◇
Péronne ●
St Michel
Rouen
Laon ▽
Trier ◇
△ Würzburg
Reims ◇
■ Nuremberg
St Denis ▽
Verdun ▽
Metz ▽
■ Eichstätt
Landévennec ▽
Toul ▽
△ Strasbourg
Passau ▽
Regensburg
Soisson
Vienna
Auxerre ▽
Melk ◇ ◇
Annegray ●
Reichenau ◇
Göttweig
Noirmoutier ●
Luxeuil ● ●
◇ Konztanz
Lure ●
Rheinau ◇
St Gall ◇
△ Mazerolles
Fontaine ●

Bay of Biscay

▽ Angoulème

Pyrenees

Milan ▽
▽ Verona
Pavia
◇ Bobbio

Adriatic Sea

Lucca ◇
▽ Fiesole

● Rome

Mediterranean Sea

Ireland before the Normans,
c. 1100

MIDE Over-kingdoms

Airthir Sub-kingdoms and territories

UA NÉILL Principal dynastic surnames

Ua Bric Lesser dynastic surnames

Inis Eógain
Ua Dochartaig

UA MÁEL DORAIG
Cenél
Conaill
MAC LOCHLAINN
Cenél Moen
Ua Gairmledaig

Ciannachta
Ua Catháin
Uí Thuirtre
Ua Flainn

ULAID
Dál nAraide

NORTHERN UÍ NÉILL
Ua Cannannáin

Fir Lurg

Cenél nEógain
UA NÉILL
Cenél MacCana
Feredaig Airthir
Mac Cathmail Ua hAnluain

MACDUINNSLÉIBE
Dál
Fiatach

Cairpre
Fir Manach

Uí
Echach
Coba
MacOengussa

Uí
Fiachrach
Muaide
Ua Dubda

Uí Briúin
UA RUAIRC
BRÉIFNE

AIRGIALLA
Fernmag
UA CERBAILL

Gailenga
Ua hEgra

Mag
Luirg
Ua Máel Ruanaid

Uá Ragallaig
Machaire
Gaileng

Fir Umaill
Ua Máille

Luigne
Ua Gadra

Lóegaire
Ua Caindelbáin

Brega
Ua Cellaig

CONNACHT

Síl Muiredaig
MacRagnaill

UA CONCHOBHAIR

Tethba
Ua Fergail

MIDE
UA MÁELSECHNAILL

• Tara
Ua Congalaig

Ua Cellaig
Uí Maine

Delbna
Ethra
MacCochláin

Fine
Gall

• Dublin

Uí
Fiachrach
Aidne
Ua hEidin

Síl
nAnmchada
Ua Matudáin

Uí
Failge
Ua Conchobhair
Failge

Uí
Fáeláin
MacFáeláin

Uí Dúnchada
MacGilla
Mocholmóc

Corco
Mruad
Ua Lochlainn
MacConmara

Ua Duinn Ua Dimmussaig

Uí Muiredaig
Ua Tuathail

Uí Máil

Ua Cennétig
Dál Cais UA BRIAIN

Loiges
Ua Mórda

LAIGIN

TUADMUMU

• Limerick

Osraige
Mac Gilla Pátraic

Éile
Ua Cerbaill

Uí
Bairrche
Ua Gormáin

Uí
Chairpre
Ua Donnabáin

Ua Máel Riain
Ua Duibir

Fothairt
Ua Nualláin

Uí
Chennselaig
MACMURCHADA

• Wexford

Corca Duibhne
Ua Failbe

Déise Muman
Ua Bric Ua Fáeláin

• Waterford

Ua Súilleáin

DESMUMU
MACCARTHAIG

Eóganacht
Locha Léin
Ua Ségda Ua Muirchertaig

Eóganacht
Glenndamna
Ua Cáim

Cenél
Lóegaire
Ua Donnchada

• Cork

Corco
Loígde
Ua hEitirscéoil

3280 — 500
1320 — 400
990 — 300
660 — 200
330 — 100
0 ft — 0 m

0   20 km

7 0

0   20 miles

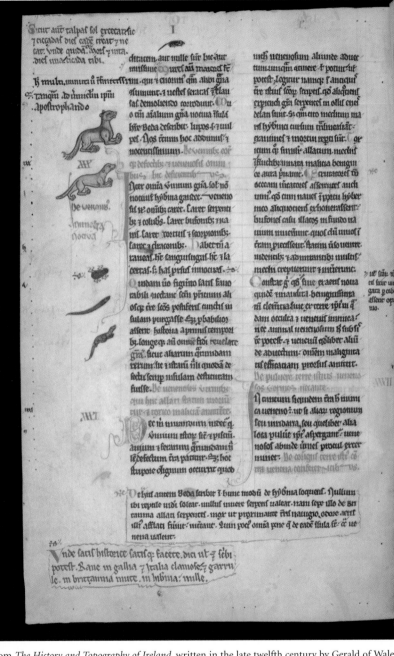

A page from *The History and Topography of Ireland*, written in the late twelfth century by Gerald of Wales. This is from the First Part, describing creatures to be found on the island. The Third Part tells readers how lazy and barbarous the Irish are and describes their 'vices and treacheries'. Gerald also wrote *The Conquest of Ireland* which includes glowing accounts of his relatives, the Geraldines, who were among the leading Norman invaders. (*National Library of Ireland / Irish Script on Screen*)

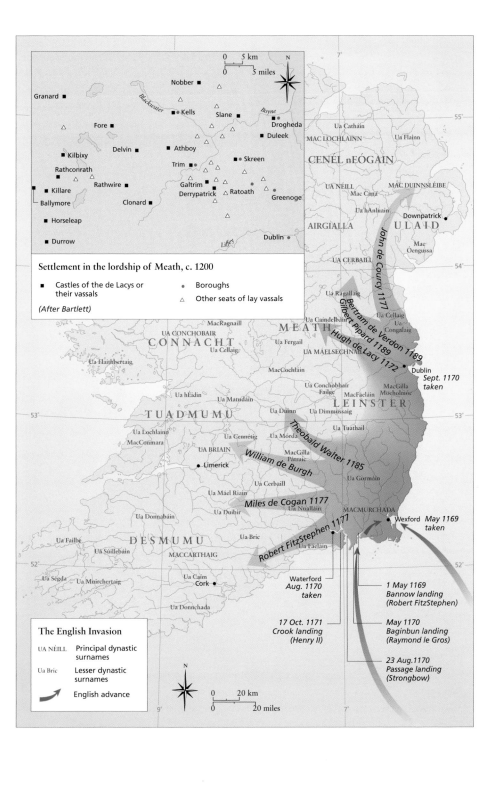

Settlement in the lordship of Meath, c. 1200

- ■ Castles of the de Lacys or their vassals
- ● Boroughs
- △ Other seats of lay vassals

(After Bartlett)

Granard ■
Nobber ■ △
△
Blackwater
△ ● Kells
Slane ■ Boyne
△ ● Drogheda
Fore ■ △ △ ● Duleek
△ △
Delvin ■ △ ■ Athboy
Kilbixy ■ △ ● Skreen
Rathconrath ■ Trim ■ ■ △
△ △
Rathwire ■ Galtrim ■ △ △
Killare ■ Derrypatrick ■ △ Ratoath
Ballymore ■ Clonard ■ ● Greenoge
△
Horseleap ■ △
Durrow ■ Dublin ●
Liffey

MAC LOCHLAINN Ua Catháin Ua Flainn

CENÉL nEÓGAIN

UA NÉILL MAC DUINNSLÉIBE
Mac Cana

Ua hAnluain Downpatrick ●

AIRGIALLA **ULAID**

Mac
Óengussa

UA CERBAILL

Ua Ragallaig

UA CONCHOBAIR MacRagnaill Ua Caindelbáin Ua Cellaig Ua Congalaig

CONNACHT **MEATH**

Ua Haithbertaig Ua Cellaig Ua Fergail

UA MAELSECHNAILL

MacCochláin

Ua Conchobair MacGilla
Failge MacFáeláin Mocholmóc

LEINSTER

Ua hÉidin Ua Matudáin Ua Duinn Ua Dimmasaig

TUADMUMU Ua Mórda Ua Tuathail

Ua Lochlainn Ua Cennétig
MacConmara MacGilla
Pátraic

UA BRIAIN

● Limerick Ua Cerbaill Ua Gormáin

Ua Máel Riain

Ua Donnabáin Ua Duibir Ua Nualláin MACMURCHADA

DESMUMU Ua Bric Ua Fáeláin ● Wexford *May 1169 taken*

Ua Failbe Ua Súillebáin

MACCARTHAIG

Ua Ségda Ua Muirchertaig Ua Caím
Cork ●

Ua Donnchada

Waterford
Aug. 1170 taken

*1 May 1169
Bannow landing
(Robert FitzStephen)*

*17 Oct. 1171
Crook landing
(Henry II)*

*May 1170
Baginbun landing
(Raymond le Gros)*

*23 Aug. 1170
Passage landing
(Strongbow)*

Dublin ●
*Sept. 1170
taken*

John de Courcy 1177
Bertram de Verdon 1189
Gilbert Pipard 1189
Hugh de Lacy 1172
Theobald Walter 1185
William de Burgh
Miles de Cogan 1177
Robert FitzStephen 1177

The English Invasion

UA NÉILL Principal dynastic
surnames

Ua Bric Lesser dynastic
surnames

→ English advance

0 5 km
0 5 miles

0 20 km
0 20 miles

Carving of a noblewoman on a cloister pillar in Jerpoint Abbey, Co. Kilkenny. Begun just before the coming of the Normans, the abbey was mostly built in the 1180s. Jerpoint, which has the most complete remains of a Cistercian community in the country, was in the heart of a thriving part of the English lordship of Ireland. (*Department of the Environment*)

An encounter between the Earl of Gloucester, with his knights, and Art MacMurrough Kavanagh, King of Leinster, and his men. This was during Richard II's successful expedition of 1394–5 to curb Art's power. However Art renounced his fealty later, prompting Richard to return in 1399 for a disastrous second expedition to Ireland. (*British Library, London / Bridgeman Art Library*)

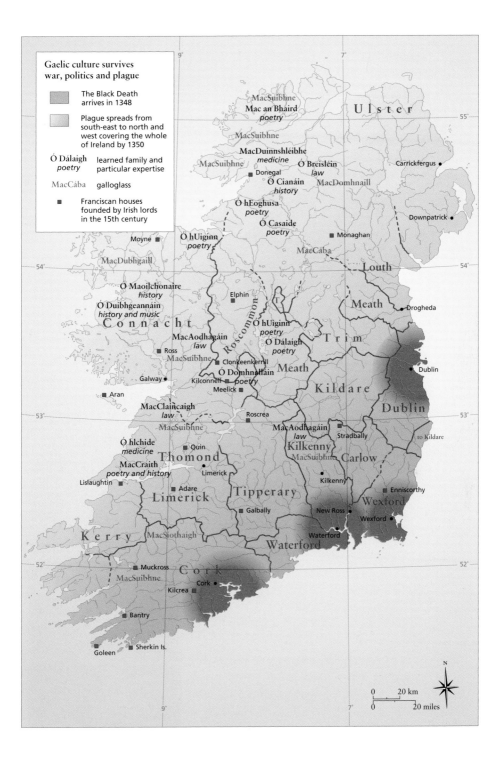

Gaelic culture survives
war, politics and plague

The Black Death
arrives in 1348

Plague spreads from
south-east to north and
west covering the whole
of Ireland by 1350

Ó Dálaigh   learned family and
poetry   particular expertise

MacCába   galloglass

■   Franciscan houses
             founded by Irish lords
             in the 15th century

MacSuibhne
Mac an Bhaird
poetry

Ulster

MacSuibhne

MacDuinnshléibhe
medicine

MacSuibhne   Ó Breisléin   Carrickfergus ●
              law
Donegal ●
Ó Cianáin   MacDomhnaill
history

O hEoghusa   Downpatrick ●
poetry
Ó Casaide
poetry   Monaghan ■

Moyne ■   Ó hUiginn
          poetry   MacCába

MacDubhgaill   **Louth**

Connacht   **Meath**

Ó Maoilchonaire   Drogheda ●
history   Elphin ■

Ó Duibhgeannáin
history and music

MacAodhagáin   Ó hUiginn   **Trim**
law   *poetry*
Ross ■   Ó Dálaigh
MacSuibhne   *poetry*   **Trim**
          Clonkeenkerrill
          Ó Domhnalláin   **Meath**
Galway ● Kilconnell ■   *poetry*
          Meelick ■   Dublin ●

                                          Kildare
Aran ■

MacClainchaigh   Roscrea ●   **Dublin**
law
MacSuibhne   MacAodhagáin   to Kildare
                                   law   Stradbally ●
Ó hIchide   Quin ■   **Kilkenny**
medicine   **Thomond**   MacSuibhne **Carlow**
MacCraith
poetry and history   Limerick ●   Kilkenny ●
Lislaughtin ■   Enniscorthy ■
                         Adare ■   **Tipperary**   **Wexford**
Limerick
                         Galbally ●   New Ross ●
Kerry   MacSíothaigh   Wexford ●
                                   Waterford ●
                         Muckross ■   **Waterford**
MacSuibhne
          Kilcrea ●   **Cork**
                         Cork ●

          Bantry ●

Goleen ■ Sherkin Is. ■

Roscommon

N

0   20 km

0   20 miles

The 'Fair Geraldine', a painting of the daughter of the most powerful man in early sixteenth-century Ireland, the Earl of Kildare, Garret Óg FitzGerald. Her black woollen gown has the large wings on the shoulders slashed to show the white silk gown with gold thread underneath. Her brother, Silken Thomas, led a rebellion in 1534–5 and was executed (with five of his uncles) at Tyburn in 1537. (*National Gallery of Ireland*)

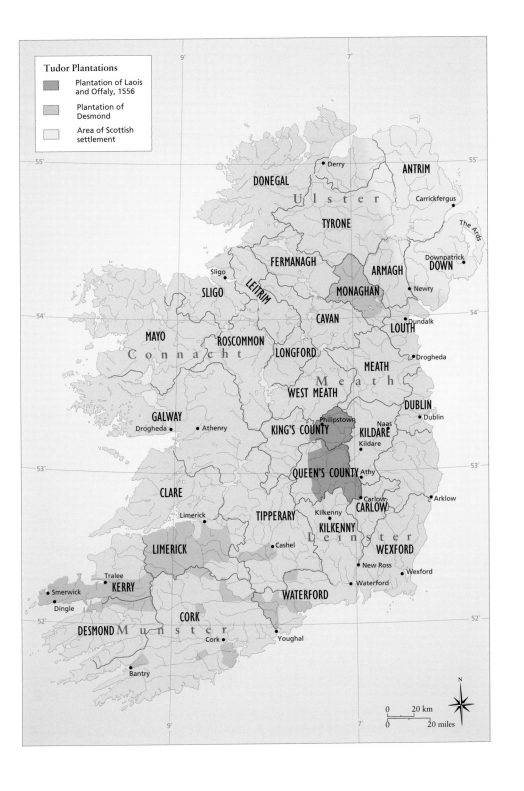

Tudor Plantations

- **Plantation of Laois and Offaly, 1556**
- **Plantation of Desmond**
- **Area of Scottish settlement**

9°
7°

Derry
ANTRIM
DONEGAL
U l s t e r
Carrickfergus
TYRONE
The Ards
55°   55°
Downpatrick
FERMANAGH   ARMAGH   DOWN
Sligo   MONAGHAN   Newry
LEITRIM
SLIGO   CAVAN
Dundalk
54°   54°
MAYO   ROSCOMMON   LONGFORD   LOUTH
C o n n a c h t   Drogheda
MEATH
WEST MEATH   M e a t h
GALWAY   DUBLIN
Drogheda   Athenry   Philipstown   Naas   Dublin
KING'S COUNTY   KILDARE
Kildare
53°   53°
QUEEN'S COUNTY Athy
CLARE   Carlow   Arklow
Limerick   Kilkenny   CARLOW
TIPPERARY   KILKENNY
L e i n s t e r
LIMERICK   Cashel   WEXFORD
New Ross   Wexford
Tralee   Waterford
Smerwick   KERRY
Dingle   WATERFORD
52°   CORK   52°
DESMOND M u n s t e r
Cork   Youghal
Bantry

N

0   20 km
0   20 miles

9°   7°

The royal arms and name of Philip II embossed on a massive bronze siege-gun recovered from the wreck of *La Trinidad Valencera*, one of the greatest ships of the Spanish Armada which foundered in Kinnagoe Bay, Inishowen, during the autumn of 1588. Don Alonso de Luzon, commander of this galleon and *Maestre de Campo*, had intended to use this gun to help him take London. He was ransomed in 1591 but his men were slaughtered near Derry. (© *Colin Martin 2008. Collection Ulster Museum, Belfast. Photograph reproduced courtesy the Trustees of National Museums Northern Ireland*)

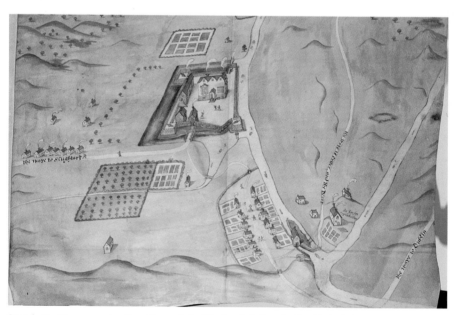

Omagh, Co. Tyrone, c. 1611. Once the capital of Turlough Luineach O'Neill, the independent Lord of Tír Eóghain for much of Queen Elizabeth's reign, Omagh was now a model town in King James I's Plantation of Ulster. It was neatly laid out adjacent to the fortified manor house erected for the servitor grantee, the retired army captain, Edward Leigh. (*Board of Trinity College, Dublin*)

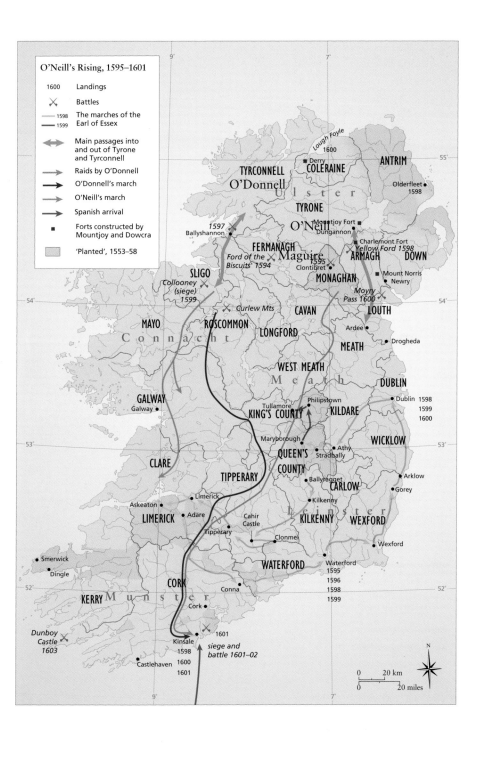

O'Neill's Rising, 1595–1601

1600	Landings
✕	Battles
—— 1598	The marches of the
—— 1599	Earl of Essex
⟷	Main passages into and out of Tyrone and Tyrconnell
→	Raids by O'Donnell
→	O'Donnell's march
→	O'Neill's march
→	Spanish arrival
▪	Forts constructed by Mountjoy and Dowcra
▨	'Planted', 1553–58

9°
7°
55°

TYRCONNELL   COLERAINE   ANTRIM
O'Donnell   Olderfleet ▪
                                        1598
U l s t e r
TYRONE
O'Neill   Mountjoy Fort ▪
Derry ▪   Dungannon ▪
                 Charlemont Fort ▪
1597 ✕   Yellow Ford 1598 ✕
Ballyshannon   Maguire   1595   ARMAGH   DOWN
FERMANAGH   ✕ ✕   Clontibret ✕
Ford of the   MONAGHAN   Mount Norris ▪
Biscuits' 1594   Newry ▪
SLIGO   Moyry
Collooney ✕   CAVAN   Pass 1600 ✕
(siege)   LOUTH
1599   ✕ Curlew Mts
MAYO   ROSCOMMON   Ardee ▪
        C o n n a c h t LONGFORD   ▪ Drogheda
                        MEATH
                WEST MEATH
                M e a t h
GALWAY   DUBLIN
Galway ▪   Tullamore Philipstown   ▪ Dublin 1598
        KING'S COUNTY   KILDARE   1599
                                           1600
        Maryborough   ▪ Athy   WICKLOW
CLARE   QUEEN'S   Stradbally
        TIPPERARY COUNTY   ▪ Arklow
Limerick ▪   Ballyragget ▪   ▪ Gorey
Askeaton ▪   ✕ Kilkenny   CARLOW
LIMERICK ▪ Adare   L e i n s t e r WEXFORD
        ▪ Tipperary Cahir   KILKENNY
                     Castle   ▪ Wexford
Smerwick ▪   ✕   Clonmel ▪
Dingle ▪   Conna ▪   WATERFORD Waterford
                                     1595
        CORK   1596
KERRY M u n s t e r   1598
        Cork ▪   1599
Dunboy   ✕
Castle   Kinsale 1601
1603   1598 siege and
Castlehaven 1600 battle 1601–02
            1601

N
0   20 km
0   20 miles

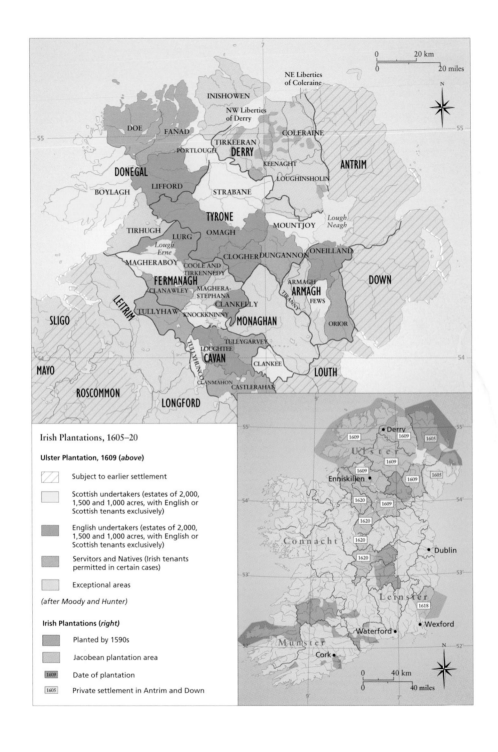

Irish Plantations, 1605–20

Ulster Plantation, 1609 (above)

Subject to earlier settlement

Scottish undertakers (estates of 2,000, 1,500 and 1,000 acres, with English or Scottish tenants exclusively)

English undertakers (estates of 2,000, 1,500 and 1,000 acres, with English or Scottish tenants exclusively)

Servitors and Natives (Irish tenants permitted in certain cases)

Exceptional areas

(after Moody and Hunter)

Irish Plantations (right)

Planted by 1590s

Jacobean plantation area

1609 Date of plantation

1605 Private settlement in Antrim and Down

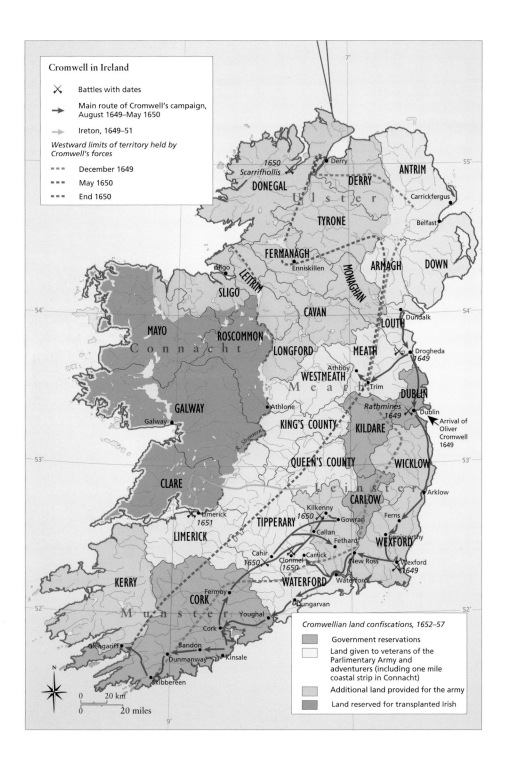

Cromwell in Ireland

✕   Battles with dates

→   Main route of Cromwell's campaign,
     August 1649–May 1650

→   Ireton, 1649–51

Westward limits of territory held by
Cromwell's forces

---   December 1649

---   May 1650

---   End 1650

1650
Scarrifhollis ✕   •Derry   **ANTRIM**

DONEGAL   **DERRY**

U l s t e r   Carrickfergus

TYRONE   Belfast•

FERMANAGH

•Sligo   **LEITRIM**   •Enniskillen   **ARMAGH**   **DOWN**

SLIGO   **MONAGHAN**

MAYO   **ROSCOMMON**   **CAVAN**

C o n n a c h t   **LONGFORD**   **MEATH**   •Dundalk

   LOUTH

Athboy•   ✕ Drogheda
     1649

WESTMEATH   M e a t h

GALWAY   •Athlone   •Trim   **DUBLIN**

Galway•   *Rathmines*   •Dublin
     1649 ✕

KING'S COUNTY   **KILDARE**   → Arrival of
     Oliver
     Cromwell
R. Shannon   1649

CLARE   **QUEEN'S COUNTY**   **WICKLOW**

L e i n s t e r

   CARLOW   •Arklow

Kilkenny•   *1650* ✕

✕Limerick   •Gowran   Ferns•
1651

TIPPERARY   •Callan   •Enniscorthy

LIMERICK   •Cahir   Fethard•   **WEXFORD**

   ✕•Carrick

Cahir✕   •Clonmel   New Ross•   •Wexford
1650   *1650*   ✕ *1649*

KERRY   **WATERFORD**   Waterford•

Fermoy•   •Waterford

CORK   •Dungarvan

M u n s t e r   •Youghal

Glengariff•   •Cork
  Bandon•
  Dunmanway•   •Kinsale

N

•Skibbereen

0   20 km
|————|————|
0   20 miles

Cromwellian land confiscations, 1652–57

▨   Government reservations

☐   Land given to veterans of the
     Parliamentary Army and
     adventurers (including one mile
     coastal strip in Connacht)

▨   Additional land provided for the army

▨   Land reserved for transplanted Irish

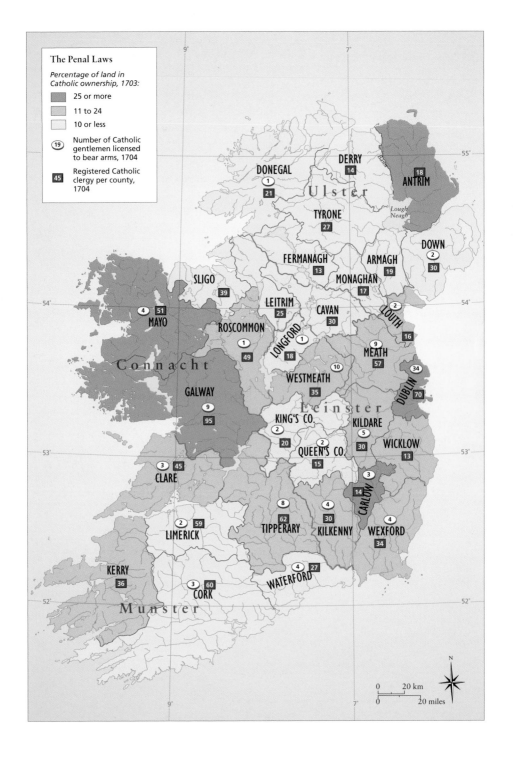

The Penal Laws

Percentage of land in Catholic ownership, 1703:

- 25 or more
- 11 to 24
- 10 or less

(19) Number of Catholic gentlemen licensed to bear arms, 1704

[45] Registered Catholic clergy per county, 1704

DONEGAL (1) [21]

DERRY [14]

ANTRIM [18]

Ulster

TYRONE [27]

DOWN (2)

FERMANAGH [13]

ARMAGH [19]

MONAGHAN [17]

DOWN [30]

SLIGO [39]

MAYO (4) [51]

Connacht

LEITRIM [25]

CAVAN [30]

LOUTH (2)

LOUTH [16]

ROSCOMMON (1) [49]

LONGFORD [18]

MEATH (9) [57]

WESTMEATH (10) [35]

Leinster

GALWAY (9) [95]

KING'S CO. (2) [20]

KILDARE (5) [30]

WICKLOW [13]

DUBLIN (34) [70]

QUEEN'S CO. (2) [15]

CLARE (3) [45]

CARLOW (3) [14]

TIPPERARY (8) [62]

KILKENNY (4) [30]

WEXFORD (4) [34]

LIMERICK (2) [59]

KERRY [36]

CORK (3) [60]

WATERFORD (4) [27]

Munster

Lough Neagh

0   20 km
0   20 miles

N

former Gaelic warriors—known as 'woodkerne'—lurked in the forests, living as bandits.

The solution, Sir Thomas suggested, was to persuade the merchants of London to colonise this wild county in Ulster. The king was delighted by this proposal. The city merchants were not so sure. A special court of aldermen met on 1 July. The representative of the Fishmongers declared: 'It were best never to entermeddle at al in this busyness ... for that it wil be exceeding chargeable.' Nevertheless, the city fathers sent a deputation to tour the county in the autumn. When the investigators returned, they recommended that the London Companies become involved in the plantation. In particular, they were impressed by the huge stretches of valuable oak forest.

The livery companies of London, descended from the medieval guilds, hammered out an agreement with the king in January 1610. The companies could afford to dictate terms—after all, the city had unwritten much of the cost of conquering Ireland during the reign of Queen Elizabeth. The capital was always the most reliable source of ready money for the crown. Fretting at the slow progress of the plantation of Ulster, King James granted the London Companies not only the entire county of Coleraine, but also the barony of Loughinsholin with its great forest of Glenconkeyne, as well as a slice of Tyrconnell including Derry and Culmore, and another slice of Co. Antrim to give more land to the town of Coleraine.

The new enlarged county was renamed the county of Londonderry. This great area of around half a million acres would henceforth be supervised by elected representatives of the London Companies, known as 'The Honorable The Irish Society'. The Society sent over to Ireland two agents, John Rowley and Tristram Beresford, along with 130 masons, carpenters and other workmen. Both Rowley and Beresford were ruthless asset-strippers who lined their own pockets, plundering the forests against orders and illegally exporting the timber for the making of barrels. Most progress was made at Coleraine, which was surrounded by a 'rampier', a massive wall constructed of clay and sods.

More agents arrived in 1613. They stamped out theft and corruption and marked out the ground for the walls of the newly founded city of Londonderry. Work began with a will on the erection of massive walls for what was to be the very last walled city to be built in western Europe. Meanwhile the lands of Co. Londonderry were being mapped by the city of London's surveyor, Thomas Raven—after whom the Ravenhill Road in Belfast is named. By the end of the year 1613 all was ready for a grand draw in London to parcel out the Irish Society's twelve proportions.

Episode 88 ～

THE LUCK OF THE DRAW

On 17 December 1613 aldermen and freemen of the city of London crowded into the Guildhall, full of expectation. This day there would be a draw for the twelve proportions of Londonderry, the county granted to the city for plantation by king James I. The fifty-five livery companies arranged themselves into twelve associations. The Goldsmiths, for example, joined with the Cordwainers, Paintstainers and Armourers. Called to order, a hush descended on the packed guildhall as the City Swordbearer, with great pomp and ceremony, conducted the draw.

By the luck of the draw, the Grocers, the Fishmongers and the Goldsmiths got the most fertile proportions. The Drapers and the Skinners were particularly disappointed: their estates included much land which was both difficult of access and infertile.

King James regarded the colonisation of six counties in the northern province of Ireland as the greatest project of his reign. He hoped that, by settling loyal British subjects there, Ulster would change from being the most lawless part of the island to being the most peaceful. Though certainly not a failure, the king's scheme was far too ambitious to bring about the realisation of his dreams.

Perhaps the greatest failing was that the land was not properly measured. The planters got far more land than they could colonise successfully. For example, Co. Londonderry was thought to contain 40,000 acres; in fact there were no fewer than *half a million* acres in the twelve estates granted to the London Companies. A man granted a thousand acres might discover that he had at least six thousand. Nearly all the planters brought over the required number of British Protestant families, but even then they could not possibly manage to farm the lands they had been granted without local Irish help.

The most important planters, the undertakers, were supposed to clear the native Irish completely off their proportions. Very few of them did so. With a nod and a wink, the ordinary Gaelic Irish were allowed to stay on to provide cheap labour or to pay useful rents for the land they worked themselves. Inevitably the king got to hear about it, and he was furious. Removing the natives was, in his words, 'the fundamental reason' for the plantation. James ordered one plantation survey after another. The survey of the London lands in 1614 appalled the king. He fired off a long and angry letter:

Having taken an exact survey of the works and plantation performed by the City of London, I cannot find that either in the one or the other they ever intended his Majesty's satisfaction and regarded the true end and drift of his favourable grant so that whatsoever they talk of great masses of wealth by them expended, naming what sums they please, yet of any real plantation or fortification to the purpose (the only means of setting and securing those parts which they have undertaken) they have little or nothing to say.

It was in vain that James raged against the undertakers. The king announced the confiscation of the undertakers' estates in 1619. Then he realised he was cutting off his nose to spite his face; the eventual outcome was that he returned the lands on condition that fines were paid. And so the grand royal plan to separate natives and newcomers had come to nothing.

It could be said that the planters themselves had been deceived by their own government. They had been told that the native population had been all but wiped out by war and famine. When these British colonists arrived in Ulster, they found that they were everywhere outnumbered by the Gaelic Irish. Some of these Irish were waiting to be moved on. Others lurked in the forests: these were landless men and former warriors known as woodkerne waiting their opportunity to attack the settlements. At Charlemont Sir Toby Caulfield was forced 'every night to lay up all his cattle as it were in ward, and do he and his what they can, the wolf and the woodkerne (within caliver shot of his fort) have oftentimes a share'.

In 1615 the agent for the Drapers' Company were building Moneymore 'as it were with the sword in one hand and the axe in the other'. In the following year the Ironmongers' agent, George Canning, informed London that his labourers were 'fearful to work in the woods except they be ten or twelve in a company'. The Lord Deputy ordered his officers to 'take up lewd kerns or such as have been rebels or idle livers'; and indeed, hundreds were rounded up and shipped off to serve in the armies of the King of Sweden. Again and again, however, woodkerne emerged from their forest and mountain retreats to plunder the settlers.

However, the disillusionment of the Protestant planters was more than matched by the deep discontent of the Catholics, Old English and Gaelic Irish alike.

Episode 89 ~

'THE HERETICS INTEND TO VOMIT OUT ALL THEIR POISON'

In the early seventeenth century the people of central and western Europe continued to be bitterly divided by religion. In the realms ruled by King James I, most people living in England, Wales and the Scottish Lowlands were Protestants supporting the Reformation. In Ireland only the British colonists in Ulster and recently arrived officials and landowners, known as the 'New English', were Protestant. The great majority of the inhabitants of Ireland remained Catholic and supported the Counter-Reformation. These were not only the native Irish but also the descendants of the Norman conquerors, known now as the 'Old English'.

The Old English as Catholics gave their allegiance to the pope. They also, very willingly, gave their allegiance to the king. James, however, demanded that he alone be recognised as the supreme governor of the church. Catholics, particularly in Dublin, who refused to attend Protestant church services were fined. If they were lawyers, they lost their right to practise. If they were public servants, they lost their jobs.

Tension rose in the capital when Conor O'Devany, the Catholic Bishop of Down and Connor, was, on trumped-up charges, convicted of treason in February 1612. A Jesuit priest watched as the bishop, a frail man in his eighties, was taken to the scaffold in Dublin to be hanged, drawn and quartered:

> Along the road by which they went there was a multitude of people of all degrees, such as were never seen at such a spectacle before; and the Catholics, despising the danger, cast themselves upon their knees to ask the bishop's blessing, which he gave them to satisfy their devotion, and the blows and the kicks of the heretics were not sufficient to deter them.

This account is confirmed by that of Barnaby Rich, a Protestant. He recalled that the bishop was followed by

> troops of citizens, not of the inferior sort alone, but of the better, and amongst the women, of the best men's wives within the city of Dublin ... [who kept up] such a screeching, such a howling, as if Saint Patrick himself had been going to the gallows.

And after the hanging, and the plucking of the victim's still beating heart from his breast and the chopping of his body into four pieces, happy was she that could but get her handkerchief dipped in the blood of the traitor. And the body being once dissevered into four quarters, they left neither finger nor toe, but they cut them off and carried them away. And to show their Catholic zeal, they tore his garments into tatters, and some others that could get no holy monuments to his person, with their knives they shaved off chips from the hallowed gallows.

The calling of a parliament confirmed the worst fears of Old English Catholics. The Lord Deputy created new parliamentary seats—thirty-four of them in the newly planted counties in Ulster—to ensure a Protestant majority. One Catholic gentleman predicted the introduction of anti-Catholic laws:

What keeps everyone in a state of suspense is the fear of the approaching parliament, which is to assemble after St John's festival, in which the heretics intend to vomit out all their poison and infect the purity of our holy religion.

After the elections in the spring of 1614 leading Old English lords had an altercation with Lord Deputy Sir Arthur Chichester as they were escorting him from church:

Two of their followers drew their swords, close by the Lord Deputy, whereupon he himself called the guard. At least five hundred swords were drawn, everyone fearing that there had been a massacre intended by papists.

On that occasion bloodshed was avoided; but, for security, the Irish parliament was summoned to meet inside the walls of Dublin Castle. Tempers rose when it was time to elect the Speaker of the House of Commons. Catholics placed their own candidate, Sir John Everard, in the chair. Whereupon the Protestants placed their own candidate, Sir John Davies, on his lap. This was not a pleasant experience for Everard, as Davies was extremely corpulent—a fellow-Englishmen remarked on how Davies 'goes waddling with his arse out behind him as though he were about to make everyone that he meets a wall to piss against.... He never walks but carries a cloakbag behind him, his arse sticks out so far.' In protest at the unseemly events in the House of Commons, the Catholic MPs—most of them Old English—walked out *en masse*.

Catholic fears of persecution proved justified. Catholics lost their jobs and paid heavy fines for refusing to take communion in Protestant churches. When the city of Waterford stubbornly continued to elect Catholics as aldermen, the Lord Deputy revoked the city's charter in 1618.

Then in 1625 James I died. Would his son, now King Charles I, show greater tolerance? At first the signs were good. In 1626 the king proposed 'matters of grace and bounty to be rendered to Ireland'. What did this mean? It looked as if Charles was prepared to allow Catholics to practise as lawyers and to be appointed to government jobs. In return the Irish parliament cheerfully voted the king subsidies of £40,000 each year for three years.

But the years that followed showed that Charles could not be trusted at all.

Episode 90 ⌒

THOMAS WENTWORTH AND THE 'GRACES'

The ambition of Charles I was to become a monarch whose power was absolute, just like the King of Spain or the Holy Roman Emperor. The problem was that parliament normally voted the money needed to pay for government, the army and the navy. To rule without the consent of parliament, therefore, Charles had to find alternative sources of income. Ireland was one of those alternative sources.

In 1626 the king presented the gentlemen of Ireland with what he called 'matters of grace and bounty'. These 'graces' were particularly appealing to the Old English Catholics because they offered religious toleration, the right of Catholics to become lawyers and hold government jobs, and—above all—secure legal titles to their landed estates. Though nothing definite was granted, the Irish parliament, which still had many Old English Catholic members, voted large sums of money to the king.

In January 1632 King Charles announced his decision to appoint as his Lord Deputy his trusted servant, Thomas Wentworth. Having taken up his post in the following year, Wentworth proved to be arrogant, overbearing and insensitive. He called his policy 'Thorough'; it had only one purpose—to make certain his master, Charles I, had supreme power in both church and state.

Wentworth called an Irish parliament to meet in July 1634. The first session was to raise money for the king, the Lord Deputy warning that he would enforce fines for failing to attend services of the Established Church if the subsidy payments 'be not freely and thankfully given'. Fully expecting the implementation of the Graces, the Irish parliament voted more generous payments to the king for the next four years.

Having got his money, Wentworth then showed his true colours. He had no intention of granting toleration to Catholics or, indeed, to Presbyterians.

More alarmingly, he would not grant the Old English landlords secure legal title to their estates, even if these lands had been in their possession for centuries. A 'Commission for Defective Titles' began a series of rather disturbing inquiries. Both the Old English and Gaelic Irish lords of Ireland began to have real fears that their lands might be taken away from them.

The province of Ulster had been planted, and some other, not particularly successful, colonisation schemes had been put into effect in the counties of Leitrim, Longford and Wexford. Now Wentworth planned to plant all of the rest of Ireland. He started with the western province of Connacht. He proposed to confiscate *all* the landed estates owned by Catholics there, give a quarter of each to the king, and return the other three-quarters of each to the owners with a secure title of ownership. On the confiscated portions Wentworth intended to settle families of loyal Protestant English—the Lord Deputy had no liking for Presbyterian Scots. He actually tried to persuade the landowners that they would be better off with just three-quarters of their estates:

> These three parts remaining will after this settlement be better and more valuable to them than the former four parts ... as well in regard of the benefit that they shall have by the plantation as of the security and settlement they shall gain in their estates.

No doubt this would be because Catholics would have enterprising Protestants living amongst them. Indeed, Wentworth was sure that the example of English neighbours would, in time, lead Old English and Gaelic Irish Catholics to convert to Protestantism.

The first step was to establish the king's title to the land of Connacht. Hand-picked grand juries in the counties of Roscommon, Sligo and Mayo duly agreed in July 1635 that the king had title. The jurors of Co. Galway, including Old English Catholics from the city of Galway, refused to bend so easily. For picking an unsympathetic jury, the sheriff was fined the huge sum of £1,000.

The plantation of Connacht never actually took place. This was mainly because Charles I was getting himself into deeper and hotter water on the other side of the Irish Sea. And, at the same time, his Lord Deputy was alienating just about every interest in Ireland. Wentworth even managed to turn many of his natural allies, the New English, against him. He described them as 'a company of men the most intent upon their own ends that ever I met with'. Many were greedy men, indeed, but no more than Wentworth himself, who seized or otherwise acquired vast estates for himself. The Lord Deputy fell out with Richard Boyle, the Earl of Cork, who had become perhaps the richest landowner in Ireland. The earl had put up a monument to his late wife in St Patrick's Cathedral in Dublin, and the Lord Deputy thought it too ostentatious. Wentworth made Lord Cork dismantle the monument, stone by stone, and take it away in boxes.

Wentworth owed his eventual fall, not to the New English, not to the Old English, not to the Gaelic Irish, but to the planters in Ulster and their friends at Westminster.

Episode 91 ∾

THE *EAGLE WING* AND THE BLACK OATH

King Charles I, refusing to rule with the consent of parliament, imposed a whole series of new and unusual taxes on his people. One of these was 'ship money', a tax on trade by sea. The burden fell heavily on the merchants and shippers of London, and they resisted payment as best they could. The king was furious, and he soon found his revenge.

The London Companies had been granted half a million acres in Ulster and had invested great sums in building the city of Londonderry, bringing over British colonists, erecting forts, developing towns, and so on. Charles hounded the London Companies relentlessly until the Court of Star Chamber condemned them to pay a fine of £70,000 and surrender their grant in 1635. The main charge was that the Londoners had failed to clear all the native Irish off their lands. This was true, but then all the planters in Ulster had failed to comply with this condition of their grants. Unlike his father, Charles I had little interest in the plantation of Ulster. His only concern was money. The London Companies had their lands formally confiscated in 1639.

Thomas Wentworth, the Lord Deputy, ruthlessly enforced the king's will. Charles aspired to supreme dominance in religious as well as in temporal affairs of state. Wentworth, after denying Catholics the right to public office, now turned on Protestants who did not toe the line. Until now the Church of Ireland had tolerated a wide range of Protestant beliefs and practices. This suited Scots very well: most of those settling in Ulster were Presbyterians who, since they did not yet have their own church here, cheerfully joined the Church of Ireland. And all over Ireland Protestants in this, the Established Church, tended to be Puritans, favouring plain forms of worship and plain dress.

Wentworth was determined to change all that. Bishops using the High Church pomp, ceremony, chanting and liturgy favoured by the king replaced the ones that Irish Protestants preferred. Henry Leslie, appointed Bishop of Down under Wentworth's regime, carried out a special visitation of his diocese in 1636. On 10 August he summoned his clergy to a meeting in Belfast. Leslie chose as his text Matthew 18 : 17: 'But if he neglect to hear the church, let him be unto thee as an heathen man and a publican.' Then the bishop castigated those clergymen who had succumbed to Presbyterianism:

> They think by the puff of preaching to blowe downe the goodly orders of our church, as the walls of Jericho were beaten downe with sheepes hornes. Good God! Is this not the sinne of Uzziah, who intruded himselfe into the office of priesthood? ... They have cryed downe the most wholesome orders of the church as popish superstitions.

Clergy present had the cheek to answer back. They did indeed regard the forms of worship prescribed in the Book of Common Prayer as popish. These clergy who refused to change their tune were then deprived of their parishes.

The excommunicated ministers sailed away from north Down with about 140 followers to make a new start in America. Their ship, the *Eagle Wing*, got almost as far as Newfoundland, but was forced by storms to return back across the Atlantic to Scotland. Others had already escaped the wrath of the bishops by taking refuge there.

Meanwhile King Charles was attempting to impose the Book of Common Prayer on Scotland. There, opposition was led by Robert Blair, former minister of Bangor, and John Livingsone, former minister of Killinchy, both of whom had been excommunicated by Bishop Leslie. Both rallied support for the Covenant, a bond of union among the King's Scottish opponents.

Scottish planters in Ulster needed no encouragement to sign the Covenant. Wentworth and Leslie lost no time in taking action against them. The bishop told the Lord Deputy: 'They do threaten me for my life, but, by the grace of God, all their brags shall never make me faint in doing service to God and the King!' Wentworth drafted a command that all Scots in Ulster over the age of sixteen, male and female, must take an 'oath of abjuration of their abominable covenant'.

The Lord Deputy had raised an army of 3,000 men in Ireland to fight for the king. Half of this force now marched north to Carrickfergus to enforce this oath—better known as the Black Oath. The troops were billeted in the homes of the Ulster Scots, to their great cost.

The Black Oath had to be taken kneeling, and if it was refused, Bishop Leslie had the power to fine, imprison and excommunicate. For Sir John Clotworthy, an English Puritan with estates in Antrim and Londonderry, this was the last straw. He resolved to go to London, there to rally his friends in the House of Commons to bring about the downfall of Wentworth.

Episode 92 ⌒

PRESBYTERIAN ANGER, CATHOLIC RESENTMENT

In 1639 Lord Deputy Wentworth sent an army northwards to force the Ulster Scots to take the Black Oath—an oath which denied support for the Scottish Covenant. The Devonshire planter, Sir John Clotworthy, as we have seen, was determined to end this tyranny. He had a seat in the House of Commons at Westminster. He also had powerful friends in the House—indeed, he was related by marriage to John Pym, the leader of the opposition to King Charles I.

On 7 November 1640 Clotworthy presented a long petition to the Commons on behalf of the Presbyterians and Puritans of Ireland. These people, he began, had 'translated themselves out of several parts of his Majesties kingdoms of England and Scotland, to promote the infant plantation of Ireland', only to be oppressed by the king's ministers and High Church bishops. Very many, he continued, were

> reviled, threatnd, imprisoned, fettered together by threes and foures in iron yoakes, some in chaines carried up to Dublin, in Starre chamber fined in thousands beyond abilitie, and condemned to perpetuall imprisonment; Divers poore women but two dayes before delivery of children were apprehended, threatnd, and terrified.... They therefore most humbly pray that this unlawfull hierarchicall government with all their appendices may bee utterly extirpate.

Much affected by Clotworthy's oratory, the House of Commons seized on the evidence he presented. Here was further ammunition against Thomas Wentworth, now the king's first minister and ennobled as the Earl of Strafford. On 11 November the House of Commons voted to impeach Wentworth. Sixteen out of the twenty-eight accusations against him related to his tyrannical rule in Ireland. In April 1641 the House of Lords found him guilty of treason, and on 12 May Wentworth was beheaded—'as he well deserved', the Earl of Cork noted in his diary.

Everything now was going wrong for Charles I. His most faithful minister had been executed; his attempts to punish the Scots had failed; his parliament was defying his will; and he was almost bankrupt. Perhaps the large Irish army, mainly made up of Catholics, raised recently by Wentworth, could help? No, it was too late: that army melted slowly away simply because there was no money to pay the men.

The Gaelic Irish lords closely monitored all these developments across the Irish Sea. Grievances discussed in both the Westminster and Irish parliaments related mainly to the Protestants and the Catholic Old English. Little wonder: only a handful of MPs represented the Gaelic Irish in the Dublin parliament.

Simply because they were further away from the centre of power in Dublin, the Gaelic Irish had not suffered so severely from religious oppression as the Old English Catholics. Nevertheless, Catholic fervour among them had grown remarkably during the first forty years of the seventeenth century. At a time when the Church of Ireland could not find enough clergy for its parishes, the numbers of Franciscans increased threefold in Ireland between 1623 and 1639. Trained in Spain, Flanders and Rome, these clergy were standard-bearers for the Counter-Reformation, rallying support for the international campaign against the Protestant heretics. One of these was the friar Turlough McCrudden, a native of Tyrone, who had returned from Flanders. A guest of the O'Hagans, he drew enormous crowds to hear his sermons. In the woody fastness of Glenconkeyne

> he told the people ... that he was come from the pope to persuade them not to change their religion, but rather go into rebellion ... and that every year the pope would send unto them holy men, lest they be seduced and reasoned by the English.... Though for a time God punished them by suffering their lands to be given to strangers and heretics, it was a punishment for their sins; and he bade them fast and pray ... for it would not be long before they were restored to their prosperities.

On the lonely settlements by the Sperrins or Glenveagh the baying of a wolf at the moon must have sent a chill down the spine of many a colonist who had never heard the sound before. The fear of the landless woodkerne lurking in the forests was better founded. The greatest threat, however, was the smouldering resentment of the native Irish who worked and farmed with the settlers. These Gaelic Irish were confronted by planters who spoke another language and who held Protestant beliefs in stark contrast with their own Catholic faith. They knew that their presence on the undertakers' proportions, the largest planter estates, was illegal. They lived in constant fear that they would be thrown off the land. With no security of tenure, their burdensome rents set by informal arrangements from year to year, and their status severely reduced, the native Irish yearned for a return of the old order.

It was the political instability across the Irish Sea that offered them a golden opportunity to realise that dream.

Episode 93 ~

OCTOBER 1641: THE PLOT THAT FAILED

Eochaid O'Hussey, the most renowned bard of Fermanagh, mourned the condition of his country, Inisfail, the Island of Destiny:

> Now is Inisfail taken at disadvantage,
> Nurse of the sons of Milesius of Spain;
> Her strength is reft, she is caught unrewarded;
> Denizens of all strange countries flock to her.
>
> No friend falls now for her sake,
> For her no fight is procured;
> Woe is me for the light in which she is today.
> No utterance is head from her.

In the reign of Charles I there were few enough Gaelic lords capable of maintaining poets in the old way. Many of these lords were teetering on the edge of bankruptcy. Ruthless adventurers, such as Richard Boyle, Earl of Cork, used English law to seize lands and enrich themselves. The government's Commission for Defective Titles, by questioning ownership, had drastically reduced the value of estates. And all felt threatened by grandiose schemes for further plantations.

It was in Ulster that the Gaelic lords felt most insecure. Even those who had been classed as 'deserving natives' in the Ulster plantation were in trouble. They found it difficult to manage their estates in the new way required by the crown. Some simply were not used to dealing with money rents from their tenants. Conn O'Neill of Clandeboye, for example, lost everything: he sold his townlands one by one to his Protestant neighbours, and his son Daniel had to live by his wits at court. In Co. Down the Hills and the Trevors acquired lands from the Magennises of Iveagh by lending money they knew could not be paid back and by charging outrageous legal fees. On the other hand, it was hardly the fault of the planters that one Magennis lord bankrupted himself by giving dowries and other gifts to all his thirteen children. Others were simply foolish. The second Earl of Antrim, Randal MacDonnell—who gave his name to Randalstown—lost £2,000 at court during one game of ninepins in 1635. And by 1640 the earl had debts of £39,377; only by mortgaging the entire barony of Cary did he save himself from ruin.

Sir Phelim O'Neill, Lord of Kinard in south Tyrone, certainly had his financial troubles—he had mortgaged his estates for £13,000. Early in 1641 he was approached by Rory O'More, who had lands in Kildare and Armagh, about the possibility of rebellion. King Charles I had suffered military humiliation at the hands of the Scots and was at loggerheads with his parliament. Surely this was the time to act? Irish officers serving abroad had offered help. During a session of the Irish parliament O'More was able to talk confidentially with the young Conor Maguire, Baron Enniskillen. As Lord Maguire later confessed in court,

> He began to lay down the case that I was in, overwhelmed in debt, the smallness of my now estate, and the greatness of the estate my ancestors had, and how I should be sure to get it again or at least a good part thereof; and, moreover, how the welfare of the Catholic religion, which, he said, the Parliament now in England will suppress, doth depend on it.

Slowly the plot matured, and on 5 October 1641 the final arrangements were made in Sir Phelim's brother's house by Lough Ross. Dublin Castle was to be seized on 23 October, while Sir Phelim O'Neill would lead a simultaneous revolt in Ulster.

In Dublin on 22 October Lord Maguire disclosed the plot to Owen O'Connolly, employed by Sir John Clotworthy on his lands in Co. Londonderry. Maguire concluded: 'And whereas you have of long time been a slave to that Puritan Sir John Clotworthy, I hope you shall have as good a man to wait upon you.' What Maguire did not know was that O'Connolly had become a Protestant convert. O'Connolly joined conspirators at the Lion public house in Winetavern Street to pick up as many details as he could and then leaped over a wall and two fences to bring the news to Lord Justice Parsons on Merchants' Quay. Parsons only half believed the story, but, just to be sure, put Dublin Castle in a high state of defence. Soon afterwards Lord Maguire and other leading conspirators were seized and imprisoned in the fortress they had planned to capture. The plot had been foiled, but that same night the rebellion in Ulster began.

Just before eight o'clock on the evening of Friday 22 October Sir Phelim O'Neill called on his neighbour Lady Caulfield at Charlemont and invited himself to dinner. Once inside, Sir Phelim and his men seized the fort and imprisoned the garrison. Then they galloped to Dungannon, which had fallen by the same ruse. Next day at dawn the O'Quinns took Mountjoy and the O'Donnellys seized Castlecaulfield.

Over the next ten years and more Ireland was to endure the most terrible violence.

Episode 94 ～

THE 1641 MASSACRES

The native Irish of Ulster, led by Sir Phelim O'Neill, rose in furious rebellion on the night of Friday 22 October 1641. Charlemont, Mountjoy, Castlecaulfield, and Dungannon fell to the insurgents within hours of each other. Sir Conn Magennis led a successful assault on Newry at nightfall on Saturday. Lurgan, in flames, capitulated on Sunday, and Lisburn came under siege.

Lisburn held out. Three times the insurgents were driven back. A herd of four hundred head of cattle driven against the gates failed to batter them down. Belfast, Antrim, Carrickfergus, Larne and Ballygally were thus given time to resist. Meanwhile, in all the rest of Ulster, only the island town of Enniskillen and the walled city of Derry were able to hold out.

On Sunday 24 October Sir Phelim issued a proclamation from Dungannon, declaring that the rising

> is no ways intended against our Sovereign Lord the King, nor the hurt of any of his subjects, either of the English or Scottish nation, but only for the defence and liberty of our selves and the Irish natives of this kingdom.

Soon after this, however, Sir Phelim and the other leaders lost complete control of their people. The Irish victories were so rapid in the first few days that the leaders did not know what to do with those who had surrendered. For example, after they had robbed and stripped the settlers in Cavan, the O'Reillys simply released them, 'turned naked, without respect of age or sex, upon the wild, barren mountains, in the cold air, exposed to all the severity of the winter; from whence in such posture and state they wandered towards Dublin'.

All authority collapsed in a climate of fear and want; the native Irish, inflamed by rumour, religious passion and a lust for revenge, fell ferociously on the planter families of Ulster. The most notorious massacre was at Portadown in the middle of November. William Clark told how Manus Roe O'Cahan drove him

> with such other English as they could find to the number of threescore persons which belonged to the said Parish of Loughgall and put them all in the Church there ... imprisoned for the space of nine days with at the least 100 men, women and children during which time manie of them were sore tortured by strangling and halfe hanging ... after which time of imprisonment hee with an 100 men, women and children or thereabouts were

driven like hogs about six miles to Porte of Doune to a river called the Band and there they forced them to goe upon the Bridge ... and then stripped the said people naked and with theire pikes and swords and other weapons thruste them down headlong in to the said river and immediately they perished and those of them that asayed to swim to the shore the rebels stood to shoot at.

Elizabeth Price confirmed that the prisoners were driven

off the bridge into the water and then and there instantly and most barbarously drowned the most of them. And those that could not swim and came to the shore they knocked on the head, and so after drowned them, or else shot them to death in the water.

Like William Clark, Mrs Price was kept alive because she was thought to be hiding money; in an effort to find it, her tormenters 'had the soles of her feet fried and burnt at the fire, and was often scourged or whipped'.

After the massacre at Portadown other Protestant settlers were herded into a house at Shewie nearby and burnt to death. Ann Smith and Margaret Clark escaped through a hole in the wall; they were knocked on the head and left for dead, but survived to give evidence of the atrocity.

Ellen Matchett described a similar incident where settlers were burnt to death in a house where they had taken refuge. She herself was 'miraculously preserved by a mastiff dog that set upon these slaughtering and bloody rebels'. She survived with others in hiding, emerging 'sometimes to get the brains of a cow, dead of disease, boiled with nettles, which they accounted good fare'.

Anne Blennerhasset saw colonists hanged from tenterhooks in Fermanagh. By the southern shore of Lower Lough Erne the Maguires slaughtered the entire garrison of Tully Castle after promising quarter. The most horrific massacre took place near Augher in south Tyrone: here nearly four hundred Scots who surrendered were put to the sword.

The bloodshed was not all one-sided. Sir William Cole and his men made a sally from Enniskillen and, having rounded up two hundred Irish, butchered them all.

The native Irish had overwhelmed most of Ulster. Now they were advancing on Dublin. Would the Old English, for centuries loyal to the crown but smarting from constant oppression, now join Sir Phelim? What would the Westminster parliament, at loggerheads with King Charles I, do to avenge the Ulster massacres?

Episode 95 ∿

THE CONFEDERATION OF KILKENNY

On 23 October 1641 the Ulster Irish had risen in revolt. In the weeks that followed thousands of British colonists had been driven out; thousands more had been massacred; and the whole of the north, apart from Enniskillen, Derry, Lisburn, Belfast and parts of Co. Antrim, had fallen to the rebels.

The victorious insurgents took Dundalk and began to lay siege to Drogheda. The Lords Justices in Dublin Castle announced the existence of 'a most disloyal and detestable conspiracy by some evil-affected Irish papists'.

The Catholic Old English gentlemen had responded to the Dublin government's call to arms. As they marched north to Drogheda, however, they wondered whether they too were being branded as 'disloyal and detestable'. For years they had been persecuted on account of their religion, and, despite their long record of loyalty to the crown, they had been threatened with the confiscation of their lands. As they approached the walled town, they turned aside. In December 1641 they had meetings with the Gaelic Irish commanders at Tara and Knockcrofty. The momentous decision they arrived at was to join the native Irish rebels of Ulster. For centuries these Old English lords, descendants of the Norman colonists, had fought loyally for the English government. Now they had been pushed too far. Richard Bellings, who had been at the meeting, knew how significant it was:

> And thus, distrust, aversion, force, and fear united the two parties which since the conquest had at all times been most opposite, and ... publicly declared that they would repute all such enemies as did not assist them in their ways.

Protestant refugees from the surrounding countryside poured into Drogheda. One defender reported:

> Miserable spectacles of wealthy men and women, utterly despoiled and undone, nay, stripped stark naked, with doleful cries, came flocking in to us by multitudes, upon whom our bowels could not but yearn.

Help came in the spring of 1642. The Westminster parliament had voted to rush troops to Ireland. The Earl of Ormond brought over a large English army and sent troops from Dublin to relieve Drogheda. His commanding officer reported: 'The number of the slain, I looked not after, but there was little mercy shown in those times.'

Meanwhile the Scots cautiously responded to an urgent plea from London to send a relief army to Ulster. On 15 April 1642 Major-General Robert Monro, after landing at Carrickfergus with 10,000 men, swept southwards with his Scots army in pursuit of the Irish. A hardened veteran of the religious wars in Germany, he simply slaughtered his captives, first at Kilwarlin Wood, then at Loughbrickland, and finally at Newry. There he shot and hanged sixty men and his troops, scouring the countryside about, made sure any Irish they caught, one officer reported, were 'cutte downe, with sume wyves and chyldrene for I promis such gallants gotis but small mercie if they come in your comone sogeris handis'.

The crown forces now held Dungannon, much of the east coast, and some southern ports. In Derry and north Donegal colonists banded together in the 'Laggan force' to win some notable victories. Nevertheless, most of Ireland fell under the control of the rebels. One after another, the counties of the west and the south joined the insurrection. The O'Flahertys of Connemara joined rebels in Mayo in February to slaughter around a hundred Protestants at Shrule.

Long promised, Irish exiles sailed from the European mainland to join their compatriots in arms. Many were experienced veterans from the Spanish army. The most distinguished was Owen Roe O'Neill, nephew of the great Earl of Tyrone; sailing from Dunkirk up the North Sea and around Scotland, O'Neill landed at Doe Castle in north Donegal in July 1642. Cardinal Richelieu released all Irishmen serving in the French army to return to fight in their native land. Many travelled with the Old English commander Thomas Preston, who sailed in to Wexford in August.

It was on 22 August 1642 that the English Civil War broke out. Now that the forces raised by the Westminster parliament were marching against Charles I's Cavaliers, the English government in all parts of Ireland was in peril. Certainly there were as many as 37,000 Protestant men in arms in Ireland. But their loyalties now were dangerously divided between king and parliament.

Leading members of the Catholic hierarchy met in Kilkenny. These clergy declared that all Catholics who did not take part in this just war would be excommunicated. In October elected men from all over the island formed the Confederation of Kilkenny. The Confederation's Supreme Council acted as the government of Ireland, appointed generals, issued writs and minted a new coinage.

There is little doubt that at this moment the Confederate Irish, working together, could have seized control of the entire island. Fatal hesitation, conflicting aims and wasting disputes, however, prevented them from achieving that objective.

Episode 96 ❧

'YOUR WORD IS *SANCTA MARIA!*'

Few periods of Irish history are as confusing as the 1640s. During most of this time the English Civil War raged. In Ireland these were years of massacres, innumerable sieges, dozens of battles, hundreds of skirmishes; this was a time of religious hatred, burnt crops, smoking ruins, when the defeated and the innocent were cut down without mercy again and again. Generals and their men changed sides, sometimes with bewildering frequency. In command in Cork, the Protestant Lord Inchiquin, known as 'Murrough of the Burnings', fought for Charles I, then for parliament, then again for Charles I, and finally became a Catholic. Major-General Robert Monro and his Scots troops in Ulster were royalists, then parliamentarians, and then royalists again.

After a string of successes the Gaelic Irish and the Old English Catholics had united to form the Confederation of Kilkenny in October 1642. The Confederates could have taken control of the whole island, but they failed to seize the moment. Instead of driving their opponents into the sea, they opened negotiations with Charles I. Their view was that King Charles was more likely to give them religious freedom than parliament's Puritans and Roundheads.

The Confederates' faith in King Charles—like almost everyone else's—was completely misplaced. Pointless negotiations dragged on for years. On behalf of the king, the Earl of Ormond negotiated a 'cessation'—that is, a truce—with the Confederates on 15 September 1643. This did not mean an end to the fighting, however. Many Protestants on both sides of the Irish Sea were horrified that the king had done a deal with Catholic 'malignants', and more of them came over to the side of parliament. The Confederation of Kilkenny, indeed, promised the king £300,000 to support the royalist war effort. One Englishman wrote:

> Most of all the Irish cessation made the minds of the people embrace [parliament]; for when ... the agreement was proclaimed, accepting the sum of £300,000 from these idolatrous butchers, and giving them, over the name of Roman Catholic subjects now in arms, a sure peace ... and to exterminate all who should not agree to that proclamation; we thought the popish party was so far countenanced, as it was necessary for all Protestants to join more strictly for their own safety.

Monro, saying he would take orders only from the Scottish government, fought on. Then, as the Roundheads began to turn the tide against the

Cavaliers in England, parliamentary armies began to make inroads into Confederate territory. One was led by Murrough O'Brien, Lord Inchiquin, who after an unsuccessful meeting with King Charles, returned to Ireland, declared for parliament, and ruthlessly drove all the Catholics out of Cork, Youghal and Kinsale.

Meanwhile divisions began to weaken the Confederate cause. The Old English Catholics, despite everything, remained loyal to Charles I. Owen Roe O'Neill, the veteran Confederate commander in Ulster, along with many other Gaelic Irish, sought complete Irish independence. The arrival in Kerry of the pope's representative, Archbishop Giovanni Battista Rinuccini, swung the pendulum in O'Neill's favour. Rinuccini brought arms, 20,000 pounds of gunpowder, 200,000 silver dollars, and a determination to stop the Confederation of Kilkenny making a deal with Charles I.

For the past four years Owen Roe O'Neill had been training his Ulster army in modern fighting methods. He was ready when Monro moved out of Antrim to march south in June 1646. With fresh Scottish reinforcements, Monro advanced with 6,000 men and six field pieces drawn by oxen. On the River Blackwater, at Benburb, O'Neill attacked from the rear. As his men were pounded by Monro's cannon, Owen Roe harangued his men:

> Let your manhood be seen by your push of pike! Your word is *Sancta Maria*, and so in the name of the Father, Son, and Holy Ghost advance!— and give not fire till you are within pike-length!

With no guns but an equal number of men, the Irish steadily pressed the Scots back to the river, slaughtering them. Monro escaped only after he had cast away his coat, hat and wig. Between one-third and one-half of the Scots were killed, the Irish sustaining only trifling losses.

When the news reached Rome, Pope Innocent X himself attended a *Te Deum* in Santa Maria Maggiore to thank God for the triumph. The Battle of Benburb was the greatest and most annihilating victory in arms the Irish ever won over the British. Monro ruefully observed: 'For ought I can understand, the Lord of Hosts had a controversie with us to rub shame in our faces.'

Yet this great victory at Benburb was thrown away. Though all the north was now at his mercy, Owen Roe instead turned south to help Rinuccini take control of the Catholic Confederation in Kilkenny. Fatally divided, the Confederates would soon be in no condition to face the victors in the English Civil War—the Roundheads and their leader, Oliver Cromwell.

Episode 97 ～

'THE RIGHTEOUS JUDGMENT OF GOD'

During the summer of 1647 the green fields of Ireland were once more drenched red with blood. At least 3,000 Irishmen were cut down at Dungan's Hill in Co. Meath and another 4,000 died at Knocknanuss Hill in Co. Cork. And these were only two battles out of an endless series of armed engagements.

By the end of 1648 the Catholic Confederation of Kilkenny had joined with Presbyterian Scots in Ulster and royalists, both English and Irish. These men, bitter enemies until recently, now united behind their king. But in England the cause of Charles I was lost. Soon he was on trial for his life, and on 30 January 1649 the king was executed. Parliament, after setting up the Commonwealth in May, could now concentrate resources on crushing opposition across the Irish Sea. Oliver Cromwell, parliament's greatest general, relished his appointment as commander-in-chief and Lord Lieutenant of Ireland. He had at his disposal a war chest of £100,000, a great train of artillery and 12,000 'Ironsides'—seasoned veterans of many victories.

As the invading army prepared to board more than a hundred vessels at Milford Haven, Irish royalists made a desperate attempt to seize Dublin to deny Cromwell a safe landing. They got to within less than a mile from the city centre, but they were driven back in what is now Baggot Street and routed at Rathfarnham.

Cromwell faced no opposition when he stepped ashore from his frigate on 15 August 1649. From the outset he made it clear that he intended to avenge the 1641 massacre of Protestants in Ulster:

> You, unprovoked, put the English to the most unheard of and most barbarous massacre without respect of sex or age, that ever the sun beheld, and at a time when Ireland was in perfect peace.

He opened his campaign by besieging the walled port of Drogheda. For an entire week Cromwell positioned his cannon with infinite care. Then, on three sides, the guns battered the walls, some firing cannon-balls weighing sixty-four pounds. After almost two days the breaches in the walls were judged large enough for an assault. Cromwell reported that he drove most of the garrison into the Mill-mount, a place very strong and of difficult access.... The governor, Sir Arthur Aston, and divers considerable officers being there, our men getting up to them were ordered by me to put all to the sword; and, indeed, being in the heat of the action, I forbade them to spare any that there were in arms in the town.

Cromwell's own estimate was that some 2,000 were put to the sword. Governor Aston was clubbed to death with his own wooden leg. Only sixty-four parliamentary troops had fallen in the fighting. The killing didn't stop there. A hundred took refuge in the tower of St Peter's; Cromwell ordered the church to be set on fire, and all inside were burned to death. All priests and friars found in the town were killed—or, as Cromwell put it, their 'heads were knocked promiscuously together'. With Cromwell at Drogheda was Lieutenant-General Edmund Ludlow; he observed:

The slaughter was continued all that day and the next, which extraordinary severity, I presume, was used to discourage others from making opposition. And truly I believe this bitterness will save much effusion of blood.

For Cromwell, the slaughter was more than this—it was God's revenge for the Ulster massacres of 1641:

I am persuaded that this is a righteous judgment of God upon these barbarous wretches, who have imbrued their hands in so much innocent blood, and that it will tend to prevent the effusion of blood for the future, which are the satisfactory grounds for such actions, which otherwise cannot but work remorse and regret.

Cromwell sent Colonel Robert Venables to the north. The royalist Colonel Mark Trevor inflicted severe losses with a cavalry attack at night outside Lisburn, but these Ironsides were not to be deflected. Soon only Charlemont, Enniskillen and Coleraine remained in royalist hands. The Lord Lieutenant himself then forged his way southwards, down the coast to the port of Wexford. Cromwell lost only about twenty men in taking the town, but another massacre followed—the total number of soldiers and townspeople slain was not far short of 2,000. Next he besieged the walled town of New Ross at the junction of the Barrow and Nore rivers. After enduring two days of bombardment, the people of the town sued for terms. One of their requests was for freedom of worship. Cromwell gave this famous reply:

For what you mention concerning liberty of conscience you mean a liberty to exercise the Mass, I judge it best to use plain dealing, and to let you know, where the parliament of England have power, that will not be allowed of.

Cromwell's subjugation of Ireland would take more than another two blood-soaked years.

Episode 98 ⮽

THE CURSE OF CROMWELL

Having taken the walled towns of Drogheda and Wexford and slaughtered their garrisons, Oliver Cromwell relentlessly pressed on. Opposed to him were the royalists, many of them Protestants and English, and the Catholic Confederation of Kilkenny. Towns along the Munster coast surrendered to him without a fight. Kilkenny capitulated at the end of March 1650. But parliament's commander-in-chief did not have everything his own way. Cromwell lost some 2,000 men during his assault on the Tipperary town of Clonmel in May 1650. A few days later he returned to England, leaving his son-in-law Henry Ireton in charge.

In the north the native Irish appointed Bishop Heber MacMahon as their leader. But it was hopeless: the parliamentarian cavalry slaughtered his men at Scariffhollis, overlooking Lough Swilly, on 21 June 1650. The victor, Sir Charles Coote, put his prisoners, senior officers included, to the sword. Later captured in Enniskillen, Bishop MacMahon was hanged and his head was then fixed on one of the gates of Derry.

In the south Ireton besieged Limerick for two months. He brought in heavy guns by sea, including mortars firing exploding shells. A battery of twenty-eight guns pounded the city for days. When citizens attempted to leave, Ireton had them hanged, including one little girl. On 27 October the city surrendered. Apart from nearly a thousand men of the garrison killed in the fighting, Ireton reckoned that about 5,000 persons had perished 'by the sword without and the famine and plague within'. Galway was the last city to submit, in May 1652.

Boats had to be dragged by oxen to the lakes of Killarney before Lord Muskerry would surrender Ross Castle in June 1652. Fighting did not actually stop until February 1653 when the western islands of Inishbofin, Inishturk and Clare Island surrendered.

The destruction of war was evident everywhere. Dr William Petty, the army's physician-general, estimated that 504,000 native Irish and 112,000 colonists and English troops had perished between 1641 and 1652. Petty reckoned that another 100,000 Irish men, women and children had been forcibly transported to the colonies in the West Indies and in North America.

Famine swept through the country, and then bubonic plague began to take its toll. Colonel Jones wrote:

It fearfully broke out in Cashel, the people being taken suddenly with madness, whereof they die instantly; twenty died in that manner in three days in that little town.

Colonel Richard Lawrence wrote:

About the years 1652 and 1653 the plague and famine had swept away whole countries that a man might travel twenty or thirty miles and not see a living creature, either man, beast, or bird, they being either all dead or had quit those desolate places.

Campaigning troops had routinely destroyed stores of food and seized the rest for their own use. Colonel George Cooke, governor of Wexford, reported in 1652:

In searching the woods and bogs we found great store of corn, which we burn, also all the houses and cabins we could find; in all of which we found plenty of corn: we continued burning and destroying for four days.... He was an idle soldier who had not a fat lamb, veal, pig, poultry or all of them, every night to his supper. The enemy in these parts chiefly depended upon this country for provision. I believe we have destroyed as much as would have served some thousands of them until next harvest.

Feeding on corpses of cattle, horses and—no doubt—people, packs of wolves grew fat and numerous. In December 1652 a public wolf hunt was organised in Castleknock on the very outskirts of Dublin. Military commanders received orders to organise wolf hunts in their area. One captain leasing land in Co. Dublin paid part of his rent in wolves' heads, each one worth £5. By March 1655 £243 5s 4d had been paid out in rewards for killing wolves. The going rate was £6 for a she-wolf, £5 for a dog-wolf, and £2 for a cub.

Retribution did not end with the fighting. People wondered when the trials and executions would stop. Despite his possession of a safe-conduct, the poet and musician Piers Ferriter was hanged at Killarney, together with a bishop and a priest. Theobald Burke, Viscount Mayo, faced a firing-squad in Galway city. In February 1653 Colonel Robert Venables reported: 'It hath pleased God to deliver into your hands the ringleader in the late bloody massacres and rebellions, Sir Phelim O'Neill.' Convicted in Dublin, he was hanged, drawn and quartered.

By 1654 more than 200 men had been tried and executed by Cromwell's special commission. Catholic priests had been given twenty days to get out of Ireland. Many who dared to stay were hunted down and put to death. For the majority of the Irish, the greatest fear was confiscation of their lands. For Cromwell was now putting into effect his threat that he would send Catholics 'to Hell or Connacht'.

Episode 99 ∾

'TO HELL OR CONNACHT'

The Gaelic poet Seán O'Connell described Cromwell's conquest of Ireland as 'the war that finished Ireland'. This was close to the truth. Much of the island had been laid waste. The government made an appeal for charitable donations for

> the great multitudes of poore, swarming in all partes of this nation, occasioned by the devastations of the country ... that frequently some [are] found feeding on carrion and weeds, some starved in the highways, and many times poore children, who lost their parents, or deserted by them, are found exposed to, and some of them fed upon by ravening wolves and other beasts of prey.

Cromwell had once declared that the Catholics of Ireland could go 'to Hell or Connacht'. In his Act of Settlement in 1652 he spelled out what he meant by this. Large numbers of people were entirely exempt from life or pardon. Of the remainder, only those who could prove 'constant good affection' to the cause of parliament could keep their estates. However, very few in Ireland could prove constant support for parliament over the past ten years. Hence almost all Catholic landowners were to lose their estates entirely and get smaller ones west of the River Shannon—in the province of Connacht.

Cromwell was not just concerned to punish. He had to find the cost of his conquest, a sum reaching £3,500,000. His soldiers were owed £1,750,000 in back pay. 'Adventurers'—men who had adventured or lent money to the government—were due to receive 2,500,000 acres of Irish land in return for their investment. It was quite clear that the only way to meet the English government's debts was to confiscate most of the land held by Catholics.

Under the Act of Settlement about 80,000 men were liable for the death penalty—that is around half the adult males then living in Ireland. In fact the government did not attempt this kind of carnage. Hundreds, not tens of thousands, were executed. Otherwise, the price paid by the Catholics of Ireland was very high.

A general search of the countryside was ordered for those who had not transplanted themselves to Connacht. Courts martial condemned to death some who had failed to move in time. Edward Hetherington, sentenced by a court sitting in St Patrick's Cathedral in Dublin, was hanged with placards on his chest and back bearing the words 'For Not Transplanting'.

Miserable groups of Catholics gathered at Loughrea in Co. Galway. Here five commissioners had to consider their claims to land in Connacht, supposed to be a specified fraction of the estates they been forced to give up. Each claimant carried with them passports and certificates issued by revenue officers. Some of these certificates survive:

Sir Nicholas Comyn, numb at one side of his body of a dead palsy, accompanied only by his lady, Catherine Comyn, aged thirty-five years, brown hair, middle stature; having no substance, but expecting the benefit of his qualification ...

Pierce, Viscount Ikerran, going with seventeen persons, four cows, five garrans, twenty-four sheep and two swine, and claiming against sixteen acres of winter corn ...

Ignatius Stacpole of Limerick, orphant, aged eleven years, flaxen haire, full face, low stature; Katherine Stacpole, orphant, sister to the said Ignatius, aged eight years, flaxen haire, full face; having no substance to relieve themselves, but desireth the benefit of his claim before the commissioners of the revenue ...

The legislation demanded the complete clearance of Catholics of every class from the counties lying between the River Boyne and the River Barrow. This proved impossible. In practice, towns such as Dublin, Drogheda, Carlow and Wexford could not survive without Catholic tradesmen. And the new owners of land wanted humble Catholic labourers to stay on to help them get their farms up and running.

Protestants who had not shown 'constant good affection' to the cause of parliament were supposed to lose some of their estates. In the end they were let off with fines, most of which were never paid. What is clear is that Catholics almost disappeared as a property-owning class east of the Shannon. Indeed, out of 380 Catholics who had owned land in Co. Wexford before the war, 297 were left with nothing at all by 1657.

In lieu of their back pay, 33,419 soldiers got what were called 'debentures'—pieces of paper entitling them to Irish land. Many sold these, usually at great loss, to land speculators. About 12,000 stayed to become Irish farmers. Quite contrary to Cromwell's plans, these men went native very quickly. They were thinly scattered across the countryside and defied an ordinance forbidding them to marry Irish girls. Many, in time, became Catholics. Forty years later a visiting Englishman commented on the survival of Irish culture: 'We cannot wonder at this when we consider how many there are of the children of Oliver's soldiers in Ireland who cannot speak one word of English.'

Meanwhile, many Irishmen who had lost everything took to the hills and bogs to live as bandits—or, as they were called at the time, 'tories'.

Episode 100 ∿

PRIESTS AND TORIES

While Cromwell still ruled, Catholic worship was illegal in Ireland. Around a thousand priests left the country; those who stayed were in peril of their lives; many were executed; and people who sheltered priests ran the risk of imprisonment. Inishbofin Island off the coast of Galway became an internment camp for priests. A Jesuit priest described conditions in 1656:

> We live, for the most part, in the mountains and forests ... to escape the cavalry of the heretics. Catholics flock to us, whom we refresh by the Word of God and consolation of the Sacraments.... In spite of all the precautions used to exercise our evangelical ministry in secret, the Cromwellians often discover it; and then the wild beast was never hunted with more fury, nor tracked with more pertinacity, through mountains, woods and bogs, than the priest!

Outlawed worship was confined to a 'Mass rock' in a remote place. Edmund O'Reilly, Archbishop of Armagh, recalled: 'I made for myself a small hut in a mountainous district, one here, another there, so that no one else should suffer for my sake.' Even so, he managed to maintain twenty-two priests in the county of Armagh: 'They visit the sick by night; they celebrate Mass before and round about dawn, and that in hiding places and recesses, having appointed scouts to look around and with eyes and ears agog to keep watch lest the soldiers come by surprise.'

The restoration of Charles II in 1660 ushered in a new era of toleration for all. Presbyterian ministers were allowed to return, and Catholic worship became public again. Catholic gentlemen who had lost their estates in Cromwell's time now hoped to get them back. Charles, however much he sympathised with them, was in no position to face down the Protestants who now owned most of the land of Ireland. The only notable Catholic who got his estates back was the Earl of Antrim.

Around 34,000 Irish Catholic soldiers left the country to serve in the armies of France and Spain. About 12,000 were transported to the West Indies—often they married black slaves there, and amongst their descendants on St Kitts and Montserrat today the Irish accent is very distinct. Other defeated soldiers and men who had lost their lands lived as outlaws. They were known as 'tories', from the Irish word *tóraidhe*, which means a 'pursuer' or bandit.

Tories continued their banditry throughout the reign of Charles II. One of the most notorious was Redmond O'Hanlon. Imprisoned for stealing horses, he bribed his way out of Armagh jail, and, according to a popular biography published in 1681, this 'Incomparable and Indefatigable Tory ... despairing of mercy or pardon ... resolved to abandon himself to all Lewdness and to become a perfect bird of Prey.' His robberies became so outrageous that landowners cut down the Glen Woods, O'Hanlon's hideout just south of Poyntzpass, and paid thirty men ninepence a day for three months to track down the outlaw. Wounded, O'Hanlon had to lie up on Ram's Island in Lough Neagh, but soon he resumed his brigandage in Co. Fermanagh. At the funeral of a gentleman he murdered in 1679 the clergyman denounced O'Hanlon as

a cunning and dangerous fellow who though Proclaimed as Outlaw with the rest of his Crew and summs of Money upon their heads, yet he raigns still and keeps all in subjection so far that 'tis credibly reported he raises more in a year by contribution à la mode de France, than the King's Land-Taxes and Chimney Money come to.

Reports of O'Hanlon's daring now appeared in London newspapers as he extended his plundering activities into Down, Leitrim and Roscommon in October 1679. Eventually Redmond O'Hanlon was shot dead by his foster-brother, who had been handsomely bribed by Dublin Castle to do the deed.

In a few years most of the tories had been rounded up and killed. Sir William Stewart of Newtownstewart, Co. Tyrone, reported in March 1683:

There was never such a winter for country sports as the last, and I have enjoyed them in much perfection. I have very good hawks and hounds, but we have not had more success in any sport than tory-hunting. The gentle-men of the country have been so hearty in that chase that of thirteen in the county where I live in November, the last was killed two days before I left home.

Later this nursery rhyme became popular:

> Ho! Brother Tadhg, what is your story?
> I went to the wood and shot a tory,
> I went to the wood and shot another,
> Was it the same or was it his brother?
>
> I hunted him in, I hunted him out,
> Three times through the bog and about and about,
> Till out of a bush I spied his head
> So I levelled my gun and shot him dead!

The disappearance of tories was a sign that Ireland was becoming more peaceful and prosperous.

Episode 101 ∾

RESTORATION IRELAND

In 1682 several writers were commissioned to compile what were described as 'statistical accounts' of districts of Ireland for a 'Grand Atlas'. The publication of the volume on Ireland fell through, but a few of these descriptions survive. They demonstrate that the island was enjoying a remarkable recovery following the destruction and dislocation of Cromwell's time. In his description of Oneilland barony in north Armagh William Brooke observed:

> The soile of this Barony of O'Nealand is very deep and fertile, being productive of all Sorts of grain, as wheat, Rye, Barly, Oats,&c. The vast quantity of wheat that is yearly carried hence into the County of Antrim, besides the maintenance of above two thousand Familys with bread ... most whereof being English, do plainly demonstrate it to be the granary of Ulster ... and as it Excells all the rest for Corn, so it challenges the preference for fruit trees, good sider being sold here for 30 shillings the hogshead.

As under the terms of their leases tenants were made to plant apple trees, Brooke predicted that 'this County twenty or thirty years hence will be little inferiour to the best sider county in England'. In and about Lurgan, he continued, 'is managed the greatest Linnen manufacture in Ireland', helping to make this barony 'a paradise of pleasure'.

William Montgomery described a peaceful and flourishing settlement in the Ards peninsula:

> The inhabitants doe Manure & Dung the land with sea oar by them called Tangle which being spread on it and plowed down makes winter grain & summer Barly grow in aboundance without weeds cocle or tares; the roads are pleasant & smooth in depth of winter.

The salt marsh was so valued for its medicinal herbs that Lord Montgomery had refused an offer of £2,000 made by the 'Netherland Dutch' to lease it.

Richard Dobbs of Carrickfergus was impressed by the industry of the people of Islandmagee;

> The people here think that no profit can be made but by ploughing, in which the men spend their whole time, except the summer in bringing home firing; and the women theirs, in spinning and making linen cloth, and some ordinary woollen for their family's use.

He was amazed at their bravery in lowering themselves by horse leathers down the cliffs at the Gobbins to collect gulls' eggs to supplement their diet of oatmeal.

These accounts help to show that it was during the Restoration era that the plantation in Ulster really took off. Every year Scots and English families strengthened the British colony in the north, and towns there at last began to grow.

Roderic O'Flaherty was probably surprised to be invited to contribute a statistical account of West Connacht. A Catholic, and a leading member of the ruling family of Connemara, he had lost nearly everything as a result of the Cromwellian confiscations. Severed from his ancestral territory, he now made a meagre living as a scholar and a writer. He explained:

> I live a banished man within the bounds of my native soil; a spectator of others enriched by my birthright; an object of condoling to my relations and friends, and a condoler of their miseries.

Normally O'Flaherty wrote in Latin—this statistical account would have to written in what was to him a foreign language, English. He also had to be very careful not to express any opinions about recent events. This landscape of the far west he was asked to describe was very different from the fertile plains on the other side of the country. Gaelic scholars of the past had felt it beneath their dignity to tell how those on the bottom rung of society scratched a living from the ground. O'Flaherty was the first to do so. He showed—in rather halting English—how hard poor people worked in order to raise corn planted in traditional ridges in the rain-soaked, thin, infertile and rock-strewn soils of windswept Connemara:

> The tract of land ... by the bay of Galway ... is good pasture for cattell; but so craggy and full of stones, and so destitute of deep mold, that in very few spots of it a plow can goe; yet the tenants, by digging, manure it so well, that they have corn for themselves, their landlords, and the market. Never was garden with more paines tilled for black seeds. They carry on horses, out of the shore, all the seaweeds cast in daily, as long as they can get it, from Michaelmas till sowing time past: and sometimes on spring tide low waters, they goe as far down as they can, man, woman and child, and cut the sea weed with knives, to have it cast up again by the sea. With this they muck the land, and dig up daily, earth to cover it, out of watery furrows which serve for conveying away the water from the ridges. This mucking and digging keeps them in action till March, before which they sow not a grain of corn. In sowing, they give so small a measure of seed as can be immagined, being sure not a grain will fail to multiply. In summer, when it grows up, they goe, man, woman and child, and ly prostrate ... to weed it with their bare hands.... Twice, perhaps, they thus weed it before it comes to an ear. The soile bears not but for two years, till they muck it again.... Here is a kinde of corn they call *bwagh*, the grain is like wheat, but more brownish and swarthy; the bread like barly bread but finer.... This land hath no help for building but thatch, and plenty of rude stones that cannot be wrought. It is destitute of wood and lime-stone.

At least the land was at peace. Some of the credit for that must be given to Charles II's viceroy, the Duke of Ormond.

Episode 102 ～

ORMOND

James Butler, the newly created Duke of Ormond, returned from exile in triumph. He entered Dublin on 27 July 1662, fifteen years to the day since he had surrendered the city to the forces of parliament. He had endured years of poverty and danger as King Charles II's most faithful servant. He had served for a time as Charles I's Lord Lieutenant of Ireland and commanded his armies; now he was returning with the same title as Charles II's viceroy. The people of Dublin trusted that he would bring with him a new era of peace, toleration and prosperity. As he made his way from Howth Castle he was greeting by great cheering crowds. 'The joy of the city', it was recorded, ' was continued by the plenty of wine that was given in the streets, the ringing of bells, bonfires and several fireworks.'

Ormond was determined to make Dublin a capital city to be proud of. He began by getting the king to upgrade the city's mayor to become Lord Mayor at a salary of £500 a year. At the king's request, Ormond created what is still the largest public park in Europe, Phoenix Park. Originally the 2,000 acres were intended for the chase: one nobleman went to England to bring back fallow deer; another travelled to Wales to fetch partridges; and the duke's son provided pheasants from his Tipperary estates. It was not long before poachers from the city hunted down every last game bird, but the descendants of the fallow deer still graze there today. Of course, Charles never came to Ireland and planned to give the park to his mistress, Barbara Villiers. Ormond talked the king out of it. The mistress, of course, was furious: she hissed in Ormond's ear that she hoped she would live long enough to see him hanged.

From the outset Phoenix Park was a public park where citizens could take their ease. Ormond liked it too, and—finding Dublin Castle dingy and dank— built himself a viceregal residence close by. Grounds were set aside nearby for a gracious home for old soldiers, the Royal Hospital at Kilmainham, and work began in 1680. It remains today Ireland's finest seventeenth-century building.

Ormond encouraged Dublin Corporation to designate St Stephen's Green for development as an elegant residential square for persons of substance; the sites were apportioned to eighty-nine speculators by lot. Over much of the city brick houses were replacing the decaying timber dwellings; the most handsome of these became known as 'Dutch Billys', though they were actually built by Huguenots, Protestants escaping from persecution in France. The Huguenots developed a flourishing silk industry in the area known as the Coombe. There they developed a unique fabric, called poplin, made from a blend of silk and wool, still favoured for men's neckties today.

The 1662 'Act to Encourage Protestant Strangers to Settle in Ireland' also attracted to Dublin Jews who had taken refuge in Tenerife. These Jews were accepted as a variety of 'foreign Protestants' and became a vibrant addition to Dublin society.

During these years Dublin acquired its first stone-lined quays, street lamps, a boys' school known as the Blue-Coat Hospital, a fine stone bridge to Ormond Quay to add to the four wooden bridges already there, a post office and a theatre in Smock Alley—though at a gala performance in 1680 the galleries collapsed, killing three people. The two cathedrals both acquired new sets of bells in 1670, and St Patrick's was given a new roof built with forty tons of oak donated by the executed Earl of Strafford's son from his Wicklow estate.

High on the list of exports was wool. The coarse long-stapled wool from Irish sheep was just what was wanted for the new draperies in the fashion houses of the European mainland. Much of it was landed at St Malo in northern France. Most Irish wool was spun and woven in the homes of the poor to clothe themselves. But Dublin and country towns such as Carrick-on-Suir, Carlow and Bandon began to specialise in weaving high-quality woollen frieze for sale to the gentry and for export overseas.

The Westminster parliament believed the flourishing Irish export trade in live cattle was damaging the English home market. In 1663 and 1667 it passed Cattle Acts forbidding the export of live cattle from Ireland. This caused much resentment, and Ormond travelled several times to London in a vain attempt to get the legislation repealed.

The damage to Irish trade was less than expected. It seems to have been more than compensated for by the rise in exports of butter. English settlers, who had no liking for Irish bog butter, knew what the overseas buyers wanted, and this probably explains why Belfast and Youghal together accounted for half of all Irish butter exported. The Dutch paid the highest prices, but the French bought the greatest quantities.

The growing prosperity of Ireland depended on peace, and this the Duke of Ormond was determined to maintain.

Episode 103 ~

WORK, FOOD AND LEISURE

The long period of peace during the reign of Charles II gave the Irish economy ample time to recover. The great majority, humble people who worked the land, had seen many changes of landlords. Gaelic noble or Cromwellian trooper, it made little difference: one landlord seemed as bad or as good as another. Working the farm without the constant fear of cattle being seized, corn being trampled and homes being burnt—that was what really improved the quality of life.

The most recent English arrivals in Ireland often wrote home to describe the characteristics of the native Irish who worked for them. One anonymous letter describes the inhabitants of the Curragh of Kildare in 1683:

The men are hardy, laborious and industrious, of healthful bodies and constitutions, able and enured to bear labour, and live to a great age, generally
to seventy and eighty....

Their women [are] generally inclined to corpulency and thick-legged,
which is occasioned by their loose garments, flat pumps and brogues, using
little or no action or exercises, in or without their houses, having easy
labour and being good nurses but bad housewives, not being used to any
sort of manual labour except spinning, which by reason of the suppleness
of their fingers they perform well.

They are great admirers of music, yet their own songs are doleful
lamentations as those of a conquered people, or as the Jews in bondage or
captivity....

They are not very lascivious, yet the ordinary sort of people take a sort
of pride in prostituting their daughters or kinswomen to their landlord's
sons ... and if the young women bear a child or children, the parents are
exceedingly fond of it ... and further, if they happen to nurse a gentleman's
child, whose parents fall into decay or want, they think themselves bound
to provide for that nursechild as for their own, it having drawn of the same
milk....

Their diet generally is very mean and sparing, consisting of milk, roots
and coarse unsavoury bread; their lodging and habit proportionable ...

Potatoes had become an important supplement to the staple diet, Sir
William Petty observed: 'Their food is bread in cakes, whereof a penny serves
a week for each; potatoes from August till May ...'. Nevertheless, oatcakes and
bread, together with dairy products, formed the usual daily fare of the Irish,
as Thomas Dineley recorded:

Dyet generally of the vulgar Irish are potatoes, milk, new milk which they
call sweet milk, bonnyclobber, mallabaune, whey, curds, large brown oatcakes of a foot and a half broad bak't before the fire, bread made of bare, a
sort of barley, peas, beans and oatmeale, wheat and rye for great days.

The food of the upper class was, of course, more luxurious and varied. Lord
Orrery's steward left notes on what was served at Castlemartyr House in west
Cork:

1679 Thursday the 3rd of July. Mr Love was the only visitor dinner & supper.
    Dinner: 1 hanch of Venison; Calves head harshed; Pulletts 2; Sallett;
Turbett; 1 shoulder & Rack of Mutton; 1 Briskett of beafe Boyled; Chickings
6; Pease; Kidney toastes; Neates tongues; Clary & Eggs; Rabitts 2.
    Supper: Water Gruell; 1 shoulder of veal Roste; Stewed Troutes; Sliced
Beafe; Beanes; Harty choakes; 1 Line & breast of Mutton.

The following day, when three Scottish officers and Mr Love joined the household at table, the bill of fare was even longer and included:

Scotch Schollops of Veale; Sallett; Harty choakes, Could Lamb; Tongue & marrowbones; Buttered Carretts; Venison Pye; Chickings 3 & 3 rabitts; Gelly; Sheepes Tongues; Ducks 3 ...

An inventory of the contents of Rathcline House, Co. Longford, the property of Viscount Lanesborough, dated April 1688, gives some idea of kitchen and outhouse equipment in a great house:

Kitchen: 1 grate and fender, 1 frying pan and dripping pan, a brass or copper boiler, 2 pair of racks ... Larder: 1 cupboard and dresser, a crackt sylebub cup, a butter tub, an iron hoop with hooks to hang meat on, 2 pailes. Bakehouse: powdering tub, etc. Dary: 12 coolers, 2 pailes, 9 bouls, 1 butter tub, one churn and stafhold, 1 cheespress, 4 chees fatts. Brewhouse: 1 brass or copper furnace sett, 2 keeves, 1 guile, 1 tundish and longeard paile, hopsive, casks etc.

The anonymous account of Kildare tells us that the Curragh, twenty-seven miles from Dublin, was becoming the playground of the rich:

Hither repairs the Lord Lieutenant or Chief Governor when His Majesty's important affairs will admit leisure to unbend and slacken from tiring cares. Hither are also seen to come all the nobility and gentry of the kingdom that either pretend to love or delight in hawking or hunting or racing, for in this clearer and finer air the falcon goes to a higher pitch or mount so often as to be scarce visible, the hounds enjoy the scent more freely ...

Ireland was still an alien country, however, especially in its continued support for the Catholic Church.

Episode 104 ～

THE POPISH PLOT

Like so many other Englishmen freshly arrived in Restoration Ireland, the anonymous author of the description of Co. Kildare in 1683 was both fascinated and repelled by the religious beliefs and practices of the native people.

This account, like many later ones, reveals that ancient pagan beliefs were intermixed with a strong Catholic piety:

> Notwithstanding all the laws and methods used to reclaim them there they still retain some customs, heathenish, barbarous and superstitious....
>
> Such are their opinion of souls departed that as the party was conditioned when alive his soul is transmigrated into some creature of like fierce disposition as a cruel man into a wolf and the like, hence the first lamb or calf that fall of that season they devote or dedicate to him ... they suppose he'll spare their herd or flock that year....
>
> At their first seeing of a child they spit in the face of it in token of good will to it ... and whereby they say that is secured from an evil eye....
>
> They are much given to credit charms, spells, incantations, divinations and attribute all diseases not very frequent or common among them to ... witchcraft. Their ignorant priests nursle them up in this that they might have matter for their exorcisms....
>
> Their wakes also over dead corpses, where they have a table spread and served with the best that can be had at such a time, and after a while attending (in expectation the departed soul will partake) they fall to eating and drinking, after to revelling, as if one of the feasts of Bacchus; the next day at their setting out to accompany it to the grave, as soon as the bearers have taken up the body, they begin their shrill cries and hideous hootings ... and if there be not enough to make out a good cry, they hire the best and deepest mouthed in all the country ... this may now be heard two miles or more.

After a long period of service in the Vatican, Oliver Plunkett returned to Ireland in 1669 as Archbishop of Armagh. The Catholic primate spent much of his time attempting to stamp out pagan superstition and disciplining clergy who encouraged the continuance of pre-Christian practices.

Meanwhile Catholics who had lost their landed estates under Cromwell pressed hard to get them back. The fact that Charles had been restored largely as a result of the action of Cromwell's former generals made it extremely difficult to meet this demand. After much wrangling, it was agreed to order the Cromwellians to give up one-third of their lands, so that these could be redistributed to loyal Catholics. But the process was slow, and only a few thousand of the dispossessed were restored to even a small portion of their estates. Decisions proved hard to enforce. For example, Patrick Sarsfield— father of the famous soldier—had testimonials from some of the most powerful in the land. The court ordered the return of most of his lands in Kildare, but Sarsfield found it impossible to get Sir Theophilus Jones out of his extensive Lucan estate.

Charles II's viceroy in Ireland, the Duke of Ormond, was an unusual man for his time. He believed in religious toleration. A fervent member of the Church of Ireland, he had nevertheless been brought up as a Catholic, and in his lifetime he had seen too much blood spilt over religion.

In the reign of Charles II two political factions had emerged in England, and the insulting names they hurled at each other stuck. Opponents of the king became known as 'Whigs', from 'whiggamore', a Scots expression denoting a rebel Covenanter. Supporters of the king became known as 'Tories', from the Irish word *tóraidhe*, meaning a bandit. Charles II had no legitimate heir, and the Whigs feared that his brother James—an avowed Catholic—would make the kingdom Catholic when he came to the throne.

In 1678 details of an alleged 'Popish Plot' were revealed in London. It was claimed that the Jesuits intended to assassinate Charles II and, with the help of the French, put James on the throne. London was soon gripped by an anti-Catholic hysteria.

Ormond was certain the plot was a complete fabrication, and he was right. When orders came from London to arrest the Catholic Archbishop of Armagh, however, the viceroy had to comply. Archbishop Plunkett was the only man named in the plot. A member of an Old English family in Co. Meath, he had made some enemies, particularly among the Franciscans in Ulster, as he imposed strict Church discipline. Ormond made sure that the archbishop was not convicted of treason when brought to trial in Dundalk. The viceroy kept Plunkett in prison, nevertheless, perhaps for his own safety.

Then in 1681 the House of Lords at Westminster voted to have Archbishop Plunkett put on trial in London.

Episode 105 ∿

THE TRIAL OF OLIVER PLUNKETT

London, 8 June 1681. A huge throng swarmed the approaches, gateway and lobby of Westminster Hall. They crowded to witness the trial of the Catholic Archbishop of Armagh, Oliver Plunkett, accused of high treason:

Clerk of the Court: Oliver Plunkett, hold up thy hand.

Unable to find a lawyer to speak for him, Archbishop Plunkett had to conduct his own defence. He pleaded that he had not been able to get his witnesses over from Ireland. The Lord Chief Justice was not impressed:

Lord Chief Justice: Look you, Mr Plunkett, it is vain for you to make this discourse now.... You shall have as fair a trial as if you were in Ireland: but for us to stay for your witnesses, we cannot do it.

Plunkett: My lord, I desire only—

Lord Chief Justice: We can't do it.

The twelve jurymen were sworn, and the Clerk of the Court read out a long indictment charging the archbishop with high treason.

Mr Heath: May it please your lordship, and you gentlemen of the jury, this is an indictment of treason against Dr Oliver Plunkett, the prisoner at the bar. It sets forth, that the two and thirtieth year of the king, at Dublin in the kingdom of Ireland, he did compass and imagine the death of the king, and to raise war to extirpate the Protestant religion in Ireland, and to establish the Romish religion there. And that to accomplish these treasons, the defendant did raise great sums of money in the kingdom of Ireland....

Attorney-General: May it please your lordship, and you gentlemen of the jury, this gentleman, as primate under a foreign jurisdiction ... issues out warrants to his clergy to make a collection of money and sent into France to further the business.... First, we call Florence MacMoyer.

Solicitor-General: Are you sworn, sir?

MacMoyer: Yes, sir.

Solicitor-General: Pray give the court and the jury an account of what you know of any plot in Ireland, to introduce the Romish religion, or to bring in the French king.

MacMoyer: Yes, I know there was a plot.

MacMoyer was only one of several priests and friars brought over by the prosecution to give evidence of the plot. All of them had been disciplined for bad behaviour by Plunkett.

Plunkett: Tell me this—

Lord Chief Justice: What is your question, Dr Plunkett? Pray tell it us.

Plunkett: I say, my lord, why did he not tell some justice of the peace that I was on such a design ... and never speak of it till now.

[*MacMoyer hesitates*]

Lord Chief Justice: What say you to the question?

[*MacMoyer hesitates*]

  What religion were you of then?

MacMoyer: I was a Roman Catholic.

Lord Chief Justice: And are you not so now?

MacMoyer: Yes, I am so.
Justice Dolben: Therefore it will be no wonder that you did not discover it.
Attorney-General: Then swear Hugh Duffy.

Duffy was a Franciscan friar who had been expelled from Rome for deliberately smashing a bust of Plunkett in the Vatican library. Now he gave the court damning evidence. This was too much for the archbishop:

Attorney-General: Pray let him have fair play to ask any questions.
Plunkett: Mr Duffy, one word with you: is not this out of malice to me, for correcting some of the clergy?

The next witness to be sworn in was Father Edmund Murphy. He had been suspended by Plunkett for constant drunkenness and disorderly conduct. Murphy was less reliable than the prosecution hoped. In court he was clearly petrified.

Lord Chief Justice: Answer me directly, did he claim to be titular primate under the pope?
Murphy: I suppose he did ...
Lord Chief Justice: You are upon your oath, you must speak the truth, and the whole truth. You must not mince or conceal anything.
Attorney-General: Upon your oath, did you converse with him about bringing in the French?
[*silence*]
Serjeant Jeffreys: Declare the truth, come!
[*silence*]
Lord Chief Justice: Come, don't trifle! What discourse have you had with the prisoner about bringing in the French, sir?
Murphy: ... It was a general expectation that all the French and Irish would come and fall upon the English nation, as I understood.
Lord Chief Justice: Pray answer the question directly; you must not come and think to trifle with the court.... You must not come to quibble and run about to this, and that, and t'other, but answer directly.

Suddenly Father Murphy reached for his hat and dashed in terror from Westminster Hall. As he was dragged back Friar MacMoyer was called again. He was questioned about the raising of money and was shown a paper signed by Plunkett:

Attorney-General: It is £500 in the whole.
Plunkett: Is it £500?

MacMoyer: It is in figure a 5 and two oos.
Plunkett: My lord, this is counterfeit, it is put in by other ink.
Justice Dolben: Like enough so.

Not one of the witnesses for the prosecution had produced any real evidence of treason. The jury now retired and returned after fifteen minutes.

Clerk of the Court: Oliver Plunkett, hold up thy hand. How say you, is he guilty of the high treason whereof he stands indicted, or not guilty?
Jury foreman: Guilty.
Plunkett: *Deo gratias*, God be thanked.

When sentenced to be hanged, drawn and quartered, the archbishop responded:

Plunkett: God Almighty bless your lordship.... I die most willingly. And with God's grace I shall give others the good example not to fear death. I do forgive all who had a hand directly or indirectly in my death and in my innocent blood. As for my religion, 'tis glorious for all my friends that I should die for it.

Episode 106 ~

'LILLIBURLERO'

Look you, Mr Plunkett, you have been here indicted of the greatest of all crimes, and that is, high treason. The bottom of your treason was your setting up your false religion ... a religion that is ten times worse than all the heathenish superstitions.

So spoke the Lord Chief Justice in Westminster Hall after the Catholic Archbishop of Armagh had been condemned. Then came the sentence:

And therefore you must go from hence to the place from whence you came, that is to Newgate, and from thence you shall be drawn through the city of London to Tyburn; there you shall be hanged by the neck, but cut down before you are dead, your bowels shall be taken out and burnt before your face, your head shall be cut off, and your body be divided into four quarters.

This was nothing short of judicial murder: not a shred of evidence had been put forward to prove treason. On 11 July 1681 Archbishop Oliver Plunkett was tied lying down with his face uppermost on a sledge, shaped like a flat-bottomed boat, and this was drawn by three horses along rough cobbles for more than two miles. In front of the sledge a fife and drum band played; then followed a company of mounted soldiers.

At Tyburn a huge crowd watched as the hangman and his assistant, a butcher, took their instruments from a cart. The prisoner was untied and taken to the gallows, where he forgave his enemies and prayed briefly. One witness recalled:

> His speech ended, and his cap drawn over his eyes ... the cart was drawn from under him. Thus he hung betwixt Heaven and Earth ... the execu-tioner ripped up his belly and breast, and pulled out his heart and bowels, threw them into the fire, ready kindled.

And what did King Charles II think of this? The French ambassador to London observed:

> I spoke to the King of England on this matter of Monsieur Plunkett and he told me he was more sorry than he could possibly express to see a man con-demned to death who was in no wise guilty, but that his enemies were watching for him to make a false step.

Indeed, King Charles had to watch his step during this wave of anti-Catholic hysteria in England, known as the Popish Plot. Charles, having no legitimate child to succeed him to the throne, took serious risks when he refused to exclude his Catholic brother James from the succession.

Perhaps the most remarkable feature of this Popish Plot is that the king's viceroy in Dublin Castle, the Duke of Ormond, succeeded in keeping this frenzy of religious hate out of Ireland. Catholic bishops had to go into genteel hiding for a time, certainly, but there was no repeat of the religious persecu-tion of Cromwell's day.

Then, rather suddenly, Charles II died in 1685. His brother was now King James II. Protestants on both sides of the Irish Sea dreaded what would come next.

They did not have to wait long. In 1687 a Catholic, Richard Talbot, was appointed Lord Deputy, the king's chief governor in Ireland. Talbot, the sixteenth child of an impoverished Kildare landowner, had been one of the very few royalist officers to escape Cromwell's massacre in Drogheda in 1649. Now created the Earl of Tyrconnell, he was a man dedicated to the Catholic cause. Protestants in Ireland referred to him as 'Lying Dick Talbot', and in England a song of derision written by Thomas Wharton—a take-off of the Irish brogue—very quickly reached the top of the 1687 hit parade:

Ho brother Teig, dost hear de decree,
Lilliburlero Bullen a la!
Dat we shall have a new Deputy?
Lilliburlero, Bullen a la!
Ho, by my Soul, it is a Talbot,
Lilliburlero, Bullen a la!
And he will cut all de English throat.
Lilliburlero, Bullen a la!

Tyrconnell did not delay in his mission. All counties but Donegal acquired Catholic sheriffs. Boroughs—that is, town and city councils—were overhauled to give them Catholic majorities. The army was purged of most of its Protestant officers. A Gaelic poet in Munster, Dáibhidh Ó Bruadair, rejoiced at the change and at the discomfiture of 'John', the archetypal English planter:

Behold there the Gael in arms in every one of them,
They have powder and guns, hold the castles and fortresses;
The Presbyterians, lo, have been overthrown,
And the fanatics have left an infernal smell after them.
Whither shall John turn? He has now no red coat on him.
Nor 'Who's there?' on his lips when standing beside the gate.
'You popish rogue' they won't dare to say to us,
But 'Cromwellian dog' is the watchword we have for him.

Catholics may have been exulting, but the Protestants of England had decided that King James would have to go. Fearing that Tyrconnell was about to send a Catholic army across the Irish Sea, they turned to William of Orange for aid.

Episode 107 ∿

THREE KINGS AND THIRTEEN APPRENTICE BOYS

Dare was an auld prophecy found in a bog,
Lilliburlero Bullen a la!
That we would be ruled by an ass and a hog.
Lilliburlero Bullen a la!

And now the auld prophecy has come to pass,
Lilliburlero, Bullen a la!
For Talbot's the hog and James is the ass.
Lilliburlero, Bullen a la!

Richard Talbot, the Earl of Tyrconnell, appointed Lord Deputy by James II, was busy clearing Protestants out of the Irish army and the country's administration. Following the birth of a male heir to the throne in June 1688, thereby ensuring the Catholic succession, the Protestant gentlemen of England became convinced that King James would have to go. William of Orange, ruler of the Dutch Republic, accepted their invitation and landed with an imposing army at Torbay in the south-west of England on 5 November 1688.

While King James was in London making frantic efforts to stop his support melting away, Protestants in Ulster were rallying for their own defence against Tyrconnell's Catholic troops. On 3 December 1688 an anonymous letter was found lying in a street in Comber, Co. Down, addressed to Lord Mount Alexander. It began:

> Good my lord, I have written to you to know that all our Irishmen through Ireland is sworn that on the ninth day of this month they are to fall on to kill and murder man, wife and child ...

Almost certainly a forgery, the 'Comber Letter' nevertheless galvanised the Protestant population of Ulster. Indeed, one of the aldermen of Derry was reading out the letter to citizens when a messenger arrived warning that Lord Antrim and his troop of soldiers was approaching. The Earl of Antrim had been ordered by Tyrconnell to place a garrison in the walled city. Fortunately for the Protestants of Derry, Lord Antrim was elderly and a little crazy, and it took weeks before he was ready to move. He insisted, for example, that all his Redshank soldiers should be over six foot tall. Nevertheless, the appearance finally of 1,200 Catholic soldiers on 7 December caused instant alarm inside the walls.

The Protestant Bishop of Derry advised citizens to admit Lord Antrim's troops. But when the Redshanks entered the Waterside and began to cross the Foyle, thirteen apprentice boys seized the keys from the main guard, raised the drawbridge at Ferryquay gate and closed the gates. This swift action by the apprentice boys, an army captain recalled, 'acted like magic and roused an un-animous spirit of defence; and now with one voice we determined to maintain the city at all hazards, and each age and sex conjoined in the important cause'.

On 23 December 1688 James fled to France, and on 13 February 1689 William and his wife Mary, a Protestant daughter of James by his first marriage, were declared joint sovereigns of England, Scotland and Ireland. Louis XIV now persuaded James to go to Ireland to recover his kingdom; the French king's plan was to keep William busy in Ireland while he overwhelmed the Dutch Republic.

On 12 March 1689 a French fleet of twenty-two ships steered into the Bandon estuary and James stepped ashore at Kinsale. From there to Cork and north to Dublin the Irish turned out to give him a rapturous welcome, as one of his officers recalled:

> All along the road the country came to meet his majesty with staunch loyalty, profound respect, and tender love as if he had been an angel from heaven. All degrees of people and of both sexes were of the number, young and old; orations of welcome were made to him at the entrance to each town, and rural maids danced before him as he travelled.

Men took off their coats and laid them in the mud before his horses' hooves. In Carlow he 'was slobbered with the kisses of the rude countrywomen, so that he was forced to have them kept away from him'.

James entered Dublin in triumph on Palm Sunday. Two harpers played on a richly decorated stage; below it friars, holding a large cross, were singing; bells rang; guns fired in salute; and there were 'about forty oyster-women, poultry- and herb-women in white, dancing'. The Lord Mayor and Corporation presented James with the keys of the city while pipers played 'The King Enjoys His Own Again'. The king dismounted and approached Dublin Castle on foot. All fell silent as James received benediction from the Archbishop of Armagh. Overhead the white standard of the Stuarts was unfurled with the motto:

> *Now or Never*
> *Now and Forever*

Then a great cheer erupted from the dense crowd. These people were pinning all their hopes on this deposed king.

Meanwhile Louis xiv had sent out another formidable fleet. Over two thousand seasoned French troops came ashore, bringing with them engineers and an impressive quantity of munitions and artillery. Very soon King James had control of the whole island—or rather, *almost* the whole island, because there were two or three places in the north which refused to accept his authority. One of these was Derry.

Episode 108 ◠

'NO SURRENDER!'

On 7 December 1688, thirteen Protestant apprentice boys closed the gates of Derry against the forces of the Catholic King James II. The mayor expelled the remaining Catholics from the city and issued this proclamation:

> We have resolved to stand upon our guard and to defend our walls, and not to admit of any papists whatsoever to quarter amongst us.

On 22 March, King James arrived from France with a large professional army sent by Louis XIV. Meanwhile the 'Jacobites'—those who remained loyal to King James—were sweeping northwards.

On 14 March 1689 the Protestant gentlemen who had declared for William of Orange had suffered a crushing defeat in Co. Down—this was to become known as the 'Break of Dromore'. Lisburn, Belfast and Antrim fell to the Jacobites without a fight, and, after a brisk engagement in a snowstorm, the Coleraine garrison, 'Williamites' who supported William, pulled west to Derry. On the other side of Ulster the men of Enniskillen, also loyal to William, kept the Jacobites at a respectful distance with their long fowling pieces.

Meanwhile, from all over the north, Protestants poured into Derry, then under the command of Lieutenant-Colonel Robert Lundy. As well as a garrison of over 7,000 men, perhaps another 30,000 colonists sought sanctuary in the city. So, in a very real sense, the fate of the entire Protestant settlement in Ulster depended on Derry's ability to hold out.

In April men from the Derry garrison were overwhelmed by James's French and Irish troops. Driven out of their trenches at Lifford and Cladyford, about fifteen miles south-west of the city, Protestant foot-soldiers were hacked down, while their cavalry support ignominiously galloped in retreat back to Derry. Thomas Ash recorded in his diary that the Williamites had been beaten 'although we were five to one against them, which caused suspicion that Colonel Lundy was a traitor to our cause'.

When Lundy, the governor of Derry, refused the support of two regiments sent out from Liverpool, that suspicion became a certainty. The citizens revolted, overthrew Lundy, and appointed as joint governors in his place Major Henry Baker and the Rev. George Walker, the Church of Ireland rector of Donaghmore. They were to provide inspired leadership, and they both humanely allowed Lundy, disguised as a common soldier, to slip away over the walls. Walker described the prospects of a successful resistance:

We had but few horse to sally out with and no forage; no engineers to instruct us in our works; no Fireworks, not so much as a hand-grenado to annoy the enemy; nor a gun well mounted in the town.

Well-mounted or not, some of the guns in the city were impressive. The largest was 'Roaring Meg', given to the city in 1642 by the Fishmongers' Company. And there was no shortage of powder and handguns.

Exhilarated by the victory at Lifford and Cladyford, King James travelled from Dublin to join his besieging army. On 18 April he advanced towards the walls and offered terms. He was greeted with cries of 'No surrender!' This was followed by a sustained barrage of shot and ball from the city walls. Just out of range, James sat motionless on his horse for several hours in the pouring rain. Then the king was persuaded to return to Dublin, where the French ambassador observed that 'His Majesty appears to me to be very mortified over his latest proceeding'.

The Jacobites were badly equipped for a long siege. One French supply officer reported that 'most of the soldiers in front of Derry have still only pointed sticks, without iron tips'. A single mortar was the only artillery piece the besiegers possessed. More heavy guns arrived later, but these were not sufficient to attempt a breach of the walls, except at very close quarters. Indeed, the defenders made several audacious sallies from the city, mortally wounding two French generals.

The defenders had entrenched themselves on a hillock to the west of the city, where a windmill stood. The Jacobite general, Richard Hamilton, resolved to drive them back, as one of his Irish officers recalled:

General Hamilton, observing that the rebels made a walking place of this entrenched ground for the preservation of their health, and that they gave great annoyance with their cannon from the said mill and with their long fowling-pieces....Whereupon he commanded, on the sixth of May, an attack to be made upon the entrenchment.

The Jacobite assault was a complete failure. As an alternative strategy Hamilton drew the net tighter, cutting the city off from much of its water supply. Just downstream the French constructed a boom, made of fir beams fastened with chains, to stretch across the Foyle. Derry was now completely cut off.

Episode 109 ～

THE RELIEF OF DERRY

Since December 1688 the citizens of Derry, loyal to King William, had been under siege. At the end of May 1689 a train of heavy guns sent by King James arrived to intensify the bombardment of the city which had not ceased since the beginning of the siege. Governor George Walker recorded that the shells from one mortar lobbed into Derry weighed 270 pounds

> and contained several pounds of powder in the shell; they plowed up our streets and broke down our houses, so that there was no passing the streets or staying within doors, but all flock to the Walls and the remotest parts of the Town, where we continued very safe, while many of our sick were killed, not being able to leave their houses.

Captain George Holmes recalled:

> One bomb slew over seventeen persons. I was in the next room one night at my supper (which was but mean) and seven men were thrown out of the third room next to that we were in, all killed and some of them in pieces.

The walls were not breached, however, and the French general, the Marquis de Pointis, ruefully concluded that

> The state of affairs is such that attacking must no longer be thought of and it will be well if without raising the siege we shall have to wait on hunger.

After months of siege the defenders were starving. Walker's memoir provides a price list for July:

> Horse-flesh 1/8d a pound; a quarter of a dog 5/6d (fattened by eating the bodies of the slain Irish); a dog's head 2/6d; a cat 4/6d; a rat 1/0d; a mouse 6d; a small flook taken in the river, not to be bought for money ...

George Holmes observed:

> I believe there died 15,000 men, women and children, many of which died for want of meat. But we had a great fever amongst us and all the children died, almost whole families not one left alive.

Because of the fever, another survivor wrote,

> [people] died so fast at length as could scarce be found room to interr them, even the backsides and gardens were filled with graves, and some thrown in cellars; some whole families were entirely extinct.

Major-General Percy Kirke had sailed into Lough Foyle on 11 June with thirty vessels. But for six weeks he waited, unwilling to risk the Jacobite guns at Culmore downstream from Derry. Another deterrent was the floating boom across the Foyle constructed by French engineers. Meanwhile a young boy carried messages from Derry to the fleet concealed in his rectum. Finally, moved by pleas for help and a stern order from his superiors, Kirke made a move on Sunday 28 July. While one warship engaged Culmore, a longboat and three small vessels sailed up the Foyle.

The wind dropped completely, but the flowing tide pushed the leading vessel, the *Mountjoy*, against the boom, snapping its chains. The ship's captain died as he ordered his men to respond to the Jacobite guns, and the *Mountjoy*, stuck fast in the mud, was freed in the recoil to drift up to the city. To the disgust of an Irish Jacobite officer, the shore gunners were drunk with brandy and fired wildly:

> What shouts of joy the town gave hereat you may easily imagine, and what pangs of heart it gave to the loyal army you may easily conceive.... Lord, who seest the hearts of people, we leave the judgment of this affair to Thy mercy. In the interim those gunners lost Ireland through their neglect of duty.

Thomas Ash, who had survived the 105 days of siege, recorded in his diary:

> Oh! To hear the loud acclamations of the garrison soldiers round the Walls when the ships came to the quay.... The Lord, who has preserved this City from the Enemy, I hope will always keep it to the Protestants.

For the Protestants, this epic defence gave inspiration for more than three centuries to come.

In the meantime large numbers of Jacobites had been tied down for months in a vain attempt to starve Enniskillen into submission. The Protestant garrison, however, had broken out of the island town to rout the Jacobites at the 'break of Belleek', relieve Ballyshannon, and bring supplies from Donegal Bay up the Erne to Enniskillen.

Then, on the day that the *Mountjoy* was breaking the boom at Derry, Lieutenant-General Justin MacCarthy arrived with a formidable Jacobite army. The men of Enniskillen—soon to be known as Inniskillingers—advanced to Lisnaskea, drove back the Jacobites in confusion, and with the battle-cry 'No Popery' closed in on MacCarthy at Newtownbutler. With his much larger army, MacCarthy should have won, but his troops were not ready for the furious onslaught of the Inniskillingers. A merciless slaughter followed.

Episode 110 ～

SCHOMBERG

On Wednesday 31 July 1689, the very day King James II's army withdrew from Derry, the men of Enniskillen overwhelmed the Jacobite army at Newtownbutler. A confused order caused the Jacobite cavalry to turn tail, and then the foot-soldiers were driven to the marshy shores of Upper Lough Erne. The French ambassador in Dublin reported to his king:

> The cavalry and dragoons fled without firing a pistol, and after some of them had burst their horses with the force of flight, they took to their feet and threw away their weapons, their swords, and jackets, that they might run more swiftly.

Of 500 men who tried to swim across the lough, only one survived. The rest were hunted down and slain. The victors ruthlessly put over 2,000 Jacobites to the sword.

For William of Orange, the steadfast refusal of Derry to surrender and the victory of Newtownbutler provided a vital breathing space—they gave him a safe base in Ireland to drive out King James in a campaign which had just begun. The Duke of Schomberg's Williamite army met no opposition as it came ashore at Ballyholme Bay in north Down on 13 August. A contemporary news-sheet reported:

> The shore was all crowded with Protestants—men, women, and children—old and young, falling on their knees with tears in their eyes thanking God and the English for their deliverance.

Schomberg first closed in on Carrickfergus Castle. Pounded by cannon from land and sea, the defenders judged it safest for them to Capitulate and Surrender; ... the Town has been so miserably defaced, by the continual playing of the Bombs for five Days together, that it looks like a dismal heape of ruine.

The Jacobites were fortunate not to be lynched as they marched out of the castle, according to George Story, a Williamite army chaplain:

The Countrey people were so inveterate against them ... that they stript most part of the Women ... and so rude were the Irish Scots, that the Duke was forced to ride in among them, with his Pistol in his hand, to keep the Irish from being murdered.

Schomberg, an elderly French Huguenot veteran, was over-cautious. As he advanced south the Jacobites were given time to burn Newry to the ground. And when he camped north of Dundalk, he refused action. With their tents pitched by a marsh, Schomberg's soldiers were ravaged by fever. As George Story tells us, around 1,700 died at Dundalk and another 1,000 in vessels taking the sick back to Belfast:

Nay, so great was the Mortality, that several ships had all the Men in them dead, and no Body to look after them whilst they lay in the Bay at Carrickfergus. As for the Great Hospital at Belfast, there were 3,762 that died in it from the first of November to the first of May.... There were several that had their limbs so mortified in the Camp, afterwards, that some had their Toes, and some their whole Feet that fell off as the Surgeons were dressing them; so that upon the whole matter, we lost nigh one half of the Men that we took over with us.

With a heavy heart, William III realised he had no choice but to go to Ireland himself. Early in June 1690 he assembled an army of continental size at Hounslow Heath in London. Then a cavalry detachment went ahead to clear the road to Chester for a train of no fewer than 3,000 ox-carts stretching for more than eighteen miles—and these were carrying just the supplies, tents and ammunition bound for Ireland. Then Sir Cloudesley Shovell's squadron of warships escorted William's fleet of about 300 vessels across the Irish Sea into Belfast Lough on 14 June. The king stepped ashore at Carrickfergus, mounted his horse and

rode through the main streets of the town, where almost numberless crowds received him with continued shouts and acclamations on till the Whitehouse.

He drove along the lough shore with Schomberg to Belfast, where, as George Story records, they were met

> by a great concourse of People who at first could do nothing but Stare, never having seen a King before in that part of the World, but after a while some of them began to Huzzah, the rest took it up (as Hounds follow a Scent).

Never before had Belfast greeted so many men of distinction: Godard van Reede, Baron de Ginkel of Utrecht; Hans Willem Bentinck, the king's close adviser; the Duke of Würtemberg-Neustadt, the German commander of the Danish force; Count Henry Nassau; Prince Georg of Daamstadt, brother of Christian v of Denmark; the Duke of Ormond; and many others.

For a brief moment in history Ireland had become the cockpit of Europe.

Episode 111 ⌒

THE BATTLE OF THE BOYNE

William of Orange stepped ashore at Carrickfergus on 14 June 1690, and a few hours later he was in Belfast. Here he accepted a verse address from Belfast Corporation urging him to 'pull the stiff neck of every papist down'. Then the pale asthmatic monarch, his face lined with the constant pain of fighting ill-health, told the citizens in halting English that he had come to see that the people of Ireland would be 'settled in a lasting peace'. William III had with him by far the largest invading force Ireland had yet seen. Some of the Dutch guns required sixteen horses to pull them, and altogether William had more than one thousand horses to draw his artillery and gun equipment. One eyewitness in Belfast described in the scene:

> The Lough between this and Carrickfergus seems like a wood, there being no less than seven hundred sail of ships in it, mostly laden with provisions and ammunition.... The great numbers of coaches, waggons, baggage horses and the like is almost incredible to be supplied from England, or any of the biggest nations in Europe. I cannot think that any army of Christendom hath the like.

The Jacobites—the forces of King James II—withdrew from Dundalk to take up battle positions on the tidal south bank of the River Boyne, just west of Drogheda. William marched south and by Monday 30 June he had deployed his troops on the north side of the river. The international composition of his army underlined the fact that it represented the Grand Alliance against France, the world's greatest power. The core of his army was made up of Dutch, Danish, French Huguenot and German veterans of continental campaigns. His English troops were mostly raw recruits, reinforced by Ulster Protestant skirmishers, described by the army chaplain George Story as being 'half-naked with sabre and pistols hanging from their belts ... like a Horde of Tartars'.

Numbering 36,000, the Williamites were at least 10,000 stronger than the Jacobites and far superior in firepower. William was superstitiously opposed to doing anything important on a Monday, but according to Sir Robert Southwell:

His Majesty at his arrival yesterday near the river about 12 of the clock, rode in full view of the Irish army, which are ranged upwards on the other side. The enemy even discovered it must be his Majesty.... They began to fire and presently one of the balls past so close to his Majesty's back upon the blade of his right shoulder as to take away his outward coat, his chamois waist-coat, shirt and all to draw near half a spoonful of blood.

That night the bandaged king held a council of war with his generals. A detachment would ride inland to the fords at Slane, to make it look as if this would be where the main attack would be. Meanwhile, when the tide was right, he would direct a frontal assault across the river.

Sending troops upstream in a feint successfully drew the French away. This advantage having been gained, the ground shook as William's artillery pounded the Jacobite positions and the Dutch Blue Guards waded up to their armpits across the river at Oldbridge, holding their weapons over their heads. The Irish Jacobite cavalry fought back fiercely, but in the end the Williamites triumphed by superior firepower and weight of numbers. The Duke of Schomberg and the Rev. George Walker, the hero of the Siege of Derry, were killed in the fighting. To Southwell's alarm, William

weares his Star and Garter and will not disguise who he is.... His Majesty was here in the crowd of all, drawing his swoard & animating those that fled to follow him, His danger was great among the enemys guns which killed 30 of the Inniskillingers on the spott. Nay one of the Inniskillingers came with a Pistol cockt to his Majesty till he called out; What are you so angry with your friends! The truth is the cloaths of friends and foes are soe much alike.

The Battle of the Boyne was not a rout; the Irish and French retired in good order to fight for more than another year. Yet the battle was decisive. It was a severe blow to Louis xiv's pretensions to European domination, and it was celebrated by the singing of a *Te Deum* in thanks to God in Catholic Vienna. James ii could no longer think of Ireland as a springboard for recovering his throne. For the English, parliamentary rule was made secure. For the Old English and the Gaelic Irish, the defeat dashed hopes of recovering the lands they had lost in the days of Cromwell. For Ulster Protestants, the battle ensured the survival of their plantation and a victory to be celebrated from year to year.

Episode 112 〜

GALLOPING HOGAN, SARSFIELD AND THE WALLS OF LIMERICK

Here from my hand as from a cup
I pour this pure libation;
And ere I drink, I offer up
One fervent aspiration—
Let man with man, let kin with kin,
Contend through fields of slaughter—
Whoever fights, may freedom win,
As then, at the Boyne Water.

Following his rout at the Boyne on 1 July 1690, King James ii dashed straight for Dublin. Here he made an ungracious speech to his Privy Council. The Irish soldiers, he said, 'basely fled the field and left the spoil to the enemies, nor could they be prevailed upon to rally ... so that henceforth I never more determined to head an Irish army and do now resolve to shift for myself and so, gentlemen, must you'.

And shift for himself he did. Next day he left for Waterford to sail for France, never to return. No wonder the Irish Jacobite commander, Patrick Sarsfield, observed: 'Change but kings and we will fight you over again.'

The Jacobite army adopted Sarsfield's plan to withdraw westwards and hold a line running along the River Shannon. William iii made his camp just north of the city at Finglas, and on Sunday 6 July the 'Deliverer' entered the city in triumph, listened to a sermon in St Patrick's Cathedral, and watched the Dublin Protestants run about 'shouting and embracing one another and blessing God for his wonderful deliverance as if they had been alive from the dead'.

King William was anxious to move on in pursuit of the Jacobites. He had reason to be worried because he had just received bad news: on the day before his victory at the Boyne the French fleet had inflicted a disastrous defeat on the English navy at Beachy Head. And he had information that Louis xiv was sending to Ireland twenty-four additional vessels with men and munitions.

During William's slow progress southwards by Waterford and Carrick-on-Suir the Jacobites worked frantically to improve the defences of Limerick. On 7 August William halted about eight miles south west of the city to await the arrival of his train of heavy guns and carts drawn by no fewer than 400 horses. But at midnight on 9 August Patrick Sarsfield stole out of Limerick with 500 men. Guided by 'Galloping' Michael Hogan through the Tipperary mountains, in the following night they surreptitiously drew near to the siege train of 153 wagons which had made camp in a meadow. The password, curiously, was 'Sarsfield'—this 'Galloping' Hogan discovered from an old woman selling apples. So, when challenged in the dark by a sentry, Sarsfield cried out: 'Sarsfield is the word, and Sarsfield is the man!'

Carters and horses were ruthlessly cut down; but the life of one gunner was spared in return for demonstrating how the cannon could be put out of action. Then 800 cannon-balls, 12,000 pounds of gunpowder, 1,600 barrels of match and 500 hand-grenades, along with tin pontoon boats, were heaped in circle and a long powder trail laid. Hogan lit the fuse. The earth shook with the explosion, the loudest man-made sound yet heard in Ireland, and people far away in Co. Clare were wakened from their beds. After a brief silence there followed the crumbling sound of the ruined Ballyneety Castle close by, crashing down from the shock waves. The holes left in the ground by the explosion can still be seen today.

King William had to wait for heavy guns from Waterford before he could begin to besiege Limerick. Using sacks of wool as protection against bullets and shrapnel, the Dutch got the cannon close to the walls of Limerick and made a breach. On the afternoon of 27 August the Williamites assaulted the breach. John Stevens, an English Jacobite unhesitatingly branding William's men as 'rebels', was one of the defenders and left a record of the events that followed:

The word was given to fire, which was performed so effectually that a considerable number of the rebels dropped.... Nothing daunted they pressed over, fresh men succeeding those that were killed or wounded.... The fight was for some time renewed and continued with sword in hand and the butt end of the musket.... The action continued hot and dubious for at least three hours ... till the enemy wholly drew off. A great slaughter was made of them ... there could not be much less than 3,000 killed.

One of the Williamite officers, a Dane, wrote in a report to his king:

The very women, prone as they are to violent passions, have since then become more furious ... they caused as much, indeed more, damage than the garrison by throwing huge stones on the assailants, of whom a great number thus perished.

It was clear there would be no quick end to this war.

Episode 113 ⌒

ATHLONE AND AUGHRIM: JUNE–JULY 1691

Saturday the 30th: in the morning we observed there was great silence in the enemy's works and day appearing we could not perceive any body in them.... Immediately the word was carried ... that the rebels had raised the siege and stole away in the dead of night.

So John Stevens, an English Jacobite, described how the 'rebels', the Williamites, withdrew from their attempt to seize the city of Limerick in August 1690. King William returned to direct affairs from London. The Jacobites, holding the River Shannon and all the land to the west of it, and delighted by their recent success, refused offers of a compromise peace.

William appointed Godard van Reede, Baron de Ginkel, as his commander in Ireland. It was a wise choice. Campaigning was a miserable affair during the persistent rains of winter. On 27 December Ginkel wrote: 'The enemy are burning all before us, and the Rapparees are so great a number that we can find neither forage nor cover, which hinders much our march.' Named from their main weapon, a short pike known in Irish as a *rapaire*, the rapparees were Irish skirmishers. They did much to frustrate Ginkel's attempts to bring the war in Ireland to a conclusion.

As well as reinforcements and fresh supplies sent by Louis xiv, the Jacobites acquired a new commander, Charles Chaumont, the Marquis de Saint-Ruth.

St Ruth had no fewer than 16,000 foot-soldiers, 3,000 cavalry and 2,000 dragoons to stop Ginkel—with a smaller force—from taking Athlone, a town at a vital crossing of the Shannon.

Ginkel launched the heaviest bombardment ever in Irish history on the night of 21 June 1691. For ten days, without let-up, the town and Jacobite fortifications were pounded and reduced to rubble. John Stevens was in the thick of the fighting in defence of the bridge over the Shannon:

> Sunday the 28th: continued playing incessantly.... The great and small shot never ceased firing.... The enemy bent thirty pieces of cannon and all their mortars in that way, so that what with the fire and what with the balls and bombs flying so thick that spot was a mere Hell on Earth, and so many cannon and mortars incessantly playing on it there seemed to be no likelihood of any man coming off alive.... We had very many men killed here.... And I think this was the hottest place that ever I saw in my time of service.

But how was the Shannon, the largest river in these islands, to be crossed? In spite of the artillery barrage, attempts to seize the bridge at Athlone failed, as the Rev. George Story recorded:

> We labour hard to gain the bridge, but what we got there was inch by inch as it were, the enemy sticking very close to it, though great numbers of them were slain by our guns.

Ginkel decided to test a ford below Athlone. On 7 June he sent three Danes under sentence of death for mutiny to try the crossing in return for their lives. Yes, they reported—after wading across and back—the river was fordable. On 30 June 1691 the assault began. A church bell gave the signal for the grenadiers to enter the water, which came up to their chests. Each man had been given a golden guinea to whet his courage.

The Jacobites, caught from behind, were completely taken by surprise. In less than half an hour Athlone fell to King William's army. St Ruth pulled back sixteen miles to the south-west, near to the village of Aughrim. There he prepared a set-piece battle on the limestone Galway plain. His plan was to lure the Williamites into a treacherous bog in front of his line.

At first these tactics seemed to work. A thick mist enveloped Ginkel's army as it moved out of Ballinasloe on Sunday 12 July. Ginkel's Huguenots were drawn into the bog, cut off and slaughtered, while the Danes strove in vain to relieve them. The Irish pikemen stood firm even when, it was reported, 'the blood flowed into their shewse', and Ulster Jacobites, led by Gordon O'Neill, spiked a battery of Williamite guns. In anticipation of a speedy victory, St Ruth cried out: 'Le jour est à nous, the day is ours, mes enfants!'

At that moment a cannon-ball, fired at extreme range, took off his head. This chance incident created total confusion in the Jacobite ranks. Guided by members of the Trench family, French Protestants who had settled in Co. Galway, Ginkel sent his cavalry by a causeway over the bog. As these horsemen made a devastating assault over this narrow stretch of dry ground, the Jacobite cavalry—the flower of the Old English gentry of Ireland—turned tail and abandoned their foot-soldiers to their fate.

Episode 114 ∿

LIMERICK: A SECOND SIEGE AND A TREATY

Fought on the plains of Galway on Sunday 12 July 1691, the Battle of Aughrim was the bloodiest battle ever fought on Irish soil. The French commander, the Marquis de Saint-Ruth, three major-generals, seven brigadiers, twenty-two colonels, seventeen lieutenant-colonels and over seven thousand other ranks were killed. When news of this victory for King William's army, commanded by Baron de Ginkel, spread north, the Protestants of Ulster set bonfires ablazing, as they would do year after year thereafter.

The French and the Irish Jacobites—supporters of James II, the deposed king now in France—decided to make a last stand in Limerick city. Patrick Sarsfield took over command from the Duke of Tyrconnell, King James's dying Lord Deputy. An intense contest ensued. The Siege of Derry two years earlier was the longest siege in this war and the most decisive. But this second siege of Limerick was a far more extensive affair, and was conducted on a scale never again equalled in Irish history.

The Rev. George Story, an English chaplain in Ginkel's army, described what happened in his journal:

September the 8th, our new Batteries were all ready; one to the left of ten Field-pieces, to shoot red hot Ball; another to the right of 25 Guns, all 24 and 18 Pounders; and in the Center were placed eight Mortars.... These stood altogether upon the North-east of the Town nigh the Island: then there were 8 Guns of 12 pound Ball each, planted at Mackay's fort; and some also towards the River on the South-west, where the Danes were posted.

Those fell to work all at a time, and put the Irish into such a fright, that a great many of them wish'd themselves in another place, having never heard such a Noise before, or I hope never shall in that Kingdom. One of the great Mortars had a shell burst in her, flinging the Mortar and Carriage from the Flooring; which is demonstration, that the firing of the Fuse before you give fire to the Mortar, is neither the readiest nor the safest way, but this was the method of all our Foreign Bombadeers....We threw Bombs, Fireballs and Carcasses all day long, and our Guns were discharged almost without ceasing; by which there appeared a considerable Breach in the Wall.

This furious bombardment continued without let-up for the next fortnight. Then Ginkel decided to storm the gaping breach in the walls, as George Story records:

> September the 22d ... For our Granadeers were so very forward, and despised all Dangers to that degree, that they put the whole Body to flight in despight of their Forts, Cannon, and all other Advantages, and pursued them so close, that a French Major who commanded at Thoumond Gate, fearing our mens entring the Town with their own, he ordered the Draw-bridg to be pluck'd up, and left the whole Party to the Mercy of our Souldiers.

By raising the drawbridge at Thomond Gate, that French officer left Jacobites stranded outside to certain slaughter:

> Those that were left behind, pressing the others forward, [threw] them down over the Fall of the Draw-bridg: then the rest cried out for Quarter, holding up their Handkerchiefs, and what else they could get: but before killing was over, they were laid in Heaps upon the Bridg higher than the Ledges of it; so that they were either all killed or taken.... The number of the dead is said to be six hundred, amongst whom we may reckone over hundred fifty four that were drowned in being forced over the Fall of the Draw-bridg.

On the following day Ginkel wrote to William's representatives in Dublin to assure them that it was impossible for him to take the city of Limerick by assault. He told them how vigorously the Irish had defended themselves the previous day: 'They do not fear fire and were very steady in the charge.' That same day, however, the French and the Irish held a council of war and agreed to ask Ginkel for a capitulation and a ceasefire. The ensuing discussions were conducted with great courtesy—helped, no doubt, by a boatload of Bordeaux wine brought over for the Williamite officers by Patrick Sarsfield. By 3 October 1691 terms had been agreed and both sides signed what became known as the Treaty of Limerick.

The articles of the treaty appeared lenient. But it was one thing for a Dutch general to sign a generous treaty to end a war. It was quite another for the Protestant gentlemen in the Westminster and Dublin parliaments to agree to those terms. With very good reason, the Treaty of Limerick was to become known as the 'Broken Treaty', and it embittered relations between the Irish and the English for more than two centuries.

Episode 115 ∿

THE WILD GEESE

On 5 October 1691 a great French fleet entered the Shannon below Limerick. Only two days earlier, the defeated Jacobites had signed the Treaty of Limerick. Patrick Sarsfield, their leader, fell silent and then said: 'Too late, our honour is pledged.... We must keep our plighted troth.'

All things considered, the treaty signed with Baron de Ginkel, King William III's general, was a fair one. Those officers and men who had surrendered and were to remain in Ireland would be pardoned. They would keep their property, provided they gave an oath of allegiance to King William and Queen Mary. If they were gentlemen, they could ride with a sword and a case of pistols and keep a gun in their houses. Catholics all over Ireland were to have freedom of worship. The same terms applied to civilians in the western counties under Jacobite control at the time of the ceasefire.

Those Jacobites who preferred to join the armies of Louis XIV could leave for France. Within a short time some 5,000 had sailed away from Limerick with the French fleet. Ginkel actually agreed to pay for the ships to take the rest, and around another 7,000 Jacobite soldiers thereupon opted to leave for France. Sarsfield was with those who crowded aboard vessels for the last sailing on 22 December.

Here in Cork harbour there was room enough for the Jacobite soldiers—but not for all their wives and children. The historian Macaulay later penned a memorable description:

> ... there still remained at the waterside a great multitude clamouring piteously to be taken on board. As the last boats pulled off there was a rush into the surf. Some women caught hold of the ropes, were dragged out into the depth, clung till their fingers were cut through and perished in the waves. The ships began to move. A wild and terrible wail arose from the

shore and excited unwanton passion in hearts steeled by hatred of the Irish race and of the Romish faith. Even the stern Cromwellian ... could not hear unmoved the bitter cry, in which poured forth all the rage and sorrow of a conquered nation.

Certainly Colonel Charles O'Kelly, one of Sarsfield's officers, recorded this departure as a tragic moment in the island's history:

And now, alas! The saddest day is come that ever appeared above the horizon of Ireland; the sun was darkened and covered over with a black cloud, as if unwilling to behold such a woeful spectacle; there needed no rain to bedew the earth; for the tears of the disconsolate Irish did abundantly moisten their native soil, to which they were that day to bid the last farewell. Those who resolved to leave it never hoped to see it again; and those who made the unfortunate choice to continue therein, could at the same time have nothing in prospect but contempt and poverty, chains and imprisonment, and in a word, all the miseries that a conquered nation could naturally expect from the power and malice of implacable enemies.

One anonymous poet in his long lament expressed in Gaelic the sorrow of many. In translation, one verse reads:

Farewell, Patrick Sarsfield, wherever you may roam,
You crossed the seas to France and left empty camps at home,
To plead our cause before many a foreign throne
Though you left ourselves and poor Ireland overthrown.

The Jacobite exiles soon became known as the 'Wild Geese'. Unlike the myriads of white-fronted, barnacle and brent geese which fly in from the north every autumn, very few of these Jacobite Wild Geese ever returned to Ireland.

Meanwhile Ginkel took his copy of the Treaty of Limerick with him to London. There he explained to the Privy Council that one clause had been mistakenly left out. That was the article which extended the terms of the treaty to the civilian population under the protection of the Jacobite army. To his horror, the Privy Council refused to allow the 'missing clause' to be reinserted. This was the first step towards the mutilation of the treaty. King William willingly signed the treaty himself. Others were not so willing.

A contemporary broadsheet entitled *A smart poem on the generous articles of Limerick and Galway* put forward the view that Ginkel had been outwitted by the Jacobite negotiators:

Hard fate that still attends our Irish war,
The conquerors lose, the conquered gainers are;
Their pen's the symbol of our sword's defeat,
We fight like heroes but like fools we treat.

Soon it became clear that members of both the Westminster and Dublin parliaments would refuse to accept the Treaty of Limerick.

The outcome of this 'Broken Treaty' was a succession of acts passed by both parliaments which collectively would become known as the Penal Laws.

Episode 116 ～

THE PENAL LAWS

Whereas, it is Notoriously known, that the late Rebellions in this Kingdom have been Contrived, Promoted and Carried on by Popish Archbishops, Bishops, Jesuits, and other Ecclesiastical persons of the Romish Clergy. And forasmuch as the Peace and Publick Safety of this Kingdom is in Danger ... which said Romish Clergy do, not only endeavour to withdraw his Majesty's Subjects from their Obedience but do daily stir up, and move Sedition, and Rebellion, to the great hazard of the Ruine and Desolation of this Kingdom ...

So began a bill put forward in the Irish parliament to exile monks, friars, Jesuits and the Catholic hierarchy in 1695. Because the Emperor Leopold of Austria, then in alliance with Britain against Louis xiv of France, objected to it, the bill was set aside. Once the war was over in 1697, however, it was passed triumphantly into law. Other penal laws against Catholics followed rapidly, one after another.

The initiative for this anti-Catholic legislation had been taken in England. As early as 1691 Westminster passed a law that no MP could sit in the Irish parliament or hold public office who had not sworn against transubstantiation—that is, the actual turning of bread and wine at the Eucharist into the body and blood of Christ. No Catholic could take such an oath, since it denied the validity of the Mass.

William viewed the strident demand for further laws against Catholics with some distaste. But in the spring of 1702 the king's horse tripped on a molehill; William was thrown to the ground, breaking his collarbone, and died shortly afterwards from complications arising from his injury. Anne, the Protestant daughter of James II, was now queen.

No longer held back by William of Orange, and encouraged by Queen Anne, both parliaments set about drafting fresh laws to restrict the rights of Catholics. The 1704 'Act to prevent the further growth of popery' was the crowning piece of this legislation. It represented the final dismantling of the terms agreed between the forces of King James and those of King William at Limerick in 1691.

These laws—known as the Penal Code—were enacted over a long period— thirty-nine years in fact. The final penal law, depriving Catholics of the vote, did not enter the statute book until 1728. The principal laws can be sum-marised as follows:

- No Catholic could buy land.
- No Catholic could have a lease on a farm for longer than thirty-one years. The rent was to be at least two-thirds of the holding's yearly value.
- When a Catholic died, his estate was not be inherited by the eldest son, but would be divided equally among all the sons. If one son became a Protestant, he could inherit the entire estate.
- No Catholic could become a barrister, a solicitor, a judge or a member of a grand jury.
- Catholics could not sit in parliament or vote in elections.
- Catholics could not hold public office—for example, a Catholic could not be a civil servant, a sheriff, or a member of a town council.
- Catholics could neither send their children abroad to be educated nor establish schools at home.
- Catholics could not be guardians of orphans.
- Catholics could not carry arms, join the army, or own a horse worth more than £5.
- Catholics were excluded from living in many important provincial towns.
- Catholics could worship freely, but their churches could not have steeples or display crosses. Priests were not to wear clerical garb or holy emblems in public; they had to register with the government and take an oath of loyalty. Archbishops, bishops, Jesuits and other regular clergy (monks and friars) had to leave the country.
- Catholic pilgrimages, especially the one at Lough Derg in Co. Donegal, were forbidden.

All legislation put forward in the Irish parliament had to have the approval of the English Privy Council. Much enthusiastic fine-tuning went on between Dublin and London. One letter from the Irish Privy Council to London explained:

The Commons proposed the marking of every priest who shall be convicted of being an unregistered priest ... remaining in this kingdom after 1st May 1720 with a large 'P' to be made with a red hot iron on the cheek. The council generally disliked that punishment, and have altered it into that of castration, which they are persuaded will be the most effectual remedy.

Actually the English Privy Council ruled out both suggested punishments as being too barbaric. It soon transpired that many of these Penal Laws were impossible to enforce. But the laws concerned with political rights, jobs and landed property were rigidly imposed, with long-term consequences. They created what became known as the 'Protestant Ascendancy'.

Episode 117 ∿

'THE MINORITY PREVAILING OVER THE MAJORITY'

What is often forgotten is that some of the Penal Laws passed in the 1690s and in the early eighteenth century applied not only to Catholics but also to Presbyterians—indeed, to all 'Dissenters' (the term generally applied to those Protestants who were not members of the Church of Ireland). Presbyterians could not be married legally except in a Church of Ireland church and in a ceremony performed by a Church of Ireland clergyman. In 1701 the Presbyterians of Belfast sent a petition to the Lord Lieutenant in Dublin demanding the repeal of this law which obliged 'persons so married publickly to confess themselves guilty of the damnable sin of fornication ... their children ... being bastards'.

Then in 1704 the English Privy Council added a clause to the 'Bill to prevent the further growth of popery'. It stated that any person holding public office must produce a certificate proving that he had received communion in a Church of Ireland church. Since Catholics were already disqualified by previous penal laws, this sacramental test was really directed at Presbyterians. When the bill became law, Dissenters could no longer be members of municipal corporations—that is, town councils—and they could not serve as officers in the army or the militia.

Ulster Presbyterians were outraged by this 'test', but at the same time they were among the most eager supporters of the 1704 Popery Bill. They kept their complaints reasonably polite. It was an English Dissenter, Daniel Defoe, who from his cell in Newgate Prison launched a fierce attack on the test. He declared that since the end of King William's war in 1691 Ulster Presbyterians

> instead of being remembered to their honour ... have been ranked amongst the worst enemies of the church, and chained to a bill to prevent the further growth of popery.... Will any man in the world tell us that to divide the Protestants is a way to prevent the further growth of popery, when their united force is little enough to keep it down? This is like sinking the ship to drown the rats, or cutting off the foot to cure the corns.

Those with fond memories of reading *Robinson Crusoe* might be a little startled to discover that its author was so very keen on the suppression of Catholics. And Catholics were those who suffered most acutely: the Penal Laws were overwhelmingly directed at them. As one Chief Justice put it very bluntly, 'The law does not suppose any such person to exist as an Irish Roman Catholic.'

Defoe's standpoint was typical of his time. Only a few eccentric Quakers and retired Dutch soldiers thought that religious toleration had anything to recommend it. William King, the Church of Ireland Archbishop of Dublin, wrote a book justifying laws depriving Catholics of their rights. He declared:

> Upon the whole, the Irish may justly blame themselves ... for whatever they have, or shall suffer in the issue of this matter, since it is apparent that the necessity was brought about by them, that either they or we must be ruined.

Similar penal laws were imposed on Huguenots in France and Protestants in Silesia. But the difference was that in Ireland the Penal Code was applied by a *minority* to a *majority*. As the eighteenth century wore on, and more enlightened views gained acceptance, this wholesale legal suppression of Catholics attracted growing critical comment. The situation inspired a terse observation from the writer Samuel Johnson:

> The Irish are in a most unnatural state, for we see there the minority prevailing over the majority. There is no instance even in the Ten Persecutions, of such severity as that which the Protestants of Ireland have exercised against the Catholics.

Edmund Burke, the Irishman who became a leading politician at Westminster in the late eighteenth century, described the Penal Laws as

> a machine of wise and deliberate contrivance, as well fitted for the oppression, impoverishment and degradation of a people, and the debasement of

human nature itself, as ever proceeded from the perverted ingenuity of man.

The Penal Laws were directed principally at Catholics of education and property. The aim was the disarming and 'dismounting' of Catholic gentlemen so that they could never again organise and conduct a rebellion. The most effective legislation deprived the Catholic elite of political and economic power. Humble Catholic farmers and labourers, humiliated though they might be, were not so severely affected, for the Penal Laws were not really concerned with the Catholic lower orders. Defeat in previous wars and rebellions had already shattered the Gaelic nobility. Now the Old English gentry—Catholic descendants of the original Norman colonists, for the most part—lost almost everything.

Those who gained from the ruin of the Catholic gentry were Protestant landowners and their relatives—those who would eventually become known as the 'Protestant Ascendancy'.

Episode 118 ⌇

THE PROTESTANT ASCENDANCY

William of Orange had done his best to keep the terms of the Treaty of Limerick—the signed agreement in 1691 which ended his war with the Jacobites. He had kept his word and, at his own expense, transported thousands of Irish soldiers to France. Out of 1,300 Catholics who registered claims to keep their property under the terms of the treaty, only sixteen had been refused.

But the Protestant gentlemen of the Irish parliament, warmly supported by Westminster, hated the terms of the treaty. When they finally got round to approving the treaty *six years* after it had been signed, it had been mutilated beyond recognition. The key clause allowing Catholics religious toleration had been dropped altogether. So too had the clause which protected civilians from confiscation of their property in specified areas of the west of Ireland.

King William's war in Ireland had cost over £6 million sterling. At least some of this vast debt could be met by taking away yet more land still held by Catholics. Close to a million acres of land were confiscated. First the government seized the estates of those Jacobites who had been killed or captured in the war. Then officers of the crown took possession of the lands of Jacobites who had chosen to go into exile in France. Estates of Catholics who stayed in Ireland and who had backed King James in any way were also duly forfeited.

The Treaty of Limerick specifically protected the property of Catholic civilians in much of the west of Ireland. The Irish parliament refused to accept that clause. So the estates of most of those Catholics were also confiscated. Even after lavish grants had been made to those who had served the crown well, there was an extraordinary amount of land suddenly made available for sale.

The result was that the bottom dropped out of the Irish land market. After all, of course, only Protestants were allowed to buy. A consortium of London merchants, adopting the curious title of 'The Company for Making Hollow Sword-Blades in England', was able to buy a great deal of confiscated land at a knockdown price. The lawyer William Conolly was one of those with ready cash and a good business head who made a fortune from dealing in land. The son of a native Irish innkeeper from Ballyshannon, he became a Protestant, the Speaker of the Irish House of Commons, and the richest man in Ireland.

In 1688 Catholics held 22 per cent of the land of Ireland. By the time that Queen Anne died in 1714 only 14 per cent was left to them. By 1780 the proportion of land owned by Catholics—three-quarters of the population—had dropped to an all-time low of 5 per cent. How can this be explained?

For a start, the Penal Laws prevented Catholics from buying land. In addition, when the head of a Catholic family died, his estate had to be divided equally among his sons. Many of those farms, when split up in this way, were no longer commercially viable. Furthermore, if one son became a Protestant, he could inherit the entire estate.

Only 5,500 Catholics officially converted to the Established Church—that is, the Church of Ireland—between 1703 and 1789. However, these converts were drawn almost exclusively from the Catholic gentry eager to avoid subdivision of their estates and to find careers for younger sons in the legal profession, which was, of course, open only to Protestants. These high-profile conversions significantly reduced the percentage of land held by Catholics. Virtually no Catholic estate of any significance was left in the entire province of Ulster when Alexander MacDonnell, the fifth Earl of Antrim, 'turned' when he reached the age of twenty-one in 1734.

The term 'Protestant Ascendancy' only appeared for the first time during debates in the Irish parliament in the 1790s. But it very neatly describes the charmed circle of Anglican (that is Church of Ireland) aristocrats, landlords, clergy and prosperous lawyers, along with their relatives, which formed Ireland's highly privileged elite in the eighteenth century.

Members of the Ascendancy showed no enthusiasm for schemes to convert the popish natives. After all, they had no interest in seeing their privileged and exclusive community expanded too much. Their view was stated with brutal clarity by Lord Drogheda:

I shall be very glad to see the Protestant religion strengthened; but what will we do for hewers of wood and drawers of water, for labouring men to plough our lands, thresh our corn, etc?

Meanwhile the island was entering a century of peace—the longest peace that modern Ireland has enjoyed. Certainly John Dunton, an English bookseller, did not witness a single act of violence during his tour across Ireland in 1698.

Episode 119 ∾

JOHN DUNTON EATS AND SLEEPS IN CONNEMARA

John Dunton, a London bookseller, arrived in Dublin in April 1698 and, keen to visit the wildest part of Ireland, headed westwards to Galway and on to Connemara. He was particularly glad that he had brought with him a plentiful supply of tobacco, for he found it ensured a welcome wherever he went:

My guide was a gentleman descended from one who had been a master of some estate, but the sins of his father in rebellion fell upon him ... he had been a soldier in the late war.... I had with me a pocket bottle of usque bagh or aqua vitae, a dram of which and a pipe of tobacco regaled him sufficiently, and with this treatment he was soe well satisfied that he never complain'd.

This gentleman, as a mark of his standing in society, had a greyhound with him, which managed to run down and kill a hare—which was just as well, since they had run out of food.

In the evening we came to a place where one of my guide's relations dwelt.... At the place we alighted the people of the house swept it immediately, and gave us a reception fuller of humanity than I could hope for from appearing so barbarous; some of them brought in back-burdens of rushes, green and fresh cutt, with which they made a long thing like a bed to repose my selfe on; I distributed some tobacco among them which highly obliged them.

I layd me down upon my couch of rushes to repose my selfe and desir'd the hare might be gotten ready for supper; I soe much doubted their cookerie that I prayed them to spare them selves the trouble of roasting it; and to let me have it boyled; presently the wife of the house, who was a woman of middle age, well flesht and ruddy complexiond, only a little colour'd with the sun ... presently tooke out an olde horse's hide and layd it on the floore, upon which she placed her querns or hand mill stones betwixt her legs which were naked, and stripping up her clothes to the bottom of her belly which exposed her thighs bare as her face, she opened a small bagg of about three pecks of dried oates and fell to grinding verie lustily....

When she had ground her oates ... with a little water she made a triangular cake against a little wodden stool like a tripod, the bakeing of which was committed to the care of her mother, an old woman who was all the while either cramming, sneezeing into her nose wipeing away the snivell with the same hands that she turn'd my oaten cake, which made my gutts wamble.... Well, the oaten cake was sett next to me, at the lower end of our stoole or table was placed a great roll of fresh butter of three pound at least, and a wodden vessel full of milk and water. Then enters the landlady's daughter with her haire finely plaited ... in her hand she brought the hare swimming in a wodden boul full of oyl of butter.... I pretended weariness and desired an egg which the daughter presently gott ready. I envited the family to sitt down with my guide.... Thus they devour'd the hare and I my egg which was the only thing I could eate after the sluttish preparations I had been witness of; well, drink I must, tho what I had seen made me nauseate everie vessel. I shut my eyes ... but for feare of making any ungratefull discoveries in my liquor, which I powr'd down eagerly enough that I might be the sooner ridd of it....

Thus supper ended and I made a dole of my tobacco to everyone againe, which they received with all the expressions of gratitude they could shew.... I had just compos'd my selfe to sleep when I was strangely surprised to heare the cows and sheep all comeing into my bed chamber. I enquired the meaning and was told it was to preserve them from the wolfe which everie night was rambling about for prey. I found the beasts lay down soone after they had enter'd ... and truly if the nastiness of theire excrements did not cause an aversion hereto, the sweetness of theire breath which I was not sensible of before, and the pleaseing noise they made in ruminating or chawing the cudd, would lull a body to sleep as soon as the noys of a murmuring brook and the fragrancy of a bed of roses.

When he returned to Dublin, Dunton was able to sell all *ten tons* of books he had brought from London. It was striking evidence that Dublin was fast becoming the second city of the British Empire.

Episode 120 ~

WOOD'S HALFPENCE AND THE DRAPIER

In the early eighteenth century Dublin was thriving. The Protestant nobility and gentry built mansions and rented houses in elegant Georgian squares. The 'quality', as Dubliners called them, wanted to be in the capital not only for the winter social season, but also for the duration of the parliamentary sessions.

The Irish parliament only represented the Protestant Ascendancy, the country's landed elite. Protestant bishops, archbishops and nobles sat in the Lords, and seats in the Commons were for the most part owned or controlled by them. MPs tended to be younger brothers, sons or nominees of the nobility. There was never more than a handful of Presbyterian MPs, and, of course, Catholics could neither vote nor be members of parliament.

Yet it was in this privileged, unrepresentative parliament that the origins of modern Irish nationalism can be found. Bills put forward in the Irish Commons had to have London's approval, and, when passed, they could be amended or, indeed, suppressed by the English Privy Council. In addition, the Westminster parliament could pass laws for Ireland. It often did so. In 1698 one Irish MP, William Molyneux, denounced these powers in a pamphlet entitled *The Case of Ireland's being Bound by Acts of Parliament in England Stated.* Undaunted, Westminster passed a Woollen Act in 1699 forbidding the export of Irish woollen goods in order to protect the interests of English producers. This drastic legislation, which killed off a thriving trade, caused an outrage which united Protestants and Catholics alike.

Born in Dublin and now Dean of St Patrick's, Jonathan Swift lived among the poor weavers of the Coombe, a congested warren of streets close to the cathedral. His concern for their welfare led him in 1720 to write, anonymously, an angry pamphlet entitled *A Proposal for the Universal Use of Irish Manufacture ... utterly Rejecting and Renouncing Everything Wearable that comes from England.* His argument was summed up in vivid and forceful language:

> Upon the whole, and to crown all the rest, let a firm Resolution be taken, by *Male* and *Female*, never to appear with one single *Shred* that comes from *England*; and let all the People say, AMEN.... I could wish our Shopkeepers would immediately think on this *Proposal*.... I think it needless to exhort the *Clergy* to follow this good Example [and] will think themselves abundantly happy when they can afford Irish Crape, and an Athlone Hat.

Then in 1722 the English government gave William Wood, a Wolverhampton ironmaster, a patent for the minting of a great quantity of halfpennies and farthings for Ireland. Wood had given King George 1's mistress, the Duchess of Kendal, £10,000 in return for using her influence, so clearly he was expecting to make a handsome profit. The Irish were certain they were going to be ruined by having debased coinage foisted on them. Once again Swift joined the fray, even though he was in the middle of writing his masterpiece, *Gulliver's Travels*:

> But Mr WOOD made his HALF-PENCE of such *Base Metal*, and so much smaller than the *English* ones, that the *Brazier* would hardly give you above a *Penny* of good Money for a *Shilling* of his; so that this sum of £108,000 in good Gold and Silver, must be given for TRASH that will not be worth above *Eight or Nine Thousand Pounds* real Value.... But this same Mr WOOD was able to attend constantly for his own Interest; he is an ENGLISHMAN and had great FRIENDS, and it seems knew very well where to give Money, to those that speak to OTHERS that could speak to the KING, and would tell a FAIR STORY.
>
> THEREFORE, my Friends, stand to it One and All: Refuse this *Filthy Trash*.

He signed himself 'M. B. Drapier', posing as a draper dealing in woollen cloth. But even the dogs in the street knew that the author was Jonathan Swift. He had become a national hero overnight. The government frantically tried to prosecute the printer, but no jury could be found to convict him. In the Irish House of Commons MPs deserted the government benches to join the opposition, now calling themselves 'Patriots', to vote overwhelmingly against 'Wood's Halfpence'. The outcome was that in 1725 the government decided that it had no alternative but to withdraw Wood's patent and his notorious halfpence.

Swift added to his hugely popular series of *Drapier's Letters*. The Patriots particularly delighted in his fourth letter in which he declared 'that by the laws of God, of nature, of nations, and of your own country, you are and ought to be as free a people as your brethren in England'. And he did not confine his strictures to the English government. He included

> our Country Landlords; who, by unmeasurable *screwing* and *racking* their Tenants all over the Kingdom, have already reduced the miserable *People* to a worse *Condition* than the *Peasants* in *France*, or the *Vassals* in *Germany* and *Poland*.

Episode 121 ∾

A MODEST PROPOSAL

Ireland in the early 1700s was an island of stark contrasts. At the top of Irish society there were men who were as rich as German princes. These were the winners in the wars and convulsions of the previous century. At the bottom rungs of society were families who owned little or nothing, cultivating the soil with spades, working for farmers, or renting patches of land. Lacking the protection of leases, these people were 'rack-rented', that is, they paid rents which were generally raised from year to year to the very limit of what they could pay.

Angered by the ruthless exploitation of the rural poor, Jonathan Swift, Dean of St Patrick's Cathedral in Dublin, launched a savage attack on the landlords in a pamphlet published in 1729. It was entitled *A Modest Proposal for Preventing the Children of Ireland, from Being a Burden to their Parents or Country; and for Making them Beneficial to the Publick*. Since he believed the landlords treated their domestic animals better than the poor people who worked for them, he set out to shock his readers with terrible irony: he suggested that the peasantry should raise their babies to be served for dinner at the tables of the rich.

> I have been assured by a very knowing American of my Acquaintance in *London*; that a young healthy Child, well nursed, is at a Year old, a most delicious, nourishing, and wholesome Food; whether *Stewed, Roasted, Baked* or *Boiled*; and I make no doubt that it will equally serve in a *Fricassée* or a *Ragoût*.
>
> I do therefore humbly offer it to *publick Consideration*, that of the Hundred and Twenty Thousand Children, already computed, Twenty thousand may be reserved for Breed; whereof only one Fourth Part to be Males; which is more than we allow to *Sheep, black Cattle*, or *Swine*; and my Reason is, that these Children are seldom the Fruits of Marriage, *a Circumstance not much regarded by our Savages*; therefore, one Male will be sufficient to serve *four Females*. That the remaining Hundred thousand, may, at a Year old, be offered in Sale to Persons of Quality and *Fortune*, through the Kingdom, always advising the Mother to let them suck plentifully in the last Month, so as to render them plump, and fat for a good Table....
>
> I grant this Food will be somewhat dear, and therefore very *proper for Landlords*; who, as they have already devoured most of the Parents, seem to have the best Title to the Children.... It will have one other Collateral Advantage, by lessening the Number of *Papists* among us.... I believe no

gentleman would repine to give Ten Shillings for the *Carcase of a good fat Child*; which ... will make four Dishes of excellent nutritive Meat....

Those who are more thrifty (*as I must confess the Times require*) may flay the Carcase; the Skin of which, artificially dressed, will make admirable *Gloves for Ladies*, and *Summer Boots for fine Gentlemen*.

As to our City of *Dublin*; Shambles may be appointed for this Purpose ... and Butchers we may be assured will not be wanting; although I rather recommend buying the Children alive, and dressing them hot from the Knife, as we do *roasting Pigs*.

Swift's *Modest Proposal* is almost certainly the most ferocious and uncomfortable pamphlet ever to have been written in the English language.

The Church of Ireland Bishop of Cloyne, George Berkeley, is remembered today as one of the greatest philosophers of the eighteenth century. He was so appalled by the wretched condition of the peasantry who lived and worked around him in Co. Cork that in 1735 he asked the landlords a series of rhetorical questions in a pamphlet he titled *The Querist*:

Whether there be upon earth any Christian or civilised people so beggarly wretched and destitute, as the common Irish?

Whether, nevertheless, there is any other people whose wants may be more easily supplied from home?

Whether, if there was a wall of brass a thousand cubits high round their kingdom, our natives might not nevertheless live cleanly and comfortably, till the land, and reap the fruits of it?

Whether an Irish lady, set out with French silks and Flanders lace, may not be said to consume more beef and butter than fifty of our labouring peasants?

Whether there be any country in Christendom more capable of improvement than Ireland?

Whether we are the only people who starve in the market of plenty?

Whether there be not every year more cash circulated at the card-tables of Dublin than at all the fairs of Ireland?

In Ireland, as in every part of Europe in the eighteenth century, the poor were particularly vulnerable to bad weather. That was demonstrated with terrible force in 1740, the year of the 'Great Frost'.

Episode 122 ∽

1740: THE YEAR OF THE GREAT FROST

During January 1740 Arctic weather descended on Ireland, so intense that vast numbers of fish were found dead around the shores of Strangford Lough and Lough Neagh. In north Tipperary a whole sheep was roasted on top of nineteen inches of ice on the River Shannon at Portumna, 'at the eating of which they had great mirth, and drank many loyal toasts'. Afterwards a hurling match was played on the ice between two teams of gentlemen. So sharp was the frost that people from Tyrone walked directly across the frozen waters of Lough Neagh as they travelled to the market in Antrim town.

Lasting seven weeks, this 'Great Frost' froze the sea around both English and Irish ports, stopping the carrying of coal across the Irish Sea to Dublin. Hedges and ornamental shrubs were torn up around the city, and fourteen men were arrested for felling trees in Phoenix Park. For the ordinary people of Ireland, this Siberian weather was a disaster. The temperature plummeted so greatly that potato stores in straw-covered clamps in the ground were turned to inedible pulp. As Michael Rivers, a Co. Waterford merchant, observed,

> [The frost] has already destroyed a great part of the potatoes that lie in the cabins that lodge them and most of the potatoes of our country that are in the ground, by which the poor are likely to suffer greatly.

Three weeks later Richard Purcell wrote from north Cork:

> The eating potatoes are all destroyed, which many think will be followed by famine among the poor, and if the small ones, which are not bigger than large peas and which be deepest in the ground, are so destroyed as not to serve for seed, there must be sore famine in 1741.... If no potatoes remain sound for seed, I think this frost the most dreadful calamity that ever befell this poor kingdom.

So many wild birds had been killed that there was an eerie silence across the land. This poem appeared in *Faulkner's Dublin Journal*:

> No lark is left to wake the morn,
> Or rouse the youth with early horn;
> The blackbird's melody is o'er
> And pretty robin sings no more.

No thrush to serenade the grove
And soothe the passions into love,
Thou sweetest songster of the throng,
Now only live in poet's song.

Huge numbers of cattle and sheep had been killed by the extreme cold. Then, for those animals which survived, there was little or no grazing—the usual rains did not follow when a thaw set in during February. 'The cattle are all dying,' it was reported from Lismore in Waterford at the end of March. In April a correspondent from north Wexford wrote to the Dublin newspaper *Pue's Occurrences*:

Without rain what is to come of us? The corn that is sowed is perishing, the corn we have in our haggards is so prodigious dear the poor cannot purchase it.... As for flesh meat they cannot smell to it, they have lost all their sheep long ago, and now their last stake, their little cows are daily and hourly dropping for want of grass.

Corn prices more than doubled; at Drogheda a mob boarded and smashed up a vessel laden with corn; and in the capital at the end of May the *Dublin Newsletter* reported:

The bakers having made but little household bread, the populace were so greatly enraged that they broke open their shops that night and on Sunday; some sold their bread and gave them money, others took it away, and in this manner they went through the city.

The drought was so severe that the streams that usually turned the water-wheels to power corn mills and woollen tuck mills dried up. In the tinder-dry conditions fires raged in many towns: 150 houses burned down in Carrick-on-Suir, Co. Tipperary, 53 in Wexford town, and 20 in the village of Moate, Co. Westmeath.

The harvest in the autumn of 1740, depleted though it was, brought some relief. Then bad weather returned. Violent gales blew in September, followed by blizzards along the east coast in October, covering Belfast in what were described as 'prodigious' quantities of snow. Two terrible storms hit the country in November, accompanied by more snow and frost. On 9 December the heavens opened with such force that floods were reported across the island, washing houses and 'whole trees' into the River Liffey, and one correspondent from Navan, Co. Meath, described 'the greatest flood in the River Boyne that was ever known in the memory of man'.

On the following day temperatures dropped and the Arctic weather returned. The only outcome now could be famine—a famine so terrible that 1741 would be remembered as the 'Year of the Slaughter'.

Episode 123 ∿

1741: THE 'YEAR OF THE SLAUGHTER'

The great frost of 1740, followed by a prolonged drought, killed livestock, destroyed stores of potatoes, and produced a harvest with a pitiful yield. A survey in Louth during January 1741 revealed that only one household in five in the county had enough food to see them through the following months. There is no reason to believe that the rest of Ireland was in any better condition.

Lord Justice Hugh Boulter, Archbishop of Armagh, started a scheme of relief in Dublin on New Year's Day 1741. Three thousand were being fed every day by mid-January. By April the numbers had reached 4,400. At first the archbishop was paying for this out of his own pocket; it cost him £18 a day. Then Dean Jonathan Swift, Bishop George Berkeley and a number of noblemen rallied round to contribute and raise funds. In Waterford nearly 2,000 were being served boiled oatmeal two days a week.

Every year energetic Dubliners rise early to climb Killiney Hill to greet the dawn on midsummer's day. As the sun rises these people look down on the fabulously expensive homes of Van Morrison, Bono of U2 and other members of Ireland's prosperous elite. Only a few of them will know why there is an obelisk at the summit, or why there are remains of a huge wall surrounding the hill. These constructions are evidence of a great relief scheme to provide work for the starving in 1741, funded by John Mapas, one of the few wealthy Catholic landowners in the area. In a similar relief scheme in Co. Kildare, organised by Lady Katherine Conolly, a huge obelisk was erected close to Castletown House.

Their bodies weakened by hunger, people fell prey to disease, including smallpox and dysentery, known then as 'the bloody flux'. *Faulkner's Dublin Journal's* correspondent wrote from Drogheda:

> We have a great mortality among the poor people, who die in great numbers from fevers and fluxes. One poor man buried eight of his family in a few days.

John Usher, a land agent at Lismore, Co. Waterford, wrote to his employer in London in February:

> A bloody flux and a violent fever rages so all over the country that scarce a day passes that we do not bury fifteen or sixteen even in this small place....

For my own part, were it not for the business of this place I would fly for my life.

Now the killing disease was typhus, an infection spread mainly by body lice. Typhus produced delirium, vertigo, a high fever, bloodshot eyes and a spotted rash. Most victims died from heart failure. From west Cork Sir Richard Cox wrote:

By all I can learn, the dreadfullest civil war, or most raging plague never destroyed so many as this season. The distempers and famine increase so that it is no vain fear that there will not be hands to save the harvest.

The Rev. Philip Skelton, curate of Monaghan parish, reported that there were

whole parishes in some places ... almost desolate; the dead have been eaten in the fields by dogs for want of people to bury them. Whole thousands in a barony have perished, some of hunger and others of disorders occasioned by unnatural, unwholesome, and putrid diet.

An anonymous author of an open letter to Archbishop Boulter described conditions in the vicinity of Cashel, Co. Tipperary:

Multitudes are daily perishing.... I have seen the labourer endeavouring to work at his spade, but fainting for want of food and forced to quit it. I have seen the aged father eating grass like a beast ... the helpless orphan exposed on the dunghill, and none to take him in for fear of infection ... the hungry infant sucking at the breast of the already expired parent ...

The wealthy and powerful also succumbed from fever. They included Sir Alexander Staples, a Dublin merchant, and three judges: Lord Chief Justice Sir John Rogerson, Prime Serjeant Bettesworth, and Chief Baron Wainwright.

The Irish called this year of 1741 *bliain an áir*, 'year of the slaughter'. Out of a population of 2,400,000, between 310,000 and 480,000 died as a direct result of famine and fever that year. A greater proportion of the population died in this *one* year than during the *six* years of the Great Famine in the 1840s when the population was more than three times larger than it was in 1741. All Europe suffered famine in 1741, but no country, except for Norway, suffered as much as Ireland.

The Duke of Devonshire, the viceroy, on government business in London, was kept informed of the famine in Ireland. He was so appalled by what he read that he at once agreed to support a plan proposed by the Charitable Musical Society. He personally sought out the composer George Frideric Handel and handed him a letter inviting him to Dublin.

Episode 124 ✺

THE FIRST PERFORMANCE OF HANDEL'S *MESSIAH*

The terrible famine of 1741 had filled the city of Dublin with emaciated and fever-ridden refugees from the countryside. The wards of the Charitable Infirmary on Inns Quay and Mercer's Hospital in Stephen Street could take no more patients. Money was needed—and quickly. The plight of those placed behind bars for debt in the city's prisons was the special concern of the Charitable Musical Society. A magnificent new Musick Hall had been opened in October 1741—why not invite the famous composer Handel over from London to give charitable performances there?

George Frideric Handel had good reasons for accepting the invitation. His last oratorio had been poorly received, and he was in severe financial difficulties. Besides, he was working on another great oratorio, the *Messiah*, composed to passages selected from the Scriptures by his friend Charles Jennens. Handel preferred to submit this composition to an audience that did not include his London critics.

Handel arrived in Dublin on 17 November and gave his first concert in the Musick Hall on 23 December. In a letter to Charles Jennens he expressed delight with his reception:

> The Musick sounds delightfully in this charming Room.... I exert myself on my Organ with more than usual success.... I cannot sufficiently express the kind treatment I receive here; but the Politeness of this generous Nation cannot be unknown to you.

Rehearsals for the *Messiah* began in February 1742. Great care had to be taken in obtaining permission for the choirs of Christ Church and St Patrick's Cathedrals to take part. It was known that Jonathan Swift, Dean of St Patrick's, was opposed to his vicars choral singing with bands. So Handel decided to call personally on the famous dean, the author of *Gulliver's Travels*. When told by his servant who was at the door, the elderly Swift responded: 'O! A German, and a genius! A prodigy! Admit him.' Permission was granted. The Lord Lieutenant, the Duke of Devonshire, gave the services of His Majesty's Band of Musick. *Faulkner's Dublin Journal* published this report on the first public rehearsal on 8 April:

> Yesterday, Mr Handel's new Grand Sacred Oratorio, called The Messiah was rehearsed at the Musick Hall in Fishamble Street, to a most Grand, Polite,

and Crowded Audience ... and was allowed by the greatest Judges to be the Finest Composition of Musick that ever was heard.

Though the tickets cost half a guinea apiece, so great was the expected audience that the stewards issued a special request to

ladies and gentlemen who are well-wishers to this noble and grand charity ... request as a favour, that the ladies who honour this performance with their presence would be pleased to come without hoops, as it will greatly increase the charity by making room for more company.

At eleven in the morning the doors were opened, and the New Room, richly decorated in white and gold and with large mirrors for the ladies, was soon filled by over seven hundred people of fashion. At noon the full choirs of the two cathedrals were ready, Mr Maclaine was at the organ, Mr Handel turned to direct His Majesty's Band, and the performance began.

So moved was Dr Patrick Delany, the Dean of Down, by Susanna Cibber's singing of 'He was despised' that he rose from his seat and cried out with passion: 'Woman, for this, be all thy sins forgiven!' *Faulkner's Dublin Journal* gave this verdict on the performance:

Words are wanting to express the exquisite Delight it afforded to the admiring crowded Audience. The Sublime, the Grand, and the Tender, adapted to most elevated, Majestick and moving Words, conspired to transport and charm the ravished Heart and Ear.

Handel and all the performers had given their services without payment, and the £400 collected in ticket money was divided evenly between the three charities. In response to entreaties, Handel put on another performance on 3 June, a pane of glass being removed from the top of each of the windows to ventilate the Musick Hall. After being lavishly entertained everywhere and enjoying a well-earned rest, Handel returned to England in August.

While he waited patiently to be appreciated in London, Handel was showered with fan mail from Ireland. Mary Delany preferred to pass on her admiration through her brother, who was a friend of the composer:

3rd December 1750. I hope you will find Mr Handel well.... His wonderful Messiah will never be out of my head; and I may say my heart was raised almost to heaven by it.... If anything can give us an idea of the last day it must be that part 'The trumpet shall sound, the dead shall be raised'.

Only a city with a large leisured class could have given Handel the patronage he received. Dublin was fast becoming the second city of the British Empire.

Episode 125 ~

THE SECOND CITY OF THE EMPIRE

During the eighteenth century Britain became a world power. Possessing a powerful navy, it conquered territory from its rivals France, Spain, Portugal and Holland, extended its control in the Indian subcontinent, developed colonies in North America, and began its settlement of Australia. Strict laws prevented Ireland trading directly with the colonies, but English vessels brought into Irish ports: tea from the Far East; sugar from the West Indies; tobacco from Virginia; fine muslin from India; and other exotic luxuries. To pay for these overseas goods and also for English coal, Ireland exported linen, corn, butter, salt pork and other farm produce.

No city in Ireland benefited more from the expansion of the British Empire than Dublin. Captain William Bligh—yes, the same captain of 'Mutiny on the *Bounty*' fame—supervised the impressive deepening of the Liffey estuary to allow vessels to come up at all tides to the new stone-lined quays. The population, which had been 58,000 in 1683, was close to 129,000 by 1772, and 182,000 (including the garrison) by 1798, making Dublin the second largest city in the British Empire.

It was in this city that the viceroy held court at Dublin Castle. In the 1750s the handsome Bedford Tower was erected there and the castle was extended and given an elegant square built of red brick and cream stone. Edward Lovett Pearce, descended from the seventeenth-century rebel leader Rory O'More, designed a magnificent new Parliament House in College Green with a line of stone columns in the new classical style. Across the island, expanding trade, a rising population and—above all—the long period of peace increased the income of the Protestant landowners. Much of the money they collected from their tenants they spent in Dublin. Here they needed to be present to attend the sessions of parliament and the law courts. And, of course, they wanted to show off by entertaining lavishly and find suitable husbands for their daughters.

As well as erecting great mansions on their estates, these gentlemen built magnificent town houses in Dublin constructed of cut stone. The first to be put up in the new Georgian style was Tyrone House, built for Marcus Beresford, Earl of Tyrone, in 1740. Then followed many others, including: Powerscourt House in William Street, built for Richard Wingfield, Viscount Powerscourt; Leinster House in Kildare Street, completed for James Fitzgerald, first Duke of Leinster, in 1745, and now the home of Dáil Éireann;

Northland House, built for the Knox family of Dungannon in 1770, and now the Royal Irish Academy; and Charlemont House, designed by and built for James Caulfield, first Earl of Charlemont of Co. Armagh, and later the Municipal Gallery of Modern Art.

Other Protestant gentlemen became urban developers. The included: Luke Gardiner, first Viscount Mountjoy, who planned and laid out Gardiner Street and Mountjoy Square; the sixth Lord Fitzwilliam of Meryon, who developed Merrion Square and Fitzwilliam Street (the longest Georgian street in the world); and Dr Bartholomew Mosse, who developed Rutland Square, now Parnell Square. On the same site Dr Mosse erected the Rotunda Lying-in Hospital—the first maternity hospital in either Britain or Ireland. The Assembly Rooms attached to the Rotunda rapidly became Dublin's social hub where concerts and other events were put on to raise funds for the hospital.

Most of these Protestant gentlemen and their families had become newly rich in only one or two generations. Visitors from England often found them to be noisy, wild, brash, extravagant and hard-living—in particular, hard-drinking. Lord Chesterfield, when he was Lord Lieutenant, was horrified by the 'beastly vice' of excessive drinking of French wine which destroyed 'the constitutions, the faculties, and too often the fortunes of those of superior rank'. Heavy drinking naturally took place on festive occasions when endless toasts were given, the most popular being to

> the glorious, pious and immortal enemy of the good and great King William, who delivered us from popery, slavery, arbitrary power, brass money, and wooden shoes.

This caused that perceptive observer of Irish society, Sir Jonah Barrington, to remark:

> Could His Majesty King William learn in the other world that he had been the cause of more broken heads and drunken men, since his departure, than all his predecessors, he must be the proudest ghost, and most conceited skeleton that ever entered the gardens of Elysium.

According to John Bush, an Englishman who visited Dublin in 1764, a 'middling drinker' would drink four bottles of claret—that is, red wine from Bordeaux—without showing any effects. No man was considered a serious drinker in Dublin who could not, he wrote, 'take off his gallon coolly'—that is, the equivalent of six modern bottles drunk at a single sitting.

Dublin, indeed, was a city of excess and extremes.

Episode 126 ⤳

DUBLIN: POVERTY, CRIME AND DUELS

Visitors to Dublin in the eighteenth century were struck by the over-indulgence and lavish lifestyle of those at the apex of society. But just a short distance from Dublin Castle the poor crowded the narrow streets and lanes. The Rev. James Whitelaw, the Church of Ireland rector ministering from St Catherine's Church in Thomas Street, described the condition of these slums:

> This crowded population is almost universally accompanied by a very serious evil—a degree of filth and stench inconceivable.... Into the back-yard of each house, frequently not ten feet deep, is flung from the windows of each apartment, the ordure and filth of its numerous inhabitants; from which it is so seldom removed, that I have seen it nearly on a level with the windows of the first floor; and the moisture that, after heavy rains, oozes from this heap ... runs into the street, by the entry leading to the staircase....
> In Joseph's Lane near Castle market, I was interrupted in my progress by an inundation of putrid blood, alive with maggots, which had from an adjacent slaughter yard burst the back door, and filled the hall to the depth of several inches....
>
> The sallow looks and filth of the wretches who crowded round me indicated their situation, though they seemed insensible to the stench.... In the garret I found the entire family of a poor working shoemaker, seven in number, lying in a fever, without a human being to administer to their wants.

He counted thirty-seven persons in one house:

> Its humane proprietor received out of an absolute ruin which should be taken down by the magistrate, a profit rent of above £30 per annum, which he extracted every Saturday night with unfeeling severity. I will not disgust the reader with any further detail.

The poor tended to cluster round two fetid streams, the Poddle and the Coombe. Their homes were frequently inundated by floods, as the young Edmund Burke observed from his family residence on Arran Quay in January 1746:

Our cellars are drowned ... the water comes up to the first floor of the house threatening us every minute.... From our doors and windows we watch the rise and fall of the waters as carefully as the Egyptians do the Nile, but for different reasons.... [It is] melancholy to see the poor people of other parts of the town emptying their cellars ... for as fast as they teem out the water, so fast does it, through some subterraneous channels, return again.

The poor were also the most frequent victims of crime. On 10 September 1778 the *Hibernian Magazine* reported:

Last Sunday morning about 3 o'clock five soldiers supposed belonging to the main guard forced an unhappy woman into an entry in Fishamble Street, and two of them guarded the pass alternately with drawn bayonets in their hands until each had gratified his brutal desires. This piece of barbarity was transacted in the presence of above twenty spectators one of whom dared not venture to the poor creature's assistance; the military heroes threatened with horrid imprecations to stab the first person to the heart who should offer to molest them.

Dublin's criminals could also be drawn from the educated classes. These included the 'pinking dindies', skilled in slashing their victims with the points of their swords which stuck out below the open end of their scabbards. They used this technique to force passers-by to hand over their purses, usually for the purpose of recouping the losses they had incurred at the gaming tables. By the same means they also snatched ladies from their protectors, and, as one observer noted, '*many* females were destroyed by that lawless banditti'.

The students of Trinity College, given a splendid façade facing the Parliament House in College Green in 1759, acquired a reputation for wild and debauched behaviour. Sons of nobles and gentlemen for the most part, they strode about wearing gowns trimmed with gold or silver according to rank. Some could afford to dine at the Eagle Tavern, home of the notorious Hell-Fire Club, or risk a duel at Lucas's Coffee-House on Cork Hill. Others would eat beefsteaks in The Old Sot's Hole at Essex Bridge or mingle with the humbler classes in the ale-houses of Winetavern Street. Generally known as 'bucks', they were often eager to join in fights in the narrow streets, wielding the heavy keys to their rooms as weapons.

Duelling was so popular amongst the Dublin gentry that duelling clubs were established. Newspapers frequently carried complaints that passers-by in the Phoenix Park were in considerable danger from stray bullets. Richard Daly, manager of the Theatre Royal, fought nineteen duels in two years—three with swords and sixteen with pistols.

When the winter season was over, the gentry deserted the capital for the countryside, where the nobility were erecting splendid mansions.

Episode 127 ↝

'THE IRISH GENTRY ARE AN EXPENSIVE PEOPLE'

The population of Ireland rose from around two million in 1700, to about two and a quarter million by 1740 and reached over five million by 1800. In consequence, the demand for land increased sharply, and this allowed landowners to raise their rents. Now the nobility and gentry could afford to knock down or abandon the uncomfortable castles and fortified houses that had been erected in more turbulent times and replace these outmoded dwellings with new luxurious mansions.

Without exception, all looked east across the Irish Sea for inspiration. The classical style became the vogue when Sir Gustavus Hume, High Sheriff of Co. Fermanagh, commissioned the German architect Richard Cassels to build his country seat on the western peninsula of Lower Lough Erne in 1728. At about the same time William Conolly, Speaker of the Irish House of Commons and the richest man in Ireland, erected what is still regarded as the most magnificent Georgian great house in Ireland, Castletown, fifteen miles west of Dublin. Almost as splendid was Carton nearby, designed by Cassels for Robert Fitzgerald, nineteenth Earl of Kildare.

It cost Armar Lowry-Corry, first Earl of Belmore, some £90,000 to build Castle Coole in Co. Fermanagh. He chartered a brig to bring Portland stone from the Isle of Wight to a specially constructed quay at Ballyshannon; from there the blocks were carted ten miles to Lough Erne to be taken by barge to Enniskillen, and more bullock carts were used for the last two miles to complete the delivery. Visiting in 1796, the French *émigré*, the Chevalier de Latocnaye, found the interior 'full of rare marbles, and the walls of several rooms are covered with rare stucco work produced at great cost, and by workers brought from Italy.... Temples should be left to the gods.' When the earl died in 1802, his estate had debts of £70,000. Lord Belmore's extravagance was exceeded by that of Frederick Hervey, simultaneously Earl of Bristol and Bishop of Derry. After visiting the Earl-Bishop's huge palace at Downhill on the rugged Londonderry coast, de Latocnaye wrote:

> Oh, what a lovely thing it is to be an Anglican bishop or minister! These are the spoiled children of fortune, rich as bankers, enjoying good wine, good cheer, and pretty women, and all for their benediction. God bless them!

During a tour of Ireland in 1732 the English historian John Loveday remarked:

The Irish gentry are an expensive people, they live in the most open hospitable manner continually feasting with one another.

Certainly there are numerous accounts of gargantuan meals and extended drinking bouts. John Boyle, fifth Earl of Orrery, wrote in 1736:

Drunkenness is the touchstone by which they try every man.... A right jolly glorious-memory Hibernian never rolls into bed without having taken a sober gallon of claret to his own share.... It is a Yahoo that toasts the glorious and immortal memory of King William in a bumper without any other joy in the Revolution than that it gives him a pretence to drink so many more daily quarts of wine. The person who refuses a goblet to this prevailing toast is deemed a Jacobite, a papist and a knave.

Beauchamp Bagenal of Dunleckney House in Co. Carlow was so fond of duelling that he kept a brace of pistols loaded upon his dinner-table. When the meal was over, the claret being produced in a cask, he would tap the cask with a bullet from one of his pistols, while he kept the other for any of his guests who failed to do justice to his wine. John Eyre, a baron living in Co. Galway, served his meals at Eyrecourt with such little ceremony that guests were expected to cut off hunks from the whole roasted ox he had hung up by its heels.

Feasts at Shane's Castle by Lough Neagh in Co. Antrim were altogether more refined. Sarah Siddons, the celebrated English actress, visited her friend Lady O'Neill there in 1783:

It is scarce possible to conceive the splendour of this almost Royal Establishment, except by recollecting the circumstances of an Arabian Night's entertainment. Six or eight carriages with a numerous throung of Lords and Ladies and gentlemen on Horseback began the day by making excursions about this terrestrial paradise, returning home but just in time to dress for dinner. The table was served with a profusion and elegance to which I have never seen anything comparable.... A fine band of musicians played during the repast. They were stationed on the Corridor, which led from the dining room into a fine Conservatory, where we plucked our dessert from numerous trees of the most exquisite fruits, and where the waves of the superb Lake wash'd its feet while its delicious murmurs were accompanied with strains of celestial harmony from the Corridor.

It would be impossible to imagine a greater contrast between such scenes of opulence and refinement and the squalor and destitution in which the peasantry lived.

Episode 128 ～

'A SORT OF DESPOT'

A rthur Young, the English agricultural improver who toured Ireland and briefly worked as a land agent there in the 1770s, formed a poor opinion of Irish landlords. He denounced them as 'lazy, trifling, inattentive, negligent, slobbering, profligate'. He was appalled by their brutality towards their tenants:

> The landlord of an Irish estate, inhabited by Roman Catholics, is a sort of despot, who yields in obedience in whatever concerns the poor, but to no law but that of his will.... Speaking a language that is despised, professing a religion that is abhorred, and being disarmed, the poor find themselves in many cases slaves even in the bosom of written liberty.... A landlord in Ireland can scarcely invent an order which a servant, labourer or cottar dares to refuse to execute. Nothing satisfies him but an unlimited submission. Disrespect, or anything tending towards sauciness he may punish with his cane or his horsewhip with the most perfect security; a poor man would have his bones broke if he offered to lift his hand in his own defence. Knocking down is spoken of in the country in a manner that makes an Englishman stare. Landlords of consequence have assured me that many of their cottars would think themselves honoured by having their wives and daughters sent for to the bed of their masters....
>
> It must strike the most careless traveller to see whole strings of cars whipt into a ditch by a gentleman's footman, to make way for his carriage; if they are overturned, or broken in pieces, no matter, it is taken in patience; were they to complain, they would perhaps be horsewhipped. The execution of the laws lies very much in the hands of the justices of the peace, many of whom are drawn from the most illiberal class in the kingdom.

In almost every locality the landlord wielded supreme power. For example, the Earl of Donegall picked all thirteen members of Belfast Corporation and chose the 'sovereign', or mayor, of the town. Counties were governed by unelected grand juries composed of landlords, their relatives and their agents, and Church of Ireland clergy. The landlords too were the magistrates presiding over local courts.

Early in the eighteenth century in particular, owners of great estates for convenience often let out their lands in large portions to 'middlemen', poorer members of the gentry, who in turn sublet farms to tenants. These middlemen were particularly hated since they did their best to extract as much rent as they could. A fortunate minority of farmers, known as 'freeholders', owned their land outright. The vast majority, however, rented their farms and were at the mercy, therefore, of landlords. The better off were 'leaseholders', that is, they had a legal document which fixed the rent and other obligations. Here, for example, is a lease signed on 21 November 1783 between Lord Welles of Dungannon and Joseph Dickson of Mullaghbawn, Co. Tyrone. The farm contained

> thirty-six acres English statute measure appertaining, situate, lying and being in the townland of Dristernan, parish of Donaghmore, barony of Dungannon ... excepting and always reserving out of this demise unto the said Thomas Lord Baron Welles, his heirs and assigns, all manner of mines, minerals, quarries of freestone, limestone, slate, and coals, all woods, underwoods, timber and trees ... all turf bogs, mosses and marl....
>
> He the said Joseph Dickson his heirs, administrators and assigns, yielding and paying ... unto the said Thomas Lord Baron Welles his heirs and assigns, the clear yearly rent or sum of thirteen shillings sterling per acre.

In addition to money rent, the tenant had also to supply labour and food from his farm. Joseph Dickson had to provide

> two days work of man and horse or four shillings sterling in lieu thereof, two couple of good fat hens ... nine bushels of good white oats ...

Joseph Dickson also had to build a forty-foot-long dwelling-house, agree to have all his corn ground at his lordship's mills (and pay the specified fees), plant a hundred apple trees, and

> cause to be made on the premises thirty perches of ditch, five feet wide and four feet deep, set with white thorn and crab quicks, at the usual and proper distance.

Until 1782, Catholics were not permitted to have leases lasting longer than thirty-one years. After that year they, along with Protestants, could name three persons in the lease, and the lease with a fixed rent continued until the last person named had died. Joseph Dickson, for example, named his two young sons as well as himself. Those who named King George III—as many did—were fortunate: he reigned from 1760 until his death in 1820. When leases expired, however, tenant farmers usually faced greatly increased rents. It was then—faced with ruin and eviction—that some of them turned to violence. In Ulster they called themselves the Hearts of Steel and the Hearts of Oak.

Episode 129 ∿

HEARTS OF STEEL, HEARTS OF OAK

Twice a year, after the 'gale days' in May and November when the rent had been paid, Lord Bandon, threw a party for the tenants of his large estate in Co. Cork. In the spring of 1793 the task of organising the revels was left to his land agent:

> None who were not tenants did I invite, except those named by you, viz., Father Morgan Flaherty, Tim McCarthy, Charles Casey, Doctor Leyne, and Father Nolan, son to Old John. These I asked as Catholics particularly attached to you.

Twenty-two favoured tenants were seated in the parlour; others in the breakfast parlour; the remainder were accommodated in a large tent on the avenue. The agent continued:

> In the parlour your claret was made free with, as Stephen tells me he opened 34 bottles. In the breakfast parlour port-wine and rum-punch were supplied in abundance; and abroad large libations of whiskey-punch. We had two quarter casks (above 80 gallons) of that beverage made the day before, which was drawn off unsparingly for those abroad, and plenty of beer besides.... Pipers and fiddlers enlivened the intervals between the peals of ordnance.... An ox was roasted whole at one end of the turf-house, on a large ash beam, by way of a spit, and turned with a wheel by Tom O'Brien ... six sheep were also sacrificed on the occasion.... All was happiness, mirth and good humour. 'God save Great George our King' was cheered within and abroad, accompanied by fiddles, pipes, etc.

Wise landlords like Lord Bandon understood that it made good sense to keep the tenantry happy. Others could be negligent or ruthless. Landlords had a habit of encouraging what was known as the 'hanging gale'—that is, allowing tenants to fall behind in payment of rent by six months or more. These tenants, having broken the terms of their leases, could then be legally evicted and replaced with others prepared to pay higher rents. When their leases expired, tenants found that they had to pay heavy sums known as 'fines' and greatly increased rents to renew their leases. Worse still, they could be evicted and replaced.

During 1770 the seething resentments aroused by such practices reached boiling-point in Co. Antrim. Tenants had been evicted by the Upton family

from their Templepatrick estate and had been replaced by speculators, including the Belfast merchant Waddell Cunningham, who had been able to outbid
them when leases expired. In the same year the leases of Lord Donegall's Co.
Antrim estate expired; leases were renewed only if heavy fines were paid—
fines many tenants could not pay.

On the morning of Sunday 23 December angry farmers gathered at the
Presbyterian meeting-house in Templepatrick and, armed with firelocks,
pistols and pitchforks, set out for Belfast. They numbered at least 1,200 as they
advanced on the town's North Gate, now North Street. Calling themselves the
'Hearts of Steel', they surged around the army barrack intent on forcing the
release of a comrade held prisoner on a charge of maiming cattle. Dr
Alexander Halliday, a leading citizen, attempted to negotiate the release of the
prisoner. A contemporary letter describes the sequel:

> The Doctor had just reached the Barrack on his embassy, passing through
> an immense multitude ... when the gate was thrown open by the military,
> who fired upon the assailants, killed five persons and wounded nine others.

In the meantime Cunningham's house in Hercules Lane (now Royal Avenue)
was burning fiercely, putting the whole town in danger. At one o'clock in
the morning the sovereign, or mayor, saw no alternative but to give up the
prisoner to prevent the destruction of Belfast.

The revolt of the Hearts of Steel spilled over into mid-Ulster, merging with
another group calling themselves the 'Hearts of Oak' which had been resisting the 'cess', a rate imposed by grand juries to pay for roads and bridges. In
March 1772, when Sir Richard Johnston of Gilford, Co. Down, captured 'the
ring-leader of this banditti', his house was besieged next day, as a witness
relates:

> They began to fire at the windows and set the offices on fire ... upon which
> Mr Morrell a dissenting minister ... desirous to prevent further bloodshed,
> drew up a window in order to speak out to them, but was saluted by four
> musket balls in his head and breast. He fell dead out of the window.

Johnston hung out a flag of truce and escaped through a back window. He
gathered together a posse of 150 men, but judged it better to await the arrival
of the army.

This was only one incident in a series of disturbances causing the Irish parliament to rush through 'An Act for the more effectual punishment of wicked
and disorderly persons in Antrim, Down, Armagh, the City and County of
Londonderry, and County Tyrone'.

Retribution swiftly followed.

Episode 130 ～

CLEARING THE LAND

In March 1772 the Hearts of Steel—tenant farmers of eastern Ulster who had risen against their landlords—issued their proclamation which blamed the 'heavy rents which are become so great a burden to us that we are not scarcely able to bear'. It continued:

> Betwixt landlord and rectors, the very marrow is screwed out of our bones.... They have reduced us to such a deplorable state by such grievous oppressions that the poor is turned black in the face, and the skin parched on their back, that they are rendered incapable to support their starving families ... that they have not even food, nor yet raiment to secure from them the extremities of the weather.

The government's response was to spread soldiers through Ulster to crush the risings. Men were tried and hanged, and some were drowned while attempting to escape to Scotland in open boats.

Most of those who had risen against their landlords were farmers who had some legal protection in the form of leases. The great majority living on the land, however, had no such protection. They sublet land from better-off farmers, and many of them walked to hiring fairs to sell their labour, particularly at harvest time. Pretty thatched cottages with windows, half-doors and chimneys were beyond their reach.

Yet the ordinary people of Ireland were almost certainly better off than they had been in the previous century. It could be said that the great theme of eighteenth-century Irish history is the contest between population growth and growth of productivity. In most years prosperity was winning the race. The land was being cultivated and grazed more intensively than it had ever been. The result was a drastic transformation of the Irish countryside.

Since the beginning of the seventeenth century the great forests of Ireland had been swept away by ruthless felling. Losing their habitat, the native red deer became extinct except in Kerry and a few other areas in the west. The last wolves were killed in the Sperrins and in Co. Carlow in the 1760s. No attempt was made to coppice trees, and the landlords recklessly squandered the woodlands not only to build homes and towns but also to export barrel-staves, boards and ship timber. For a time ironworks and tanneries had flourished. Sir Richard Boyle, the first Earl of Cork, had grown rich by making charcoal and smelting iron in Munster. Sir Charles Coote of Cavan once employed 2,500 men in his iron-founding concern, and it must have been a prodigal consumer of wood—it took two and a half tons of charcoal to make one ton of bar iron. Tanners, such as Thomas Waring, five times sovereign of Belfast between 1652 and 1666, had a tannery in the town in Waring Street and others at Toome, Derriaghy and Lurgan. Tanners preferred to strip bark from living oak, and eventually their depredations deprived them of their raw material.

As early as 1718 it was noted that wood was 'extraordinary dear' in Ballyclare, Co. Antrim. In 1780 a mighty tree forty-two feet in girth, known as the Royal Oak, was felled on Lord Conway's estate near Antrim. Part of it was sawn up to build a fifty-ton vessel for Lough Neagh, but—as a striking illustration of the soaring price of wood products—the bark alone of this single oak was sold for £40. Cities such as Dublin, Cork, Waterford and Limerick could not have existed if they had not been able to import coal from Britain.

An exotic vegetable, the potato, had been introduced in the sixteenth century. Increasingly it formed a crucial part of the Irish diet. Almost certainly the potato improved the health of the people because—though nobody knew it at the time—it provided vitamin C, which had previously been somewhat lacking in the Irish menu. Scurvy, which had in past times plagued the people of Ireland, now largely disappeared.

The potato, which tolerates a wide range of soils, was considered the best crop for clearing land. The favoured implement for preparing and cultivating new land was the loy, from the Irish *láighe*, a spade with a long shaft, one footrest and a narrow iron blade—this was ideal for cutting and turning the sod. Potatoes were grown on raised ridges known—by those who never had to do the job themselves—as 'lazy beds'. Sods were carefully turned over (with elaborate local variations in technique), ashes spread over these as fertiliser, and potatoes planted on top and then covered with mould from the adjacent furrow. Potatoes became part of the rotation with barley and sometimes flax, if the soil could be made fertile enough.

Previously the hillsides had been forested or used only for summer grazing. Now the growing population was settling here all year round and farming the land intensively.

Episode 131 ～

THE PEASANTRY

As the population rose during the eighteenth century every available scrap of land was being dug over or ploughed, and hillsides, previously kept only for summer grazing, were now being cultivated almost to the summits.

Of course, the labour of removing furze and heather and the prising out of rocks or stumps was unremitting. In his book *The Antient and Present State of the County of Down*, published in 1744, Walter Harris described farming above Dromara on the slopes of Slieve Croob:

> The face of the Country hereabouts is rough, bleak and unimproved; yet produces the Necessaries of Life sufficient to support a large Number of Inhabitants, who have little other Bread Corn but Oats, of which they make great Quantities of Meal to supply not only themselves, but the neighbouring Markets. They are an industrious hardy People, and may be properly said to *eat their Bread in the Sweat of their Face*, the Courseness of the land obliging them to great Labour. The Coldness of the Soil occasions their Harvests to be late; yet by due Care and Culture it yields Rye and great Quantities of Flax. The Plenty of cheap firing got out of Bogs and Mosses throughout this whole Country does not a little contribute to the Service of the Linen Trade.

Coastal farms could draw on the bounty of the sea to fertilise the thin leached soils of the west. Seaweed was rightly seen as an excellent manure and was gathered on every shore. Native Irish-speakers carefully distinguished between the various species, while English-speakers referred to seaweed as wrack, sea-bar and kelp. Knotted, bladder and saw-wrack were carefully cultivated—the rectangular plots or 'cuts' marked out with boulders, giving anchorage for the weed, can still be seen today, especially in Strangford Lough and the shore line at the foot of the Mourne Mountains. Storms blew in kelp from the deeps. Shells and shell-sand cast onto peaty, acid soils much improved fertility—indeed, onion-growing today on the Dingle peninsula in Kerry would hardly be possible without the shell-sand laboriously spread there to sweeten the soil by the peasantry more than two centuries ago.

Better-off farmers—known as 'strong farmers'—lived in the thatched stone cottages, whitewashed with lime, now considered to be characteristically Irish. The majority had much humbler dwellings, often no more than single-room cabins—there was no point in erecting more permanent houses for those who rented land from year to year, often forced to move on the following season. The English traveller C. T. Bowden described homes he saw in Co. Tipperary in 1790 as 'less calculated for any of the comforts or conveniences of life than the huts of the savages I have seen in the back settlements of North America'. Here there were no beds; instead the whole family would sleep on rushes strewn on the mud floor. Furniture consisted of little more than a deal table, an iron 'cruisie' filled with fish oil to provide light, a couple of three-legged stools, and an iron pot for boiling potatoes on an open fire. A rush mat served as a door, and smoke had to find its way out without a chimney. Beggars had to make do with even less, as the English agricultural writer Arthur Young observed in the 1770s:

> A wandering family will fix themselves under a dry bank and with a few sticks, furze, fern, etc., make up a hovel much worse than an English pigsty, and support themselves how they can, by work, begging, and stealing.

Even in quite substantial dwellings farm animals were allowed to roam freely, as the Chevalier de Latocnaye discovered when he spent a night in 1796 with peasants in Co. Waterford:

> Half a dozen children almost naked were sleeping on a little straw, with a pig, a dog, a cat, two chickens and a duck. I never before saw such a sight. The poor woman ... spread a mat on a chest, the only piece of furniture in the house and invited me to lie there.... It rained very hard ... so I lay down on this bed of thorns. The animals saluted the first rays of the sun by their cries.... I transported myself in imagination into the Ark, and fancied myself Noah.... The dog came to smell me ... the pig also put up her snout to me and began to grunt; the chickens and the duck began to eat my powder-bag, and the children began to laugh. I should add that I had no small difficulty in making my hostess accept a shilling.

The surprising fact is that houses like this were even to be found in the area at the heart of Ireland's flourishing textile industry.

Episode 132 ～

'SUPERFINE CLOTH, OF HOME MANUFACTURE'

It is not widely known that eighteenth-century Ireland was an industrial country. There were few tall smoking chimneys and 'dark satanic mills', it is true. But in every town of any size, and right across the island, people were busy producing yarn and cloth.

Even though an act of 1699 prohibited the export of Irish wool, the home market continued to flourish as the country's population rose. And, of course, smuggling made many prosperous. Cloth was stuffed into small butter casks, known as firkins, and sent out illegally to Portugal and the West Indies. It was rumoured that the O'Connell family of Cahirciveen in Co. Kerry grew rich in this way.

Merchants bought wool at the great fairs of Ballinasloe in Co. Galway and Mullingar in Co. Westmeath and employed people in their cabins and cottages to comb it and spin it into yarn. Some homes were big enough to accommodate a loom, but most of the spun yarn was taken to weavers in the larger towns such as Clonmel and Carrick-on-Suir in Co. Tipperary; Carlow town; Doneraile, Bandon, Mitchelstown and Mallow in Co. Cork; and Mountmellick and Maryborough in Queen's County. In 1769 Arthur Young found 400 weavers in Carrick-on-Suir making broadcloths and ratteens, and by the end of the century there were some 3,000 employed in the town; the industry had been helped, no doubt, by the removal of the export prohibition in 1780.

Kilkenny, then regarded as the largest inland town in Ireland, made frieze, flannels, druggets, worsteds and blankets for the British army. John Holroyd, the Earl of Sheffield, wrote in 1785:

The amount of the consumption of woollens in Ireland ... is very great; and perhaps no country whatever, in proportion to the number of inhabitants, consumes so much. The lower ranks are covered in the clumsiest woollen drapery, and although the material may not be fine, there is an abundance of it. Besides coat and waistcoat, the lower classes wear a great coat, both summer and winter, if it can possibly be got. Not only their clothing but their stockings seem to contain a double quantity of wool, and the women among the peasantry seem to depend on other charms than elegance and ornament: they also wear the clumsiest woollens. There is no intention of insinuating that they always wear stockings, but that which covers their persons, and their petticoats, and also their cloke, if they have one, contain much wool, and all of the gloomiest colours; linen or cotton gowns are seldom to be seen among the common peasantry in Ireland.

A colony of French Protestants in Portarlington in Queen's County manufactured gloves, silk and lace. These Huguenots were particularly numerous in Dublin, where they made the city famous for 'tabinet' or poplin, a fine cloth of mixed wool and silk.

In the capital, full-time weavers, then called 'manufacturers', worked in districts known as Pimlico, the Spitalfields, and the Coombe in the Earl of Meath's Liberty, where they erected a Weavers' Hall in 1750. An anonymous author, writing in 1759, described the wide variety of cloth produced, with a bewildering range of names:

We have in Dublin, superfine, fine, and middling Cloathes, Serges, Druggets, Drabs, Ratteens ... Callimincoes, Everlastings, German-Serges, Stuffs, Camlets, Poplins, etc., all very well finished, and some to the utmost Nicety; as are also Velvets, plain and flowered; Hair and Worsted Shags; Silks of different Kinds and Patterns; Silk Handkerchiefs and Ribbands. It was with real Satisfaction that I have seen some pieces of superfine Cloth, of Home-manufacture, equal to any imported.... We shall, in a few Years, have scarce any Occasion of deriving these costly Commodities from other Countries.... Gold, and Silver Lace and Fringe, fine Hats, millinery Articles, Saddlers' Goods, Cloaks, Watches, Cutlery-Wares, Fire-Arms, Coaches, Post-Chaises, Chariots, etc., are extremely well and neatly finished in Dublin.

Much of the raw material for Dublin's flourishing hat manufacture came from a flat sandy headland in north Co. Londonderry. At Magilligan the salt spray from the sea damaged crops, and in order to prosper the people had to supplement their income in other ways. Here the sand dunes and marram grass were home to the most extensive rabbit warren in Ulster. The local people, trapping the animals with ferrets and nets, sold the carcasses for about fourpence each and found buyers eager to take the skins for the capital's felt and hatting trade. In the 1750s the Gage family, leasing Magilligan from the Church of Ireland, tripled the rent to 120 dozen rabbit skins and restricted the killing season to the months from November to February. By the end of the century the annual take was around 30,000 animals, selling at thirteen shillings a dozen.

Most of Ireland's manufactures were bought by Irish people themselves. But Ulster's largest industry, linen, was also directed at the export market.

Episode 133 ~

ULSTER'S DOMESTIC LINEN INDUSTRY

From very early times the Irish had grown their own flax and made their own linen; it gets scant attention in Gaelic records, however, since it was produced by people who were low-born. This type of linen was still being made for local sale in the eighteenth century; however, its width was too narrow for the export market.

Some of the leading Ulster planters, such as the Clotworthys of south Antrim, encouraged their tenants to grow and spin flax to help tide them over hard times. The government too was keen to foster an industry that did not conflict with English commercial interests; in 1696 it removed duties on 'brown', or unbleached, Irish linen bound for the English market. The Irish parliament paid a large grant to the French Huguenot Louis Crommelin to establish a colony of skilled weavers in Lisburn in 1698. Although these foreign weavers were scattered by a terrible fire which destroyed Lisburn in 1707, they had already taught others about the latest continental techniques.

The Irish parliament set up the Linen Board in 1710: it awarded grants to inventors; gave subsidies to bleachers; paid tuition fees at spinning schools; and gave out—free—thousands of spinning-wheels to the poor. The board put up a Linen Hall in Dublin city in 1728, and the Ulster origin of most of the cloth is underlined by the names of the streets adjoining it: Coleraine Street, Lurgan Street, Lisburn Street. Here linen brought from the north in solid-wheeled carts was sold to English drapers, and it was not until the 1780s that Dublin ceased to be the main point of export for Ulster cloth.

The making of linen in Ulster was a domestic industry, carried on in the home by people who divided their time between farming and the production of yarn and cloth. Planted in the spring in heavily manured soil and producing a delicate blue flower in early summer, flax was ready for harvesting about the middle of August. It was pulled, not cut, and then tied in sheaves, or 'beets', and allowed to dry in stooks for a few days. Then the beets were weighed down in a pond or a dammed stream, known as a 'lint-hole', and allowed to rot or 'ret' for about a fortnight.

Now for the worst job of all: strong men plunged up to their oxters in the stinking lint-hole and, with special forks, heaved the wet flax out, ready to be spread out over the fields to dry. And after the flax had dried there was still more back-breaking work before it was ready for the spinning-wheel. For it was only after the flax was 'broken', 'scutched' and 'hackled'—each process in itself intensely laborious—that the fibres could be made into yarn. Long fibres produced fine linen yarn, while short fibres, or 'tow', were suitable only for sacking and coarse cloth.

The native Irish had spun yarn from a distaff with a weighted stone, or whorl, but this was being rapidly replaced by a treadle-operated spinning-wheel of Dutch design—the spinning-wheel most of us think of as being distinctively Irish. There can have few homes in the whole of the northern half of Ireland where the hum of the spinning-wheel did not blend almost every night with the soft song of the 'spinster'.

The yarn, wound on what was known as a 'clock reel', was ready then for the weaver—usually a man, for weaving was heavy work. Preparing the loom was a tricky job, as one account from Co. Armagh explains:

There is considerable skill and knowledge required for putting up a loom properly, mounting her, and giving her a complete rig. Sometimes a weaver can do this for himself, but often he possesses not the necessary knowledge, nor the way to carry it into practice. And hence, in almost every country district, there are some of clearer heads and readier hands who become a sort of professors in this line.

When the loom was tackled, the warp threads had to be dressed with flour and water, fanned dry with a goose wing, and then rubbed with tallow. Only then was the weft ready to be placed in the shuttle. Linen cloth was woven into a 'web', a roll of cloth one yard wide and twenty-five yards in length.

It goes without saying that the completed web was not yet ready for the dressmaker. It had to be thoroughly cleaned of its tallow and flour, and then bleached white. Cleaning and bleaching were almost as labour-intensive as the making of the cloth itself.

It was to speed up this finishing of the linen cloth that drapers began to build massive water-powered machines across the Ulster countryside.

Episode 134 ∿

WASH-MILLS, BLEACH-GREENS AND BEETLING ENGINES

In 1776 the English agricultural improver Arthur Young watched the linen market at Lurgan, Co. Armagh:

> When the clock strikes eleven the drapers jump upon stone standings, and the weavers instantly flock about them with their pieces.... The draper's clerk stands by him, and writes his master's name on the pieces he buys, with the price.... At twelve it ends; then there is an hour for measuring the pieces, and paying the money; for nothing but ready money is taken; and this is the way the business is carried on at all the markets. Three thousand pieces a week are sold here, at 35s each on an average ... and per annum £273,000 and this is all made in a circumference of not many miles.

Early in the eighteenth century weavers bleached their own 'pieces' or 'webs', each one yard wide and twenty-five yards long. The linen had to be boiled and rinsed between seven and twelve times, and then laid out on the grass to be whitened by the sun and the rain. Each weaver had his own secret recipe for aiding the bleaching process, usually incorporating sour milk, urine and manure. Even then, linen was not ready for sale until the weave had been closed and given a sheen by being hammered on a flat stone with a wooden club known as a 'beetle'.

Not only was this exhausting, but it long delayed the time when a family could get hard cash for its webs. Not surprisingly, these finishing processes were the first to become mechanised as drapers began damming the streams to drive engines by water power.

In the seventeenth century corn mills turned by horizontal wheels transferred to more efficient vertical wheels. The power transmitted from the wheel down the axle could be harnessed to an impressive array of labour-saving machines by the linen drapers. These drapers, in short, ensured that Ulster had an important and early role to play in Europe's first industrial revolution.

The heart of the industry was the 'linen triangle', extending from Dungannon, east to Lisburn, and south to Armagh; then, as output increased, Newry was drawn in. Within this area, and later beyond it, drapers dammed every available river and stream and constructed mill-races for their great water-wheels. On the River Callan in Co. Armagh there were no bleach-works until 1743, and yet by 1771 there were thirty-six bleach-yards along its banks finishing nearly three million yards of cloth. By 1795 it was reckoned that there were in Co. Armagh fifty-one bleach-yards, each covering around three acres and operating two or three wheels and finishing 162,500 pieces of linen.

After being boiled in an alkaline solution for twelve hours, ten times over, the linen was then steeped in a sulphuric acid solution and then washed again. Rub-boards—corrugated wooden boards which were pushed backwards and forwards by water power while wet soaped cloth was drawn between them— were a local invention. The wash-mills, first introduced in the 1720s, dwarfed the very largest machines to be found in a modern launderette. Two massive feet, each weighing around a quarter of a ton, were suspended from a great wooden frame and swung to swirl and squeeze the cloth.

In between these repeated operations the linen webs were laid out in fields to bleach in the sun, wind and rain. In the middle of many Ulster fields curious round stone huts with conical roofs can still be seen. These were watch-houses to keep an eye on the bleaching linen webs to prevent them being stolen. These were necessary, as a report from the *Belfast News-Letter* of 11 April 1783 makes clear:

At the assizes for the county of Down ... the following persons were capitally convicted ... Stephen Gordon, otherwise McGurnaghan (to be executed at Castlewellan on Monday next the 14th inst.) for stealing linen out of the bleachgreen of George and Walter Crawford of Balleivy; George Brown (to be executed at Downpatrick 1st June next) for stealing linen out of the bleachgreen of Samuel McAlester of Lisnamore; John Wright (to be executed at Banbridge on Monday 21st inst.).

The beetling engine was a striking improvement on hand-beating with a wooden club. A row of heavy beams dropped in regular succession on the cloth, the stamping process bringing out the natural lustre of the fibres, and giving the necessary sheen to high-quality ducks, hollands, hucks, buckrams, interlinings, and umbrella and book-binding cloth. As pounding one piece could last up to a fortnight and beat out a thunderous tattoo reminiscent of a huge Lambeg drum, the beetling mill had to be placed some distance from the main works.

The success of rural linen industry provided a good living for the rapidly rising population in central and southern Ulster. Many, however, were restless and sought a better life across the Atlantic Ocean.

Episode 135 ✑

'A VAST NUMBER OF PEOPLE SHIPPING OFF FOR PENNSYLVANIA AND BOSTON'

Ulster linen drapers could drive a hard bargain, but they acquired a reputation for straight-dealing. Not all were prosaic, hard-nosed businessmen. In 1795 Friend Thomas Stott of Dromore sent a pack of linen to his fellow-Quaker, Friend James Gilmour. Included was his bill, written in Ulster Scots verse:

> This morn', Frien' James, we sent a wheen
> Of good thick lawns and cambrics thin
> To Maister Mirries at Belfast
> (As we've been wont this sometime past).
> The hail are packed in ae stout kist
> That nothing hurtful might maelist.

> The lawns we fear ye'll no think cheap
> Though we by them smal' profit reap.
> The cambrics, tho' they luk but lean,
> Will make a shift to haud their ain.
> On baith to this bit paper joined
> The bill o' parcels ye will find.
> An' we hae placed the fair amount
> Right cannily to your account,
> Which, if we cast the figures straight,
> Is just of pounds four score and eight,
> Five Irish siller shillins smug
> And six bawbees—to buy a mug.

Weavers, too, composed verse during the long hours they spent at the loom. Not all were content, however. Ulster landlords were able to raise the rents year after year, and the county grand juries increased the local tax, known as the 'cess'. Clergy of the Church of Ireland increased the burden of tithes, the compulsory payment farmers of every religion had to make to the Established Church. Rents quintupled in many areas between 1710 and 1770, and yet in the same period the average price of linen cloth rose only by twenty per cent. The sense of hopelessness created by these circumstances is encapsulated in the words of Ulster's most famous ballad of emigration:

> For the rent is getting higher, and I can no longer stay,
> So fare well unto ye bonny, bonny Slieve Gallon Brae....
> But these days are now all over, for I am far away,
> So fare well unto ye bonny, bonny Slieve Gallon Brae.

The prospect of a better life in America undoubtedly had a very strong appeal for these industrious but poverty-stricken tenants.

In the year 1718 eleven Ulster Presbyterian ministers and nearly three hundred members of their congregations petitioned Samuel Shute, the governor of New England, for a grant of land. Shute gave every encouragement, and that summer five ships left Derry quay for Boston. This was the start of a momentous migration across the Atlantic, and it got under way just at the time that the coming of Scots into Ulster had almost completely stopped.

From the outset the authorities were alarmed because they believed the island would be drained of Protestants. William King, Archbishop of Dublin and a key member of the government, wrote in 1718: 'No papists stir.... The papists being already five or six to one, you imagine in what condition we are like to be in.' In the following year a Co. Monaghan land agent wrote a letter from the town of Clones to his employer:

There is a hundred families gone through this towne this week past for New England.... I believe we shall have nothing left but Irish at last; but I hope your honour's estate will be safe enough, for they complayne most of the hardships of the tythes makes them all goe, which is true, for the Clergy is unreasonable.

In July 1728 Thomas Whitney, a seaman waiting, wrote:

Here are a vast number of people shipping off for Pennsylvania and Boston, here are three ships at Larne, 5 at Derry two at Coleraine 3 at Belfast and 4 at Sligo, I'm assured within these eight years there are gone above forty thousand people out of Ulster and the low part of Connacht.

In November of the same year Primate Hugh Boulter, deputising for the viceroy, informed the British government: 'The humour has spread like a contagious distemper.... The worst is that it affects only Protestants, and reigns chiefly in the north, which is the seat of our linen manufacture.'

And why did Catholics not cross the Atlantic? The truth was that the mainly Puritan colonies of New England did not as yet welcome Catholic immigrants. In any case, most Catholics would have found it too difficult to raise the capital required. Presbyterians complained about taxes and rents, Penal Laws which excluded them from town councils, and being forced to contribute to a church to which they did not belong. Certainly the Presbyterian ministers played a leading role in organising emigration. Ezekiel Stewart of Portstewart observed in 1729:

The Presbiteirin ministers have taken their shear of pains to seduce their poor Ignorant heerers, by Bellowing from their pulpits against Landlords and the Clargey, calling them Rackers of Rents and Scruers of Tythes.... Two of these Preachers caryed this affair to such a length that they went themselves to New England and caryed numbers with them.

The greatest attraction, however, was that America offered Ulster Presbyterians access to cheap land.

Episode 136 ∽

THE VOYAGE OF THE *SALLY*

FOR THE CITY OF PHILADELPHIA IN AMERICA

The good ship *SALLY*, burthen three hundred tuns, mounted with twelve carriage guns and six swivels, with small arms in proportion, Captain James Taylor, Commander, will be clear to sail from hence by the 15th day of April next for Philadelphia aforesaid.... She is a fine new ship, and proves to be one of the fastest sailing vessels belonging to North America, and shall be amply provided with proper accommodations for passengers; and as the Captain is well known to be well experienced in that trade, those who take their passage with him, may depend on the best usage. Dated at Belfast, March 1, 1762.

It was this advertisement that John Smilie of Greyabbey read in the *Belfast News-Letter*. Like so many Ulster Presbyterians, he saw America as a land of opportunity at a time when farm rents at home were rising fast. John bade farewell to his father on 18 May; he was in no danger of missing his ship, for the *Sally* was delayed, waiting no doubt for a full complement of passengers. Coming into Belfast through Ballymacarrett, he approached the Lagan mouth, spanned by the twenty-one arches of the Long Bridge, described three years before as 'the longest in His Majesty's dominions'. Here the stallion 'Tickle Me Quickly' stood at the County Down end, ready to cover mares at the cost of 'half a guinea, and a shilling'. John found High Street thronged with dealers and traders, while importers, shipping agents and sugar refiners in the entries were not short of customers.

Crossing the Farset stream by one of the High Street bridges, John Smilie walked to Donegall Street, and here Mr James Sinclaire, the agent, arranged his passage. The fare was generally around £5, and it is quite likely that Smilie became an 'indentured servant', agreeing to work without pay for a fixed term on an American plantation in return for a free passage.

On Monday 24 May 1762 the *Sally* weighed anchor, nosed past Carrickfergus and Whitehead, and sailed northwards by the Antrim coast, to steer west beyond Rathlin into the open Atlantic. In a letter describing his voyage John Smilie began:

Honoured father ... On the 31st we lost Sight of Ireland, having been detained 'till then by Calms and contrary Winds.... We had our full Allowance of Bread and Water, only for the first Fortnight; then we were reduced to three Pints of Water per day; and three Pounds and a Half of Bread per week.

Grasping shipowners would keep food and water at a bare minimum, and unscrupulous masters would dole them out unfairly, but it was only when adverse weather conditions delayed the voyage that passengers would starve. During a fortnight of storms the *Sally* was blown off course.

We had a South-West Wind, which drove us so far North, that our weather became extremely cold, with much Rain and hard Gales of Wind: On the 5th of July we had a hard Squal of Wind which lasted 3 Hours, and caused us to lie to; on the 6th we had a Storm which continued 9 Hours, and obliged us to lie to under bare Poles; on the 12th we espied a Mountain of Ice of prodigious Size.

Britain was then at war with France and Spain, and Captain Taylor—disregarding the perilously low stock of food and water on board—eagerly pursued enemy merchant vessels in the hope of taking a prize. After ten weeks at sea, for the remaining twelve days of the voyage each of the passengers had to survive on just two and half biscuits, half a naggin of raw barley and twelve pints of water.

Hunger and Thirst had now reduced our Crew to the last Extremity; nothing was now to be heard aboard our ship but the Cries of distressed children, and of their distressed Mothers, unable to relieve them. Our Ship was now truly a real Spectacle of Horror! Never a day passed without one or two of our Crew put over Board; many kill'd themselves by drinking Salt Water; and their own Urine was a common Drink; yet in the midst of all our Miseries, our Captain shewed not the least Remorse or Pity. We were out of Hopes of ever seeing land. August 29th we had only one Pint of Water for each Person ... and our Bread was done; But on that Day the Lord was pleased to sent the Greatest Shower of Rain I ever saw, which was the Means of preserving our Lives.

A few days later the *Sally* reached Philadelphia, after a passage of fourteen weeks and five days during which sixty-four passengers died. Despite the hazards of the Atlantic crossing, however, the numbers leaving Ulster continued to rise, reaching a peak in the 1770s.

Episode 137 ～

THE AMERICAN REVOLUTION AND IRELAND

The journey of emigrants across the Atlantic in the eighteenth century could be perilous. In 1729, for example, 175 people died on board two vessels from Belfast during the crossing; and in 1741 the *Seaflower* sprang her mast *en route* to Philadelphia and forty-six passengers died, six of their corpses being eaten in desperation by the survivors. For many Ulster Presbyterians, however, these were risks worth taking. As David Lindsay explained to his Pennsylvanian cousins in 1758, 'The good Bargins of yar lands doe greatly encourage me to pluck up my spirits and make redie for the journey, for we are now oppressed with our lands at 8s an acre.'

During a severe economic downturn in the early 1770s migration to America reached a new peak of about ten thousand a year. In April 1773 the *Londonderry Journal* reported:

> Their removal is sensibly felt in this county—This prevalent humour of industrious Protestants withdrawing from this once flourishing corner of the kingdom seems to be increasing....Where the evil will end, remains only in the womb of time to determine.

The Governor of North Carolina, Arthur Dobbs of Carrickfergus, was only one of many colonial land developers anxious to attract Ulster families to what was known as the 'back country'. Ulster Presbyterians—known as the 'Scotch-Irish'—were already accustomed to being on the move and defending their land; woodkerne, tories and rapparees at home had prepared them for frontier skirmishing with Pontiac and other native Americans. The settlers' pugnacious attitude is tersely expressed in an urgent message sent by the backwoodsman James Magraw to his brother in Paxtang: 'Get some guns for us—There's a good wheen of ingens about here.'

Magraw was writing from the Cumberland valley, where the fertile soil attracted many Scotch-Irish pioneers. From there they pushed south into Virginia to the Appalachian Mountains and fanned out over the South Carolina Piedmont, and then on to West Virginia and through the Cumberland Gap into Kentucky and Tennessee. By now around quarter of a million Ulster Protestants had emigrated to the American colonies, which then had a European population of no more than a million.

On 14 June 1774 Thomas Wright wrote a letter from Bucks County to his friend Thomas Greer in Co. Tyrone:

The Colonies at present is in a very dissatisfied position by reason of the impositions of Great Britain; Boston is entirely blocked up since the first of this month that no vessel is to pass or repass.... Some here is apprehensive the event will be attended with much bloodshed.

Wright's prediction was accurate—the Boston Tea Party was the beginning of the American Revolution and a very bloody war.

On 13 April 1778 the American privateer John Paul Jones sailed his ship *Ranger* into Belfast Lough and engaged *Drake*, a Royal Navy sloop stationed there. After an obstinate fight of forty-five minutes off the Copeland Islands the British vessel struck its colours and was seized. The American War of Independence, now more than two years old, had been brought to the very shores of Ireland.

Stewart Banks, the sovereign, or mayor, of Belfast, applied to Dublin Castle for help. The viceroy, Lord Harcourt, replied that all he could spare were half a company of invalids and a troop or two of cavalry—but without any horses. As Lord Charlemont recalled, 'Abandoned by the Government in the hour of Danger, the inhabitants of Belfast were left to their own defence, and boldly and instantly undertook it.' A Volunteer company formed on St Patrick's Day now took on an urgent role, and recruitment was brisk.

When the American Revolution broke, the sympathy of the northern Protestants was with the colonists. As the Presbyterian minister William Steel Dickson said in a sermon in Belfast, 'There is scarcely a Protestant family of the middle classes amongst us who does not reckon kindred with the inhabitants of that extensive continent.' John Hancock, from Co. Down, was the first to sign the American Declaration of Independence; and other signatories included Thomas McKean from Ballymoney, and Charles Thomson from Maghera, who served as Secretary of Congress and later designed the Great Seal of the United States. Men of Ulster Presbyterian stock, known as the Scotch-Irish, played a pivotal role in the revolutionary armies, and at the height of the war George Washington observed: 'If defeated everywhere else, I will make my last stand for liberty among the Scotch-Irish of my native Virginia.' Indeed, Lord Harcourt informed London that Ulster Presbyterians were 'Americans ... in their hearts ... talking in all companies in such a way that if they are not rebels, it is hard to find a name for them'.

In that year, 1778, however, France had joined the war on the side of the American colonists, and Ulster Protestants had no difficulty in recognising the traditional enemy.

Episode 138 ～

'FREE TRADE—OR ELSE!'

> Where are the legs with which you run?
> *Hurroo! Hurroo!*
> Where are the legs with which you run?
> *Hurroo! Hurroo!*
> Where are the legs with which you run?
> When you went to carry a gun?
> Indeed, your dancing days are done!
> Och, Johnny, I hardly knew ye!

By 1778 the British government's position was desperate. The American colonists in revolt had now been joined by France, and soon Spain would add her support. Even though the Penal Laws had made it illegal, the government recruited great numbers of Irish Catholics to fight on the other side of the Atlantic.

> With drums and guns, and guns and drums
> The enemy nearly slew ye;
> My darling dear, you look so queer,
> Och, Johnny, I hardly knew ye!

Ireland was stripped of troops to fight in America, and the coffers of the Irish administration in Dublin were empty. No money could be found to form a militia for home defence purposes. The island was completely defenceless against a possible French invasion, as Lord Charlemont explained:

> Ireland was hourly threatened with invasion—The Enemy was at our Doors, and Administration had no possible Means of Assistance—Unsupported by England and destitute both of Men and Money they shuddered at the idea of a most trifling Incursion—They feared and consequently hated the Volunteers, yet to them alone They looked for Assistance, for Safety.

The first Volunteer corps had been formed in Belfast in April 1778. Soon every county in Ireland followed Belfast's example until by the following year there were 40,000 Volunteers drilling to defend Ireland—entirely self-financed and out of the control of government. Only landlords, substantial farmers and professional men could afford to pay around £1 15s for a musket, buy a uniform and suffer loss of earnings while drilling and on manoeuvre. Nevertheless, the

Volunteers were democratically organised: officers were elected by the ranks, and, for example, a man who had just paid £25,000 for an estate in Larne was content to serve as a private in his local company.

In fact the French never came. The Volunteers soon realised that they now possessed considerable muscle which they could flex to extract concessions from the beleaguered British government. In particular, they wanted the government to remove laws imposed by England on Ireland, forbidding the export of wool, glass, leather and other goods. Supporting the Volunteers, the 'Patriot' opposition in the Irish parliament forced through 'short money bills'—voting money to the government for six months only.

On 4 November 1779 the Volunteers organised a massive demonstration in College Green in front of the Parliament House. The *Dublin Journal* published this account:

> Thursday being the anniversary of the birth and landing in England of his Majesty King William the Third, of glorious memory ...
>
> At noon the ... volunteer corps belonging of the county and city of Dublin, assembled in St Stephen's Green ... the whole dressed in scarlet faced with black velvet, silver epaulets and buttons, white waistcoats and breeches, small half gaiters, and white cross belts with silver breast plates ... Luke Gardiner, Esq; commander of the united corps for the day....
>
> The enemies to Ireland ... must confess, no troops in Europe are better disciplined, and none in the world so well appointed. This independent, this Irish army, this martial phaenomenon, must create the wonder and admiration of mankind, when they are informed that the first nobility, most respectable senators, and principal men, for fortune and character, formed the ranks of it.
>
> In this order they proceeded through the city, amidst the acclamations of multitudes, and surrounded the equestrian statue of King William on College-green, where, after a grand salute, they fired three vollies with admirable regularity.... The statue preparatory to this occasion, was new painted, and ornamented with ribbons and from each side of the pedestal hung large labels, on which the following words were inscribed in capital letters:
>
> East.–THE VOLUNTEERS OF IRELAND.
> The Motto,
> QUINQUAGINTA MILLIA JUNCTA,
> PARATI PRO PATRIA MORI.

... translated from Latin that means: '50,000 joined together, ready to die for their fatherland' ...

West.–THE GLORIOUS REVOLUTION.
North.–SHORT MONEY BILLS, A FREE TRADE—OR ELSE !!!!!
South.–RELIEF TO IRELAND.

The numbers of spectators on this occasion were almost incredible. Every avenue that leads into College-green, were so crowded that all free intercourse subsided until the whole was over....

If the scene during the day was busy and beautiful the evening was brilliant and illustrious. A general illumination took place, attended by every mark of real rejoicing. The different corps of our Volunteers ... dined with their commanders and officers. Harmony, affection, and public spirit reigned among them, and truly constitutional, Hibernian toasts were drank.... Bells and bonfires likewise lent their assistance, but we are sorry to say that squibs and crackers, bouncing about, terrified several ladies.

What would the government do now?

Episode 139 ～

THE DUNGANNON CONVENTION

By the autumn of 1779 the British administration in Dublin had been reduced to a state of helplessness. News had come in of catastrophic defeats at the hands of American colonists; a French invasion was daily expected; the treasury in Dublin was empty; and the defence of the island was entirely dependent on 50,000 independent Volunteers demanding drastic political change. In the Irish parliament the 'Patriot' opposition commanded a crushing majority. On 24 November, Walter Hussey Burgh, MP, urged his fellow-Patriots to stand firm, declaring that the bonds of slavery imposed by a foreign parliament must be broken:

Talk not to me of peace; Ireland is not in a state of peace; it is smothered war. England has sown her laws like dragon's teeth and they have sprung up in armed men.

Lord North's government at Westminster had no choice but to capitulate completely. Prohibitions on the export of Irish wool, cut glass, leather and other items were removed, and legislation was introduced to allow Irish ships to trade directly with Jamaica and other colonies of the British Empire.

For some Patriots and Volunteers, this was only the beginning of a campaign to win for Ireland 'legislative independence'. The aim was not to make Ireland an independent state but to raise the island from being a colony to being an equal partner with Britain. To achieve this, two statutes would have to be changed or repealed altogether. One was Poynings' Law, first enacted in the fifteenth century: in practice, this measure made it possible for the government of the day in London to change or even suppress bills passed by the Irish parliament. The other was the Declaratory Act of 1720, by which Westminster declared that it could enact laws for Ireland—a power most often used to regulate Irish trade.

Until these statutes had been changed, it was believed, Ireland would continue to be treated as a subservient colony. Nowhere was this felt more strongly than in Ulster, the province where around half of all Ireland's Volunteers were based. Since the government gave not the slightest indication of making any concessions, Volunteer commanders met at Armagh and agreed new tactics. In accordance with this decision, delegates from every Volunteer company in Ulster were summoned to Dungannon in Co. Tyrone.

On the morning of 15 February 1782 242 delegates, representing 143 Volunteer companies, marched two by two along the streets of Dungannon, lined by the local light infantry company, to the parish church. William Irvine, colonel of the Lowtherstown Company in Fermanagh, took the chair. Between noon and eight o'clock that evening propositions were solemnly debated and voted on. The motions passed were a clarion call for legislative independence:

Resolved unanimously, that a claim of any body of men, other than the King, Lords and Commons of Ireland, to make laws to bind this kingdom, is unconstitutional, illegal, and a Grievance.

Resolved (with one dissenting voice only), That the powers exercised by the privy Councils of both kingdoms, under, or under colour or pretence of, the law of Poynings, are unconstitutional and a Grievance.

These were but two of twenty resolutions approved. In addition to these, the assembled Volunteers agreed to send a public address of support to the Patriots in the Irish parliament. Like the American Declaration of Independence, it pulsates with the spirit of the eighteenth-century Enlightenment:

MY LORDS AND GENTLEMEN,
We thank you for your noble and spirited, though hitherto ineffectual efforts, in defence of the great constitutional and commercial rights of your country. Go on. The almost unanimous voice of the people is with you; and

in a free country, the voice of the People must prevail. We know our duty to our Sovereign, and are loyal. We know our duty to ourselves, and are resolved to be Free. We seek for our Rights, and no more than our Rights; and, in so just a pursuit, we should doubt the Being of a Providence, if we doubted of success.

The Dungannon Convention also debated the prickly question of Catholic rights. Luke Gardiner, Dublin's leading Volunteer commander and a Patriot MP, had successfully steered a motion through the Irish parliament to remove some of the most damaging legal disabilities—above all, Catholics were now able (for the first time in nearly ninety years) to buy land outright. Only two delegates refused to support the resolution adopted by the Volunteers:

> ... that, as men and as Irishmen, as Christians and as Protestants, we rejoice in the relaxation of the penal laws against our Roman Catholic fellow-subjects.

The resolution was supported by Captain the Rev. Robert Black: 'I rejoice to hear a motion in favour of our Roman Catholic brethren; Sir, I am proud to second it as a Protestant Dissenting clergyman, as an Irish Independent Volunteer.'

Few of the delegates at Dungannon could have predicted that legislative independence would be won just a few weeks hence.

Episode 140 ~

'I AM NOW TO ADDRESS A FREE PEOPLE'

> Our freedom's declared, we'll chase dull sorrows,
> All cares we'll banish to feast and banquet,
> With bonfire smoke we'll darken the skies.
> What mortal so grave in aged Hibernia!
> As to hate the frolic by fate allotted
> To groaning, moaning widows and wives.

The Dungannon Convention of Volunteer delegates in February 1782 had electrified the whole of Ireland. The resolutions calling for Ireland's legislative independence were enthusiastically ratified by meetings all across the

island. Two Patriot MPs, Henry Grattan and Henry Flood, rallied support with
fiery speeches.

> Dungannon's great oak from whose trunk honey dropped,
> Whose branches spread over the four wide provinces,
> Ye topers now honour with port and claret!
> Hallo! *Go maidin geal* toast sweet Harry Flood
> In copious, flowing, logical tide.

Henry Grattan seized his opportunity when the Irish parliament opened on
16 April 1782. Following catastrophic defeat in the American War of
Independence, Lord North's Tory government at Westminster was forced to
resign. On the opening of the parliamentary session in Dublin, the public galleries and the bar of the House of Commons in College Green were packed, so
great was the anxiety to hear what the new government intended. As soon as the
Speaker had taken the chair, the Secretary of State, John Hely Hutchinson, read
out the Address from the Throne, which outlined the Whig government's inten-
tions. This, rather vaguely, stated that the government intended to make concessions. Grattan then rose to make a carefully rehearsed speech which made the
assumption that all the demands of the Patriots and the Volunteers would be
met:

> I am now to address a free people: ages have passed away, and this is the
> first moment you could be distinguished by that appellation.
>
> I have spoken on the subject of your liberty so often, that I have nothing
> to add, and have only to admire by what Heaven-directed steps you have
> proceeded until the whole faculty of the nation is braced up to the act of
> her own deliverance.
>
> I found Ireland on her knees, I watched over her with a paternal solicitude;
> I have traced her progress from injuries to arms, and from arms to liberty.
> Spirit of Swift! Spirit of Molyneux! Your genius has prevailed! Ireland is
> now a nation! In that new character I hail her! And bowing to her august
> presence, I say, *Esto perpetua.*

... 'Esto perpetua' means 'may it be forever'...

> She is no longer a wretched colony, returning thanks to her governor for his
> rapine, and to her king for his oppression.... Look to the rest of Europe, and
> contemplate yourself, and be satisfied. Holland lives on the memory of past
> achievements; England has sullied her name by an attempt to enslave her
> colonies. You are the only people—you, of the nations of Europe, are now
> the only people who excite admiration.... For acknowledging American lib-
> erty, England has the plea of necessity; for acknowledging the liberties of
> Ireland she has the plea of justice.

Grattan then proposed an amendment to the address of thanks to the king, which in effect was a demand for full legislative independence for the Irish parliament. Grattan's speech had such a powerful effect that not a single MP voted against the amendment.

The alarmed Chief Secretary, Richard Fitzpatrick, wrote to London:

> Debate it can hardly be called, since that implies discussion.... Grattan's speech was splendid in point of eloquence, all declamation, and what there was weak in argument, his manner I think, though certainly very animated, disgusting to the last degree from affectation.

Nevertheless, feelings were running so high in Ireland that the Prime Minister, Lord Shelburne—himself owner of a huge estate in Munster—felt that all demands would have to be conceded. In a matter of weeks the necessary legislation was passed in London: no longer could Westminster pass laws for Ireland; and no longer did bills in the Irish parliament need to be approved by the English Privy Council. The Volunteers and the Patriots had won. Ireland appeared to enjoy an equal status with Britain in the British Empire. That summer a huge Volunteer parade in Dublin's Phoenix Park celebrated the triumph. A grateful Irish House of Commons voted Grattan, a comparatively poor man, the huge sum of £50,000 so that he could buy himself an estate to become a country gentleman. For the remainder of its existence the Irish legislature would become known as 'Grattan's Parliament'. This was a period of apparent prosperity, when Dublin reached its climax as a glittering Georgian capital, adorned with elegant new streets and magnificent new public buildings, including the Four Courts and the Custom House.

Henry Flood's nose was out of joint: Flood was not at all pleased that Grattan had pushed him out of the limelight. He now became the champion of those Volunteers who wanted to bring about radical reform of the Irish parliament itself.

Episode 141 ⁓

THE FAILURE OF REFORM

The eighteenth-century Irish parliament in College Green was even more unrepresentative of the people than the Westminster parliament. For a start Catholics—three-quarters of the population—were ineligible to sit as members of parliament, and until the final decade of the century they were unable to vote; even a Protestant married to a Catholic could not vote. Only a handful of Presbyterians ever got elected, and there were no Presbyterians in the Irish House of Lords.

There was no secret ballot, and in county elections landlords or their agents simply told the tenants how to vote—or risk eviction. Out of a total of 300 MPS, 234 were elected from boroughs, that is, towns with their own councils. Only a few, such as Dublin and Cork cities, had reasonably large electorates. Some fortunate towns, such as Lisburn, had a 'potwalloper' franchise—in other words, any man with a pot, a hearth to place it on, and a house could vote—only if he was a Protestant, of course.

Most boroughs were owned by landlords, and it was they who decided who would be elected. Belfast was typical: Lord Donegall appointed all thirteen members of the Corporation, and they alone elected two members to sit in the Irish Commons. Some boroughs had no inhabitants at all: Bannow, Co. Wexford, was just a pile of sea sand without a single house; at Clonmines, in the same county, there was but one solitary house; and at Harristown, Co. Kildare, there nothing other than a single tree. Yet those boroughs each returned two members to parliament.

The Irish Volunteers, with considerable justification, felt that they represented the Protestants of Ireland rather better than parliament. They had played a pivotal role in forcing the British government to grant the Irish parliament legislative independence in 1782. Now they called for a radical reform of the Irish parliament. The campaign was kicked off by the Volunteers of Lisburn in 1783 and was enormously boosted when two young aristocrats, Hercules Rowley and John O'Neill, were elected by the freeholders of Co. Antrim. Both men were Volunteers and committed to the cause of reform.

The reformers turned to the great orator Henry Flood for leadership. A Volunteer reform convention was held in every province, the first in Ulster at Dungannon on 8 September. These in turn elected 160 delegates to meet in Dublin on 10 November 1783. On that day the delegates met at the Royal Exchange and then marched in procession through the streets, escorted by the city and county Volunteers, with drums beating and colours flying, as thousands of spectators cheered them on to the Rotunda. Flood inspired the delegates with his speeches:

Is there a man who will say that the constitution wants no reform? Will any man be found to say, that the constitution is perfect, when he knows the honour of the peerage may be obtained by any ruffian who possesses borough interest?

After many days debate the delegates agreed on a programme, and on 29 November Flood, still in his Volunteer uniform, presented his parliamentary reform bill to the Commons.

For some time members of the Irish parliament had been alarmed at the presence of armed Volunteers just a mile from College Green. They were outraged by Flood's instructions to the delegates not to disband until they knew the outcome of the bill. Even supporters of parliamentary reform felt that an attempt was being made to overawe parliament by military force. The Attorney-General, Barry Yelverton, was not slow to express his objections:

> I do not mean to go into the discussion of the bill, but ... I will say, if it originates with an armed body, it is inconsistent with the freedom of debate for this house to receive it. We sit not here to receive propositions at the point of the bayonet. When the Volunteers with that ... rude instrument the bayonet probe and explore a constitution which requires the nicest hand to touch, I own my respect and veneration for them is destroyed.

Instead of expanding on the merits of his bill for parliamentary reform, Flood was forced to defend the conduct of the Volunteers, pointing out that Yelverton himself was a Volunteer:

> Why did not the right honourable gentleman make a declaration against them?... He was then one of their body—he is now their accuser ... he cannot now bear to hear of Volunteers—but I will ask him, and I will have a starling taught to holla it in his ear, Who got you the free trade? Who got you the constitution? Who made you a nation?—the Volunteers.

Most MPs, however, agreed with the Attorney-General. Flood's bill was heavily defeated. What would the Volunteers do now? They were too law-abiding even to think of attempting to overawe parliament by force. They simply went home. Their moment was over. The Irish parliament would not be reformed.

Episode 142 ∽

'FOURTEENTH JULY 1789; SACRED TO LIBERTY'

The defence of Ireland against a possible French invasion had depended entirely on the Volunteers. By 1784, however, the British government had given its recognition to the United States of America and regular troops were returning to Ireland from across the Atlantic. The Volunteers, no longer the only armed body on the island, now proved unable to exert pressure on the Irish parliament to make itself more representative of the people. Above all, the Volunteers were bitterly divided on whether or not Catholics should be given political rights.

Over most of Ireland, Protestants were in a small minority, concerned to defend their privileges. Many would have agreed with the Rev. John Rodgers, who in a sermon to Volunteers at Ballybay, Co. Monaghan, urged his congregation 'not to consent to the repeal of the Penal Laws, or to allow of a legal toleration of the popish religion.... Popery is of a persecuting spirit and has always marked her steps, wherever she trod, with blood.' John Wesley, who visited Ireland many times, was inclined to agree. In 1780 he had written to the *Freeman's Journal* in Dublin in favour of retaining the remaining Penal Laws: 'I would not have the Roman Catholics persecuted at all. I would only have them hindered from doing hurt: I would not put it in their power to cut the throats of their quiet neighbours.'

Only east of the River Bann in Ulster did Protestants have such an overwhelming majority that they had no fear of their Catholic neighbours. Here Presbyterians of Antrim and Down had a long tradition of defending their rights against tithe-collectors, clergy and landlords of the Church of Ireland, the Established Church. The Enlightenment had taken deep root in Belfast, still barely one-tenth the size of Dublin but growing fast. Here an energetic and confident middle class passionately debated new political ideas coming in with their cargoes from Scotland, America and France.

The Belfast delegates to the Volunteer Convention in Dublin in 1783 were bitterly disappointed that they had failed to convince their fellow-Volunteers that Catholics should be given the vote. In the following year the Belfast 1st Volunteer Company defiantly invited Catholics to join their ranks, the first in Ireland formally to do so. Then in May 1784 they attended Mass at St Mary's Chapel, which Protestants of Belfast had largely paid for, since the several hundred Catholics in the town were too poor to meet the cost.

Across Ireland the campaign to make parliament more representative of the people slowly fizzled out. Parliamentary reform was, after all, an out-landish and largely irrelevant concept even in Enlightenment Europe—where, it should be remembered, Britain, Ireland and Holland were about the only countries with elected legislative assemblies. Then, in July 1789, that changed dramatically:

> Ah! ça ira, ça ira, ça ira,
> Les aristocrates a la lanterne!
> Ah! ça ira, ça ira, ça ira,
> Les aristocrates on les pendra!

News of the French Revolution electrified the citizens of Belfast. Their views were reflected in the *Belfast News-Letter*, which described it as 'the greatest event in human annals' and continued:

> Twenty-six millions of our fellow-creatures (near one-sixth of the inhabit-ants of Europe) bursting their chains, and throwing off in an instant, the degrading yoke of slavery—it is a scene so new, interesting and sublime, that the heart which cannot participate in the triumph, must either have been vitiated by illiberal politics, or be naturally depraved.

The example of France spurred the Presbyterians of Belfast to campaign anew for the reform of parliament. A Northern Whig Club was formed in 1790, and in the following year it organised a great celebration of the second anniversary of the fall of the Bastille.

On 14 July 1791 the Belfast Volunteers, including a troop of light dragoons and the artillery corps trailing brass six-pounders, set out from the Exchange. The *Belfast News-Letter* described the banners they bore, including:

> A portrait of MONSIEUR MIRABEAU, (borne by two young volunteers) [and] ... The GREAT STANDARD, elevated on a triumphal car, drawn by four horses, with two volunteers as supporters; containing, on one side of the canvass, eight feet and a half long by six in depth, a very animated rep-resentation of *The Releasement of the Prisoners from the Bastile* ... Motto at the bottom of the painting—'*Fourteenth July, 1789; Sacred to Liberty.*' The reverse contained a large figure of Hibernia in reclining posture, one hand and foot in shackles, a Volunteer presenting to her a figure of Liberty....
>
> After three o'clock they moved forward in this order, passing through every street of any consequence in the town; and when arrived at the White Linen Hall, three *feu de joyes* were fired by the Battalion companies, answered between each by seven guns from the Artillery.

As yet there were few indications that for some present this was the first step towards rebellion.

Episode 143 ⌒

THE UNITED IRISHMEN

On 14 July 1791 the Volunteers and leading citizens of Belfast had formed a great circle inside the quadrangle of the White Linen Hall, and there they unanimously agreed to a declaration to the National Assembly of France:

> We meet this day to commemorate the French Revolution, that the remembrance of this day may sink deeply into our hearts ... with a sympathy which binds us to the human race in a brotherhood of interest, of duty, and of affection....
>
> If we be asked, what is the French Revolution to us? We answer;— MUCH.
>
> Much as Men.—It is good for human nature that the grass grows where the Bastile stood. We do rejoice at an event which seemed the breaking of a charm that held *universal* France in a Bastile of civil and religious bondage....
>
> AS IRISHMEN. We too have a country, and we hold it very dear— so dear to us its *Interest,* that we wish all *Civil and Religious Intolerance* annihilated in this land....
>
> Go on then—Great and Gallant People!—to practise the sublime philosophy of your legislation ... and not by conquest, but by the omnipotence of reason , to convert and liberate the World—a world whose eyes are fixed on you; whose heart is with you; who talks to you with all her tongues. You are, in very truth, the Hope of this World.

The success of the French in ending despotic power in their country—so far, with comparatively little loss of life—seemed to demonstrate to Belfast radicals that rapid political change was possible. Certainly this was the view of a group of young Protestants who met in Peggy Barclay's tavern in Crown Entry on Friday 14 October 1791. They invited up from Dublin Theobald Wolfe Tone, a lawyer who had deeply impressed northern reformers with his recent pamphlet *An Argument on Behalf of the Catholics of Ireland.* Tone gave them a name for their new organisation: the Society of United Irishmen:

In the present great aera of reform, when unjust governments are falling in every quarter of Europe ... when all government is acknowledged to originate from the people ... we think it our duty, as Irishmen, to come forward, and state what we feel to be our heavy grievance, and what we know to be its effectual remedy.

WE HAVE NO NATIONAL GOVERNMENT—we are ruled by Englishmen, and the servants of Englishmen.... Such an extrinsic power ... can be resisted with effect solely by unanimity, decision, and spirit in the people,—qualities which may be most exerted most legally, constitutionally, and efficaciously, by that great measure essential to the prosperity and freedom of Ireland—AN EQUAL REPRESENTATION OF ALL THE PEOPLE IN PARLIAMENT....

Impressed by these sentiments, we have agreed to form an association, to be called THE SOCIETY OF UNITED IRISHMEN; and we do pledge ourselves to our country, and mutually to each other, that we will steadily support, and endeavour by all due means to carry into effect the following Resolutions—

First, resolved.—that the weight of English influence in the government of this country is so great as to require a cordial union among all the people of Ireland....

Second.—that the sole constitutional mode by which this influence can be opposed, is by a complete and radical reform of the representation of the people in parliament.

Third.—that no reform is practicable, efficacious, or just, which shall not include Irishmen of every religious persuasion.

All the founder members were Protestants. Dr William Drennan, an obstetrician who first planned the society, was the son of a Presbyterian minister in Rosemary Street; the secretary, Roberts Simms, owned a papermill in Ballyclare; Thomas McCabe was a watch and clock maker in Belfast; Samuel Neilson had a woollen warehouse in Bridge Street; Samuel McTier, married to Drennan's sister Martha, was an unsuccessful businessman; and Henry Joy McCracken, son of a Rosemary Street sea captain, was a commercial traveller in cotton. These men were not revolutionaries—at least, not yet. They passionately believed that they would win the day by argument, by the force of reason.

The Society rapidly spread to towns close to Belfast, among Presbyterian farmers in Antrim and Down, to Dublin and beyond. To promote the radical cause, in 1792 the United Irishmen launched the *Northern Star*, with Samuel Neilson as editor; it soon became the most widely read newspaper in Ireland.

Wolfe Tone found these Belfast reformers remarkably ignorant of their Catholic fellow-countrymen; yet what drove them forward was a fervent determination to win political rights for Catholics. In addition, Belfast Protestants knew little enough about the culture of the Irish-speaking people of the countryside. It was a new-found fascination with this mysterious indigenous culture that led them to organise a uniquely important event— the Belfast Harp Festival of 1792.

Episode 144 ᠊ᢁ

THE BELFAST HARP FESTIVAL OF 1792

Shortly before he died in 1774 the poet Oliver Goldsmith wrote this memoir on the most celebrated of the Irish harpists:

Of all the bards this country ever produced, the last and the greatest was CAROLAN THE BLIND. He was at once a poet, a musician, a composer, and sung his own verses to his harp. The original natives never mention his name without rapture.... He was possessed of an astonishing memory.... Being once at the house of an Irish nobleman, where there was a musician present who was eminent in the profession, Carolan immediately challenged him to a trial of skill.... The musician accordingly played over on his fiddle the fifth concerto of Vivaldi. Carolan, immediately taking his harp, played over the whole piece after him without missing a note ... but their astonishment increased when he assured them he could make a concerto in the same taste himself, which he instantly composed, and that with such spirit and elegance that it may compare (for we have it still) with the finest compositions of Italy.

The Italian musician was Geminiani, and the harpist's composition is known to us today as 'Carolan's Concerto'. Turlough O'Carolan died in 1738, and thereafter the possibility loomed that an ancient art would be lost altogether.

Dr James McDonnell, Belfast's leading physician, was determined to do what he could to preserve the harping tradition. Though a Protestant, he had been born a Catholic near Cushendall, Co. Antrim, and his early education was a distinctly Gaelic one. He had been taught to play the harp by the renowned blind harpist Arthur O'Neill. McDonnell never lost his love of music, and in 1791 he threw himself into a project to hold a harp festival in

Belfast in the following year. Performers had to assemble in Belfast on 10 July 1792, and the newspaper advertisements promised what were called 'premiums' to cover their expenses. McDonnell wrote to his former teacher, Arthur O'Neill, begging him to be present.

O'Neill received McDonnell's letter while he was staying with the O'Reillys of Cavan. At first he refused the invitation, as he recorded himself:

> In consequence of my rheumatism I felt my own incapacity, as I had not the use of the two principal fingers of my left hand.... Mr O'Reilly would take no excuse, and swore vehemently that if I did not go freely, he would tie me on a car, and have me conducted to assist in performing what was required in the advertisement before mentioned.

All but three of the ten harpists who came to Belfast were blind, including the only woman, Rose Mooney. Except for the fifteen-year-old Willian Carr, all were elderly—the most senior, Denis Hempson, was almost a hundred years old. The festival had been arranged to coincide with the third anniversary of the fall of the Bastille when great numbers of Volunteers were expected to be present in the town to celebrate the French Revolution.

At one end of the Assembly Room in the Exchange a platform had been erected, and the appearance of the somewhat decrepit and largely unkempt performers with their attendants must have seemed strange to the audience which, we are assured, was composed of 'Ladies and Gentlemen of the first fashion in Belfast and its vicinity'.

Wolfe Tone, one of the founder members of the United Irishmen, was on a visit from Dublin and went to hear the harpists. His journal indicates that he was not impressed:

> July 11th ... All go to the Harpers at one; poor enough; ten performers; seven execrable, three good, one of them, Fanning, far the best. No new musical discovery; believe all the good Irish airs are already written....
> July 12th ... Lounge to the Harpers....
> July 13th ... The Harpers again. Strum. Strum and be hanged.

Unlike Wolfe Tone, the nineteen-year-old Edward Bunting, assistant organist at St Anne's Church, had been deeply moved by the experience. Bunting travelled back with the aged harpist Denis Hempson to his home in Magilligan, and there he began his life's work of transcribing Irish airs and songs. In 1796 Bunting published his first collection of Irish harp music, including sixty-six airs never before printed. It was an incalculable service to Irish culture. The book caused a sensation. Mrs Martha McTier, from her home at Cabin Hill in east Belfast, wrote to her brother Dr William Drennan, then in Dublin:

Have you got the Irish music—it is the rage here.... It would be worth your while to try if you could hear him play his Irish music—sugar plumbs or sweetys is his greatest temptation, for he despises both money and praise, and is thought a good hearted original.

Thomas Moore later drew on Bunting's pioneering work, adding matchless words to the collected airs in his immensely popular *Irish Melodies*.

In the same year as the Harp Festival, 1792, revolutionary France declared war on kings and aristocrats. The shock-waves were soon felt in Ireland.

Episode 145 ～

AT WAR WITH FRANCE

Allons enfants de la patrie,
Le jour de gloire est arrivé;
Contre nous de la tyrannie
L'étandard sanglant est levé.

It is April 1792. Revolutionary France has declared war on Austria and Prussia. For the French, this is an ideological war, a war to bring an end to the inherited privileges of kings and aristocrats and the tyranny of the clergy. For the Irishman Edmund Burke, on the other hand, the French now threaten all Europe with terror and the tyranny of the 'swinish multitude'.

Burke's predictions become true. The mob rules. Priests and suspects are massacred in their hundreds in the prisons of Paris. Daniel O'Connell, a young Catholic Irishman who witnesses the slaughter, concludes: 'Liberty is not worth the shedding of a single drop of blood.' This sentiment will remain his guiding principle for the rest of his life.

The Reign of Terror has begun. The men of Marseilles are on the march:

Aux armes citoyens!
Formez vos bataillons!
Marchons! Marchons!
Qu'un sang impur
Abreuve nos sillons.

Early in 1793 King Louis XVI is on trial for his life. On 21 January, before an immense crowd in Paris, he is guillotined. In Belfast, reading of these bloody events, Martha McTier writes: 'I am turned, quite turned against the French.'

Many members of the United Irishmen, the radical society that had been inspired by the early achievements of the French Revolution, agree with Mrs McTier. Others do not agree with her: they are excited by news of French victories as the revolutionary armies sweep the Prussians and Austrians back over the frontiers and surge north towards Holland. The French are now offering to help all those seeking to throw off the yoke of kings and aristocrats. Is there a possibility that revolutionary France could help the Irish to win their freedom?

William Pitt the Younger has been Prime Minister of Britain since 1783. Since he brought Britain into the war in February 1793 his armies have faced one humiliating defeat after another. As one by one Britain's allies are knocked out of the war, Pitt becomes ever more anxious about his vulnerable western flank—Ireland. He must do everything to prevent discontented Irishmen turning to France for help. He must win the sympathy of Irish Catholics, and to do that he needs the help of the Irish parliament.

Ever since 'legislative independence' had been won in 1782 Westminster can no longer pass laws for Ireland. But Pitt has made sure that the parliament in Dublin has less power than it thinks it has. The British government of the day still appoints the Lord Lieutenant and other government ministers in Dublin Castle. Only the king—advised, of course by Pitt—can create peerages, make appointments and award pensions. Irish MPs are not slow to look for comfortable jobs and titles for themselves, their sons and their relatives. In this way Pitt has effectively bought himself a secure majority in the Irish House of Commons. He now uses this power to help Irish Catholics.

On 2 January 1793 at St James's Palace King George III receives members of the Catholic Committee from Ireland. William Pitt, Edmund Burke and the Irish 'Patriot' leader Henry Grattan have all spoken persuasively to His Majesty, who is not usually noted for his tolerance of Catholics. The king seems in the best of humour, however, as John Keogh hands him a petition seeking a redress of Catholic grievances. The committee's paid secretary, the United Irishman Wolfe Tone, is delighted:

> Their appearance was splendid and they met with ... a most gracious reception.... His Majesty was pleased to say a few words to each of the delegates in his turn.... With the manner of the Sovereign the delegates had every reason to be content....
>
> Keogh ... was prodigiously fine; he wore silk stockings and a round sharp-buckled tie-wig, with two rows of hard curls that were extremely well powdered.

Back in Ireland the members of the Protestant Ascendancy are horrified. Hearing rumours of concessions to Catholics, Dublin Corporation issues its definition of what it thinks is best for Ireland:

A Protestant King of Ireland; a Protestant Parliament; a Protestant hierarchy; Protestant electors and Government; the Benches of Justice, the Army and the Revenue, through all their branches and details, Protestant; and the system supported by a connexion with the Protestant realm of England.

But Pitt is determined. On 10 January the Lord Lieutenant announces to the Irish parliament:

His Majesty trusts that the situation of His Majesty's Catholic subjects will engage your serious attention and in the consideration of this subject relies on the wisdom and liberality of his Parliament.

That parliament, entirely Protestant, duly enacts legislation to give Catholics the vote in parliamentary elections. *All* the Penal Laws passed against Catholics nearly a century ago have been removed—*except* for one important one: Catholics still cannot sit as members of parliament. Will the Catholics ever be fully emancipated?

Episode 146 ∽

EARL FITZWILLIAM'S FAILURE

There cannot be a permanency in the Constitution of Ireland unless the Protestants of Ireland will lay aside their prejudices, forgo their exclusive pre-eminence, and gradually open their arms to the Roman Catholics.

This was the view of Henry Dundas, Minister of War and right-hand-man of the British Prime Minister, William Pitt. It was an opinion certainly shared by William, Earl Fitzwilliam, who arrived in Dublin as Lord Lieutenant of Ireland on 4 January 1795. Fitzwilliam gave every encouragement to Henry Grattan, the 'Patriot' leader, to bring forward a bill to repeal the last of the Penal Laws, that which prevented Catholics being elected as members of parliament. Fitzwilliam wrote back to London: 'I have little doubt the Catholic business will be carried easily.'

Fitzwilliam's confidence proved to be unfounded. Leading members of the Irish government made loud protests, and, above all, King George III declared that he would regard anyone who supported Catholic Emancipation as his personal enemy. Pitt, who was privately in favour of Emancipation but had no wish to be put out of power, firmly refused Fitzwilliam permission to back Grattan's bill. Fitzwilliam was so furious that he published his private correspondence on the issue, stating that 'I am at a loss to conjecture what benefits will accrue to the British Empire by deferring consideration of this question.'

For his defiance, Fitzwilliam paid the penalty: he was swiftly removed as viceroy of Ireland. Thomas Hussey, Catholic Bishop of Lismore, noted grimly: 'The disastrous news of Earl Fitzwilliam's recall is come, and Ireland is now on the brink of civil war.' Huge crowds of Dubliners lined the Liffey quays as far as Ringsend to bid Fitzwilliam farewell, as the *Belfast News-Letter* reported:

> At length the trying hour of separation arrived. Every sensation that could wring the heart, was experienced by all ranks and conditions. The multitude saw the yacht ride proudly before them, ready to take away with her their darling, and the hopes and prospects of Ireland.... They saw his Lordship, ashamed to betray the most amiable weakness, and with his handkerchief, endeavouring to conceal pure tears springing from an undefiled heart ...

Grattan put forward his Emancipation bill, and in support, George Knox, the Dungannon MP, warned the Irish Commons:

> Much of the real, and no small share of the personal, property of the country is in Catholic hands.... If we drive the rich Catholic from the Legislature and from our own society, we force him to attach himself to the needy and disaffected.... Take, then, your choice; re-enact your penal laws, risk a rebellion, a separation or an Union, or pass this Bill.

Without government support, however, the bill was easily defeated. Disgusted and disillusioned, members of the Society of United Irishmen abandoned peaceful methods and began to plan a rebellion. They were joined in this endeavour by members of the Catholic Committee. Their only hope of success was to persuade revolutionary France to send them military aid. Wolfe Tone, one of the United Irish leaders, had already decided that this was the only option. But he was caught talking to a French spy in a coffee-house in Dublin. Tone was fortunate not to be hanged. However, he had relatives in high places, and instead he was allowed to go into exile in America. In May 1795 he took his family to Belfast, and while waiting for his ship he was lavishly entertained by his Presbyterian supporters:

But, if our friends in Dublin were kind and affectionate, those in Belfast, if possible, were still more so.... Parties and excursions were planned for our amusement; and certainly the whole of our deportment and reception at Belfast very little resembled those of a man who escaped with his life only by a miracle.... I remember particularly two days that we passed on the Cave Hill. On the first Russell, Neilson, Simms, McCracken, and one or to more of us, on the summit of McArt's fort took a solemn obligation ... never to desist in our efforts until we had subverted the authority of England over our country and asserted her independence.

On 13 June Tone embarked on board the *Cincinnatus* and sailed to America. His Belfast friends had raised enough money for him to buy a tobacco farm in New Jersey. But they continued to send him further supplies of money to enable him to seek French help. Early in 1796 he set out for France and landed at Le Havre on 1 February. By December Wolfe Tone would be an adjutant-general in the French army, ready to sail to Ireland with a great invasion fleet.

Meanwhile the outbreak of bloody sectarian warfare in Co. Armagh ensured that the middle-class businessmen and intellectuals of the United Irishmen would acquire the field army of infuriated peasants they would need to launch their rebellion.

Episode 147 ∿

PEEP O' DAY BOYS AND DEFENDERS

In the late eighteenth century Co. Armagh was certainly the most densely populated rural area in Ireland. Here the linen industry flourished, and competition to rent land became fierce in the vicinity of market towns, bleach-greens and the water-powered wash-mills, dye-works and beetling mills. Few Catholics were drapers, but many were handloom weavers, competing with their Protestant neighbours. Trade rivalry easily became sectarian rivalry. Rents for the tiny farms here were the highest in Ireland, and Protestants, living on oatmeal, perhaps supplemented with bacon once a week, often felt that Catholics, able to survive on potatoes and buttermilk, could unfairly outbid them by paying higher rents.

Here in mid Ulster the ideas of the Enlightenment had made little headway. Memories of seventeenth-century dispossession and massacre remained stubbornly alive.

Drunken affrays in the vicinity of Markethill, between gangs of weavers calling themselves the Nappach Fleet, the Bawn Fleet and the Bunkerhill Defenders had become openly sectarian by 1786. The combatants regrouped, Protestants becoming 'Peep o' Day Boys' and Catholics 'Defenders'. For the next ten years and more sectarian warfare raged in Co. Armagh. Better armed, the Peep o' Day Boys at first swept all before them. These were described by a local landlord, the Earl of Gosford, as 'a low set of fellows ... who with Guns and Bayonets, and Other weapons Break Open the Houses of the Roman Catholics, and as I am informed treat many of them with Cruelty'. According to John Byrne, a Catholic dyer from Armagh city, some Protestant gentlemen lent arms to Catholics 'to protect themselves from depredations of these fanatick madmen; and many poor creatures were obliged to abandon their houses at night, and sleep in turf-bogs, in little huts made of sods; so great was the zeal of our holy crusados this year'.

In November 1788, when a Catholic mob near Blackwatertown taunted the Benburb Volunteers for marching to 'The Protestant Boys' and 'The Boyne Water', it was fired on. Five were killed. In the following July more lives were lost when Volunteers made a successful assault on Defenders assembled on Lisnaglade Fort near Tandragee.

'For heaven's sake dont forget the Powder & Ball with all Expedition,' the Drumbanagher magistrate John Moore wrote to Lord Charlemont in July 1789. He had no hesitation in giving out arms to 'the Protestant Boys that have none', because Defenders 'are now beginning their Night Depredations and Lye in Wait behind Ditches, to murder and Destroy Every protestant that appears'.

The sectarian violence fanned out to the uplands of south Armagh. Here the Catholics—still speaking Gaelic and wearing mantles—had the advantage of numbers and turned on the Protestants with a ferocity not seen for more than a century. A horrific climax was reached when Defenders attacked a school-master and his family in Forkill on 28 January 1791, an event graphically described by the Rev. Edward Hudson, Presbyterian minister of Jonesborough:

In rushed a Body of Hellhounds—not content with cutting & stabbing him in several places, they drew a cord round his neck until his Tongue was forced out—It they cut off and three fingers of his right hand—Then they cut out his wife's tongue and ... with a case knife cut off her Thumb and four of her fingers one after another ... she I fear cannot recover—there was in the house a Brother of hers about fourteen years old ... his Tongue those merciless Villains cut out and cut the calf of his leg with a sword.

The magistrate John Moore wrote: 'The whole country for Ten Mile Round is in absolute Rebellion & Confusion. Where it will end God only knows.'

In September 1795 Defenders assembled near Loughgall at a crossroads known as the Diamond to face the Peep o' Day Boys in battle. When the Protestants were reinforced by a Co. Down contingent called the Bleary Boys, the Defenders took their priest's advice and agreed to a truce. Both sides withdrew, but on 21 September a fresh body of Defenders arrived from Co. Tyrone, determined to fight. The Peep o' Day Boys, on home ground, quickly reassembled and took position on the brow of a hill overlooking the Diamond. William Blacker, a Trinity College student home on vacation, spent his time melting lead from the roof of Castle Blacker, making bullets for the Peep o' Day Boys. Then, he tells us, the Protestants opened fire

> with cool and steady aim at the swarms of Defenders, who were in a manner cooped up in the valley and presented an excellent mark for their shots. The affair was of brief duration.... From the bodies found afterwards by the reapers in the cornfields, I am inclined to think that not less than thirty lost their lives.

The victorious Protestants then marched into Loughgall, and there, in the house of James Sloan, the Orange Order was founded.

Episode 148 ～

'I WILL BLOW YOUR SOUL TO THE LOW HILLS OF HELL'

> Then heigho the lily-o,
> The royal, loyal lily-o,
> There's not a flower in Erin's bower
> Can match the Orange lily-o.

Following their rout of the Catholic Defenders at the Battle of the Diamond in September 1795, the victorious Protestants founded the Orange Order. This was a defensive association of lodges: like the Defenders, it was oath-bound, used passwords and signs, was confined to one sect, and its membership was made up mainly of weaver-farmers. William Blacker was one of the very few of the landed gentry who joined the order at the outset. He remembered the assemblage of men, young and old, some seated on heaps of sods or rude blocks of wood, some standing in various attitudes, most of them armed with guns of every age and calibre.... There was a stern solemnity in the reading of the lesson from Scripture and administering the oath to the newly admitted brethren.

Blacker did not approve, however, of the immediate outcome of the Battle of the Diamond:

Unhappily ... A determination was expressed of driving from this quarter of the county the entire of its Roman Catholic population.... A written notice was thrown into or posted upon the door of a house warning the inmates, in the words of Cromwell, to betake themselves 'to Hell or Connaught'.

A sample of what was called 'placarding' was sent by General Dalrymple to Dublin Castle. It warned a woman of Keady and her brother that they must not be informers,

otherwise Be all the Secruts of hell your house Shall Be Burned to the Ground. Both his Soul & your Shall be Blwed To the Blue flames of hell. Now Teak this for Warnig, For if you Bee in this Contry Wednesday Night I will Blow your Soul to the Low hils of hell And Burn the House you are in.

The 'wreckers' smashed looms, tore up linen webs, and destroyed great numbers of homes. In just two months some seven thousand Catholics were driven out of Co. Armagh. Many did flee to Connacht. Lord Altamont reckoned that four thousand had taken refuge in Co. Mayo, and his brother concluded:

Be assured that no circumstance that has happened in Ireland for a hundred years past, has gone so decidedly to separate the mind of this country from the Government.... The Emigration from the North continues; every day families arrive here with the wreck of their properties.

Lord Altamont built a town in the coastal region west of Murrisk in Co. Mayo for these Catholic weavers. He named it Louisburgh, after his daughter Louisa, and descendants of these refugees are living in the town to this day.

Lord Gosford, Deputy Lieutenant of Armagh, summoned the magistrates of the county to a special meeting on 28 December 1795. These men had been either unable or unwilling to uphold the rule of law. Gosford did not beat about the bush:

It is no secret, that a persecution ... is now raging in this county; neither age nor sex, etc., is sufficient to excite mercy, much less to afford protection. The only crime which the wretched objects of this ruthless persecution are charged with, is a crime of easy proof; it is simply a profession of the Roman Catholic faith.... A lawless banditti have constituted themselves judges of this new species of delinquency, and the sentence they have denounced is equally concise and terrible—it is nothing less than a confiscation of all property, and an immediate banishment.

Gosford concluded by saying that he was 'as true a Protestant as any gentleman in this room', adding that 'The supineness of the magistracy of Armagh is become a common topic of conversation in every corner of the kingdom.'

Meanwhile the United Irishmen had become a secret oath-bound revolutionary body pledged to fight for an Irish republic with the aid of the French. Now tens of thousands of Defenders clamoured to be part of the coming revolution. Far from shattering the movement, the Protestant intimidation hastened recruitment by scattering highly political Catholics to the west and the south. Executed in dozens and transported in thousands to Botany Bay in the 1795 autumn assizes, the Defenders did not flinch—not even when they were excommunicated by the Catholic Archbishop of Dublin, John Thomas Troy.

Until now the United Irishmen had been confined to middle-class radicals in Belfast, Bangor, Lisburn, Dublin and Cork, and Presbyterian farmers in the counties of Antrim and Down. Towards the end of 1795 their leaders made the decision to accept into their organisation tens of thousands of Catholic Defenders fired by sectarian zeal. The United Irishmen now had the field army they required—but could they control the actions of their rank and file, bent on revenge?

For the present the United Irishmen had only one concern: when would the French arrive?

Episode 149 ～

'THE FRENCH ARE IN THE BAY'

On 24 February 1796 Theobald Wolfe Tone walked to the Palais de Luxembourg in Paris. There, somewhat to his surprise, he was immediately given an audience with Lazare Carnot, one of the three Directors who now ruled France. Carnot listened intently and agreed to send an expedition to Ireland. To his delight, Tone was given the rank of adjutant-general in the French army. The distinguished general Lazare Hoche, who had been placed in charge of the expedition, received his instructions on 19 June:

> We intend, Citizen General, to restore to a people ripe for revolution the independence and liberty for which it clamours. Ireland has groaned under the hateful yoke of England for centuries. The Defenders ... are already secretly armed.... Detach Ireland from England, and she will be reduced to a second-rate power.

The only hope of reaching Ireland without confronting the Royal Navy was to set out in mid-winter when British patrols would be in port. Great quantities of arms, intended for distribution to the United Irishmen and the Defenders, were loaded onto the forty-three warships, seventeen of them ships of the line. Then Wolfe Tone and 45,450 men—crack troops who had never been defeated—stepped on board. On the morning of 15 December 1796 the fleet sailed out of the Breton port of Brest.

Right from the start, the expedition ran into trouble. As it was heading for the open sea the seventy-four-gun ship of the line, the *Séduisant*, struck a rock and all but forty-five of its crew of 1,300 were drowned. Soon after this the *Fraternité*, carrying General Hoche, sailed out of sight and never managed to rejoin the invasion fleet.

On 20 December General Grouchy, second-in-command, decided to open the package containing secret orders. The fleet was to sail to west Cork, to Bantry Bay.

> O the French are on the sea, says the Shan Van Vocht;
> O the French are on the sea, says the Shan Van Vocht;
> O the French are in the bay, they'll be here without delay,
> And the Orange will decay, says the Shan Van Vocht.

Tone described the progress of the expedition in his journal:

> December 21st ... this morning at day-break we are under Cape Clear, distant about four leagues, so I have at all events once more seen my country.... It is most delicious weather, with a favourable wind and everything in short that we can desire except our absent comrades.... What if the General should not join us?

On the following day the French *were* in the bay, Bantry Bay. But the fatal decision was made not to attempt a landing until General Hoche appeared. By the time it had been agreed to make a landing on Christmas Day a violent storm was buffeting the fleet.

December 24th ... This infernal easterly wind continues without remorse. Well, let it blow and be hanged!...

December 25th—Last night I had the strongest expectations that today we should debark, but at two this morning I was awakened by the wind.... The wind continues right ahead so that it is absolutely impossible to work up to the landing-place, and God knows when it will change.

By now the fleet was in full view of those on shore and the news swept through the country. The Catholic Bishop of Cork, Francis Moylan, in his Christmas Day address, urged his flock not to join the French:

Charged as I am by that Blessed Saviour, whose birth with grateful hearts we this day solemnise, with the care of your souls; it is incumbent on me to exhort you to that peaceable demeanour which must ever mark his true and faithful disciples.... Be not deceived by the lure of equalising property which they hold out to you. They come only to rob, plunder and destroy....

If the sway of our impious invaders were here established, you would not, my beloved people, enjoy the comfort of uniting with the celestial spirits in Heaven ... in singing: 'Glory to God on High and on earth peace to men of goodwill'.

Tone's journal expressed his disappointment at the damaging effect of the disastrous delay:

Had we been able to land the first day and march directly to Cork, we should infallibly have carried it by a coup de main; and then we should have a footing in the country, but as it is — ?... I see nothing before me, unless a miracle be wrought in our favour, but the ruin of the expedition, the slavery of my country and my own destruction.... I have a merry Christmas of it today.

Next day the storm became so fierce that orders were issued to cut cables and return to France. Tone wrote:

December 26th ... Well, England has not had such an escape since the Spanish Armada, and that expedition, like ours, was defeated by the weather.

Even without the French, however, the rising would still go ahead.

Episode 150 ∾

'NOTHING BUT TERROR WILL KEEP THEM IN ORDER'

December 1796 had been a month of grave anxiety for the British Empire. France had launched a fleet carrying more than 45,000 men to Ireland at a time when there were fewer than 13,000 regular troops on the island. Only atrocious weather had prevented a landing. Now the government acted swiftly: an Insurrection Act effectively allowed the imposition of martial law in disturbed districts; Yeomanry corps, almost entirely composed of Protestants, were raised in every county; and conscription into the militia of young men, mostly Catholics, was stepped up.

But news of the appearance of the French had electrified the United Irishmen and their Defender allies. Recruitment in Ulster doubled during the first four months of 1797, and as Defenderism spread southwards deep into the province of Leinster government spies were reporting that there were over 300,000 men ready in arms to rise against the crown.

The government now acted to disarm the people. It began with Ulster. 'Nothing but terror will keep them in order ...', Lieutenant-General Gerard Lake wrote on taking up his post in Belfast; 'it is plain every act of sedition originates in this town.' On 13 March he proclaimed martial law, ordering the immediate surrender of all arms and ammunition. Military searches began at once in Belfast and Carrickfergus, spreading out to Loughbrickland next day, and Armagh in the week following. In the first ten days alone more than 5,000 firearms were seized, together with an immense number of pikes. Spies had penetrated the inner counsels of the United Irishmen, and thanks to their information Lake was able to arrest almost all the leading northern revolutionaries. Seven tumbrels left Belfast filled with prisoners to be escorted by a troop of dragoons to Dublin.

'The flame is smothered, but not extinguished,' Lake declared as he applied harsher regulations in May. In the countryside the Yeomanry were let loose, striking terror by burning houses and flogging suspects. The Presbyterian minister Robert Magill watched men being flogged at Broughshane, Co. Antrim:

I saw Samuel Bones of Lower Broughshane receive 500 lashes—250 on the back and 250 on the buttocks. I saw Samuel Crawford of Ballymena receive 500 lashes. The only words he spoke during the time were 'Gentlemen, be pleased to shoot me'; I heard him utter them. I saw Hood Haslett of Ballymena receive 500 lashes ...

Almost fifty United Irish prisoners were executed, including several Presbyterian ministers. The most notorious conviction was that of William Orr of Farranshane near Antrim. Held at Carrickfergus for a year, Orr was charged with administering unlawful oaths. Even the packed jury found the evidence conflicting and recommended the prisoner to mercy. But Orr was executed on 14 October 1797 on the Gallows Green outside the town. His 'Dying Declaration' was printed and distributed in thousands:

> If to have loved my Country, to have known its Wrongs, to have felt the Injuries of the persecuted Catholics and to have united with them and all other Religious Persuasions in the most orderly and least sanguinery Means of procuring redress;—If these be Felonies I am a Felon, but not otherwise.

By the end of 1797 Lake's ruthless campaign had almost obliterated the United Irishmen in Ulster, where previously they had been strongest. No attempt was made to disarm the Orangemen; indeed, as recruits for the Yeomanry, they provided an invaluable addition to government forces.

Far from snuffing out rebellion in the south, however, General Lake helped to provoke it there in 1798. In November 1797 Britain's most distinguished soldier, General Sir Ralph Abercromby, was appointed commander-in-chief in Ireland. Two months later a tour of army units quickly convinced him that the crown forces in Ireland were out of control and that there was a very real risk that their reckless brutality would drive the people into rebellion. On 26 February he issued his report to all officers:

> The Irish army is in a state of licentiousness which must render it formidable to everyone but the enemy—this is proved by the very disgraceful frequency of courts martial.

Leading members of the Irish government were outraged:

> I resent the peevish indiscretion of this Scotch beast ...

> For God's sake, what is doing with our Commander-in-Chief. I wish he stayed with the Negroes on Martinico ...

> Poor creature, I pity him. He is quite in his dotage ...

> A public and indiscriminate censure—almost an invitation to a foreign enemy ...

Because Abercromby refused to retract the conclusions of his report, he was forced to resign. General Lake took his place. Abercromby's bloodless but effective methods were dropped in favour of a more strenuous policy, chillingly summed up by Lake himself: '... other vigorous and effectual measures.... You make think me too violent, but I am convinced it would be a mercy in the end.' The actions he authorised were to do much to drive an inflamed people into open rebellion.

Episode 151 ∾

'CROPPIES, LIE DOWN!'

In Dublin the traitors were ready to rise
And murder was seen in their lowering eyes.
With poison, the cowards, they aimed to succeed
And thousands were doomed by Assassins to bleed.
But the Yeomen advanced, of Rebels the dread
And each Croppy soon hid his dastardly head.
Down, down, Croppies, lie down!

Indeed, the 'Croppies'—those who cropped their hair short in the French revolutionary style—were ready to rise in the spring of 1798. Given information by a spy, Town Major Henry Sirr, Dublin's police chief, seized ten United Irish leaders on 12 March in the house of Oliver Bond, a woollen merchant in the city. From the captured papers it was evident that rebellion was imminent.

But other leaders were still at large, including the rebel commander-in-chief, Lord Edward Fitzgerald, brother of the most distinguished Irish peer, the Duke of Leinster. Famous for his military exploits when serving with the British forces during the American War of Independence, Lord Edward had acquired his revolutionary ideas from his father-in law, Philippe Égalité ('Equality Philip'), the now executed Duke of Orléans.

Meanwhile other United Irishmen, including Wolfe Tone and Napper Tandy, were in Paris attempting to persuade Napoleon Bonaparte to send help to Ireland. But Napoleon preferred to plan an invasion of England. 'What would these gentlemen have?' he asked. 'France is revolutionised! Holland is revolutionised! Italy is revolutionised! Switzerland is revolutionised! Europe will soon be revolutionised. But this it seems is not enough to content them.' But then the great general turned to Wolfe Tone and said: '*Mais, vous êtes brave* ... but, you are brave.'

Hearing that there would not be an expedition, Lord Edward decided in any case that the rebellion would begin without the French on 23 May. United Irishmen and their Defender allies would converge in three columns on the capital while he himself led an attack on Dublin Castle. He listed his requirements: fifty hammers, fifty groove irons, 150 hooks for scaling ladders, and so on.

Facing a string of humiliating defeats abroad at the hands of the French and a number of alarming naval mutinies in English ports, the government made frantic efforts to prevent rebellion in Ireland. General Gerard Lake, the newly appointed commander-in-chief, unleashed regular troops, together with units of the Yeomanry and Fencibles, on the population of Leinster. Troops flogged blacksmiths until they revealed where pikes were hidden. In the village of Ballitore, Co. Kildare, a Quaker lady, Mary Leadbeater, recorded in her diary:

> They set fire to some cabins near the village—took P. Murphy ... apparently an inoffensive man, tied him to a car opposite to his own door, and these ... officers degraded themselves so far as to scourge him with their own hands. James Carney, tied to a tree, underwent a similar punishment—the torture was excessive—they did not recover soon.... The village, so peaceful, exhibited a scene of tumult and dismay—the air rang with the shrieks of sufferers, and the lamentations of those who beheld them suffer. These violent measures caused a great many pikes to be brought in.

It was at Athy, Co. Kildare, on 1 May 1798 that the triangle made its first appearance. On this apparatus Colonel Campbell tied suspects, one at a time, and flogged them until they revealed where arms had been hidden. Thomas Rawson was one of the interrogators, as a survivor remembered:

> Rawson would seat himself in a chair in the centre of a ring formed around the triangles, the miserable victims kneeling under the triangle until they would be spotted over with the blood of others.

Other commanders had with them 'travelling gallows' for half-hanging men until they would give information. Captain Swayne was credited with the invention of 'pitch-capping'—pitch was mixed with gunpowder, then placed on a suspect's head and set on fire. The flames were not extinguished until the whereabouts of arms had been revealed.

> I met with Napper Tandy, and he took me by the hand,
> And he said, 'How's poor ould Ireland, and how does she stand?'
> 'She's the most distressful country that ever yet was seen,
> For they're hanging men and women there for the Wearin' o' the Green.'

Captain John Edwards of the Bray Yeomanry protested that troops were attacking people in Co. Wicklow simply because they were wearing green:

> Where is the man whose blood will not boil with revenge who sees the petticoat of his wife or sister cut off her back by the sabre of the Dragoon— merely for the crime of being green, a colour certainly with them innocent of disaffection.

Huge quantities of arms were seized, but the infuriated country people were now flocking to the rebel army in their thousands.

Episode 152 ∾

'ROUSE, HIBERNIANS, FROM YOUR SLUMBERS'

The boys will all be there, says the Shan Van Vocht;
The boys will all be there, says the Shan Van Vocht;
The boys will all be there, with their pikes in good repair,
And Lord Edward will be there, says the Shan Van Vocht.

But Lord Edward Fitzgerald would *not* be there. On 19 May 1798, just four days before tens of thousands of United Irishmen were due to rise up in rebellion, he was cornered in Dublin. Lord Edward, the rebel commander-in-chief, had been lying in bed in an upstairs room in a house in the Liberties recovering from a bout of influenza. That afternoon his revolutionary uniform was brought to him: a bottle-green braided suit with silk lace and a crimson cape, and a Cap of Liberty two feet long. Then suddenly at seven in the evening Dublin's police chief, Major Swan, and a Yeomanry officer, Captain Ryan, burst into the room. Swan declared: 'You know me, my lord, and I know you. It will be vain to resist.' Lord Edward, however, leaped from his bed and stabbed Swan three times. Swan fired his pistol, but only hit Lord Edward's shoulder and ran bleeding down the stairs crying: 'Ryan, Ryan, I am basely murdered.'

Ryan, wielding a swordstick, now faced Lord Edward's revolutionary stiletto. The two rolled down the stairs in deadly conflict. Stabbed fourteen times in the stomach by Lord Edward, Captain Ryan—the man who had written the most popular loyalist ballad of the year, 'Croppies, Lie Down'—soon bled to death. Lord Edward Fitzgerald was led away, and he too was shortly to die: while in prison awaiting trial, his wounded shoulder became affected by gangrene, and he expired a fortnight later.

Every other United Irish leader of any importance had either been hanged or been thrown into jail. The last to be arrested was Samuel Neilson, the Belfast wool merchant, now a hopeless alcoholic; it was he who had unwittingly led the police to Lord Edward's hideout. But it had been Neilson in a sober moment who had thought up the ingenious plan to signal the start of the rebellion—simply stop the government coaches carrying the mail and other vital army communications, and when the coach failed to appear at the usual time, then it was time to lift the pikes out of the thatch.

On 23 May 1798 many of the coaches leaving Dublin were stopped and destroyed on roads radiating out of the capital. What was to be the bloodiest conflict in Ireland in modern times had begun:

> Rouse, Hibernians, from your slumbers!
> See the moment just arrived,
> Imperious tyrants for to humble,
> Our French brethren are at hand.

Revolutionary sentiments abounded and were freely expressed:

Revenge! Glorious revenge! Your name is as sweet as liberty!

Irishmen! ... Arm yourselves and rush like lions on your foes!

Vengeance, Irishmen, on your oppressors!

Vengeance! Arise, then, United Sons of Ireland!

> *Vive la*, United Heroes,
> Triumphant always may they be.
> *Vive la*, our gallant brethren
> That have come to set us free.

In fact the French were not on their way to Ireland; and without well-known leaders, the planned attack on Dublin Castle came to nothing. But tens of thousands armed themselves, and in the first thirty-six hours fourteen engagements were fought in Co. Kildare. First of all the town of Prosperous fell to the insurgents, and Captain Swayne, the inventor of the pitch-cap, was shot in his bed with a blunderbuss and his body burnt in a barrel of tar. In Clane, Catholics though they were, forty-eight members of the militia were piked or shot or burnt to death by the insurgents. At Old Kilcullen the 9th Dragoons charged with sabres drawn, only to transfix themselves on insurgent pikes. Their commander, Captain Erskine, thrown from his horse and breaking his leg, was stabbed to death by an old beggar-woman wielding a rusty clasp-knife.

Perhaps a thousand pikemen charged down the main street of Naas, the headquarters of the third largest garrison in Ireland, but were driven back and slaughtered by cannon firing rounds of grapeshot. Lord Gosford, who famously had denounced Orange atrocities in his native Co. Armagh, was in command. He reported: 'The cavalry took advantage of their confusion, charged in amongst them, and pursued them all over the country in almost every direction and killed a great number of them.'

Meanwhile the United Irish army of Co. Meath had planted the Tree of Liberty at Dunshaughlin, captured firearms and 9,000 ball cartridges, and made camp at the seat of the High-Kings of Ireland, the Hill of Tara. The problem was that most of the insurgents had no idea how to use the captured guns. And on 26 May three companies of Scotch Fencibles and Lord Fingall's Yeomanry attacked and decimated the great rebel force.

In fact the rebellion of 1798 had hardly begun.

Episode 153 ～

THE BOYS OF WEXFORD

Towards the end of May 1798 it looked as if the rebellion of the United Irishmen had been crushed. General Sir Ralph Dundas, in spite of fierce loyalist criticism in Dublin, offered a pardon to the rebels of Co. Kildare. Huge numbers of people came forward, and the heap of surrendered pikes on the Curragh was described as being as high as the Royal Exchange. But the Limerick commander, General Sir James Duff, had not heard of the capitulation. Making a forced march of a hundred miles northwards over two days and two nights, his militia and dragoons fell upon the unarmed rebels on the Curragh and slaughtered at least 350 of them.

Other incidents helped to sustain the rebellion. On 25 May at Dunlavin Green on the Wicklow–Kildare border the militia took prisoners from the local jail, men who had taken no part in the rising, and summarily executed them:

> In the year of one thousand seven hundred and ninety-eight
> A sorrowful tale the truth unto you I'll relate
> Of thirty-six heroes to the world were left to be seen,
> By a false information were shot on Dunlavin Green.

Next day militiamen in south Co. Wicklow marched twenty-eight suspects from Carnew town prison to the local handball alley, where, one by one, they were shot by firing-squad.

The people of Co. Wicklow and north Co. Wexford had by now become convinced that they were all going to be slaughtered. This impression was reinforced by the activities of a group of loyalists known as the 'Black Mob', led by the notorious Hunter Gowan. Men were flogged to death, homes and haggards were burnt, suspects were tortured with burning pitch-caps, and Hunter Gowan himself stirred the punch at a local celebration in Gorey with the amputated finger of one of his victims. Archibald Hamilton Jacob, an Enniscorthy magistrate, toured the countryside with an executioner equipped with a hanging-rope and a cat-o'-nine-tails. At Ballaghkeen he flogged a man to death, and in Enniscorthy he hanged a man and had his body dragged backwards and forwards through the market place.

Thousands of terrified people took to the hillsides and ditches. Many turned to their local priests for leadership. One of them was Father John Murphy, whose chapel at Boulavogue had been burnt down. After seizing a great quantity of arms at Camolin in north Wexford, Father Murphy and his followers made camp nearby on Oulart Hill.

On 27 May the North Cork Militia made ready to attack the rebels on Oulart Hill. Gaelic-speaking Catholic men from Cork, fighting for the crown, faced English-speaking rebels led by a Catholic priest. The militiamen, unused to army footwear, asked permission to attack in their bare feet. The militia were completely overwhelmed as they surged uphill. Out of 109 men, the only survivors in the government force were Colonel Foote and three of his soldiers.

Hearing of the victory at Oulart Hill, thousands more joined Father Murphy. At one o'clock on the afternoon of Whit Monday what was described as a 'black cloud' of between nine and ten thousand insurgents descended on the walled town of Enniscorthy in central Co. Wexford. After fierce fighting by the Duffrey Gate the pikemen prevailed in the narrow streets. At four o'clock half the town was in flames and the garrison withdrew, leaving loyalists to their fate.

In Wexford army discipline collapsed as masses of insurgents approached the town. Mrs Brownrigg took her two children on board a vessel in the harbour, hoping to sail for Wales. But, quite rightly, she did not trust the owner Captain Dixon:

Great God! What a night that was. The Horns of the Rebels I heard very plainly, for the ship just lay about half way from Ferry Bank and Wexford.... At the first dawn of day, May the thirtieth, the bridge was set on fire from the Ferry Bank side; all our crew were or pretended to be asleep. I woke them and if I doubted their principles before could no longer doubt them. A wonderful scene of confusion now ensued. Boats of every description put off from the shore, and our ship and every other in the harbour was filled with women and children, some naked, several that had been in Enniscorthy the day before entirely frantic.... All this time, of course, the Rebels were advancing and increasing in numbers.... Captain Dixon got into his boat ... saying he would *try* what he could do to save our lives in a manner that showed he had little to hope. We were then I suppose, about forty women and children put into the hold of the ship on Coals with which it was loaded, and sat expecting immediate death.

Soon after these dramatic events a republic would be proclaimed in Wexford.

Episode 154 ∿

THE BATTLE OF NEW ROSS

> It was early, early in the spring,
> When small birds tune, and thrushes sing,
> Changing their note from tree to tree,
> And the song they sang was old Ireland free.

On the last day of May 1798 huge numbers of rebels poured into Wexford town. The loyalist Charles Jackson remembered:

We passed through crowds of rebels, who were in the most disorderly state, without the least appearance of discipline. They had no kind of uniform but most of them in the dress of labourers, white bands round their hats and green cockades being the only marks by which they were distinguished. They made a most fantastic appearance, many having decorated themselves with parts of the apparel of ladies, found in the houses they had plundered. Some wore ladies' hats and feathers, others, caps, bonnets and tippets.... Their arms consisted chiefly of pikes of an enormous length, the handles of many being sixteen or eighteen feet long. Some carried rusty muskets. They were accompanied by a number of women shouting and huzzaing for the Croppies and crying, Who now dare say 'Croppies, lie down?'

General Sir William Fawcett sent the Meath Militia and eighteen gunners trailing three howitzers to relieve Wexford. But four miles outside the town, at a place called the Three Rocks, they were ambushed and overwhelmed by the rebel pikemen. The field guns were captured, all seventy militiamen were shot or hacked to death, and only one officer and two men survived to report the disaster to General Fawcett.

Meanwhile the insurgents broke into Wexford town jail to release United Irish prisoners. One of them was found stuck half-way up the prison chimney where he had been attempting to hide himself. He was Bagenal Harvey, a local Protestant landlord, and he was now appointed commander-in-chief of the rebel army. In the presence of perhaps 15,000 insurgents the first Irish Republic was proclaimed and green flags were unfurled, some emblazoned with a golden harp and others with the words 'Erin go Bragh' (Ireland Forever) inscribed on them.

Harvey planned to take the rebellion beyond the county. The first assault was to be on New Ross, a key garrison town on the River Barrow guarding the passage to the counties of Carlow, Kilkenny and Waterford. Every forge in Wexford was set to work making pike blades, and the Bull Ring in the centre of the town rang to the sound of smiths' hammers.

It took almost a week to take the rebel army to New Ross. First they camped at the Three Rocks, where they danced to the tune of the French revolutionary song, the *Carmagnole*. Then they moved on westwards, as one fleeing loyalist put it, 'moving with slow but irresistible progress ... like an immense body of lava'. They halted at Corbet Hill overlooking New Ross. The delays gave Major-General Henry Johnston time to prepare, though the town's medieval walls had not been repaired since they had been breached in 1649 by Oliver Cromwell. Luke Gardiner, now Colonel Lord Mountjoy, arrived with a substantial force of the Dublin Militia.

Shortly after dawn on 5 June waves of pikemen and musketeers, led by John Kelly, the 'Boy from Killane', surged down Corbet Hill and swept aside the red-coats guarding Three Bullet Gate. Men of the 4th and 5th Dragoons charged the insurgents as they entered the main street only to be transfixed by pikes. A woodcutter's daughter ran about the dead and dying cavalry men, cutting off their cartridge cases with a billhook and passing them to the rebels. One of those killed was Lord Mountjoy, who had done more than anyone else in the Irish parliament to have Penal Laws against Catholics removed.

After seven hours continuous fighting in the intense heat of that June day, almost all of New Ross had fallen to the United Irishmen. Now the exhausted insurgents turned aside to look for food and drink, and many lay down to sleep. Still in control of a small corner of the town, General Johnston rallied his men. 'Will you desert your general?', he shouted. 'Will you desert your fellow-countrymen?' Taken completely by surprise, the rebel army was shattered by this counter-attack. No prisoners were taken, and even sleeping insurgents were shot or bayoneted. About a hundred wounded rebels were burnt to death when a building serving as a temporary hospital was set on fire. Major Vesey, now commanding the Dublin Militia, admitted: 'The carnage was shocking, as no quarter was given, the soldiers were too much exasperated and could not be stopped.'

The fury of the soldiers would have been all the greater had they known of a rebel atrocity that day, the massacre of loyalists a few miles away at Scullabogue.

Episode 155 ~

THE REBELLION SPREADS NORTH

Following the victory of the crown forces at New Ross, Co. Wexford, on 5 June 1798, James Alexander was given the task of disposing of the dead. He reported:

> The rebel carcasses lay in the streets unburied for three or four days; some perforated over and over with musket balls or the bayonet; some hacked with swords; some mangled and torn with grapeshot and worse still with *pigs*, some of which I have seen eating the brains out of the cloven skulls and gnawing the flesh about the raw wounds! Many rebels were reduced to ashes ... and many partly burned and partly roasted.

Sixty-two cartloads of bodies were thrown into the River Barrow, in addition to those buried with quicklime in mass graves. Almost 3,000 bodies had been disposed of.

But there were more to be buried. Not far from New Ross at Scullabogue, the insurgents held a large number of loyalists prisoner in a house and a thatched barn. Most of them were Protestants, though there were also a few Catholics among them. On the same day that the battle took place in the town several of these prisoners were brought out and lined up on the lawn in front of the house. Having been made to kneel down, four at a time, they were shot; thirty-five men were killed in this way. The insurgents then set fire to the barn.

The prisoners inside, including twenty women and children, twice managed to break open the door, and on both occasions they were forced back by pikes. One two-year-old child crawled out from under the door, but the poor creature was piked to death. For two days after the event the insurgents turned over the charred bodies, over a hundred in number, in search of coins.

Had the United Irishmen of Ulster heard in time of this ghastly atrocity, they might have acted very differently. Once the very heart of the United Irish conspiracy, the province had been very effectively disarmed in 1797. Nearly all the leaders had been seized. But a humble Presbyterian weaver from Templepatrick, Jemmy Hope, was determined to raise the standard of revolt:

> 'I will not desert my neighbours,' said I, 'though I do not like the road; I'll travel it, however, as clean as I can.'

Hope was joined in Belfast by Henry Joy McCracken, just released from Kilmainham Jail for fear he might die after a fellow-prisoner had thrown a basin of boiling water over him. As the second-largest garrison in Ireland, Belfast was an impossible target. Instead McCracken and Hope planned to attack Antrim town on 7 June, the day the magistrates of the county were due to meet there:

> Army of Ulster! Tomorrow we march on Antrim. Drive the garrison of Randalstown before you and haste to form a junction with your Commander-in-Chief. Henry Joy McCracken. 1st Year of Liberty, 6th day of June 1798.

As darkness fell on Wednesday 6 June armed United Irishmen met at the Cold Well near Larne and in the small hours moved into the town, driving a party of Tay Fencibles back to their barracks. Then as dawn came they drew off to join their comrades on Donegore Hill. They had fired the first shots of the rebellion in Ulster.

Next day the Ballymoney United Irishmen gathered at Kilraghts and then, with other parties, advanced on Ballymena. Joining them was a contingent from Crebilly, wearing green cockades; as they marched north through Broughshane they were cheered by children bearing green branches representing the Tree of Liberty. However, thanks to General Lake's sweeps for weapons the year before, very few had firearms. According to the yeoman Samuel McSkimin, many had no weapons at all and the rest only had 'pitchforks, peat spades, scythes, bayonets, sharpened harrow-pins fixed on poles, old rusty sword blades and reaping hooks'. Entering by Church Street, they nevertheless forced the surrender of Ballymena after a brisk battle by placing tar-barrels against the Market House. Meanwhile Randalstown fell to the insurgents by a similar device—the Yeomanry were smoked into submission when straw was set on fire underneath the Market House. One party was sent to break down the bridge at Toome to prevent the military from further west from crossing the River Bann. This task took fourteen hours of hard manual labour. The main contingent at Randalstown then hastened to reach Antrim to join McCracken in his attack on the town.

That morning, 7 June, McCracken gathered his men at Craigarogan Fort near Roughfort north of Belfast. As they advanced through Dunadry and Muckamore the United Irish army kept spirits high by singing the *Marseillaise*. They had only one cannon, however, a brass six-pounder long hidden under the floor of Templepatrick meeting-house and insecurely mounted on the wheels of an old carriage.

What McCracken did not know was that the authorities in Belfast, thanks to efficient informers and spies, knew what his plans were in perfect detail.

Episode 156 ∽

REBELLION IN COUNTY ANTRIM

An Ulsterman I'm proud to be,
From Antrim's Glens I've come,
And though I've laboured by the sea,
I've followed fife and drum.
I've heard the martial tramp of men,
I've watched them fight and die,
And well do I remember when
I followed Henry Joy.

At nightfall on 6 June 1798 Major-General George Nugent, in command in Belfast, received news from an informer that Henry Joy McCracken would attack Antrim town on the following day. An order was quickly sent to Blaris military camp near Lisburn, and early in the day Colonel Henry Clavering led out two companies of militia and 150 light dragoons trailing two six-pounders and two modern howitzers. They sped north by a route along the eastern shores of Lough Neagh towards Antrim. Two hours after McCracken's United Irishmen had marched out from Roughfort, Colonel James Durham advanced from Belfast by the same road with 250 men of the Monaghan Militia, a troop of 22nd Dragoons and men of the Royal Irish Artillery taking with them two field guns.

Meanwhile Major Daniel Seddon, in command in Antrim, had discovered to his alarm that many in the town had left to join the rebels. He immediately issued orders that their houses should be burnt. Thatch was blazing as the insurgents approached from the south by Scotch Street. McCracken delayed fatally for half an hour to allow his other three rebel columns to converge on the town from other parts of the county. This gave time for Clavering's troops to enter the town on the north side.

It was not until 2.45 p.m. that McCracken gave the order to advance. Preceded by fifes and a single drum, the United Irish recruits from Templepatrick, Carnmoney and Roughfort marched into Scotch Street with around eighty musketeers, followed by a single six-pounder cannon and the rest of the force armed with pikes and pitchforks. The newly arrived government troops positioned two cannon and fired badly aimed canisters of grapeshot at the insurgents, doing little more than casting gravel in their faces. Then the cavalry charged the rebels, only to be greeted by two rounds of grapeshot and a deadly retaliation by pikemen. As McCracken's men fought towards the town centre, men from Ballyclare fought their way forward down Bow Lane. It was in this last action that Lord O'Neill—once the darling of the Presbyterian freeholders now in combat against him—was killed near the Market House. Colonel Durham's force had now arrived and bombarded the town from Sentry Hill; his men then swiftly poured into the streets, scattering the insurgents.

The soldiery finished off any wounded rebels they found and summarily executed thirty others captured in arms. It was only three days later that Antrim's streets were cleared and the bodies thrown into sandpits on the shore of Lough Neagh. Samuel Skelton, Lord Massereene's agent, recalled:

As a cart-load of dead and dying arrived at the sandpit a yeoman officer asked the driver 'Where the devil did these rascals come from?' A poor wretch raised his gory head from the cart and feebly answered 'I come frae Ballyboley.' He was buried with the rest.

McCracken, Jemmy Hope and a few others attempted to rally the fleeing insurgents, but to no avail.

> It was for Ireland's cause we fought,
> For home and sire we bled,
> Our numbers were few but our hearts beat true,
> And five to one lay dead.
> And many the lassie mourned her lad
> And mother mourned her boy,
> For youth was strong in that gallant throng
> That followed Henry Joy.

Elsewhere in Co. Antrim rebels in arms anxiously awaited news. Great numbers had gathered at Bellair Hill at Glenarm. On the preceding Sunday their leader, the Rev. Robert Acheson, had preached to them in Glenarm meeting-house on a text from the Gospel of St Luke: 'Be not afraid of them that kill the body'. Ten thousand occupied Ballymena and, beating drums and blowing conch-shells and tin trumpets, noisily greeted fresh arrivals with cries of 'Ballymena's our own!' 'Hurrah for the United Irishmen!' 'Friends from Clough!' 'More friends from Clough!'

Here a Committee of Public Safety kept guard over loyalist prisoners almost suffocating in the Market House dungeon, known as the Black Hole. Under the direction of James Dickey, a deranged lawyer from Crumlin, some suspects and prisoners, although they had offered no provocation, were stabbed to death, and taverns and homes of the wealthy were wrecked in the search for plunder. Ballymena held out longest, but when news of the defeat at Antrim arrived the insurgents melted away, throwing their pikes into ditches.

After hiding out on Slemish and the Cave Hill, McCracken from the slopes of Collin Mountain watched Saintfield burn and heard the distant guns at Ballynahinch. The Co. Down uprising had begun.

Episode 157 ∾

REBELLION IN COUNTY DOWN

On Friday 8 June 1798 a number of armed United Irishmen from Killinchy came to Saintfield and laid siege to a farmstead owned by the McKee family, thought to be informers. Next morning they set fire to the building, and the entire household perished in the flames—a deed for which eleven were subsequently hanged. It was a grim beginning to the rebellion in Co. Down.

On the following day Colonel Chetwynd Stapylton approached Saintfield with the Newtownards Yeomanry cavalry and 270 York Fencibles. About 4.30 p.m. the insurgents ambushed this force, Richard Frazer of Ravarna leading a charge of pikemen from the demesne woods on the Comber Road. Before he was driven off, Stapylton lost three officers, five sergeants, one clergyman, two drummers and forty-five other ranks. A York Fencible was heard to recall that 'for danger and desperation this skirmish exceeded anything he had before witnessed'.

Other actions that day were not so successful. Men from Bangor and Donaghadee were driven out of Newtownards by volleys from the Market

House and survivors were forced to spend the night on Scrabo Hill. An attack on Portaferry Market House was beaten back when insurgents came under flanking fire from a revenue vessel anchored near the quay. News of the victory at Saintfield spread rapidly, however, and United Irishmen hurried to join the rebel camp here at the Creevy Rocks.

On Sunday 10 June the Rev. Thomas Ledlie Birch preached to the insurgents on the Creevy Rocks. He took his text from Ezekiel: 'Cause them that have charge over the city to draw near, even every man with his destroying weapon in his hand.' But who was to command them? The Co. Down leader, the Rev. William Steel Dickson, had been arrested at Ballynahinch five days earlier. Eventually Henry Munro, a Scottish merchant from Lisburn, agreed to head the Down insurrection. Munro ordered his rebel army south to Ballynahinch, where a new camp was made at Montalto on Ednavady, with an entrenched forward position on Windmill Hill.

On 11 June Major-General George Nugent issued a proclamation in Belfast warning that unless the rebels laid down their arms and released their prisoners he would

> proceed to set fire to and totally destroy the towns of Killinchy, Killyleagh, Ballynahinch, Saintfield and every cottage and farmhouse in the vicinity of those places, carry off the stock and cattle and put everyone to the sword who may be found in arms.

Nugent was as good as his word: on the following day the Ballynahinch insurgents could see columns of smoke rising into the still air as the troops set fire to farmhouses and haggards and burnt Saintfield to the ground.

The weather was perfect that day as it had been for weeks. James Thomson, then a boy of twelve and later the father of the great scientist Lord Kelvin, accompanied women carrying food to the rebel encampment. Here he found

> a considerable number sheltering themselves from the scorching rays of a burning sun under the shade of the trees.... They wore no uniforms; yet they presented a tolerably decent appearance being dressed, no doubt, in their 'Sunday clothes' ... The only thing in which they all concurred was the wearing of green: almost every individual having a knot of ribbons of that colour, sometimes mixed with yellow in his hat ... and many ... bore ornaments of various descriptions and of different degrees of taste and execution; the most of which had been presented as tributes of regard and affection and as incentives to heroic deeds, by females whose breasts beat as high in patriotic ardour as those of their husbands, their sweethearts and their brothers.... On a sudden an alarm was given.... In a moment all was bustle through the field.

The experiences of a humble participant in the fighting are captured in a contemporary ballad:

> My name is George Campbell, at the age of eighteen
> I joined the United Men to strive for the green
> And many a battle I did undergo
> With that hero commander, brave General Munro.

Nugent began pounding the rebel positions with his eight guns, which included two howitzers firing exploding shells. The insurgents on Windmill Hill were overwhelmed, and one of them, Hugh McCulloch, a grocer from Bangor, was captured and hanged from one of the mill's sails.

At nightfall the Monaghan Militia occupied Ballynahinch. Awed by Nugent's artillery, many insurgents deserted the field of battle that night. Those remaining launched a dawn attack on the militia, which, a survivor recalled,

> did not fail to salute us with a brisk fire. We ran up like bloodhounds and the Monaghans fled into the town where they kept up a kind of broken fire, although only about twenty of us were armed with muskets.

At about seven o'clock on the following morning the rebel ammunition ran out and Nugent's army overwhelmed the United Irish on Ednavady Hill. The rebellion in Ulster was now over, and in the south too the tide had turned against the United Irishmen.

Episode 158 ～

VINEGAR HILL

> Have you heard of the Battle of Ballynahinch
> Where the people oppressed rose up in defence?
> When Munro left the mountains his men took the field,
> And they fought for twelve hours and never did yield.

Contrary to the balladmaker's proud claim, the Presbyterian United Irishmen did in fact yield on 13 June 1798. No quarter was given as the cavalry in relentless pursuit hacked down those in flight through lanes and byways. Betsy Gray of Gransha, who had stayed on the field of battle, was overtaken and killed with her brother George and her lover Willie Boal. She was the first to die, shot through the eye by a yeoman from Annahilt.

Two days later troops captured the rebel commander, Henry Munro. Condemned and then taken to the market place in Lisburn, he prepared himself to meet his Maker. An officer present recalled:

> I stood very near him when at the foot of the gallows, and he settled his accounts as coolly as if he had been in his own office, a free man.... This done, he said a short prayer.

The reprisals following the Battle of Ballynahinch were fearful, but they could not equal in ferocity those that were about to take place in the province of Leinster.

Co. Wexford remained the storm centre of the rebellion. In the hardest-fought battle of the insurrection, the United Irishmen had been repulsed at Arklow on 9 June. From several directions, columns of regular troops, militia and yeomen closed in, the largest being led by General Gerard Lake, the commander-in-chief.

Rebel atrocity marked the final stages. Dragged from the prisons of Wexford town, loyalists in a ghastly ritual were cruelly slaughtered. Each prisoner was made to kneel on the bridge spanning the River Slaney, and there they were piked to death. Ninety-seven prisoners were butchered, some left bleeding to death on the bridge, and others having their bodies hurled down into the river. Then the pikemen were called away—they were needed to defend Vinegar Hill.

The Wexford insurgents had made their main camp on a hill just outside the town of Enniscorthy: Vinegar Hill. General Lake rejected all suggestions from fellow-officers that he should attempt to impose a surrender—he wanted a great military victory. Twenty thousand rebels, almost all armed only with pikes, massed on the hill. The outcome could not be in doubt. Lake had 10,000 troops and twenty pieces of artillery, together with 400 requisitioned coaches loaded with ammunition and equipment. For four days his forces encircled the hill, and at 7 a.m. on the morning of the fifth day, 21 June, his heavy guns opened up. For an hour the pikemen withstood the hail of grapeshot and the new exploding shells fired by Lake's howitzers.

Then the rebel army broke, the cavalry advanced, cutting down retreating insurgents in their hundreds, and, after capturing a rebel hospital in Enniscorthy, the crown forces set fire to it with all the patients still inside. Following the recovery of Wexford town, courts martial meted out the death sentence to scores of 'Croppies'—so named because the United Irishmen had cropped their hair short in the French revolutionary fashion.

> When I was marching o'er Wexford Hill
> O! who could blame me to cry my fill?
> I looked behind me and I looked before
> But my tender mother I ne'er saw more.
>
> When I was mounted on the gallows high,
> My aged father he was standing by;
> My aged father he did me deny,
> And the name he gave me was the Croppy Boy.

One of the last to be executed in Ulster was Henry Joy McCracken. His sister Mary Ann had bought him a passage to America and sent him tools and clothes so that he could disguise himself as a carpenter. But a former customer recognised him as he crossed the green at Carrickfergus. He was arrested and put on trial in Ann Street in Belfast, where the crown attorney offered him his life if he would name his co-conspirators; but he refused, whispering to his sister: 'You must be prepared for my conviction.' On 17 July he was taken to the Market House on the corner of High Street and Cornmarket, the ground for which had been given to Belfast by his great-great-grandfather. Then, Mary Ann recalled,

> I took his arm and we walked to the place of execution.... Harry begged I should go. Clasping my arms around him (I did not weep till then), I said I could bear any thing but leaving him.... Fearing any further refusal would disturb the last moments of my dearest brother, I suffered myself to be led away.

Though Michael Dwyer still held out with a small band of dedicated followers in the Wicklow Mountains, the rebellion effectively was over.

Or was it? On 23 August 1798 three frigates sailed into Killala Bay in a remote corner of north Co. Mayo. The French had come.

Episode 159 ∼

THE RACES OF CASTLEBAR

> O the French are on the sea, says the Shan Van Vocht,
> O the French are on the sea, says the Shan Van Vocht,
> O the French are in the bay ...

On 22 August 1798 the French were indeed in the bay, Killala Bay. Here in remote north Mayo General Jean Humbert, with 1,099 men, disembarked from three frigates and began to distribute leaflets to local people who had come to stare at them:

Liberty, Equality, Fraternity, Union! Irishmen ... After several unsuccessful attempts, behold Frenchmen arrived amongst you.... The moment of breaking your chains is arrived.... Union! Liberty! The Irish Republic!— Such is our shout. Let us march!

> Erin's sons be not faint-hearted,
> Welcome, sing then *Ça ira*;
> From Killala they are marching,
> To the tune of *Vive la.*

Many Mayo men joined the French, though a proclamation written in English meant nothing to these Irish-speakers. Few had even heard of the United Irishmen, and some were sure the French had been sent by the pope. One French officer declared:

God help these simpletons. If they knew how little we care for the pope or his religion, they would not be so hot in expecting help from us: we have just sent away *Mr Pope* from Italy, and who knows we may find him again in this country.

Meanwhile the newly appointed viceroy, Lord Cornwallis, led a great army out of Dublin and sent an advance party of 3,000 troops aboard a fleet of barges on the Grand Canal to take them westwards.

Humbert, after taking Ballina, took his men twenty-five miles south by a narrow bridle track skirting Nephin mountain. He headed for Castlebar, where at an hour before midnight on 26 August General Gerard Lake took command. Then, at 7 a.m. in the morning of 27 August, Humbert found himself faced by formidable opposition: a front line manned by the Kilkenny Militia, commanded by the Marquis of Ormond, and the Royal Irish Artillery with four curricle guns; a second line of Fraser Fencibles from the Highlands, with two cannon, and a corps of Galway Yeomen; a third line consisting of four companies of Longford Militia commanded by Lord Granard; and, in reserve, squadrons of carabineers and Lord Roden's Foxhunters.

With only one small cannon and his Irish allies fleeing after the first shot, Humbert ordered his grenadiers to charge with fixed bayonets. Outgunned and greatly outnumbered, the French nevertheless overwhelmed the first two lines. The militia threw down their arms and scattered. Lord Ormond 'begged and beseeched' his men to rally, but in vain, and he finally broke down in tears. The flight of the crown forces had been so precipitate that the battle ever after was known as the 'Races of Castlebar'.

The victorious Humbert held a victory ball in Castlebar and proclaimed a Republic of Connacht. But few of the local Irish joined him. He fought his way north-west, intent on reaching Ulster (which he mistakenly thought was still in rebellion), until he reached Drumahair in Co. Leitrim. There he heard that the Defenders and United Irishmen of the counties of Westmeath and Longford had risen in revolt. He rushed to join them. By now, however, the government forces had become so formidable that defeat was inevitable. On 8 September 1798 at Ballinamuck, Co. Longford, the French and their Irish allies made a last stand. Humbert and his men surrendered. They were treated courteously. The Irish who had joined the French suffered terrible retribution.

Humbert knew that two more French expeditions were due to sail. They were too late. On 16 September a French corvette sailed into Rutland harbour in Co. Donegal. The veteran United Irishman Napper Tandy stepped ashore, only to find, remarkably, that the local postmaster was old friend. The postmaster assured Tandy that the rebellion was over. The two men shared several bottles, and French officers carried Napper Tandy, unconscious with drink, back on board and sailed away.

A much larger French expedition, made up of ten ships of the line under the command of Admiral Jean-Baptiste Bompart, reached Lough Swilly in north Donegal on 12 October. But the Royal Navy, directed by Sir John Warren, was already there. During a violent storm, in perhaps the greatest sea battle ever fought in Irish waters, the French were overcome. Seven French ships struck their colours, and one of the first to step ashore from the captured flagship at Buncrana was the United Irish leader, Theobald Wolfe Tone.

Taken in chains to Dublin, Wolfe Tone faced a military court in the Royal Barracks on Saturday 10 November 1798. He was allowed to read out a long statement. He began:

It is not my intention to give the court any trouble. I admit the charge against me in the fullest extent; what I have done, I have done, and I am prepared to stand the consequences.

Episode 160 ↶

THE UNION PROPOSED

The great object of my life has been the independence of my country; for that I have sacrificed every thing that is most dear to man.... Whatever I have said, written, or thought on the subject of Ireland I now reiterate: looking upon the connexion with England to have been her bane I have endeavoured by every means in my power to break that connexion.... I have failed in the attempt; my life is in consequence forfeited and I submit; the court will do their duty and I shall endeavour to do mine.

With these words Theobald Wolfe Tone ended his address to a military court in Dublin on 10 November 1798. Denied his request to be shot by firing-squad as a soldier, instead of being hanged as a traitor, he cut his throat. His partly severed windpipe was sewn up in the hope that he could still be hanged, but after a week he died. He was buried in the family plot at Bodenstown, Co. Kildare.

At least 20,000 men, women and children had met with violent deaths during the great Irish rebellion of 1798. Most of them were from poor farming and labouring families. Few had any real understanding of what the United Irishmen meant by an Irish republic. They had fought against the crown for a bewilderingly wide range of motives: hunger for land; revenge; adventure; sectarian hatred; and a desire to be rid of high rents, taxes and tithes.

Wolfe Tone had plotted to sever Ireland's connection with England. The Prime Minister, William Pitt, on the other hand, was determined to bind the island ever more closely to Britain. For Pitt the last straw was the inability of the Ascendancy—the Protestant gentry and nobility of Ireland—to maintain law and order at a time when the Empire was in peril.

On 28 May 1798, only days after the start of the rebellion, Pitt wrote formally to the Irish viceroy, to inform him that he intended to press forward with a bill to unite the kingdoms of Great Britain and Ireland under one legislature at Westminster. Pitt's main concern was Britain's safety during a deadly war with revolutionary France. So far in this conflict, Britain had suffered a string of catastrophic defeats. French expeditions to Ireland had shown how vulnerable Britain's western flank could be. But Pitt also was certain that a union of the two kingdoms would bring prosperity and contentment to Ireland. Ireland would no longer be a colony but a partner with Britain—perhaps a junior partner, but a partner nevertheless.

Absolutely central to Pitt's scheme was the emancipation of the Catholics. Penal legislation passed in the late seventeenth and early eighteenth centuries had largely been repealed. In fact there were only two significant penal laws left by 1798: Catholics were still excluded from certain senior public positions; and Catholics could not be members of parliament. Pitt was convinced that the stability of Ireland depended on bringing in from the cold the Catholics with education and money. Get rid of the last Penal Laws—emancipate them—and Catholics could then become part of the governing elite. He planned to include Catholic Emancipation in his Union Bill.

Since 1782 Westminster could not make laws to bind the kingdom of Ireland. So a union of the two kingdoms had, in effect, to be a treaty, approved by both parliaments. The Prime Minister knew that he could count on Westminster MPs to agree with him that Ireland could be more safely ruled from London rather than from Dublin. He hoped that the Irish Protestant Ascendancy—badly frightened by the rebellion—would also take this view.

Pitt and his cabinet colleagues completely underestimated the difficulty of persuading the Irish parliament to vote itself out of existence. For a start, some members of the Irish government, loyal supporters of Pitt until now, vehemently opposed a union. Others, including the Lord Chancellor—'Black Jack' Fitzgibbon, the Earl of Clare—made it plain that they would support a Union bill only if it did *not* include Catholic Emancipation. Lord Clare said that he would not help to create a 'popish democracy'. Since King George III then very forcefully declared himself opposed to further concessions to Catholics, Pitt—with a heavy heart—dropped Catholic Emancipation from his bill. The viceroy of Ireland, Lord Cornwallis, was bitterly disappointed. He wrote: 'I certainly wish that England could now make a union with the Irish nation, instead of making it with a party in Ireland.'

In October 1798 a senior public servant in Dublin Castle, Under-Secretary Edward Cooke, wrote to William Pitt to warn him that a Union bill might well be lost in the Irish parliament. It would be necessary, Cooke added, to have the Union 'written-up, spoken-up, intrigued-up, drunk-up, sung-up and bribed-up'.

So, indeed, it proved.

Episode 161 ~

'JOBBING WITH THE MOST CORRUPT PEOPLE UNDER HEAVEN'

On 22 January 1799 the public galleries of the Irish House of Commons were packed. This was the first opportunity the Irish parliament had to express its opinion on the government's proposal to unite Britain and Ireland under one parliament at Westminster. Feelings ran high. The debate lasted for twenty-one uninterrupted hours. No fewer than eighty MPs addressed the House. Tempers flared. One government supporter reported to London: 'You would have thought you were in a Polish diet. Direct treason spoken, resistance to law declared, encouraged and recommended.'

Abuse was heaped by the opposition on Robert Stewart, Lord Castlereagh, whose job it was as Chief Secretary to recommend the Union Bill. William Plunkett, after denouncing Castlereagh as 'a green and sapless twig' (because he had failed to father children), then declared:

> For my part I will resist it to the last gasp of my existence and with the last drop of my blood. And when I feel the hour of my dissolution approaching, I will, like the father of Hannibal, take my children to the altar and swear them to eternal hostility against the invaders of their country's freedom.

When it came to a division at dawn on 23 January, the government defeated the opposition by a single vote. This was not enough to ensure the enactment of such a momentous measure. Exceptional effort would have to be put in to win a comfortable parliamentary majority in the final vote.

A pamphlet warfare raged. At least 248 pamphlets penned during these months on the subject of the proposed union survive. Titles included:

> *Irish salvation promulged, or The effects of an union with Great Britain candidly investigated in an evening's conversation between a farmer and a schoolmaster*

> *Alarum to the people of Great Britain, and Ireland; in answer to a late proposal for uniting these kingdoms. Shewing the fatal consequences of such an union*

> *Keep up your spirits, or Huzza for the empire!! Being a fair, argumentative defence of an union addressed to the people of Ireland. By a citizen of the Isle of Man*

The wedding and bedding, or John Bull and his bride, fast asleep, a satirical poem containing an history of the happy pair from their infancy to the present period, with reasons for and means used to accomplish their union; also The matchmakers, with their rueful lamentation on the loss of the bride-cake

For the next year the Lord Lieutenant, Lord Cornwallis, and his Chief Secretary, Lord Castlereagh, used every means in their power to win over a parliamentary majority for the Union. Castlereagh announced that the government would compensate every borough-owner—that is, every man who controlled a town or village returning members to the Irish parliament. Each would receive the very generous compensation payment of £15,000 per borough. Above all, the government made lavish promises of 'places' and 'pensions'—that is, of well-paid government jobs for MPs and their relatives, and annual payments to be made by the crown. Some MPs were raised to the peerage or promoted, for example from a baronage to an earldom. In a few cases direct money bribes were made. The viceroy wrote in despair: 'My occupation is now of the most unpleasant nature, negotiating and jobbing with the most corrupt people under Heaven.... I despise and hate myself every hour for engaging in such dirty work.'

This lavish use of what was then called 'patronage' may not have been ethical, but, strictly speaking, it was not illegal. What we now know, however, is that the Prime Minister, William Pitt, did in desperation resort to illegality: he used Secret Service funds, unauthorised, to pay for bribes and propaganda. Melodramatically, he sent Castlereagh £5,000 in Bank of England notes all cut in half and sent to Ireland by two separate messengers ... and, of course, in those days Castlereagh would not have had Sellotape to stick them back together again. In all, a total of £32,556 6s 11d was sent to buy support in various ways for the Union Bill in Ireland. This was entirely illegal, and most of Pitt's fellow cabinet ministers were kept in the dark about it.

To keep up the morale of its supporters, Dublin Castle gave a lavish dinner every day for twenty or thirty members, who could then be rushed to the debating chamber when urgently required. As the alcohol flowed freely, Sir Jonah Barrington recalled, Under-Secretary Edward Cooke 'with significant nods, and smirking innuendoes began to circulate his official rewards to the company [until] every man became in a prosperous state of official pregnancy ... fully resolved to eat drink, speak, and *fight* for Lord Castlereagh'.

By the beginning of 1800 it was becoming clear that Castlereagh would get the large majority he needed.

Episode 162 ～

THE PASSING OF THE ACT OF UNION

When the Irish House of Commons met on 15 January 1800, the Chief Secretary, Lord Castlereagh, again put forward a resolution to bring about the unification of Great Britain and Ireland under a single parliament at Westminster. In a packed House, a furious debate ensued. Sir Boyle Roche spoke in support of the bill. This colourful MP had once famously asked: 'Why should we put ourselves out of our way to do anything for posterity, for what has posterity ever done for us?' Now he said: 'Sir, there is no Levitical decree between nations, and on this occasion I can see neither sin nor shame in marrying our own sister.' Another MP, John Egan, announced his opposition to the Union, and speaking in defence of retaining the Irish parliament, he declared: 'It would be the glory of my life to spill the last drop of blood I have in my veins.' Egan, a bankrupt barrister, had refused an offer of a well-paid post as governor of Kilmainham Jail if he would support the bill. Now, overcome by emotion or too much claret, he bellowed across the floor: 'Ireland—Ireland forever! And damn Kilmainham!'

The great 'Patriot' orator, Henry Grattan, had not been a member of the Irish Commons for some years. At midnight he bought the parliamentary seat of Wicklow borough for £1,200, and as soon as he had become its MP he galloped through the darkness and arrived at dawn in the House of Commons—which had been debating all day and all night—dressed in his old blue Volunteer uniform, with red cuffs and collar. Looking very ill, he was allowed to speak sitting down and, in a two-hour declamation, charged the government with bribery and deceit. Waving his finger at Lord Castlereagh, he said:

> The thing which he proposes to buy is what cannot be sold—liberty. He proposes to you to substitute the British parliament in your place.... Against such a body, were I expiring on the floor, I should beg to utter my last breath and record my dying testimony.

Crowds rioted in Dublin's streets; Castlereagh had to be restrained by his friends from challenging Grattan to a duel; and Grattan actually did fight a duel with another MP, leaving a bullet in the arm of Isaac Corry, the Chancellor of the Exchequer.

The Grand Lodge of Ireland tried to be neutral on the issue, but most rank-and-file Orangemen hated the Union bill—they were certain it would be accompanied by Catholic Emancipation. No fewer than thirty-six lodges from the counties of Armagh and Louth sent in petitions against the Union. Indeed, Prime Minister William Pitt had all but promised to put forward a bill to allow Catholics to sit in parliament. For this reason most educated Catholics warmly supported the Union—with one notable exception, Daniel O'Connell, a young barrister, who spoke powerfully against it.

And what about the rest of the population? Lord Cornwallis, the viceroy, observed: 'The mass of the people do not care one farthing about the Union.' He was correct. The great majority were simply thankful to have survived the slaughter of the recent rebellion and had little interest in the parliamentary debate.

The crucial vote came on 26 May, and the Union Bill was carried comfortably by a majority of sixty votes. The debate ended with Grattan's emotional attack on the Union. But Ireland still had a future, he said:

> I see her in a swoon but she is not dead. Though in her tomb she lies helpless and motionless, still there is on her lips a spirit of life and on her cheek a glow of beauty.... While a plank of the vessel sticks together I will not leave her. Let the courtier present his flimsy sail and carry the light barge of his faith with every breath of wind. I will remain anchored here, with fidelity to the fortunes of my country, faithful to her freedom, faithful to her fall.

Meanwhile Pitt had no difficulty in persuading Westminster to pass an identical Union Bill. The royal assent was given on 2 July 1800, and the Irish parliament in College Green closed forever on 2 August. On 1 January 1801 the Act of Union came into force. From public buildings was unfurled the new Union Flag, incorporating the red diagonal cross of St Patrick on a white background.

From now on Ireland would be ruled from London. A hundred Irish MPs entered the Commons, and thirty-two peers joined their equals in the House of Lords at Westminster. Now the name of the state was 'The United Kingdom of Great Britain and Ireland'. There would be complete free trade between Britain and Ireland. The Church of Ireland was now united with the Church of England to become one 'Established' Church.

As year succeeded year in the early nineteenth century attitudes towards the Union underwent a change: the majority of the people, initially indifferent about the new system, became passionate supporters or opponents of it.

Episode 163 ⌒

ROBERT EMMET

King George III held an official entertainment at Windsor Castle on 28 January 1801. On the throne since the year 1760, the king in his old age had become rather deaf. He asked Lord Melville, the War Minister, to repeat what he had just said. The minister reminded His Majesty that his Prime Minister, William Pitt, had promised Catholic Emancipation—that is, the repeal of the law which prevented Catholics from becoming members of parliament.

King George was outraged. He shouted out, so that no one there could fail to hear him: 'The most Jacobinical thing I ever heard of! I shall reckon any man my personal enemy who proposes any such measure!'

The Act of Union had been in force only for a month. William Pitt had all but promised to grant Emancipation as soon as the act had been passed. Now, without the king's agreement, he could not do that. Pitt felt he had no choice but to resign. The failure to give Catholic men of property the same rights as Protestants of their own class would, over time, gravely weaken support for the Union. Catholic gentlemen and their descendants would form an alternative elite in Ireland, presenting a formidable challenge both to the Protestant Ascendancy and the Westminster government.

Meanwhile there was a more immediate threat to the Act of Union—the threat of revolution. Almost every day spies brought in alarming reports of conspiracies to bring down the government with the help of the French. On 16 November 1802 Bow Street Runners arrested thirty men in a public house at Lambeth in London. Their leader was an Irishman, Colonel Edward Despard; he and six others were tried for treason, convicted and hanged. Other Irish revolutionaries in Britain now hurried back to Ireland. Several offered their services to Robert Emmet, busily preparing for an insurrection in Dublin.

Robert Emmet, son of the surgeon to the Lord Lieutenant, had helped to revive the Society of United Irishmen after the rebellion of 1798. In 1799 he travelled to France. In Paris he joined his brother, Thomas Addis Emmet, who, along with other Irish exiles, was attempting to persuade Napoleon to send an expedition to Ireland. Robert Emmet then returned to Ireland in October 1802. He had repeated assurances of French help ringing in his ears. Using a legacy of £2,000 left to him by his father, Emmet began in great secrecy to prepare an Irish rebellion. Many veterans of the 1798 insurrection were living in Dublin, and these now threw themselves into the conspiracy.

Emmet put his plans into operation with such care that the government had not the slightest idea that a rebellion was in preparation in the capital.

Sympathetic businessmen provided more money, and with these funds Emmet bought or rented premises at strategic points around Dublin. In Emmet's main depots in Patrick Street, Thomas Street and Marshalsea Lane the walls rang to the sound of beaten metal as throngs of men prepared weapons for the coming revolution. This activity aroused no suspicion since tradesmen were always clanging and banging in this congested part of Dublin. The armoury grew to an impressive size. Emmet, an enthusiastic inventor, designed rockets to be launched all at once from special batteries, and hollowed-out beams packed with gunpowder to be pulled into the middle of streets to halt cavalry charges. In one depot alone Emmet had 240 hand-grenades made to his own design, formed of ink bottles filled with gunpow-der and encircled with buckshot; a hundred larger grenades made from wine bottles covered with canvas; thousands of pikes; numerous rockets and flares; explosive beams; and fire-balls made of flax, tar and gunpowder which would stick to walls when thrown and burn fiercely when ignited.

Still the government suspected nothing. Thomas Russell, a founder mem-ber of the United Irishmen who had been Wolfe Tone's closest friend, now returned from France. Russell agreed to travel to Ulster to seek the support of the Presbyterian farmers there. Trusted leaders from the counties of Wicklow, Kildare and Wexford quietly rallied their men. And Michael Dwyer, the leg-endary rebel leader who had been holding out in the heart of the Wicklow Mountains since 1798, promised his support.

Then, on Saturday 16 July 1803, an accidental explosion at Emmet's Patrick Street depot could not fail to attract the attention of the authorities. Fearing suffocation, one of the workmen thrust his fist through a window, severed an artery, and bled to death. Someone called the fire brigade. Emmet's men refused to let the firemen in. This explosion, however, seemed to indicate that Emmet's cover had been blown.

Episode 164 ～

'NOW IS YOUR TIME FOR LIBERTY!'

Saturday 23 July 1803 was the date fixed by Robert Emmet for the over-throwing of British rule in Dublin. The day began badly: at 10 a.m., in a College Green warehouse, the Dublin leaders advised him to call off the rebel-lion. An hour later Emmet met the leaders from Co. Kildare in the White Bull Inn in Thomas Street. They demanded to see the arms that were being held in readiness. Emmet took them to a depot and showed them great numbers of pikes, grenades, rockets and his specially designed exploding hollowed-out beams. They were not impressed. Where were the firearms? They left and turned back other Kildare insurgents on the road to Dublin.

Emmet was quite unable to take advantage of the gross incompetence of the authorities. General Henry Fox, the commander-in-chief, refused to take seriously several disturbing reports brought to him. Desperately Emmet attempted to raise more money to buy firearms: £500 was delivered at five in the afternoon, but the man entrusted with the money absconded. Emmet was able to buy only six additional blunderbusses.

Men intent on joining the rebellion gathered around the Marshalsea Lane depot. There were few enough of them, and most of the 240 loaves of bread Emmet had ordered were never eaten. As the men waited they fell to carousing in the local taverns. Then one of the conspirators accidentally mixed the fuses that had been prepared with those that were still unprepared. It proved impossible to distinguish them. Emmet's combat rockets—his key weapons—were now useless.

Emmet's plan was to drive six carriages—decked out to look as if they were on official business and manned by rebels armed with blunderbusses—through the gates of Dublin Castle, seize the viceroy and other officers of the state, and set up a provisional government of an Irish Republic. Ned Conlon duly hired six hackney coaches with their drivers, but as they were approaching Thomas Street they were stopped by a soldier. Conlon panicked, shot the soldier, and the terrified drivers rushed off, taking their coaches with them.

Emmet had expected at least 2,000 men. By eight o'clock there were only eighty rebels, most of whom, as one later admitted, had been in the Yellow Bottle tavern 'drinking and smoking, in the highest spirits, cracking jokes, and bantering one another, as if the business they were about to enter on was a party of pleasure'. Pikes were taken out in bundles from the Thomas Street depot, but there were only eighteen blunderbusses, four muskets and one sword, which Emmet carried himself. As one rebel leader, Miles Byrne, recalled:

Emmet, Malachy, one or two others, and myself, put on our green uniform, trimmed with gold lace, and selected our arms. The insurgents, who had all day been well plied with whiskey, began to prepare for commencing an attack upon the castle; and when all was ready, Emmet made an animated address to the conspirators. At eight o'clock precisely we sallied out of the depôt, and when we arrived in Thomas-street, the insurgents gave three deafening cheers.

The consternation excited by our presence defies description. Every avenue emptied its curious hundreds, and almost every window exhibited half-a-dozen inquisitive heads, while peaceable shopkeepers ran to their doors, and beheld with amazement a lawless band of armed insurgents ... but when the rocket ascended ... those who, a few minutes before, seemed to look on with vacant wonder, now assumed a face of horror, and fled with precipitation....

'To the castle!' cried our enthusiastic leader, drawing his sword ... but when we reached the market-house, our adherents had wonderfully diminished, there being not more than twenty insurgents with us.

Emmet then stopped to address the people:

Turn out my boys, now is your time for liberty! Liberty, my boys—now turn out!

Firing his pistol in the air he made a last attempt to rally support. Then, realising the cause was lost, he told his men to disperse. When Emmet reached his home in Rathfarnham on Dublin's outskirts, his housekeeper, Anne Devlin, called out: 'Who's there?' He replied: 'It's me, Anne.'

She responded bitterly: 'Oh, bad welcome to you. Is the world lost by you, you coward that you are, to lead the people to destruction, and then to leave them?'

'Don't blame me, the fault is not mine,' was Emmet's response.

Meanwhile, as night closed in, the fighting continued in the streets of Dublin, degenerating into a drunken riot. A coach carrying Lord Kilwarden, his daughter and his nephew, the Rev. Richard Wolfe, tried to make its way through the mob. Kilwarden attempted to assert his authority, exclaiming: 'It's me, Kilwarden, the Chief Justice of the King's Bench', whereupon an insurgent shouted: 'You're the very man I want!' and drove his pike into Kilwarden, mortally wounding him. His daughter was taken to safety, but the clergyman Wolfe was hacked to death. It was an ignominious and inglorious end to Robert Emmet's rebellion.

Episode 165 ⁓

'LET NO MAN WRITE MY EPITAPH'

Following the swift collapse of his rebellion in Dublin on 23 July 1803, Robert Emmet went into hiding. Soon afterwards yeomen questioned his housekeeper in Rathfarnham, Anne Devlin. As they prodded her arms and shoulders with bayonets, covering her with blood, she declared: 'I have nothing to tell. I will tell nothing.' They put a noose around her neck, and she declared defiantly: 'You may murder me, you villains, but not one word about him will you ever get from me. The Lord Jesus have mercy on my soul.' Then they half-hanged her until she fainted.

Finally, on 25 August, thanks to an informer, Emmet was arrested. On 19 September 1803 he was brought to Green Street Courthouse in Dublin. The evidence presented by the prosecuting counsel, Standish O'Grady, was overwhelming. Emmet had instructed his lawyers to make no defence. Convicted of treason, Emmet was asked: 'What have you, therefore, now to say, why judgment of death and execution should not be awarded against you according to law?'

Emmet's long speech from the dock, frequently interrupted by the presiding judge, Lord Norbury, ended with these words:

My lords, you are impatient for the sacrifice.... Be yet patient! I have but a few words to say ... My race is run. The grave opens to receive me and I sink into its bosom. I am ready to die.... I have but one request to ask at my departure from this world: it is *the charity of its silence.* Let no man write my epitaph.... When my country takes her place among the nations of the earth, then, and not till then, let my epitaph be written.

On the following day he was hanged in Thomas Street. After thirty minutes his corpse was cut down and the executioner cut his head from his body, crying out: 'This is the head of a traitor, Robert Emmet. This is the head of a traitor.'

Meanwhile Thomas Russell had been attempting to stir the Presbyterians of the north into rebellion. At Castlereagh in north Down Russell conferred with delegates of the United Irishmen. A spy reported to Dublin that men were drilling at Carnmoney, Newry, Ballynahinch and Knockbracken. He added that, although 'in many parts anxious for a rising, yet they cannot see how it is to be effected, having no system amongst them. Arms they have but few.'

There was a miserable turnout as Russell raised the standard of revolt by the Buck's Head dolmen near Loughinisland, Co. Down. The dispirited rebels quickly returned to their homes. Hearing of the collapse of the rebellion in the south, Russell dashed down to Dublin. There he was arrested while attempting to organise the rescue of Robert Emmet from Kilmainham Jail. Convicted of treason, he was hanged in front of Downpatrick Jail on 21 October 1803. The twenty-third man to be executed after Emmet's rebellion, Thomas Russell joined the swelling ranks of Irish revolutionary martyrs and became the subject of one of Ulster's best-known recitations, 'The Man from God Knows Where'.

Meanwhile tens of thousands of Irishmen were taking the king's shilling:

'Oh Mrs McGrath,' the sergeant said,
'Would you like to make a soldier out of your son Ted,
With a scarlet coat and a big cocked hat,
Now Mrs McGrath, wouldn't you like that?'
Wid yer too-ri-aa, fol-the diddle-aa, Too-ri-oori-oo-ri-aa,
Fol-the-diddle-aa, Too-ri-oo-ri-aa. Láv beg, the cracker, O.

Almost half the entire British army was made up of Irish recruits. Their commander in the Peninsular War was Arthur Wellesley, the future Duke of Wellington, himself an Irishman—though he did observe that just because you were born in a stable did not mean that you were a horse. These Irishmen did much to turn the tide against Napoleon in Portugal and Spain. Thousands of them died at the lines of Torres Vedras, at Salamanca and Vittoria.

'Oh then were ye drunk or were ye blind
That ye left yer two fine legs behind?'

Many Irishmen fought in Wellington's army at the Battle of Waterloo on 18 June 1815. The longest European war of modern times was over at last. Thousands of men, discharged from the army, streamed back to Ireland. Many were dreadfully maimed:

'Oh I wasn't drunk and I wasn't blind
But I left my two fine legs behind,
For a cannon ball on the fifth of May
Took my two fine legs from the knees away.'

'Oh then Teddy me boy,' the widow cried,
'Yer two fine legs were yer mammy's pride;
Them stumps of a tree wouldn't do at all
Why didn't ye run from the big cannon ball?'
Wid yer too-ri-aa ...

These men returned to swell the ranks of the poor in Ireland, an island once again alarming the ruling classes by its turbulence.

Episode 166 ∾

CARAVATS AND SHANAVESTS

While the long war against Napoleon continued to rage, Ireland seemed to prosper as never before. The island became an important provider of wheat, barley, oats, salt pork, butter and other supplies needed by troops and sailors.

Meanwhile the Irish population was rising fast. The great majority of the poor lived in the countryside, and their search for land to rent became ever more desperate. The landless labourers and cottiers turned their anger not on the landlords—often absent from their estates, in any case—but on the better-off tenant farmers who were able to outbid them for land. The result was a fierce and savage class war which for years swept the fertile lands of Munster and south Leinster.

In the eighteenth century, because of their habit of disguising themselves with white sheets, rural vigilantes were known generally as 'Whiteboys'. In the early nineteenth century secret societies and feuding gangs adopted a bewildering range of names, including: Caravats, Shanavests, Threshers, Terry Alts, Dowsers, Dingers, Bootashees, Bogboys, Three-Year-Olds, Moll Doyle's Children, Polleens, Gows, Moyle Rangers, Coffees, Ruskavellas, Black Hens, Quilts, Blue-Belt Boys. Some of these were just local names for 'Caravats', poor labourers, river boatmen, quarrymen and military deserters who followed the lead of Nicholas Hanley. Hanley strutted about with a brace of pistols in his belt and a blunderbuss in his hands and committed a whole string of mail-coach robberies and attacks on farmers in Co. Tipperary. He was nicknamed after his elegant cravat, or 'caravat'. In the winter of 1805 for his numerous crimes he was hanged in Clonmel before a violent crowd of supporters—wearing cravats—and an opposing, baying crowd of tenant farmers led by Paudeen Gar Connors, noted for his battered old waistcoat, or 'shanavest'. Hanley coolly traded insults with Paudeen Gar from the scaffold, and as the rope was put around his neck he threw his cravat to his devoted followers.

For six years and more after that a fierce warfare raged between Caravats and Shanavests. The intense violence spread out from Tipperary: south to Co. Waterford, west to Limerick and Cork, and east to the province of Leinster as far north as Co. Kildare. Typically the Caravats made raids at night—perhaps a dozen men in a band, armed, mounted, and with blackened faces and disguised by wearing women's clothes. Cases were reported of people having their ears cut off, of gang rapes, and of houses being burnt down with all the inhabitants inside. Many Caravat captains adopted the pseudonym 'John Doe'. Waterford Caravats were led for a time by a woman, Joan Lacy, who persuaded her men to murder the lover who had jilted her and, for good measure, to kill his entire family as well.

Caravats murdered farmers in dozens, often for refusing arms, horses, bridles and food. Other victims included millers, shopkeepers, publicans, yeomen and priests. Caravats would travel up to sixty miles and often in large numbers—one band in Co. Waterford was thought to be 3,000 strong. Some Caravats simply took to the hills. The most legendary was the north Cork outlaw 'Brennan on the Moor':

> 'Tis of a famous highwayman a story I will tell,
> His name was Willie Brennan and in Ireland he did dwell.
> 'Twas on the Kilworth Mountains he commenced his wild career,
> Where many a gallant gentleman before him shook with fear.
> Bold Brennan on the Moor, Brennan on the Moor.
> A brave undaunted robber was bold Brennan on the Moor.

Outnumbered though they were, Shanavests were better armed, and they organised efficient vigilante patrols exacting brutal revenge. They bonded themselves by terrifying oaths and elaborate passwords. In daylight, Caravats and Shanavests most frequently clashed at fairs. Often they arrived in formation, firing shots and yelling slogans, sometimes led in by musicians. Battles at fairs could involve thousands. The traditional shillelagh, or faction stick, was replaced by the 'clogh alpeen', an ashplant weighted with lead. Other weapons included homemade swords and spears, and whatever firearms could be got—the sawn-off shotgun was particularly favoured. Hundreds died.

Eventually the government flooded the wide area affected with troops until by December 1810 there were more soldiers in the region than there had been during the rebellion of 1798. A special commission opened at Clonmel, Co. Tipperary, on 1 February 1811, and magistrates began by sentencing twenty men to be executed, and seventeen to be transported to Botany Bay, or flogged or imprisoned. Rural violence subsided as a result, but only temporarily.

Just four years later the Battle of Waterloo ended the longest European conflict of modern times. The long wartime boom came abruptly to a halt, heralding a period of dramatic change in the Irish countryside.

Episode 167 ❧

RIBBONMEN, ORANGEMEN AND ROCKITES

The day came out, they did repair
In multitudes to Garvagh fair;
Some travelled thirty miles and mair
To burn the town of Garvagh.

On Monday 26 July 1813 during the Lammas Fair some 400 Catholic 'Ribbonmen', armed with bludgeons and intent on destroying the tavern where the Orange lodge met, converged on Garvagh in Co. Londonderry. They planned to avenge a defeat at the previous fair. As trading was drawing to a close a whistle was blown. The Ribbonmen tied long white handkerchiefs round their waists and began stoning the King's Arms.

But the Orangemen were ready. Inside the tavern, thronged with Protestants, they had their Yeomanry muskets cocked and primed. The Ribbonmen were met with a volley of gunfire. A 'mountainy man' from Foreglen fell dead, several others were desperately wounded, and the rest of the Ribbonmen, lacking the firearms needed for a counter-attack, fled to the open countryside.

Had it not been celebrated in an Orange ballad, the 'Battle of Garvagh' might be long forgotten. It was merely one of several sectarian clashes during the early years of the nineteenth century, not only in Ulster but over many parts of Ireland. Ribbonmen, in effect, were the Defenders of earlier times, organised to be a Catholic counterweight to the Orange Order. The Ribbon oath began with these words:

I ... Do Swear in the presence of My Brethren and by the Cross of St Peter and of Our Blessed Lady that I will Aid and Support Our holy Religion by Destroying the Heriticks and as far as my power & property will Go not one Shall be excepted ...

Tensions were heightened by the first major drive in more than a century to convert Irish Catholics to Protestantism. This was largely funded by wealthy English Evangelicals. By 1816 there were twenty-one Methodist missionaries operating out of fourteen stations across Ireland. Anglicans, Baptists and Presbyterians had their own missionary organisations. Over a period of ten years the Religious Tract and Book Society alone distributed 4,400,000 tracts. Between 1806 and 1823 the Hibernian Bible Society issued 218,000 copies of the New Testament and 104,000 Bibles. Over much of rural Catholic Ireland this missionary campaign caused deep resentment.

Meanwhile the Catholic poor were convinced that the day of reckoning for Protestants was fast approaching. Indeed, it was widely believed that Protestants would get their comeuppance in the year 1825, as a spy reported to the government:

> They spoke of a prophecy to be fulfilled in the year 1825, for the overthrow of the tyranny of Orangemen and government, and that there will be but one religion.

The prophecies of Pastorini, the pseudonym of an eighteenth-century English Catholic bishop, foretold the violent destruction of Protestant churches in the year 1825. Cheap editions and summaries circulated freely as the year of doom approached. It was widely believed that the 'locusts from the bottomless pit'—the Protestants—were about to meet their end. This ballad appeared in Limerick in 1821:

> Now the year 21 is drawing by degrees,
> In the year the locusts will weep,
> But in the year 23 we'll begin to reap.
> Good people, take courage, don't perish in fright,
> For notes will be of nothing in the year 25,
> As I am O'Healy, we'll daily drink beer.

These prophecies were accompanied by sectarian attacks. Half a dozen Protestant churches were burnt in the counties of Limerick, Cork and Kerry in the early 1820s, and these acts were usually claimed by 'Captain Rock'—and so these Catholic vigilantes became known as 'Rockites'. Indeed, a Catholic priest in Limerick reported that he had pursued and captured, redhanded, men he described as 'Lady Rocks'—they had disguised themselves by wearing women's clothes. In April 1823 a large band of over 100 Rockites burnt down the village of Glenosheen in Co. Limerick, a village inhabited exclusively by Palatines, Protestants of German origin.

In Ireland this 'millenarianism'—the belief that the world would shortly come to an end—was fuelled, as elsewhere, by the unemployment and distress caused by economic dislocation following the end of the Napoleonic Wars. This manifesto was posted in Co. Limerick in January 1822:

> Hearken unto me, ye men of Ireland, and hear my voice!... Your eyes shall have no pity on the breed of Luther.... Behold, the day of the Lord

cometh.... Their children also shall ye dash to pieces. Before their eyes their houses shall be spoiled, and their wives ravished.... You see misery upon misery is come upon us.... We have nothing left but to die valiantly or starve.... Lament and mourn, ye heretics, for the day of your destruction is come.

Catholic clergy and educated Catholic gentlemen were deeply embarrassed by this sectarianism of their co-religionists. They sought now to harness this discontent towards a peaceful, constitutional campaign for Catholic Emancipation.

Episode 168 ～

EMANCIPATION REFUSED

On 28 January 1801 George III publicly declared his opposition to Catholic Emancipation.

By 1806 Pitt was dead, and, soon after, George III was gnashing his gums impotently in his strait-jacket. Now it was the Prince Regent who declared that he was opposed to further concessions to Catholics. Most Tories agreed with him. As one Tory backbencher put it, 'I care no more for a Catholic than I care for a Chinese.'

The Whigs were in favour of Emancipation, and when they came to office in 1806, with Lord Grenville as Prime Minister, they prepared a bill to grant more rights to Catholics. This provoked so much royal displeasure that Grenville resigned in 1807. For the second time in less than seven years a Westminster government had been brought down by the issue of Catholic Emancipation.

These developments brought much satisfaction to Ireland's elite, the Protestant Ascendancy. Many Protestant gentlemen had hated the Union because it seemed likely that it would be accompanied by Catholic Emancipation. Now they discovered that the sky had not fallen in. Catholics were still not allowed in parliament. Even better, Ireland seemed to be governed in much the same way as it had been before the Union. Though there was not a word about it in the text of the Act of Union, the British government decided that it would continue to have a separate executive in Dublin Castle: there would still be a viceroy, an Irish Chief Secretary, an Attorney-General, and so on. There would still be plum jobs for Protestants in a separate Irish civil service. And educated and propertied Protestants continued to monopolise power in city and town corporations, to rule the thirty-two counties through unelected grand juries, to be the officer class in the Yeomanry and militia, and to have the pick of legal appointments. This was in spite of the fact that most of the Penal Laws against Catholics had long since been repealed.

In 1828 it was shown that in Ireland, of 1,314 offices connected with the administration of justice open to Catholics, only 39 were held by Catholics. Out of another list of 3,033 public offices, Catholics held only 134 posts. Irish Protestant opposition to the Union now rapidly melted away.

From January 1801 Irish MPs took their seats at Westminster. They were a pretty uninspiring lot. Fifty per cent of Irish MPs never made a single speech in the House of Commons in the nineteen years between 1801 and 1820. There were a few energetic exceptions. One was Richard 'Humanity Dick' Martin, the MP for Co. Galway: his act of 1822 for the protection of cattle from cruelty was the first legislation for animal protection ever to be enacted.

'Humanity Dick' was a supporter of Catholic Emancipation. But the most determined champion of Catholic rights at Westminster was Henry Grattan, who had been the most renowned orator of the old Irish parliament. He declared:

> The question is not whether we shall show mercy to the Roman Catholics, but whether we shall mould the inhabitants of Ireland into a *people*: for as long as we exclude Catholics from natural liberty, and the common rights of man, we are not a *people*.

Again and again Grattan presented petitions, put forward motions in the House of Commons and drafted relief bills. He made his last attempt in 1819; it was defeated by just two votes.

Grattan died in 1820. In the following year a Catholic Emancipation Bill did pass in the Commons, but it was defeated in the Lords. Had the Lords passed this bill, the future history of the United Kingdom would probably have been very different.

Catholic men of education and property, originally keen supporters of the Union, felt deceived and humiliated. It had become quite clear that a completely new approach would be needed to persuade Westminster to carry Emancipation. Inspirational leadership was needed. The man who provided it was Daniel O'Connell.

Episode 169 ⟶

THE CATHOLIC ASSOCIATION

In 1823, after more than twenty years of futile campaigning for Catholic rights, Richard Lalor Sheil was full of despair:

> I do not exaggerate when I say that the Catholic question was nearly forgotten. No angry resolutions issued from public bodies; the monster abuses of the Church Establishment, the frightful evils of political monopoly ... the unnatural ascendancy of a handful of men over an immense and powerful population ... were gradually dropping out of the national memory.... It was a degrading and unwholesome tranquillity. We sat down like galley-slaves in a calm.... The country was palsied to the heart.

Again and again, Westminster had refused Emancipation, that is, to remove the last of the Penal Laws, to allow Catholics to become members of parliament.

In January 1823 Sheil invited Daniel O'Connell to dinner. Drawn from a family of comfortable Catholic landowners in Kerry, O'Connell had established a reputation as a brilliant barrister. Over the years there had been many differences between himself and Sheil, but now the two agreed to be reconciled. Why not make one more effort, O'Connell suggested—unite all in favour of Emancipation into one organisation, the Catholic Association. With some hesitation, Sheil agreed.

The Catholic Association, based at first in Dublin, had a slow start. Six times meetings had to be abandoned because the agreed quorum of ten members could not be found. Then in 1824 O'Connell proposed that, while full members should continue to pay an annual fee of one guinea, the association should seek associate members paying a penny a month or a farthing a week. The whole movement was transformed. O'Connell had discovered that people have a much stronger sense of belonging to an organisation if they contribute towards it.

Great numbers of middle-class Catholics set up local committees, appointed collectors for various districts, posted receipt books, wrote articles for newspapers, and kept very strict accounts. Then Bishop James Doyle of Kildare and Leighlin, well known for his 'patriotic' views, sent O'Connell a list of priests who might be prepared to help. The Catholic Church became involved and made it easy to collect the pennies and farthings at chapel gates. In the first year £20,000—then a very large sum—was raised in what quickly became known as the 'Catholic Rent'. The poor had been given a stake in a national movement. The money was used to organise petitions, to buy schoolbooks for poor children, and to pay legal expenses.

The government was greatly alarmed. O'Connell had become a national figure. Up and down the country he electrified audiences with his witty and powerful oratory. Half a million Irish people were contributing to the Catholic Rent. Attempts to prosecute O'Connell for seditious libel failed. The Duke of Wellington wrote to Robert Peel, the Home Secretary: 'If we cannot get rid of the Catholic Association, we must look to civil war in Ireland sooner or later.' The government decided to suppress the Catholic Association in the spring of 1825; and, to make sure it was not accused of partiality, it banned the Orange Order as well.

But O'Connell was a brilliant lawyer: declaring that he could drive a coach and four through any act of parliament, he founded the 'New Catholic Association', which remained strictly within the law. The problem for the government was that this movement was peaceful, constitutional and orderly. Indeed, O'Connell should be remembered as one of the great pacifists of nineteenth-century Europe.

The initiative was now seized by a group of Catholics in Waterford city, led by Thomas Wyse and Father John Sheehan. A general election had been called in 1826. Owning vast estates in Co. Waterford, the Beresford family had always ensured that their tenants voted for its candidates. And the Beresfords were notoriously opposed to Catholic Emancipation. Could at least one MP for Waterford be elected who would be in favour of Emancipation?

First a candidate had to be found. The young liberal Protestant gentleman, Henry Villiers Stuart, was so delighted to be asked that he flung aside his hiking boots and abandoned his walking holiday in the Austrian Tyrol to dash back to Waterford. Indeed, he was to contribute £30,000 towards his own election expenses. But the real problem was how to persuade the 'forty-shilling freeholders', who constituted the great majority of the electorate, to risk eviction by defying their landlords to vote against the Beresfords.

Perhaps never before in Ireland had an election campaign been organised with such meticulous attention to detail. Committees were formed to transport, feed and house the voters. Priests and laymen patrolled with shillelaghs to make sure that all supporters remained sober. The Beresfords lavished silver shillings on voters to keep them loyal. O'Connell joined Villiers Stuart in Co. Waterford, and both men were drawn three miles by voters harnessed to their coach. They were aware that they were making history.

Episode 170 ∽

THE 'INVASION' OF ULSTER

During the general election of 1826 Henry Villiers Stuart, who had agreed to stand as a candidate in favour of Catholic Emancipation in the county of Waterford, needed large numbers of voters to defy their landlords, particularly the Beresfords, and risk eviction. Daniel O'Connell, the leader of the Catholic Association, who was there to rally support, described his reception in the constituency and the prevailing attitude among the electorate:

> We breakfasted at Kilmacthomas, a town belonging to the Beresfords, but the people belong to us. They came out to meet us with green boughs and such shouting you can have no idea of. I harangued them from a window of the inn, and we had a good deal of laughing at the bloody Beresfords. Judge what the popular feeling must be when in this, a Beresford town, every man their tenant, we had such a reception.

In those days there was no secret voting, and as polling got under way it was clear that Villiers Stuart was going to win. The head of the Beresford clan, the Marquis of Waterford, turned to his faithful huntsman and said: '*Et tu, Brute?*' Not recognising this quotation from Shakespeare's *Julius Caesar*, the old man nevertheless replied, his voice broken with emotion: 'Long life to yer honour, I'd go to the world's end with yer honour, but sure, please your lordship, I cannot go agin my country and religion.'

Villiers Stuart was elected along with another pro-Emancipation candidate, and his opponent, Lord George Beresford, had the humiliation of being relegated to third place. Elsewhere tenant farmers defied their landlords successfully to return pro-Emancipation candidates in the counties of Monaghan, Louth and Westmeath. The tenant farmers had risked all in defying their landlords—unthinkable in other parts of the United Kingdom. Many, indeed, suffered eviction, and to help them make a new start, great sums had to be drawn from the Catholic Rent—money collected in pennies and farthings from supporters.

Still Westminster would not give in. King George IV instructed his Prime Minister, Lord Liverpool, to stand firm against Emancipation, as his father, George III, had done: 'The sentiments of the king upon Catholic Emancipation are those of his revered and excellent father; from those sentiments the king can and never will deviate.' But Lord Liverpool had a seizure in his drawing-room in April 1827. He was replaced as Prime Minister by George Canning, who had a Co. Londonderry background and was known to be in favour of Emancipation. Canning, however, dropped dead five months later, whereupon Lord Goderich became Prime Minister. But the arguments in his cabinet room were so bitter that he dissolved in floods of tears, and in January 1828 he resigned. There was nothing for it, the king concluded, but to ask the Duke of Wellington to form a government.

Passions now ran high in Ireland. In the autumn of 1828 Jack Lawless, one of O'Connell's most energetic lieutenants, announced what he called 'the invasion of Ulster'. His plan was to advance from town to town in the province, rallying support for Emancipation. On 17 September Lawless arrived in Carrickmacross, Co. Monaghan, and declared that he would go on to enter Ballybay, then a Presbyterian town, with 50,000 followers. Some 8,000 Orangemen rallied in the town, as the *Northern Whig* reported:

> They were generally armed with muskets; but failing these, swords, bayonets, pitch-forks, scythes, &c. &c. were in requisition. A set of more determined men, perhaps, never appeared in any cause. It is well known that many of them made their wills, and settled their affairs before they left their houses in the morning.

General Thornton, in command of a body of foot-soldiers, all the county police and a troop of lancers, galloped towards Carrickmacross and persuaded Lawless to take a circuitous route. Nevertheless, supporters from the two sides clashed on the Rockcorry road:

> A conflict ensued immediately ... the termination was awfully fatal. One Catholic was run through the body with a sword or bayonet, and died on the spot. Another had his leg shattered by a musket ball, and is lying with little hopes of recovery.

The *Northern Whig*, a Belfast newspaper which supported Emancipation, concluded:

> Mr Lawless's procedure was impolitic in the highest degree.... As to his reconciling the Catholics and Orangemen—the idea is Quixotic.

Lawless abandoned his plan to march to Armagh. Protestants celebrated at great demonstrations, 40,000 gathering at Tandragee alone. Some Orangemen marched to the Moy, where all but two families were Catholic. Their approach, the *Newry Telegraph* reported,

> was announced by drums, fifes, bugles, and by playing party tunes, such as 'Holy Water', 'Croppies lie down', and 'Kick the Pope before Us' ... till two in

the morning, when they marched back, playing the same tunes, huzzaing, and firing shots.

Support for Emancipation was hard to find among ordinary Protestants in Ulster, but O'Connell's movement was only a few months away from complete victory.

Episode 171 ～

THE CLARE ELECTION

In response to entreaties from King George IV, the Duke of Wellington agreed to become Prime Minister in January 1828. He was expected to hold the line against Catholic Emancipation, that is, the repeal of the penal law which prevented Catholics sitting in parliament. Wellington selected an Irishman, William Vesey Fitzgerald, MP for Co. Clare, to be President of the Board of Trade. In those days an MP appointed to the cabinet had to stand for re-election in his constituency.

Fitzgerald expected no opposition. After all, he himself supported Catholic Emancipation. He was wrong. Daniel O'Connell, the charismatic leader of the Catholic Association, agreed to stand against Fitzgerald. But how could a Catholic stand? A careful scrutiny of the law showed that there was nothing to stop a Catholic being elected—it was just that the oath prescribed for MPs was an impossible one for any Catholic to take. This O'Connell made clear in his election address:

> You will be told I am not qualified to be elected: the assertion, my friends, is untrue.… It is true that, as a Catholic, I cannot, and of course never will, take the oaths prescribed to members of parliament.…
>
> The oath at present required by law is, 'That the sacrifice of the mass, and the invocation of the Blessed Virgin Mary, and other saints, as now practised in the Church of Rome, are impious and idolatrous'. Of course I will never stain my soul with such an oath: I leave that to my honourable opponent, Mr Vesey Fitzgerald. He has often taken that horrible oath.… I would rather be torn limb from limb than take it.

O'Connell's journey from the capital to Ennis, the county town, was a triumphal procession. At the chapel of Corofin on the Sunday before the poll the aged Father John Murphy threw off his vestments after Mass and called upon his people in Irish to sacrifice themselves for O'Connell, their faith and their fatherland. Richard Lalor Sheil described the scene:

> It was a most extraordinary and powerful display of the externals of elo-quence.... His intonations were soft, pathetic, denunciatory, and conjur-ing.... Shouts of laughter attended his description of a miserable Catholic who should prove recreant to the great cause, by making a sacrifice of his country to his landlord.
>
> The close of his speech was peculiarly effective. He became inflamed by the power of his emotions, and while he raised himself to the loftiest atti-tude to which he could ascend, he laid one hand on the altar ... and as his eyes blazed and seemed to start from his forehead, thick drops fell down his face, and his voice rolled through lips livid with passion and covered with foam.... The multitude burst into shouts of acclamation, and would have been ready to mount a battery roaring with cannon at his command.

Two days later Father Murphy led the freeholders of his parish into Ennis and polled them to a man in favour of Daniel O'Connell. Their landlord, Sir Edward O'Brien, stood aghast. After all, these voters, those who had holdings worth forty shillings or more, risked eviction from their farms by going against him. As he saw he was going down to defeat, Vesey Fitzgerald wept openly. Meanwhile O'Connell joked with the crowd in a rich Munster accent:

> Arrah, bhoys, where's Vasy Vijarld at all, at all ... sind the bell about for him. Here's the cry for yez:—
>> Stholen or sthrayed,
>> Losht or mishlaid,
>> The President of the Boord of Thrade!

When a priest announced that a forty-shilling freeholder who had voted against O'Connell had just dropped dead, the crowded square of Ennis became totally silent, and the entire body knelt down in prayer.

Huge numbers packed the town. The three thousand freeholders qualified to vote were accompanied by perhaps ten times that number, this huge con-course being made up of wives, children, relations, supporters and friends. Around 150 priests were in the town organising and arranging feeding and accommodation.

When the results were announced, O'Connell was declared the winner, having polled 2,057 votes to 982 for Vesy Fitzgerald, with 300 additional votes for him ruled out because of a printer's error on the ballot paper. O'Connell beseeched the landlords of the county not to avenge themselves on the wretched forty-shilling freeholders, and he concluded:

Wellington and Peel, if you be true to old England, for I love and cherish her ... all shall be forgotten, pardoned and forgiven upon giving us Emancipation, unconditional, unqualified, free, and unshackled.

Robert Peel, the Home Secretary, after reading a letter from Vesey Fitzgerald reporting the election result, observed:

We were watching the movements of tens of thousands of disciplined fanatics, abstaining from every excess and indulgence, and concentrating every passion and feeling on one single object.... Is it consistent with common prudence and common sense to repeat such scenes and to incur such risks of contagion?

He was rapidly coming to the conclusion that Catholic Emancipation would have to be conceded.

Episode 172 ∽

'SCUM CONDENSED OF IRISH BOG!'

Following his famous victory in the Clare election in July 1828, Daniel O'Connell made a triumphal return to Dublin. Here ballad-singers had a new version of an old favourite:

We have good news today, says the Shan Van Vocht,
And the parsons feel dismayed, says the Shan Van Vocht.
Now the Bible saints won't pray, but curse both night and day
Since O'Connell gained the day, says the Shan Van Vocht.

What was to be done? The Prime Minister, the Duke of Wellington, was aghast when his old comrade in arms, the Marquis of Anglesey, now the Lord Lieutenant of Ireland, announced his conversion to Catholic Emancipation: 'Lord Anglesey is gone mad. He is bit by a mad papist.'

Robert Peel, the Home Secretary, had long been O'Connell's bitter adversary. Denouncing him as 'Orange Peel', O'Connell had notoriously likened Peel's smile to the shine of a silver plate on a coffin. Now Peel became convinced that, for the sake of peace in Ireland, Catholics should be allowed to take seats in parliament. He also persuaded Wellington to change his mind. That meant wigs on the green: when Wellington introduced his Emancipation Bill in February 1829, the Earl of Winchelsea accused him of seeking to introduce popery into every government department. The Prime Minister reached for his duelling pistols. The Iron Duke and the earl met at dawn on Battersea Fields. Fortunately both were unscathed, and, honour satisfied, they shook hands.

The Emancipation Bill became law in April 1829—but there was a sting in the tail. The property qualification for voting in county elections in Ireland was raised from forty shillings to £10. O'Connell never quite lived down the accusation that he did not fight hard enough to prevent the disenfranchise-ment of the forty-shilling freeholders, the men who had risked the wrath of their landlords to get him elected in Clare.

And so for the first time since the Reformation a Catholic took his seat in the House of Commons. The year 1830 saw the return of the Whigs to power after decades of opposition. The burning issue now was reform of parliament. O'Connell's support was crucial to get the Reform Bill through, and during the session of 1831 he spoke in the House no fewer than 283 times in favour of the measure.

O'Connell's next great objective was repeal of the Union, which meant, in effect, the restoration of the Irish parliament, closed down in 1800. But it was hard enough to get sufficient support for that proposal from Irish MPs, let alone from those representing the rest of the United Kingdom. Though he quarrelled with the Whigs endlessly, O'Connell realised that, as reformers, they were more likely than the Tories to produce beneficial measures for Ireland. His view was that he would test the Union: if governments were pre-pared to give justice to Ireland, then he could set his demand for repeal to one side. 'The people of Ireland', he declared, 'are ready to become a portion of the Empire, provided they be made so in reality and not in name alone; they are ready to become a kind of West Britons if made so in benefits and in justice; but if not, we are Irishmen again.'

Reform certainly was needed. Irish farmers—Catholics and Presbyterians, as well as Anglicans—were still forced by law to pay the tithe, a compulsory payment for the upkeep of the Established Church. Now Irish farmers violently resisted tithe collection. In 1832 this 'Tithe War' resulted in 242 homicides, 300 attempted murders, thousands of assaults on persons and property, and widespread intimidation of juries.

The government's response in 1833 was to put through a stringent coercion act, which included the suspension of trial by jury. O'Connell hated this measure and denounced 'the base, bloody and brutal Whigs'. Nevertheless, he did not want the Tories in power, especially with Peel as Prime Minister. In turn the Whigs realised that they needed O'Connell, and the forty MPs he had with him, to stay in power. In 1835 at Lichfield House in London the new Whig leader, Lord Melbourne, and O'Connell made a gentleman's agreement to back each other in parliament. When news of what became known as the 'Lichfield House Compact' came out, the *Times* newspaper was outraged and published a scathing piece of verse which began:

> Scum condensed of Irish bog!
> Ruffian—coward—demagogue!
> Boundless liar—base detractor!
> Nurse of murders—treason's factor!
> Of pope and priest the crouching slave,
> While thy lips of freedom rave;
> Of England's fame the vip'rous hater,
> Yet wanting courage for a traitor.
> Ireland's peasants feed thy purse,
> Still thou art her bane and curse ...

In fact O'Connell's alliance with the Whigs was to last for six years. It resulted in a radical change in the way Ireland was governed.

Episode 173 ⌒

A SOCIAL LABORATORY

When the new Union Flag was unfurled for the first time on 1 January 1801, it was assumed that, now Ireland was part of the United Kingdom, the island would be ruled in just the same way as England, Scotland and Wales. But was this possible? The British ruling classes tended to regard Ireland as a place apart, inhabited by turbulent and backward people, constantly threatening the violent overthrow of law and order.

The first sign that Ireland would be treated differently was the retention of a separate administration in Dublin Castle. There would still be a Lord Lieutenant residing in the Viceregal Lodge in Phoenix Park. And he still had the support of a Chief Secretary, other ministers, and a separate civil service. This was not the case in Wales or Scotland.

A startling fact is that during the first fifty years of the nineteenth century ordinary law was in force in Ireland for only five years. During the other forty-five years the government adopted special powers—then generally known as 'coercion'—to suspend trial by jury, to hold people without trial, and to send in armed forces to restore order. The Protestant Ascendancy, for long the ruling class of Ireland, could be forgiven for thinking, with much satisfaction, that nothing much had changed.

Yet the Act of Union had been introduced because the British government had lost confidence in the ability of the Protestant Ascendancy to govern Ireland. In time successive governments, both Whig and Tory and, later, Liberal and Conservative, steadily undermined the power base of the Ascendancy. With differing degrees of enthusiasm, Westminster governments strove to be neutral and to detach themselves from dependence on Ireland's Protestant elite.

To achieve this, governments had to take on responsibilities they would not think of accepting on the other side of the Irish Sea. Such a proactive approach could be very much to the benefit of the Irish people. Indeed, some historians argue that British governments were using Ireland as a 'social laboratory' for trying out national education, publicly funded hospitals, independent policing, unemployment relief schemes, and the like, long before these improvements were introduced into the rest of the United Kingdom.

The man who really set this process rolling was Robert Peel. Peel arrived in Dublin as Chief Secretary at the age of twenty-four in September 1812. A virulent opponent of Catholic Emancipation, he soon attracted the vituperative denunciation of Daniel O'Connell, who depicted him as 'a raw youth squeezed out of the workings of I know not what factory in England before he had got rid of the foppery of perfumed handkerchiefs and thin shoes'. Yet O'Connell's contemptuous soubriquet 'Orange Peel' was unjustified, for Peel was determined to show no favour to sectional interests in the government of Ireland. He sent out an order that members of the Yeomanry were not to appear at Orange parades in their uniforms. Seeing that the Yeomanry—for the most part Protestant gentlemen and farmers—rarely acted with impartiality when called in to restore order, Peel decided to create a new force which would command respect from all sides of the community. In 1813 he proposed that the viceroy should appoint a specialist force of police to be sent into the most disturbed districts. Though the Prime Minister, Lord Liverpool, objected that this was 'not English', Peel obtained parliament's permission. The Peace Preservation Force, which later became the Irish Constabulary, came into being in 1814—the first police force in any part of the United Kingdom. It soon proved its worth, often coping where soldiers were unable to do so. Since the new police force was independent of local landlord control, its very existence began a significant erosion of the power of the Ascendancy. Peel was determined that there should be no 'jobs for the boys', stating emphatically that 'We ought to be crucified if we ... select our constables from the servants of our parliamentary friends.'

A terrible famine, followed by a typhus fever epidemic, swept the country in 1816 and 1817. About 65,000 people died, but the death toll might have been much higher had not Peel acted promptly. He set up a central committee and gave it the authority to distribute nearly £50,000—which he extracted from a very reluctant Exchequer—to local relief committees. This kind of intervention was unheard of in other distressed parts of the United Kingdom. Peel followed this up by instituting local boards of health to establish and manage publicly funded fever hospitals.

After Peel left Ireland in 1818 there were few more such attempts at dynamic impartiality until the Whigs came to power in 1830. Grateful for the support of O'Connell as the Great Reform Bill was being steered through parliament, the Whigs felt obliged to do more for Ireland. If the Whigs really could give 'Justice to Ireland', O'Connell concluded, then his demand for repeal of the Union could be parked for a long time to come.

Episode 174 ~

THE TITHE WAR

Perhaps the most hated tax in early nineteenth-century Ireland was the tithe, which earmarked about one-tenth of the produce of the land for the upkeep of the clergy of the Established Church. This was considered most unjust by those farmers who were not members of that church, in particular Catholics, who formed never less than three-quarters of the population.

The tithe was usually collected in kind in the form of corn, eggs, poultry and the like, which made its levying both highly visible and open to abuse. Then in 1823 the Tithe Composition Act set up a procedure for 'commutating' payment in kind into payment in cash. This created fresh injustice: the new valuations were based on the average price of corn over the seven years leading up to November 1821. Since then the price obtained for corn in the market had fallen sharply, plunging by almost 25 per cent between 1820 and 1830. Resentment intensified because lands previously exempt were now included. In the parish of Castlecomer, Co. Kilkenny, for example, tithe had formerly been levied on 2,000 acres, but under the new system 12,000 were liable for payment.

The harvest of 1829 had been very poor, and in the following year angry farmers in south Leinster began to meet at hurling matches to organise resistance. On 13 December 1830 in the Kilkenny parish of Graiguenamanagh some cattle seized for non-payment of tithe were put up for sale. Though a large crowd was present, there were no buyers. The farmers had hit on a highly effective way of dislocating the collection of tithe. The example of the farmers of Graiguenamanagh was soon followed in the surrounding parishes of Goresbridge, Powerstown, Gowran and Borris.

Sir John Harvey, Inspector-General for Leinster, rushed some 400 police-men, supported by the militia, to Co. Kilkenny. But, he reported, seizures for tithe 'proceeded very slowly or not at all, and so few cattle will be at the sale'. The 'tithe hurlers' refined their tactics: boys acting as sentinels warned of approaching police by blowing hunting horns; livestock were then all locked up (these, through a legal point, could not be distrained) and only let out at night to graze. In Co. Cork people celebrated by singing 'The Barrymore Tithe Victory':

> We cannot, we will not—we'll go to the auction,
> And let us then see which foul fiend of the faction
> Will purchase your cow, Kate, at cant or at fair,
> Or guarded by Lancers in fine hollow square.

At a meeting in Maryborough in Queen's County (now Portlaoise in Co. Laois) on 10 February 1831 Pat Lalor declared to wild cheers from a great crowd that he would no longer pay tithes but would allow the parson to seize his goods, and that he was sure no man could be found to bid for them. He was right: great numbers of local people gathered for the sale of his cattle and sheep in March 1831, but there was not a single bid, and the rector's agent had no choice but to buy them himself. The animals were taken under guard to Dublin and shipped to Liverpool. Even there no buyer could be found, and eventually the animals perished from starvation. The 'tithe hurlers' had branded the dis-trained cattle with the word 'TITHE' and, on the day of the sale, circulated printed notices in Liverpool including an extract from Lalor's speech.

James Doyle, the Catholic Bishop of Kildare and Leighlin, now came in behind the tithe hurlers. In an open letter he declared that tithes were no longer legally binding, because a quarter of the money collected was supposed to be set aside for the poor, and it was not. His letter was quoted from plat-forms at innumerable meetings:

An indomitable hatred of oppression is like a gem upon the front of our nation which no darkness can obscure. To this firm quality I trace their hatred of tithe: may it be as lasting as their love of justice.... Can Ireland, the poorest nation in Europe, support the most affluent and luxurious priesthood which does not profess the religion of the people, nor minister to the wants of the poor?

As the movement spread throughout Leinster and much of Munster, blood began to flow. On 22 May 1831 at a fair in Castlepollard, Co. Longford, police opened fire, killing seventeen people:

> They drew up round the market-house their chief he made them fire,
> While the astonished flying crowd on all sides did retire.
> 'Twas human blood they wanted—their deadly aim they took,
> And Castlepollard streets with gore were running like a brook.

On 18 June at Newtownbarry, Co. Wexford, during a tithe sale where no one could be found to bid, the Yeomanry shot dead fourteen people in a stone-throwing crowd. On 14 December 1831 tithe hurlers laid an ambush to await a force accompanying a process-server at Carrickshock, two miles from Knocktopher, Co. Kilkenny. Twelve policemen and three of the ambushers were killed:

> Who could desire to see better sport
> Than Peelers groaning among the rocks,
> Their skulls all fractured, their eyeballs broken,
> Their fine long noses and ears cut off.

Deprived of income, many Anglican rectors were in difficulties. One clergyman wrote: 'I have now but one woman servant, and I believe I am not the only clergyman in the same situation, reduced from comfort to absolute poverty.' He was fortunate: other Protestant clergy, including the incumbents of Naas, Co. Kildare, and Golden, Co. Tipperary, were murdered.

The turbulence and violence increased and spread in 1832 in what was now described as the 'Tithe War'. There were reports of a meeting in Co. Longford involving 120,000, and another in Co. Cork at which 200,000 were believed to be present. Under the Peace Preservation Act, the government 'proclaimed' the most disturbed districts and imposed heavy fines and prison sentences on leaders of the movement. Daniel O'Connell, for his part, hated the privileges of the Established Church, but he was anxious to remain within the law. His great object now was repeal of the Act of Union, and in a letter to the people of Kilkenny he declared that the anti-tithe meetings 'are illegal' and added: 'We are on the fair road to Repeal, and only by Repeal can church taxes and tithes be abolished…. The conduct of the people of Kilkenny will only harm Repeal.'

In addition to passing legislation giving itself fresh special powers, the government cut the costs of the Established Church by suppressing ten of its bishoprics. The Prime Minister, Lord Melbourne, ruefully admitted that the movement had succeeded 'in practically abolishing tithes by force and is compelling the state to make up the loss to the clergymen from the public purse'. Seizure of livestock and forced collection continued, but the government felt obliged to vote £1 million to make up the shortfall. O'Connell succeeded in getting the government to reduce the tithe by a quarter in 1838 and making landlords responsible for its collection. The country calmed down, but the tithe remained a corrosive issue for many years to come.

Episode 175 ~

'PROPERTY HAS ITS DUTIES AS WELL AS ITS RIGHTS'

For most of the 1830s Daniel O'Connell and Irish MPs supporting him had helped the Whig governments carry through a series of momentous reforms. In return the Whigs did much to change how Ireland was governed. In particular, they undermined the power of Ireland's exclusive elite, the Protestant Ascendancy.

In 1831 Chief Secretary Edward Stanley established a national system of primary education, with teachers' salaries almost entirely paid by the government. By 1840 nearly a quarter of a million young people were receiving formal education in just under two thousand of these schools, known as 'National Schools'. England was not to have a national system of education for another thirty years.

Passionate Anglican though he was, Stanley sought to have Catholics and Protestants educated together. The object of government policy, he said, was to have in Ireland 'a system of education from which should be banished even the suspicion of proselytism, and which, admitting children of all religious persuasions, should not interfere with the peculiar tenets of any'. This was a view shared by the Catholic Bishop of Kildare and Leighlin, James Doyle, who had written in 1826:

I do not know of any measures which would prepare the way for a better feeling in Ireland, than uniting children at an early age and bringing them up in the same school, leading them to commune with one another and to form those little intimacies and friendships which often subsist through life.

The Catholic Church at first cautiously welcomed integrated National Schools, but the Presbyterians of Ulster were hostile from the outset. The Anglicans of the Established Church then announced that they intended to educate their children separately. And, finally, after Bishop Doyle had died in 1834, the Catholic Church also insisted on Catholic National Schools for Catholic children. The government could not resist such pressure, and so all the National Schools became denominational.

In 1835, the year in which Daniel O'Connell's alliance with the Whigs was formalised, Thomas Drummond took up his post as Under-Secretary—in effect, the head of the Irish civil service. Employed for many years by the Ordnance Survey, this Scot had come to know Ireland well. He had seen the wretched condition of the peasantry and had been appalled by the tyranny of the landlords. Now he had a chance to make a difference. The answer to unrest, he believed, was not coercion and repression, but the creation of an administration which would win popular confidence by being impartial.

In 1833, four years after Catholic Emancipation, there was still not a single Catholic judge or paid magistrate. All the high sheriffs with one exception, the overwhelming majority of paid magistrates and grand jurors, the five inspectors-general and the thirty-two sub-inspectors of police were all Protestant. In just a few years Drummond was able to change all that. Catholics were appointed to important legal posts, and Drummond drafted a Constabulary Bill, successfully steered through parliament in 1836, which eliminated the baleful influence of local men of property, set new standards of professionalism, and encouraged Catholics to join up and be promoted. The Irish Constabulary rapidly gained acceptance in the countryside and reduced levels of crime. When Tipperary magistrates in 1838 demanded harsh measures to suppress disorder, Drummond knew that the trouble had been caused by the eviction of poor farmers. In his reply to the magistrates Drummond wrote:

> Property ... has its duties as well as its rights.... To the neglect of these duties in times past is mainly to be attributed that diseased state of society in which such crimes can take their rise ... and it is not in the enactment and enforcement of statutes of extraordinary severity, but chiefly in the better and more faithful performance of those duties ... that a permanent remedy for such disorders is to be sought.

Drummond also played a major part in reducing the influence of the Orange Order. In 1835 a parliamentary select committee produced a 4,500-page report on the institution. For MPs the alarming conclusion was not only that the Yeomanry was controlled by the Orangemen, but also that the army was full of lodges; this was especially worrying, as the British Grand Master, the Duke of Cumberland, was King William iv's brother and a field marshal. To prevent stern action by parliament, Cumberland dissolved the army lodges in February 1836, and the Grand Orange Lodge of Ireland closed itself down in the following April. The Orange Order continued in Ireland, but it was largely deserted by the upper classes. Almost another fifty years were to pass before the institution recovered its prestige and influence.

Daniel O'Connell, however, was becoming increasingly dissatisfied with the results of his alliance with the Whigs. The time had come, he believed, to demand repeal of the Union.

Episode 176 ～

THE REPEALER REPULSED

For ten years Daniel O'Connell had worked along with Whig governments to achieve justice for Ireland. By 1840, however, his patience had run out. The crop of reforms had been miserable enough, he believed. A Poor Law, with harsh provisions, had been enacted in 1838, completely ignoring thoughtful recommendations made by high-powered committees in Ireland. Following an impressive report which denounced unrepresentative local government as incompetent and unfair, only ten elected corporations had been created in Ireland in 1840.

O'Connell now launched a great campaign for repeal of the Union and the restoration of the Irish parliament. O'Connell decided to begin with Ulster. He had once toasted the 'immortal memory' of William of Orange by drinking a tumbler of Boyne water, and he never ceased to hope that northern Presbyterians would join him. In January 1841 he accepted an invitation to speak in Belfast.

The Rev. Dr Henry Cooke, now the main spokesman for Presbyterians, declared that repeal was 'just a discreet word for Romish ascendancy and Protestant extermination'. He promptly challenged O'Connell:

When you *invade* Ulster, and unfurl the flag of *Repeal*, you will find yourself in a new climate.... I believe you are a great bad man, engaged in a great bad cause—and as easily foiled by a weak man, armed with a good cause, as Goliath, the Giant of Gath, was discomfited by the stripling with no weapon but a sling and two pebbles from the brook.

The original plan for a procession into Ulster was dropped. The government, for its part, was taking no chances. It engaged two steamers to take north detachments of the 99th Regiment from Dublin; the Enniskillen Dragoons were called to Belfast; and the artillery arrived with four pieces of cannon.

Immense hostile crowds congregated in Dromore, Hillsborough and Lisburn. But they had to be satisfied with burning O'Connell in effigy, for on Saturday 16 January he slipped through incognito. O'Connell did indeed find himself in a new climate in Belfast. He did not even dare leave the safety of Kern's Hotel in Donegall Place to attend Mass at St Patrick's the following morning. It was not until Tuesday 19 January that O'Connell faced the public in the open. On the balcony of Kern's Hotel he threw off his green cloak to reveal a splendid suit of Repeal frieze, with a white velvet collar and Repeal buttons. But he could not be heard, as the *Belfast News-Letter* reported:

> Yells, hisses, groans, cheers, and exclamations of all descriptions were blended together in the most strange confusion imaginable ... 'Ha, Dan, there's Dr Cooke coming'—'No Pope'—'No Surrender'—'Come out of that ye big beggarman, till we shake hands with ye'—'Put out the Ballymacarrett weavers ...—'Dan O'Connell for ever'—'Hurrah for Repeal', etc.

That evening, as O'Connell attended a soirée in the May Street Music Hall, a stone-throwing battle raged outside, while a

> still larger body of people traversed the town, shouting and yelling...they smashed the windows of several houses, confining their rage, principally, to the residences of persons to had been accessory to the late Repeal.

A well-aimed stone broke through a window and sliced through a blind to shatter the great chandelier in Kern's Hotel. Meanwhile the office of the *Vindicator*, the Belfast Repeal journal, also came under attack, as was recorded by a journalist inside the building:

> While we write, they are after being repulsed by the police, in the fifth attempt to break open the door; and there is scarcely a whole pane in the front of the office.

Next morning, escorted by four cars full of police and a body of police cavalry, O'Connell left Belfast for Donaghadee. As he approached the cross-channel vessel a woman threw a cup of tea at him. At the gangplank O'Connell attempted polite conversation with an old fisherman, saying: 'You have very pretty girls here.' The old man replied: 'Yes, but none of them are Repealers.'

Two days later Dr Cooke addressed a 'Grand Conservative Demonstration' in Belfast:

Look at the town of Belfast. When I was myself a youth I remember it almost a village. But what a glorious sight does it now present—the masted grove within our harbour—our mighty warehouses teeming with the wealth of every climate—(*cheers*)—our giant manufactories lifting themselves on every side.... And all this we owe to the Union.... Mr O'Connell ... look at Belfast, and be a Repealer—if you can.

The Orange lodge in Comber, Co. Down, soon had a new marching song:

> O'Connell he does boast of his great big rebel host,
> He says they are ten million in number.
> But half of them you'll find they are both lame and blind,
> For we're the Bright Orange Heroes of Comber.

Undeterred, O'Connell threw himself into organising a series of 'monster meetings' to seek repeal of the Union.

Episode 177 ⌒

MONSTER MEETINGS

The Repeal and the Repeal alone is and must be the grand basis of all future operations, hit or miss, win or lose. The people will take nothing short of that.... I say there can be no other basis of association save the Repeal, the glorious Repeal.

In declarations such as this Daniel O'Connell made his programme clear during the general election campaign of 1841. He was seeking the repeal of the Act of Union and the restoration of the Irish parliament. Could he repeat the brilliant success of his campaign for Catholic Emancipation in the 1820s? The problem was that the election of 1841 brought the Tories to power, with O'Connell's bitter adversary, Sir Robert Peel, as Prime Minister.

Once again the peasantry of Ireland contributed to a fighting fund, known as the 'Repeal Rent', collected mostly in pennies and farthings. With indefatigable energy O'Connell addressed a series of 'monster meetings' across the country. The excitement was intense. Vast numbers travelled great distances to hear O'Connell, the 'Agitator', the 'Emancipator', the 'Liberator'.

A German traveller, Jacob Veneday, reported O'Connell's arrival at the Athlone monster meeting of 15 June 1843:

Now there arose a cry such as never before had greeted my ears; now all hats were raised in the air, and there burst forth the unanimous shouts: 'Hurrah! hurrah! hurrah! Long live O'Connell! Long live the Liberator!' A hundred thousand voices sent forth these salutations to the man whose magic power had circled them around him. He sat on the box-seat of a carriage drawn by four horses, and answered the salutation with head, hand, and cap.... How he made his way I do not even to this day comprehend, for there was not room for a person to fall, much less to walk. 'Make way for the Liberator!' was the charm word which accomplished the wonder that otherwise had been an impossibility.

Meetings were usually followed by public banquets. At Mallow, Co. Cork, before the dinner speeches, a singer performed one of Thomas Moore's 'melodies':

> Oh, where's the slave so lowly,
> Condemned to chains unholy,
> Who, could he burst
> His bonds accursed,
> Would pine beneath them slowly?

O'Connell then leaped to his feet and raising his arms wide, cried out 'I am not that slave!' Then all in the room raised their arms in the same way, exclaiming again and again: 'We are not those slaves! We are not those slaves!'

The greatest meeting of all was on the Hill of Tara on the feast-day of the Assumption, 15 August 1843. Even *The Times*, a newspaper fiercely hostile to O'Connell, reported the audience at Tara to be around a million. The fields for miles around were filled with vehicles. The mounted escort, told off in lines of four by volunteer 'Repeal police', was estimated at 10,000 horsemen. It took O'Connell's open carriage two hours to make its way through the vast crowd. The carriage was preceded by a car on which a harper sat on a throne playing Thomas Moore's 'The Harp that Once through Tara's Halls'. Vigilant laymen and priests made sure that there was no disorder, no shillelaghs, no strong drink. During O'Connell's speech the vast audience shouted, laughed, groaned and exulted at appropriate moments in response to his stentorian oratory—including those who were too far away to hear what was being said.

The English writer Bulwer Lytton attended a monster meeting and described the scene in verse:

> Once to my sight the giant thus was given:
> Walled by wide air and roofed by boundless heaven,
> Beneath his feet the human ocean lay,
> And wave on wave flowed into space away.

Methought no clarion could have sent its sound
E'en to the centre of the hosts around;
And, as I thought, arose a sonorous swell,
As from some church tower swings the silvery bell;
Aloft and clear from airy tide to tide,
It glided easy as a bird may glide;
To the last verge of that vast audience sent,
It played with each wild passion as it went:
Now stirred the uproar, now the murmurs stilled,
And sobs or laughter answered as it willed.

Peaceful meetings of such enormous size were unheard of in other parts of Europe. Only meticulous planning and organisation made it possible to hold more than forty monster meetings across Ireland during the year 1843 without any violent incidents.

And how did Peel's government respond? Thomas, Earl de Grey, the viceroy, urged the Prime Minister to stand firm: 'Let whatever you do be strong enough.... Let no morbid sensibility, or mawkish apprehension of invading the constitution ... be allowed to weigh.' Peel had every intention of following this advice. O'Connell announced that the climax of his Repeal campaign would be a monster meeting on 8 October 1843. It would be held at Clontarf, the site of Brian Boru's victory over the Vikings in the year 1014. The government, however, was determined that this meeting would not take place.

Episode 178 ~

A NATION ONCE AGAIN?

At 3.30 in the afternoon of 7 October 1843 a messenger arrived hotfoot from Dublin Castle to the offices of the Loyal National Repeal Association in Dublin. There Daniel O'Connell read out the Lord Lieutenant's proclamation to committee members. The monster meeting, due to take place next day north of the city at Clontarf, had been 'proclaimed'—in other words, it would be an illegal assembly. What was to be done?

All his life Daniel O'Connell had believed passionately in staying within the law. 'Liberty is not worth the shedding of a single drop of blood,' he had once said. Now tens of thousands were making their way to Clontarf. This was arranged to be the greatest of his 'monster meetings', a massive peaceful demonstration to demand repeal of the Act of Union. O'Connell did not hesitate: the meeting would be called off. All the committee members agreed.

The government feared that O'Connell's campaign would end in violence. Extra troops had been rushed to Ireland. Additional warships rode at anchor in Dublin Bay. Sir Robert Peel, the Prime Minister, should have known O'Connell better. O'Connell dictated an address to the Irish people, directing them to obey the proclamation. Within minutes it was dispatched to the printer.

In spite of his strict compliance with the law, on 30 May 1844 O'Connell was sentenced to one year's imprisonment in Richmond Penitentiary in London. Instead of putting O'Connell in a cell, the bewildered governor deferentially made over his handsome residence to the great man. Then in September the sentence was overturned in the House of Lords and O'Connell was released. Nevertheless, now approaching seventy, O'Connell was no longer the man he had been. The millions who had devotedly followed him were left in a state of bewilderment. The Repeal movement began to run into the sands.

Meanwhile, over much of western and central Europe, the old order faced a growing challenge. Kings, emperors and privileged aristocrats, brought into the sun again after Waterloo, had to cope with rising discontent. The seeds of liberty, equality and fraternity, planted over vast areas during the years of Napoleon's greatest triumphs, had sprouted and grown. Germans, Italians, Poles and a host of other peoples demanded national self-determination with an ever more powerful voice. Romantic nationalism saw the forging of new identities and threatened to rock the sprawling multinational great powers to their foundations.

Thomas Davis was one young man powerfully affected by this political romanticism. Son of an English surgeon and an Irish mother, and a Protestant, Davis turned to Irish history rather than to the Rights of Man for inspiration. He threw himself into O'Connell's Repeal movement and joined with two other young activists, John Blake Dillon and Charles Gavan Duffy, to found a newspaper to promote the cause. The *Nation* began publication in October 1842 and quickly outsold all other newspapers in Ireland; since it was widely circulated throughout Repeal reading rooms, it may have a readership of a quarter of a million.

Davis and his associates formed a group within the Repeal movement called Young Ireland—a conscious imitation of Giuseppe Mazzini's Young Italy. Repeal of the Union was, to Young Ireland, only the first step towards full national independence. The pages of the *Nation* carried passionate songs written by Davis to instil a love of national freedom:

When boyhood's fire was in my blood
I read of ancient freemen,
For Greece and Rome who bravely stood,
Three hundred men and three men.
And then I prayed I yet might see
Our fetters rent in twain,
And Ireland, long a province, be
A NATION ONCE AGAIN.

Davis viewed the history of Ireland as a six-hundred-year struggle against the foreigner. In 'The West's Asleep' he reminded the people of Connacht of their ancestors' resistance over the centuries:

And if, when all a vigil keep,
The West's asleep, the West's asleep—
Alas! and well may Erin weep,
That Connaught lies in slumber deep.
But—hark!—some voice like thunder spake:
'*The West's awake, the West's awake*'—
Sing, oh! hurra! let England quake,
We'll watch till death for Erin's sake!

Unlike Daniel O'Connell, Young Ireland believed that it was not wrong to shed blood for Ireland's freedom. In April 1843 the *Nation* published a song by John Kells Ingram commemorating those who had fought and died in the rebellion of 1798:

Who fears to speak of Ninety-Eight?
Who blushes at the name?
When cowards mock the patriots' fate,
Who hangs his head in shame?
He's all a knave, or half a slave,
Who slights his country thus;
But a *true* man, like you, man,
Will fill your glass with us.

O'Connell would have nothing to do with any talk of armed insurrection. Bitter exchanges with the Young Irelanders inevitably followed.

Episode 179 ◌

'THE MISERY OF IRELAND DESCENDS TO DEGREES UNKNOWN'

In their prospectus of the *Nation*, the Young Ireland newspaper launched in 1842, the editors explained:

> Nationality is their first great object—a Nationality which will not only raise our people from their poverty ... but inflame them and purify them with a lofty and heroic love of country ... a Nationality which may embrace Protestant, Catholic and Dissenter—Milesian and Cromwellian—the Irishman of a hundred generations and the stranger who is within our gates ... a Nationality which would be recognised by the world and sanctified by wisdom, virtue and prudence.

By 1844 members of Young Ireland and Daniel O'Connell were quarrelling openly. Young Ireland believed that O'Connell's movement had become too closely tied in with the Catholic Church. Protestants were being alienated, especially after O'Connell had denounced the plan for Queen's Colleges in Belfast, Cork and Galway as 'godless colleges' because of their secular character. Young Ireland wanted armed insurrection to end the Union to be given serious consideration. O'Connell would not hear of it. By 1845 these bitter disputes had become increasingly irrelevant, for Ireland was on the brink of a national catastrophe.

While the Napoleonic Wars still raged, Ireland gave every indication of flourishing under the Act of Union. Then, after Waterloo, markets with the European mainland opened up again and agricultural prices began to fall, and they continued to fall for years to come. The Corn Law, enacted by Westminster in 1815, failed to stop the collapse in prices for wheat, barley, oats, butter, salt pork and other farm produce. In this protracted depression, almost everyone getting a living from the land was in difficulties.

Landlords had been able to increase rents very considerably during the war. In Co. Cavan, for example, the Hodson estate raised rents by 257 per cent between 1806 and 1812. Then, in response to the sharp and prolonged fall in the prices tenant farmers could get for their produce, most landlords lowered their rents for a time—but only slightly. The Co. Tyrone estates of the Royal Schools did not reduce rents at all until 1843. The Marquis of Downshire actually increased the income from his Co. Down estates by 5 per cent in the years after 1815.

Landlords had little incentive to lower rents. The demand to rent land—even miserable scraps of mountain and bog—was too strong. The plain fact was that Ireland's population had increased at an extraordinary rate: it had actually quadrupled between the famine of 1741 and the census of 1841. With the possible exception of Finland, nowhere else in Europe experienced such an increase. The 1841 census recorded 8,175,124 people, and the population was probably 8,500,000 by 1845—and this was in spite of the fact that well over 1,500,000 had emigrated since the Union in 1801.

In some respects early nineteenth-century Ireland was not a backward country. Agricultural output may have been lower than in England, but it was as good as that of France. Life expectancy too was similar to that of France. Ireland became more than ever a granary for Britain, supplying the rapidly growing industrial towns across the Irish Sea with their daily bread. Agricultural output, indeed, increased by 80 per cent during the first forty-five years of the nineteenth century. The problem was that population increase was greatest among the poorest classes, the cottiers and labourers. By the 1840s official government inquiries reported that some two million were living in a state of extreme poverty. Forty per cent of Ireland's population lived in wretched one-roomed cabins. These people desperately competed with one another to rent scraps of land, often too small to feed them adequately over a year.

The French writer Gustave de Beaumont was appalled by what he had seen during his tour of Ireland in 1837:

I have seen the Indian in his forests, and the negro in his chains, and thought, as I contemplated their pitiable condition, that I saw the very extreme of human wretchedness; but I did not then know the condition of unfortunate Ireland....

In all countries, more or less, paupers may be discovered; but an entire nation of paupers is what never was seen until it was shown in Ireland....

The misery of Ireland descends to degrees unknown elsewhere. The condition which in that country is deemed superior to poverty, would in any other be regarded as a state of frightful distress; the miserable classes of France, whose lot we justly deplore, would in Ireland form a privileged class. And these miseries of the Irish population are not rare accidents; nearly all are permanent, and those which are not permanent are periodic.

Every year, nearly at the same season, the commencement of a famine is announced in Ireland, its progress, its ravages, its decline.

By 1731, when this was painted, Dublin had become the second city of the British Empire. This shows a splendid state ball in Dublin Castle being opened by the Lord Lieutenant, the Duke of Dorset, and his duchess. The ballroom, decorated by the architect Edward Lovett Pearce, was described in a letter as 'finely ordered with paintings and obelisks'. (*The Art Archive*)

An eighteenth-century water-powered bleach-mill in County Down. Lengths of linen are pegged on the grass to bleach in the open; men are working on cloth in a long wooden trough; in the wing of the mill from which smoke is issuing, linen webs are being boiled and bucked; and the adjacent wing houses rub-boards, the beetling-engine and the wash-mill. (*Linen Hall Library*)

Cruikshank's illustration showing the arrest of the United Irish commander, Lord Edward Fitzgerald, in the Dublin Liberties, on 19 May 1798. The shot being fired here by Town Major Henry Sirr only struck the rebel lord's shoulder but eventually proved fatal. Captain Ryan (author of the loyalist ballad 'Croppies, Lie Down'), clinging to Lord Edward's left leg, bled to death from the fourteen stab wounds he received from his assailant's revolutionary stiletto. (*Mary Evans Picture Library*)

The Light Company of the Dublin Militia advancing with its band on the insurgents making a last stand on Vinegar Hill, Co. Wexford, 21 June 1798. This hill, just outside Enniscorthy, had been the most important encampment in the country for the United Irishmen who had begun their rebellion on 23 May. (*National Library of Ireland*)

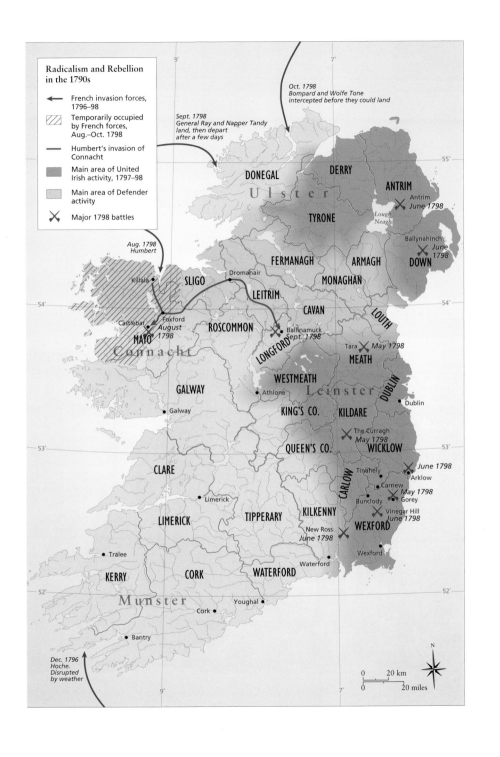

Radicalism and Rebellion
in the 1790s

← French invasion forces,
1796–98

▨ Temporarily occupied
by French forces,
Aug.–Oct. 1798

— Humbert's invasion of
Connacht

■ Main area of United
Irish activity, 1797–98

▨ Main area of Defender
activity

✕ Major 1798 battles

Oct. 1798
Bompard and Wolfe Tone
intercepted before they could land

Sept. 1798
General Ray and Napper Tandy
land, then depart
after a few days

Aug. 1798
Humbert

DONEGAL

DERRY

ANTRIM

U l s t e r

Antrim
June 1798

TYRONE

Lough
Neagh

Ballynahinch
June
1798

FERMANAGH

ARMAGH

DOWN

Dromahair

MONAGHAN

Killala

SLIGO

LEITRIM

Castlebar

Foxford
August
1798

ROSCOMMON

CAVAN

LOUTH

Ballinamuck
Sept. 1798

MAYO

C o n n a c h t

LONGFORD

Tara

May 1798

MEATH

WESTMEATH

L e i n s t e r

GALWAY

Athlone

DUBLIN

Galway

KING'S CO.

KILDARE

Dublin

The Curragh
May 1798

QUEEN'S CO.

WICKLOW

CLARE

Tinahely

June 1798

CARLOW

Carnew

Arklow

May 1798

Limerick

Bunclody

Gorey

KILKENNY

Vinegar Hill
June 1798

LIMERICK

TIPPERARY

New Ross
June 1798

WEXFORD

Tralee

Wexford

KERRY

CORK

WATERFORD

Waterford

M u n s t e r

Youghal

Cork

Bantry

Dec. 1796
Hoche.
Disrupted
by weather

N

0   20 km

0   20 miles

Portrait of Daniel O'Connell at the height of his career, painted by John Gubbins. Known as the 'Liberator', O'Connell brilliantly orchestrated the campaign which achieved Catholic Emancipation in 1829. Though he failed to persuade Westminster to repeal the Act of Union, O'Connell is remembered as one of the great pacifist leaders of nineteenth-century Europe. (*Dublin City Council / Mansion House*)

Those left destitute after their potato crops had been destroyed by blight clamour at the gates of a workhouse in 1846. Conditions were even worse by September 1847 when the government closed down soup kitchens and decreed that famine relief could only be obtained within the workhouses. Many of the starving died inside the workhouses: outdoor relief was refused, and within the overcrowded buildings deadly fevers flourished among the inmates. (*Getty Images*)

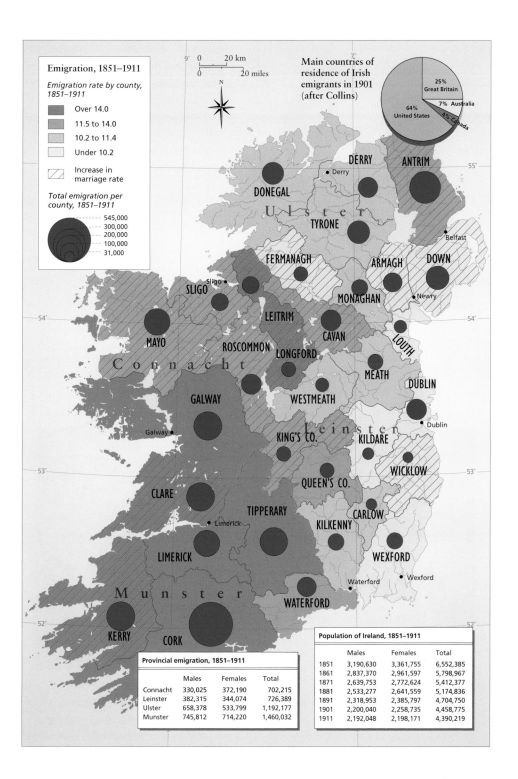

Emigration, 1851–1911

Emigration rate by county, 1851–1911

- Over 14.0
- 11.5 to 14.0
- 10.2 to 11.4
- Under 10.2
- Increase in marriage rate

Total emigration per county, 1851–1911

- 545,000
- 300,000
- 200,000
- 100,000
- 31,000

Main countries of residence of Irish emigrants in 1901 (after Collins)

- 64% United States
- 25% Great Britain
- 7% Australia
- 4% Canada

0   20 km
0   20 miles

N

Ulster

DERRY · Derry
ANTRIM
DONEGAL
TYRONE
Belfast
FERMANAGH
ARMAGH
DOWN
SLIGO · Sligo
MONAGHAN · Newry
LEITRIM
CAVAN
LOUTH
MAYO
ROSCOMMON
LONGFORD
MEATH
DUBLIN
GALWAY
WESTMEATH
Galway ·
Leinster
KING'S CO.
KILDARE
· Dublin
WICKLOW
CLARE
QUEEN'S CO.
TIPPERARY
CARLOW
· Limerick
KILKENNY
LIMERICK
WEXFORD
Munster
· Waterford   · Wexford
KERRY
WATERFORD
CORK

Connacht

Provincial emigration, 1851–1911			
	Males	Females	Total
Connacht	330,025	372,190	702,215
Leinster	382,315	344,074	726,389
Ulster	658,378	533,799	1,192,177
Munster	745,812	714,220	1,460,032

Population of Ireland, 1851–1911			
	Males	Females	Total
1851	3,190,630	3,361,755	6,552,385
1861	2,837,370	2,961,597	5,798,967
1871	2,639,753	2,772,624	5,412,377
1881	2,533,277	2,641,559	5,174,836
1891	2,318,953	2,385,797	4,704,750
1901	2,200,040	2,258,735	4,458,775
1911	2,192,048	2,198,171	4,390,219

Charles Stewart Parnell, the charismatic leader of the Irish Parliamentary Party who, as president of the Land League, led tenant farmers close to victory and, in command of a highly disciplined party, persuaded Prime Minister W. E. Gladstone to put forward a Home Rule Bill in 1886. When his relationship with Mrs Katharine O'Shea became public knowledge in 1890, his fall from power rapidly followed. (*The Art Archive*)

Shipwrights—known as 'Islandmen'—pour out of Harland & Wolff's Belfast shipyard on Queen's Island at the end of a working day in 1911. The *Olympic* had been launched the year before, as the largest ship in the world, leaving a vacancy in the high gantry in the background. Its even larger sister ship, the ill-fated *Titanic*, can be seen there, nearing completion. (*Ulster Museum, Belfast. Photograph reproduced courtesy the Trustees of National Museums Northern Ireland*)

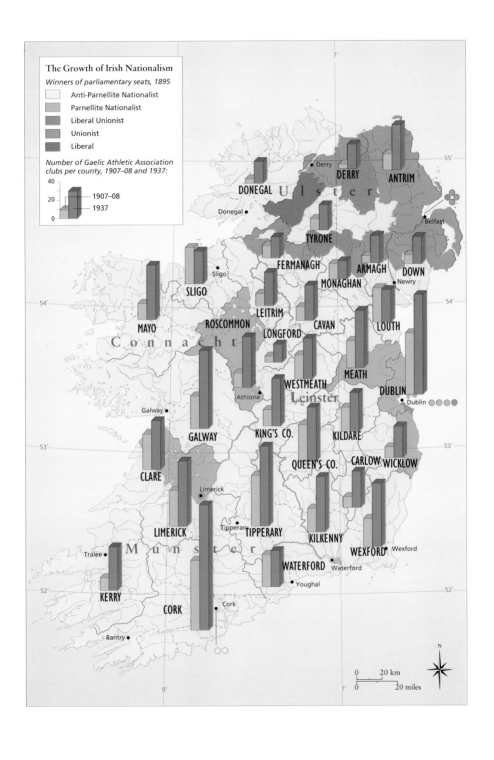

The Growth of Irish Nationalism

Winners of parliamentary seats, 1895

- Anti-Parnellite Nationalist
- Parnellite Nationalist
- Liberal Unionist
- Unionist
- Liberal

Number of Gaelic Athletic Association
clubs per county, 1907–08 and 1937:

40

20

0

1907–08

1937

Ulster

DONEGAL

DERRY

ANTRIM

Donegal •

• Derry

Belfast •

TYRONE

FERMANAGH

ARMAGH

DOWN

MONAGHAN

Newry •

Sligo •

SLIGO

LEITRIM

CAVAN

LOUTH

MAYO

Connacht

ROSCOMMON

LONGFORD

MEATH

Galway •

WESTMEATH

DUBLIN

Athlone •

Leinster

Dublin •

GALWAY

KING'S CO.

KILDARE

CLARE

Limerick •

QUEEN'S CO.

CARLOW

WICKLOW

LIMERICK

Tipperary •

TIPPERARY

KILKENNY

WEXFORD

Wexford •

Tralee •

Munster

WATERFORD

Waterford •

KERRY

Youghal •

CORK

Cork •

Bantry •

0   20 km

0   20 miles

N

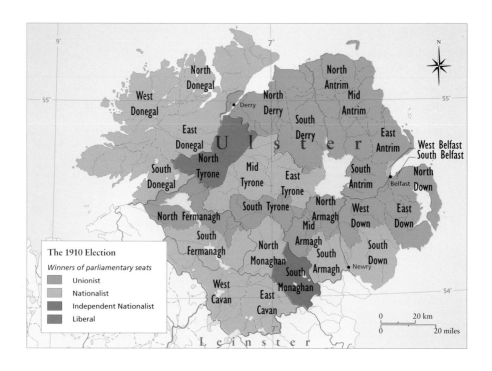

The 1910 Election

Winners of parliamentary seats

- Unionist
- Nationalist
- Independent Nationalist
- Liberal

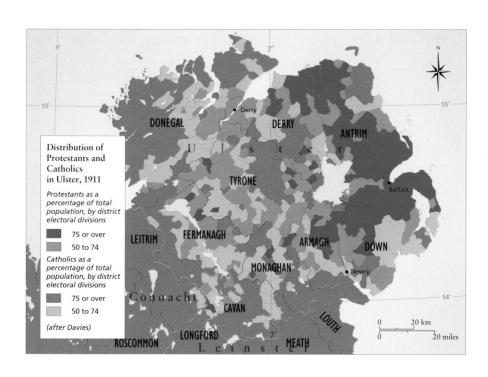

Distribution of Protestants and Catholics in Ulster, 1911

Protestants as a percentage of total population, by district electoral divisions

- 75 or over
- 50 to 74

Catholics as a percentage of total population, by district electoral divisions

- 75 or over
- 50 to 74

(after Davies)

Recruiting posters such as this one did much to persuade tens of thousands of Irishmen to join up in the early stages of the Great War. By early 1916 at least 210,000 had been recruited in Ireland. Around 28,000 Irishmen died in action during the war. (*Alamy*)

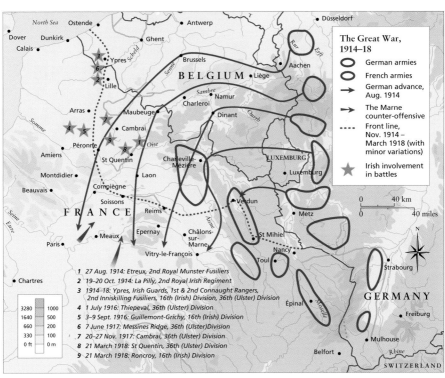

The Great War, 1914–18

- ⭕ German armies
- ⭕ French armies
- → German advance, Aug. 1914
- → The Marne counter-offensive
- ---- Front line, Nov. 1914 – March 1918 (with minor variations)
- ★ Irish involvement in battles

1   27 Aug. 1914: Etreux, 2nd Royal Munster Fusiliers
2   19–20 Oct. 1914: La Pilly, 2nd Royal Irish Regiment
3   1914–18: Ypres, Irish Guards, 1st & 2nd Connaught Rangers, 2nd Inniskilling Fusiliers, 16th (Irish) Division, 36th (Ulster) Division
4   1 July 1916: Thiepeval, 36th (Ulster) Division
5   3–9 Sept. 1916: Guillemont-Grichy, 16th (Irish) Division
6   7 June 1917: Messines Ridge, 36th (Ulster)Division
7   20–27 Nov. 1917: Cambrai, 36th (Ulster) Division
8   21 March 1918: St Quentin, 36th (Ulster) Division
9   21 March 1918: Roncroy, 16th (Irish) Division

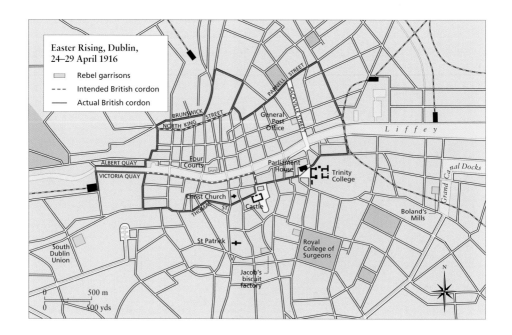

Easter Rising, Dublin,
24–29 April 1916

Rebel garrisons
Intended British cordon
Actual British cordon

PARNELL STREET

SACKVILLE STREET

BRUNSWICK STREET
NORTH KING STREET

General
Post
Office

L i f f e y

Four
Courts

ALBERT QUAY

VICTORIA QUAY

Parliament
House

Trinity
College

Grand Canal Docks

Christ Church

THOMAS ST

Castle

Boland's
Mills

South
Dublin
Union

St Patrick

Royal
College of
Surgeons

Jacob's
biscuit
factory

N

500 m
0
500 yds
0

Dublin under martial law, May 1916. In addition to those insurgents who had surrendered on Saturday 29 April, several hundred suspects who had taken no part in the rebellion were rounded up, taken away by military escort (as in this photograph) and interned, many of them at Frongoch camp in north Wales. (*Topfoto*)

Sectarian rioting at the corner of York Street and Donegall Street in Belfast in 1920. Violence had first broken out on 21 July, and in the ensuing days several thousand 'disloyal' workers (Catholics and socialists) were driven by loyalists out of the two shipyards and all the major engineering works in the city. Between July 1920 and July 1922 the death toll in the six north-eastern counties (which became Northern Ireland in December 1920) was 557. (*Belfast Telegraph*)

Arthur Griffith with his wife Maud at 22 Hans Place in London where he led the Irish delegation. A few days later, on 6 December 1921 in 10 Downing Street, Prime Minister David Lloyd George persuaded Griffith to be the first Irishman to sign the Anglo-Irish Treaty. Three days later the President of Dáil Éireann, Eamon de Valera, issued an open letter denouncing the treaty. (*Getty Images*)

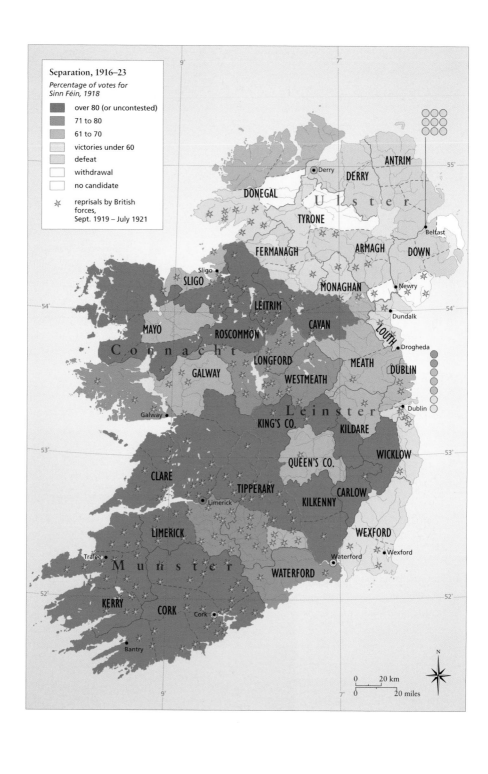

Separation, 1916–23

*Percentage of votes for
Sinn Féin, 1918*

- over 80 (or uncontested)
- 71 to 80
- 61 to 70
- victories under 60
- defeat
- withdrawal
- no candidate

✳ reprisals by British
forces,
Sept. 1919 – July 1921

ANTRIM

Derry   DERRY

DONEGAL   U l s t e r   55°

TYRONE   Belfast

FERMANAGH   ARMAGH   DOWN

Sligo   MONAGHAN   Newry

SLIGO

LEITRIM   54°

MAYO   CAVAN

ROSCOMMON   Dundalk

C o n n a c h t   LOUTH   Drogheda

LONGFORD   MEATH

GALWAY   WESTMEATH   DUBLIN

Galway   L e i n s t e r   Dublin

KING'S CO.   KILDARE

53°   WICKLOW   53°

QUEEN'S CO.

CLARE

TIPPERARY   CARLOW

Limerick   KILKENNY

LIMERICK   WEXFORD

Tralee   Waterford   Wexford

M u n s t e r

WATERFORD   52°

KERRY   CORK

Cork

Bantry

N

0   20 km

0   20 miles

Eamon de Valera resigned as President of Dáil Éireann following the narrow vote in favour of the Anglo-Irish Treaty there in January 1922. Here he denounces the treaty at a meeting in Dublin's O'Connell Street on 24 February. Differences over the treaty led to the outbreak of civil war by the end of June 1922. (*Bettmann/Corbis*)

Soldiers from the 25th Rifle Battalion saving turf in neutral Éire in 1942. As a result of a drastic reduction of coal imports from Britain, during the 'Emergency' turf once more became a crucial source of domestic fuel. However, turf proved incapable of raising sufficient steam to propel rail locomotives. (*Hanley Collection, Military Archives, Cathal Brugha Barracks*)

Dr John Charles McQuaid, newly consecrated as Archbishop of Dublin, gives his first blessing to well-wishers on 27 December 1940. A theological conservative, McQuaid exercised considerable influence on successive governments for many years to come. (*Courtesy of Dublin Diocesan Archives*)

The historic handshake: Taoiseach Seán Lemass, who had fought in the GPO in 1916, meets Prime Minister Terence O'Neill at Stormont on 14 January 1965. Seeking improved relations with Britain was a key part of Lemass's economic strategy, and that included establishing regular contacts between Dublin and Belfast. As it turned out, O'Neill was taking a greater political risk than Lemass. (*Public Record Office of Northern Ireland*)

The East Park, Shannon Free Zone, Co. Clare, part of the Shannon development scheme created to attract foreign investment to the south-west. A comprehensive package of incentives and a well-developed infrastructure proved highly successful in bringing in branches of multinational concerns. (*Shannon Development Photo Library*)

Farringdon Gardens, Belfast, the day after the imposition of internment on 9 August 1971. In this street and in Velsheda Park and Cranbrook Park in Ardoyne about 240 houses were destroyed by fire. That Tuesday 10 August, the most violent day since 1969, eleven people were killed in the city alone, including Father Hugh Mullan, shot while administering the last rites to an injured man in Ballymurphy. (*PA Photos*)

The funeral in west Belfast of Bobby Sands who died on the sixty-sixth day of his hunger strike in the Maze Prison H Blocks on 5 May 1981. At least one hundred thousand people—nearly one-fifth of the entire Catholic population of Northern Ireland—crowded the route of the cortège from St Luke's Church in Twinbrook to Milltown Cemetery. (*Pacemaker Press International*)

Left to right: Tánaiste Dick Spring, Fianna Fáil leader Charles J. Haughey, Taoiseach Garret FitzGerald and SDLP leader John Hume at the New Ireland Forum which met between May 1983 and May 1984 in Dublin Castle. Prime Minister Margaret Thatcher rejected the Forum's selection of recommendations but went on to sign the Anglo-Irish Agreement with FitzGerald and Spring in November 1985—an agreement initially rejected by Haughey because it 'copper-fastened partition'. (*Photocall Ireland*)

Left to right: Taoiseach Bertie Ahern, former US senator George Mitchell and Prime Minister Tony Blair at Stormont after the signing of the Good Friday Agreement in April 1998. No American politician and no British prime minister had ever before devoted so much time and concentrated energy to seeking a solution for Northern Ireland. Ahern displayed a similar commitment equalled only by a previous Taoiseach, Garret FitzGerald. (*Topfoto*)

The Celtic Tiger roars: cranes on the Dublin skyline in February 2005. Output had grown by a remarkable 52 per cent between 1995 and 2002, and by 2001 output per person was 127 per cent of the EU average. A high proportion of total US investment in Europe was made in the Republic, where low corporate taxes played a pivotal role in attracting transnational enterprises. (*Photocall Ireland*)

Episode 180 ~

'SO MUCH WRETCHEDNESS'

At the beginning of the nineteenth century poor farmers and labourers had supplemented their incomes by spinning and weaving wool and linen in their homes. Thirty years later cheap printed and dyed cloth from the steam-powered mills and factories of Manchester and Leeds flooded into Ireland, supplemented by the output of Belfast's linen mills. Spinning-wheels and handlooms found it impossible to compete. A vital supplement to the family incomes of labourers, cottiers and small farmers was being destroyed. Joseph Nicholson of Bessbrook, Co. Armagh, observed:

> To one unacquainted with Ireland the small earnings of the poorer females— frequently not more than two pence a day, working diligently from morning till night, for months together—must appear very extraordinary.

As Thomas Beggs, a Co. Antrim weaver-poet who died during the Famine, wrote:

> But the guid auld times are gane out o' sight,
> An' it mak's the saut tear aften start to mine e'e;
> For lords o' the Mill and Machine ha'e decreed
> That bodies like me maun beg their bread.

The Ordnance Survey Memoirs, written by army officers as they mapped Ireland in the 1830s, tell the same story:

> Parish of Laragh, Co. Cavan: The manufacture of coarse linen has almost ceased within the parish ... the flying shuttle seldom resounds ...
> Parish of Pomeroy, Co. Tyrone: A good weaver can only earn about 5s a week and a spinner must work hard to earn 2d a day ...
> Parish of Currin, Co. Monaghan: The ruins of the extensive bleachfields, which are observable around the district, testifying by their magnitude the outlay of vast capital in their erection, very few of which unfortunately are now in operation.

No memoirs survive for southern parishes, where the hand spinning and weaving of wool had been so important, but the story was much the same. The collapse of domestic industry left the vast majority of people in the congested countryside utterly dependent on what the overworked soil would

yield. The handloom weavers of fine cloth in Dublin were also steadily driven
to the wall by imports. Industrial concerns in towns across the country wilted
and died. Ploughshares, sickle and scythe blades, harrow pins and the like were
forged more cheaply by the steam-hammers of Coventry and Birmingham than
they could be beaten out on the anvils of local Irish blacksmiths. Mr and Mrs
S. C. Hall, in their 1841–3 publication on Ireland's scenery and character,
observed the squalor and lack of employment in Navan, a town in the heart
of Ireland's most fertile county, Co. Meath:

> The towns ... into which the poor have been driven, are thronged with
> squalid countenances; starvation stalks at noonday through the streets; and
> perhaps in no part of the world could be found so much wretchedness
> 'huddled' together in an equal space as in the town of Navan. All around
> the suburbs, the cabins are filthy to the last degree; a very large proportion
> of them have no other outlets for smoke but the broken windows; the roofs
> of many have fallen in.

So dependent were the vast majority on the cultivation of the land that
stands of trees could be found only within the walled demesnes of the gentry.
Writing in 1839, after his visit to Ireland, the French social commentator
Gustave de Beaumont noticed:

> Formerly Ireland was a vast forest.... It is now almost destitute of trees; and
> when, on a fine day in spring, it appears, though bare, full of sap and youth,
> it seems like a young and lovely girl deprived of her hair.

He described a typical Irish cabin, the dwelling place of two-fifths of the
population:

> Imagine four walls of dry mud, which the rain, as it falls, easily restores to
> its primitive condition; having for its roof a little straw or some sods, for its
> chimney a hole cut in the roof, or very frequently the door, through which
> the smoke finds an issue. One single apartment contains the father,
> mother, children, and sometimes a grandfather or grandmother; there is no
> furniture in this wretched hovel; a single bed of hay or straw serves for the
> entire family. Five or six half-naked children may be seen crouched near a
> miserable fire, the ashes of which cover a few potatoes, the sole nourish-
> ment of the family. In the midst of all lies a dirty pig, the only thriving
> inhabitant of the place, for he lives in filth....
>   This dwelling is very miserable, still it is not that of the pauper, properly
> so called; I have just described the dwelling of the Irish farmer and agricul-
> tural labourer....

All being poor, the only food they use is the cheapest in the country—potatoes.

It was the total dependence of so many millions on this one item of food that led to the greatest tragedy in modern Irish history.

Episode 181 ∼

THE CENSUS OF 1841

In 1837 Patrick McKye, a National School teacher, wrote a letter to Dublin Castle on behalf of the people of West Tullaghobegley, the parish comprising Gweedore, Co. Donegal. The inhabitants, he informed the viceroy, 'are in the most needy, hungry, and naked condition of any people that ever came within the precincts of my knowledge'. There, among a population of some 9,000, was to be found only one cart, one plough, sixteen harrows, eight saddles, twenty shovels, seven table-forks, twenty-seven geese, eight turkeys, three watches and two feather beds. In the whole parish there was not a single wheel-car, not a pig, not a clock, and not a pair of boots. And there were neither fruit trees nor crops of turnips, parsnips, carrots or clover. McKye continued:

> None of their either married or unmarried women can afford more than one shift, and the fewest number cannot afford any ... nor can many of them afford a second bed, but whole families of sons and daughters of mature age indiscriminately lieing together with their parents, and all in the bare buff. Their beds are straw—green and dried rushes or mountain bent: their bed cloathes are either coarse sheets, or no sheets, and ragged filthy blankets.... If any unprejudiced gentleman should be sent here to investigate ... I can shew him about one hundred and forty children bare naked, and was so during winter, and some hundreds only covered with filthy rags, most disgustful to look at.

Long storms had ruined their crops and now they faced starvation. Many could afford only one meal every three days, and McKye found

> their children crying and fainting with hunger, and their parents weeping, being full of grief, hunger, debility and dejection, with glooming aspect, looking at their children likely to expire in the jaws of starvation.

Patrick McKye could have been writing about almost any part of Ireland's Atlantic seaboard. This beautiful but barren coastland and its adjacent islands had only acquired a dense population over the previous century. There only by unremitting labour had the people had made the thin and leached soil fertile by spreading shell sand and seaweed on the ground.

The first thorough census in Ireland was completed in 1841. The population of the island was enumerated as 8,175,124. Ninety years earlier the number of people in Ireland had been no more than 2,500,000. This was an astonishing growth considering that at least 1,500,000 had emigrated since the end of the war with Napoleon in 1815. No great plague or epidemic had checked the natural tendency of the population to grow.

Just across the Irish Sea, Britain was fast becoming the greatest industrial power on earth. The burgeoning populations of the manufacturing and coalmining towns there eagerly bought up food from Ireland's farms. Irish landlords and farmers prospered from this trade, but this intense economic activity concealed a drawback—competition from mass-produced British imports had all but destroyed the ability of the Irish poor to supplement their incomes by selling cloth and knitwear made in the home.

In the 1840s the gap between the rich and the poor was yawning wide. The 1841 census reported that two-fifths of the houses in Ireland were single-roomed mud cabins without windows. Only seven out of every hundred farms in Ireland were of thirty acres or more—and this at a time when in Scotland a farm of sixty acres was considered small. Only a quarter of the rural population was made up of farmers; the rest were wretchedly poor labourers and cottiers. As the population rose the land was sublet into smaller and smaller scraps—in the western province of Connacht 64 per cent of holdings were of less than five acres.

Most of the produce of even the tiniest plots of land had to be set aside to pay rent. More than ever, the Irish depended on the potato. The potato provided more nourishment per acre than any other crop. By the 1840s half the population of Ireland was almost totally dependent on the potato for sustenance. The precarious position of so many people was recognised by the Devon Commission, which reported to the government in 1845:

> It would be impossible adequately to describe the privations which they habitually and silently endure.... In many districts their only food is the potato, their only beverage water ... their cabins are seldom a protection against the weather ... a bed or a blanket is a rare luxury ... and nearly in all their pig and a manure heap constitute their only property.

Such people were fatally vulnerable when a previously unknown disease struck the potato crop in Ireland in August 1845.

Episode 182 ~

PHYTOPHTHORA INFESTANS

On 13 September 1845 the editor of the *Gardeners' Chronicle* held up publication to make a dramatic announcement:

> We stop the Press with very great regret to announce that the potato Murrain has unequivocally declared itself in Ireland. The crops about Dublin are suddenly perishing.... Where will Ireland be in the event of a universal potato rot?

The potato 'murrain' or blight was *phytophthora infestans*, a microscopic fungus spread by the wind and the rain, particularly during mild and humid weather. This previously unknown disease, brought from America, rapidly turned the potato stalks black and reduced the tubers in the soil to a stinking pulp. As the crop was being lifted during the autumn of 1845 reports of failure came from across the island. A Belfast newspaper, the *Vindicator*, predicted on 22 October:

> The failure of the potato crop in Ireland ... is now confirmed.... A large portion of the crop turns out to be quite useless for purposes of food. A dearth is inevitable; and a famine is extremely probable.... The Irish peasantry rely almost exclusively upon potatoes for their subsistence; and when the crop fails, they have nothing to fall back upon but grass, nettles, and seaweed.

The failure of the potato crop in 1845 was not total, however. Parts of Ulster and much of the Atlantic coast escaped. Over the whole island between one-quarter and one-third of the crop had been lost. The real worry was whether or not the potatoes successfully saved would escape the blight. Soon the worst fears were confirmed. News began to come in that potatoes were rotting in clamps and stores. The medical officer for Coleraine workhouse reported: 'Nothing else is heard of, nothing else is spoken of.... Famine must be looked forward to.'

Sir Robert Peel, the Tory Prime Minister, acted swiftly by the standards of the day. In November 1845 he set up a central relief commission, and, fearing criticism from his colleagues, he secretly arranged the purchase of £100,000 worth of maize—then known as 'Indian corn'—from the United States. As the cargoes arrived from February 1846 onwards Peel made more money available and ordered the army commissariat to set up depots across the country to store 44 million pounds of corn. The plan was not to give out the corn free, but to sell it at cost price. The effect was to keep down the price of other food-stuffs. This 'yellow meal', as the Irish called it, was at first condemned as 'Peel's brimstone'. But a government halfpenny pamphlet, telling people how to cook it, sold in tens of thousands. Peel also set up a scientific commission which issued completely useless advice on how to protect stored potatoes from infection. The experts of the day were quite unable to find a way of halting the blight.

The Prime Minister also put bills through parliament in January 1846 to fund public works for the destitute so that they could earn money to buy food. Then, in June 1846, Peel committed an act of political suicide. With the aid of the Whig opposition, he brought about the repeal of the Corn Laws in an attempt to encourage the importation of cheap grain into Ireland. For the Tory grandees this was unforgivable treachery. The Duke of Wellington was outraged: 'Rotten potatoes have done it all,' he expostulated; 'they put Peel in his damned fright.'

Peel had no choice but to resign. In July the opposition Whig leader, Lord John Russell, formed a government. Russell turned for advice to Charles Trevelyan, the civil servant at the head of the Treasury. Trevelyan recom-mended a drastic reduction in the distribution of subsidised food and a major extension of public works. Free market forces must not be disrupted by government interference. The poor must work for their food. In his memo-randum to the cabinet on 1 August 1846 Trevelyan advised that 'The supply of the home market may safely be left to the foresight of private merchants.'

At the same time a disaster on an unprecedented scale was unfolding in Ireland. One of the many who recorded it was the Rev. Samuel Montgomery, rector of Ballinascreen, Co. Londonderry. He made this entry in the parish register:

On the three last days of July and the first six days of August 1846 the potatoes were suddenly attacked, when in their full growth, with a sudden blight. The tops were first observed to wither and then, on looking to the roots, the tubers were found hastening to Decomposition. The entire crop that in the Month of July appeared so luxuriant, about the 15th of August manifested only blackened and withered stems. The whole atmosphere in the Month of September was tainted with the odour of the decaying potatoes.

Underneath his signature he wrote this prayer:

Increase the fruits of the earth by Thy heavenly benediction.

This time no part of Ireland escaped.

Episode 183 ～

'GIVE US FOOD, OR WE PERISH'

When the potato blight struck for a second time in 1846, every part of Ireland was affected. Father Theobald Mathew, after travelling from Dublin to Cork, wrote to Charles Trevelyan, head of the Treasury, on 7 August:

> I beheld with sorrow one wide waste of putrefying vegetation. In many places the wretched people were seated on the fences of their decaying gardens, wringing their hands and wailing bitterly the destruction.... The food of a whole nation has perished.

What should the government do? Trevelyan devised a new system of public works in August. To fit in with Trevelyan's free market philosophy, warmly shared by the Whig government, the works were not to compete with capitalist enterprise, and they were confined to building walls, roads, bridges, causeways and fences. The new relief works were to be financed entirely out of rates—Irish property was to pay for Irish poverty. It was not until October that this cumbersome bureaucracy (eventually numbering 12,000 officials) could issue tickets giving employment to those considered sufficiently destitute.

Commissary-General Sir Randolph Routh suggested that the Irish ports should be closed to stop the further export of corn. This proposal was firmly rejected by Trevelyan, who told Routh on 3 September: 'Do not encourage the idea of prohibiting exports, perfect Free Trade is the right course.' For once, Routh dared to disagree with his superior. By the end of the harvest 60,000 tons of oats alone would have left the country, he explained. But Trevelyan, fully supported by Prime Minister Lord John Russell, vehemently opposed such a radical step: 'We beg of you not to countenance in any way the idea of prohibiting exportation.... There cannot be a doubt that it would inflict a permanent injury on the country.'

All this time the depots providing subsidised Indian corn, set up by Peel's Tory government in the previous year, were being closed down. Too late in the day Trevelyan decided to attempt to buy corn abroad. The harvest across Europe in 1846 had been very poor, and there was no surplus for sale. The American maize harvest had already mostly been bought up. Even if corn could be purchased, it would not be ready for transportation until December, a month when American rivers were mostly frozen over. And yet oats, wheat and barley, grown and harvested in Ireland, continued to be shipped out of the country across the Irish Sea.

On 3 October 1846 the Repeal journal, the *Vindicator*, made a simple appeal:

'Give us food, or we perish,' is now the loudest cry that is heard in this unfortunate country. It is heard in every corner of the island—it breaks in like some awful spectre on the festive revelry of the rich—it startles and appals the merchant at his desk, the landlord in his office, the scholar in his study, the minister in his council-room, and the priest at the altar. 'Give us food, or we perish.' It is a strange popular cry to be heard within the limits of the powerful and wealthy British empire.... Russia wants liberty, Prussia wants a constitution, Switzerland wants religion, Spain wants a king, Ireland alone wants food.

Lord John Russell's government opposed such a simple solution: the starving must buy food with money earned on public works. But there were agonising delays before many of the relief schemes opened. The relief works were hampered by a shortage of handcarts and wheelbarrows, a lack of engineers to direct operations, and heavy falls of snow. The longest and most severe winter in living memory had begun.

During the first weeks of 1847 the weather deteriorated even further. From the north-east blew 'perfect hurricanes of snow, hail and sleet' which caused the famished labourers on the relief works to collapse from exposure.

On 17 January George Dawson, wrote from Castledawson, Co. Londonderry, to Sir Thomas Fremantle, a former Irish Chief Secretary:

My dear Fremantle,
    ... I can think of nothing else than the wretched condition of this wretched people.... I do not exaggerate when I tell you that from the moment I open my hall door in the morning until dark, I have a crowd of women and children crying out for something to save them from starving. The men, except the old and infirm, stay away and show the greatest patience and resignation. I have been obliged to turn my kitchen into a bakery and soup shop to enable me to feed the miserable children and mothers that cannot be sent away empty. So great is their distress that they actually faint on getting food into their stomachs.... Death is dealing severely and consigning many to an untimely tomb.... I see enough to make the heart sick.... Hundreds will die of starvation.

And, as we shall see, during that terrible winter of 1846–7 conditions were even worse in the west and the south.

Episode 184 ⌒

THE FAMINE IN SKIBBEREEN

After visiting Skibbereen, a village on the coast of west Cork, Nicholas Cummins, a local magistrate, wrote to the Duke of Wellington on 22 December 1846:

My Lord Duke,
... Being aware that I should have to witness scenes of frightful hunger, I provided myself with as much bread as five men could carry, and on reaching the spot I was surprised to find the wretched hamlet apparently deserted.
I entered some of the hovels to ascertain the cause. In the first, six famished and ghastly skeletons, to all appearances dead, were huddled in a corner on some filthy straw.... I approached with horror, and found by a low moaning they were alive.... Suffice to say, that in a few minutes I was surrounded by at least 200 of such phantoms, such frightful spectres as no words can describe.... Their demoniac yells are still ringing in my ears, and their horrible images are fixed upon my brain.... The same morning the police opened a house on the adjoining lands ... and two frozen corpses were found, half devoured by rats.... Within 500 yards of the cavalry station at Skibbereen, the dispensary doctor found seven wretches lying unable to move. One had been dead many hours ...

The situation had not improved in January 1847 when the *Cork Examiner* sent its reporter to Skibbereen:

In huts I have visited, I have seen children reduced to skeletons, in some instances; in others bloated beyond expression by hideous dropsy, and creeping around the damp wet floors of their miserable cabins, unable to stand erect....
It is too late to rescue the hundreds of diseased and stricken wretches from destruction—their fate is sealed without a hope—their earthly sufferings will speedily terminate.

In the following month Elihu Burritt, an American writer and philanthropist, crossed the Atlantic from his home in Boston to see for himself what could be done for the starving people. On 20 February the parish priest took him through the town of Skibbereen:

We saw, in every tenement we entered, enough to sicken the stoutest heart.... Half-naked women and children would come out of their cabins, apparently in the last stages of famine fever, to beg 'a ha'penny, for the honour of God!' As they stood upon the wet ground, one could almost see it smoke beneath their bare feet, burning with the fever.

We entered the graveyard, in the midst of which was a small watch-house. This miserable shed had served as a grave where the dying could bury themselves.... And into this horrible den of death, this noisome sepulchre, living men, women, and children went down to die....

Here they lay side by side on the bottom of one grave. Six persons had been found in this fetid sepulchre at one time, and with only one able to crawl to the door to ask for water. Removing a board from this black hole of pestilence, we found it crammed with wan victims of famine, ready and anxious to perish.

Next day Dr O'Donovan, the dispensary doctor, took Burritt to another part of the town of Skibbereen:

In one of these straw-roofed burrows eight persons had died in the last fortnight, and five more were lying upon the pestiferous straw. In scarcely a single one of these most inhuman habitations was there the slightest indication of food of any kind to be found, nor fuel, nor anything resembling a bed....

A faint glimmering of light from a handful of burning straw would soon reveal the indistinct images of wan-faced children grouped together, with large plaintive still eyes looking out at us like the sick young of wild beasts in their dens. Then the groans, and the choked, incoherent entreaties for help ... would apprise us of the number and condition of the family....

Let the reader group these apparitions of death and disease into the spectacle of ten feet square, and then multiply it into three-fourths of the hovels in this region and he will arrive at a fair estimate of the extent of is misery.

Cork, February 28, 1847. While waiting for the steamer, I wrote an earnest appeal to the people of New England for aid for the starving Irish. I trust my earnest entreaties will not be in vain.

Burritt's entreaties were not in vain. His harrowing descriptions of Skibbereen helped to raise $100,000 in Boston to buy provisions for the starving Irish. The us government lent a warship to take over this food, and it arrived in Cork harbour in April 1847.

The state of Skibbereen was by no means unique. Indeed, in many other parts of the country, particularly in more inaccessible places further west, the death toll during the Famine was even higher than in west Cork. And those Americans who had given so generously were not to know that the worst of the Famine was still to come.

Episode 185 ～

FEVER

The Religious Society of Friends, better known as the Quakers, believed there was a simple answer to starvation. Acting with a directness which would not shame the most modern relief agency, the Quakers set out to feed the people. In January 1847, as the Great Famine was moving into its third year, the *Illustrated London News* described how the Society of Friends' 'soup house' in Cork city was providing nourishment to the destitute

> at a loss, or rather cost, of from £120 to £150 per month to supporters of the design. The present calls are for from 150 to 180 gallons daily, requiring 120 pounds of good beef, 27 pounds of rice, 27 pounds of oatmeal, 27 pounds of split peas, and 14 ounces of spices, with a quantity of vegetables. Tickets, at one penny each, are unsparingly distributed.

Meanwhile the government's cumbersome scheme of public works was breaking down—the starving were simply too weak and sick to earn enough to feed their families. An Act for the Temporary Relief of Destitute Persons in Ireland, passed in February 1847, was, in effect, an open admission by Lord John Russell's Whig government that its policies had failed. Henceforth relief would be provided by the free distribution of soup.

A formidable new bureaucracy had to be created and some 10,000 account books, 80,000 record sheets and 3 million ration tickets had to be printed before the new machinery could be set in motion. However, once they were fully in operation, the government soup kitchens saved more lives than any other measure taken during the Famine. By July 1847 more than 3 million people were being fed every day.

For many, however, the soup kitchens had come too late. People, weakened by starvation, were falling victim to fever and dying in their thousands. Deaths resulted principally from typhus and relapsing fever transmitted by lice; the 'bloody flux' or bacillary dysentery; 'famine dropsy' or hunger oedema; and scurvy. Fever struck not only the emaciated frames of the starving but also those who ministered to the sick and dying: in one year, for example, seven doctors died of fever in Cavan town, and Lord Lurgan, chairman of the Board of Guardians of Lurgan Union Workhouse, was a high-profile victim of typhus fever. Hordes of the poor brought disease eastwards to Dublin and Belfast in particular. Dr Andrew Malcolm, who worked day and night to treat those stricken by fever, recalled the influx of the starving into Belfast:

Famine was depicted in the look, in the hue, in the voice, and the gait. The food of a nation had been cut off; the physical strength of a whole people was reduced; and this condition, highly favourable to the impression of the plague-breath, resulted in the most terrible epidemic that this Island ever experienced.

The hospitals in the town were overflowing, the *Belfast News-Letter* reported in July 1847,

Yet hundreds ... are daily exposed in the delirium of this frightful malady, on the streets, or left to die in their filthy and ill-ventilated hovels.... It is now a thing of daily occurrence to see haggard, sallow and emaciated beings, stricken down by fever or debility from actual want, stretched prostrate upon the footways of our streets and bridges.

The fine summer of 1847 ensured that the grain harvest was excellent and kept the blight at bay. But the acreage planted with what few tubers had survived two years of famine was so small that the poor still faced mass starvation. Nevertheless, the government declared the Famine was over in September 1847. In the same month the distribution of soup stopped in almost all districts. Henceforth the burden of relief was to fall entirely on the workhouses financed by Irish ratepayers. This was, unquestionably, the harshest decision made by Westminster during the Famine.

The destitute were refused relief outside the workhouse. To gain admission, applicants had to accept the harsh institutional discipline and work at breaking stone, etc., and husbands were separated from wives, and mothers from their children. But because nothing else was offered to them, the starving crowded into the workhouses. In the densely packed buildings fever spread with fearful rapidity. The condition of Enniskillen workhouse was typical. The roof of the temporary fever hospital fell in on 7 January 1848, and it still had not been fixed when Temporary Inspector d'Arcy reported on 2 March. He came upon twenty-nine patients sharing beds in one small room; and, he continued,

Immediately previous to my visit there had been *five children in one bed, three of whom were in fever and two in small-pox*.... No statement of mine can convey an idea of the wretched condition the inmates of this house were in; I have frequently heard the horrors of Skibbereen quoted, but they can hardly have exceeded these.

Little wonder, then, that, for many of the starving, flight from Ireland overseas seemed the only option.

Episode 186 ～

EMIGRATION

In 1848 Michael Rush of Ardglass, Co. Down, wrote to his parents in America:

Now my dear father and mother, if you knew what hunger we and our fellow-countrymen are suffering, you would take us out of this poverty Isle.... If you don't endeavour to take us out of it, it will be the first news you will hear by some friend of me and my little family to be lost by hunger, and there are thousands dread they will share the same fate.

In eleven years, during and after the Famine, Ireland sent abroad over two million people, more than had migrated over the preceding two and a half centuries. About 1,200,000 left the country between 1846 and 1851. For the vast majority, America was the preferred destination. Strict controls imposed by the United States government on its passenger vessels pushed fares up, but lax standards on British ships kept fares to Canada as low as £6 for a man, his wife and four small children. Vessels carrying timber from the St Lawrence to British ports had not enough cargo to take back even to serve as ballast; owners therefore gladly accepted destitute Irish into their holds, usually at Liverpool, the cheapest point of departure. These were the infamous 'coffin ships', grossly overcrowded and inadequately provided with food and clean water.

Some ships sailed directly from Irish ports, 11,000 from Sligo alone, for example. One ship leaving Westport, Co. Mayo, foundered with the loss of all on board, within sight of land, watched with horror by those who had just bidden them farewell. A typical 'coffin ship' was the barque *Elizabeth and Sarah*, built in 1762, which sailed from Killala, Co. Mayo, in July 1846 with 276 passengers. By law this vessel should have carried 12,532 gallons of water, but all it had was 8,700 gallons in leaky casks. Each passenger should have been provided with seven pounds of rations per week, but in fact no food was ever given out. All but thirty-two passengers had to sleep on the bare decks, and no toilets of any kind were provided. Forty-two died during the voyage, and the state of the vessel when it was towed into the St Lawrence in September was described as 'horrible and disgusting beyond the power of language to describe'.

Fever flourished in the filthy and congested conditions on board these ships. The *Larch*, sailing from Sligo with 440 passengers, lost 108 at sea, most of them killed by typhus fever. All ships coming up the St Lawrence were required to stop at the quarantine station on Grosse Isle. Many died there. On

Grosse Isle Robert Whyte attended the funeral of the wife of an emigrant from Co. Meath:

> After the grave was filled up the husband placed two shovels in the form of a cross and said, 'By that cross, Mary, I swear to avenge your death. As soon as I earn the price of my passage home I'll go back and shoot the man that murdered you—and that's the landlord.'

Another woman buried on Grosse Isle was the wife of John Ford, an emigrant from Co. Cork, whose grandson was to become the most distinguished founder of the modern automobile industry.

By the middle of the summer of 1847 the line of ships waiting for inspection at Grosse Isle was several miles long. Delays were inevitable, and fever continued to spread among those cooped up on board. The *Agnes*, for instance, arrived with 427 passengers, but after a quarantine of fifteen days only 150 were left alive. The vast majority arriving in Canada walked south to the United States. Many did not make it. It has been estimated that in the single year of 1847 a total of 17,000 emigrants perished at sea (mainly from typhus), 5,300 died on Grosse Isle, and nearly 16,000 more died in British North America, most of them while making their way on foot to the United States.

Great numbers simply crossed the Irish Sea. During the first five months of 1847 300,000 Irish paupers landed in Liverpool, pouring into a city which, until then, had a population of 250,000. Since there were not enough town police to control this Irish multitude, 20,000 citizens were sworn in as special constables and 2,000 soldiers were brought in and encamped at Everton. The immigrants brought 'famine fever' with them, and before the year was out 60,000 people in Liverpool had contracted typhus.

Meanwhile the *Glasgow Herald* reported:

> The streets of Glasgow are at present literally swarming with vagrants from the sister kingdom, and the misery which many of these poor creatures endure can scarcely be less than what they have fled or been driven from at home.

Other Irishmen, excited by events in other parts of Europe, took up arms against the government.

Episode 187 ~

THE BATTLE OF WIDOW McCORMACK'S CABBAGE PATCH

The year 1848—the Year of Revolutions. First, revolution in Sicily. Then, revolution in Naples. Next, on 23 February in Paris, as Victor Hugo recalls:

> A shot rang out, from which side is not known. Panic ... and then a volley. Eighty dead on the spot. A universal cry of fury ... Vengeance!

King Louis-Philippe takes flight. France becomes a republic. Vienna falls to the revolutionaries in March ... so does Berlin ... and Budapest ... and Munich (where the mad King Ludwig runs off with an Irish dancing-girl) ... the pope is chased out of Rome. Every single city in central Europe with a population of 100,000 or more is convulsed by revolution in 1848. The old order is shaken to its foundations.

And what about Ireland? Here the Young Irelander Charles Gavan Duffy declares:

> Ireland's opportunity, thank God and France, has come at last! We must die rather than let this providential hour pass over us unliberated!

John Mitchel, a Presbyterian solicitor from Co. Down, is convinced that, though God had sent the potato blight, the British created the Famine. In his newspaper, the *United Irishman*, he preaches revolution.

But this is no time for a revolution in Ireland. Hundreds of thousands have died. And starvation and fever will kill many more before the year is out. Mitchel is arrested in May, convicted of treason-felony and transported to Van Diemen's Land (Tasmania). Charles Gavan Duffy is arrested in July. Other members of Young Ireland, planning rebellion, are apprehended and held in chains. William Smith O'Brien, a Protestant landlord from Limerick and an MP, agrees to raise the standard of revolt.

At first the prospects look good. Enthusiastic Young Ireland meetings take place in the counties of Meath and Limerick, and 50,000 assemble on the mountain-side at Slievenamon in Co. Tipperary. O'Brien tours the counties of Wexford and Kilkenny, and by the time he reaches Mullinahone in Co. Tipperary he has 6,000 men armed with pitchforks, pikes and fowling pieces.

But O'Brien has made no arrangements to feed his rebel army. He tells his followers to go home and get enough food for four days and 'oatmeal, bread and hard eggs'. These people cannot do that. Soon, though, he is joined on 27 July by Terence Bellew McManus, a Fermanagh man, with volunteers brought over from Liverpool, O'Brien has no more than forty men following him. As they march towards Slievenamon they confront a force of police at Ballingarry on Saturday 30 July. The constables take refuge in Widow McCormack's house, a two-storey stone farmhouse standing in a cabbage garden. The police barricade the windows, using Mrs McCormack's mattresses and furniture, tearing down her mantelpieces, and taking doors off their hinges.

Then Widow McCormack comes up the road: she is frantic—her four young children are inside. O'Brien calls a truce so that the children can be brought to safety. He and McManus open the garden gate, walk up the path and O'Brien climbs onto a window-sill, shakes a constable's hand, and says that it is not their lives but their arms they want. Then some insurgents begin throwing stones. The police fire two volleys. A man falls dead; another is severely injured; O'Brien is shot in the leg; and the rebels flee from the scene. The Young Ireland rebellion is over.

The Battle of Widow McCormack's Cabbage Patch is Ireland's sole contribution to the Year of Revolutions. The English historian Thomas Carlyle writes:

> Ireland is like a half-starved rat, that crosses the path of an elephant. What must the elephant do? Squelch it—by heavens—squelch it.

The government has rushed special repressive legislation through parliament and flooded the island with troops. But, showing remarkable restraint, the authorities do not 'squelch' the Young Irelanders. Not a single person is executed. O'Brien is arrested and condemned to be transported to Van Diemen's Land. One of the earliest photographs taken in Ireland shows him sitting proudly in a good suit with his jailers holding an enormous key. He and John Mitchel are treated as 'gentleman felons' and given separate cabins on board their prison ships and supplied with books and a servant each.

That summer the potato blight returns with deadly force. News of the rebellion causes charitable contributions from Britain to dry up. Hundreds of thousands of starving people have no choice but to become inmates of the workhouses. Officially the Famine is over, but people continue to die. As late as June 1851 there are as many as 263,000 men, women and children in the workhouses.

The year 1851 is a census year. The terrible toll of the Famine is revealed. The population of Ireland in 1841 was given as 8,175,124. In 1851 it is 6,552,385. The Census Commissioners, taking into account the normal rate of increase, reckon that a loss of at least two and a half million has taken place.

Episode 188 ~

THE FENIAN BROTHERHOOD

In attempting to calculate the impact of the Great Famine, modern scholars refer to 'excess mortality'. They reckon that there were 1,082,000 'excess deaths', not counting 'averted births', that is, unborn babies who died when their mothers died. The western province of Connacht suffered most, with much of Munster and southern Ulster not far behind. Those who died were drawn from the lowest rungs of society, the cottiers and rural labourers and their families.

One point of view is that no European government had ever created such an elaborate system of relief to deal with a natural disaster. Another is that the British government, hidebound by the free market economic theories of the day, failed the starving by refusing to provide enough direct relief. In later years critics were to point out that, after workhouse debts had been cancelled in 1853, the overall balance of the government's contribution was only £7 million, and that £69.3 million was expended on the Crimean War between 1854 and 1856. Landlords were able to collect three-quarters of their rents. Some had thrown themselves into providing relief, but the government took no action to restrain the many who took the opportunity to cast the impoverished off their estates. Captain Arthur Kennedy, the Poor Law inspector in Kilrush Union who witnessed evictions in Co. Clare, afterwards recalled:

> I can tell you ... that there were days in that western county when I came back from some scene of eviction so maddened by the sights of hunger and misery I had seen in the day's work that I felt disposed to take the gun from behind my door and shoot the first landlord I met.

Evictions soared in 1847 and reached a peak in 1850. The police kept records from 1849, and their figures show that some 50,000 families were permanently dispossessed between 1849 and 1850, accounting for around a quarter of a million people. And this figure does not include the tens of thousands who voluntarily abandoned their holdings to flee the country.

Between 1845 and 1855 2,100,000 chose to escape from Ireland; of these, 1,500,000 went to the United States. Many of those who survived to make a new life for themselves in America, and, indeed, closer at home across the Irish Sea, would foster a bitter hatred of the British government. These exiles and their descendants would make a potent contribution to the Irish revolutionary cause.

James Stephens had been present at the Battle of Widow McCormack's Cabbage Patch, the Young Irelanders' pathetic attempt at revolution in the summer of 1848. He fled the country to avoid arrest and settled in Paris. Here Stephens mixed with other revolutionary exiles, Italians in particular, and became an eager student of revolutionary strategy.

In 1856 Stephens returned to Ireland with the intention of reviving the revolutionary movement. Adopting the code name 'An Seabhac Siubhlach', meaning 'The Wandering Hawk', he set out on foot and met great numbers of sympathisers, many of whom had been in the now defunct Young Ireland movement. With his long hair and clothes bought in Paris, Stephens frequently was mistaken as an actor. After his walk of some three thousand miles, mostly in the south and the west of the country, Stephens became convinced that there was enough potential in the country to make a fresh attempt at rebellion. For the moment, however, Ireland 'was politically dead ... she had given up the ghost, and was at last, to all intents and purposes, one of England's reconquered provinces'. Action was needed immediately, he believed:

> The attempt ... should be tried in the very near future if we wanted at all to keep our flag flying; for I was as sure as of my own existence that if another decade was allowed to pass without an endeavour of some kind or another to shake off an unjust yoke, the Irish people would sink into a lethargy from which it would be impossible for any patriot ... to arouse them.

Arrogant, quarrelsome, egotistical, jealous and boastful, Stephens nevertheless impressed others with his dedication and philosophy. He was convinced that the Irish in America could be persuaded to provide crucial support and that another European war would in time provide Ireland with its opportunity.

At his lodgings behind Lombard Street in Dublin, on St Patrick's Day 1858, Stephens founded a secret society dedicated to the establishment of an Independent Democratic Republic of Ireland, later to be known as the Irish Republican Brotherhood. Stephens applied what he had learned in Paris: to reduce the danger of being exposed by informers, the organisation was divided into cells or 'circles' in which no member should be known to any other members except those in their own circles. For all its apparent weakness, the IRB, soon popularly known as the Fenian Brotherhood, would certainly keep the Irish revolutionary tradition alive.

Episode 189 ～

'THE GREEN FLAG WILL BE FLYING INDEPENDENTLY'

On 10 November 1861 great numbers gathered in the sleet and rain for a remarkable funeral in Dublin. Terence Bellew McManus of Fermanagh, who had been present at the Battle of Widow McCormack's Cabbage Patch in 1848, who had been transported as a convicted felon to Van Diemen's Land, and who had escaped captivity to reach California, had died in poverty in San Francisco. McManus's body had been disinterred by the Fenian Brotherhood of America, been given a lying-in-state in St Patrick's Cathedral in New York, and was now being taken to a final resting place in Glasnevin cemetery. Men on horseback, wearing black scarves and armlets and equipped with batons, held back the crowds estimated to total between 20,000 and 30,000. The coffin, held aloft by four pall-bearers, was followed by carriages carrying veterans of the 1848 rebellion (including its leader, William Smith O'Brien, released from captivity), 8,000 members of the National Brotherhood of St Patrick, and men of the Dublin trades, in full regalia, and all marching with military precision, while a band played the 'Dead March' from *Saul*. After the formal funeral oration given by torchlight at the cemetery, the radical priest Father Patrick Lavelle of Partry, Co. Mayo, gave an impassioned impromptu address, frequently interrupted by cheers.

The funeral was a triumph for James Stephens, the founder of the Irish Republican Brotherhood. Not only had he upstaged moderate nationalists, but he had also successfully defied the authority of the Catholic Church. Archbishop Paul Cullen of Dublin had forbidden the use of formal religious rites and had refused a lying-in-state in the Pro-Cathedral, expecting thereby to downgrade the status of the funeral as a public event.

McManus's funeral was propaganda coup for the IRB. This secret oath-bound organisation, pledged to establish an Irish Republic by force of arms, now gathered recruits at dizzying speed, particularly among working men in Dublin and shop assistants, tradesmen, labourers and farmers' sons in the countryside. It was particularly strong in west Cork, where Jeremiah O'Donovan Rossa had incorporated his Phoenix Society in Skibbereen into the national organisation. The movement had many adherents amongst the Irish in British cities. And a vigorous sister organisation led by John O'Mahony in America, the Fenian Brotherhood, led journalists to apply the word 'Fenians' to members of the IRB.

Stephens staked everything on Irish-American support. But the outbreak of the American Civil War in 1861 upset his plans. In this, the bloodiest conflict of the nineteenth century, Irishmen fought Irishmen. For example, John Mitchel, who had escaped from captivity in Van Diemen's Land to settle in Knoxville, Tennessee, lost two sons fighting for the Confederates. General Ulysses Grant, who led the Union to victory, was—like Mitchel and many other Civil War officers—of Ulster Presbyterian stock. The right moment to act seemed to be in 1865, when the war came to an end. Great numbers of disbanded soldiers, particularly in the Union armies, were eager to play their part in helping the Irish in the home country to win their freedom.

At this crucial moment Stephens faltered. He hesitated and alienated others by his dictatorial, quarrelsome approach. Greatly assisted by informers, the government seized the initiative in September 1865. Most of the leaders were arrested, and troops were put on high alert. The only encouraging news was the dramatic rescue of Stephens from prison on 24 November, with the aid of two prison warders and a rope ladder.

To make matters worse, the Fenian Brotherhood in America was rent in two. One wing, led by Colonel John Roberts, decided on an immediate attack on Canada, the nearest part of the British Empire. In February 1866 Roberts issued a stirring declaration:

> We promise that before the summer sun kisses the hill-tops of Ireland, a ray of hope will gladden every true Irish heart. The green flag will be flying independently to freedom's breeze.

On the night of 31 May 1866 a force of 800 American Fenians, calling themselves the 'Irish Republican Army', assembled at Buffalo, crossed the Niagara River and seized Fort Erie on the Canadian shore. They routed a Canadian force at Lime Ridge, but the United States government, enforcing a neutrality agreement, cut them off, and the invasion force withdrew and dispersed. About sixty Fenians were captured. The exploit was commemorated in a song which quickly achieved wide currency:

> Deep in Canadian Woods we've met,
> From one bright island flown,
> Great is the land we tread, but yet
> Our hearts are with our own....
> Ireland, boys, Hurrah!
> Ireland, boys, Hurrah!
> We'll toast old Ireland, dear old Ireland,
> Ireland, boys, Hurrah!

Meanwhile, during a visit to New York, Stephens was effectively deposed, and was replaced as 'Head Centre', or leader, by Colonel Thomas Kelly. Kelly crossed the Atlantic to rally the Fenians for an Irish rebellion.

Episode 190 ～

'GOD SAVE IRELAND!'

'Twas down by the glenside, I met an old woman,
A plucking young nettles, she ne'er saw me comin'
I listened a while to the song she was humin'
Glory O, Glory O, to the bold Fenian men.

O n the evening of 5 March 1867 a proclamation was delivered to the *Times* newspaper in London:

THE IRISH PEOPLE TO THE WORLD

... History bears testimony to the intensity of our sufferings.... Our war is against the aristocratic locusts, whether English or Irish, who have eaten the verdure of our fields—against the aristocratic leeches who drain alike our blood and theirs. Republicans of the entire world, our cause is your cause.... Avenge yourselves....
Herewith we proclaim the Irish Republic.

That night the Fenian rising began. It was doomed from the outset. The government had been kept extremely well informed by John Corydon, a man who had infiltrated the highest ranks of the Brotherhood. The movement was crippled by the arrest of key leaders, which left local bands of insurgents confused and without direction. Every attempt over previous weeks to seize arms had been frustrated. In Co. Cork rebels took the coastguard station of Knockadown and captured the police barracks in Ballyknockane, where they derailed the Dublin express. Otherwise all was failure.

The constabulary dispersed groups of rebels in Drogheda's Potato Market, at Drumcliff churchyard in Co. Sligo, at Ballyhurst in Co. Tipperary, and repelled attacks on barracks at Ardagh and Kilmallock in Co. Limerick. Dublin produced the largest Fenian turnout. Marching out of the city, several hundred men found themselves confronted at Tallaght by fourteen constables under the command of Sub-Inspector Burke. The Fenians fired about fifty shots, but not one of them found their mark. The police returned the fire, wounding one man, and the insurgents scattered.

The Irish Constabulary had been able to suppress the Fenian rising without seeking the assistance of the military. Queen Victoria was so pleased that she renamed the force the 'Royal Irish Constabulary'. Vigorous condemnation of the rising came from within the Catholic hierarchy, most notably from Bishop David Moriarty of Ardfert (Kerry) who called down 'God's heaviest curse, his withering, blasting, blighting curse' upon the militant republicans, whom he characterised as 'miscreants', 'criminals' and 'swindlers', declaring that for their punishment 'eternity is not long enough nor Hell hot enough'.

So complete was the failure of the rising that when *Erin's Hope*, a 200-ton ship from New York, sailed into Sligo Bay in May 1867, the thirty-eight Irish-American officers on board quickly learned that there was not the slightest hope of support in the locality. Sailing on round the Irish coast the ship was finally arrested by the authorities at Dungarvan, Co. Waterford. In the hold the police found 5,000 modern breech-loading and repeating rifles, three artillery pieces and 1,500,000 rounds of ammunition.

With the help of informers the government rounded up and convicted great numbers of Fenians. Just as they had done in 1848, those in power showed restraint. Sentences of death were commuted to terms of imprisonment with hard labour. There were, therefore, no martyrs for the cause in Ireland. It was a different matter in England.

On 11 September 1867 police in Manchester arrested two men who were acting suspiciously in a doorway. One of them was none other than the head of the Fenian Brotherhood, Colonel Thomas Kelly. A week later around thirty Fenians ambushed an unescorted prison van taking Kelly and other convicts to Belle Vue Jail. Inside the van Police Sergeant Brett refused to open the door. A Fenian, Peter Rice, fired his revolver through the grille, mortally wounding the sergeant. A prisoner took the keys from the dying policeman, and Kelly escaped.

Arrests followed, and five faced trial for their lives. Four were found guilty of murder: William Allen, Philip Larkin, Michael O'Brien and Edward Condon. None had fired the fatal shot, but all openly confessed that they were part of the rescue mission. All made speeches from the dock. Michael O'Brien said: 'Look to Ireland; see the hundreds of thousands of its people in misery and want. See the virtuous, beautiful and industrious women who only a few years ago—aye and yet—are obliged to look at their children dying for want of food.' Edward Condon cried out: 'I have nothing to regret, to retract or take back. I can only say: God Save Ireland!' As *The Times* reported, the other prisoners all called out 'in chorus and with great power: "God Save Ireland!"'

Condon was given a last-minute reprieve because he was an American citizen. On the morning of 23 November 1867 Allen, Larkin and O'Brien were hanged before an immense crowd in Manchester. It was almost the last public hanging in England. A few days later T. D. Sullivan, opposed though he was to militant republicanism, composed a song echoing Condon's words, a song which became a kind of national anthem over the next fifty years:

> God save Ireland, said the heroes,
> God save Ireland said they all.
> Whether on the scaffold high,
> Or the battle field we die,
> O, what matter when for Ireland dear we fall.

The Fenians had their martyrs after all.

Episode 191 ~

THE GROWTH OF BELFAST

At 1.30 p.m. on Tuesday 10 July 1849 the Belfast Harbour Commissioners, members of the Town Council, the principal gentry and merchants of Belfast, and officers and men of the 13th Regiment stepped on board the royal mail steamer *Prince of Wales*. They had come to open the new channel running from the Garmoyle Pool in Belfast Lough to the quays, which would enable large vessels to come up the Lagan at any state of the tide. Then, at the signal of a ship's bell, a flotilla of vessels, led by the tug *Superb*, moved into the centre of the river. A military band played on board the commissioners' vessel, and then William Pirrie, chairman of the commissioners, made a short speech, poured a libation of champagne into the river 'as a rite of inauguration', and named the new cut the Victoria Channel. Then, as the *Belfast News-Letter* reported,

> Along the whole line of the opposite quay, loud huzzas from a dense multitude of spectators rent the air.... A scarlet flag, inscribed with the words 'The New Channel Opened', was then unfurled from the mizzen-mast head, amidst the huzzas of her living freight. The booming of cannon announced the completion of the auspicious event, and 'Rule Britannia' resounded from the deck.

The completion of the channel was a vital step in the continuing rapid development of Belfast; and its achievement was all the more remarkable in that it had been carried out during the last great famine in western Europe.

A month later Queen Victoria, Prince Albert and the Prince of Wales, having already visited Cork and Dublin, sailed up the new channel to be rapturously received by the citizens of Belfast. They drove up High Street past 'thousands of gaily-dressed and animated spectators, whose acclamations, as the cortège passed by, rose like the roar of the wind in the forest'. Oil paintings of the queen and Prince Albert adorned the balcony of McGee's the tailors; 'Welcome' was inscribed in immense gold letters over the Northern Bank; and in High Street a thirty-two-foot-high triumphal arch had been erected with the words 'Caed Mille Failthe' magnificently misspelt in dahlias. The queen viewed an exhibition of the province's principal industry, 'from flax in the growth to the splendid damask', in the White Linen Hall. As she drove through the streets a poor woman ran beside the carriage crying: 'Och, the Lord love her purty face, for goodness is in her. Look at the way she bows and smiles to everybody— God save your Majesty and the whole of yez—hurra!' On the Lisburn Road the workhouse children gave three shrill cheers, and after inspecting the new Queen's College by the Malone turnpike and Mulholland's mill in York Street the royal party re-embarked as the staff of the Donegall Arms prepared a banquet given by the mayor 'of the most *recherché* kind', including 'all the delicacies of the season'.

At this time Belfast was recovering from an epidemic of cholera, which had moved like a dark cloud across the continent as the last embers of the revolutions in central Europe were being extinguished. Over much of Ireland the Famine still raged, but here in the north-east Belfast was well on the way to becoming one of the great trading and manufacturing cities of the western world. A report of 1852 pointed out that Belfast had outstripped Dublin to become the first port in Ireland, not only in value but also in tonnage.

The mud and sleech dredged up to create the Victoria Channel had been dumped to create an artificial island adjacent to east Belfast which, during the royal visit, had been renamed Queen's Island. Here Robert Hickson, a Liverpool engineer who managed a large ironworks upstream at Cromac, decided to build ships with the iron he was finding difficult to sell at a profit. He engaged Edward Harland, a twenty-three-year-old engineer from Newcastle-upon-Tyne.

This appointment was of momentous importance for the industrial future of Belfast. Harland launched his first ship in October 1855, and his craft soon caused a sensation in the shipping world because of their revolutionary design. In 1858 Harland bought out Hickson, with the financial backing of Gustav Schwabe, a partner in John Bibby & Sons of Liverpool, who had been deeply impressed by the young man's engineering prowess. Schwabe's nephew, Gustav Wolff, had already joined Harland as a personal assistant. During the American Civil War business was brisk for the partnership of Harland & Wolff, formed in 1861, because the Confederate States were eager to buy fast steamers capable of outrunning the Union blockade. When Schwabe created the White Star Line in 1869, he ordered all his ocean-going vessels from Harland & Wolff, now on its way to becoming the biggest ship-building firm in the world.

But, as we shall see, Belfast, for all its success, was an Irish town with Irish problems.

Episode 192 ～

PARTY FIGHTS

'Twas on the Twelfth day of July, in the year of '49,
Ten hundreds of our Orangemen together did combine,
In memory of King William, on that bright and glorious day,
To walk all round Lord Roden's park, and right over Dolly's Brae.

When members of the Orange Order announced that they intended to march from Rathfriland to Tollymore Park, Lord Roden's estate in Co. Down, the government was alarmed. The return route chosen was a long one, veering north back to Rathfriland through the townland of Magheramayo, inhabited almost exclusively by Catholics. Major Arthur Wilkinson believed the Protestants were 'epicures to choose it instead of keeping on a good road'.

Early on Thursday 12 July 1849 Wilkinson's troops, together with a body of constabulary, took up position at Dolly's Brae, a defile on the route where there had been trouble the previous year. During the afternoon they were joined by up to a thousand Ribbonmen, Catholics in an organisation mirroring the Orange Order, all armed with pitchforks, pikes and muskets. At 5 p.m. around 1,400 Orangemen, fully armed, marched out of Tollymore, with bands playing, accompanied by dragoons and some anxious magistrates. As they approached Dolly's Brae, Constabulary Sub-Inspector James Hill later told the inquest, 'I addressed every file of the procession as it passed, asking them, for God's sake, to pass on quietly, and not to fire a shot, even for fun.' Then, Wilkinson recalled, 'There went bang a shot in front, but I don't know where it came from no more than the man in the moon.' There followed, Hill continued, 'a succession of shots from both sides ... a regular blazing away, helter-skelter.... Shots were tearing up the ground where the men were.... I ordered a few of the police for God's sake to fire and they did.... At that time the gun balls were flying, I should say in hundreds, from the Protestant party.'

Resident Magistrate George Fitzmaurice rode along the line of Orangemen urging them to stop shooting, but to no effect. Then at the end of the procession he found Catholic homes being attacked and one of their owners wounded. He stated in evidence: 'I said to them, there's a man lying on the road. Go back, perhaps he's not dead, and afford him some assistance. They roared out—"He's not one of our party."'

Not a single Orangeman was either killed or wounded, and, except for a policeman accidentally bayoneted by a fellow-constable, the forces of law and order were also unscathed. A government inquiry later estimated that at least thirty Catholics had been killed.

Intense rioting in 1857 showed that traditional fears and rivalries, far from wilting when transferred from the countryside, found new strength in the narrow streets of working-class Belfast. The violence in 1857 began on Monday night, 12 July, when mobs hurled stones and insults at each other across wasteland by Albert Street and Catholics at Millfield beat two Methodist ministers with sticks. On the following night Sandy Row Protestants made a determined attack on the Pound, smashing windows with long poles and setting houses on fire. When the mills stopped work on Saturday afternoon, the police were swept aside as the mobs clashed in ferocious combat. Sporadic gunfire continued during the night, and on Sunday afternoon Head-Constable Henderson from Quadrant Street saw a ditch 'closely lined with men, having guns levelled, firing without intermission'.

Sectarian passions were inflamed again in August by street preaching from the Custom House steps. The journalist Frankfort Moore, then a young child, was present on the occasion and later recalled that there was a 'warm interchange of opinion on a basis of basalt'. A policeman ordered his nurse: 'Take them childer out o' this or I'll not be tellin' ye. Don't ye see he's read the Riot Act. Heth! You're a gierl bringin' them wee'uns intill a crowd like thon!'

Riots regularly erupted every summer in Belfast, given added force by new arrivals pouring in to seek work in the building trade, the mills, the docks, the engineering works and the shipyard. The riots of August 1864 were so fierce that Dublin Castle sent up a special train of twenty-seven wagons carrying two field guns and substantial reinforcements. Then the funeral of one victim of police gunfire was turned into a massive parade of loyalist strength on 18 August. When the procession turned unexpectedly into Donegall Place, Belfast's most fashionable street, the forces of the crown could do little more than hold back Catholics massing in Castle Place. According to the *Northern Whig*, 'The guns fired continuously, the bullets pierced the air, whirr after whirr, in a continuous volley.' Only what Frankfort Moore called 'the usual autumn monsoon' brought this violence to an end.

Episode 193 ⌇

'MY MISSION IS TO PACIFY IRELAND'

In December 1868 the leader of the Liberal Party, William Ewart Gladstone, was engaged in his favourite form of relaxation—chopping down trees on his estate. A messenger arrived to tell him that Queen Victoria had asked him to form a government. 'Very significant,' he said, and then resting on his axe, declared with great passion: 'My mission is to pacify Ireland.'

Gladstone had long been troubled by foreign criticism of the way that Britain governed Ireland. As a young man he had written to his wife:

> Ireland, Ireland! That cloud in the west, that coming storm.... Ireland forces upon us these great social and great religious questions—God grant that we may have courage to look them in the face.

Gladstone had been strongly moved by the desperate courage of the Fenian Brotherhood and by the defiance in the dock of the 'Manchester Martyrs', the three Fenians condemned to the scaffold in 1867. Now he was Prime Minister; he promised 'justice for Ireland', but did he know how to provide that justice?

Gladstone began in 1869 by knocking away one of the principal pillars of the Union: he disestablished the Anglican Church of Ireland. He considered it unjust that a church with only 700,000 adherents out of a population of 5,750,000 should continue to occupy its privileged position as the official state church. Above all, disestablishment removed the tithe, the hated enforced contribution made by farmers of all religions to the state church.

Next, Gladstone put through a Land Act in 1870. The main purpose was to make the 'Ulster custom', which compensated tenants for improvements made to their holdings, enforceable by law throughout Ireland. Actually the act was not much use and proved a solicitor's nightmare; but at least Gladstone had established the principle that parliament should do something to protect tenants as well as uphold the rights of landed property.

Almost certainly the most valuable measure for Ireland in these years was the introduction of the secret ballot in all elections in 1872. No more could landlords, landlords' agents and employers scrutinise the electoral preferences of voters. At last those enfranchised could cast their votes as they wished without fear of eviction or retaliation.

Secret ballot was first put to the test in the general election of 1874. The results had dramatic consequences for both British and Irish politics. Liberal representation in Ireland received a deadly blow from which it never recovered. The Liberals had largely been displaced by fifty-nine MPs who described themselves as 'Home Rulers'.

Isaac Butt was the unlikely leader of a new movement seeking the restoration of the Irish parliament. Son of a Co. Donegal clergyman, Butt was for a time a Professor of Political Economy, an Orange Tory Dublin councillor, a Conservative MP and a barrister. His opinions changed, and his brilliant defence of Young Ireland and Fenian prisoners won him the respect of a wide range of Irish nationalists. On 19 May 1870, in a Dublin hotel, the Home Government Association had been formed to demand, in Butt's words, 'full control over our domestic affairs'.

Since the Famine and the death of Daniel O'Connell in 1847 Irish politics had become somewhat humdrum and unexciting. Attempts in the 1850s and 1860s to create a robust independent Irish party, to champion the rights of tenant farmers in particular, had proved disappointing. For nearly a quarter of a century the issue of repeal of the Act of Union had been all but dead. Now it was revived by an uneasy alliance of disgruntled Liberals and Conservatives, former Repealers, and Fenians searching for an alternative to futile revolution. Seeking support for a Catholic university, members of the hierarchy, after some hesitation, also gave their support to the new association.

Any feeling of elation at their success in the 1874 election soon deserted the Home Rule MPs. On the eve of the election the *Belfast News-Letter* had declared:

Home rule is simple Rome rule, and, if home rule were accomplished tomorrow, before that day week Rome rule would be evident.

It was a view firmly believed by the great majority of Irish Protestants. They did not hesitate to express their implacable opposition to an Irish parliament. In any case, the same election put Gladstone and the Liberals out of office. Benjamin Disraeli now headed a Conservative government more interested in imperial adventure than in Ireland's problems. Isaac Butt's moderate attempts in the House of Commons to bring Ireland back on the agenda got nowhere.

Then on 22 April 1875 a tall, bearded young man, a Protestant landlord from Co. Wicklow, made his first appearance in the House of Commons. Returned as a Home Ruler in a by-election in Co. Meath, Charles Stewart Parnell would soon transform the Irish political landscape.

Episode 194 ∿

'KEEP A FIRM GRIP OF YOUR HOMESTEADS'

On the evening of Thursday 22 April 1875 Joseph Biggar, the Home Rule (or Nationalist) MP for Co. Cavan, was delivering a long, boring speech to an almost empty House of Commons. This was quite deliberate. Biggar, a Presbyterian pork butcher and secretly a sworn member of the Irish Republican Brotherhood, was filibustering: this was to delay the passage of a coercion bill for Ireland. English MPs found Biggar's Belfast accent difficult enough to understand at the best of times. Reading long extracts from dry reports, he droned on until, after almost four hours on his feet, he said he was 'unwilling to detain the House at further length' and sat down.

During this interminable speech the newly elected MP for Co. Meath, Charles Stewart Parnell, entered the chamber for the first time. Parnell was impressed. Soon, along with a couple of other members, he joined Biggar in what became known as 'obstruction', that is, holding up the business of parliament to force the government to pay attention to Irish problems.

Isaac Butt, leader of the Irish Home Rule MPs, strongly disapproved of this ungentlemanly tactic of obstruction. But this filibustering was popular with constituents back in Ireland, and Parnell was fast becoming a prominent figure. Butt, the founder of the Home Rule movement, was now being edged aside by members of the party he had created, the Irish Parliamentary Party. At this point a severe economic crisis provided Parnell with the opportunity to become the undisputed leader not only of the Irish Party but of all nationalists in Ireland.

Unremitting rain throughout August 1877 destroyed the oats and rotted the potatoes in the ground, especially in the west and north-west. Many smallholders could not pay their rents, and for the first time for many years tenant farmers were being evicted in their hundreds. The harvest of 1878 was also poor, but that of the following year was disastrous, the worst since the Famine. The year 1879 was the wettest and coldest since records began. Between March and September rain fell on 125 days out of a six-month total of 183, that is, two days out of every three. Turf cut from the bogs had no chance to dry. Above all, the potato crop was ravaged by blight—the yield was reduced by more than two-thirds.

Smallholders in the west, still dependent on the potato for their staple diet, faced starvation. Thousands were evicted. The *Freeman's Journal* reported on the condition of Co. Mayo at the end of August:

The prospect of an abundant harvest is at an end; the chance even of a tolerable one hangs dangerously in the balance. The lightnings of Sunday night, the rains and winds which have raged either daily or nightly ever since, have left the footprints of their vengeance deep behind them. The two props of the Mayo farmer's homestead have collapsed miserably upon his head. The potatoes are bad, the turf is worse.

Many families owed two or three years' rent. This time, however, as they received their eviction notices, the tenant farmers planned to resist. Galvanised and organised by the editor of the *Connaught Telegraph*, James Daly, at least 10,000 assembled at Irishtown, Co. Mayo, on 20 April 1879 to demand action. Most MPs in the Irish Party greeted news of this peasant defiance with alarm. Not so Charles Stewart Parnell: he realised that his party could be swept aside if it ignored the anger of humble people in the countryside facing ruin. He readily accepted an invitation to address a meeting to be held at Westport, Co. Mayo. Parnell was about to draw the respectable Home Rulers into an alliance with poor farmers and militant republicans to engage in a titanic struggle with the privileged landed elite.

The rain poured in torrents on 8 June 1879 as thousands came in from all parts of Co. Mayo to a field on the edge of Westport town. Many wore green ribbons and rosettes, eighty arrived in a body on horseback, and some held aloft banners proclaiming 'The Land for the People!', 'Down with the Land Robbers!' and 'Ireland for the Irish!' They had come despite the open condemnation of the Catholic Archbishop of Tuam, John MacHale. And they had come to listen to Parnell, a landlord and a Protestant who spoke in an upper-class accent. He openly urged them to flout the law:

You must show the landlords that you intend to keep a firm grip of your homesteads and lands. You must not allow yourselves to be dispossessed as you were dispossessed in 1847.

These tenant farmers had every intention this time of resisting eviction. Organised soon after in the Land League, they launched what became known as the 'Land War'.

Episode 195 ∾

THE LAND WAR

In March 1879 John Devoy, the head of Clan na Gael, the main Fenian organ-isation in America, met Charles Stewart Parnell, the Irish Party MP, in northern France. There in secret Devoy explained what he described as a 'new departure': the Fenians would abandon plans for armed revolt and support the drive for Home Rule, provided Parnell backed the campaign of tenant farmers against the landlords. Though he was careful not to put it in writing, Parnell did not hesitate to give his approval.

Michael Davitt played a pivotal role in brokering this deal between repub-lican revolutionaries and constitutional nationalist politicians. A Fenian recently paroled from a term of penal servitude after conviction for illegal arms dealing, Davitt was to make sure that Parnell would lead a great national campaign to break the power of the landlords.

During that year of 1879 drenching rain, a succession of bad harvests and the reappearance of potato blight had brought many families—particularly in the west of Ireland—to the brink of starvation.

Co. Mayo took the lead in defying the landlords and in the formation of the Irish National Land League in October 1879. A poster explained its aims:

First—To put an end to Rack-renting, Eviction, and Landlord Oppression. Second—To effect such a radical change in the Land System of Ireland as will put it in the power of every Irish Farmer to become the owner, on fair terms, of the land he tills.

Such excitement had not been witnessed in Ireland since Daniel O'Connell's monster meetings for repeal of the Union more than thirty years before. Huge numbers of country people, threatened with eviction, unemployment and star-vation, assembled to hear fiery speeches from Land League agitators. Economic conditions worsened in the hard winter of 1879–80, and once again torrential rains in the ensuing spring and summer threatened to ruin the harvest. As the general election of 1880 approached, the *Fermanagh Times* declared:

The question of the hour is a sad one—destitution. It is echoed from the Giant's Causeway to the Cove of Cork. Go where we may, throughout Ireland to-day, we hear the wail of distress for food.

The Land League demanded substantial rent reductions, and if these were refused, tenants were urged to refuse to pay the rent. The Liberal leader, W. E.

Gladstone, declared that eviction notices were now falling like snowflakes. This seemed all too true. How could evictions be stopped without recourse to violence? The Land League's answer was to make life impossible for any farmer who took over an evicted man's holding. Michael Davitt, at a meeting in Knockaroo, Co. Mayo, made reference to a holding from which the occupier had been just evicted:

> This farm I trust will not be tenanted by any man.... If such a traitor to your cause enters this part of the country, why, keep your eyes fixed upon him—point him out—and if a pig of his falls into a boghole, let it lie there.

Charles Stewart Parnell, president of the Land League, had returned from a spectacularly successful whistle-stop tour of America during which he had delivered speeches to Irish-Americans in sixty-two towns and cities, addressed Congressmen in the House of Representatives, and raised great sums for famine relief and for the Land League. Now he gave his full support for the approach recommended by Davitt. At Ennis, Co. Clare, on Sunday 19 September, even though it was four o'clock in the morning, hundreds were waiting for him when he arrived. A procession formed up with lighted torches and a band to escort him to his hotel. Later in the day, speaking to a crowd that had now swollen to 12,000, Parnell asked:

> Now, what are you going to do with a tenant who bids for a farm from which his neighbour has been evicted? (*A voice*: Shoot him!) Now I think I heard somebody say, 'Shoot him,' but I wish to point out to you a very much better way, a more Christian, a more charitable way which will give the lost sinner an opportunity of repenting. When a man takes a farm from which another has been evicted, you must show him on the roadside when you meet him, you must show him at the shop counter, you must show him in the fair and at the market place and even in the house of worship, by leaving him severely alone, by putting him in a sort of moral Coventry, by isolating him from the rest of his kind as if he were a leper of old, you must show him your detestation of the crime he has committed.

Soon afterwards this advice was followed with striking effect in Co. Mayo. Here by Lough Mask, Captain Charles Boycott was to experience at first hand the formidable power of the Land League.

Episode 196 ∾

THE RELIEF OF CAPTAIN BOYCOTT

On 18 October 1880 *The Times* published a letter from Ireland. It was from Captain Charles Boycott, an army captain from Norfolk, who had an estate surrounding Lough Mask House in Co. Mayo and also acted as agent for Lord Erne's extensive properties in the province of Connacht. After several seasons of atrocious weather, tenants had been unable to pay the rent. Boycott had issued eviction orders but, as he explained to the press, his process-server had been intimidated and driven back. Now, he told readers, a howling mob had coerced all his workers to leave him; the blacksmith and the laundress refused to work for his family; and shopkeepers in nearby Ballinrobe would not serve him. In its editorial *The Times* concluded: 'The persecution of the writer, Mr Boycott, for some offence against the Land League's code, is an insult to the government and to public justice.'

Loyalists in Ireland agreed, and the *Belfast News-Letter* headed a campaign to send an expedition to rescue Captain Boycott. Ulster Protestants clamoured to be part of a rescue expedition and to lift his potatoes and thresh his corn. When arrangements were made to hire a special train to take hundreds of loyalists to Connacht, the anxious Irish Chief Secretary, W. E. Forster, wrote to the Prime Minister, W. E. Gladstone: 'This would be civil war, we know the whole countryside would be up against them.' Forster rushed a thousand additional troops to Connacht to reinforce the police protecting Boycott. Then he announced that there would be no special train, and he strictly limited the rescue team to fifty men. And so twenty-five Orangemen from Co. Cavan and twenty-five Orangemen from Co. Monaghan boarded a train at Clones on 11 November. At Athlone each volunteer was issued with a revolver. As the Orange labourers marched out of the station at Claremorris between lines of soldiers with bayonets fixed, a great crowd of local people subjected them to a storm of groans, hissings, hootings and booing.

As darkness fell the rain lashed down in blinding sheets. The owners of carriages hired by the police refused to allow their vehicles to convey the Orangemen. The Ulstermen had no choice but to walk to Ballinrobe, a walk which took them five hours. Next morning, after spending the night in the infantry barracks, the men tramped the final four miles to Lough Mask House. The cavalcade of Orangemen, infantry, cavalry and police was described by the *Daily News* correspondent as being 'like a huge red serpent with black head and tail'. At the iron gates to Lough Mask House, Captain

Boycott gave no greeting to the fifty labourers who had come so far to salvage his crops.

The Cavan and Monaghan labourers sang Orange songs around campfires they had built and then settled down for the night in rain-sodden tents supplied by the army. Captain Boycott rather meanly charged the Orangemen nine-pence a stone for their potatoes. Despite a torrential rainstorm accompanied by gale-force winds, the men were up early. The task ahead was formidable: they had to lift two acres of potatoes, eight acres of turnips and seven acres of mangolds. Twenty acres of corn had already been cut, but the sheaves had still to be threshed.

Meanwhile the Land League imposed a strict discipline on the local people. They followed the instructions given by the *Connaught Telegraph*:

> Be calm, be cool and, at the same time, resolute and determined.... Treat those mailed and buckshot warriors with silence and contempt.... Show the world over by your calm, but resolute demeanour, that you are worthy of your name and traditions.

To the great disappointment of foreign correspondents—some of them from as far away as the Russian Empire and the United States—there were no incidents of violence.

After two weeks, on Friday 26 November, the work was finished. To rein-force the current nationalist joke that the clerk of the weather had joined the Land League, the worst storm that Mayo had endured in many years burst over the area. The Orangemen had a sleepless last night as their tents in the encampment were ripped to shreds by the howling winds.

The relief of Captain Boycott was proclaimed a victory by loyalists. But it had cost £10,000 to save crops that were not worth a tenth of that sum. To rescue every beleaguered landlord in this way would be quite impossible. The French newspaper *Le Figaro* reported: 'The bright Irish have invented a new word, they are currently saying to *boycott* somebody, meaning to ostracise him.'

Boycotting now swept the country. Any landlord attempting to evict tenants suddenly found himself powerless. Evictions fell sharply. The Land League was the real victor in this episode which had captured the imagination of the world.

Episode 197 〜

ASSASSINATION IN THE PHOENIX PARK

Back in 1847 the Tenant Right League summarised its demands as the 'three Fs': fair rent, fixity of tenure, and free sale. In 1881 W. E. Gladstone, the Prime Minister, seeing the great power of the Land League, decided to grant these three demands in a new Land Act. From now on land courts, and not the landlords, would decide what a fair rent would be—the first rent control in United Kingdom history. 'Fixity of tenure' ensured that tenants could not be evicted provided they had paid the rent. Finally, 'free sale' gave the tenant a clear right to sell the interest in his holding to an incoming tenant without landlord interference.

Charles Stewart Parnell, leader of the Irish Parliamentary Party, cautiously welcomed the act. The problem was that many tenants, their crops ruined by bad weather, were quite unable to pay their rents. In any case, the ultimate aim of the Land League was to get rid of the landlords altogether. While Parnell advised farmers to 'test the act', the Irish countryside remained turbulent. There were so many violent incidents that the Irish Chief Secretary, W. E. Forster, pushed through a coercion act giving special powers to the police and military. In reaction, the speeches of Irish MPs and Land League members were so ferocious that in October Parnell and other prominent leaders were imprisoned in Kilmainham Jail in Dublin.

This only made the situation worse. Parnell's sisters, Anna and Fanny, formed the Ladies' Land League which openly organised extreme action. The high-profile prisoners meanwhile issued a 'no rent' manifesto from their prison cells. The country slid more and more out of government control. Finally, on 2 May 1882, in what became known as the 'Kilmainham Treaty', the leaders were released on condition that they called a halt to the turbulence in the countryside. In return Gladstone promised an arrears bill which by the end of the year would give protection from eviction to more than 100,000 tenants who were behind with their rent. This was too much for Forster: he resigned.

On 6 May, four days after the release of Parnell and his associates, Lord Frederick Cavendish took his first walk as the new Irish Chief Secretary in Dublin's Phoenix Park, in the company of Under-Secretary Thomas Burke. It was a fine evening, the park was full of people, and the two gentlemen stopped to watch a game of polo. Suddenly a number of men came up from behind, stabbed the Chief Secretary and Under-Secretary to death with twelve-inch surgical knives, and then made their escape in a waiting cab.

The assassins were members of a group calling themselves the 'Invincibles'. Eventually they were caught and brought to justice. This appalling act shook Parnell and caused him to distance himself from the more extreme agitators. He now set about concentrating on constitutional politics to obtain Home Rule for Ireland. For that he needed the co-operation of the Liberals. Many Liberals, however, were convinced that Parnell was up to his neck in conspiracy with murderers. On 22 February 1883 Foster made a blistering attack on Parnell in the House of Commons. He accused him of conniving at the assassinations. 'It's a lie,' Parnell cried out, but it was years before Liberals felt they could work with him.

Rather later than some other European states, the United Kingdom was gradually becoming more representative, more democratic. In December 1884 Gladstone gave the vote to all male heads of households. The Irish electorate leaped from under a quarter of a million to nearly three quarters of a million. In the following year it was decided that, in spite of a steady fall in population due mainly to emigration, Ireland would be allowed to keep all its 103 seats at Westminster. Ireland had been serioiusly underrepresented at the time of the Union. Now it was overrepresented. Very soon Ireland would be deciding what government would be in power in London.

On 8 June 1885 there was to be a division in the Commons on an additional tax on wines and spirits. Parnell summoned all absent Nationalists to Westminster by telegram, and all thirty-nine Irish Parliamentary Party MPs trooped through the lobby to vote against the Liberal government. Gladstone's administration lost by 263 votes to 252. As one MP remembered, 'a collection of bores and the bored became a mass of screaming, waving, gesticulating lunatics', and Lord Randolph Churchill emitted hysterical yells 'like a wild animal fastening its teeth on the prey'.

Lord Salisbury, with Parnell's help, now formed a Conservative government. His majority was too slim for comfort, however, and in November he called an election.

For Ireland, that general election of 1885—the first to be conducted on the new franchise—was certainly the most momentous of the century.

Episode 198 ᕆ

THE FIRST HOME RULE BILL

No one could predict the outcome of the general election of 1885 in Ireland. The number of voters had been tripled by the Reform Act of the year before. Party scrutineers were fiercely vigilant during the extraordinary turnout, which reached over 93 per cent in some divisions.

Liberal representation on the island was completely wiped out. The Irish Parliamentary Party leaped to eighty-six seats, one of these being won in Liverpool by T. P. O'Connor. Because the Conservatives and Liberals were so evenly matched in numbers, Charles Stewart Parnell, at the head of the most disciplined political party in the United Kingdom, could call the shots. At first Parnell was inclined to keep the Conservatives in power. But it was unlikely that the new Prime Minister, Lord Salisbury, would ever concede Home Rule. And what about Gladstone, the Liberal leader?

In December 1885 the political journalist Thomas McKnight visited a leading Liberal, Sir Edward Cowan, at Craigavad in north Down. Ulster Liberals had just completed the magnificent Reform Club at the entrance to Royal Avenue in Belfast. Now there was not a single Liberal MP representing Ireland. McKnight had some grim news for his host: producing a letter, he announced abruptly: 'Gladstone has gone over to the Home Rulers.' Cowan replied incredulously: 'Impossible! Absurd!' But McKnight presented his proof:

> I put Mr Gladstone's letter in Sir Edward's hands. He read it slowly and then hesitated to speak.
> What do you think of it?', I asked.
> 'I must candidly say that I do not like it.'
> 'Nor I. It means to us utter ruin.'

The news of Gladstone's conversion to Home Rule immediately brought Liberals and Conservatives together in Ulster. Solid Protestant opposition in the north to Home Rule had not really entered into the calculations of either Parnell or Gladstone. Parnell duly transferred the Irish Party's support to the Liberals. With some distaste Queen Victoria accepted Gladstone as her Prime Minister for the third time on 30 January 1886, disinclined as she was to 'take this half-crazy and in many ways ridiculous old man for the sake of the country'.

It would be quite wrong to conclude that Gladstone had gone over to Home Rule simply to get back into power. For years he had immersed himself in books on Irish history, and it is clear that deep conviction was behind his decision to take his party along this treacherous course.

The Conservative politician Lord Randolph Churchill wrote to a friend in February: 'I decided some time ago that if the Grand Old Man went for Home Rule, the Orange card would be the one to play.' And play that card he did. Churchill was billed as the principal speaker at a 'Monster Meeting of Conservatives and Orangemen' in Belfast's Ulster Hall on 22 February. When he put in at Larne, Churchill proclaimed to cheering supporters: 'Ulster will fight, and Ulster will be right.' Then, after enjoying a selection of loyal airs played by the Ballymacarrett Brass Band and the Britannic Flute Band, the audience in the Ulster Hall listened to Churchill for one and a half hours with rapt attention:

> On you it primarily rests whether Ireland shall remain an integral portion of this great empire sharing in its glory ... or whether, on the other hand, Ireland shall become the focus and the centre of foreign intrigue and deadly conspiracy.

He urged loyalists to organise so that Home Rule might not come upon them 'as a thief in the night'.

Not since the second reading of the Great Reform Bill in 1832 were the Commons and its public gallery so packed as when Gladstone introduced the Home Rule Bill on 8 April 1886. The journalist Frank Harris recorded the occasion:

> The house was so thronged that members sat about on the steps leading from the floor and even on the arms of the benches and on each other's knees.... Every diplomat in London seemed to be present; and cheek by jowl with the black uniforms of bishops, Indian princes by the dozen blazing with diamonds lent a rich Oriental flavour to the scene.

Gladstone spoke for two and a half hours. Harris described his demeanour:

> His head was like that of an old eagle—luminous eyes, rapacious beak and bony jaws.... His voice was a high, clear tenor; his gestures rare but well chosen; his utterance as fluid as water.... He seemed so passionately sincere and earnest that time and time again you might have thought he was expounding God's law conveyed to him on Sinai.

By later standards, the Prime Minister was offering a very limited form of devolution—little more than control over the police, civil service and the judiciary. But, whatever their private reservations, the Nationalist MPs gave Gladstone their full backing. Parnell knew that all his party's disciplined energy would be needed to secure the passage of the bill. In stark contrast, within the Liberal ranks there was rebellion.

Episode 199 ⁓

'IS THEM 'UNS BATE?'

In a speech to Liberals in Portsmouth in 1886 Charles Stewart Parnell held up a map of Ireland. The Conservative constituencies—those opposed to Home Rule—had been coloured in in yellow. He said in mocking tones:

> This yellow patch covered by my forefinger represents Protestant Ulster— and now they say they want a separate parliament for this little yellow patch up in the north-east!

Yet Parnell, leader of the Irish Parliamentary Party, was forced to pay attention to the Ulster question as the crucial vote in the House of Commons approached. In his final speech in support of the Home Rule Bill he said to MPs:

> We cannot give up a single Irishman. We want the energy, the talents and the work of every Irishman to ensure that this great experiment shall be a successful one. The best system of government for a country I believe to be the one which requires that government should be the result of all the forces within that country.

Not all the forces in Ireland, however, wanted an Irish parliament. The 1881 census returns showed that there were 866,000 Protestants in Ulster, and almost all—Conservatives and Liberals alike—passionately opposed Home Rule. The strength of their feeling would soon be manifest.

It was a rebellion within the Liberal government's ranks, however, that defeated Home Rule. Like the Conservatives, the Liberal dissidents feared that Home Rule would begin the dismemberment of the Empire. On the night of 8 June 1886 ninety-three Liberal MPs voted with the Conservatives against the bill; and as a result of their defection from party ranks, Home Rule was defeated by a margin of thirty votes.

In Belfast the journalist Frankfort Moore received the news by electric telegraph:

> As I made my way homeward on [that] lovely June morning ... although it was only four o'clock, I was met by groups of working men who had risen two or three hours before their usual time ... to learn the result of the division in the House of Commons; and when I told them that the bill had been defeated, the cheers that filled the air at the news surprised the policemen at the corners.... I met scores of the same class ... in the ultra-Protestant

Sandy Row ... to put to me in their own idiom and staccato pronunciation the burning question:

'Is them 'uns bate?'

And when I assured them that the unspeakable Nationalists had been beaten by a good majority, once more cheers were raised. I was slapped familiarly on the back by half-dressed 'Islandmen' (the shipwrights) with shouts of 'Bully wee fella!' as though the defeat of the measure was due to my personal exertions.

Later in the day, to lament the bill's failure, Catholics in Belfast set fire to their chimneys. Protestants left their work early, and, while Orange bands played loyalist airs, they lit bonfires and tar-barrels in jubilation. No wonder the *Belfast News-Letter* noted that the combined result was a pall over the town 'as thick as a London fog'.

Differences of opinion on Home Rule ignited a fresh conflagration of inter-communal violence in Belfast on a scale not seen before. The trouble began five days before the vote on the bill when Catholic navvies at work on the Alexandra Dock drove out a Protestant, warning him that 'neither he nor any of his sort should get leave to work there, or earn a loaf there or any other place'. On the following day nearly a thousand shipwrights descended on the navvies. The few who stood their ground were badly beaten, and others took refuge in the water. One young man drowned. The mayor, Sir Edward Harland, telegraphed Dublin Castle requesting reinforcements. Rural constables disembarking at the railway stations followed Town-Inspector Thomas Carr through a maze of unfamiliar streets to the Shankill Road. Here Protestants had extended their demonstrations against Home Rule to sacking Catholic-owned public houses. In the words of the government inquiry,

Mr Carr and his party, as they advanced up the street, were furiously attacked by the mob.... The police—a number of whom had firearms—charged, by Mr Carr's orders, three times; once with fixed bayonets; but the mob kept up the attack with unabated fierceness. Some of the streets of Belfast are paved with small paving stones, popularly called 'kidneys', and these formidable missiles were rooted from the street by the women and handed to the men.

Almost every policeman in Mr Carr's party was struck with stones, by the tremendous fusillade of these weapons which was kept up by the mob.

When Carr, himself severely injured, got to his feet, he read the Riot Act. Then he ordered his men to fire buckshot over the heads of the rioters, who at last dispersed.

Next day, 9 June, the violence reached new levels of intensity.

In fact the Belfast riots of 1886 had only just begun.

Episode 200 ~

THE BELFAST RIOTS OF 1886

On Wednesday 9 June 1886, the day after the Home Rule Bill had been defeated, a mob of around two thousand Protestants drove back members of the Royal Irish Constabulary. The police had been attempting to stop the looting of a liquor store on Belfast's Shankill Road. Three magistrates, seventy-two constables, several police officers and a reporter took refuge in Bower's Hill barracks. The besieged came under ferocious and prolonged attack. According to the *Belfast News-Letter*, 'kidney pavers' had been 'strewn over the road by a number of vicious young women who carried them in their aprons ... and when the stone-throwing waned for a moment girls and women came to the front and uttered the most desperate threats to the men who desisted'. A salvo of paving stones destroyed the telegraph apparatus, and in desperation the defenders opened fire on the mob. Seven of those outside were killed. At 10 p.m. the Highland Light Infantry came to the rescue and found several children unconscious from the drinking of looted alcohol.

Many Protestants were convinced that Gladstone's Liberal government was intent on punishing them for opposing Home Rule. On the following Sunday the Rev. Hugh Hanna said from his pulpit in St Enoch's Presbyterian Church:

> It was right that the loyalty of the land should celebrate as it did that God has given us.... But that celebration has cost us dear. It incurred the wrath of a government that has been traitorous to its trusts.... The armed servants of that government are sent to suppress rejoicing loyalty by the sanguinary slaughter of a people resolved to resist a wicked policy.

The fact that most of the police were southern Catholics, officered though they were by Protestants, only reinforced this conviction.

Battles between loyalists and the police continued to rage all through the summer. Fighting the constabulary became a kind of sport. The journalist Frankfort Moore recorded this conversation:

> 'Who have you there, Bill?'
> 'A policeman.'
> 'Hold on, and let me have a thump at him.'
> 'Git along out of this, and find a policeman for yourself.'

Sectarian mobs clashed ferociously at the brickfields on 13 July; the police killed two rioters with buckshot; a soldier was shot dead on the Shankill; and a Head Constable was mortally wounded. Later in the summer the return of a Sunday school excursion accompanied by an Orange band attracted a stone-throwing mob in Donegall Street. In retaliation, Protestants attacked Catholic children returning from *their* outing the next day. Frankfort Moore was there. He had seen riots in Cape Town, Trafalgar Square and rural Ireland, but, he believed,

> None of the principals in these actions knew anything of strategy, compared with those who engineered the sacking of York Street upon that dark night in August, 1886.... Scarcely a light was to be seen; still I had no difficulty in making out the movements of the dense crowds surging in every direction, and shot after shot I heard above the shouts that suggested something very like Pandemonium. Once or twice I was carried along in the rush of people before a police charge.... I felt that I had learned something of the impotence of every arm except artillery in the case of street fighting.

Thirteen died violently that weekend. On the following Saturday almost all Catholics were driven from the shipyards, and the police, trapped in Dover Street, killed three people as they shot their way to safety. The riots continued until mid-September, when torrents of rain began to fall. As Frankfort Moore observed,

> That rain lasted, as a shower does in Ulster, for three days, and, as a dreadful rascal who had taken part in the campaign told me a long time afterwards, that rain 'took the heart out of the fighting'.

The official death toll was thirty-one, though the actual number killed, according to surgical reports on the riots, was probably around fifty.

Intercommunal violence blighted other Ulster towns, including Derry, Portadown and Ballymena. But these clashes were on a small scale by comparison with those that convulsed Belfast. And yet the official government inquiry on the riots observed that, in normal times, crime in Belfast was lower than in any other comparable urban centre in the United Kingdom. By 1886 Belfast, though still officially designated a town, had become Ireland's largest city. Its prosperity contrasted sharply with that of Dublin, with its limited range of industries and poverty-ridden tenements. Belfast's citizens could compare their condition very favourably with that of tenant farmers and agricultural labourers impoverished by atrocious wet seasons and a protracted agricultural depression. One publication of the time, *The Industries of Ireland*, found that

> Here in these crowded rushing thoroughfares, we find the pulsing heart of a mighty commercial organisation, whose vitality is ever augmenting, and whose influence is already world-wide.

Official recognition that Belfast was a city seemed somewhat overdue.

Episode 201 ~

BELFAST: AN IMPERIAL CITY

On Saturday 13 October 1888 Charles Vane-Tempest-Stewart, sixth Marquis of Londonderry and Lord Lieutenant of Ireland, made a grand state visit to Belfast to give it official recognition as a city. It was somewhat late in the day. In fact Belfast was now Ireland's largest city, and by 1900 it would be, after London and Liverpool, the third most important port in the United Kingdom, at that time the greatest trading state on earth.

This was a city of superlatives. Tall, ornate warehouses in Bedford Street and in Donegall Square signalled that Belfast was the world centre of the linen industry. In 1895 H. O. Lanyon, president of the Belfast Chamber of Commerce, made this estimation based on the previous year's production:

I find the length of yarn produced in the year amounts to about 644,000,000 miles, making a thread that would encircle the world 25,000 times. If it could be used as a telephone wire, it would give us six lines to the sun, and about 380 besides to the moon. The exports of linen in 1894 measured about 156,000,000 yards, which would make a girdle for the earth at the Equator three yards wide, or cover an area of 32,000 acres, or it would reach from end to end of the County of Down, one mile wide.

The York Street Flax Spinning and Weaving Company, the largest of its kind in the world, sold fronting linens, interlinings, sheets, printed dress linens and lawns, damask tablecloths and napkins, glass cloths, elastic canvas, drills, ducks, hollands, cambrics, and a great range of handkerchiefs, and clothing for Latin America described as 'Creas, Platillas, Bretanas, Silesias, Irlandas etc.'

Skilled men who had served apprenticeships could earn as much as three times the wages of mill workers and so-called 'unskilled' labourers. Some sought employment in engineering works making linen machinery, including Mackies, the largest such enterprise in the world. Most found work in the shipyards. Harland & Wolff had become the greatest shipyard in the world, launching the largest vessels on earth.

Immense crowds gathered adjacent to Queen's Island on 14 January 1899 to watch the launch of a great liner, the *Oceanic*. This vessel had been ordered by the White Star Line as a competitor to rival North German Lloyd's *Kaiser Wilhelm der Grosse* and Cunard's *Campania* and *Lucania* in the lucrative transatlantic passenger market. Two guns gave the signal to the shipwrights to stand aside, the general manager waved the launch flag, and—released by a hydraulic trigger—the *Oceanic* began to move. As the great vessel slid down, the Dublin-based *Freeman's Journal* reported:

> Pieces of timber as large almost as forest trees rose into the air like chips in a wind and fell in showers on the water. Presently the great hawsers, which held the two immense bow chains in sections, began to break and fly in the air.

Then the ship settled, the *Belfast News-Letter* observed, 'like a gull alighting with graceful curve on the water'.

Thirteen feet longer than Brunel's *Great Eastern*, the *Oceanic* was the mightiest ship afloat and the largest man-made moving object ever constructed up to that time anywhere in the world. Close by, Workman Clark, known affectionately as the 'wee yard', specialised in building refrigerated and whaling vessels, but it too on several occasions launched massive liners.

By the end of the nineteenth century Belfast also had the largest tobacco factory, tea-machinery and fan-making works, handkerchief factory, coloured Christmas card printing firm, dry dock and spiral-guided gasometer in the world. The city was also a world centre for the manufacture of fizzy drinks, or, as they were then called, aerated waters. This was an extraordinary achievement, considering that the water was obtained by boring artesian wells through the foul sleech of Cromac.

The products of Cantrell & Cochrane, the biggest aerated waters factory in the world, included: Aromatic Ginger Ale, Fruit Flavoured Lemonade, Sparkling Montserrat, Club Soda and Refreshing Seltzer, Kali and Lithia Waters. One of the firm's advertisements declared:

> The popping of Cantrell and Cochrane's corks is heard in the bungalows of the British cantonment in the Far East, and its sparkle is familiar to the Vice-Regal entourage up in the hot season refuge of the Anglo-Indians at Simla. Dons and seignorinas quaff this liquid boon in the tropical climes of South America; the West Indies welcome it as a treasure; Afric's 'sunny fountains' are out-rivalled in their very habitat by its gleam; the Antipodes have taken this gift of the Mother Empire with gratitude.

Nowhere else in Ireland had enjoyed such economic success under the Act of Union. Three-quarters of Belfast's population was Protestant, utterly opposed to Home Rule. But three-quarters of Ireland's population as a whole was Catholic, ever more determined that the island should have a parliament of its own in Dublin.

Episode 202 ⌒

COMMITTEE ROOM 15

On 2 May 1888 Mary Gladstone, daughter of the Liberal Party leader, watched in admiration as Charles Stewart Parnell skilfully parried questions put to him by the most distinguished lawyers in the state. She recorded in her diary:

> Parnell before Commission. Attorney-General's manner odious in cross-examination. Insolent, ungentlemanlike, treating Parnell like dirt. He [Parnell] really exhibited all the fruits of the Spirit.... His personality takes hold of one, the refined delicate face, illuminating smile, fire-darting eyes, slightly tall figure.

The Conservative government had appointed a special commission of three judges to investigate charges made in *The Times* that Parnell, leader of the Irish Parliamentary Party, had approved of the murders in Dublin's Phoenix Park in 1882. In a blaze of publicity, the commission sat no fewer than 128 times, examined 445 witnesses and asked 150,000 questions. Then in February 1890 Parnell triumphed: the letters supposed to have been written by him were found to be forgeries. The forger, Richard Pigott, fled to Spain and, in a Madrid hotel room, shot himself.

Parnell was now at the height of his power and influence. Known widely as 'the Uncrowned King of Ireland', he had created the most disciplined party ever to sit at Westminster; he had persuaded the Liberal Party to champion Irish Home Rule; and now he had humiliated his Conservative detractors. But there was a dark cloud on the horizon.

On Christmas Eve 1889 Parnell had been served with papers naming him as co-respondent in a suit for divorce filed by Captain William O'Shea. Indeed, for the past eight years Parnell had been in a relationship with O'Shea's English wife, Katharine. He had fathered three of her children, two of whom survived. O'Shea, though not a convinced Home Ruler, had been foisted by Parnell on the constituents of Co. Galway in 1886. But this had not been enough to placate the captain.

At first Irish Party MPs seemed unconcerned, and they re-elected Parnell as their leader. But the divorce trial revealed unedifying details: how Parnell had adopted false names, disguised himself, and shinned down fire-escapes in efforts to conceal his relationship. Mary Gladstone now changed her opinion of the Uncrowned King: '... and he had lived the life of lies all these years! A heartbreaking revelation! Blot out his name!' Her eighty-year-old father,

W. E. Gladstone, observed that he had known eleven Prime Ministers and that every single one of them had been an adulterer. But he had to listen to the Nonconformists, the core support of the Liberal Party he led. The *Methodist Times* declared that if the Irish kept Parnell as leader, they would be branded as 'an obscene race utterly unfit for anything except a military dictatorship'.

Gladstone allowed a letter he had written to the Irish Party to be published. In it he observed of Parnell: 'His continuance at the present moment in the leadership ... would render my retention of the leadership of the Liberal Party ... almost a nullity.' Meanwhile Archbishop Croke of Cashel wrote in angry despair: 'I have flung him away from me forever. His bust which for some time has held a prominent place in my hall I threw out yesterday.' But the Catholic hierarchy for the present hesitated to make public condemnation. It was Gladstone's letter which persuaded thirty-one Irish MPs to call a special meeting of their party. After all, without Gladstone as leader, the Liberals might drop the demand for Home Rule.

The Irish Party gathered round the huge horseshoe table in Committee Room 15 at Westminster on 1 December 1890. Parnell saw with dismay that a team of shorthand reporters from the *Freeman's Journal* were there with pencils poised. For six days Parnell, sitting in the chair, defended himself tenaciously. Tempers flared. One MP shouted: 'Crucify him!'

At one point it was feared that Parnell would produce a revolver from his pocket to shoot his ablest critic, Timothy Healy. Healy declared that Parnell's power had completely gone: 'Place an iron bar in a coil and the bar becomes magnetised. The party was that electric coil, there stood the iron bar. The electricity is gone and the magnetism with it.' When Parnell's supporter John Redmond observed that Gladstone was now master of the party, Healy hissed venomously: 'Who is to be the mistress of the party?' His face contorted with emotion, Parnell rose and held his clenched fist inches from Healy's face, declaring: 'Better appeal ... Better appeal to that cowardly little scoundrel there who dares in an assembly of Irishmen to insult a woman.'

That Saturday afternoon in Committee Room 15, on 6 December 1890, Parnell's fate was sealed. Forty-five MPs withdrew, leaving Parnell with only twenty-eight supporters. The party he had built was sundered. It would remain shattered for years to come. And as for Parnell, he had less than a year to live.

Episode 203 ~

'KEEP OUR NOBLE KINGDOM WHOLE'

Ousted as leader of the Irish Parliamentary Party, Charles Stewart Parnell refused to accept his fate. He returned to Dublin on 9 December 1890, and here in the Rotunda a huge audience assembled to greet him. One young woman remembered:

> Everywhere around there was a sea of passionate faces, loving, admiring, almost worshipping that silent, pale man. The cheering broke out again and again; there was no quelling it. Parnell bowed from side to side, sweeping the assemblage with his eagle glance.

Next morning a crowd in O'Connell Street rushed towards the offices of the *United Irishman*, now held by Parnell's opponents. Suddenly a carriage sped to the scene, stopping so suddenly that the horse collapsed on the road. Parnell leaped out, his eyes blazing, and smashed open the door with a crowbar to seize back control of the newspaper.

But Dublin was not Ireland, and Parnell was immediately put to the test in the North Kilkenny by-election. Everywhere, because of his liaison with Katharine O'Shea, he was denounced as an adulterer. An English journalist observed:

> It was no longer the dignified, self-possessed Charles Stewart Parnell of old.... Mr Parnell's face was thinner than I had ever seen it. The lustre of the eyes was gone.... The 'Uncrowned King' is breaking down.

At Castlecomer local coalminers threw lime into his eyes. When the votes were counted, the anti-Parnellite candidate had won handsomely. Further defeats were to follow. His cause was lost.

On 25 June 1891 Parnell married Katharine before a registrar in Sussex. For years he had begun letters to her with the words 'My own Wifie' and signed them 'Your own Husband'; now she was, indeed, his wife—but not for long. He returned to campaign indefatigably in Ireland.

Clearly unwell, he returned to Sussex. He took to his bed on the evening of 6 October. 'Kiss me, sweet Wifie, and I will try to sleep a little,' he said. They were the last words he uttered. During the night coronary thrombosis struck. He was only forty-five years old.

The rift between the Parnellites and the anti-Parnellites was not healed by his death. As the general election of 1892 approached, the two wings of the Irish Party clashed bitterly. The Catholic Church had by now thrown its weight behind the anti-Parnellites. The parish priest of Roundwood, Co. Wicklow, did not mince his words:

> Parnellism is a simple love of adultery and all those who profess Parnellism profess to love and admire adultery. They are an adulterous set, their leaders are open and avowed adulterers, and therefore I say to you, as parish priest, beware of these Parnellites when they enter your house, you that have wives and daughters, for they will do all they can to commit these adulteries, for their cause is not patriotism—it is adultery—and they back Parnellism because it gratifies their adultery.

Meanwhile Gladstone, the Liberal leader, now aged eighty-two, once more declared that, if his party defeated the Conservative government, he would bring forward a Home Rule Bill. This galvanised the Ulster Unionists. Determined to erase the memory of the vicious rioting which had so besmirched the opposition to the First Home Rule Bill in 1886, Unionist leaders planned a dignified demonstration.

This time 12,000 delegates were to meet indoors on the plains of Stranmillis in Belfast in a huge specially constructed convention hall on Friday 17 June 1892. Delegates had a choice of twenty-four doors and eight aisles by which they could reach their numbered seats. There they could read mottoes round the hall, including 'In union is our strength and freedom', 'Keep our noble kingdom whole' and (perhaps surprisingly) the slogan of the 1798 rebels, 'Erin go Bragh' (Ireland Forever). The *Northern Whig* declared: 'There were the rugged strength and energy of the North, still Liberal, still Conservative, on his occasion and in this cause they know but one name—that of Unionist.'

The Church of Ireland Archbishop of Armagh, Robert Knox, began the proceedings by asking God to send down 'Thy Holy Spirit to guide our deliberations for the advancement of Thy Glory, the safety of the Throne, and the integrity of the Empire'. Then, led by a male-voice choir, all sang the versified Psalm 46: 'God is our refuge and our strength'.

The Liberal Unionist Thomas Sinclair gave the most effective speech:

> Cost what it may, we will have nothing to do with a Dublin parliament (*loud cheers*). If it be ever set up, we shall simply ignore its existence (*tremendous cheering*).... If Mr Gladstone, in mad wantonness, can induce parliament to pass it into law, Ulstermen will be idiots, if they do not utterly repudiate it (*loud applause*).

Gladstone won the election. And he was indeed determined to induce parliament to pass his Second Home Rule Bill into law.

Episode 204 ❧

THE SECOND HOME RULE BILL

The general election of July 1892 delivered a crippling blow to those who remained faithful to the memory of their former leader, Parnell. Only nine Parnellites, led by John Redmond, were elected, while seventy-one anti-Parnellites, now led by Justin McCarthy, were returned. Nevertheless, the Liberals had been able to form a government, and Gladstone, now re-elected for his fourth term as Prime Minister, drafted a fresh Home Rule Bill to give Ireland a parliament of its own.

No bill in the nineteenth century occupied so much parliamentary time. Fighting the provisions clause by clause, Unionists—as the Conservatives and Liberal dissidents opposed to Home Rule now called themselves—spoke 938 times for a total of almost 153 hours over 82 days. The Liberals and Nationalists, that is, Parnellites and anti-Parnellites, made 459 speeches, lasting over 57 hours in all. In the protracted debates the Parnellites and anti-Parnellites were unable to prevent their bitter quarrel breaking out in public. McCarthy wrote: 'It is all a conflict of jealousies and hates and the national cause is forgotten.... I feel terribly depressed.'

On 28 March 1893 representatives of the Belfast Chamber of Commerce met Gladstone in a vain attempt to persuade him to change his mind. Next day Adam Duffin, the Liberal Unionist MP, wrote to his wife:

Dearest—
    As I expected we did not get much change out of Gladstone yesterday.... The old man was jumping with impatience....
    We shall defeat this conspiracy.... George Clark says the old man is mad & we ought to publish the fact & give no other answer! I say he is bad. He has the look of a bird of prey and the smile of a hyena.

Arthur Balfour, the former Conservative Chief Secretary, came to Belfast, and on 4 April he stood for four hours on a great platform in front of the Linen Hall to watch a march-past of 100,000 loyalists. Thomas McKnight remembered:

Such a display the city had never before seen.... There was one vast sea of heads ... as the various bodies, most of them with bands and banners, filed past. A copy of the Home Rule Bill was burnt publicly and stamped upon amid great cheering.

All this effort notwithstanding, the House of Commons passed the bill by a majority of thirty-four votes on 2 September 1893. The House of Lords was packed when it gave its verdict six days later. It was said that only two Unionist peers were absent without valid excuse—one shooting lions in Somaliland, the other killing rats in Reigate. The Lords threw out the bill by 419 votes to 41. A constitutional crisis should have followed this rejection of the will of the elected representatives of the people. But the Liberals had not the stomach to renew the fight. The Nationalists in turn were too demoralised by their bitter internal quarrels to conduct an effective campaign outside Westminster. As Michael Davitt, the anti-Parnellite MP, put it, 'I feel almost ashamed to go before an educated English audience while we are showing ourselves so unworthy of Home Rule.'

Exhausted and dispirited, Gladstone retired in 1894, replaced by Lord Rosebery. He made it clear that he would not bring forward a new Home Rule Bill. Archbishop Croke of Cashel wrote that 'The hope of attaining a legislature for our country within measurable time is no longer entertained by reasoning men.'

In 1895 the Unionists returned to office. The new Prime Minister, Lord Salisbury, had no doubt that that his government should leave 'Home Rule sleeping the sleep of the unjust'. Salisbury had once told supporters that the Celtic Irish were unsuited to self-government and that democracy

works admirably when it is confined to people who are of Teutonic race.... You would not confide free representative institutions to the Hottentots, for example.

The Conservatives were to be in power without a break for the next ten years. Lord Salisbury had stated firmly that what Ireland needed was twenty years of resolute government. His nephew, Gerald Balfour, who served as Irish Chief Secretary, was determined to provide that. In particular, firm coercive measures suppressed any manifestation of disorder in the countryside. At the same time, Balfour was keen to show that Westminster could govern Ireland well, making a devolved parliament in Dublin unnecessary. Some came to describe this Conservative policy as 'killing Home Rule with kindness'. Actually, since the Nationalists were in disarray, there did not seem to be much Home Rule to kill, and so the kindness could be rationed to no more than what the British electorate considered just.

As the nineteenth century drew to a close, Ireland was remarkably peaceful and calm. One reason for this, undoubtedly, was that so many young Irish men and women siphoned off discontent from the countryside simply by leaving the island altogether.

Episode 205 ᔕ

'THE COUNTRY IS BLEEDING TO DEATH'

> So farewell to my friends and relations,
> Perchance I shall see you no more,
> And when I'm in far distant nations,
> Sure I'll sigh for my dear native shore.

Between 1851 and 1921 two and a half million people emigrated from Ireland. No other country in Europe experienced such an outflow—the rate of emigration from Ireland was triple that of the nearest rivals, Norway, Sweden and Scotland. The census figures showed that a quarter of those aged between the ages of five and twenty-four had left the island for abroad.

This remarkable exodus largely explains why Ireland was the only country in Europe to experience a fall in population in the second half of the nineteenth century and the early twentieth century. The Irish had formed one-third of the United Kingdom's population in 1841; by 1911 the proportion had fallen to one-tenth.

Emigration was highest in areas where there was little alternative employment apart from working on the land. The west consistently provided the highest proportion of emigrants. Living standards had risen remarkably since the Great Famine of the 1840s, in spite of acute destitution during the 1880s. The truth was that opportunities abroad were unrivalled. And the habit of emigration had already become ingrained earlier in the century.

Sons and daughters of farmers dominated the emigrant lists. Unlike all other emigrating peoples from Europe, except the Swedes, as many female Irish emigrated as males. Indeed, the province of Connacht exported more women than men. Those most likely to leave were aged between twenty and twenty-four, not yet married, and ready to enter the labour market.

Irish emigrants left with distinct advantages. Though a high proportion came from Irish-speaking districts, the majority—thanks to the effectiveness of the National Schools—could not only speak English but also read and write in English. By the beginning of the twentieth century nine-tenths of Irish emigrants were literate. National School teachers often helped children to write specimen letters to prospective employers overseas. Irish girls were in strong demand for domestic service in the United States, not least because they could read and write grocery lists.

The most important emigrant port was Cóbh in Cork harbour, then called Queenstown. Leinster emigrants chose Dublin, and those from Ulster left from Derry and Belfast. Few expected to see their departed loved ones again. One Donegal man remembered how 'the shouting, the roaring, and the lamentation of the people on the quays would deafen you'.

Families generally raised the money themselves for the fare, which for a steerage passage across the Atlantic was usually four guineas. Every emigrant felt obliged to send money home by postal order not only to help their parents pay the rent and shopkeepers' bills, but also to fund the fares for younger brothers and sisters to come after them.

For the vast majority, America was the preferred destination. In 1880 Robert Vere O'Brien, a land agent, observed: 'I think they all set towards the west, more or less. In my part of the country I think they have got as many relations in Boston as they have in Clare.'

The United States now applied strict immigration controls. From 1882 onwards convicts, lunatics, idiots and destitutes were excluded. Along with tens of thousands from other parts of Europe, Irish immigrants sailing into New York harbour stood anxiously in lines to undergo medical and other screening checks on Ellis Island. Shipping companies were obliged to take back across the Atlantic those who failed to gain admission.

Views were mixed on the impact of emigration back in Ireland. In evidence to the Dudley Commission in 1908, witnesses bemoaned the departure of the strong and healthy, while 'the delicate bird in every clutch' and 'the cripples and the paralytics' stayed at home. A shopkeeper from Drumcliff, Co. Sligo, concluded:

> As soon as their children reach the adult age, through the scarcity of employment, they join their uncles and aunts and cousins in the United States, one son remaining on the farm; and if the parents do not get him married before they die, he generally sells out and goes too. Thus the country is bleeding to death.

Emigration, simply by reducing the population on the land, did at least ensure a steady increase in the average size of the family farm. And emigrants' remittances assumed a vital role in the Irish economy, particularly in impoverished western districts. A Co. Leitrim curate commented:

We are living on credit, and on the returns from America. Our incomes are microscopic in their smallness.... Wiped out [the farmers] would have been long ago but for American aid.

However, as the twentieth century opened, the Conservative government was to put through revolutionary legislation which, for most farmers, would make the payment of rent a thing of the past.

Episode 206 ∿

KILLING HOME RULE WITH KINDNESS

'Are ye right there, Michael are ye right,
Do you think that we'll be home before the night?'
'We've been so long in startin', that ye couldn't say for sartin.'
'Still, ye might now, Michael, so ye might.'

At Lahinch the sea shines like a jewel,
With joy you are ready to shout,
When the stoker cries out: 'There's no fuel,
And the fire's taytotally out' ...

Percy French, a Board of Works employee from Roscommon who became a hugely popular 'parlour' songwriter, poked fun at the shortcomings of the West Clare Railway. There is no doubt, however, that the extension of the railway network brought about a vast improvement in the quality of life of the Irish people. By 1880 2,370 miles had been opened. The 1890s and early twentieth century saw another surge in railway construction. The Conservative government, in power for most of these years, did something which then would have been unthinkable in other parts of the United Kingdom: it subsidised public transport. The construction of light railways provided much-needed employment and, extending to towns such as Clifden in Connemara and Cahirciveen in Co. Kerry, reached out to remote communities. Local people looked in awe at, for example, the erection of a great viaduct over the estuary at Ballydehob for the Skibbereen to Schull railway in west Cork.

It was now possible to introduce standard time, known as Dublin Mean Time (which was 25 minutes behind Greenwich Mean Time until 1916).

Connected by light rail, places such as Bundoran, Co. Donegal, and Mulranny, Co. Mayo, became popular seaside resorts. Remote rivers and loughs became accessible to English fishermen, now able to alight, for example, from the station at Ballynahinch, Co. Galway, where in 1892 eighty-six men found employment as bailiffs, watchers and gillies. In the far west, lobsters, brought in by currachs and sailing boats known as hookers, glothogues and pookhauns, arrived in creels at railways stations ready to be rushed to the London market.

Railways greatly stimulated the production of eggs. In 1892 seventeen tons of eggs, or 244,800 a week, were loaded onto the Leitrim Railway at Manorhamilton, Dromahair, Glenfarne and Belcoo—a total of some 13 million eggs a year from these four small towns alone.

This was all part of a Conservative policy which has been described as 'constructive Unionism'. It was begun by Chief Secretary Arthur Balfour, who set up the Congested Districts Board in 1891 to provide regeneration in the west. His brother, Gerald, was appointed Chief Secretary in 1895. In that year he explained to his constituents in Leeds: 'The government would, of course, be very glad if they were able by kindness to kill Home Rule.'

The Congested Districts Board, as extended by Gerald Balfour, subsidised local craft industries such as handloom weaving and knitting, improved roads and built new harbours; the pier at Killybegs, Co. Donegal, for example, still bears the inscription 'CDB'. The innovative and resourceful Irish Unionist Sir Horace Plunkett enthusiastically backed Gerald Balfour's schemes. Plunkett had set up co-operative dairies or 'creameries' which greatly improved the collection, quality and marketing of Irish dairy produce—indeed, many are still operating today. Gerald Balfour appointed him head of a new Department of Agriculture and Technical Instruction, which, incidentally, led directly to the construction of major technical colleges in Belfast and Dublin.

Was good money thrown after bad? Some economists think so. And, since the Nationalists were still deeply divided between Parnellites and anti-Parnellites, kindness could be strictly limited, since there wasn't much Home Rule to kill. In any case, the Irish had to pay themselves for these improvements. Indeed, in 1896 a government commission reported that Ireland had been overtaxed since the Act of Union had been implemented in 1801.

Gerald Balfour's most lasting achievement was the introduction of democracy into the Irish countryside. Until his Local Government Act of 1898 rural Ireland had been ruled by grand juries, unelected self-perpetuating bodies composed mainly of local landlords and their relatives. On the eve of their abolition Nationalists held only 47 out of a total of 704 positions on grand juries. Now they were replaced by county councils and urban and rural district councils. The electorate for these new bodies was very large and—for the first time in Ireland—included women. Nothing did more than this major reform of local government to familiarise the Irish people with the working of representative institutions and to strengthen support for democracy in the years to come.

At one stroke Gerald Balfour had destroyed the political power of the old Protestant Ascendancy in the Irish countryside. Nationalists won huge majorities in local elections, and Unionists only just managed to achieve a majority in the province of Ulster. However, it was left to Balfour's successor, George Wyndham, to knock aside the last pillars of the Ascendancy.

Episode 207 ∿

'DE-ANGLICISING THE IRISH PEOPLE'

Parnell's creation, the Irish Parliamentary Party, remained shattered and demoralised in the years following the defeat of the Second Home Rule Bill in 1893. John Dillon, elected leader of the anti-Parnellites in 1896, described the behaviour of two of his fellow-MPs in 1898. One of them 'appeared yesterday in a horrible state of intoxication and voted in the wrong lobby', and another 'has been drunk for several days and was in a most beastly condition while I was moving the adjournment yesterday.... An increasing number of them are pre-pared to throw themselves into oceans of whiskey and into nothing else.'

Just two years later, however, in January 1900, the Irish Party reunited under the leadership of the Parnellite John Redmond. But as long as the Conservatives remained in office there could be no hope of a separate Irish parliament.

A great-grandson of Lord Edward Fitzgerald, George Wyndham seemed to have inherited some of his forebear's revolutionary zeal on taking office as Irish Chief Secretary in November 1900. Mafeking had been relieved in the South African War, the 'Khaki Election' had been won, and the time seemed right to demonstrate to all the benefits of the imperial connection to Ireland. This was an island, Wyndham felt certain, best governed in the manner of a crown colony. He told his mother that Ireland was the 'Cinderella' of the Empire, 'poor and hurt ... but one of the first family'. In a letter to a friend he outlined his hopes for Ireland:

If only we could turn the river of imperialism into this backwater spawned over by obscene reptiles: if one could change these anaemic children into full-blooded men! They are part of the Aryan race.... 'Ireland a nation'. Yes & ah! no.

Wyndham declared his preference for 'surgery' rather than 'medicine'. And surgery he did indeed apply—to the Ascendancy, the landlords of Ireland. Wyndham triumphed over his critics because, for once, Nationalists and Unionists found themselves in agreement. On 2 September 1902 the landowner Captain John Shawe-Taylor wrote to the press inviting landlord and tenant representatives to seek a final solution to the Irish land question. Lord Dunraven chaired a conference which gathered together Unionists, including the Irish Unionist leader, Colonel Edward Saunderson, while John Redmond headed a delegation of Nationalists.

All agreed to recommend that a massive scheme of land purchase be undertaken at once by the government. To Wyndham's delight, a unanimous paean of praise for Dunraven's report from Nationalists, Unionists and the British press forced the government's hand. In 1903 Westminster passed Wyndham's Land Bill. This encouraged landlords to sell entire estates, the immense sum being advanced to the tenants by the Treasury. Tenants were to pay back the government in annuities over sixty-eight and a half years; these annual payments were actually lower than the rents previously demanded.

Wyndham's Land Purchase Act was an immediate success, though it took further legislation in 1909 to compel all landlords to sell. Most landlords were glad to be relieved of their estates. They no longer had the stomach to stand up to impudent and unruly tenants. Happy to pocket lump sums from the Treasury, they kept only their demesnes, many later managed by organisations such as the National Trust, An Taisce, the Irish Georgian Society and the K Club. Others cleared off immediately, never to return.

The land issue virtually dropped out of the Irish Question. In revolutionary France they guillotined the aristocrats; in eastern Europe the landlords fled before the advancing Soviet armies in 1944 and 1945; in Mao's China the landlords faced execution in their tens of thousands; in Ireland landlords, clutching their cheques, disappeared in just a few years with hardly a murmur.

Wyndham despised Ulster Unionists. In 1904 he observed: 'My contact with the Ulster members is like catching an "itch" from park pests.' In that year Wyndham alienated them completely. A plan to give Ireland devolution was being drafted in Dublin Castle. As an Irish Nationalist MP gleefully pointed out, 'devolution' was simply the Latin word for Home Rule. Wyndham denied having seen the devolution proposals. He was lying. He resigned in the spring of 1905, to dissolve rapidly in alcohol thereafter.

Not only Wyndham's career but also the Conservative policy of 'killing Home Rule with kindness' was in ruins. The majority of the Irish had no wish to embrace the imperial dream. They wanted to rule themselves. The resilient strength of Irish national feeling found powerful expression in a lecture given in 1892 by Dr Douglas Hyde, entitled 'The Necessity for De-anglicising the Irish People'. He declared:

I wish to show you that in anglicising ourselves wholesale we have thrown away with a light heart the best claim which we have upon the world's recognition of us as a separate nationality.

His words were to have a powerful impact.

Episode 208 ❧

TWO NATIONS?

Modern nationalism, which could be said to have originated in revolutionary France, sped along rapidly extending railway lines to engulf every part of Europe by the end of the nineteenth century. In the course of that century some nationalities such as the Greeks, Serbs and Romanians won their independence; the Italians united themselves into one kingdom in 1870; and in the following year the Germanic peoples allowed themselves to be conquered into unity by the Prussians. Over much of the rest of the European mainland, however, ancient dynasties held sway over the sprawling empires of Austria-Hungary, Russia and Turkey. The Habsburg, Romanov, Hohenzollern and Ottoman dreams of imperial glory conflicted profoundly with the mounting demand for national self-determination.

As modern communications steadily eroded parochial sentiment, peoples discovered their national identity. Poets and other writers, historians, musicians and artists fed a multiplicity of national passions. Every nationality emphasised its individuality and distinctiveness, generally using language as the badge of identity. Some, such as the Poles, separated by three powerful empires, seemed to yearn in vain for freedom. For others, independence appeared to be just around the corner.

The prospect of national liberation revealed a grave difficulty: nationalities were rarely neatly divided from one another. Often impelled by raw and aggressive racism, peoples in their struggle for freedom competed with each other for the same territory. The Czechs laid claim to Slovakia, on the grounds that it was part of the state originally created by King Wenceslas; but the Magyars also claimed Slovakia as an integral part of the lands of King

Stephen, the first Christian King of Hungary. Few thought of asking the Slovaks what they wanted. The Magyar gentry, who ruled all of the eastern half of the Austro-Hungarian Empire, regarded the Slav peoples who formed a majority there as inferior, subject peoples. The great Hungarian nationalist Lajos Kossuth looked on his people as a master race, describing the Croats as 'not enough for a single meal' and telling the Serbs that 'the sword shall decide between us'. Kossuth neglected to mention that his mother was a Slovak.

Ireland too formed part of a great empire. Indeed, Irishmen had done much to extend British dominions. At the top of the equivalent of the British hit parade of 1900 was 'What do you think of the Irish now?', an acknowledgment of the part played by Irish soldiers in defeating the Boers. But uncomfortably close comparisons can be made with developments in central Europe and the situation in Ireland. A quarter of the country's population was Protestant, and, while still happy to be described as Irish, they looked on themselves as part of one large British family. The *Ulster Journal of Archaeology* ran a series of articles which informed readers that Protestants in Ulster were Anglo-Saxon in race, possessing the inherited virtues of thrift, capacity for hard work and respect for law and order. Using words such as 'staunch' and 'stalwart' to describe themselves, northern Protestants by the beginning of the twentieth century had largely accepted this theory.

Certainly the majority of Ulster Protestants could claim that their ancestors were Scottish and English planters of the seventeenth century. But they tended to overlook the fact that many native Irish, particularly in eastern Ulster, had dropped the 'O' and 'Mac' from their surnames, become Protestants, and intermarried with the colonists. The Evangelical Revival had been far more successful in converting Catholics than the Catholic Church cared to admit. This was a time when Irish was fast being supplanted by English. As surnames were anglicised, translated or given pseudo-translations, the memory of ancestral connection was often lost. Many Donnellys in the Coleraine district became Donaldsons; some Laverys on the eastern shore of Lough Neagh became Armstrongs; many of the McBrin family of Co. Down changed their name to Burns, an Argyll surname; some names were easily confused and amalgamated, such as the Scottish Border surname Kerr and the Irish surname Carr; and the O'Carrolls of Dromore, Co. Down, almost all changed their name to Cardwell.

Three-quarters of the island's inhabitants were Catholic, and almost all saw themselves as part of a distinct nationality, deserving some form of self-government. By the beginning of the twentieth century most Catholic Irish largely accepted Protestants' assumption of racial separateness. They were, after all, emphasising their Celtic and Gaelic origins and laying claim to inherent characteristics such as hospitality, passion and love of poetry. These assumptions overlooked the fact that a great many Irish Catholics had Norman, English and, indeed, planter blood flowing in their veins.

The fact that the peoples of Ireland had become irretrievably blended did not prevent the emergence of the belief that the island was inhabited by two distinct nations. The late nineteenth and early twentieth centuries were to witness a vibrant cultural revival, a fresh and passionate assertion of national identity.

Episode 209 ∿

CULTURAL REVIVAL

On 25 November 1892 Dr Douglas Hyde gave a lecture to the Irish National Literary Society, entitled 'The Necessity for De-anglicising the Irish People'. He concluded:

> I would earnestly appeal to everyone, whether Unionist or Nationalist ... to set his face against the constant running to England for our books, literature, music, games, fashions and ideas. I appeal to everyone ... to help the Irish race to develop in future upon Irish lines ... because upon Irish lines alone can the Irish race once more become what it was of yore—one of the most original, artistic, literary, and charming people of Europe.

Hyde, the son of a Church of Ireland clergyman and brought up among Irish speakers in Co. Roscommon, believed passionately that the Irish people were turning their backs on a unique and glorious heritage and, as a result, losing their claim to a separate identity.

The Great Famine of the 1840s, by starvation, fever and emigration, had dealt a severe blow to the Irish language—whose speakers were, of course, largely drawn from the poorest and most vulnerable classes. The 1851 census showed that the proportion of Irish-speakers had fallen to just over 23 per cent. That proportion had dropped to 14.5 per cent by 1891. The decline had been hastened by the tendency for native speakers to regard the language as a badge of poverty and social inferiority. National Schools taught through English and were not allowed to have Irish on the curriculum until 1878. Catholic clergy were given little encouragement to use Irish when training at St Patrick's College, Maynooth.

Disappointment at the rejection of two Home Rule Bills in 1886 and 1893 helped to galvanise a new generation to restore respect for the language and for a distinctive Irish culture. Hyde provided the inspiration. In 1889 he had written:

If we allow one of the finest and richest languages in Europe, which, fifty years ago, was spoken by nearly four millions of Irishmen, to die without a struggle, it will be an everlasting disgrace and a blighting stigma upon our nationality.

Eoin MacNeill, a native of the Glens of Antrim who had learned Irish in Connemara, agreed. He was largely responsible for the formation of the Gaelic League in July 1893. The organisation declared that its object was 'to keep the Irish language spoken in Ireland'. The new movement was particularly successful in the towns and where Irish had died out. After fifteen years the League had 599 branches spread throughout the island. It failed to arrest the steady decline of the Gaeltacht, the Irish-speaking areas, but the status of the language had been turned around. Dignity had been restored to the Irish language—once denounced by the *Morning Post* as 'kitchen kaffir' and by the *Daily Mail* as a 'barbarous tongue'.

The Gaelic League declared itself to be non-political and non-denominational. There is no denying, however, that the great numbers of mainly young people who met in its branches for the most part had advanced nationalist views. It was through the Gaelic League that future revolutionaries, including Patrick Pearse, Eamon de Valera and Seán T. O'Kelly, acquired their separatist principles. O'Kelly, indeed, joined the Irish Republican Brotherhood and was ordered to use his position in the League to infiltrate its central organising committee with IRB members.

The Gaelic Athletic Association also became a nursery for future republican activists. P. W. Nally, who co-founded the movement with Michael Cusack in 1884, was not only a renowned Co. Mayo athlete but had also had served a term of prison for his political activities. Indeed, at least four of the seven men who attended the inaugural meeting were Fenians. The GAA, set up for 'the preservation and cultivation of the national pastimes of Ireland', was arguably the most popular and enduring product of the Irish cultural revival. Michael Cusack, an Irish-speaker from Co. Clare, gave the organisation a firm foundation based on parishes, counties and provinces, while Maurice Davin, who once held the world hammer-throwing record, drafted rules which won general acceptance. Davin also persuaded Archbishop Croke of Cashel to become the GAA's patron. Its success can be measured by the fact that over most of the island throughout the twentieth century the leading games were hurling and Gaelic football.

The drive to reinforce a separate identity was underscored by the GAA rules banning 'foreign games' (including cricket, rugby and tennis) and excluding members of the crown forces, including the Royal Irish Constabulary. Hyde and MacNeill, however, became increasingly alarmed by a growing tendency of 'Irish-Irelanders' to refuse to accept Protestants as true Irishmen. D. P.

Moran, the acerbic editor of the *Leader*, bluntly stated that the Irish nation was Catholic—if Protestants refused to accept the majority culture, then the only solution was partition, 'leaving the Orangemen and their friends in the north-east corner'.

At the beginning of the twentieth century the establishment of a Dublin parliament seemed but a dream. By 1912 Home Rule appeared to be just round the corner.

Episode 210 ∾

HOME RULE PROMISED

In the momentous general election of 1906 the Liberals won their greatest victory. But their triumph dashed the Irish Parliamentary Party's expectation of Home Rule. The Conservative and Unionist vote crashed so dramatically that Sir Henry Campbell-Bannerman, the new Prime Minister, had no need of Irish Nationalist support. Indeed, one leading Liberal, Herbert Asquith, made it clear in his election address that 'it will be no part of the policy of the new Liberal government to introduce a Home Rule Bill in a new parliament'.

Younger nationalists had become impatient with the party's reliance on the Liberals. Some transferred their allegiance to a new party founded in 1905: Sinn Féin. The name Sinn Féin—which means 'Ourselves'—had been suggested by Máire Butler, Sir Edward Carson's cousin. The party, founded by Arthur Griffith, a Dublin journalist, called on Irish MPs to abstain from Westminster, to set up an assembly in Dublin and use passive resistance to undermine British rule in Ireland. Looking anxiously over his shoulder, the Nationalist MP John Dillon wrote to his leader, John Redmond, in 1908: 'An effort must be made to put some life into the movement. At present it is very much asleep, and Sinn Féiners, Gaelic League, etc., etc., are making great play.'

Little did Dillon know that at that moment, to his party's advantage, the United Kingdom was entering the most dangerous constitutional crisis since the Glorious Revolution of 1688. For three years the House of Lords had been rejecting or emasculating bills sent up from the Commons. Campbell-Bannerman had died in 1908; Asquith had become Prime Minister; and David Lloyd George, the Chancellor of the Exchequer, made ready for a robust struggle with the peers of the realm. As expected, the 'People's Budget', introduced in 1909 to wage, in Lloyd George's words, 'implacable warfare against poverty and squalidness', was haughtily rejected by the Lords. Asquith had no choice but to take the issue to the people.

In the general election of January 1910 the Liberals were so reduced in numbers that they now needed the support of the Irish Party to stay in power. The Lords, with no choice but to accept the budget, then faced a Parliament Bill designed to deny peers the right to reject bills outright. When the Lords threw out this bill, once again the issue could only be solved by an election. The outcome of the election of December 1910 was almost identical to that at the beginning of the year. The Liberal government still needed the Nationalists to stay in office.

In gratitude for the Irish Party's support throughout this crisis, Asquith promised Home Rule. And in 1911 the peers bowed to the inevitable and passed the Parliament Act. Henceforth the Lords could reject bills only for three successive parliamentary sessions—roughly two years. If Asquith kept his promise, Ireland seemed sure to have its own parliament by 1914.

Irish Unionists were horrified. They had chosen Sir Edward Carson as their leader in 1910. One of the most brilliant lawyers of his day, Unionist MP for Trinity College Dublin and a former Conservative minister, Carson had become a household name in 1895 when he brought down the playwright Oscar Wilde. On 23 September 1911 he addressed 50,000 men from Unionist Clubs and Orange lodges at Strandtown in east Belfast:

> With the help of God, you and I joined together ... will yet defeat the most nefarious conspiracy that has ever been hatched against a free people.... We must be prepared ... the morning Home Rule passes, ourselves to become responsible for the government of the Protestant Province of Ulster.

The Conservatives threw caution to the winds and gave full backing to Unionist resistance. Their leader, Andrew Bonar Law, whose father had been a Presbyterian minister in Coleraine, came to Belfast on Easter Tuesday 1912. Seventy special trains brought in 100,000 loyalist demonstrators who, after marching past the platforms at the Balmoral showgrounds, listened to prayers by the Church of Ireland Archbishop of Armagh and the Presbyterian Moderator, and joined in singing Psalm 90. After the unfurling of the largest Union Flag ever woven Bonar Law assured them that they were like their fore-bears besieged in Derry:

> Once more you hold the pass, the pass for the Empire. You are a besieged city. The timid have left you; your Lundys have betrayed you; but you have closed your gates. The Government have erected by their Parliament Act a boom against you to shut you off from the help of the British people. You will burst that boom.

Two days later, on 11 April 1912, Asquith introduced the Home Rule Bill in the Commons. Redmond told the House with evident emotion:

If I may say so reverently, I personally thank God that I have lived to see this day.

Episode 211 ～

THE COVENANT

O God, our help in ages past,
Our hope for years to come,
Our shelter from the stormy blast,
And our eternal home ...

The Ulster Hall, Belfast, Saturday 28 September 1912. The Protestants of Ulster had set aside this day, 'Ulster Day', to show the world their deter-mination—to demonstrate their detestation for the Liberal government's Third Home Rule Bill now before parliament. After prayers and lessons the Presbyterian minister Dr William McKean rose to deliver his sermon. He took as his text a verse from the First Epistle to Timothy: 'Keep that which is committed to thy trust':

We are plain, blunt men.... The Irish Question is at bottom a war against Protestantism; it is an attempt to establish a Roman Catholic ascendancy in Ireland to begin the disintegration of the Empire by securing a second parliament in Dublin.

All over Ulster people emerged from churches and meeting halls to sign 'Ulster's Solemn League and Covenant'. They were pledging themselves

to stand by one another in defending for ourselves and our children our cherished position of equal citizenship in the United Kingdom and in using all means which may be found to defeat the present conspiracy to set up a Home Rule Parliament in Ireland.

At noon prominent Ulster Unionists, led by Sir Edward Carson, walked to the City Hall. Its Portland stone gleamed in the sun. Greeted by the Lord

Mayor, aldermen and councillors in their scarlet and ermine robes, Carson entered the vestibule and advanced towards a circular table directly under the dome. There, with a silver pen, he was the first to sign the Covenant. When he re-emerged, the reverential hum of the vast crowd changed to tempestuous cheering.

At 2.30 p.m. a procession of bands from every Protestant quarter of Belfast converged on the City Hall. All played different tunes simultaneously, producing an extraordinary cacophony. The *Pall Mall Gazette* described the scene:

> Seen from the topmost outside gallery of the dome, the square below, and the streets striking away from it were black with people. Through the mass, with drums and fifes, sashes and banners, the clubs marched all day. The streets surged with cheering.

Bowler-hatted stewards struggled to regulate the flow of men eager to sign. A double row of desks stretching right round the City Hall made it possible for 550 to sign simultaneously. Some signed in their own blood. Signatures were still being affixed after 11 p.m. Women signed their own declaration. Altogether 471,414 men and women who could prove Ulster birth signed either the Covenant or the declaration—over 30,000 more women, in fact, than men.

At 8.30 p.m. a brass band advanced towards the Ulster Club in Castle Place playing 'See the Conquering Hero Comes'. Its staff major and spear-carriers had almost to carve a way through the surging mass to accompany Carson in a waiting motor-brake to the docks. The vehicle was pulled down High Street by hundreds of willing hands. The *Pall Mall Gazette* reported:

> With a roaring hurricane of cheers punctuated on every side by the steady rattle of revolver shots, onward swept this whole city in motion with a tumult that was mad.

At Donegall Quay a fusillade of shots saluted Sir Edward as he stepped aboard the SS *Patriotic*. From the upper deck he shouted out:

> I have very little voice left. I ask you while I am away in England and Scotland and fighting your battle in the Imperial Parliament to keep the old flag flying (*cheers*). And 'No Surrender!' (*loud cheers*).

As the vessel steamed into the Victoria Channel, bonfires in Great Patrick Street sprang into life; a huge fire on the Cave Hill threw a brilliant glare over the sky; fifty other bonfires blazed from hills and headlands around Belfast Lough; and salvos of rockets shot up into the air.

Denounced as 'a silly masquerade' by the *Irish News*, 'an impressive farce' by the *Freeman's Journal*, and by the *Manchester Guardian* as 'anarchic hectoring by the ascendancy party', the signing of the Covenant and the attendant celebrations did show that Ulster Protestants were in earnest.

In fact they were more in earnest than the general public—and, indeed, the government—then realised. As early as November 1910 the inner committee of the Ulster Unionist Council secretly sought a quotation from a German arms manufacturer for 20,000 rifles and a million rounds of ammunition. In March 1911 the UUC, including Carson himself, voted its first cash allocation for the buying of rifles. Carson urged the Council's inner circle: 'I am convinced that unless a steady supply is started, we will be caught like rats in a trap.'

The gun was returning to Irish politics. Meanwhile the Nationalist camp was being severely dislocated by the outbreak of a fierce class struggle in Dublin.

Episode 212 ∿

THE GREAT DUBLIN LOCK-OUT

Dublin, once the second city of the Empire, had struggled to prosper under the Union. Apart from Guinness's Brewery and Jacob's biscuit factory, it had failed to acquire industries of any size. And by the start of the twentieth century doctors, lawyers, public servants and other members of the middle classes, commuting by electric tram, had moved out to the suburbs. The once elegant Georgian terraces they left behind decayed to become shabby tenements rented out room by room to the families of the poor.

The majority of the men made a meagre living as casual labourers, carters and dockers. Women earned pittances as domestic servants and washerwomen, or became prostitutes seeking business from the many soldiers stationed in the city. Disease flourished in the crowded, damp and draughty tenements. Dublin's death rate was the highest in the United Kingdom.

Labour unrest over much of Europe spilled over into Ireland. Jim Larkin, a union leader from Liverpool, led a great dock strike in Belfast in 1907. He then moved to Dublin where he founded the Irish Transport and General Workers' Union. The leading figure in the Dublin Employers' Federation, William Martin Murphy, set out to smash Larkin's union. Owner of the Dublin tramways, the *Irish Independent* newspaper and much else besides, Murphy began by offering his employees a stark choice: leave the ITGWU or lose your jobs. On 21 August 1913 he dismissed a hundred men.

This action was regarded by the trade unionists as a 'lock-out'. Given courage by Murphy, other employers also locked out their workers. A titanic class struggle had begun. Larkin called all the tramway workers out on strike on 26 August. As the future playwright Seán O'Casey remembered, 'While all Dublin was harnessing itself into its best for the Horse Show, the trams suddenly stopped. Drivers and conductors left them standing wherever they happened to be.... They came out bravely, marching steadily towards hunger, harm and hostility.'

Every night Larkin stiffened the resolve of the workers by his fiery oratory. Countess Markievicz recalled:

Listening to Larkin, I realised that I was in the presence of something that I had never come across before, some great primeval force, rather than a man. A tornado, a storm-driven wave, the rush into life of spring and the blasting breath of autumn, all seemed to emanate from the power that spoke.

The authorities banned a meeting in O'Connell Street fixed for Sunday 31 August. But on the afternoon of that day Larkin, wearing Count Markievicz's frock coat, evaded the watching police and entered the Imperial Hotel opposite Nelson Pillar—a hotel owned, incidentally, by Murphy. Ernie O'Malley was there and described what happened next:

Jim Larkin, to keep a promise, appeared on the balcony of the hotel, wearing a beard as a disguise. He spoke amidst cheers, and hoots for the employers. Police swept down from many quarters, hemmed in the crowd, and used their heavy batons.... I saw women knocked down and kicked.... I could hear the crunch as the heavy sticks struck unprotected skulls.

Heavy-handed action by the police, who killed one man, resulted in a special government inquiry. The dispute paralysed the city. Murphy now had 404 employers behind him.

The strikers and their families were starving. British trade unionists sent a steamship every week loaded with food. Better-off sympathisers helped to run soup kitchens. George Russell, the writer from Portadown who signed himself 'Æ', fired off an angry letter to the newspapers:

It remained for the twentieth century and the capital city of Ireland to see four hundred masters deciding openly upon starving one hundred thousand people, and refusing to consider any solution except that fixed by their pride....

You may succeed in your policy and ensure your own damnation by your victory. The men whose manhood you have broken will loathe you, and will always be brooding and scheming to strike a fresh blow. The children will be taught to curse you. The infant being moulded in the womb will have breathed into its starved body the vitality of hate. It is not they— it is you who are blind Samsons pulling down the pillars of the social order.

As the lock-out continued the leaders decided to send some of the starving children to be cared for a time by families in Liverpool. The Archbishop of Dublin objected that the children might be sent to homes which were not Catholic: 'The Dublin women now subjected to this cruel temptation to part with their helpless offspring ... can be no longer held worthy of the name of Catholic mothers.'

Touring England, Larkin failed to get the sympathetic strikes he needed to win. On 18 January 1914 the Union advised the men to return to work. Larkin declared: 'We are beaten. We make no bones about it.'

Meanwhile, throughout this labour dispute—in effect a struggle within the nationalist camp—the issue of Home Rule never dropped out of sight.

Episode 213 ᴄ

THE CURRAGH 'MUTINY'

'Traitor!', roared Sir William Bull across the floor of the House of Commons. Prime Minister Herbert Asquith had just made it clear that Home Rule would be pushed through the Commons by the guillotine. That day, 13 November 1912, tempers flared. Conservative and Unionist MPs chanted: 'Resign! Resign!... Civil war! Civil war!' Ulsterman Ronald McNeill, MP for East Kent, hurled a bound copy of the Standing Orders at Home Secretary Winston Churchill, striking him on the head. Nevertheless, early in 1913 the bill passed the Commons.

Ulster Unionists had pledged themselves to use 'all means which may be found necessary' to stop Home Rule. 'All means' included the formation of the Ulster Volunteer Force in January 1913. By the end of the year the UVF had grown to 90,000 men—and this did not include the Motor Car Corps, the Signalling and Dispatch Rider Corps, the Ballymena Horse, the Medical Corps and the Nursing Corps. In Dublin Patrick Pearse, headmaster of St Enda's boys' school, declared: 'Personally I think the Orangeman with a rifle is a much less ridiculous figure than the nationalist without a rifle.' The Irish history professor Eoin MacNeill agreed, and presided over a crowded meeting in the Rotunda concert hall in Dublin on 25 November 1913. There it was agreed to form the Irish Volunteers. What were these Volunteers for? The stated object was somewhat vague: 'to secure and maintain the rights and liberties common to all the people of Ireland'.

We now know that no fewer than twelve out of thirty men on the Irish Volunteers' executive were members of the secret Irish Republican Brotherhood, dedicated to armed rebellion. Tom Clarke, an IRB ex-convict, wrote enthusiastically from Dublin to Joe McGarrity, the Clan na Gael leader in Philadelphia:

> Joe, it is worth living in Ireland these times—there is an awakening.... Wait till they get their first clutching the steel barrel of a business rifle and then Irish instincts and Irish manhood can be relied upon.

In fact there were few enough rifles as yet for the Volunteers to clutch.

Meanwhile Asquith desperately sought a resolution. In 1912 one of his Liberal backbenchers, T. C. Agar-Robartes, had moved an amendment to the Home Rule Bill to exclude from its operation the four most Protestant counties in Ulster, saying: 'I have never heard that orange bitters will mix with Irish whiskey.' But his amendment had been decisively rejected. Now Asquith and his cabinet drafted a variety of partition proposals. John Redmond, leader of the Irish Party, responded: 'Irish nationalists can never be the assenting parties to the mutilation of the Irish nation.... The two nation theory is to us an abomination and a blasphemy.' But Redmond did support Asquith's amendment allowing each Ulster county to opt out of Home Rule for six years. Then Sir Edward Carson, the Unionist leader, let him off the hook: 'We do not want sentence of death with a stay of execution for six years.'

That was on 9 March 1914. Ten days later Carson challenged the government to 'come and try conclusions with us in Ulster.... I am off to Belfast.... I go to my people.'

Carson had gone to set up a Provisional Government of Ulster. Asquith felt he had to take decisive action to prevent the UVF seizing control of the province. Winston Churchill, now First Lord of the Admiralty, ordered a naval cordon into position: two light cruisers to Belfast Lough, and seven battleships and eight destroyers to the Clyde. Colonel John Seely, the War Minister, rushed troops northwards.

Then fifty-eight cavalry officers at the Curragh army camp in Co. Kildare announced that they would prefer to be dismissed rather than lead their men against Ulster loyalists. The War Minister appeared to cave in to this so-called 'mutiny': he gave the officers a written assurance that the government did not intend to crush political opposition in the north. Asquith dismissed Seely, but it was too late. Fully alerted, the UVF moved its headquarters to a heavily sandbagged position at Captain James Craig's home, 'Craigavon', in east Belfast.

Meanwhile barges steamed from Hamburg eastwards along the newly constructed Kiel Canal to Danish waters in the Baltic. Here in great secrecy Major Fred Crawford, on behalf of the UVF, prepared to take on board 24,000 modern rifles and 5 million rounds of ammunition. Then he steamed out in a gale into the North Sea. To avoid recognition, in the dark he transferred the 216 tons of arms to a coal-boat, the SS *Clydevalley*, off the coast of Wexford on 19 April. As Crawford approached Ulster, members of the UVF Motor Car Corps received a momentous order:

> Your car should arrive at Larne in the night of Friday–Saturday 24th–25th instant *at 1 a.m. punctually but not before that hour* for a very secret and important duty.

Episode 214 ❧

TO THE BRINK OF CIVIL WAR

During the small hours of Saturday morning 25 April 1914 members of the Ulster Volunteer Force unloaded from the SS *Clydevalley* 216 tons of modern rifles and ammunition at Larne, Bangor and Donaghadee. There was no interference: the authorities futilely directed their attention to a decoy ship, the SS *Balmerino*, in Belfast Lough. Motor-cars sped through the night distributing the arms to prepared dumps all over Ulster. It was the first significant use of the internal combustion engine in military history.

An Englishman, Captain Wilfrid Spender, played a key role in the operation. His wife Lilian recorded in her diary:

> W. had told me he would have to be away that night ... seeing after the big Test Mobilisation ... which was being kept a profound secret until the last moment.... His post was to be at Musgrave Channel, assisting at the Hoax which took in all the Customs officers, & kept them occupied all night, watching the *Balmerino* which of course contained nothing but coal!
>
> I was anxious, & we occupied ourselves as best we could, by catechising one another in First Aid & Home Nursing.

The gun had returned centre-stage to Irish politics. The UVF, now impressively armed, unwittingly did much to revitalise militant separatism. The Irish

Republican Brotherhood, almost defunct at the beginning of the century, recruited a new generation of activists. The Irish Party leader, John Redmond, suspected that republican militants were in control of the Irish Volunteers. He insisted on taking over control of the Volunteers in June 1914, but the IRB were not so easily pushed aside.

If the UVF could arm themselves without retribution, then why not the Irish Volunteers? Erskine Childers, a former clerk of the House of Commons who had written the first modern thriller, *The Riddle of the Sands*, passionately supported Home Rule. An expert sailor, he and the journalist Darrell Figgis took the yacht *Asgard* to Hamburg. There he bought a consignment of 1,500 Mauser rifles; almost antiques, these single-shot weapons, loaded with black powder cartridges, were nevertheless deadly.

On 26 July 1914, in a blaze of publicity, the *Asgard* steered into Howth harbour, just north of Dublin. Some Volunteers openly shouldered rifles on the road. Soldiers made ineffective attempts to disarm them. Returning to Dublin, the troops responded to taunts and stones from a hostile crowd at Bachelor's Walk by opening fire. Four people were killed and thirty-eight wounded. The impression that nationalists and unionists were being treated differently had been viciously reinforced.

Meanwhile Prime Minister Herbert Asquith faced a bewildering array of problems: suffragettes on hunger strike in prison; a threatened general strike; and the assassination of Archduke Franz Ferdinand in Sarajevo. But Ireland, Asquith was certain, was the most intractable problem.

Asquith might refer to his own 'masterly inactivity' and the merits of his policy of 'wait and see', but actually he did not know what to do. Then King George V stepped in. He called an all-party conference on Asquith's Home Rule Bill at Buckingham Palace on 21 July. In his opening address he said:

> For months we have watched with deep misgivings the course of events in Ireland ... and today the cry of civil war is on the lips of the most responsible and sober-minded of my people.... To me it is unthinkable ... that we should be brought to the brink of fratricidal strife upon issues apparently so capable of adjustment ... if handled in a spirit of generous compromise.

According to Winston Churchill, the conference 'toiled round the muddy byways of Fermanagh and Tyrone', but there was no spirit of generous compromise, and the talks broke down. Sir Edward Carson certainly thought that civil war was unavoidable: 'I see no hopes of peace. I see nothing at present but darkness and shadows.... We shall have once more to assert the manhood of our race.'

But it was not to be in Ireland but in France that the manhood of both the Ulster Volunteers and the Irish Volunteers would be asserted. The generals of the German and the Austro-Hungarian armies were wrong to think that England would be paralysed by civil war in Ireland. On 3 August 1914 German troops began to pour across the Belgian border. That night John Redmond rose to his feet in the House of Commons:

> I say to the government that they may tomorrow withdraw every one of their troops from Ireland.... The armed Catholics in the South will only be too glad to join arms with the armed Protestant Ulstermen.

No wonder the Foreign Secretary, Sir Edward Grey, replied with profound relief: 'The one bright spot in the very dreadful situation is Ireland.'

Men of both the Ulster Volunteer Force and the Irish Volunteers would fight and die together on the same side in what quickly became known as the Great War.

Episode 215 ⁓

'FAITHFUL TO ERIN, WE ANSWER HER CALL!'

On 3 August 1914 the German army swept into neutral Belgium. Next day the United Kingdom of Great Britain and Ireland was at war. Redmond's face adorned a recruiting poster which exhorted:

> Your first duty is to take your part in ending the war. Join an Irish regiment to-day.

Carson sent a similar message in a telegram to members of the UVF:

> All officers, non-commissioned officers and men who are in the Ulster Volunteer Force ... are requested to answer immediately His Majesty's call, as our first duty as loyal subjects is to the King.

Recruiting posters festooned gable walls and hoardings:

> Fight for Ireland! Remember Belgium!

> Have YOU any women-folk worth defending? Remember the Women of Belgium. JOIN TO-DAY.

I'll go too! The real Irish spirit!

THE CALL TO ARMS : IRISHMEN DON'T YOU HEAR IT?

Daddy—What did you do in the war?

On one poster entitled 'For the Glory of Ireland' an Irish colleen, holding a rifle and pointing towards Belgium in flames, asks a young man with a shillelagh under his arm: 'Will you go or must I?' And a postcard was issued which showed a child declaring: 'I'm going to kill *all* the Germans and make sausages out of them!'

One of the best-known songs of the Great War featured an Irish county:

> It's a long way to Tipperary,
> It's a long way to go ...

—but it was a long way *from* Tipperary to the killing fields of Flanders. A massive recruiting drive was launched throughout Ireland, and during August 1914 men of the Irish National Volunteers and the Ulster Volunteers, who so recently seemed about to fight each other, now rushed forward to take the king's shilling. In Belfast the *Irish News* published this verse:

> Bless the good fortune which brings us together,
> Rich men and poor men, short men and tall;
> Some from the seaside and some from the heather,
> Townsmen and countrymen, Irishmen all;
> Faithful to Erin, we answer her call!

The same newspaper carried this report on 10 August:

TYRONE'S FINE EXAMPLE
NATIONAL AND ULSTER VOLUNTEERS MARCH TOGETHER
ROUSING SCENES

The Ulster Volunteers and Irish National Volunteers united at Omagh on Friday night in giving a most hearty send-off to the final draft of the Army Reserve of the Royal Inniskillings, who left the town about half-past nine o'clock, and a scene of an unparalleled description was witnessed when the procession of both bodies of Volunteers and military marched through the town together.... Subsequently, as both bodies of Volunteers paraded the town, they met one another and respectfully saluted.

Sir Edward Carson, the Unionist leader, declared: 'England's difficulty is not Ulster's opportunity.... We do not seek to purchase terms by selling our patriotism.'

The new Secretary for War, Lord Kitchener, testily remarked that he did not 'trust one single Irishman with a rifle in his hands one single yard', but he quickly changed his mind and announced: 'I want the Ulster Volunteers.'

Carson never liked Kitchener and had been heard to describe him as 'that great stuffed oaf', but he called on Kitchener at the War Office. The interview began badly. Kitchener asked: 'Surely you are not going to hold out for Tyrone and Fermanagh?' Carson snapped back: 'You're a damned clever fellow telling me what I ought to be doing.'

Nevertheless, Carson offered the services of the Ulster Volunteer Force without conditions, and, to his surprise, Kitchener agreed to keep the UVF together, with its command structure virtually intact, in one division—the 36th (Ulster) Division. The problem was that Kitchener—a blimpish member of the Irish landlord class with almost no political acumen—refused to create a separate division for Irish nationalists.

Redmond had already pledged the support of the Irish National Volunteers in the defence of Ireland. On 20 September 1914 he went further. In a speech to his Volunteers at Woodenbridge, Co. Wicklow, he said:

> I say to you—Go on drilling and make yourselves efficient for the work, and then account yourselves as men, not only for Ireland itself, but wher- ever the fighting line extends, in defence of right, of freedom and religion in this war (*cheers*).

This was too much for some of the Volunteers. They might be prepared to defend Ireland, but they would not fight outside the country for the British Empire. Led by Eoin MacNeill, they left the National Volunteers to form their own organisation, which resumed its original title, the Irish Volunteers. Only 11,000 followed MacNeill; the remaining 170,000 volunteers remained loyal to Redmond and to Irish participation in the war.

By early 1916 at least 210,000 Irishmen had joined up. One-third of those in the UVF enlisted. Although Ulster supplied just above half the recruits for the island, 57 per cent of recruits from Ireland as a whole were Catholic. In the Belfast–Antrim area Catholics were actually more likely to take the king's shilling than their Protestant neighbours.

Nearly 28,000 men—and, indeed, boys—who had joined up in Ireland were never to return.

Episode 216 ～

THE CONSPIRATORS PREPARE

In September 1914, after a hard day, Prime Minister Herbert Asquith opened his diary and lifted his pen:

> The Irish on both sides are giving me a lot of trouble just at a difficult moment.... I sometimes wish we could submerge the whole lot of them and their island for say, ten years, under the waves of the Atlantic.

The Great War was a month old. Irish Home Rule had to be pushed off centre-stage where it had been for so long. What would be his interim solution? Asquith announced it on 18 September. He had already told the Commons that the UVF's patriotic spirit had made the coercion of Ulster 'unthinkable'. Now he declared that the Home Rule Bill would become law, though it would not be implemented until after the war. The Irish Party MPs cheered and chanted and waved a green flag in the Commons. Carefully avoiding details, Asquith added that, later on, he would make special provision for Ulster. The Conservative opposition leader, Andrew Bonar Law, made a speech so vitriolic in denunciation that, as Asquith explained in his diary, he and his fellow government ministers left while he was still speaking 'lest they should be unable to overcome their impulse to throw books, paper-knives, and other handy missiles at his head'.

At that stage Asquith, along with most of the general public, expected the war to be over by Christmas. But as the months rolled by the earlier war of movement congealed into a bloody and inconclusive slogging match in the trenches. In a vain Allied attempt to break the deadlock at Gallipoli, southern Irishmen of the 10th Division fell in their thousands at Suvla Bay in August 1915.

Protected by the Royal Navy and far out of range of Zeppelins, the farms, mills, workshops and shipyards of Ireland strove to meet the insatiable demands of the Allied war effort. Never before had the Irish people been so prosperous. Rarely had Ireland known such peace at home.

Very soon after the outbreak of war the Irish Republican Brotherhood had decided on rebellion. Sir Roger Casement, in America when the war broke out, took the advice of the Clan na Gael leader, John Devoy, and called on the German ambassador in Washington. Casement, a Co. Antrim Protestant knighted for his services as an imperial consul, soon after was in Berlin urging Chancellor Bethmann-Hollweg to send German arms to ensure the republican rebels' success.

On 1 August 1915 Patrick Pearse, son of an English stonemason and an Irish mother, and now headmaster of St Enda's School, stood in Dublin's Glasnevin cemetery. There he spoke at the graveside of Jeremiah O'Donovan Rossa, a founder member of the IRB:

> Life springs from death; and from the graves of patriot men and women spring living nations. The Defenders of this Realm have worked well in secret and in the open. They think that they have pacified Ireland. They think that they have purchased half of us and intimidated the other half. They think that they have foreseen everything, think that they have provided against everything; but the fools, the fools, the fools!—they have left us our Fenian dead, and while Ireland holds these graves, Ireland unfree shall never be at peace.

Pearse was the propagandist, the front man. Behind him were the real organisers of revolution: Tom Clarke, a Dungannon-born IRB ex-convict; Seán MacDermott, a Leitrim farmer's son who had been a tram-driver in Belfast; and Joseph Mary Plunkett, the sickly son of a papal count from Kimmage in Dublin. Plunkett and Casement between them convinced the Kaiser's government to send arms to Ireland.

On 17 March 1916 a meeting of the German naval high command took place in Berlin. The decision was taken to send to Ireland a vessel loaded with 20,000 rifles and a million rounds of ammunition. The minutes of the meeting record:

> The enterprise does not seem to be without hope. Even if the English succeeded in suppressing the rebellion quickly ... we can still count on a strong moral effect.... The attempt must be made to fulfil the urgent wish of the General Staff ... that a substantial force will be tied up in Ireland, far from the European mainland.

In accordance with this decision, Captain Karl Spindler, commanding the *Aud*, disguised as a neutral tramp steamer, sailed into Tralee Bay on 20 April 1916. But there was a problem: thanks to Russian co-operation, the British Admiralty had cracked the German radio codes. Vigilant Royal Navy sloops cornered the *Aud*, and after it had been brought into Cork harbour Spindler scuttled his vessel with all its arms.

Meanwhile Casement, brought to Banna strand in Co. Kerry by U-boat, was within a short time arrested and sent to Dublin, where he was identified. The prospects for a successful rebellion were diminishing with every day that passed.

Episode 217 ～

'WE'RE GOING TO BE SLAUGHTERED'

James Connolly had developed his revolutionary socialist views during a grim upbringing in working-class Edinburgh. In 1916 he was commandant of the Irish Citizen Army, founded in Dublin in 1913 to protect strikers against the police. Though his army numbered no more than 130 men and boys and a handful of women, Connolly prepared for a revolution in Dublin.

Alarmed that a premature revolt would lead to a government crackdown, the leaders of the Irish Republican Brotherhood, among them Patrick Pearse, revealed their plans to begin an uprising on Easter Sunday 1916. Connolly had often denounced these 'wrap-the green-flag-round-me' republican conspirators. But in January he agreed to join them and accepted the position as commandant of the insurrection in Dublin.

The IRB had kept Eoin MacNeill in the dark. MacNeill, president of the Irish Volunteers—who, unlike the much larger National Volunteers, were opposed to helping Britain in the Great War—refused to support a rising which had no prospect of success. Learning of the imminent rebellion on Saturday afternoon 22 April, he jabbed an old bayonet he used as a poker into his living-room fire and declared: 'I'll stop all this damned nonsense.'

MacNeill did his best. He inserted a notice in the *Sunday Independent*:

All orders given to the Irish Volunteers for tomorrow Easter Sunday are hereby rescinded and no parades, marches or other movements of Irish Volunteers will take place. Each individual Volunteer will obey this order in every particular.

Government officials in Dublin Castle assumed that the rebellion which they knew was in preparation had now been called off. After all, the German ship bringing 20,000 rifles to the IRB had been captured, and Sir Roger Casement—the man thought to be the leader of the conspiracy—was in custody. But the Military Council of the IRB decided to go ahead, postponing action to Easter Monday.

'Heroism has come back to the earth.... The old heart of the earth needed to be warmed with the red wine of the battlefields....' For Patrick Pearse, this rising would be a blood sacrifice to keep militancy alive:

We may make mistakes in the beginning and shoot the wrong people, but bloodshed is a cleansing and sanctifying thing, and the nation which regards it as a final horror has lost its manhood.... Life springs from death and the nation which regards it as a final horror has lost its manhood.

The other revolutionary leaders nursed the strong hope that the people would join them and that Germany would make a fresh attempt to send help. Nevertheless, as they marched out from Liberty Hall on the quays over to O'Connell Street on Easter Monday, Connolly turned to a Citizen Army man and said: 'Bill, we're going to be slaughtered.' 'Is there no hope at all?', the man asked. 'None whatever,' replied Connolly and then gave the command: 'Company halt! Left wheel! The GPO ... *charge!*'

The military plan was to seize prominent buildings in the centre of Dublin. People protesting that they only wanted to buy stamps were shooed out of the General Post Office, now the insurgent headquarters. The men ran up a tricolour on one flagpole of the building and a green banner with the inscription 'IRISH REPUBLIC' on another. At 12.45 p.m. Pearse, the insurgent commander-in-chief, stood outside and read aloud the 'Proclamation of the Irish Republic':

IRISHMEN AND IRISHWOMEN: In the name of God and of the dead generations from which she receives her old tradition of nationhood, Ireland, through us, summons her children to her flag and strikes for her freedom.

Having organized and trained her manhood through her secret revolutionary organization, the Irish Republican Brotherhood, and through her open military organizations, the Irish Volunteers and the Irish Citizen Army ... and, supported by her exiled children in America and by gallant allies in Europe ... she strikes in full confidence of victory....

We place the cause of the Irish Republic under the protection of the Most High God....

Dublin Castle had been taken completely unawares. On this beautiful Bank Holiday Monday most troops were relaxing out of the city, many of them at the Fairyhouse races. Other buildings seized by insurgents included: the Four Courts, the South Dublin Union, Jacob's Biscuit Factory, the Royal College of Surgeons, and Boland's Bakery.

In St Stephen's Green Countess Constance Markievicz, resplendent in her Citizen Army uniform with green puttees, tunic, riding breeches, and slouch hat with ostrich feather, brandished her revolver. Here an elderly guest of the Shelbourne Hotel, Michael Cavanagh, decided to intervene in the proceedings. The Citizen Army wanted his lorry full of theatrical effects, and he was not prepared to allow this. He approached insurgents with a raised finger: 'Go and put back that lorry or you are a dead man. Go back before I count four.

One, two, three, four—' There was a burst of firing, and Cavanagh fell to the ground. The writer James Stephens ran forward in a vain attempt to help the dying man; in recollecting the incident, he concluded: 'At that moment the Volunteers were hated.'

Episode 218 ~

EASTER WEEK

During the afternoon of Easter Monday 24 April 1916 a party of Lancers trotted into Dublin's O'Connell Street to investigate reported disturbances. As they approached the Nelson Pillar, Volunteers in the General Post Office opened fire. Four of the soldiers fell dead. Soon afterwards, Ernie O'Malley, an eighteen-year-old medical student, saw local people looting public houses, while in the middle of O'Connell Street

> Seated on a dead horse was a woman, a shawl around her head, untidy wisps of hair straggled across her dirty face. She swayed slowly, drunk, singing: 'Boys in khaki, boys in blue, here's the best of jolly good luck to you.'

Over much of the centre of Dublin insurgents had seized the initiative. Already, however, the crown forces were recovering control. An attack on Dublin Castle, begun by shooting dead an unarmed policeman in cold blood, had failed in spite of the fact that a mere handful of soldiers had been available to defend it. Only two railway stations had been seized, and the Shelbourne Hotel, looming high over St Stephen's Green, had not been taken. Military barracks ringing the city now filled up with soldiers returning from the races. Troops were brought in from the Curragh Camp in Co. Kildare.

Above all, the people had not risen in support. The poor poured out of the tenements and concentrated their energies on looting the shops. The numbers of Irish Volunteers and Citizen Army men and boys numbered less than two thousand. They had no artillery or machine-guns, and their rifles, for the most part, were antiquated single-shot German Mausers.

South of the city centre, at Boland's Mills, Commandant Eamon de Valera sent men up to Mount Street Bridge to hold back any approaching troops. Here Michael Malone took command. He ordered houses overlooking the bridge to be barricaded with bicycles, furniture and sacks of flour. On

Wednesday morning a column of 2,000 soldiers, most of them recently disembarked Sherwood Foresters, advanced with fixed bayonets from Ballsbridge. With just a few men Malone inflicted devastating fire on the soldiers. Again and again officers with their swords flashing in the sun ordered their men to advance against these hidden snipers. One resident, Mrs Ismena Rohde, witnessed the slaughter: 'The poor fellows fell in rows without being able to return a shot. It was ghastly for those who saw it.' An English visitor also left a vivid record:

A poor girl ran out on to the bridge while yet the bullets from rifles and revolvers were flying thickly from both sides. She put up both her hands, and almost instantly the firing ceased.... The girl picked up the soldier....

It was a throbbing incident that brought tears to the eyes.... She pushed an apron down his trousers to staunch the blood. He was shot in the small of the back and in the thigh. He was a Sherwood Forester, and the little girl was crying over him.

The British army deployed the same tactics in the streets as they used on the Western Front—and with similar results. Sustaining around 230 casualties, the Sherwoods eventually prevailed, and Malone was shot dead.

Everywhere the insurgents were on the defensive, sleepless and suffering heavy losses.

The government had proclaimed martial law on Tuesday. On Wednesday a fishery protection vessel, the *Helga*, steamed up the Liffey to shell rebel positions. Artillery pieces in the grounds of Trinity College proved much more effective. On Thursday their shells fell with increasing intensity on O'Connell Street. Snipers on the roofs and squads equipped with automatic weapons closed in on the insurgents. James Connolly was no longer able to exercise command. Severely wounded, he survived on injections of morphine provided by a captured doctor in the GPO. Michael O'Rahilly, better known as 'The O'Rahilly', took over command. Pounded by howitzers firing shrapnel and incendiary shells, much of O'Connell Street became engulfed in a firestorm. The O'Rahilly's nephew, Dick Humphries, fighting as a Volunteer alongside his uncle, recalled:

Suddenly some oil works near Abbey Street is singed by the conflagration, and immediately a solid sheet of blinding death-white flame rushes hundreds of feet into the air with a thunderous explosion which shakes the walls. It is followed by a heavy bombardment as hundreds of drums explode. The intense light compels one to close the eyes.... Millions of sparks are floating in masses for hundreds of yards around O'Connell Street and as a precaution we are ordered to drench the barricades with water again.... Crimson-tinged men moved around dazedly. Above it all the sharp crack of rifle fire predominates, while the deadly rattle of the machine-gun sounds like the coughing laughter of jeering spirits.

When during Friday further intensive shelling set the GPO's roof ablaze, it was clear to all defenders that the end was near.

Episode 219 ~

EXECUTIONS AND INTERNMENT

At 8 p.m. on Friday 28 April 1916 Patrick Pearse, the rebel commander-in-chief, ordered the evacuation of the burning General Post Office in Dublin's O'Connell Street. The O'Rahilly led a futile charge down Henry Street. He and many of his men fell in a hail of bullets.

At 12.45 p.m. on Saturday Elizabeth O'Farrell, a nurse who had been with the insurgents in the GPO throughout this Easter week, took a hastily made Red Cross insignia and a white flag and stepped out into the open:

I waved a small white flag which I carried and the military ceased firing and called me up to the barrier.... I saw, at the corner of Sackville Lane, The O'Rahilly's hat and a revolver lying on the ground.

She spoke to a senior army officer:

'The commandant of the Irish Republican Army wishes to treat with the commandant of the British forces in Ireland.'
    'The Irish Republican Army?—the Sinn Féiners, you mean,' he replied.
    'No, the Irish Republican Army they call themselves and I think that is a very good name too.'

Soon after this the insurgent leaders signed an unconditional surrender, and on Sunday the last of the Volunteers and Citizen Army combatants emerged from Boland's Mills, Jacob's Biscuit Factory, St Stephen's Green and Marrowbone Lane. Angry Dubliners spat on them as they were led away.

For almost a week a self-appointed group of fewer than 2,000 members of the Irish Volunteers, the Irish Citizen Army and the Irish Republican Brotherhood had fought the forces of the most extensive empire the world has ever seen. The rebellion had occurred in the depths of the bloodiest conflict mankind had yet experienced—and at a time when over 145,000 Irishmen engaged in deadly conflict in the trenches. At least 450 people, many of them innocent civilians, had been killed; 2,600 had been wounded; and much of central Dublin had been reduced to rubble.

Martial law had been proclaimed on Easter Tuesday, and on Friday General Sir John Grenfell Maxwell arrived to take charge in Dublin. His forces arrested 3,430 men and 79 women, and on 2 May the first courts martial began. Condemned to death, Patrick Pearse, Tom Clarke and Thomas MacDonagh were taken to the disued Kilmainham Jail and, on 3 May, shot at dawn in the Stonebreaker's Yard. Four more faced the firing-squad on 4 May. The authorities executed seven more on 5, 8 and 12 May. The severely wounded James Connolly had to be strapped to a chair in front of the firing-squad.

Altogether ninety men were condemned to death. Maxwell eventually agreed to commute all but fifteen of these sentences. Countess Constance Markievicz pleaded at her trial: 'I am only a woman, you cannot shoot a woman, you must not shoot a woman.' Maxwell agreed. Eamon de Valera, commandant at Boland's Mills, avoided execution, partly perhaps because he could claim American citizenship. Sir Roger Casement, arrested in Co. Kerry on the eve of the rising, however, was hanged at Pentonville on 3 August.

The press described the insurrection as the 'Sinn Féin rebellion'. This was incorrect. Arthur Griffith's Sinn Féin was then a separatist party opposed to violent methods. Nevertheless, Griffith, together with Eoin MacNeill, the Irish Volunteers' president who had attempted to stop the rising, were among those interned by Maxwell's orders. Most were transferred to Frongoch, a barbed-wire encampment in north Wales.

Meanwhile nationalist opinion in Ireland underwent a seismic change. The government had carefully avoided inflicting the ultimate penalty on those convicted in the country in the wake of the uprisings of 1848 and 1867. The executions after the Easter Rising, following secret military trials, each announced in a blaze of publicity, shocked the public who had earlier condemned the rebellion. Even the Unionist leader, Sir Edward Carson, declared: 'No true Irishman calls for vengeance.' He recognised that a whole new cohort of republican martyrs was being created. Postcards commemorating the dead sold briskly, and new nationalist ballads, usually set to music-hall tunes, gained a wide currency:

> God rest gallant Pearse and his comrades who died
> Tom Clarke, MacDonagh, McDermott, MacBride
> And here's to Jem Connolly who gave one hurrah
> And placed the machine-guns for Erin-go-Bragh.

Meanwhile the position of the Irish Parliamentary Party now became desperate. Its leader, John Redmond, found himself condemned for his unreserved support for Britain in the war. He pleaded for immediate implementation of Home Rule, enacted in 1914 but suspended until the end of fighting in Europe.

The Prime Minister, Herbert Asquith, sent over Lloyd George to see if agreement could be forged. But Lloyd George spoke with a forked tongue: to the Unionists he promised permanent exclusion of Ulster counties, but his promise to the Nationalists only temporarily excluded those counties. The fate of the Irish Party was being sealed.

Episode 220 ⁓

SACRIFICE AT THE SOMME

In 1916 on the Western Front, Tom Kettle, a former Nationalist MP, now a lieutenant in the Dublin Fusiliers, received news of the Easter Rising. In a letter home he gave his opinion of the insurgents: 'These men will go down in history as heroes and martyrs; and I will go down—if I go down at all—as a bloody British officer.' Shortly afterwards Kettle found himself at the River Somme, ready to take part in a great offensive. And just after dawn on 1 July, in front of Thiepval Wood and astride the River Ancre, men of the Ulster Division waited as the six-day Allied artillery barrage reached a horrific climax. Captain Percy Crozier was there:

> Jimmy Law comes round from Brigade with a chronometer to synchronise the time, as everything has to be done to the second.... 'Don't you go and get shot to-day, Jimmy; your mother would never forgive me.'...
> The men fall in, in fours.... A pin could be heard to drop.

At 7.30 a.m. officers blew their whistles and the men advanced into no-man's land at a steady marching pace. But the massive bombardment had neither cut the wire nor knocked out the German machine-gun nests. North of the Ancre the attack proved a disastrous failure: troops were caught by crossfire in a deep ravine. One German soldier recalled: 'We just had to load and reload. They went down in their hundreds. You didn't have to aim, we just fired into them. If only they had run, they would have overwhelmed us.' Opposite Thiepval Wood, however, the Ulster Division advanced with astonishing speed, reaching the German fourth line. But dangerously overextended, exposed to relentless fire and mistakenly shelled from their own side, whole companies disappeared. By nightfall all gains had been lost.

'Blacker's Boys'—men from the Armagh, Monaghan and Cavan Ulster Volunteers—returned with only 64 out of 600 men who had gone over the top. Seventeen-year-old Private Herbert Beattie wrote home to Belfast:

> Dear Mother,
>   Just to let you know I am safe and thank God for it for we had a ruf time of it in the charge we made. Mother, don't let on to V. Quinn mother or Archers mother that they must be killed wounded for they are missen of roll call, and tell Hugh the fellow that youst to run along with E. Ferguson called Eddie Mallin he youst to have Pigens if Hugh dus not no him McKeown nows him tell them he was killed, tell them ther is not another grosvenor Rd fellow left but myself. Mother wee were tramping over the dead i think there is onley about 4 hundred left out of about 13 hundered ... Mother if god spers me to get home safe i will have something uful to tell you if hell is any wores i would not like to go to it Mother let me here from you soone as you can....
>   This is all I can say at present from your loving son Herbie.
> Mother xxxxxxxxxxxxxxxxxxxxxx
> Father xxxxxxxxxxxxxxxxxxxxx
> Show my Father this letter and tell him to writ

Emma Duffin, daughter of a Unionist MP, waited to treat the wounded at Le Havre. She wrote in her diary:

> The big push began and the trains came and came.... I was sent on duty on the station platform; if the hospital had not made me realize the war I realized it that night; under the big arc lights in the station lay stretchers 4 deep ... huddled together, their arms in slings, and their heads bound up, the mud from the trenches sticking to their clothes and the blood still caked on them.

During the first day of the Battle of the Somme, the bloodiest day in the history of the British army, the United Kingdom sustained over 54,000 casualties. The Ulster Division suffered a loss of 5,700 killed or wounded.

In fact the Battle of the Somme had only just begun. It raged on inconclusively and bloodily all through the summer into the autumn. In the September offensive by the villages of Guillemont and Ginchy the 36th (Ulster) Division fought side by side with the 16th Division, composed overwhelmingly of southern Irishmen. Lieutenant Kettle wrote:

We are moving up to-night into the Somme. The bombardment, destruction and bloodshed are beyond all imagination, nor did I ever think the valour of simple men could be quite as beautiful as that of my Dublin Fusiliers.... The big guns are coughing and smacking their shells.

In a trench he wrote a poem for his little daughter Betty, which ended:

> So here, while the mad guns curse overhead,
> And tired men sigh, with mud for couch and floor,
> Know that we fools, now with the foolish dead,
> Died not for flag, nor King, nor Emperor,
> But for a dream, born in a herdsman's shed,
> And for the secret scripture of the poor.

Days later Kettle himself was lying dead on the battlefield.

Episode 221 ∾

THE RISE OF SINN FÉIN

In December 1916 David Lloyd George, who had just ousted Herbert Asquith as Prime Minister, released the remaining Irish internees. Convicted republicans remained in jail.

In the same month James O'Kelly, MP for North Roscommon, died. He had been perhaps the most colourful character in the Irish Parliamentary Party. O'Kelly had joined the French Foreign Legion, had fought in Algeria and Mexico, had helped to defend Paris against the Prussians in 1870, had been with American troops fighting against Sitting Bull, and had been a military prisoner in Cuba. But O'Kelly had rarely, if ever, visited his constituency of North Roscommon.

For more than forty years the Irish Party, virtually without opposition, had represented the nationalists of Ireland. Then, in February 1917, those disgusted by the moderation of the party decided to put up their own man in the by election which followed O'Kelly's death. Their candidate was hardly an ideal choice: George Plunkett, a papal count, who had published a study of the Renaissance painter Botticelli, and who was now described as 'a very feeble old man', so decrepit he was declared fit only to be in charge of a Christmas tree.

But three of the count's sons had fought in the Easter Rising, and one of them, Joseph Mary Plunkett, had been executed. Michael Collins and other released internees revived the Irish Volunteers and threw themselves into a campaign to get Count Plunkett elected:

The West's Awake! Men of North Roscommon, Ireland expects you to strike a blow for our small nationality and return Count Plunkett as your representative, and free ... your countrymen from prison chains....

Canvassers had to struggle through snow drifts three metres high. An observer described Plunkett's campaigners as having icicles hanging from their hair, and one car-driver was frozen so severely that he had to be lifted off his seat. One speaker, after battling eleven miles on foot through the snow, told voters that 150,000 Irishmen who had followed the Irish Party's advice were 'feeding the worms in Gallipoli and Flanders'.

Count Plunkett polled almost twice as many votes as his rival. The Irish Party was shaken to its core. Its leader, John Redmond, was stopped just in time from issuing this despairing statement:

The people have grown tired of the monotony of being served for twenty, thirty ... or forty years by the same men in parliament.... Let the Irish people replace us, by all means, by other, and, I hope, better men, if they so choose.

The Easter Rising of 1916 had been erroneously described by journalists as the 'Sinn Féin rebellion'. But Sinn Féin, a separatist but non-violent party founded in 1906 by Arthur Griffith, had not been involved. However, the name stuck, and those now seeking an independent Ireland had no objection. Immediately after being elected Count Plunkett announced that he would follow Sinn Féin policy and would therefore refuse to take his seat in Westminster.

In effect, Count Plunkett, ex-internees, Irish Volunteers and other advanced nationalists formed a new Sinn Féin in 1917—an umbrella party catering for a wide range of people from disgruntled Home Rulers to out-and-out militant republicans. Arthur Griffith, recently released from jail, agreed to lead the party. For the present there was no suggestion of renewing the armed struggle.

Thousands of nationalists, particularly young people, clamoured to join the new Sinn Féin. By July 1917, the police reported, 336 Sinn Féin clubs flourished across the island. Sinn Féin was clearly on the crest of a wave. This became particularly apparent during two further by-elections in 1917.

PUT HIM IN TO GET HIM OUT
JOE McGUINNESS, THE MAN IN JAIL FOR IRELAND

McGuinness, a republican prisoner in Lewes Jail, defeated the Irish Party candidate in South Longford in May. Then Major Willie Redmond MP, brother of the Irish Party leader, fell mortally wounded on the battlefield of Messines on the Western Front; men of the Ulster Division, fighting alongside southerners in the 16th Division, carried him back from no-man's land. A by-election followed in Willie Redmond's constituency of East Clare. And the Sinn Féin candidate was Eamon de Valera, the only surviving male commandant of the 1916 rising.

Armed Volunteers paraded the streets and formed escorts, and de Valera, freshly released from prison, spoke without restraint:

> You have no enemy but England.... Although we fought once and lost, it is only a lesson for the second time.... Every vote you give now is as good as the crack of a rifle in proclaiming your desire for freedom.

The result of the election was a foregone conclusion, though few predicted the wide margin of de Valera's victory. Arthur Griffith now stepped aside to allow de Valera to become the president of Sinn Féin.

Behind the scenes Sinn Féin activists squabbled with each other over what should next be done. Then the government swiftly provided the bonding solution required.

Episode 222 ∽

THE FIRST DÁIL

In a desperate attempt to find a way of implementing Home Rule while the Great War still raged, Prime Minister David Lloyd George called an Irish Convention. The conference, which met in Trinity College Dublin from the summer of 1917 to the spring of 1918, proved futile. The rising separatist party, Sinn Féin, refused to attend. In any case, northern and southern Unionists fell out. At a crucial meeting of the Ulster Unionist Council in 1916 it had been agreed to seek partition of the six north-eastern counties. Unionists in the Ulster counties of Donegal, Cavan and Monaghan accepted this majority decision with heavy hearts. According to one Unionist MP, 'Men not prone to emotion shed tears.'

Southern Unionists, not wanting to be cut off from the support of northern Protestants, campaigned vigorously to stop partition. They came close to clinching a deal with John Redmond, leader of the Irish Parliamentary Party. The Ulster Unionist MP Adam Duffin wrote in disgust to his wife on 28 November: 'The Southern Unionist lot ... want to capitulate & make terms with the enemy lest a worse thing befall them. They are a cowardly crew & stupid to boot.'

Redmond died in March 1918, and when his successor, John Dillon, failed to hammer out an agreement, the Convention dissolved.

At that moment Field Marshal Lüdendorff's storm-troopers dramatically broke through on the Western Front and surged towards Paris. By this time recruitment in Ireland had fallen to a trickle. A contemporary anti-recruiting song caught the prevailing sentiment:

> Sergeant William Bailey's looking very blue,
> *Too-ra-loo-ra-loo-ra-loo-ra-loo ...*
> Some rebel youths with placards
> Have called his army blackguards
> And told the Irish boyhood what to do.
> He's lost his occupation,
> Let's sing in jubilation
> For Sergeant William Bailey, *too-ra-loo.*

In 1916 Westminster had introduced conscription in Great Britain. Now it was about to be imposed in Ireland. Nationalists of every variety closed ranks to resist conscription. Dillon led his MPs out of Westminster in protest. Catholic bishops described the Conscription Act as 'an oppressive and inhuman law which the Irish people have a right to resist by every means that are consonant with the law of God'. A general strike, highly effective in all parts of the country outside the north-east, paralysed transport.

In May 1918 the newly arrived viceroy, Lord French, announced the existence of a 'German Plot'. Police arrested seventy-three prominent Sinn Féiners. Knowing that it would only strengthen their cause, Sinn Féin activists still at large made no attempt to avoid arrest. In fact not a shred of solid evidence had been presented to show that Irish nationalists were conspiring with Imperial Germany.

Lloyd George gave up the unequal task, and, as Winston Churchill remarked, the government ended up with 'no law and no men'. Then, on the eleventh hour of the eleventh day of the eleventh month of 1918, the Great War ended. It is estimated that 28,000 Irishmen had given their lives in the Allied cause.

A long overdue general election followed in December 1918. For the first time all men aged twenty-one and over had the vote. Women—provided they were aged over thirty and were householders or married to householders—

also got the vote. At a stroke the Irish electorate had been tripled. The 1918 election proved to be the most momentous of the twentieth century.

Sinn Féin had a spectacular triumph: it won 73 seats. The Irish Party lay in ruins: it won only six seats, and four of these had been the result of an electoral pact with Sinn Féin in Ulster. Helped by a much-needed redistribution of seats, Irish Unionists raised their representation from 18 to 26. Lloyd George's wartime coalition swept the boards across the Irish Sea; and of great significance for the future of Ireland was that now more than half of all MPs were Conservatives.

Countess Constance Markievicz had the honour of being the first woman ever elected to the House of Commons. But she, like all the Sinn Féin MPs, abstained from Westminster. Instead they convened on 21 January 1919 in Dublin's Mansion House as 'Dáil Éireann', the Assembly of Ireland. Reporters outnumbered the elected representatives, since thirty-four Sinn Féin MPs still languished in jail. At that historic meeting the Dáil unanimously approved a Declaration of Independence:

> Whereas the Irish people is by right a free people:
> And Whereas for seven hundred years the Irish people has ... repeatedly protested in arms against foreign usurpation:
> And Whereas English rule in this country is ... based upon fraud and maintained by military occupation against the declared will of the people:
> And Whereas the Irish Republic was proclaimed in Dublin on Easter Monday, 1916, by the Irish Republican Army acting on behalf of the Irish people ...
> Now, therefore, we, the elected Representatives of the ancient Irish people, do, in the name of the Irish nation, ratify the establishment of the Irish Republic.…

Would the peacemakers in Paris also ratify the Irish Republic?

Episode 223 ⌒

RETURN TO VIOLENCE

On 21 January 1919 Dan Breen and eight other Irish Volunteers ambushed two constables escorting a cart carrying gelignite at Soloheadbeg in Co. Tipperary. Volunteers shot dead the policemen, both of them middle-aged men well known in the locality, at point-blank range. On the following Sunday Monsignor Ryan declared from his pulpit in Tipperary town: 'God help poor Ireland if she follows this deed of blood.'

The attack at Soloheadbeg took place on the same day as the first meeting of Dáil Éireann. Would the elected representatives sanction such acts of violence? There had been no talk of a renewed armed conflict. For the present Dáil deputies put their faith in their 'Message to the Free Nations of the World', an appeal to the Paris Peace Conference.

Seán T. O'Kelly, representing the Dáil, took up residence in the Grand Hotel in the Boulevard des Capuchines. There he entertained lavishly and circulated the Dáil's Declaration of Irish Independence. But O'Kelly's voice was all but drowned by the clamouring of others. At the conference dozens of delegations—including one led by Ho Chi-Minh seeking independence for the Vietnamese in French Indo-China—lobbied for the self-determination of their nationalities. There was a further problem: the Irish republicans in their 1916 Proclamation had claimed the now defeated Imperial Germany as an ally.

With the help of a duplicate key, Eamon de Valera, the President of the Dáil, escaped from Lincoln Prison in February. Off he went to the United States in a vain attempt to seek the backing of Congress for Irish independence. The Dáil set up an administrative apparatus and appointed ministers in an effort to supplant British government institutions. Over much of the country Dáil courts, assisted by republican police, operated remarkably well. But all that Prime Minister David Lloyd George had to offer was Home Rule and partition.

The Dáil Minister for Finance, Michael Collins, became convinced that independence would have to be fought for. Collins lost patience with fellow Sinn Féin deputies who were opposed to further violence. In May 1919 he wrote:

> The policy now seems to be to squeeze out anyone who is tainted by strong fighting ideas.... It seems to me that official Sinn Féin is inclined to be ever less militant and ever more political and theoretical.... It is rather pitiful...

He and Cathal Brugha, the Defence Minister, encouraged local groups of Irish Volunteers, now officially designated the Irish Republican Army, to wage war on the Royal Irish Constabulary. In the words of a stirring rebel song:

> I'll take my Short revolver
> And my bandolier of lead,
> And live or die I can but try
> To avenge my country's dead....

> I've always hated slavery
>   Since the day that I was born,
> So I'm off to join the IRA
>   And I'm off tomorrow morn.

Soon RIC men, for the most part Catholics popular in their districts, found themselves in mortal peril, liable to be shot down in cold blood. The terror spread as ordinary people, who failed to obey a decree to shun the police, faced punishment at the point of a gun.

As well as supervising Volunteer brigades throughout the country, Collins created an elite of skilled assassins in Dublin, known as the 'Squad'. During the day Collins would appear for photo-calls as he raised money for the 'Dáil Loan' to finance the alternative republican government. At nightfall he crept into the headquarters of the Dublin detective force. There, with the assistance of detectives acting as double agents, he pored over secret British papers. Having identified civil servants and police most threatening to his cause, Collins then sent out his Squad to assassinate them.

The government's answer was to fight insurrection with repression. It imposed military rule on the most disturbed districts. By the end of August 1919 7,000 troops were on active service, administering martial law. On 12 September 1919, the same day that Collins's Squad shot dead an unarmed detective in Dublin, Lloyd George declared the Dáil illegal. By suppressing an elected body representing a majority of the Irish people, the Prime Minister unwittingly handed the initiative to Collins, Brugha and the militants within Sinn Féin.

The year 1920 witnessed an alarming upsurge in violence. Some police now retaliated with unauthorised reprisals. On 20 March RIC men in plain clothes and blackened faces murdered Tomás MacCurtain, Lord Mayor of Cork and commandant of the 1st Cork Brigade of the IRA. Other policemen resigned. To replace them, the government raised recruits in Britain. IRA propaganda portrayed them as the scrapings of English jails. Actually most were men demobilised from the British army, and all had to supply a reference, then known as a 'character'. Many wore khaki trousers since there not enough of the dark green RIC uniforms to go round. The new recruits quickly became known as 'Black and Tans', the name of a pack of hounds in Co. Tipperary.

When Lloyd George unleashed the Black and Tans on the Irish countryside, he signalled the bankruptcy of his Irish policy.

Episode 224 ◡

TERROR AND REPRISAL

However much Prime Minister Lloyd George might attempt to deny it, he had a war on his hands in Ireland in 1920. Michael Collins's assassination squad liquidated detectives, spies, government agents and public servants with cold-blooded efficiency. IRA men attacked police barracks, burnt over five hundred abandoned stations and destroyed income tax offices in twenty-two counties.

From the end of 1919 the government had been enlisting temporary recruits to the RIC, known as the Black and Tans. In July 1920 it added an Auxiliary Division, composed of demobilised army officers. These men, given no police training and free from normal military discipline, now brought further terror to the Irish countryside.

The IRA formed 'flying columns', mobile units each composed of around thirty-five men, serving for up to a week at a time. Tom Barry, a Great War veteran and commandant of the West Cork Brigade, led a particularly active flying column:

> This prison scum in brown and black
> No tanks or war equipment lack
> Yet o'er the sea they'll ne'er get back
> If they're caught by Barry's Column.

With increasing frequency, the Auxiliaries and Black and Tans saw the dead or mutilated bodies of their comrades brought back to their barracks. Unable to get at the real culprits, they wreaked their vengeance on the ordinary people. On 21 September Volunteers shot an RIC head constable in Balbriggan, Co. Dublin. That night lorry-loads of Black and Tans overran the town, setting fire to shops and houses and—unprovoked—bayoneting two citizens to death in their nightshirts.

Similar reprisals followed in the towns of Milltown Malbay, Lahinch and Ennistymon in Co. Clare. Here one man was shot to death and cremated in the blazing ruins of his own house; and another was killed when he tried to help a neighbour whose house had been set on fire. One eyewitness wrote:

You never saw anything so sad as the sight in the sandhills that morning. Groups of men and women, some of them over seventy years, practically naked, cold, wet, worn-looking and terrified, huddled in groups. I met two mothers with babies not three weeks old, little boys, partly naked, leading horses that had gone mad in their stables with the heat, and then when we got near the village ... distracted people running in all directions ... with the awful thought haunting them that the burned corpse might be some relative of their own.... Every evening there is a sorrowful procession out of the village. The people too terrified to stay in their houses sleep out in the fields.

Shortly afterwards Black and Tans wrecked and burnt houses in Trim, Co. Meath, and Mallow, Co. Cork. For a time this reign of terror seemed to work. Winston Churchill exulted in recent successes in a speech delivered at Dundee:

We are going to break up this murder gang. That it will be broken up utterly and absolutely is as sure as the sun will rise tomorrow morning.... Assassination has never changed the history of the world and the government are going to take care it does not change the history of the British Empire.

On 25 October Terence McSwiney, who had succeeded the murdered Tomás MacCurtain as Lord Mayor of Cork and commandant of the 1st Cork Brigade of the IRA, died at Brixton prison after seventy-four days on hunger strike. An eighteen-year-old medical student, Kevin Barry, was hanged in Mountjoy Jail on 1 November after shooting dead a soldier of the same age. A week later Lloyd George declared: 'We have murder by the throat!'

But did he? On the morning of Sunday 21 November Michael Collins sent out members of his 'Squad' to the Gresham Hotel and other places in Dublin. They shot dead twelve British officers, some in front of their wives. One victim was simply a veterinary officer. That afternoon Auxiliaries and RIC men opened fire on a crowd watching a Gaelic football match between Dublin and Tipperary. They killed twelve civilians, including a woman, a child and a Tipperary player. The horrors of that 'Bloody Sunday' concluded with the killing of three men held by Auxiliaries in the guardroom of Dublin Castle.

On 28 November two lorries filled with Auxiliaries ran into an ambush prepared by Tom Barry's flying column at Kilmichael near Macroom, Co. Cork. Seventeen of the eighteen Auxiliaries were killed, almost certainly a majority of them after they had surrendered. Barry recorded that he drilled his men up and down the road among the burning lorries and mutilated corpses to stiffen morale shaken by the carnage.

Auxiliaries exacted vengeance on 11 December. They sacked the centre of Cork city, destroying the City Hall, the Corn Exchange, the Carnegie Free Library and most of Patrick Street. In 1921 worse was to come.

Episode 225 ∿

'THE DREARY STEEPLES'

The sustained slaughter of the Great War seemed to accustom men to the regular use of violence to advance a multiplicity of causes. After the Armistice blood continued to flow. Foreign intervention against the Bolsheviks only intensified the miseries of civil war in Russia. There millions died. In the streets of northern Italy squads of fascist ex-servicemen and revolutionary socialists fought each other with knuckledusters and revolvers for supremacy. Spartacists and Freikorps threatened to stifle the infant Weimar Republic in its cradle. Admiral Horthy crushed Communists in Budapest with an army invading from Transylvania. In the new states emerging from four collapsed European empires ethnic rivalries flared into violent struggles. By the shores of the Aegean Sea Greeks and Turks slaughtered each other in their thousands.

And what about Ireland? What about Ulster? Such questions deeply concerned Winston Churchill as he addressed fellow-MPs in 1920:

> Then came the Great War. Every institution, almost, in the world was strained. Great Empires have been overturned. The whole map of Europe has been changed. The position of countries has been violently altered. The modes of thought of men, the whole outlook on affairs, the grouping of parties, all have encountered violent and tremendous changes in the deluge of the world. But as the deluge subsides and the waters fall short we see the dreary steeples of Fermanagh and Tyrone emerging once again. The integrity of their quarrel is one of the few institutions that has been unaltered in the cataclysm which has swept the world.

A *Daily News* correspondent reported that 'Soldiers who fought for the Allies as they return home are becoming converted by the thousand into Sinn Féiners.' Many became leading activists in the IRA, now in deadly conflict with the forces of the crown. Other ex-servicemen—recruits for the Black and Tans and the Auxiliaries—recklessly spread terror over much of the southern countryside. And as the War of Independence edged into Ulster it detonated a sectarian conflict there more vicious and lethal than all the northern riots of the previous century put together.

The trouble began in Derry city in April 1920. Here nationalists, for the first time ever, had won a majority in the Corporation. Loyalists, fearing abandonment by a British government, revived the pre-war Ulster Volunteer Force. Intense sectarian rioting spread out from Long Tower Street and Bishop Street. Catholics burned Protestants out of the Bogside after

Protestants had set fire to Catholic homes in the Waterside. In June the UVF seized control of the Diamond and Guildhall Square. The *Derry Journal* reported: 'The Long Tower, an exclusively Catholic district, was kept for hours under a deadly fire from the City Walls.... At least three men were shot dead.' Troops rushed in. Imposing a curfew and directing heavy machine-gun fire into the Bogside, the soldiers killed six more people. And as shootings, assassinations and reprisals continued, despite the presence of the army, the death toll for the city eventually reached forty.

In Co. Fermanagh Lieutenant-Colonel George Liddle formed a loyalist vigilante patrol at Lisbellaw. On the night of 8 June his men succeeded in driving back an IRA assault on the local constabulary barracks. Captain Sir Basil Brooke, the Fermanagh landlord awarded the Military Cross during the war, took out UVF rifles from their place of concealment in Colebrooke House and took command. He later recalled: 'I had thought my soldiering days were over.... I was to become a soldier of a very different sort ... but I had the added stimulant of defending my own birthplace.'

Trouble also erupted in the Belfast shipyards on 21 July 1920, the first full day back at work after the July holiday break. It was also the day of the funeral of a Banbridge RIC divisional commander, shot dead by the IRA in Cork. Men shouted enthusiastic support for the call to drive out 'disloyal' workers. Hundreds of apprentices and rivet boys from Workman Clark marched into Harland & Wolff's yard. One Catholic worker remembered: 'The gates were smashed down with sledges, the vests and shirts of those at work were torn open to see if the men were wearing any Catholic emblems, and woe betide the man who was.... One man ... had to swim two or three miles.'

Meanwhile loyalists forced out virtually the entire Catholic populations of Banbridge and Dromore in Co. Down. Much of Belfast plunged into outright intercommunal warfare, most ferociously in east Belfast. In the ensuing days expulsions continued from all the major engineering firms. A committee headed by Bishop Joseph MacRory estimated that 10,000 Catholic men and 1,000 women had been driven from their work in the city.

IRA assassins murdered a police district inspector in Lisburn on 22 August. Protestants spent the next three days burning Catholic-owned property and drove out almost all Catholic residents of the town.

The violence seemed to have reached a climax. But in fact the destruction and killing in Belfast was only just beginning.

Episode 226 ᔔ

PARTITION

Liberal though he was, David Lloyd George headed a coalition government in 1920 which was overwhelmingly Conservative. Several prominent members of his cabinet on the eve of the Great War had pledged themselves to 'use all means which may be found' to prevent the setting up of a Home Rule parliament. By now, it was true, these Conservatives were prepared to accept Home Rule, but only if loyal Ulster remained within the United Kingdom.

At a crucial meeting of the Ulster Unionist Council in 1916 it had been agreed to seek partition of the six north-eastern counties. Since 1914 the balance of power had tilted away from Irish nationalists—especially because of, as Arthur Balfour, Lord President of the Council, put it, 'the blessed refusal of Sinn Féiners to take the Oath of Allegiance in 1918'. The absence of 73 Sinn Féin MPs left only half a dozen demoralised Irish Party MPs in the Commons. And so Ulster Unionists essentially got the constitutional arrangement they desired.

In 1920 Ireland acquired a new frontier—through the decision of parliament, not by international accord. The Treaty of Versailles of 1919 allowed the exact positioning of Germany's borders in Upper Silesia, Schleswig, Marienwerder and Allenstein to be agreed after holding 'plebiscites' or referendums. Should Westminster also apply American President Woodrow Wilson's principle of self-determination by holding a referendum in Ulster? The cabinet committee on Ireland hastily dismissed this proposition. Balfour argued that referendums were only suited to vanquished enemies: 'Ireland is not like a conquered state, which we can carve up as in central Europe.'

The British government, however, could not ignore the prevailing spirit of the times. This, in part, explains the complexity of the solution it offered. The bill for 'the Better Government of Ireland' proposed two Irish parliaments, one for the six north-eastern counties to be called Northern Ireland, and another for the remaining twenty-six counties to be known as Southern Ireland. Both parts of Ireland were to continue to send representatives to Westminster. Without taking the trouble to consult Irish nationalists on the matter, Lloyd George assumed that they would find two Home Rule parliaments less objectionable than a straightforward exclusion of the north-east.

Ulster Unionists publicly declared they were making a 'supreme sacrifice' by accepting a Home Rule parliament in Belfast. Actually the whole arrangement suited them very nicely. Those in the six north-eastern counties had no wish to see the Ulster counties of Cavan, Monaghan and Donegal included in Northern Ireland. If they had been so inclined, the Unionist majority would be perilously thin, as the Co. Down MP, Captain Charles Craig, bluntly told the House of Commons: 'A couple of members sick, or two or three members absent for some accidental reason, might in one evening hand over the entire Ulster parliament and the entire Ulster position.'

Unionists soon got to like the idea of having their own parliament in Belfast. After all, the Labour and Liberal parties might form a government one day and decide to end partition. Having a parliament in Belfast might offer a protection against such an awful eventuality. As Charles Craig pointed out, 'We believe that if either of those parties, or the two in combination, were once more in power our chances of remaining a part of the United Kingdom would be very small indeed.'

Did Northern Ireland have to engulf the entire counties of Antrim, Down, Armagh, Londonderry, Tyrone and Fermanagh? Tyrone and Fermanagh then had nationalist majorities. In 1914 the Ulster Unionist leader, Sir Edward Carson, had argued that the four most Protestant counties, with a population greater than that of New Zealand, would make a perfectly viable unit. He kept quiet on that issue now. Poor Law Unions, rather than counties, could have been used as a better guide to drawing the frontier.

On 23 December 1920 the Government of Ireland Act entered the statute book. Northern Ireland came into being, with elections due on 24 May 1921. Carson privately hated partition and had no liking for devolution in Northern Ireland: 'You cannot knock parliaments up and down as you do a ball, and, once you have planted them there, you cannot get rid of them.' But Carson was not going to fall out with the Ulster Protestants now. Instead he pleaded ill-health and graciously handed the leadership over to his faithful lieutenant, Sir James Craig. Craig threw himself enthusiastically into Northern Ireland's first election:

Rally round me that I may shatter our enemies and their hopes of a republic flag. The Union Jack must sweep the polls. Vote early, work late.

The Union Jack did sweep the polls. Forty Unionists returned; and only six Sinn Féin and six Nationalists. By then it had become starkly obvious that the Government of Ireland Act had not solved the Irish Question. The most intense violence for more than a century now convulsed the whole island.

Episode 227 ~

'STRETCH OUT THE HAND OF FORBEARANCE'

In January 1921 the Irish War of Independence entered its most terrible phase. On New Year's Day British soldiers burned down seven houses in Midleton, Co. Cork. Reprisals of this kind, all too familiar over the previous six months, now had full government approval for the first time. It was a clear admission by the Prime Minister, David Lloyd George, that he had no remedy other than naked force.

Sinn Féin, representing a clear majority of the Irish people, contemptuously rejected the 1920 Government of Ireland Act. To them it was a 'Partition Act', offering a divided island and miserably weak devolved powers. The IRA fought on with relentless ferocity. Nearly 50,000 troops, police, special constables, Black and Tans and Auxiliaries in turn set pity aside. During the first six and a half months of 1921 at least 700 civilians died violently. Some fell caught in the crossfire. The IRA executed more than a hundred fellow Irish men and women, condemned as 'spies'. On a corpse found on the roadside in Co. Cork was pinned a label reading:

Convicted Spy. The penalty for all who associate with Auxiliary Cadets, Black and Tans and RIC. — IRA. Beware.

The crown forces killed even more Irish people in cold blood. Herbert Asquith, a former Prime Minister, declared from the opposition benches: 'Things are being done in Ireland which would disgrace the blackest annals of the lowest despotism in Europe.'

On 25 May 1921 over a hundred IRA volunteers entered the Custom House in Dublin, Ireland's finest Georgian building, and set fire to it. Troops quickly surrounded the men, killed five of them and captured seventy. The loss of men and arms represented a severe setback for the IRA. Avoiding roads and railways, troops operated across country with increasing success. But the government's ruthless repression attracted mounting criticism both at home and abroad. Lloyd George desperately sought a way out.

When George V offered to open the Northern Ireland parliament, Lloyd George seized the opportunity to offer an olive branch to Sinn Féin. The king's decision to go to Belfast was a brave one—ferocious sectarian battles raged there every day and night. Civil servants, Lloyd George and Jan Christian Smuts, the South African Prime Minister, carefully touched up the text of the king's speech. Lady Craig, wife of Northern Ireland's new Prime Minister, Sir James Craig, recorded in her diary:

> June 22nd. The great day.... The King and Queen have the most wonderful reception.... Even the little side streets that they will never be within miles of are draped with bunting and flags, and the pavement and lampposts painted red, white and blue, really most touching.... Trusted men stationed in each house, and on every roof top ...

In Belfast City Hall King George addressed only the Unionist MPs, senators and their wives. Nationalists and Sinn Féiners held to their pledge 'not to enter the north-eastern parliament'. But the king intended his speech to reach far beyond the walls of the City Hall:

> I speak from a full heart when I pray that my coming to Ireland today may prove to be the first step towards an end of strife amongst her people, whatever their race or creed.
>   In that hope, I appeal to all Irishmen to pause, to forgive and forget, to stretch out the hand of forbearance and conciliation, and to join in making for the land which they love a new era of peace, contentment and good will.

Back at the docks the king said to Craig: 'I can't tell you how glad I am I came, but you know my entourage were very much against it.'

George V's entourage had reason to be anxious. On the following day the IRA blew up the train carrying the king's cavalry escort back to Dublin, killing four men and eighty horses. June had been a violent month: RIC men killed at Swatragh, Co. Londonderry; special constables shot dead in Newry and Belfast; ten Catholics murdered, apparently in reprisal, by members of the Special Constabulary; intense intercommunal warfare and expulsions in Belfast's York Street, New Lodge Road and Tiger's Bay.

But the king's appeal had been heard. The IRA had had enough. Michael Collins later told a government minister: 'You had us dead beat. We could not have lasted another three weeks.' A truce was agreed on 9 July 1921, to come into force on 11 July. During those intervening three days the Black and Tans murdered a justice of the peace in Cork; the IRA killed two unarmed Catholic policemen and three unarmed soldiers in Co. Cork; and republicans assassinated three fellow-Irishmen as spies in the midlands, placing a label on one of the bodies: 'Sooner or later we get them. Beware of the IRA.'

A truce was one thing. A lasting settlement was quite another.

Episode 228 ∿

THE TREATY

On 14 July 1921 Eamon de Valera, President of Dáil Éireann, made his way to No. 10 Downing Street. A truce between the IRA and the British army had just come into force. Prime Minister David Lloyd George knew that this was a historic moment. Frances Stevenson, his private secretary and, indeed, his mistress, recalled:

> I have never seen David so excited as he was before De Valera arrived, at 4.30. He kept walking in and out of my room.... As I told him afterwards, he was bringing up all his guns! He had a big map of the British Empire hung up on the wall in the Cabinet room, with its great blotches of red all over it. This was to impress De Valera with the greatness of the British Empire and to get him to recognise it, and the King.

De Valera was not impressed. All that was agreed was that a delegation from the Dáil should go to London in the autumn to discuss terms.

De Valera refused to lead the delegation. He said this was to ensure unity at home. But was it because he knew that that he could not bring back from London the holy grail of a thirty-two-county republic? Arthur Griffith was chosen instead to lead the delegation of five, with Michael Collins as his deputy.

On Tuesday 11 October the Irish, wildly cheered on by supporters on the pavements, made their way from their base at 22 Hans Place to No. 10 Downing Street. Once inside, they faced a formidable team of seven cabinet ministers across the table. The Dáil representatives agreed on the following tactic: if the British would allow Ireland to leave the Empire, then the Irish would accept the existence of Northern Ireland. If not, then they would insist on 'essential unity', that is, a united Ireland. Weeks of deadlock followed.

Deftly Lloyd George worked separately on Griffith and Collins. He advanced a suggestion made by his principal secretary at the negotiations, Tom Jones, that a boundary commission could revise the frontier with Northern Ireland. The Irish in turn pressed de Valera's proposal that an independent Ireland could be 'externally associated' with the Empire. Further deadlock ensued.

The crucial development occurred on 5 December. Churchill subsequently recalled: 'After two months of futilities and rigmarole, unutterably wearied Ministers faced an Irish delegation themselves in actual desperation, and knowing well that death stood at their elbows.' It was in this highly charged atmosphere that Lloyd George suddenly fished an envelope out of his pocket. One of the Irish delegates asked Collins: 'What is this letter?' Collins replied: 'I don't know what the hell it is!' Then the Prime Minister said: 'Do you mean to tell me, Mr Collins, that you never learnt of this document from Mr Griffith?'

Lloyd George passed over the letter. It revealed that three weeks earlier Griffith had signed a document declaring that he would not break off negotiations simply because of disagreement on Northern Ireland. The Prime Minister asked Griffith if he was breaking faith. Griffith threw his pencil across the room, exclaiming: 'I have never let a man down in my whole life and I never will!'

Lloyd George then declared that he had promised to inform the Northern Ireland Prime Minister, Sir James Craig, immediately of the Irish delegates' response. Melodramatically Lloyd George held up two envelopes, one in either hand:

> Here are the alternative letters which I have prepared, one enclosing Articles of Agreement reached by His Majesty's Government and yourselves, and the other saying that the Sinn Féin representatives refuse to come within the Empire. If I send this letter it is war, and war within three days. Which letter am I to send? Whichever letter you choose travels by special train to Holyhead, and by destroyer to Belfast. The train is waiting with steam up at Euston. Mr Shakespeare [the Prime Minister's special envoy] is ready. If he is to reach Sir James Craig in time we must know your answer by 10 p.m. tonight. You can have until then, but no longer, to decide whether you will give peace or war to your country.

Actually it was 2.10 in the morning, on 6 December 1921, before the Irish delegation finally signed. Churchill handed round cigars, recalling afterwards: 'Michael Collins rose looking as if he was going to shoot somebody, preferably himself. In all my life I have never seen so much passion and suffering in restraint.' Later that day, on his way back to Ireland, Collins wrote home:

> Think—what have I got for Ireland? Something she has wanted these past seven hundred years. Will anyone be satisfied at the bargain? Will anyone? I tell you this—early this morning I signed my death warrant.

Three days later newspapers published an open letter from de Valera in which he stated:

> My friends, Irishmen ... the terms of the agreement are in violent conflict with the wishes of the majority of the nation.... I cannot recommend the acceptance of the Treaty either to Dáil Éireann or the country.

Episode 229 ~

THE SPLIT

The Anglo-Irish Treaty signed on 6 December 1921 in London went far beyond Home Rule. The Irish Free State was to become a Dominion, just like Canada. If Northern Ireland refused to come in, then the border would be redrawn by a Boundary Commission. Britain retained three naval bases. Dáil deputies had pledged themselves to a Republic. Now they were asked to take an oath of fidelity to King George v.

The Dáil cabinet accepted the Treaty, but by a margin of only one vote—and President de Valera himself opposed it. Now the debate was taken to the Dáil. Arthur Griffith, who had headed the Irish delegation in London, proposed the motion to approve the Treaty. The following extracts from the official account of Dáil proceedings reveal some of the more dramatic moments in the long and frequently acrimonious discussion that followed.

> *Deputy Griffith*: We have brought back the flag; we have brought back the evacuation of Ireland after 700 years by British troops and the formation of an Irish Army (*applause*).... We took an oath to the Irish Republic, but, as President de Valera himself said, he understood that oath to bind him to do the best he could for Ireland. So do we. We have done the best we could for Ireland.

> *Commandant Seán Mac Eoin*: A Chinn Chomhairle, I rise to second the motion.... In doing so, I take this course because I know I am doing it in the interests of my country which I love. To me symbols, recognitions, shadows, have little meaning.... I hold that this Treaty between the two nations gives us not shadows but real substances, and for that reason I am ready to support it.

> *President de Valera*: I am against this Treaty.... I wanted, and the Cabinet wanted, to get a document we could stand by.... That document makes British authority our masters in Ireland.... If the representatives of the Republic should ask the people of Ireland to do that which is inconsistent with the Republic, I say they are subverting the Republic. It would be a surrender ... to sign our names to the most ignoble document that could be signed....
>
> I have been brought up amongst the Irish people. I was reared in a labourer's cottage here in Ireland. I have not lived solely amongst the intellectuals—whenever I wanted to know what the Irish people wanted, I had

only to examine my own heart and it told me straight off what the Irish people wanted....

You have an oath to the Irish Constitution which will have the King of Great Britain as head of Ireland. You will swear allegiance to that King....

Mrs Pearse: It has been said here on several occasions that Pádraig Pearse would have accepted this Treaty. I deny it. As his mother I deny it, and on his account I will not accept it.

Deputy Collins: What I want to make clear is that it was the acceptance of the invitation that formed the compromise.... In my opinion it gives us freedom, not the ultimate freedom that all nations desire and develop to, but the freedom to achieve it (*applause*).

Madame Markievicz: Now, personally, I being an honourable woman, would sooner die than give a declaration of fidelity to King George or the British Empire.... I believe we never sent cleverer men over than we sent this time, yet they have been tricked. Now you all know me, you know that my people came over here in Henry viii's time, and by that bad black drop of English blood in me I know the English personally better than the people who went over on the delegation (*laughter*).
Deputy: Why didn't you go over?
Madame Markievicz: Why didn't you send me?

Deputy Childers: If Ireland's destiny is to be irrevocably linked with England in this Treaty ... the association ... is that of a bond slave.

Deputy O'Higgins: Deputy Childers ... did not tell us as an authority on military and naval matters, how we are going to break the British Army and Navy and get these better terms.

Mrs Clarke: Arthur Griffith said he had brought back peace with England, and freedom to Ireland. I can only say it is not the kind of freedom I have looked forward to.... God, the tragedy of it!

Deputy Cathal Brugha: The Head Quarters Staff ... worked ... patriotically for Ireland, with one exception—
Deputies: Shame! Get on with the Treaty!
Deputy Brugha: ... The gentleman I refer to is Mr Michael Collins.
Deputy Dan MacCarthy: Now we know the reason for the opposition to the Treaty ... (*applause*)
Deputy Brugha: ... Mr Michael Collins does not occupy that position in the Army that newspaper men said he occupied—
Seán MacGarry: I think we have had enough.

On 7 January 1922 the vote was taken: 64 votes for the motion and 57 against it. The Treaty had been approved by a majority of seven.

This was the 'Treaty split'. Passions now ran so high that, six months later, the Irish Free State would be plunged into civil war.

Episode 230 ∾

TROUBLES NORTH AND SOUTH

When Dáil Éireann accepted the Treaty on 7 January 1922, Eamon de Valera, bitterly opposed to it, stood for re-election as its President. In a bitter exchange, Arthur Griffith, for the Treaty, and Erskine Childers, against it, demonstrated in the Dáil the tension felt by all:

> *Deputy Griffith*: Now (*striking the table*) I will not reply to any Englishman in this Dáil (*applause*)....
> *Deputy Childers*: My nationality is a matter for myself....
> *Deputy Griffith*: ... I will not reply to any damned Englishman in this Assembly....
> *Deputy Childers*: ... I am not going to defend my nationality.... If he had banged the table before Lloyd George in the way he banged it here, things might have been different (*cries of 'Order' and applause*).

De Valera failed to be re-elected and Griffith became President in his place. De Valera then rose to leave the room with all his supporters. Collins led the trading of insults as they left:

> *Deputy Collins*: Deserters all! We will now call on the Irish people to rally to us. Deserters all! ...
> *Deputy Ceannt*: Up the Republic!
> *Deputy Collins*: ... Deserters all to the Irish nation in her hour of trial! We will stand by her.
> *Madame Markievicz*: Oath breakers and cowards!
> *Deputy Collins*: Foreigners—Americans—English!
> *Madame Markievicz*: Lloyd-Georgeites!

De Valera and his supporters would not return to the Dáil until 1927. A Provisional Government of the embryonic Irish Free State, an administrative body recognised by the British, was formed with Collins as Chairman. Desperately he and Griffith strove to prevent civil war.

And how was the Treaty received in Northern Ireland? The main Unionist concern was the means by which Lloyd George been able to get Sinn Féin to agree to remain within the Empire. This had been effected by Article XII, which provided for a Boundary Commission. Convinced that this could tear great lumps out of Northern Ireland, Prime Minister Craig went immediately to London to protest. Tom Jones, a cabinet secretary, reported to his superior: 'Sir James Craig was closeted with the PM.... He then went off to his Doctor to be inoculated—I suppose against a Sinn Féin germ. Anyhow, yesterday he charged the PM with a breach of faith.... Carson ... wrote a nasty letter.' Failing to get any satisfaction, Craig returned to Belfast to write a bitter missive to the Lord Privy Seal, Austen Chamberlain:

> What attitude will the British Government adopt if the government of Northern Ireland finds it necessary to call upon their friends and supporters—more especially the members of the Loyal Orange Institution—to come to their assistance by means of arms, ammunition and money from Great Britain, the Dominions and other parts of the world?... Violence is the only language understood by Mr Lloyd George and his Ministers.

In London Article XII of the Treaty was judged to be a political masterstroke. In Ulster it immediately magnified uncertainty and unrest. The truce of July 1921 had not stopped the killing in Northern Ireland. At peace in the south for the moment, the IRA used the truce to step up its campaign in the north. Then, in January 1922, whatever their views on the Treaty, IRA units united in an all-out attempt to destabilise Northern Ireland.

In Belfast loyalists attacked Catholic districts, now reinforced by IRA volunteers. Both sides perpetrated assassinations and reprisals of frightful barbarity. Altogether sixty-one people died in Belfast in the violence of March 1922. Isolated Catholic and Protestant families were particularly vulnerable, and intimidation, house-burning, rioting and murder drew the lines between the two communities in the city more tautly than ever. Atrocity followed atrocity, counter-assassination followed almost every death, and large areas of Belfast were virtually at war.

During the War of Independence the British government had not sent the notorious Black and Tans into the six north-eastern counties. Instead it had raised a Special Constabulary: A Specials, full-time and uniformed like the RIC; B Specials, by far the largest section, part-time, uniformed and unpaid, serving only in their own areas; and C Specials, an unpaid reserve force. From the outset the Special Constabulary had been an almost exclusively Protestant force. Whole units of the pre-war Ulster Volunteer Force, with their commanders, now joined the Specials. The *Westminster Gazette*, certainly not a radical publication, concluded that this 'is quite the most inhuman expedient the government could have devised [because] all the eager spirits who have driven nationalist workmen from the docks or have demonstrated their loyalty by looting Catholic shops will be eligible'.

The British government handed over control of the Specials to the Northern Ireland government. By the spring of 1922 the very survival of Northern Ireland seemed to be at stake. Craig responded to the crisis by greatly expanding the B class of the Special Constabulary. Protestant farmers and workers for the most part, on duty in their spare time and with no pay, the B Specials now bore the main brunt of the campaign to restore order in Northern Ireland.

Episode 231 ∽

CIVIL WAR

Robert McElborough, a gas worker, described conditions in east Belfast in the spring of 1922:

> I was taken off meter work and was told by the superintendent to keep the lamps in Seaforde Street and the Short Strand in repair.... Anyone who lived in the area remembers the cross-firing that was kept up day and night. No one would venture out and trams passed this area at full empty, or with passengers lying flat on the floor....
> I can't tell you how I got the cart into this area. I ran with it and got safely into Madrid Street ... with rifles cracking overhead.... It was the snipers on the roofs and back windows who were the danger. Anyone seen on the streets within the range of their gun was their target, and they found out later through the press what side he belonged to. I had seen men who were going to work shot dead as a reprisal for some other victim. My only dread was when I was standing on the ladder putting up a lamp, bullets that I suppose were meant for me went through the lamp reflector.

Conditions were little better in the Ulster countryside. On 5 April 1922 the government set up the Royal Ulster Constabulary, an armed police force closely modelled on the now disbanded Royal Irish Constabulary. In addition, more men joined the Special Constabulary—by the early summer there were no fewer than 50,000 regular and part-time policemen, that is, one policeman for every six families in the region.

On 7 April 1922 the Civil Authorities (Special Powers) Bill became law. This gave the Home Affairs minister authority to detain suspects without charge and to set up courts of summary jurisdiction. On 22 May the IRA assassinated W. J. Twaddell, Unionist MP for Woodvale. This led to the immediate imposition of internment. All 200 men arrested in the first sweep were Catholics, most of them held on board the *Argenta*, an old ship moored in Larne Lough.

Murders, ambushes and incendiary attacks continued unabated. Then, quite suddenly, this internecine conflict calmed down. The reason for this was that civil war had broken out in the south.

Arthur Griffith, Michael Collins and the newly formed Provisional Government desperately tried to prevent disagreement over the Anglo-Irish Treaty of December 1921 from descending into a civil war. A majority of senior IRA commandants supported the Treaty but most of the rank-and-file Volunteers did not. As British troops pulled out, the anti-Treaty IRA—soon to be known as the 'Irregulars'—began to occupy abandoned army barracks. On 14 April Irregulars seized the Four Courts, the Kildare Street Club and other prominent buildings in Dublin. Rory O'Connor, the anti-Treaty IRA commander in the Four Courts, when asked whether he supported military dictatorship, replied: 'You can take it that way if you like.' The anti-Treaty political leader, Eamon de Valera, told an audience in Thurles, Co. Tipperary, that if the Treaty was enforced, its opponents would

> have to wade through Irish blood, through the blood of soldiers of the Irish government, and through, perhaps, the blood of the members of the government in order to get Irish freedom.

A trade union leader recalled: 'We spent two hours pleading with de Valera, with a view to averting the calamity of civil war, and the only statement he made was this: "The majority has no right to do wrong."'

The citizens of the Irish Free State gave their verdict in a general election on 16 June 1922: pro-Treaty Sinn Féin, 58; anti-Treaty Sinn Féin, 36; Labour, 17; Farmers' Party, 7; Independents, 10.

The Irregulars refused to accept this verdict. Then, on 22 June, the IRA shot dead Field Marshal Sir Henry Wilson on the doorstep of his London home. Lloyd George's cabinet demanded that action be taken against the Irregulars if the terms of the Treaty were not to be broken.

In Dublin, shortly after midnight on Wednesday 28 June, troops of the Provisional Government's National Army, fully equipped for battle, took up their positions on the quays. Uniformed men trundled a field gun down the slope of Winetavern Street. Across the Liffey Irregulars in the Four Courts waited to see whether Irishmen would fire on Irishmen. Underneath the copper dome Father Albert told the assembled Irregulars to say an act of contrition. Tears ran down his cheeks as the men kneeled in the light of candles.

The dull yellow lights on the tram standards glowed through a steady drizzle as Commandant Emmet Dalton of the National Army stood by the field gun. Only a year before he had been fighting the British alongside the men now facing him across the river.

At 4.29 a.m. the field gun opened fire. Moments later a torrent of bullets poured from both sides of the Liffey. The Irish Civil War had begun.

Episode 232 ∽

GREEN AGAINST GREEN

Just after dawn on Wednesday 28 June 1922 the National Army of the Irish Free State, with an eighteen-pounder borrowed from the British, began shelling the Dublin Four Courts. Here, from the dome and the roof, the Irregulars, IRA men opposed to the Treaty, responded with sustained machine-gun and rifle fire.

By Thursday afternoon the relentless artillery bombardment had made a breach in the walls. Two thousand National Army troops—popularly known as 'Staters'—surged across Whitworth Bridge for the final assault. On Friday morning a temporary truce allowed twenty doctors, brought up on a horse-drawn coal dray, to treat the wounded of both sides. Inside the Four Courts, Ernie O'Malley ordered his men to pour paraffin on the scattered lawbooks. By midday the conflagration reached two lorry-loads of gelignite sticks stacked in the Public Record Office. A huge explosion rocked the city. An eye-witness recorded:

Black as ink, shot up, 400 feet into the sky, a giant column of writhing smoke and dust.... It spread into an enormous mushroom some 200 feet up and glared in the sun with lurid reds and browns, through which could be seen thousands of white snowflakes, dipping, sidling, curtsying, circling, floating as snowflakes do.

Documents going back to the twelfth century drifted over the city.

On Saturday afternoon the Four Courts garrison surrendered. The Irregulars now took the unequal fight to O'Connell Street. Cathal Brugha emerged from the burning Hammam Hotel and fell mortally wounded in a hail of bullets.

Sidelining Eamon de Valera, Liam Lynch took command of the Irregulars and carried the conflict to the countryside. At first former comrades in arms showed a reluctance to kill each other. A Kilkenny land agent wrote to his employer:

> There was a terrible battle here today between the Staters and Irregulars. They were shooting at one another all day, and it was a terrible battle. They stopped for a cup of tea and both sides admired your ladyship's chrysanthemums.

But this war between brother and brother soon surpassed the War of Independence for savagery. The bitterness and hostility generated by the conflict found open expression:

> Take it down from the mast, Irish traitors!
> The flag we republicans claim.
> It can never belong to Free Staters,
> You brought on it nothing but shame.

Limerick and Waterford cities fell to government troops on the same day, 20 July. Cork followed on 11 August. On 12 August President Arthur Griffith died suddenly. Ten days later the commander of the National Army, Michael Collins, fell mortally wounded in west Cork. His convoy had run into an Irregular ambush at Bealnablath, close to the area where he had spent his childhood.

The two leading signatories of the 1921 Treaty lay dead. William T. Cosgrave now headed the government. His cabinet did not flinch from adopting draconian special powers when the Irregulars launched a systematic campaign of assassination. On 7 December men from the anti-Treaty Dublin Brigade killed Seán Hales, a west Cork TD. Next morning, in reprisal, came the execution of four men who had surrendered at the Four Courts—one for each province: Liam Mellows, Rory O'Connor, Richard Barrett and Joe McKelvey:

> You've taken our brave Liam and Rory,
> You've murdered young Richard and Joe,
> Your hands with our blood is still gory
> Fulfilling the work of the foe.

Executions continued—seventy-seven in all before the war's end. Included was the anti-Treaty publicity officer, Erskine Childers, an Englishman.

The Irregulars began the Civil War far better armed than the whole IRA had been during the War of Independence. And the quality of the National Army recruits was low, as one of its generals, Eoin O'Duffy, admitted:

> We had to get work out of a disgruntled, undisciplined, and cowardly crowd. Arms were handed over wholesale to the enemy, sentries were drunk at their posts, and ... a whole garrison was put in clink owing to insubordination, etc.

But the Irregulars lacked sufficient support on the ground, as one of their leaders explained to Lynch:

> Our principal weakness then is that we have lost by the opposition of the people, our cover, our sources and intelligence, our supplies, transport.... The republican forces may have military successes, they cannot hope to beat the people.

So it proved. In daring amphibious operations the Provisional Government landed troops behind Irregular lines in the counties of Cork and Kerry. Then, on 10 April 1923, Lynch died fighting in the Knockmealdown Mountains in Co. Waterford. The surviving republican leaders faced the inevitable. On 24 May they issued a ceasefire order and allowed de Valera to publish this message:

> Military victory must be allowed to rest for the moment with those who have destroyed the Republic.

Episode 233 ∽

DIVIDED ULSTER

> Holy Mary, Mother of God,
> Pray for me and Tommy Todd,
> I'm a Fenian, he's a Prod,
> Holy Mary, Mother of God.

The outbreak of a vicious civil war in the Irish Free State in the summer of 1922 had been a remarkable stroke of good fortune for the Northern Ireland government. IRA units disengaged or withdrew from the north to fight each other south of the border. Incidents of violence—horrific though many of them were—steadily declined, and by 1923 it could be said that the region was at peace.

The price in blood for Northern Ireland's survival had been heavy. Between July 1920 and July 1922 the death toll had been 557 men, women and children— 303 Catholics, 172 Protestants, and 82 members of the security forces. In Belfast 236 people had been killed in the first months of 1922 alone. The remarkable fact is that there was not a single sectarian murder in Belfast between 1923 and 1933.

After the horrors of 1922 Northern Ireland enjoyed a remarkable calm, with perhaps the lowest 'ordinary' crime rate in Europe. But the 'Troubles' had left a bitter legacy, and intercommunal tensions had not been significantly reduced.

The people of Ulster liked to think their problems were unique. They were, but close parallels could be drawn between Northern Ireland and states emerging after the First World War from collapsed empires in central Europe. In a vain attempt to get him to agree to an all-Ireland parliament, the Prime Minister, David Lloyd George, had once written to Craig: 'The existing state of central and south-eastern Europe is a terrible example of the evils which spring from the creation of new frontiers.' No doubt it had been in reaction to a similar lecture that Craig had emerged from Downing Street in December 1921, saying: 'There's a verse in the Bible which says Czecho-Slovakia and Ulster are born to trouble as the sparks fly upwards.'

Whether or not the Northern Ireland Prime Minister understood the full implications of his remark is difficult to say. Czecho-Slovakia contained 4,600,000 Germans, Poles, Ruthenes and Hungarians out of a total population of 14,300,000. And here Czechs and Slovaks spoke the same language, though in different dialects; and in spite of appalling dangers threatening them, the devout Catholic peasants of Slovakia fiercely resented the domination of the urbanised Czech sceptics of Bohemia and Moravia. Only two-thirds of the inhabitants of Poland spoke Polish. Here, unlike Northern Ireland, language was the badge of distinction. Yugoslavia, however, provided a closer parallel, in that it was the ethnic tensions in the region that constantly threatened to destroy the new state. Mirroring the situation in Ulster, Bosnians, Croats and Serbs spoke the same language but remained bitterly divided by memories of past wrongs, cultural traditions and religion. Ethnic groups in Yugoslavia claimed to be able to distinguish each other by smell—just as people in Ulster had their own equally bogus means of identifying 'the other sort'.

Northern Ireland started out with assets that most of the new central European states did not possess. The evils of landlordism had largely been swept away. Like Czecho-Slovakia, but unlike most of the other new states, Northern Ireland had a developed industrial base, experience of representative institutions, and a substantial middle class from which competent public servants could be recruited. And, unlike Czecho-Slovakia, Northern Ireland had a powerful neighbour ready to provide support in times of crisis.

In September 1921 Craig had said in the Northern Ireland House of Commons:

We have nothing in our view except the welfare of the people.... Every person inside our particular boundary may rest assured that there will be nothing meted to them but the strictest justice. None need be afraid.

A year later this magnanimity had been severely eroded by the IRA campaign and mounting criticism from the British press. By the end of 1922 Craig's Protestant supporters had come to the conclusion that Catholics were aiming for nothing less than the destruction of Northern Ireland. Any Unionist MP offering compromise and concession risked annihilation at the polls.

Catholics formed one-third of the population. Their elected representatives refused to take their seats in the Northern Ireland parliament. Nationalist councils had given their allegiance to the Irish Free State. Catholics felt they were now much worse off than they had been under the direct rule of Westminster. More Catholics than Protestants had been killed in the recent violence. And Catholic relief organisations estimated that in Belfast between 8,700 and 11,000 Catholics had been driven out of their jobs, that 23,000 Catholics had been forced out of their homes, and that about 500 Catholic-owned businesses had been destroyed.

Craig and his colleagues now had to face this daunting challenge: how to govern fairly a population deeply divided for generations and possessing clashing political aspirations.

Episode 234 ❧

'NOT AN INCH!'

In 1922 the Northern Ireland government not only had to bring violent conflict to an end, it had also to establish its authority. It began by suppressing twenty-one nationalist-controlled local authorities which had pledged their allegiance to Dáil Éireann. Then in July the government rushed through a bill to abolish proportional representation in local government elections.

The London government hesitated: it had introduced PR in Ireland in 1920 to ensure the fair representation of minorities. But Lloyd George's rapidly disintegrating coalition government did not have the stomach to face down the Unionist cabinet in Belfast. And so, after two months' delay, the bill received the royal assent.

Nationalists paid a heavy price for refusing to co-operate with the commission which rearranged local government boundaries in the months that followed. The result was that local Unionist branches throughout the province, with the enthusiastic co-operation of Richard Dawson Bates, the Home Affairs minister, dictated the positioning of electoral boundaries with meticulous care to their own complete satisfaction.

The outcome of this blatant exercise in gerrymandering could be seen most obviously west of the River Bann. In Omagh Rural District Council, for example, Nationalists cast 5,381 more votes than Unionists, but the new electoral boundaries gave Unionists there a majority of eighteen.

Westminster seemed too absorbed by crises abroad to intervene. Joseph Devlin, the West Belfast MP, came to the conclusion that the Nationalists he led had no alternative but to end abstention and take their seats in the Northern Ireland parliament. Meanwhile William T. Cosgrave, premier of the Irish Free State, concentrated his energies entirely on ruthlessly crushing republicans in a savage civil war.

Not until the spring of 1924 did Cosgrave feel that he could turn his eyes northwards. Article XII of the Anglo-Irish Treaty of December 1921 provided for a Boundary Commission to revise the frontier between Northern Ireland and the Free State. Justice Richard Feetham represented Britain. Cosgrave appointed his Education minister, Eoin MacNeill to represent the Free State. And since Prime Minister Sir James Craig refused to have anything to do with the commission, Britain asked the Unionist journalist J. R. Fisher to represent Northern Ireland as the third commissioner.

Most nationalists expected large chunks of Northern Ireland to be assigned to the Free State. Certainly Craig and his colleagues feared as much. In April 1925 Craig called a snap election to demonstrate Unionist solidarity while the commission was at work. He coined an emotive rallying-cry: 'Not an inch!'

Craig need not have worried. This commission, unlike those determining German, Danish and Polish frontiers after the First World War, did not have to hold a referendum in border areas. Article XII vaguely allowed 'economic and geographical conditions' to be taken into account as well as 'the wishes of the inhabitants'. Feetham and Fisher argued that Newry and Derry were economically tied to Belfast.

Two against one: all was revealed when Fisher leaked the report's recommendations to the press. On 7 November 1925 the *Morning Post* published a 'forecast' of the Boundary Commission's report. Its map showed that slices of Donegal and Monaghan would be awarded to Northern Ireland, that Crossmaglen was the only town of any size assigned to the Free State, and that the population of Northern Ireland would be reduced by a mere 1.8 per cent.

MacNeill resigned. Cosgrave and Craig hurried over to London to confer with Stanley Baldwin, the British Prime Minister. There they agreed to suppress the Boundary Commission and to maintain the existing border. Craig returned to Belfast on 5 December to a magnificent reception. Shipyard workers gave him a gold-mounted portion of a foot rule—the inch he had not surrendered. The Northern Ireland parliament presented Craig with a large silver cup with the words 'Not an inch' inscribed on the plinth.

Nationalists had been forced to accept that, whether they liked it or not, they were all citizens of Northern Ireland. By 1928 ten Nationalists sat on the opposition benches along with three Labour MPs and a couple of independents.

Nationalists got no reward for returning fully to constitutional politics. In the whole period of devolved rule up to 1972 the only bill Nationalists successfully sponsored was the Wild Birds Protection Act. Then in 1929 Craig—now elevated to the peerage as Lord Craigavon—abolished PR in Northern Ireland parliamentary elections. The impact proved most severe not on Nationalists but on the smaller parties. Nationalists, nevertheless, regarded this as another slap in the face for the minority. In 1932 Devlin addressed the governing party in the House of Commons:

> You had opponents willing to co-operate.... We sought service. We were willing to help. But you rejected all friendly offers.... You went on the old political lines, fostering hatreds, keeping one-third of the population as if they were pariahs in the community.

Episode 235 ~

NORTHERN IRELAND: DEPRESSION YEARS

There is a happy land, far, far away
Where they eat bread and jam three times a day.
O how we sweetly sing, dancing round the gravy ring,
O how we'd love to be far, far away.

Hunger marked the years between the two world wars in Northern Ireland. During the winter of 1920 the brief post-war boom had juddered to a halt. By 1922 the unemployment rate reached 23 per cent, and for the rest of the 1920s on average one-fifth of all insured workers had no jobs. For Northern Ireland the Depression began early—the 'roaring twenties' had no meaning here. The slump developed into a protracted depression.

No one had predicted this. Was the Unionist government to blame? No—Westminster had not really given it enough power to provide significant help. And Belfast and Derry were not alone: Glasgow, Liverpool, Manchester and Tyneside all suffered in the same way.

The basic problem was that the First World War had brought about traumatic changes in world trading conditions. Dangerously dependent on exporting a limited range of products, Northern Ireland found that other states now built ships, constructed machinery and wove cloth in more effective competition. Then on 23 October 1929 security prices on the Wall Street stock market crumbled in a wave of frenzied selling.

The collapse of business confidence after the great speculative orgy of 1928–9 resulted in an unrelieved world depression lasting ten years. The shock waves surged east across the Atlantic: in June 1931 came the collapse of Austria's leading bank; in August 1931 there were six million out of work in Germany; in January 1933 the volume of international trade was barely one-third of what it had been on the eve of the Wall Street Crash.

In Belfast grass grew on the slipways of Harland & Wolff. Queen's Island did not witness the launch of a single ship between 10 December 1931 and 1 May 1934. Workman Clark, the 'wee yard', had no choice but to close down forever in January 1935.

> Datsie-dotsie, miss the rope, you're outie-o,
> If you'd've been, where I have been,
> You wouldn't have been put outie-o,
> All the money's scarce, people out of workie-o,
> Datsie-dotsie, miss the rope, you're outie-o.

As the economic crisis worsened the Lord Mayor of Belfast, Sir Crawford McCullagh, received a blizzard of letters desperately requesting help; for example, 'I think I am not getting fair play.... As a Champion Side Drummer and the most known man in the procession I think I should get a start somewhere.' A failed businessman also wrote: 'I am both Orange and Freemason.... I am appealing to you Sir Crawford.... I am without food both Wife and myself for these past Four days.'

The feelings of frustration and anger eventually found expression in the Northern Ireland parliament. On 30 September 1932 Jack Beattie, Labour MP for Pottinger, leaped to his feet in the House of Commons and threw the mace on the floor, shouting: 'I am going to put this out of action.... The House indulges in hypocrisy while there are starving thousands outside.' In support, Tommy Henderson, Independent MP for Shankill, roared above the tumult: 'What about the 78,000 unemployed who are starving?'

The insured unemployed got the dole, the 'b'roo', for six months only. Then they had to survive on 'outdoor relief' provided by the Board of Guardians.

This relief, which had to be earned by work on the roads, was the lowest for any city in the United Kingdom.

On Monday 3 October 1932 60,000 unemployed, Protestants and Catholics together, marched to a torch-lit rally at the Custom House. Their bands—careful to avoid party tunes—played the hit of the day, 'Yes, We Have No Bananas'. Protests, banned by the government, reached a climax on Tuesday 11 October. At Templemore Avenue, the *Belfast Telegraph* reported, police drew their batons:

> They formed up in marching order, whilst at their lead rushed a man wearing a cap, shouting wildly, 'Fall in and follow me'.... As the crowd continued to advance an order was given: 'Draw-Ready-Charge!' Men in the crowd went down like ninepins, and the rest fled helter skelter. [On the Lower Falls] constables wearing bandoliers filled with bullets and with rifles at the ready were speedily jumping out of caged cars.... Batons were useless and the police were compelled to fire.

On the Falls Road two men, one a Protestant and another a Catholic, fell mortally wounded. News of the fighting reached the Shankill. The *Irish Press* journalist James Kelly reported: 'I remember a woman with a shawl come running to the people I was talking to. She shouted: "They're kicking the shite out of the peelers up the Falls. Are youse going to let them down?"' Shankill Protestants swiftly ran to the aid of the Lower Falls rioters.

Soon after these events the government, highly alarmed, forced the Belfast Guardians to announce substantial increases in relief. Peace returned, but prosperity did not.

Episode 236 ～

'AN EMPTY POLITICAL FORMULA'

Kevin O'Higgins, the Irish Free State's first Home Affairs minister, described the Provisional Government as

> simply eight young men ... standing amidst the ruins of one administration, with the foundations of another not yet laid, and with wild men screaming through the key-hole. No police was functioning through the country, no system of justice was operating, the wheels of the administration hung idle, battered out of recognition by the clash of rival jurisdictions.

That was in 1922. By the end of May 1923 the government had crushed the anti-Treaty forces. A heavy price had been paid: perhaps as many as 4,000 killed; a debt of £17 million; the cost of destruction, a further £30 million; and a legacy of bitterness for decades to come. The defeated republicans would not forget that seventy-seven of their number had been executed on the orders of military courts. And 12,000 republicans languished in jail, including in solitary confinement their leader, Eamon de Valera.

Could democracy survive in the Free State, the British Commonwealth's youngest dominion? In central and eastern Europe democracy proved a tender flower: it had already been trampled underfoot in Italy, Poland, Hungary and Romania. In Dáil Éireann the Labour Party, the Farmers Party and independents played a crucial role in tending the young Irish plant, scrutinising the work of the government.

W. T. Cosgrave headed the governing pro-Treaty party, Cumann na nGaedheal, which means 'club (or party) of the Irish'. Anti-Treaty Sinn Féin formed the second-largest party. But its deputies refused to sit in the Dáil because, thanks to the Anglo-Irish Treaty of 1921, they would have to take an oath of fidelity to the king. De Valera, released from prison, became certain that abstention was self-defeating. On 16 May 1926 in Dublin's La Scala Theatre he formed a new political party, Fianna Fáil, literally the 'Soldiers of Destiny'. It differed from Sinn Féin in that it accepted the legitimacy of the Free State and forsook violence as a means of achieving its aims. It was slightly worrying, however, that Seán Lemass approvingly described Fianna Fáil as 'a slightly constitutional party'. At first only twenty-one of the abstentionist TDs joined de Valera.

Then in the general election of June 1927 Fianna Fáil won 44 seats, leaving hardline Sinn Féin with only five. Clearly the anti-Treaty electorate preferred de Valera's approach. Cumann na nGaedheal, with 47 seats, urgently needed the support of smaller parties and independents to stay in power. De Valera and his supporters had been prepared to embark on a civil war in 1922 in preference to accepting an oath to the crown. Now what was he to do? Hardline republican militants in effect decided the issue. On 10 July 1927 three gunmen shot and mortally wounded Kevin O'Higgins, now the Minister for Justice and External Affairs, as he walked to Mass in Booterstown, Co. Dublin.

Cosgrave, in response, pushed through legislation to make it easier to act against fringe republican militants. He also got support for a bill under which all Dáil candidates would have to swear to take their seats if elected. After much agonising, but no doubt tempted by the prospect of power, de Valera announced that Fianna Fáil deputies would fulfil the constitutional formalities, but only because the oath was, in his words, 'an empty political formula'. But if it had been an empty formula, many asked, why had republicans gone to war in 1922 rather than take it?

On 11 August 1927 Fianna Fáil deputies arrived at the Dáil in a body. Revolvers bulged in their pockets, and in a phone box one TD assembled a tommy gun, but there was no violence. And what about the oath? When presented with it, de Valera put a blank piece of paper over the oath, signed it, and said to the clerk: 'Remember, I have signed no oath.'

However unconvincing de Valera's tortuous thinking, he and his supporters had taken a crucial step towards the preservation of democracy in Ireland. Cosgrave, now staying in power with a perilously thin majority, deserves at least as much credit for allowing irreconcilable opponents he had defeated in a civil war the opportunity to become a government in the future.

Between 1918 and 1923 Ireland had undergone a revolution. So had many other European countries at the same time. But in Ireland this was a political revolution only, not a social one. The Irish revolution had swept away not only the British ruling elite but also the men of the Irish Parliamentary Party who had, until 1918, fully expected to become the government of the country. The new elite, veterans of the Easter Rising and the War of Independence, and thankful that Ireland had survived civil war, had no desire to turn Irish society upside down. This was particularly true of the members of Cumann na nGaedheal.

Episode 237 ᔓ

THE ECONOMIC WAR

During the summer of 1929 crowds from all over Ireland flocked to Co. Clare to see the great hydroelectric scheme at Ardnacrusha reach completion. Over four years a huge labour force, working from four special camps, had been busy building concrete weirs, bridges and dams to harness the power of the River Shannon. The contractor, Siemens-Schuckert, proudly displayed over 5,000 photographs of its prestige development back in Germany.

The 'scheme'—as everyone called it—provided a striking indication of the extent to which the Irish Free State had settled down since the Civil War of 1922–3. The ruling party, Cumann na nGaedheal, was understandably proud of its achievements. The President of the Executive Council, W. T. Cosgrave, and his colleagues aimed, above all, at stability. They had no intention of promoting sweeping changes in Irish society. Cosgrave's deputy, Kevin O'Higgins, said before being murdered by the IRA in 1927 that he and his colleagues were 'the most conservative revolutionaries that ever put through a successful revolution'.

The Shannon Scheme, which by 1937 supplied 87 per cent of the state's electricity needs, proved to be the only adventurous economic step taken by the Cumann na nGaedheal government. Aware that Britain took around 90 per cent of the Free State's exports, ministers had no wish to antagonise the former ruler by imposing irritating import duties. Taxes remained low, and welfare services were pared back to a bare minimum. All this suited the largely middle-class and mainly conservative Protestant minority; indeed, Cosgrave went out of his way to attend functions organised by men who had so recently been Unionists.

Then in October 1929, the same month that the Shannon Scheme began generating electricity for sale, the Wall Street stock market crashed. As the numbers of unemployed leaped alarmingly, the Cosgrave administration's knee-jerk response—like Brüning's government in Germany—was to cut the pay of the police, civil servants and teachers and to reduce old age pensions.

Cosgrave called a general election in February 1932. The number out of work had now risen to over 100,000. Election posters proclaimed:

WE WANT NO 'REDS' HERE! KEEP THEIR COLOUR OFF YOUR FLAG!
Vote for Cumann na nGaedheal

The almost hysterical government campaign against 'Reds', in a conservative state where support for communism and left-wing socialism was probably weaker than anywhere else in Europe, seemed a poor response to an economic crisis.

The government lost the election. Eamon de Valera took office, forming a Fianna Fáil administration with the support of the Labour deputies. It could be said that Cosgrave's greatest achievement was the impeccable manner in which he accepted loss of office and encouraged the civil service, the army and the Gardaí to work on loyally for men he had fought and imprisoned during the Civil War.

De Valera brought some improvement to the state's infant social services, subsidised council house building and raised payments to the unemployed. Socially, he proved to be just a little less conservative than Cumann na nGaedheal. Politically, however, de Valera was a radical. He had taken the republican side in the civil war in 1922 in opposition to the 1921 Anglo-Irish Treaty. Now he set about dismantling that Treaty.

In April 1932 de Valera removed the oath of allegiance to the crown from the constitution. Then in July he withheld the land annuities from Britain—these were repayments made by farmers for money lent to them by previous British governments to buy out their landlords. The United Kingdom responded by slapping a 20 per cent duty on two-thirds of the Free State's exports. De Valera in turn retaliated by imposing heavy import duties on

British imports and by erecting a high tariff barrier behind which he hoped native Irish industries would flourish. The so-called 'Economic War' had begun.

These developments swiftly led to further dislocation of the Free State economy. Angry farmers, businessmen and workers, injured by the interruption of trade, began to organise in opposition to the Fianna Fáil government. The Army Comrades' Association, formed by ex-servicemen in February 1932, now attracted recruits with dizzying speed. Members paraded in blue shirts and adopted the fascist salute.

After a snap election de Valera returned to office, this time with an overall Fianna Fáil majority, on 24 January 1933. Six days later Adolf Hitler took power in Germany. In all of central and eastern Europe just one democracy, Czecho-Slovakia, remained alive. Fascist leagues rampaged through the streets of Paris, Brussels, Madrid, Lisbon and Oslo.

In the Irish Free State democratic institutions came under perilous attack from two opposite directions. On one side was the IRA, its members freed from imprisonment by de Valera in 1932 and now flexing their muscles with knuckledusters and revolvers; and on the other was the fascist-saluting and club-wielding Blueshirts, now led by Eoin O'Duffy, recently dismissed as Garda Commissioner by de Valera.

Episode 238 ⌒

DEMOCRACY IN PERIL

In 1932 Eamon de Valera, freshly elected as President of the Executive Council, lifted the previous government's ban on the IRA and released IRA prisoners. Members of the IRA showed de Valera little gratitude. Openly brandishing arms, they intimidated shopkeepers who sold children sweets imported from England; attacked vans carrying Cadbury's cocoa; smashed open hundreds of barrels of Bass beer because it was British brewed; and, with the slogan 'no free speech for traitors', violently broke up meetings held by their political opponents. Their Chief of Staff and future Nobel Peace Prize winner, Seán MacBride, declared his opposition to democratic institutions: 'I have very little faith in the mass of constitutional republicans nor in the opinion of the mass of the people.'

On the other side of the political divide were the IRA's most hated opponents, the Blueshirts. Adopting the uniform style and straight-armed salute of fascists overseas, the Blueshirts claimed to be protecting the state from extremists. De Valera feared that they were infiltrating the army and the Gardaí and plotting to seize power by force. We now know that the Blueshirt leader, Eoin O'Duffy, when still Commissioner of the Garda Síochána, certainly had plotted a *coup d'état* in 1932 to prevent Fianna Fáil from coming to power.

In July 1933 O'Duffy announced that a march would take place in the following month to the front of Leinster House. Was this to overawe the Dáil, to take power by force, as Mussolini had by marching on Rome in 1922? De Valera acted quickly. Police carried out raids on the homes of Blueshirt leaders and found weapons in some of them. The Gardaí recruited a new special force. Uniformed police swamped the area around Leinster House. Finally the government banned the march and O'Duffy—hardly acting in the manner of a potential Duce—called it off.

Meanwhile Cumann na nGaedheal, which had governed Ireland for ten years, joined forces with the small Centre Party and—more ominously—with the Blueshirts. The name assumed by the new party was 'Fine Gael', meaning the 'Family of the Irish'. Shocked by de Valera's political and economic confrontation with the United Kingdom, some in Fine Gael were deeply attracted now to anti-democratic ideas. Ernest Blythe, an Ulster Presbyterian Irish-language enthusiast and a former Cumann na nGaedheal minister, urged that parliamentary democracy be replaced by a corporate body, an arrangement which would involve 'a drastic limitation of the powers of parliament, and the creation of a voluntary disciplined public service organisation'.

Most politicians in Fine Gael, however, observed with alarm how O'Duffy toured the country making wild speeches, usually under the influence of drink, and provoking riots and disturbances wherever he went. One Fine Gael TD, James Dillon, stood behind O'Duffy on a platform in west Cork:

> He was speaking very rapidly. It dawned on me that they were hanging on his words in a kind of obsessed way and I suddenly realized that he was speaking without any verbs.... It dawned on me that if this fellah told them to go and burn the town, they'd do it. I thought: 'We've got to get rid of this man—he could be dangerous.' I remembered Hitler.

Fortunately for Fine Gael, O'Duffy quarrelled incessantly and resigned in September 1934 to set up his own party. Ferocious battles between Blueshirts and the IRA continued, but the fascist threat to Irish democracy, such as it was, faded rapidly.

Then de Valera, somewhat belatedly, turned his full attention to the IRA. Some squalid IRA murders—including that of the elderly Vice-Admiral Henry Boyle Somerville who had committed the crime of writing references for boys in west Cork applying to join the Royal Navy—gave de Valera his opportunity.

He banned the IRA in 1936, imprisoned activists under the 1931 Public Safety Act, and—when the IRA began a bombing campaign in England in January 1939—he adopted further draconian powers.

By 1937 de Valera had reduced the original 1922 Free State constitution to tatters. The abdication of Edward VIII created a useful opportunity for the drafting of a new constitution, 'Bunreacht na hÉireann'. Approved by referendum by an uncomfortably small majority, the 1937 constitution changed the name of the state to Éire and the title of the premier to Taoiseach.

De Valera also ended the destructive economic war with Britain in the 1938 Anglo-Irish Agreement. Prime Minister Neville Chamberlain, worried by developments in central Europe, proved eager to end all disputes with his western neighbour. For de Valera, this agreement was a triumph. Britain dropped the retaliatory duties; the dispute over land annuities was settled by an Irish lump-sum payment of £10 million; and the Royal Navy gave up its bases at Berehaven, Lough Swilly and Cóbh.

Neither the 1937 constitution nor the agreement of 1938 were to the liking of the Northern Ireland government.

Episode 239 ～

'FORGET THE UNHAPPY PAST'

> Devalery had a canary
> Up the leg of his drawers
> And when it got down
> It sat on the ground
> And whistled 'The Protestant Boys'.

Eamon de Valera, taking office in the south in February 1932, caused much alarm in the northern Unionist camp. Intercommunal tension mounted. And an observation by Cardinal Joseph MacRory did not help. When the Church of Ireland announced plans to celebrate the coming of St Patrick 1,500 years before, the cardinal publicly declared:

> The Protestant Church in Ireland—and the same is true of the Protestant Church anywhere else—is not only not the rightful representative of the early Irish Church, but it is not even a part of the Church of Christ.

In June 1932 special trains and buses returning with Catholic pilgrims from the Eucharistic Congress in Dublin came under loyalist attack at Loughbrickland, Portadown, Kilkeel, Lisburn and Belfast. Tension increased as the marching season got under way. Resolutions included denunciations of 'the unchanging bigotry of Rome' and 'the arrogant, the intolerant and un-Christian pretensions fulminated by Cardinal MacRory'.

During the autumn of 1932 unemployed Protestants and Catholics in Belfast united in massive demonstrations against the infamous 'outdoor relief' system. But sectarian feeling rapidly reappeared thereafter. The Twelfth demonstrations of 1933 provided more opportunities for divisive speeches. As reported in the *Fermanagh Times*, this is what Sir Basil Brooke, the Minister of Agriculture, said at Newtownbutler:

> There were a great number of Protestants and Orangemen who employed Roman Catholics. He felt he could speak freely on this subject as he had not a Roman Catholic about his place.... He would point out that the Roman Catholics were endeavouring to get in everywhere.... He would appeal to Loyalists, therefore, wherever possible, to employ Protestant lads and lassies.

Brooke's neighbour, Captain T. T. Verschoyle, a prominent Co. Fermanagh landlord, condemned the speech: 'He who sows the wind shall reap the whirl-wind.... It remains to be seen whether the Colebrooke Hitler will receive a well-merited rebuke from a responsible member of the government.'

There was no rebuke. When the Nationalist MP Cahir Healy raised the issue of Brooke's speech at Stormont, Craigavon replied: 'There is not one of my colleagues who does not entirely agree with him, and I would not ask him to withdraw one word.' He added:

> I have always said I am an Orangeman first and a politician and Member of this Parliament afterwards.... The Hon. Member must remember that in the South they boasted of a Catholic State.... All I boast is that we are a Protestant Parliament and a Protestant State.

In 1935 feelings ran high again. Dr John MacNeice, Church of Ireland Bishop of Down and Connor, made this appeal on the eve of the Twelfth:

> Forget the things that are behind. Forget the unhappy past. Forget the stories of the old feuds, the old triumphs, the old humiliations.

At the Belmont 'Field', Grand Master Sir Joseph Davison referred directly to the bishop's appeal:

Are we to forget that the flag of Empire is described as a foreign flag and our beloved King insulted by Mr De Valera? Are we to forget that the aim of these people is to establish an all-Ireland Roman Catholic State, in which Protestantism will be crushed out of existence?

That night, as the procession returned, fierce fighting broke out in York Street in Belfast. The violence continued, and the army had to be called in. It was nearly the end of August before the rioting ceased, by which time eight Protestants and five Catholics had been killed, and over 2,000 Catholics had been driven from their homes.

In de Valera's 1937 constitution, Articles 2 and 3 claimed the constitutional right of the Dublin government to exercise jurisdiction over the whole of Ireland. Numerous clauses were bound to be repugnant to Protestants. Article 44 recognised the main Protestant churches, the Jewish congregation and other denominations, but gave 'special' recognition to the Catholic Church. Other articles enshrined Catholic social teaching on the family and made divorce, contraception and the publication of immoral literature not only illegal but unconstitutional.

Craigavon called a general election in February 1938 to show his contempt for de Valera's Ireland. The contest was fiercest in the constituency of Dock in Belfast, where the sitting Labour MP, Harry Midgley, championed the Popular Front in the Spanish Civil War then raging. The Nationalist candidate, James Collins, vociferously backed Franco and was denounced by Midgley as 'a killer of babies'. Feelings ran high:

> Vote, vote, vote for Harry Midgley,
> In comes Collins at the door—I-O!
> For Collins is the one who's goin' to have some fun,
> And we don't want Midgley any more—GET OUT!

In fact neither Midgley nor Collins won the seat—it was captured by a Unionist. The Unionists, overall, had won a crushing majority. Craigavon had made his point to de Valera.

Episode 240 ~

'CRYING FOR A HAPPIER LIFE'

The world depression of the 1930s caused destitution everywhere; and, by western European standards, Ireland was hit hard. In the Irish Free State the numbers on the unemployment register reached 145,000 in 1936. In Northern Ireland 101,967 had no work in July 1935, and in February 1938 29.5 per cent of insured industrial workers were unemployed.

Harold Binks, a trade union official, remembered seeing barefoot children waiting at the Albert Bridge pens in Belfast to get the unwanted, unsterilised milk from cows about to be shipped to England. The vigorous efforts—not always successful—to ensure the pasteurisation of milk in Belfast were not mirrored in Dublin. There a government committee reported that the Dublin slums were crammed with children crippled as a result of drinking contaminated milk. Dr Robert Collis, a Dublin paediatrician, estimated that about 40,000 people in Dublin were attempting to feed themselves on sixpence a day. He had grown tired of giving medicine to poor children who really needed food.

People living on the land had a better life expectancy than their city counterparts. But depressed prices ensured that a great many farmers lived in extreme poverty. Northern Ireland's farms were exceptionally small: a third of them contained ten acres or less. The income of small farmers was reckoned to be lower than an unemployed man received on the dole. In the Irish Free State, which became Éire in 1937, fewer than a fifth of farms were fifty acres or more in size.

Many of those attempting to make a living on the land gave up the struggle: they voted with their feet by leaving the island altogether. Nearly half a million people—most of them young and from the countryside—left the twenty-six counties during the 1920s and 1930s. The Fianna Fáil governments, eager to uphold rural values, erected 16,526 labourers' cottages. The same energy was not shown in Dublin. Here, in 1938, 111,950 people lived in 6,307 tenements, half of them deemed to be irreparably unfit for habitation. Governments could not face the expense of buying out the slum landlords. In 1936 the *Irish Press*, Fianna Fáil paper though it was, concluded:

> If this is the second century of slumdom, it is also the 14th year of a self-governed state, when the babies of 1916 are still, as men and women, crying for a happier life for their babies, crying for simple shelter.

Dublin Corporation did build 7,637 houses between 1933 and 1939. Belfast Corporation in the entire period between the two world wars put up only just over 2,000 council houses. And even this feeble effort had been attended by scandals involving profiteering and the use of inferior materials. Co. Fermanagh did not see a single dwelling built by public enterprise in these years.

Overcrowding, malnutrition and general poverty kept death rates from disease alarmingly high. A government survey reported that 60 per cent of Dublin mothers were unable to breastfeed because they were so undernourished. There the infant mortality rate was 90 per 1,000. In Belfast it was even higher: 96 per 1,000 compared with 59 per 1,000 in Sheffield. Anne Boyle, a resident of the Oldpark district, remembered:

> There was so much infant mortality that it seemed as if every week blue baby coffins were coming out of every street. I had three brothers and a sister dead before they were two years old, out of eleven of us.

At Stormont Professor R. J. Johnstone told fellow-MPs: 'Maternity is a more dangerous occupation in Northern Ireland than in the Free State or in England.' He was right: maternal mortality actually *rose* by one-fifth between 1922 and 1938. And the most feared disease, the main killer of young adults was tuberculosis. Dr Noël Browne, later Éire's Minister for Health, remembered that his afflicted brother was

> unwanted, crippled and unable to fend for himself or communicate his simplest needs, except to the family; he was unable to mix with his peers. It is impossible to imagine the awesome humiliation and desperation of his life.

In Belfast Anne Boyle recalled:

> There were twenty-eight in my class at school, and when I was about twenty-five I would say that half of those girls were dead, mostly from tuberculosis.... I remembered the sexton of Sacred Heart chapel, Paddy McKernan; all he had was four daughters, and those four daughters died within a couple of years. They were teenage girls.

There seemed to be no promise of an end to the Depression. Then on 3 September 1939, when Kilkenny triumphed over Cork in the All-Ireland Hurling Final in Croke Park, Prime Minister Neville Chamberlain told listeners on the BBC that the United Kingdom was at war.

Episode 241 ~

THE EMERGENCY

On 3 September 1939 Britain and France declared war on Germany. Members of the Dáil and the Seanad had been sitting all night to listen to the Taoiseach, Eamon de Valera, and to approve his decision that Éire would remain neutral. After supporting an Emergency Powers Bill to give the government special powers 'in time of war' to secure the public safety, they came out of Leinster House to attend six o'clock Mass. That afternoon a fierce thunderstorm swept Croke Park as Kilkenny defeated Cork in the All-Ireland Hurling Final. The same storm brought down a British four-engined Sunderland flying-boat, forcing it to land just off Skerries eleven miles north of Dublin. The local Gardaí brought the crew ashore by dingy and, after deciding quickly not to intern the airmen, allowed them to get fuel from the local petrol station and fly away. The incident was not reported in the press. That night the British liner *Athenia* was torpedoed by the German submarine U-30 off the coast of Donegal with a loss of 112 lives.

Could Ireland really remain neutral? German U-boats were menacing Allied shipping all around Ireland's coasts. On 9 September the 6,000-ton *Olive Grove* was torpedoed off Co. Cork, and on 25 September a U-boat shelled and sank the British steamer *Hazleside* off Schull; the first man to die was Denis Treacy from Arklow, hit in the face by a shell. Nevertheless, the people of Éire supported neutrality. The only Dáil deputy to argue that Britain should be supported in this war was James Dillon, and he was forced to resign from Fine Gael soon after.

Certainly Éire's defences were miserably inadequate. At the beginning of September 1939 the army had only 6,000 regular soldiers, poorly trained and equipped. Plans to mobilise more men largely failed through lack of money, and by May 1940 there were still only 13,500 men. In that year it was reported in confidence that there was 'almost a complete absence of the most important weapons, namely anti-tank weapons, anti-aircraft weapons and automatic weapons' and 'a very considerable deficiency of artillery and mortars'. On 15 May 1940 Colonel Liam Archer of Irish Intelligence told Guy Liddell, MI5's Director of Counter-Intelligence, that Irish resistance would not last a week if the Germans landed. Early in 1942 the Air Corps had just six slow-flying Lysanders and three obsolete Gloucester Gladiator fighter biplanes. The navy consisted of one armed trawler, *Fort Rannoch*, and *Muirchú* (this latter vessel was in fact the gunboat *Helga*, used against insurgents in Dublin in 1916 and subsequently bought from the British and renamed).

At first the principal threat seemed to be the enemy within. On Saturday 23

December 1939 a man called with a Christmas parcel at the Magazine Fort in Phoenix Park. When the guard stepped out to accept it, IRA men seized the fort, and over the next two hours, using a dozen lorries, the raiders made off with a great quantity of small arms and a million rounds of ammunition. Though most of the ammunition was later recovered, this was clear evidence that de Valera was wrong when he said that he had broken the power of the IRA.

On the night of 22 May 1940 the Gardaí raided the Dublin home of an IRA agent, Stephen Held. They discovered a radio transmitter, a uniform, $20,000, coded messages, and evidence that Dr Herman Görtz, a German spy parachuted into Co. Meath, had been staying in the house. It became clear that there was close collaboration between the Third Reich and the IRA. Little resulted from this alliance. Though Görtz remained at liberty for more than a year, most other German spies were quickly captured after arrival. A plan to take two IRA leaders, Seán Russell and Frank Ryan, from Germany to Ireland by U-boat was abandoned after Russell died on board. That there were collaborators ready to welcome the Germans is clear. They included Dan Breen, the War of Independence veteran, and Iseult Stuart; and three northern nationalists, Senator Thomas McLaughlin, Peadar Murney and John Southwell, who decided at a meeting with the German Minister in Dublin, Edouard Hempel, 'to place the Catholic minority in the north under the protection of the Axis powers'.

On 26 June 1940 Malcolm MacDonald, on behalf of the British government, handed de Valera a one-page memorandum. The Germans had swept through the Netherlands, Belgium and Luxemburg, driven the remnants of the British army to Dunkirk, and accomplished the surrender of France. Winston Churchill was now British Prime Minister. The paper offered a declaration accepting the principle of a united Ireland if Éire joined the war effort. De Valera was not tempted, mainly because he did not think Britain would be successful in obtaining 'the assent thereto of the Government of Northern Ireland'.

On the night of the Japanese attack on Pearl Harbor Churchill sent a final message to de Valera: 'Now is your chance, now or never, a nation once again.' But not only did the Taoiseach refuse his request to make the Treaty ports available again to Britain; he even sent a formal protest to the USA when American troops landed in Northern Ireland in January 1942. However, Sir John Maffey, the British Representative in Dublin, quietly came to the conclusion that a neutral Éire was actually, on balance, helpful to the Allies. The Irish army Intelligence unit, G2, headed by Colonel Dan Bryan, regularly sent to Britain weather reports and intercepted German communiqués. Germans who crash-landed were all interned, but in time most surviving British airmen were either put on the train to Belfast or allowed to fly away after their machines had been repaired. Approximately 70,000 southern Irish men and women joined the British armed forces, and no attempt was made to stop them (they won 780 decorations, including seven Victoria Crosses). Travel permits were freely issued, and some 200,000 Éire citizens worked in British factories during the war. And Irish food exports to the UK proved vital.

Churchill's policy was to 'keep Éire lean'. The result was acute shortages of fuel and raw materials. By 1942 more than 26,000 were employed on 803 bogs to supply turf, but this was not enough to prevent power cuts and transport paralysis. German aircraft did accidentally drop bombs on Éire: in the worst incident 34 were killed, 90 were injured and 300 houses were destroyed or damaged in Dublin's North Strand on 31 May 1941.

To maintain a strict neutral stance, the government imposed a rigorous censorship on the press, Radio Éireann, the post and telephones. It could not, however, prevent citizens listening in to the BBC. Nevertheless, the people were not informed about the death camps, and when the *Sunday Independent* published a report on the horrors of Belsen, de Valera described it as 'anti-national propaganda'. Perhaps the most startling evidence of a refusal to acknowledge Nazi tyranny was a report in the *Irish Press* on 1 April 1943: 'There is no kind of oppression visited on any minority in Europe which the six-county Nationalists have not endured.'

Episode 242 ～

THE BLITZ AND AFTER

'Ulster is ready when we get the word and always will be,' Lord Craigavon, Northern Ireland's Prime Minister, had boasted as the war approached. Very soon, however, the government proved itself unequal to the demands of total war. Sir Wilfrid Spender, the Cabinet Secretary, thought that Craigavon was a premier whom 'true friends would advise to retire now' because he was incapable of doing 'more than an hour's constructive work in a day'. Lady Londonderry simply observed that the Prime Minister was 'ga-ga'. The only new recruit to the cabinet was John MacDermott, appointed as Minister of Public Security. Sir Richard Dawson Bates, Minister of Home Affairs, was frequently drunk and simply refused to reply to army correspondence. Edmond Warnock resigned as his parliamentary secretary because the government 'has been slack, dilatory and apathetic'.

When Craigavon died on 24 November 1940, his replacement, John Miller Andrews, kept the old guard in office, and under his direction the government was no more capable than before of coping with the exigencies of war. On

30 November a single unobserved German plane flew high over Belfast; the crew brought back high-definition photographs of suitable targets, demonstrating that the entire city was defended by only seven anti-aircraft batteries. France had fallen, and British cities endured relentless German attack from the air. Yet the government still did little to protect citizens in Northern Ireland: people in Belfast were told that they could use the underground toilets in Shaftesbury Square and Donegall Square North in the event of an air-raid; and the plan to evacuate 70,000 children from the city was activated only in July 1940, and of the 8,800 who turned up, more than half had returned by the spring of 1941.

On the night of 7–8 April a small squadron of German bombers inflicted damaging blows to Harland & Wolff and Belfast's docks. Later a Luftwaffe pilot gave this description on German radio:

> We were in exceptional good humour knowing that we were going for a new target, one of England's last hiding places. Wherever Churchill is hiding his war material will go.... Belfast is as worthy a target as Coventry, Birmingham, Bristol or Glasgow.

Air crews reported that the city's defences were 'inferior in quality, scanty and insufficient'.

On Easter Tuesday 15 April 1941 180 German bombers, predominantly Junkers 88s and Heinkel 111s, flew from northern France, over the Irish Sea and towards Belfast. At 10.40 p.m. the sirens wailed, and over the next five hours the bombers dropped 203 metric tons of bombs and 800 firebomb canisters on the city. At 1.45 a.m. a bomb wrecked the city's telephone exchange, cutting off all contact with Britain and the anti-aircraft operations room. It was not the industrial heartland but the congested housing north of the city centre that received the full force of the attack.

In response to a desperate appeal made by railway telegraph at 4.35 a.m., Eamon de Valera authorised fire-engines from Dublin, Dún Laoghaire, Drogheda and Dundalk to speed northwards. Since the water mains had been cracked in so many places, little could be done. At least 900 citizens died: no other city in the UK, except London, had lost so many lives in one air-raid. Spender felt that Belfast's fire brigade made a poor showing, and John Smith, the city's chief fire officer, was found beneath a table in his office, weeping and refusing to come out. An American, seconded by the Lockheed Aircraft Corporation to Shorts, was not impressed by his fellow-workers; in a letter to his parents in California he wrote:

> All I can say is that the tough Irish must come from S. Ireland because the boys up in N. Ireland are a bunch of chicken shit yellow bastards—90% of them left everything and ran like hell. Short and Harlands, the aircraft

factory that builds Stirlings here, had 300 Volunteer fire fighters in the plant, after the raid they were lucky to get 90 of them.

The German bombers returned in even greater force to Belfast on the evening of Sunday 4 May. In the words of one pilot, 'Visibility was wonderful. I could make out my targets perfectly.' The Luftwaffe concentrated attack on the harbour, the shipyards, the aircraft factory, the docks and the city centre. Ernst von Kuhren, a war correspondent, broadcast his impressions afterwards:

> When we approached the target at half-past two we stared silently into a sea of flames such as none of us had seen before.... In Belfast there was not a large number of conflagrations, but just one enormous conflagration which spread over the entire harbour and industrial area.... Here the English had concentrated an important part of their war industries because they felt themselves safe, far up in the North, safe from the blows of the German airforce. This has come to an end.

The death toll for this May raid was 191, a low figure explained by two facts: firstly, in this Sabbatarian city the centre was largely deserted when the attack began; secondly, a very large number of people had already fled to the countryside. By the end of the month 220,000 had left the city, and every evening tens of thousands left Belfast to sleep in the open in the safety of the countryside.

In January 1941, almost a year before the USA entered the war, American 'civilian technicians' had been coming to Northern Ireland. They began to develop Derry as the most important anti-submarine base in the North Western Approaches, and Lower Lough Erne as a key flying-boat base. On 26 January 1942, shortly after Hitler had casually declared war on the richest nation on earth, the first American troops stepped ashore at Belfast's Dufferin Quay. The USA took over the defence of Northern Ireland, and, now that the Wehrmacht was largely engaged against the Soviet Union, American troops prepared in comparative safety for Operation Torch, the invasion of North Africa, and then for the D-Day landings in Normandy. Altogether some 300,000 Americans were stationed at one time or another in Northern Ireland.

In April 1943 Unionist backbenchers ousted Andrews, and Sir Basil Brooke became Prime Minister. Brooke came to power as Northern Ireland belatedly strove to feed the insatiable Allied war machine. Altogether Harland & Wolff launched almost 170 Admiralty and merchant ships and repaired or converted about 30,000 vessels, in addition to manufacturing over 13 million aircraft parts, over 500 tanks and thousands of guns. Short & Harland by the end of the war had completed almost 1,200 Stirling bombers and 125 Sunderland flying-boats. By VE-Day, 8 May 1945, the mass unemployment of the inter-war years was but a memory.

Episode 243 ～

THE INTER-PARTY GOVERNMENT

On hearing of Adolf Hitler's suicide, the War of Independence veteran and Fianna Fáil TD Dan Breen openly shed tears. As for the Taoiseach, Eamon de Valera, he decided to express his condolences on the death of the Führer by calling on the German Minister in Dublin, Edouard Hempel, on 2 May 1945. Joseph Walshe, Secretary to the Department of External Affairs, remembered:

> Literally on bended knees, we asked him to remember all the Irish-Americans who had lost their lives, but because he had been up to the United States Embassy two weeks previously to condole on the death of Roosevelt, he was afraid of being accused of being partisan.

His Assistant Secretary was surely right to observe that de Valera had made a 'ghastly mistake'. The UK Representative in Éire, Sir John Maffey, reported that in the public mind the Taoiseach's 'condolences took on a smear of turpitude'. Churchill, never reconciled to Éire's neutrality, said in his victory broadcast:

> If it had not been for the loyalty and friendship of Northern Ireland we should have been forced to come to close quarters with Mr de Valera or perish forever from the earth. However, with a restraint and poise to which, I say, history will find few parallels, His Majesty's Government never laid a violent hand upon them ... and we left the Dublin Government to frolic with the Germans and later the Japanese representatives to their hearts' content.

De Valera's radio broadcast in response was warmly welcomed as statesman-like by Irish listeners but not by many beyond Éire's frontiers. The state found itself isolated and marginalised, and the Taoiseach's insistence on raising the issue of partition at every diplomatic opportunity merely produced irritation among those dealing with the ruin and tensions in the world following the most terrible conflict in history.

In power without a break since 1932, Fianna Fáil seemed incapable of restoring Éire's fortunes. Emigration rose from 24,000 in 1945 to 40,000 in 1948. In spite of this, the level of unemployment climbed; and, to add to the government's woes, atrocious weather during the summer of 1946 ruined much of the wheat harvest, and the winter of 1946–7 was remembered as the worst of the twentieth century. The butter ration was reduced from four ounces to two ounces per week, and bread rationing was imposed in 1947.

Although he had enjoyed a comfortable majority since the election of 1944, de Valera decided to go to the country in February 1948. His principal reason for doing so was the appearance and expansion of a new republican party. Clann na Poblachta (meaning 'Family of the Republic') had been formed in July 1946 by people who had been campaigning on behalf of members of the IRA interned during the Emergency. Seán MacBride, the party leader, had been a Chief of Staff of the IRA, and, indeed, twenty-two out of twenty-six on the first executive committee had been in the IRA at various times since the Anglo-Irish Treaty of 1921. This was a republican party with a difference, however, in that it attracted to its ranks young radicals and social reformers who put together an inspiring programme of regeneration.

In the election Clann na Poblachta won ten seats. De Valera was confident he could form a coalition government, but he was wrong. Instead all the opposition TDs came together to form what became known as the 'inter-party government'. Made up of deputies from Fine Gael, Clann na Poblachta, Labour, Clann na Talmhan (the farmers' party) and twelve independents, this could certainly be described as a rainbow coalition.

MacBride became the Minister for External Affairs and refused to have Richard Mulcahy, the former Civil War general and leader of Fine Gael, as Taoiseach. Instead John A. Costello, a former Attorney-General, agreed to lead the government. Son of the executed 1916 leader Major John MacBride and Maud Gonne, Seán MacBride, speaking fluent French, seemed at first to cut quite a dash in diplomatic circles. Meanwhile de Valera, out of power for the first time in sixteen years, toured the United States, Australia, New Zealand and India, denouncing the political partition of Ireland. MacBride felt that his anti-partitionist credentials were impeccable and refused to be upstaged: he vehemently denounced partition at the newly created Council of Europe. However, at a time when the Cold War was threatening to become a hot war during the Berlin Airlift, world statesmen refused to be moved by the strident denunciations of British rule in Northern Ireland by these two Irishmen.

'If any country is attacked by Communists, we're in it,' MacBride told George Garrett, the US envoy to Dublin. The minister was keen to be seen as a valiant Cold War warrior. He threw himself behind the Irish hierarchy's fund-raising campaign to help prevent the election of a communist/socialist coalition in Italy. The inter-party government directly contributed more than £4,000; in all, £60,000 was raised from people in Ireland who no doubt concluded that they played a pivotal role in saving Italy from the wicked rule of infidel left-wingers by helping to secure an election victory for the Christian Democrats. However, Americans and western Europeans alike were not impressed when MacBride turned down an invitation to join NATO on the grounds that it was a military alliance which included the UK, and that to join would be 'repugnant and unacceptable' since 'six of [Ireland's] north-eastern counties are occupied by British forces'. Senior civil servants were deeply embarrassed by the minister's crude attempt to trade action on partition for membership of an international body.

It was Costello, not MacBride, who made the most dramatic alteration in the state's relationship with the rest of the world. No doubt Fine Gael could not long have resisted Clann na Poblachta's insistence that de Valera's External Relations Act of 1936 (which removed all reference to the British crown but kept the state in the Commonwealth) would have to go. It is still not certain whether or not the cabinet had formally agreed to it before the Taoiseach's visit to Canada in the summer of 1948.

The Taoiseach arrived in Montreal on 30 August 1948. Then at a dinner, after the toast to 'The King' had been given, the Canadian Minister for External Affairs asked: 'Doesn't that cover you?' Costello responded that it did not 'because we were not real members of the Commonwealth'. Finally on 5 September the *Sunday Independent* appeared with the headline 'EXTERNAL RELATIONS ACT TO GO'. Was this just an inspired guess? In any case, Costello decided to announce his government's decision to repeal the act at a press conference in Ottawa on 7 September.

Most citizens thought the right place to declare that Éire was about to become a republic was on Irish soil, not in Canada. When the state formally became the Republic of Ireland on Easter Monday 1949, the occasion elicited tepid enthusiasm at best. Indeed, the whole episode revealed an embarrassing amateurishness in the highest circles of government.

Episode 244 ⌥

THE MOTHER AND CHILD CRISIS

Like Ireland, India became a republic in 1949 but, unlike Ireland, remained in the Commonwealth. This option was not considered by Taoiseach John A. Costello and his inter-party government. Fortunately the British allowed the new Irish Republic to retain the privileges of its former membership: the Irish did not have to carry visas or passports to the UK, and no change was made to advantageous trade arrangements.

Largely composed of elderly and middle-aged men who had long languished in opposition, and of the idealistic young men of Clann na Poblachta, the inter-party government was impatient to put into effect its ambitious programme to revitalise the country.

Much was achieved. The number of houses built with state aid jumped from 1,600 in 1947 to 14,000 in 1953. The Independent TD James Dillon proved a particularly dynamic and colourful Minister for Agriculture. In 1949 he launched his Land Rehabilitation Project to bring back into full production 4 million acres largely lying idle. Since one aim of the Marshall Plan was to make Europe self-sufficient in food, Dillon's ambitious scheme helped the state to obtain £6 million in grants and £46 million in loans from the government of the United States.

Dr Noël Browne, employed in Newcastle sanatorium in Co. Wicklow, had campaigned vigorously as a Clann na Poblachta candidate in Dublin South-East. His manifesto referred to 'the slow rot and death each year of approximately 4,000 young Irish men and women from TB'.

Duly elected, Browne at the age of thirty-two was appointed Minister for Health on the same day he first entered the Dáil. Immediately he threw himself into a drive to wipe out tuberculosis. He had strong personal reasons for doing so: TB had killed both his parents and three of his sisters and left his brother a helpless cripple; and he himself had contracted the disease while a medical student in Trinity College, losing the use of one of his lungs. The death rate in Éire from tuberculosis was 124 per 100,000 compared with 80 in Northern Ireland, 79 in Scotland and 62 in England and Wales.

The immediate problem was the acute lack of beds for sufferers. Browne found the additional space in sanatoria by using not only the interest but also the capital of the money allocated from the Hospital Sweepstake Fund. Expenditure on TB increased fourfold. He launched mass vaccination with BCG, which lowered the incidence of childhood tuberculosis in particular. By 1952 115,992 vaccinations had been carried out in schools, factories and mobile units. J. G. Browne, the County Manager for Roscommon, met the minister to discuss his part in setting up the first regional sanatorium in Castlerea:

> He sprang up from his desk and hurried across the room, shaking my hand warmly, and thanked me for attending so early.... He then set me a deadline; June 30th. It was tough going.... I lost half a stone weight in the process, but it was a labour of love, because (I met him regularly at that time) he was so enthusiastic and appreciative and was obviously working so hard himself.

The battle to defeat tuberculosis, the 'white death', was being rapidly won. Browne was already moving on with the aim of improving state health facilities for mothers and children.

Browne was largely unaware that his high-profile campaign against TB had been observed with some distaste by the Catholic hierarchy and the medical profession. In particular, John Charles McQuaid, Archbishop of Dublin and son of a doctor, was hostile to the extension of state medical provision. In 1943 he had effectively broken up the Anti-Tuberculosis League, fearful that it was becoming a pressure group for state-sponsored health reform. Then in 1947 the Fianna Fáil government introduced a Health Bill, to modernise the Irish health service in respect of mother and child welfare and infectious diseases. Privately the bishops drafted a comprehensive condemnation, claiming that to give such power to the public authorities 'is entirely and directly contrary to Catholic teaching'. De Valera delayed making a response and was let off the hook by the fall of his government in 1948.

Costello was such a devout Catholic that he had an altar built in his house and had declared: 'I am an Irishman second: I am a Catholic first.' He also was to say: 'If the hierarchy give me any direction with regard to Catholic social teaching or Catholic moral teaching, I accept without qualification in all respects the teaching of the hierarchy and the church to which I belong.' At the first cabinet meeting of the inter-party government it had been agreed to send a telegram to the Vatican indicating their desire

to repose at the feet of your Holiness the assurance of our filial loyalty and of our devotion to your August Person, as well as our firm resolve to be guided in all our work by the teaching of Christ, and to strive for the attainment of a social order in Ireland based on Christian principles.

In 1950 Browne decided to draft a Health Bill similar to that of 1947: it was to provide free but voluntary ante-natal and post-natal care for mothers, and give free medical care to all children up to the age of sixteen. On 10 October 1950 James Staunton, secretary to the hierarchy, wrote to Costello to say that if Browne's scheme was adopted, it would 'constitute a ready-made instrument for future totalitarian aggression'. Staunton went on to declare the bishops' belief that the state 'may help indigent or neglectful parents; it may not deprive 90 per cent of parents of their rights because of 10 per cent necessitous or negligent parents'. He continued:

Education in regard to motherhood includes instruction in regard to sex relations, chastity and marriage. The State has no competence to give instruction in such matters. We regard with the greatest apprehension the proposal to give to local medical officers the right to tell Catholic girls and women how they should behave in regard to this sphere of conduct at once so delicate and sacred....

Doctors trained in instruction in which we have no confidence may be appointed as medical officers under the proposed service, and may give gynaecological care not in accordance with Catholic principles.

A month passed before Costello passed on this letter to Browne. With his civil servants, the minister drafted a prompt reply which the Taoiseach refused to send. Nothing happened until March 1951, when Browne sent a pamphlet to the bishops explaining the Mother and Child Scheme. McQuaid responded at once, repeating 'each and every objection' that had been made in October.

On 6 April Browne gave a prearranged broadcast (in Irish as well as in English) on Radio Éireann to explain the scheme. Just before going on air he read the hierarchy's detailed denunciation of the scheme. Then he attended a cabinet meeting where he discovered that not a single minister supported him. The ministers voted to drop the scheme. Five days later, on the insistence of his party leader, Seán MacBride, he was forced to resign. Browne took his revenge by allowing the *Irish Times* to publish all the confidential correspondence on the crisis.

An intense debate on church–state relations ensued inside and outside Dáil Éireann, and particularly in the press. It was not surprising that Browne, contemptuously dismissed by MacBride with a flick of cigarette ash, went over to the opposition and was joined by another Clann TD, Jack McQuillan. The inter-party government disintegrated soon afterwards.

Episode 245 ~

'WHAT WE HAVE WE HOLD'

On 2 June 1941 the Rev. Dr J. B. Woodburn, the retiring Moderator of the Presbyterian General Assembly, gave a warning in his sermon:

After the big Blitz of a few weeks ago I was inexpressibly shocked by the sight of people I saw walking in the streets. I have been working 19 years in Belfast and I never saw the like of them before—wretched people, very undersized and underfed down-and-out looking men and women. They had been bombed out of their homes and were wandering the streets. Is it creditable to us that there should be such people in a Christian country?...

We have got to see that there is more talk of justice.... If something is not done now to remedy this rank inequality, there will be revolution after the war.

But there were no barricades on the streets when peace returned. After its decisive victory in the polls in July 1945 Clement Attlee's Labour government began at once to implement its radical programme. Unionists at Westminster, horrified at the prospect of high taxation and increased government control, voted consistently with the Conservative opposition. But Unionists in Stormont voted, often enthusiastically, *for* welfare legislation opposed by their Westminster party colleagues. The explanation is that the Treasury in London agreed that Northern Ireland would enjoy the same standards of social services as those prevailing in the rest of the United Kingdom, provided parity of taxation was maintained.

The outcome was the most striking advance in the material welfare of the people of Northern Ireland, Protestants and Catholics alike, in the twentieth century. After the German raids 53.3 per cent of Belfast's housing stock was destroyed, damaged or deemed unfit for habitation. Billy Grant, the first working-class government minister, set up the Housing Trust and supervised an impressive increase in council house building. Even before the war was over, Stormont acted decisively to treat victims of TB and eventually to extirpate this disease which was responsible for almost half the deaths in the 15–25 age group. The National Health Service—open to all, totally free and almost completely comprehensive—came into operation in Britain in July 1948. Almost identical legislation followed in Northern Ireland in the same year. Sweeping away the Poor Law, this new service had, because of past neglect, a greater impact in Northern Ireland than in any other region of the UK.

Unseemly religious wrangling caused delays and prevented the main substance of Britain's 1944 Education Act being replicated in Northern Ireland until 1947. Protestant clergy and their supporters bitterly resented the scrapping of the 1930 Education Act's insistence on Bible instruction in state schools. And, since the Catholic hierarchy insisted on separate Catholic schools, the dual system continued. Indeed, the 1947 Education Act ensured that young people in the region would be educated separately for longer than before.

Nevertheless, the changes were profound: for the first time free and compulsory education was available to all; and for those who obtained the necessary entrance qualifications, free places (with grants for most students) were provided at university level. Academic selection, by means of the 'eleven plus' qualifying examination, kept intact the grammar schools (with most costs covered by the state and able to charge fees trifling by comparison with public schools in Britain), and so inequalities continued, though at a reduced level.

Once it had crossed the Irish Sea, the tidal wave which had swept Attlee and Labour to power in 1945 produced only a gentle ripple in Northern Ireland. There was only a modest increase in MPs of various socialist persuasions at Stormont. The Prime Minister, Sir Basil Brooke (later raised to the peerage as Viscount Brookeborough), and his Unionist government continued to enjoy a comfortable majority. The task of keeping the unionist camp together was helped by the refusal of the constitutional question to disappear below the horizon. Nationalist MPs and senators set up the Irish Anti-Partition League on 15 November 1945 in Dungannon, 'with the object of uniting all those opposed to partition into a sold block'. Nationalists abandoned their erratic abstentionism in the hope of winning support for their cause from the Labour government at Westminster. This hope was not realised. Herbert Morrison, a member of Attlee's government, said to de Valera that 'to expect us to coerce Ulster was expecting too much, especially in view of the troubled world in which we all lived'.

When John A. Costello announced that Éire would become a republic in September 1948, Attlee did not hesitate to reassure Brooke that his government had not changed its stance. On 28 October Attlee told MPs at Westminster: 'The view of his Majesty's government in the United Kingdom has always been that no change should be made in the constitutional status of Northern Ireland without Northern Ireland's free agreement.' This guarantee he enshrined in the Ireland Act of 1949.

Meanwhile Brooke went to the polls in February 1949 in what was dubbed the 'Chapel Gate Election' by the *Belfast Telegraph* because collections were taken after Mass outside many southern churches for Anti-Partition League candidates. With the slogan 'What we have we hold', in a campaign marked by noisy sectarian clashes, Brooke increased his majority substantially.

Some nationalists concluded that violent methods were the only ones which would work. In December 1956 a revitalised IRA launched 'Operation Harvest', a campaign of attacks along the border, but it proved little more than a minor irritant. The reality was that these generally were quiet years in Northern Ireland. The horrors of depression remembered from the 1930s did not return. Except for unemployment black spots in Derry, Strabane and west Belfast, the economy appeared to be doing well. Despite much flagrant discrimination, Catholics as well as Protestants enjoyed a rise in living standards. But Northern Ireland remained heavily dependent on traditional export industries, and, as the 1950s drew to a close, these were in trouble.

On 16 March 1960, as the RUC band played 'Waltzing Matilda', 20,000 spectators cheered vociferously as Dame Pattie Menzies broke a bottle of Australian red wine against the bows of the *Canberra* and the 45,270-ton P & O liner entered Belfast Lough. Few realised that this was the end of an era: this was the last liner to be built at Belfast. Owing to a lack of further orders, the workforce shrank severely. Linen still employed 76,000 in 1951. When the Korean War ended in 1953, however, the industry—now competing with synthetic fibres—moved into terminal decline. Brookeborough seemed to have no answer to an alarming rise in the numbers of unemployed and to election successes by socialist candidates. In February 1963 his Unionist colleagues forced him to stand down.

Episode 246 ᕽ

THE VANISHING IRISH

The census of 1951 showed that the population of the Republic of Ireland had increased by 0.2 per cent since 1946; despite high levels of emigration, this was the first gain to be recorded since reliable enumerations had begun in 1841. After that the sheer scale of the outflow more than wiped out a rise in the rate of natural increase. Between 1951 and 1956 net migration totalled nearly 200,000 people, the average annual loss of 39,353 persons being the highest recorded since 1900. In the year 1957 over 58,000 left the state. The population recorded in 1956 was just below 2,900,000, the lowest figure recorded for the twenty-six counties since 1841. Britain was by far the most favoured destination; between 1946 and 1952 only 16 per cent went overseas, mostly to the USA.

During the war Britain's fear of the spread of infectious diseases obliged de Valera's government to set up health embarkation centres in Dublin. Approximately 55,000 people were deloused there between 1943 and 1947. James Deeny, the government's chief medical adviser took J. J. McElligott, Secretary to the Department of Finance, to these centres, starting with the Globe Hotel in Talbot Street:

> In various rooms doctors in white coats were examining the people for lice. This was the health embarkation scheme in action. From the Globe Hotel we went to Iveagh Baths. There I saw something I will not forget. The baths had been emptied. On the floor of a pool were large sherry half casks. Men with rubber aprons and wellington boots were hosing people down and bathing them with disinfectant in the casks. All around were naked men, seemingly in hundreds. The place was full of steam and the smell of disinfectants.
>
> Now naked men *en masse* are not a pretty sight and the atmosphere of shame, fear and outrage was easy to feel.... A fellow with an electric iron was killing the lice in cap-bands and braces since steam disinfection, which the clothes were receiving, would perish leather and rubber. McElligott, a man with proper sensibilities, promptly came over faint and had to be taken outside and revived in the fresh air.

These procedures, along with travel permits, were discontinued after 1947, and the UK placed no restrictions on Irish immigration when Éire became a republic in 1949. The Dublin government abandoned all attempts to regulate the outflow in 1952. The haemorrhage of people was greatest in the west and north-west. Co. Leitrim headed the list for the years 1951–6, with a rate of 23.1 per 1,000, an all-time high.

What should the government do? Could it arrest this spectacular surge in emigration? A particularly worrying aspect was that the migrants were young and that the rise was largely accounted for by the doubling in the numbers of women leaving between 1946 and 1951—for every 1,000 males emigrating there were 1,365 females. The strong demand in Britain for nurses largely explains why 72 per cent of female emigrants were under the age of twenty-four; most of these young women left Ireland in order to take up training in nursing.

The Catholic Church was particularly worried about the 'moral welfare' of girls crossing the Irish Sea, and this was the main reason why it set up the Catholic Emigrant Welfare Bureau under the auspices of Archbishop John Charles McQuaid. The Vocational Commission went so far as to recommend that emigrants should have to pay 'at least five hundred pounds' before they were allowed to leave.

Emigration was a key issue in the 1948 election which brought the first inter-party government to power. Seán MacBride, the new Minister for External Affairs, read with approval a memorandum from his department which concluded that 'the most effective method of protecting the interests of young female migrants is the imposition of an age limit below which girls would not be allowed to emigrate'; this ban was, he felt, 'the only satisfactory solution of the problem'. Rejecting MacBride's proposal, the government instead put its faith in the Commission on Emigration and Other Population Problems, established in March 1948.

The commission sat for six years, and by the time the report was published in April 1954 the second inter-party government was in office. In December 1949 *Dublin Opinion* included a cartoon showing the '*Dublin Opinion* Commission on Emigration' and bearing the caption 'The Commission furnishes its report after having sat for five seconds. The people emigrate because they think they will do better elsewhere. They will return when they think they will do better here.' This indeed could be regarded as a succinct summary of the Emigration Commission's findings.

In counties such as Kilkenny, where mixed farming and dairying predominated, emigration rates were relatively low because work was available all the year round. In western counties, where holdings were small, overcrowded and with much poor land, and where incomes could be supplemented only with ill-paid temporary work provided by local authorities, the only hope for young men to improve their prospects was to go to Britain. In Tuam, for example, the commissioners reported, 'some of the men stated that plenty of work was available on the small family holding but completely without payment'. The modest prosperity of the village of Lahardane in Mayo, they continued, seemed to depend almost entirely on remittances, mostly from America.

One twenty-nine-year-old man in Tullow, Co. Carlow, preparing to leave, told the commissioners that all nine of his brothers and sisters were working in Britain. He and others demonstrated that relatives and friends gave valuable advice on wages, available work in Britain, and places where migrants could find accommodation. One commissioner said he was told that 'the lure of England, emphasised by the "grand" appearance of the returned emigrants when they came home on holidays, was a main factor' in female emigration. Young men due to inherit small, infertile farms did not constitute ideal prospective husbands. The commissioners reported:

> For the female emigrant, improvement in personal status is of no less importance than the higher wages and better conditions of employment abroad, and some of the evidence submitted to us would suggest that the prospect of better marriage opportunities is also an influence of some significance.

This in turn encouraged young men to leave. In Sligo, the commissioners added, the poor prospects of males 'prevented them from marrying, and in some areas prospective partners were difficult to find'.

This great outflow naturally led to major distortions in social patterns. 'In short,' John A. O'Brien concluded in *The Vanishing Irish*, a book published in 1954, '64 per cent of Ireland's population is single, 6 per cent widowed and only 30 per cent married—the lowest in the civilised world.'

Episode 247 ∾

THE YEARS OF STAGNATION

On St Patrick's Day 1943 the Taoiseach, Eamon de Valera, said on Radio Éireann:

> The Ireland which we have dreamed of would be the home of a people who valued material wealth only as a basis of right living, of a people who were satisfied with frugal comfort and devoted their leisure to the things of the spirit; a land whose countryside would be bright with cosy homesteads, whose fields and villages would be joyous with the sounds of industry, with the romping of sturdy children, the contests of athletic youths, the laughter

of comely maidens; whose firesides would be forums for the wisdom of serene old age. It would, in a word, be living the life that God desires that men should live.

During the ensuing years these words sounded increasingly hollow. The fields and villages of rural Ireland were rarely joyous with the sounds of industry; the laughter of comely maidens was heard less often as so many packed their bags to take up nursing training in England; and, dissatisfied with constant frugality, athletic youths left to become 'McAlpine's Fusiliers', working on building sites across the Irish Sea.

'No one shouted Stop', the journalist John Healy declared in frustration and despair, contemptuous of the 'Celtic mistery of the politicians of the day'. In *The Death of an Irish Town*, published in 1968, he looked back at what had happened to his home town of Charlestown, Co. Mayo. Out of his senior class of twenty-two boys in 1944, thirteen had emigrated abroad, six had left for Dublin and Westmeath, and only three remained in Charlestown. He continued:

> We had people and we exported them faster than cattle and like cattle, and while fathers, sons and daughters cried all the way to the train and the bus and the ship, the flow back of emigrant cheques and money orders evaporated the maternal and wifely tears so that on the threshold of the Post Office or The Hibernian Bank below in Main Street you could smile a little more with every passing week.

'The big and fatal tide wave of emigration is over now,' Healy admitted. 'Today a few leave Charlestown every year, but it is merely the muscular spasms of a corpse.' Dublin had become 'a monstrously swollen head on a shrunken body, a gross cancer which feeds and devours its body'.

In 1973 Hugh Brody published a detailed sociological study in *Inishkillane*, a name he coined (to protect its identity) for a rural parish in the south-west. Brody painted a black picture of hopelessness resulting from decades of emigration. The parish priest had conducted a survey to show that nearly 90 per cent of those born between 1940 and 1945 had already left the parish. By 1950, Brody concluded, 'the population began to experience serious imbalances.... Hundreds of other rural parishes are in much the same predicament as Inishkillane.' He counted 231 households in the parish and observed that 'An extraordinarily large number of these homes are occupied by acutely isolated people.' He found that there were 32 bachelors, 4 spinsters, 3 widowers and 13 widows 'living entirely alone'; 21 bachelors and 10 spinsters living with siblings; and 23 couples who lived alone—'a total of 115 chronically isolated people, between them occupying 80 houses'. Inevitably the incidence of mental illness was very high. He continued:

Since the girls now refuse to stay in the countryside, the last son of a family who stays at home is unlikely to marry. In the parish today, therefore, one son in each family is faced with a choice between staying celibate at home and emigrating with the chance of marriage.... Some girls dutifully return for Christmas and summer holidays, but virtually none come to marry.

'The conditions for covert liaisons and flirtations are absent,' he added. 'Those who have decided to stay at home do so in the full realisation that the decision almost certainly entails a life of chastity.'

Since the state had exported so many young people dissatisfied with conditions at home, it was unlikely that those remaining would elect governments capable of pursuing radical economic policies. By appointing Seán MacEntee as Minister for Finance in 1951, de Valera ensured that only traditional conservative solutions would be applied to the Republic's economic plight. The severely deflationary budget of 1952 increased income tax by a shilling in the pound and raised the prices of bread, butter, tea, sugar, alcoholic drink and petrol. This not only added to the general air of gloom but also presented An Foras Tionscail, the underdeveloped areas board set up in 1952 by Seán Lemass, with an almost impossible uphill task.

Independent TDS withdrew their support in 1954, and the ensuing election put a second inter-party government in office, a coalition of Fine Gael, Labour and Clann na Talmhan with John A. Costello again as Taoiseach. The new administration failed to seize the opportunity offered, and the Finance minister, Gerard Sweetman, applied the same pre-Keynesian medicine with even greater enthusiasm than MacEntee. The publication of census statistics in 1956, showing that the population of the state had fallen to an all-time low, forced Costello to go to the country in March 1957. Fianna Fáil returned to office with 78 seats. This was de Valera's greatest electoral triumph. But the incoming Taoiseach was seventy-four years old and almost blind, and he disappointed many by retaining most of his 'old guard' in his cabinet. While he remained it was unlikely that adventurous new policies would be applied. The siege economy, cowering behind its high tariff wall, would not be dismantled.

At a time when the rest of western Europe was enjoying spectacular growth, the Republic's economy remained in the doldrums. Agricultural employment, comprising 40 per cent of the workforce in 1950, suffered a decline of almost a quarter over the next ten years. Between 1951 and 1961 25,000 jobs were lost in the construction industry. Real wages failed to rise, and, indeed, an industrial worker earned less in 1958 than he or she earned in 1950. Few attempts were made to find more distant markets: the UK still took nearly 90 per cent of the state's exports, and since these were overwhelmingly agricultural, the returns were kept down by low prices on the British market arising from the system of farm deficiency payments in operation there.

Largely as a result of pressure from his own party, de Valera stepped down on 17 June 1959. On that same day he was elected President of Ireland by a comfortable majority. Seán Lemass succeeded as Taoiseach without a contest. Veteran politician though he was, Lemass would inaugurate the radical change in direction that the state desperately needed.

Episode 248 ∾

CHURCH AND STATE AND THE IRA

The controversy over Dr Noël Browne's Mother and Child Scheme in 1951 proved a gift to propagandists of the Ulster Unionist Party. Catholic bishops continued to supply ample material to allow Lord Brookeborough, Prime Minister of Northern Ireland, and in particular Harry Midgley, Education minister from 1949, to lard their speeches with scathing comments.

Eamon de Valera, Taoiseach again in 1951, proved more adroit than his inter-party predecessors in dealing with the Catholic hierarchy. Nevertheless, his Fianna Fáil government was forced to include a means test in the 1953 Health Act, and it would be many years before the state could be said to have a national health service. The ban imposed on Catholics entering Trinity College, first imposed by Archbishop John Charles McQuaid of Dublin in 1944, was adopted by other dioceses in the country. Joseph Walsh, Archbishop of Tuam, gave direct instructions that in his diocese, as from 1 October 1953, all dance halls—whether or not in the control of the clergy—should close not later than midnight in winter and 1 a.m. in summer. This arrangement was quickly adopted in many other dioceses. Nor did the hierarchy hesitate to pronounce on foreign affairs. Both Bishop Michael Browne of Galway and Bishop Cornelius Lucey of Cork publicly supported Senator Joe McCarthy in his notorious witch-hunt against communists in the USA. Cardinal John D'Alton, Archbishop of Armagh, rebuked the Fianna Fáil government when it voted that communist China should be considered for membership of the UN.

The hierarchy was particularly exercised by the dangers of 'evil literature'. Frequent pronouncements in Lenten pastorals encouraged the Censorship of Publications Board to greater efforts: about a hundred books a year were banned in the 1930s, but between 1950 and 1955 the annual average was six hundred. After a discussion with McQuaid in November 1953 on the issue of publications 'objectionable on moral grounds', de Valera directed Gerry Boland, the Minister for Justice, 'to put an end to the sale of books of the kind in question'. Revenue officers had to seize all paperback novels 'with titles, jacket designs, or illustrations suggestive of indecent content'. McQuaid wrote to the Taoiseach afterwards to thank him for his efforts 'to prevent the diffusion of evil books'. Authors having their works banned included John Steinbeck, André Gide, Ernest Hemingway, Graham Greene, George Orwell, Seán O'Faolain, Liam O'Flaherty and Seán O'Casey. Even so, the standing committee of the hierarchy felt obliged to write again to de Valera in January 1958 about 'the necessity for effective defence of the public interest' arising from the 'increase in evil publications'.

However, the bishops could not prevent the emergence of a lively home-grown literature mocking prevailing attitudes. And at times politicians stood up to them. On 13 May 1957 in the Co. Wexford village of Fethard-on-Sea Catholics began a boycott of their Protestant neighbours. The conflict was caused by the break-up of a mixed marriage. The Protestant wife took her two children to Belfast and offered her Catholic husband a reunion only if he would agree to the children being brought up as Protestants. During the boycott a Protestant music teacher lost eleven out of her twelve pupils; two Protestant shopkeepers lost their Catholic customers; and the Catholic teacher at the local Church of Ireland National School resigned.

The Catholic Bishop of Ferns, James Staunton, rejected an appeal from the Church of Ireland to express disapproval. Bishop Browne described the boycott as 'peaceful and moderate', adding that 'there seems to be a concerted campaign to entice or kidnap Catholic children and deprive them of their faith'. De Valera, who had always been at pains to maintain good relations with the Protestant minority, did not hesitate to condemn the boycott. In a long statement in the Dáil he said that 'I regard this boycott as ill-conceived, ill-considered and futile.... I regard it as unjust and cruel to confound the innocent with the guilty.' However, the clergy did not respond to his appeal to all 'to bring this deplorable affair to a speedy end'. Bishop Browne, indeed, repeated his defence of the boycott, which dragged on for several more months.

North of the border narrowness of vision was just as apparent. Lieutenant-Colonel Samuel Hall-Thompson, Minister of Education, endured three years of rancorous denunciation from Protestant clergy before his Education Act became law in 1947. 'There are no sacrifices we will not make, in order that our Protestant form of inheritance will be made secure,' the Church of Ireland Dean of Belfast declared while making an appeal for a £20,000 fighting fund to oppose the bill, condemning in particular the sections scrapping compulsory Bible instruction. A former Education minister, the Rev. Professor Robert Corkey, asserted that state schools would be thrown open to 'Jews, Agnostics,

Roman Catholics and Atheists'. In 1949, when Brookeborough told a Grand Orange Lodge meeting that he would amend the scheme, Hall-Thompson, not surprisingly, resigned. And every year overtly sectarian remarks were routinely included in speeches delivered by sash-wearing dignitaries on 12 July.

At least the Catholic bishops, the Orange Order, and the Dublin and Belfast governments were at one in condemning the IRA. In January 1956 the Catholic hierarchy issued a detailed statement, including a declaration 'that it is a mortal sin for a Catholic to become or remain a member of an organisation or society, which arrogates to itself the right to bear arms or to use them against its own or another state'.

On 10 June 1954, having previously observed that the sentry had no ammunition in his Sten gun, members of the IRA, led by Seán Garland, broke into Gough Barracks in Armagh and seized 250 rifles, thirty-seven Sten guns, nine Bren guns and forty training rifles. Taken in a lorry back over the border, the arms were quickly dispersed and hidden. It took more than another two years before the organisation launched 'Operation Harvest', an armed assault along the frontier. In driving sleet it began at midnight on 11 December 1956. A BBC transmitter was destroyed; Magherafelt courthouse was burnt to the ground; a Territorial Army building in Enniskillen was wrecked; and in Newry a B Special hut was set on fire—all in all, an unimpressive achievement for an operation involving around 150 volunteers.

Over the next few years the IRA campaign continued fitfully. The high points were usually glorious failures, the most memorable being an attack on Brookeborough RUC barracks on New Year's Day 1957. The volunteers' mine failed to explode, and in the ensuing gun battle Seán South of Garryowen in Limerick city and Fergal O'Hanlon of Monaghan were mortally wounded. Their funerals attracted huge numbers of mourners, and songs commemorating them became enormously popular. Brookeborough's government interned 256 men and one woman. Critical of the inter-party government's hostility to the IRA, Seán MacBride of Clann na Poblachta forced a general election early in 1957. Four Sinn Féin TDs were among those elected. De Valera, returned to power, reintroduced internment in the Republic in July 1957 with devastating effect. Seán Lemass set up military tribunals in 1961. There had been 366 incidents by the end of 1957; but, squeezed both north and south, the IRA was rendered powerless. On 26 February 1962 the IRA Chief of Staff, Ruairí Ó Brádaigh (one of those who had been elected Sinn Féin TDs in 1957), called off the campaign.

Episode 249 ∽

NEW BROOMS NORTH AND SOUTH

In 1956 the *Irish Times*, on the fortieth anniversary of the Easter Rising, reflected: 'If the present trend disclosed continues unchecked ... Ireland will die—not in the remote unpredictable future, but quite soon.' In the same year Dr T. K. Whitaker was appointed Secretary to the Department of Finance at the unusually young age of thirty-nine. With his colleagues, he began work on a document which attempted to find ways of revivifying the Republic's economy. As he remembered in December 2006, 'I was spurred on by a cartoon in *Dublin Opinion* showing Ireland a still beautiful but somewhat bedraggled lady asking a fortune teller "Have I a future?"'

Whitaker presented his paper, *Economic Development*, to de Valera's government in May 1958. In the opening section he wrote of a vicious circle

> of increasing emigration, resulting in a smaller domestic market depleted of initiative and skill, and a reduced incentive, whether for Irishmen or foreigners, to undertake and organise the productive enterprises which alone can provide increased employment opportunities and higher living standards.

The answer, he argued, was to reduce and perhaps even eliminate protective import duties in an orderly way and to entice overseas concerns to set up in Ireland by sweeping away the regulations which had been discouraging them. As Whitaker explained later, 'Protectionism, both in agriculture and industry, would have to give way to active participation in a free-trading world.'

The Tánaiste, Seán Lemass, cautiously welcomed the report which, it could be argued, was the state's first cohesive economic strategy document, a blueprint for the rapid modernisation. Most of the recommendations were incorporated in the White Paper *Programme for Economic Expansion* published in November 1958. This called for the staged abandonment of high protective tariffs and a five-year economically productive investment programme, with a target growth of 2 per cent per year.

Only when de Valera bowed out in June 1959 did Lemass as Taoiseach throw himself with enthusiasm behind the implementation of the programme. The results were more spectacular than anyone in the Department of Finance could hope. The repeal of the restrictive Control of Manufactures Acts of 1932–4 allowed multinational firms to set up branches in the state with the same advantages as existing native manufacturers. These international firms exported much of their output, contributing heavily to the rise of the Gross National Product by an average of 4.5 per cent annually between 1959 and 1963. Emigration, which had been 44,427 in 1961, dropped to 12,226 in 1963, and by 1966 the population had risen by 66,000 above that of 1961.

It must be admitted that Lemass had a fair wind behind him: the advanced economies were doing particularly well, and large corporations were looking for suitable places in which to invest and expand. The Taoiseach was largely able to silence the agonised howls of protest from employers and workers in industries previously cosseted by tariffs by pointing to the emergence of the EEC and its British-led counterpart EFTA. Nevertheless, Lemass showed considerable prowess in the way that he listened carefully to the advice of a talented cadre of senior civil servants to achieve a productive consensus, made sure that the public were kept fully informed about what he was doing, and brought employers and the trade unions together in the National Industrial and Economic Council to harmonise industrial relations. Lemass had been the architect of de Valera's siege economy in the 1930s. It was a formidable task therefore to persuade his colleagues in Fianna Fáil that the time had come for an about-turn, to consign to the waste-bin the ideals of self-sufficiency—so dear to de Valera—outlined originally by Arthur Griffith at the start of the century.

The Northern Ireland government had no need to overcome ideological objections to opening up the region to overseas capital. Here the problem was staple export industries: engineering and shipbuilding were contracting and the linen industry, for long the most important industrial employer, was in a nose-dive towards near oblivion. Lord Brookeborough's Finance minister, Captain Terence O'Neill, had shown flair and a professional approach in attracting multinationals to set up branches in Northern Ireland. This, however, was not enough to prevent unemployment from rising to 7.5 per cent in 1962. Brookeborough's solution was to go cap-in-hand to London to ask for short-term subsidies for the ailing industries. The report of a working party chaired by Sir Robert Hall, published in October 1962, poured scorn on this approach. This led directly to Brookeborough's fall and the appointment of O'Neill as Prime Minister in March 1963.

A few days after his appointment O'Neill told the Ulster Unionist Council: 'Our task will be literally to transform Ulster.... To achieve it will demand bold and imaginative measures.' Later he said that his main aims were not only to make the region 'economically stronger and prosperous' but also 'to build bridges between the two traditions within our community'. In short, O'Neill was the first Northern Ireland Prime Minister to state clearly that reconciliation was a central part of his programme.

O'Neill proposed to achieve both his principal aims by economic modernisation through planning—an approach condemned by Brookeborough,

O'Neill recalled, 'as a socialist menace'. The new Prime Minister's Whitaker was Tom Wilson, a professor of political economy at Glasgow University, who submitted his report at the end of 1964. Like Lemass, O'Neill worked closely with hand-picked civil servants of ability and imagination, including Jim Malley, Cecil Bateman and Ken Bloomfield. The government implemented Wilson's recommendations straight away: a Ministry of Development was set up in January 1965; as previously recommended by Sir Robert Mathew in 1962, Belfast's growth was to be restricted to encourage growth beyond the city; a motorway would be extended to Dungannon; a new city would be created between Portadown and Lurgan; and Larne, Bangor–Newtownards, Carrickfergus–Carnmoney, Antrim–Ballymena and Derry were designated as additional growth points.

Very soon O'Neill's fresh economic strategy seemed to be working. Multinational firms, including Grundig, British Enkalon, ICI, Michelin and Goodyear, were induced to establish branches in Northern Ireland. As was already happening in the Republic, international trade was so buoyant that capital came in search of labour. In addition, foreign businesses were able to use Northern Ireland to obtain unhindered access to the burgeoning British market and were attracted by generous incentives provided by the Ministry of Commerce. Both the Republic and Northern Ireland had other attractions for multinational executives: English spoken everywhere; familiar social institutions; apparent political stability; and inexpensive access to beautiful countryside, golf courses and uncrowded boating and angling centres.

In Northern Ireland the run-down in employment opportunities in the older industries meant that O'Neill's government had to run hard to avoid simply standing still. Still, manufacturing growth rate in the 1960s was 5.7 per cent, well ahead of the rest of the UK, and by the end of 1969 no fewer than 29,000 new jobs in manufacturing had been created. O'Neill put his faith in this drive for greater prosperity to improve community relations. But could improved living standards alone achieve this?

O'Neill visited Catholic schools and hospitals, making sure he was photographed in the company of nuns; he met Cardinal William Conway, Archbishop of Armagh; and when Pope John XXIII died on 3 June 1963, he sent condolences to Rome, had the Union Flag flown at half-mast, and declared that the pope 'had won widespread acclaim throughout the world because of his qualities of kindness and humanity'—in contrast to the Rev. Ian Paisley, who on the following day in the Ulster Hall excoriated 'the Iscariots of Ulster' who had expressed sympathy to the Vatican, assuring his packed audience that 'This Romish man of sin is now in Hell.' Undaunted, O'Neill began preparations to ease north–south relations by inviting Lemass to Stormont.

Episode 250 ⌇

THE O'NEILL–LEMASS MEETING, 14 JANUARY 1965

On the night of 13–14 January 1965 in Belfast St Brendan's Church collapsed and two ships collided in the lough. Gale-force winds gusting to
eighty miles an hour and accompanied by torrential rain swept Ulster.
Captain Terence O'Neill lay awake for another reason. He, the Prime Minister
of Northern Ireland, had invited the Taoiseach of the Irish Republic, Seán
Lemass, to Stormont—and he had not informed his cabinet colleagues.

Shortly after midday the Taoiseach stepped out of his Mercedes. 'Welcome
to the North,' O'Neill said. There was no reply. Lemass finally broke his silence
in the lavatory of Stormont House: 'I'll get into terrible trouble for this.' The
Taoiseach then relaxed and became more garrulous over a splendid lunch.
Ken Whitaker, who accompanied him, remembered: 'Our hosts thought the
occasion worthy of champagne. The atmosphere was most friendly. I imagine
Dr Paisley's worst fears would be confirmed if I were to say that the red wine
we drank was Châteauneuf-du-Pape!'

Cabinet ministers smiled bravely for the cameras. They had just been
summoned that morning. Only Brian Faulkner, Minister of Commerce, had
met Lemass before; he subsequently recalled:

> The first thing Lemass said to me was 'I hear you had a great day with the
> Westmeaths a few weeks ago.' 'That's right indeed, I didn't realise you knew.'
> 'Ah,' he said, 'the boys told me.' He said, 'Have you had a day with Charlie
> lately?'

Charlie was the Taoiseach's son-in-law, Charles Haughey, and Faulkner's
reminiscences about regular hunt meetings with him helped to break the ice.
After discussions on possible north–south co-operation on tourism and economic matters, Lemass then left to return to Dublin.

'I think I can say a road block has been removed,' the Taoiseach said to
waiting reporters when he arrived back in Dublin. Lemass had fought with
Patrick Pearse in the GPO in 1916; he had been a member of Michael Collins's
'Squad' which had assassinated fourteen suspected British secret service
agents in Dublin on 'Bloody Sunday', 21 November 1920; and he had fought
with the Irregulars opposed to the 1921 Anglo-Irish Treaty. He had said in an
Oxford Union debate in 1959 that the British government should declare that
it would like to see partition ended 'by agreement among the Irish'. In the

same speech, however, he asked: 'Is it not common sense that the two existing communities in our small island should seek every opportunity of working together in practical matters for their mutual and common good?'

Lemass had every reason to accept O'Neill's invitation. Better relations with Britain were vital to the success of his economic strategy. Application to join the European Economic Community by both the UK and the Republic had been rejected in 1963, but it was confidently expected that acceptance would come in the near future. The only hope for membership was a determined retreat from protectionism. Back in April 1960 an Anglo-Irish trade agreement had started the process, and unilateral tariff reductions made in 1963 and 1964 had not caused the sky to fall in. Quite the contrary: the rise in the value of exports by 35 per cent in 1959–60 had encouraged Lemass to launch the Second Programme for Economic Expansion in 1964; an enlarged role for foreign enterprise was bringing in multinational firms promoting export-led growth; the numbers of visitors from America and the European mainland had increased fourfold to 1,200,000 in 1964; and emigration was ceasing to sap the nation's strength.

On the day after the O'Neill–Lemass meeting a car, trailing a very large Ulster flag, drove to Stormont, where Ian Paisley's followers held up placards which read: 'IRA murderer welcomed at Stormont'; 'Down with the Lundys'; and 'No Mass, no Lemass'. The former cabinet minister Edmond Warnock issued a statement castigating O'Neill 'for doing within a couple of months what all our enemies failed to achieve in forty years. He has thrown the whole Ulster question back into the political arena.' In fact no widespread hostile reaction greeted the meeting. O'Neill returned the Taoiseach's visit by going to Dublin, and in November he went to the electorate, increasing the Unionist vote substantially.

The O'Neill–Lemass meeting was little more than a signal that the two premiers wished for an improvement in relations between north and south. But O'Neill fatefully believed that economic advance would, almost alone, heal the bitter divisions between Catholics and Protestants in the region. His gestures of friendship to nationalists were not followed up by practical reforms which would begin to eradicate the institutional unfairness which had prevailed for decades. Paisley, in his campaign 'O'Neill Must Go', warned the Prime Minister that he would reap the whirlwind. Nervous of traditional unionist reaction, O'Neill, by raising Catholic expectations, brought about intense frustration by lack of action. This was to cause him to reap a whirlwind quite different from that envisaged by Paisley.

The introduction of the welfare state, helped by transfers from the Treasury in London, had magnified unfairness. Vastly increased expenditure by local authorities in particular had increased opportunities for discrimination in job appointments and in the allocation of council houses. O'Neill did nothing to undo the meticulous manipulation of local government boundaries to Unionist advantage, begun in 1923. Owing to his party's fear that more Nationalist councillors would be elected, he did not follow Britain's lead, given as far back as 1949, to introduce universal suffrage in local government elections. As late as 1969 Catholics held only six senior judicial posts out of a total of sixty-eight. There were twenty-two public boards by 1969, with 332 members in all, but only 49 were Catholics. Only 15.4 per cent of 8,122 employed in the publicly owned electricity, gas and water industries were Catholics. Geoffrey Copcutt, the Englishman appointed to head the design team for the new city between Portadown and Lurgan, resigned because the plans did not include a special development plan for Derry, a predominantly Catholic city with acute unemployment—and gerrymandered to ensure a permanent Unionist majority in the Corporation. Copcutt also supported Derry's bid to be the home of a second university. O'Neill provoked outrage by implementing the recommendation of the Lockwood Committee (which had no Catholic as a member) in 1965 that Coleraine should be the site for the university. And the decision to name the new city Craigavon was hardly likely to promote intercommunal harmony.

The Unionist government failed to take warning from the Divis Street riots in Belfast in 1964—localised and short-lived though they were—which demonstrated that savage political and sectarian animosity remained virulently alive. Meanwhile the 1947 Education Act had done much to create a new Catholic middle class which was, in the words of the Cameron Commission in 1969, 'less ready to acquiesce in the situation of assumed (or established) inferiority and discrimination than was the case in the past'. In the past nationalists had simply demanded an end to partition. Now they put forward a more sophisticated demand that British standards be applied to eliminate unfairness. A civil rights movement was already in formation when O'Neill met Lemass, a movement influenced, with the help of vastly improved communications, by the black civil rights campaign in America, by protests against the Vietnam War and nuclear weapons, and later by direct action in the streets in Paris and Prague. At the same time more and more loyalists were becoming convinced that O'Neill was conceding too much to Catholics.

In 1963 O'Neill had set out in an optimistic spirit to regenerate the economy of Northern Ireland. Just six years later the region was in a state of near-revolutionary crisis. The unchained sectarian dragon leaped from its cage as fear, suspicion, atavistic hatred and memory of ancient wrongs gushed to the surface, inaugurating thirty years of destruction, conflict, forced population movement, mutilation and slaughter.

EPILOGUE

An island on the north-western edge of the Eurasian landmass, Ireland had from the eighth millennium BC attracted successive waves of people advancing westwards to make it their home. Newcomers and their descendants had brought in new technologies and ideas and in time had mixed in with the descendants of those who had arrived before them. The related cultures, from the English Pale in the east to the most remote Gaelic lordships, were all a product of importation and blending over the centuries. Until the end of the fifteenth century AD Europeans were unaware that they could find fresh lands by venturing further west into the Atlantic. Then the age of exploration across the oceans began. The quickening of economic life in western Europe in the sixteenth and seventeenth centuries had much to do with the exploitation of overseas discoveries. The Elizabethan conquest of Ireland made the island a colonial opportunity for the British in the reign of James I as much as Mexico and Peru became ones for the Spanish. In Ireland this opportunity was ruthlessly exploited throughout the seventeenth century and beyond.

The tragedy was that the arrival of 'New English' administrators and planters from across the Irish Sea coincided with the deadly struggle for supremacy between the supporters of the Reformation and the Counter-Reformation. A much greater blending of these newcomers and indigenous inhabitants occurred than is even realised or admitted today. Nevertheless, particularly in Ulster but in varying degrees across the whole island, conflict arising from religious division blighted the country's development for centuries.

By the late twentieth century the memory of earlier convulsions and past wrongs was fading fast in the Republic. In Northern Ireland, however, the memory of previous dispossessions and bloodletting remained virulently alive. Here intercommunal suspicion and clashing political aspirations, combined with institutional unfairness, plunged the region into near chaos. A vibrant civil rights movement, inspired by direct action on the streets overseas, dissolved into sectarian conflict, bloodshed and destruction in 1969. Although troops were sent into Northern Ireland on active service that August, it was not until the spring of 1972 that London stood down Stormont to impose direct rule.

In October 1972 Secretary of State William Whitelaw published his proposed solution: the restoration of devolution, but with an administration in which unionists and nationalists shared power; an acceptance that the

Republic had a legitimate interest in the affairs of Northern Ireland; and decisive action to eliminate unfairness. With refinements, all ensuing Westminster governments and their official oppositions mutually agreed that this was the blueprint for peace. In time Dublin too came to accept that this formula was the most realistic one available. In December 1973 at Sunningdale in Berkshire Whitelaw got representatives of an elected assembly to accept power-sharing and a Council of Ireland. The Sunningdale agreement, however, was rejected by an overwhelming majority of Protestants in the general election of February 1974, and then the power-sharing executive was destroyed by the loyalist strike in May.

Two more decades of savage bloodshed followed, on occasion spilling over into the Republic, Britain and the European mainland. The 'Troubles' in Northern Ireland became the longest-running conflict in Europe since the end of the Second World War. By the end of the millennium a total of 3,651 men, women and children had lost their lives in Northern Ireland as a direct result of the violence. Though shorter-lived, the much bloodier ethnic slaughter accompanying the break-up of Yugoslavia in the 1990s grimly demonstrated what could happen in an all-out conflict in Northern Ireland.

The region turned a corner with the paramilitary ceasefires of the autumn of 1994. Certainly hatreds remained, and the deep divisions in Northern Ireland's society were periodically demonstrated by confrontations at Drumcree, outside Holycross School in Belfast, at Harryville in Ballymena, and by further killings and paramilitary violence. Nevertheless, the 'peace process' was under way. Only in 1998 was Whitelaw's solution accepted by a majority in Northern Ireland—with much truth the SDLP deputy leader, Séamus Mallon, described the Good Friday Agreement that year as 'Sunningdale for slow learners'.

The era of terrorism and sectarian murders seemed to be over in spite of repeated false political starts. The horror of '9/11' across the Atlantic did much to dissipate any lingering romantic attachment in America to the Irish militant tradition. Finally, in May 2007, a power-sharing government was in place with a realistic prospect of functioning for more than just a few months. Reflecting in March 2008 on the delight in London greeting this event ten months earlier, Max Hastings, who had reported the Troubles on the ground during the most violent years, felt 'the irony that the fanatics, reformed or otherwise, now crow atop the Ulster dunghill, while the political corpses of decent men, Protestant and Catholic alike, lie mouldering among the weeds'.

The restoration of peace in the north was hastened in no small way by the transformation of the south. As long as the 'Free State' appeared to be poverty-stricken and priest-ridden, representatives of the northern majority had rarely felt the need to reconsider their position. At the same time, northern nationalists had to face the fact that, as the south cantered forward towards previously undreamed-of prosperity, Dublin governments were quietly consigning to the dustbin the rhetoric of their predecessors on the urgent need to end partition.

By the middle of the twentieth century it had become plain that a miserably weak economy and a falling population reduced by emigration could no longer be blamed on British colonial misrule. Then, under Seán Lemass in the 1960s, a remarkable turnaround began. Multinational firms eagerly took advantage of inducements and the staged reduction in tariffs to set up in the Republic. Employment resulting from the influx of foreign capital not only soaked up the large numbers leaving the farming sector but, in addition, virtually wiped out net emigration as a distinctive feature of Irish life.

In 1972 86 per cent of citizens had voted in favour of joining the EEC. The Republic's successful application for membership provided an opportunity to widen export markets and benefit from the Community's support funds. Many of the expected benefits of membership were postponed by the quintupling of oil prices and alarming fluctuations in the world economy. The high rate of natural increase—six times the EEC average—meant that even a slight contraction in the demand for labour would result in a vigorous leap in the number of unemployed. By 1977 116,000 were out of work.

In his first televised address as the new Taoiseach in January 1980 Charles Haughey warned that belt-tightening was essential: 'As a community we have been living beyond our means.... We have been living at a rate which is simply not justified by the amount of goods and services we are producing.' By the calculations of many, the state was teetering on the brink of bankruptcy: the exchequer borrowing requirement was more than a fifth of GNP by the end of 1981. Emigration from the Republic averaged 25,000 a year in the 1980s. Between them, Fine Gael and Labour coalitions and Haughey's Fianna Fáil administrations applied the strong medicine of expenditure cuts and tax increases required.

It is now widely agreed that rigorous control of the public finances in the 1980s laid firm foundations for the 'Celtic Tiger'. Even as the cuts were still being applied, Irish GDP rose by 36.6 per cent between 1987 and 1993 (in the European Union as a whole the increase was 13.3 per cent). Unemployment, which had reached 17 per cent in the mid-1980s, fell to 4.4 per cent by 2000. Early in the new millennium living standards were reckoned to be higher than those in the United Kingdom. The OECD observed of the Republic in 1999: 'It is astonishing that a nation could have moved all the way from the back of the pack to a leading position within such a short period, not much more than a decade in fact.'

The creation of a Single Market from 1987 onwards in the European Union resulted in transfers from the Structural and Cohesion Funds amounting to over £6 billion; this probably hoisted the Republic's GNP by between 2 and

3 per cent. The Industrial Development Agency had tax breaks, generous grants and an English-speaking workforce to woo overseas enterprises, most of them American; these included Intel, Microsoft, Hewlett Packard, Kodak and Pfizer. The arrival of the American company Apple in the 1980s was an indicator that a highly important accelerant was the rise of the knowledge-based economy. Any competitive disadvantage which Ireland possessed when traditional manufacturing still held sway, because of its small domestic market and an island's cost of access for imports and exports, rapidly disappeared. When wealth in the advanced economies was increasingly being created intellectually, circumstances changed to give the country a competitive advantage.

One American commentator observed: 'Ireland's well-educated workforce today offers multinational businesses perhaps Europe's best ratio of skills to wages.' This was not a situation which could last, but there is no doubt that without a determined drive to upgrade the state's education provision there would have been no 'Celtic Tiger'. The vast majority of those who had exported themselves in the 1940s and 1950s had acquired no more than elementary education at National School and, without formal skills, tended to enter the British labour market on the lowest rung. The ground was prepared by Patrick Hillery, appointed Minister for Education in 1959. Then in September 1966 his successor Donogh O'Malley made his celebrated announcement that the government would make free post-primary education available to Intermediate Certificate level for all children in 'academic' secondary, vocational and comprehensive schools. It is highly doubtful that this sweeping reform had been fully approved in cabinet; but in any case the scheme was given full sanction in December. The appearance of yellow school buses soon afterwards seemed to demonstrate to people in rural districts in particular that the era of population haemorrhage was drawing to a close.

Meanwhile Northern Ireland's economy was in a parlous condition. In 1969 output per head in the region was still around one-fifth higher than in the Republic. Then, the eruption of violence frightened foreign investors away, and, in addition, the leap in oil prices in 1973–4 effectively killed off the briefly flourishing synthetic fibre industry. Yet in 1984 the average material living standard in Northern Ireland was still more than 25 per cent above the level in the Republic. How can this be explained? The answer is that massive financial transfers from the Treasury in London prevented a fall in living standards. As the private sector continued to shrivel, citizens depended to an extraordinary degree on employment in the public service. Economists were heard to remark that Northern Ireland had become the most dependent economy in the world with the exception of Western Samoa. By 1995 living standards north and south were about equal. Then, as the Celtic Tiger began to roar, the Republic left Northern Ireland trailing further and further behind.

Between 1995 and 2005 the Republic's exports quadrupled, output increased by 350 per cent, and personal disposable income doubled. In 2004 the *Economist* concluded that Ireland's quality of life was the best in the world. That assessment has to be treated with caution. Other European states, such as France, Italy, Germany and Belgium, had an infrastructure—particularly in roads, public transport, health provision and the extension of broadband— which was vastly superior to the one the Republic possessed. Very little was done to reduce to reduce dependence on non-renewable energy sources. Too much emphasis was being placed on the value of property in the form of bricks and mortar. In the *Sunday Tribune* on 22 July 2001 Diarmuid Doyle listed thirty unpleasant facts about life in the Republic, authenticated by official reports, in an article ironically titled 'Aren't We a Great Little Country?' They included:

Irish people have the worst life expectancy in the European Union.... Ireland has the lowest number of acute hospital beds per capita in the EU.... More than 60 patients a day are having to wait on trolleys for up to six hours in the casualty departments of Dublin's acute hospitals.... Proportionately, more people live in poverty in Ireland than in any industrialised country outside the United States.... Ireland has the highest rate of child poverty in the EU.... Twenty-three per cent of the Irish population cannot perform basic literacy tasks like reading a bus timetable.... Dublin has a higher murder rate than London....

In the *Irish Times* on 13 February 2008 Vincent Browne concluded that his nation was divided by wealth. In 2007 there were between forty and fifty private jets based in Ireland, 140 registered helicopters, about 25,000 leisure boats and some 33,000 millionaires in the country. The Bank of Ireland Private Banking Limited reported that in 2006 the top 2 per cent of the population held 30 per cent of the wealth. 'Meanwhile', Browne continued, 'almost 7 per cent of the population are living in consistent poverty, that is, almost 300,000 living in consistent poverty, that is, living on incomes of less than the equivalent of about €11,000 for a single person *and* being unable to afford two pairs of strong shoes, or unable to afford a meal with meat or chicken or fish every second day.'

Certainly the hectic race towards greater prosperity had its downside. Beautiful riverscapes had been ruined by crude dredging in an economically questionable drive to improve farm drainage. Tens of thousands of Italians cluster around the shores of Lake Como, but the water there is pristine. In Ireland, however, loughs in areas of low population, bombarded by urban sewage and agricultural effluent, suffered acute blooms of deadly green-blue algae—the visual impact but not the pollution later eased by an invasion of the alien zebra mussel—and the citizens of Galway had for a time to endure a contaminated water supply. Archaeologists in the field were forced to devote almost all their attention to rescue operations as new roads advanced on ancient sites. The abolition of domestic rates following Lynch's electoral triumph in 1977 had left local authorities weak and badly funded. The inevitable outcome was bin charging and a plague of illegal fly-tipping. The 'brown envelope' culture attached to planning permission proved difficult to eradicate and contributed to a proliferation of unsightly developments and ugly homes erected in the 'Irish hacienda' and 'Toblerone' styles.

In the twenty-six counties democracy between the world wars had survived a civil war and the threats posed by Blueshirts and IRA activists. In the final decades of the twentieth century it was imperilled again by financial corruption and the abuse of power. When Taoiseach Charles Haughey broadcast to the nation in January 1980 to declare that the community was living beyond its means, his personal overdraft with one bank had reached £1 million, and it emerged over the course of time that he had been in receipt of very large payments for favours rendered.

Nevertheless, life in Ireland was incomparably better for the great majority than it had been when Taoiseach Seán Lemass had shaken hands with Prime Minister Terence O'Neill in January 1965. The corruption infecting political life did not spread to other institutions which played a key role in the development of the state, in particular the civil service, the judiciary and the banks. The country experienced a remarkable social, cultural and economic transformation over a very short period of time. Archbishop John Charles McQuaid in his 1971 Lenten pastoral had declared: 'Civil divorce is evil, and contraception is evil … a curse upon the country.' By then, however, the Catholic Church's moral monopoly was already being corroded by secularisation and modernisation. Three years later, following the highly publicised 'contraception train' from Belfast, the Dáil made a hesitant first step by making birth control available by prescription. Eventually all attempts to restrict availability were abandoned, and by 1991 the Republic was importing ten million condoms a year. Then followed a stream of revelations about the double lives of Bishop Eamon Casey and of Father Michael Cleary, and about the sexual abuse of children by Brendan Smyth, Seán Fortune and other clergy and members of religious orders in Industrial Schools, Magdalene Laundries and elsewhere. All this did much to diminish respect for the church, particularly as members of the hierarchy were so hesitant in making apologies. Vocations dropped by nearly a hundred per cent between 1966 and 1996, and between 1970 and 1995 the number of religious in the state declined by over a third. Eighty-five per cent attended church at least once a week in 1990, but just seven years later this percentage was down to sixty-five. Civil divorce, rejected by two-thirds in the 1986 referendum, was accepted—admittedly by a tiny majority—ten years later.

Broadcasters and the print media did much to create a more open, liberal and tolerant society. In *The Late Late Show* Gay Byrne introduced for discussion topics previously considered taboo. Dermot Morgan and Gerry Stembridge on RTÉ radio satirised Haughey and other politicians with devastating effect in *Scrap Saturday*. Meanwhile on BBC Radio Ulster David Dunseith vigorously challenged bigotry on *Talk Back*. A group of young lawyers-turned-comedians, calling themselves The Hole in the Wall Gang, lampooned Ulster stereotypes on *Talk Back* and in 1995 made a particularly effective attack on sectarianism in BBC Northern Ireland's *Two Ceasefires and a Wedding*. In the Republic homosexuality was decriminalised in 1993. The position of women in the workplace steadily improved, and growing numbers of women were appointed to public boards and promoted to senior positions in the civil service, the professions and the judiciary. The election of Mary Robinson, and then Mary McAleese, as President of Ireland, and Mary Harney as Tánaiste, would have astonished earlier generations. Male politicians prevailed overwhelmingly north of the border, but there too the Women's Coalition and Sylvia Herman demonstrated that change was possible.

The people of Ireland faced the new millennium with a confidence that had not been apparent before. The stereotypical view of a quaint island, as portrayed in such films as *The Quiet Man* and *Darby O'Gill and the Little People*, had been swept aside by (among others) Ryanair, which pioneered low-cost air travel; Riverdance, a troupe which captivated international audiences when Ireland hosted the Eurovision Song Contest; Bono and U2, and Van Morrison, who had good claim to be in the top tier of rock and rhythm-and-blues musicians; Paddy Maloney and The Chieftains, who brought Irish traditional music to a world stage; actors with international reputations, including Liam Neeson and Pierce Brosnan; and Séamus Heaney, who not only won the Nobel Prize for Literature but also became the world's best-selling living poet writing in English.

In the Republic a succession of tribunals exposed the misdemeanours of politicians, financiers, developers and businessmen. Though many felt the process was cumbersome and monstrously expensive, and that those named were let off too lightly, these tribunals appeared to be making sure that this dark episode would not easily be repeated. During the spring of 2008, while so many were anxiously awaiting the outcome of the credit crunch, at least the public finances were in good condition.

In Northern Ireland a whole generation had at last grown up with little or no experience of political violence. Given the breathing space of real peace, the northern economy made a remarkable recovery. Early in the new millennium levels of unemployment in the region had dropped to historically low levels. Construction firms, for example, developed a prowess sufficient to win numerous valuable contracts overseas. Visible signs of progress down the Lagan valley and into Belfast included: the expansion of the Sprucefield complex south of Lisburn; the development of the Titanic quarter as a financial centre, with Citibank leading the way; the transformation of a run-down part of Belfast city centre to become the 'Cathedral Quarter'; the success of Ikea (throwing open its doors in December 2007) in attracting bus- and car-loads of customers from as far away as Kerry; and the opening of the Victoria Centre in March 2008. The north–south bodies, envisaged in the Good Friday Agreement, began constructive work. Relations between Belfast and Dublin, and between the governments of the Republic of Ireland and the United Kingdom, had never been better.

After the expansion of the European Union to include more states from central and eastern Europe, only Ireland, the United Kingdom and Sweden permitted an unrestricted inflow of migrant workers. Once again people began to move from east to west, and soon more people in Ireland were speaking Polish and Cantonese or Mandarin than Irish in everyday conversation. Even in the quietest western villages the person behind the counter in the corner shop or filling station was likely to be from Poland or Lithuania. Towns such as Ballybofey, Co. Donegal, acquired their own dedicated Polish-speaking internet cafés. The census of 2006 in the Republic showed that, out of a population of some four million, around 400,000 were born outside the island. Sometimes immigrants and migrant workers were treated with as much unkindness as the Irish who had previously settled in cities overseas. On the whole, however, these fresh waves of newcomers settled in comfortably, well on their way to becoming 'New Irish'. The town of Gort, Co. Galway, for example, became virtually an outpost of Brazil without provoking the slightest opposition from local people.

I conclude by recalling an incident which reminds me that for long we Irish have been more concerned about what divides us than with what we have in common.

A quarter of a century ago, keen to catch fish in Lough Melvin, I launched a ten-foot flat-bottomed boat at Kinlough, Co. Leitrim. Soon a vicious westerly storm blew up and, unable to row back, I was in imminent danger of being swamped. My only hope was a small island ahead of me. I made it.

Then I realised that this was a place where cultures had met, clashed and blended. The island is an artificial one, a crannog, constructed during the Iron Age. On it is the ruined castle of the McClancys where in 1588 the Armada castaway Francisco de Cuellar and his men in a snowstorm successfully resisted the English Lord Deputy, Sir William Fitzwilliam. Looking behind me I could see a line of buoys across the lough marking the unlikely frontier between the Irish Republic and Northern Ireland.

Later I reflected that, in addition to arctic char and salmon, this lough is home to four distinct species of trout—sonaghan, gillaroo, ferox and brown trout. Though they spawn in the same rivers, they do not interbreed. In short, there is more genetic diversity in the trout of this medium-sized lake in the north-west of Ireland than there is among all humans living on this earth.

JONATHAN BARDON
31 March 2008

REFERENCES

Where the title of a book, article or pamphlet is not given, the complete reference will be found in the bibliography.

EPISODES

1. Viney, 2003, pp 15–60; Cabot, 1999, pp 50–65; Waddell, 2000, pp 8–11.
2. Woodman, 1981, p. 92; Waddell, 2000, pp 11–16; Bardon, 1992, pp 2–3; M. J. O'Kelly in Ó Cróinín (ed.), 2005, pp 65–8.
3. Waddell, 2000, pp 25–53; Harbison, 1988, p. 25; Bardon, 1992, pp 5–6.
4. Waddell, 2000, pp 57–65, 68–72.
5. Waddell, 2000, pp 179–222, 225–75; Harbison, 1988, pp 114, 153.
6. O'Kelly, 1954, pp 105–55; Waddell, 2000, pp 218–21.
7. Mallory & McNeill, 1991, p. 156; Bardon, 1992, p. 9; James Carney in Ó Cróinín (ed.), 2005, pp 460–66.
8. Waddell, 2000, pp 314–16, 325–354; Barry Raftery in Ó Cróinín (ed.), 2005, pp 140–70.
9. Kinsella, 1970, pp 61–3; James Carney in Ó Cróinín (ed.), 2005, pp 468–72; Mac Niocaill, 1972, pp 3–4.
10. Cary & Warmington, 1929, p. 43; Bardon, 1992, pp 10–11; Barry Raftery in Ó Cróinín (ed.), 2005, pp 175–6.
11. Marsh, 1966, pp 23, 29, 34; Kathleen Hughes in Ó Cróinín (ed.), 2005, pp 301–9.
12. Marsh, 1966, p. 44; Kathleen Hughes in Ó Cróinín (ed.), 2005, pp 309–15.
13. Mac Niocaill, 1972, pp 42–9; Byrne, 1973, pp 41–2, 122–3; Dáibhí Ó Cróinín in Ó Cróinín (ed.), 2005, pp 231–4; Ó Corráin, 1972, pp 28–42; O'Meara, 1982, p. 110.
14. James Carney in Ó Cróinín (ed.), 2005, pp 451–2; T. M. Charles-Edwards, ibid., pp 337–50; Byrne, 1973, pp 13–15; Gantz, 1981, p. 1.
15. Nancy Edwards in Ó Cróinín (ed.), 2005, pp 238–54.
16. O'Meara, 1982, p. 102; Kelly, 1997, pp 219–47; Nancy Edwards in Ó Cróinín (ed.), 2005, pp 265–73; Donnchadh Ó Corráin, ibid., p. 582.
17. Roger Stalley in Ó Cróinín (ed.), 2005, pp 726–7; Adamson, 1979, p. 19; McNally, 1965, p. 127; Diarmuid Ó Laoghaire in McNally, 1965, p. 44.
18. McNally, 1965, pp 125–6; William O'Sullivan in Ó Cróinín (ed.), 2005, pp 526–30.
19. Dáibhí Ó Cróinín in Ó Cróinín (ed.), 2005, p. 217; McNally, 1965, p. 125; Adamson, 1979, pp 19, 74–5.
20. Todd, 1867, pp 3, 51, 224–7; de Paor, 1964, p. 132.
21. Bardon, 1984, p. 2; Todd, 1867, p. 52; *Annals of Ulster*, AD 919.
22. F. J. Byrne in Ó Cróinín (ed.), 2005, pp 630–31; Todd, 1867, pp 79–81.
23. Bardon, 1984, p. 4; Todd, 1867, pp 159–61, 179, 191–3; Dasent, 1911, p. 327.

24. Olivia O'Leary in Bardon, 1984, p. 28; Patrick F. Wallace in Ó Cróinín (ed.), 2005, pp 814–40; Ó Corráin, 1972, pp 131–50.

25. Ó Corráin, 1972, pp 150–74; Scott & Martin, 1978, p. 25; Orpen, 1994, p. 11.

26. F. X. Martin in Cosgrove (ed.), 1987, pp 47, 73; Orpen, 1994, pp 23, 25; Scott & Martin, 1978, p. 27.

27. Scott & Martin, 1978, pp 57, 65, 67; Orpen, 1994, p. 111.

28. Scott & Martin, 1978, pp 77, 78; F. X. Martin in Cosgrove (ed.), 1987, pp 82–7.

29. Scott & Martin, 1978, pp 97, 103; F. X. Martin in Cosgrove (ed.), 1987, p. 57; O'Meara, 1982, p. 106.

30. Scott & Martin, 1978, pp 115, 177; F. X. Martin in Cosgrove (ed.), 1987, p. 99.

31. Scott & Martin, 1978, p. 237; Orpen, 1968, II, p. 236; Bardon, 1984, p. 8.

32. O'Donovan (ed.), 1856, AD 1210; Sweetman & Handcock, 1886, p. 169; Bardon, 1984, p. 8.

33. James Lydon in Cosgrove (ed.), 1987, pp 166–7; Deane (ed.), 1991, I, pp 150–52.

34. R. E. Glasscock in Cosgrove (ed.), 1987, p. 222; Kevin Down, ibid., pp 455– 60, 465, 469, 471, 475.

35. Freeman (ed.), 1983, pp 3, 57–8, 131–133; Orpen, 1968, III, p. 276.

36. Freeman (ed.), 1983, AD 1315; James Lydon in Cosgrove (ed.), 1987, p. 284; Sayles, 1956, pp 95–100; Bardon, 1985, p. 4.

37. Freeman (ed.), 1983, pp 251, 253, 259, 261, 263, 281, 283, 317, 325; O'Connor, 1959, p. 25.

38. Kelly, 2001, pp 3, 12, 24, 34, 47.

39. Hayes-McCoy, 1937, p. 32; *Calendar of State Papers, Henry VIII: Correspondence*, III, p. 11.

40. James Lydon in Cosgrove (ed.), 1987, p. 271; J. A. Watt, ibid., pp 371–2.

41. J. A. Watt in Cosgrove (ed.), 1987, pp 388–9.

42. Dorothy M. Carpenter in Haren & de Pontfarcy (eds), 1988, pp 100, 106–12.

43. Dorothy M. Carpenter in Haren & de Pontfarcy (eds), 1988, pp 109–11, 115–16.

44. Lydon, 1963, pp 141–6; E. Curtis, 'Unpublished Letters from Richard II in Ireland, 1394–5', *Proceedings of the Royal Irish Academy*, XXXVIII (1927).

45. Cosgrove (ed.), 1987, pp 531–40; Lydon, 1963, pp 143–146; Katharine Simms in Lydon (ed.), 1981, pp 230–31.

46. Edwin C. Rae in Cosgrove (ed.), 1987, pp 768–9; Simms, 1977, p. 140.

47. D. B. Quinn in Cosgrove (ed.), 1987, pp 645, 649; Connolly, 2007, pp 4–5.

48. MacCorristine, 1987, pp 16, 26, 54; Connolly, 2007, pp 86–90.

49. MacCorristine, 1987, pp 110, 117, 121, 130–31; Maxwell, 1923, pp 94–5.

50. J. A. Watt in Lydon (ed.), 1981, p. 209; Ellis, 1985, p. 187; Maxwell, 1923, pp 122, 123–4, 126.

51. *Calendar of State Papers, Henry VIII: Correspondence*, III, p. 15; Lennon, 1994, pp 148–52; Maxwell, 1923, pp 98–9, 103–4, 112–14.

52. Maxwell, 1923, p. 101; *Calendar of the Carew MSS*, III, pp 199, 421; Lennon, 1994, pp 155–9.

53. Maxwell, 1923, p. 145; G. A. Hayes-McCoy in Moody, Martin & Byrne (eds), p. 75, 78–9.

54. Bardon, 1992, pp 68, 75–77; Bagwell, 1885, II, pp 54–5; Falls, 1950, p. 87.

55. Bagwell, 1885, II, pp 54–6, 103; O'Donovan (ed.), AD 1567; G. A. Hayes-McCoy in

Moody, Martin & Byrne (eds), 1986, p. 85.

56. Canny, 1976, pp 73–6; Quinn, 1966, p. 108; Bagwell, 1885, II, pp 244, 258; O'Donovan (ed.), AD 1574.

57. Bagwell, 1885, II, pp 302, 305; Canny, 1976, pp 90–91; Bardon, 1992, pp 83–6.

58. G.A. Hayes-McCoy in Moody, Martin & Byrne (eds), 1978, p. 87; Lennon, 1994, pp 214–15, 223–5; Maxwell, 1923, p. 169.

59. Lennon, 1994, pp 225–7; Falls, 1950, pp 143–5; Maxwell, 1923, pp 170–71.

60. Sténuit, 1972, pp 118–23; Fallon, 1978, pp 129, 136.

61. Fallon, 1978, pp 80, 90, 105; Allingham, 1897, pp 63, 66; Bagwell, 1890, III, pp 186, 189.

62. Allingham, 1897, pp 61–70; Bagwell, 1890, III, p. 186.

63. Allingham, 1897, p. 61; Maxwell, 1923, pp 314–15, 316–318.

64. Maxwell, 1923, pp 315, 317–18; Dunlevy, 1989, pp 41–2, 47–51.

65. Bagwell, 1890, III, p. 137; O'Clery (ed.), 1893, pp 7–19.

66. O'Clery (ed.), 1893, pp 19–39.

67. Chambers, 1998, pp 41, 85, 87.

68. Lennon, 1994, pp 237–49; Chambers, 1998, pp 108, 113–26, 130, 150.

69. Lennon, 1994, p. 261; Bagwell, 1890, III, p. 186, 224, 244; Hayes-McCoy, 1969, pp 100, 103.

70. Bagwell, 1890, III, p. 254; Falls, 1950, p. 195; Silke, 1970, pp 29–32.

71. Falls, 1950, pp 203, 214; Hayes-McCoy, 1969, pp 114–19; Bagwell, 1890, III, pp 282, 296.

72. Falls, 1950, pp 222, 224, 228, 239, 241; Bagwell, 1890, III, p. 343.

73. John McCavitt in Mac Cuarta (ed.), 1993, pp 7–8; Docwra, 1849, pp 237–45; Moryson, 1617, Book 2, p. 137.

74. Docwra, 1849, p. 250; Moryson, 1617, Book 2, pp 223–4; Falls, 1950, p. 277; Silke, 1970, p. 79.

75. O'Donovan (ed.), AD 1601; *Calendar of the Carew* MSS, IV, pp 195–6; *Calendar of State Papers, Ireland, 1601–3*, p. 185; Jonathan Bardon, 'The Battle of Kinsale', BBC Radio Ulster, 1982.

76. O'Donovan (ed.), AD 1601; Moryson, 1617, Book 3, pp 177, 197, 199, 225, 283, 285; Docwra, 1849, pp 258, 260; Robinson, 1984, p. 38.

77. McCavitt, 2005, pp 59, 80; John McCavitt in Mac Cuarta (ed.), 1993, pp 10–11; McCavitt, 1998, pp 115–25.

78. Walsh, 1986, pp 37, 46; *Calendar of State Papers, Ireland, 1606–8*, p. 270; McCavitt, 2005, pp 87–8.

79. *Calendar of State Papers, Ireland, 1606–8*, p. 270; Walsh, 1996, pp 59, 60, 64; McCavitt, 2005, pp 95–9.

80. McCavitt, 2005, p. 98; Walsh, 1996, pp 66–7, 69, 73.

81. Walsh, 1996, p. 75; *Calendar of State Papers, Ireland, 1606–8*, pp 270, 273, 276, 281.

82. Hill, 1869, pp 13, 27; Perceval-Maxwell, 1973, pp 49–50; Bardon, 1992, pp 120–22; Report of the Plantation Commissioners, 1611, typescript copy, Lambeth Palace Library, cod. 630, fol. 144.

83. Hill, 1869, p. 66; Plantation Commissioners' Report, 1611, cod. 630, fol. 144.

84. Bardon, 1992, pp 118–20; *Calendar of State Papers, Ireland 1606–8*, pp 275, 504–6; ibid., 1608–10, pp 7, 15, 17, 27, 34; Moody, 1939, p. 31.

85. Moody, 1939, p. 31; Robinson, 1984, p. 63.
86. Gillespie, 1985, pp 31, 34; Perceval-Maxwell, 1973, pp 26–9, 326.
87. Perceval-Maxwell, 1973, pp 26–7, 46; Moody, 1939, pp 70, 369.
88. Moody, 1939, pp 160–61, 229; Gilbert (ed.), 1879, I, pp 319, 324.
89. McCavitt, 1998, pp 175–6, 183–4.
90. Aidan Clarke in Moody, Martin & Byrne (eds), 1978, pp 235, 245–64.
91. Aidan Clarke in Moody, Martin & Byrne (eds), 1978, pp 265–9; Reid, 1867, I, pp 180–82, 189, 237; Gillespie, 1985, pp 68–72.
92. Gilbert (ed.), 1879, I, p. 374; Aidan Clarke in Moody, Martin & Byrne (eds), 1978, pp 270–88; Michelle O Riordan in Mac Cuarta (ed.), 1993, pp 82–6; Elliott, 2000, pp 73–4.
93. Bardon, 1992, p. 126; Raymond Gillespie in Brady & Gillespie (eds), 1986, p. 195; Raymond Gillespie in Mac Cuarta (ed.), 1993, pp 107–21.
94. Gilbert, 1879, I, p. 363; Bardon, 1992, pp 136–8; Hilary Simms in Mac Cuarta (ed.), 1993, pp 124–8.
95. Patrick J. Corish in Moody, Martin & Byrne (eds), 1978, pp 292–3; Stevenson, 1981, p. 112.
96. Patrick J. Corish in Moody, Martin & Byrne (eds), 1978, pp 299–316; Hayes-McCoy, 1969, pp 179, 193; Stevenson, 1981, p. 233.
97. Patrick J. Corish in Moody, Martin & Byrne (eds), 1978, pp 324–5, 340–48.
98. Patrick J. Corish in Moody, Martin & Byrne (eds), 1978, III, pp 346–7; Stevenson, 1981, pp 276–7; Bagwell, 1890, III, pp 300–1; Ellis, 2000, pp 8, 37, 64.
99. Ellis, 2000, pp 83, 94, 131, 249.
100. Ellis, 2000, pp 163, 227; Patrick J. Corish in Moody, Martin & Byrne (eds), p. 385; Moody, 1937, pp 21, 23–4, 27.
101. Bardon, 1992, pp 148–9; Ellis, 2000, p. 249; O'Flaherty, 1846, pp 56–9.
102. Somerville-Large, 1981, p. 133; Craig, 1980, pp 29–67.
103. MacLysaght, 1969, pp 413–16.
104. MacLysaght, 1969, pp 313–19.
105. Jonathan Bardon, 'Oliver Plunkett', BBC Radio Ulster, 1977.
106. Jonathan Bardon, 'Oliver Plunkett' BBC Radio Ulster, 1977; Macrory, 1980, p. 114; Ellis, 1989, p. 12.
107. Haddick-Flynn, 2003, pp 63, 65, 83; Macrory, 1980, p. 124.
108. Macrory, 1980, pp 212, 214–15, 236, 238, 286; Bardon, 1992, pp 154–7.
109. Macrory, 1980, pp 214–15, 236, 238, 253, 291, 313–15.
110. Macrory, 1980, pp 314–315; Story, 1691, p. 52, 56–9.
111. Bardon, 1985, p. 10; Southwell, Public Record Office of Northern Ireland, T440, Letter XIV, Duleek, 2 July 1690, p. 38.
112. Ellis, 1989, frontispiece, pp 123–4; Haddock-Flynn, 2003, pp 134–44; Murray, 1912, pp 176–83.
113. Murray, 1912, pp 208–9; Haddick-Flynn, 2003, pp 167–72, 180–81; Hayes-McCoy, 1969, pp 238–59; Diarmuid Murtagh in Hayes-McCoy (ed.), 1964, pp 59–67; Story, 1691, pp 94–103.
114. Diarmuid Murtagh in Hayes-McCoy (ed.), 1964, pp 68–9; Story, 1691, pp 67–9; Haddock-Flynn, 2003, pp 189–92; Hayes-McCoy, 1969, pp 259–70; Story, 1691, pp 210, 217–18.

115. Haddock-Flynn, 2003, pp 197–8; J. G. Simms in Moody, Martin & Byrne (eds), 1986, p. 507.
116. Bardon, 1982, p. 26; Ranelagh, 1981, p. 116.
117. Reid, 1867, III, pp 7, 30; Lecky, 1892, I, p. 170.
118. Bardon, 1992, p. 170.
119. MacLysaght, 1969, pp 329–33.
120. Deane (ed.), 1991, pp 341–5, 345–50; Beckett, 1966, pp 156, 165–6.
121. Deane (ed.), 1991, pp 386–91, 784–5; O'Connor, 1959, pp 95–6.
122. Dickson, 1997, pp 14, 19, 20, 22–4, 27, 33.
123. Dickson, 1997, pp 35–8, 46, 48, 50, 51–2, 69.
124. Bardon, 1984, p. 20; Townsend, 1852, pp 5–30; Day, 1991, p. 262.
125. Maxwell, 1936, pp 73–8, 101–2.
126. Maxwell, 1936, pp 140–41, 143, 150–51; Bardon, 1984, p. 20.
127. Latocnaye, 1984, pp 187, 201; Bardon, 1992, pp 195, 197–9; Maxwell, 1949, p. 21.
128. Beckett, 1966, p. 176; Maxwell, 1949, pp 176–7; Crawford & Trainor (eds), 1969, pp 36–7.
129. Maxwell, 1949, pp 183–4; Crawford & Trainor (eds), 1969, pp 38–9; Bardon, 1982, p. 34.
130. Dickson, 1966, p. 74; McCracken, 1971, pp 29, 73, 78, 83–4, 118, 137.
131. Bardon, 1992, p. 191; Maxwell, 1949, pp 122, 123, 125.
132. Maxwell, 1949, pp 236–9; Maxwell, 1936, pp 253–4, 264–5; Bardon, 1992, pp 192–3.
133. Crawford, 1972, p. 31; Bardon, 1992, pp 179–82.
134. Young, 1892, I, pp 128, 131; Crawford, 1972, p. 75; Bardon, 1992, pp 184–7.
135. Crawford, 1972, p. 77; Dickson, 1966, p. 33; Bardon, 1992, pp 176–8.
136. Bardon, 1985, p. 6; Dickson, 1966, p. 289.
137. Dickson, 1966, p. 208; Crawford & Trainor (eds), 1969, p. 53; Joy, 1817, p. 138; Public Record Office of Northern Ireland, Educational Facsimile, *Volunteers*, p. 141; O'Connell, 1965, pp 28, 63.
138. O'Connor, 1959, p. 338; Public Record Office of Northern Ireland, Educational Facsimile, *Volunteers*, p. 141 (*Dublin Journal*, 7 Nov. 1779).
139. O'Connell, 1965, p. 186; Joy, 1817, pp 181–3; Public Record Office of Northern Ireland, Educational Facsimile, *Volunteers*, p. 152.
140. O Lochlainn, 1984, p. 86; Grattan, 1854, 70–77; O'Connell, 1965, p. 325.
141. Wright, 1870, II, pp 474–7; A. W. P. Malcomson in Bartlett & Hayton (eds), 1979, pp 145, 153.
142. Bardon, 1992, p. 217; O'Connell, 1965, p. 354; Joy, 1817, pp 348–50.
143. Joy, 1817, pp 349–53, 358–60.
144. O'Connor, 1959, pp 180–82; McNeill, 1988, pp 78–85.
145. McNeill, 1988, p. 91; MacDermot, 1969, pp 87, 97–8.
146. Lecky, 1892, III, pp 326–38; MacDermot, 1969, p. 145.
147. Miller, 1990, pp 30, 34, 49, 71, 80–94, 113, 121–32.
148. O Lochlainn, 1962, p. 140; Miller, 1990, pp 125, 129; Bardon, 1992, p. 227.
149. Elliott, 1989, p. 297; Zimmermann, 1967, p. 133; MacDermot, 1969, pp 192, 196–8, 201–2.
150. Dickson, 1960, pp 109, 111, 112, 119, 180; Pakenham, 1962, pp 50–56, 70.
151. Zimmermann, 1967, pp 307–8; Pakenham, 1962, pp 23, 30, 71–2, 85; O'Connor, 1959, p. 338.

152. Zimmermann, 1967, pp 133, 160; Pakenham, 1962, pp 92, 96, 117.
153. Zimmermann, 1967, p. 140; Pakenham, 1962, p. 178.
154. Zimmermann, 1967, p. 161; Pakenham, 1962, pp 179, 194, 206, 208.
155. Pakenham, 1962, p. 209; Stewart, 1995, pp 72–7; Dickson, 1960, pp 135, 138.
156. W. R. Hutchinson in Hawthorne (ed.), 1966, p. 28; Dickson, 1960, p. 135; Stewart, 1995, pp 86–121, 123–35.
157. Dickson, 1960, pp 142, 143, 147, 228; Zimmermann, 1967, p. 156; Stewart, 1995, pp 222–34.
158. Zimmermann, 1967, pp 156, 161; Maxwell, 1880, p. 215; McNeill, 1988, p. 181.
159. Zimmermann, 1967, pp 133, 160; Pakenham, 1962, pp 296, 306–7; Elliott, 1989, p. 392.
160. Elliott, 1989, pp 392–3; Beckett, 1966, p. 271; Geoghegan, 1999, p. 21.
161. Beckett, 1966, p. 272; www.actofunion.ac.uk; Geoghegan, 1999, pp 62, 85, 105.
162. O'Connor, 1959, p. 184; Geoghegan, 1999, pp 99, 110, 115; Beckett, 1966, p. 273.
163. Bardon, 1992, p. 241; Elliott, 1982, 293–7; Geoghegan, 2002, pp 116–27.
164. Geoghegan, 2002, pp 165–82.
165. Geoghegan, 2002, pp 193, 244, 253, 265; Elliott, 1982, p. 312; O Lochlainn, 1984, pp 142–3; author inspired to include 'Mrs McGrath' by Bruce Springsteen, *Seeger Sessions*.
166. Paul E. W. Roberts in Clark and Donnelly (eds), 1983, pp 64–98.
167. Carson, 1976, script; Sean Connolly in Roebuck (ed.), 1981, p. 169.
168. Watson, 1960, p. 401; O'Farrell, 1971, p. 74.
169. MacDonagh, 1991, pp 205, 214.
170. MacDonagh, 1991, pp 225–7; *Northern Whig*, 2, 9 Oct. 1828, 16 July 1829; Norman Harrison in Hawthorne (ed.), 1966, p. 42.
171. MacDonagh, 1991, pp 250–54.
172. MacDonagh, 1991, p. 269; Beckett, 1966, pp 312–23.
173. Beckett, 1966, p. 298; S. J. (Sean) Connolly in Vaughan (ed.), 1989, pp 58–60; Oliver MacDonagh, ibid., pp 193–216.
174. Bardon, 2000, pp 34–6; O'Donoghue, 1965, pp 14–28; O'Donoghue, 1966, pp 69–96; Zimmermann, 1967, pp 203–5; O'Donoghue, 1972, pp 84–108.
175. D. H. Akenson in Vaughan (ed.), 1989, pp 530–37; All Children Together manifesto, 1974.
176. *Repealer Repulsed*, pp 12, 27, 38, 110; *Northern Whig*, 22 Jan. 1841.
177. MacDonagh, 1991, pp 481, 510–12, 514.
178. Deane (ed.), 1991, 1, p. 1288; ibid., II, p. 54.
179. Maloney, 1995, p. 102; Foster, 1988, pp 310–17; Beaumont, 2006, pp 130–31.
180. McCutcheon, 1980, p. 293; Crawford, 1972, p. 84; Day & McWilliams, 1998, pp 44, 94; Beaumont, 2006, pp 122, 128–9.
181. Hill, 1845, p. 20; Woodham-Smith, 1985, p. 24.
182. Woodham-Smith, 1985, pp 40, 48, 53, 139; Killen, 1995, pp 35–6; Public Record Office of Northern Ireland, Educational Facsimile, *The Great Famine*, n.d., p. 15.
183. Woodham-Smith, 1985, pp 91, 123, Killen, 1995, pp 71–2; Public Record Office of Northern Ireland, Educational Facsimile, *The Great Famine*, n.d., p. 7.
184. Jonathan Bardon, *The Famine in Skibbereen*, Modern Irish History: People and Events, BBC Radio Ulster, 1978; Woodham-Smith, 1985, pp 162–3.

185. Killen, 1995, p. 97; Bardon, 1982, p. 97; *Belfast News-Letter* 30 Apr. 1847; Board of Works, Distress, Jan. 1848, pp 107–8.

186. Speed, 1976, p. 63; Woodham-Smith, 1985, pp 216–17, 225, 238; Handley, 1947, p. 25.

187. Woodham Smith, 1985 p. 335; O'Farrell, 1971, p. 112.

188. J. S. Donnelly jr in Vaughan (ed.), 1989, pp 337, 351–2; Kee, 1989, II, p. 10.

189. Kee, 1989, II, pp 18–19, 29; Bill Meek in Hawthorne, 1966, pp 88–91.

190. Bill Meek in Hawthorne, 1966, p. 87; Newsinger, 1994, pp 54–5, 62–63; Kee, 1989, II, pp 39–48.

191. *Belfast News-Letter*, 13 July 1849; Bardon, 1982, pp 100–1.

192. Zimmermann, 1967, p. 311; *Newry Telegraph*, repr. in *Belfast News-Letter* 20 July 1849; Bardon, 1992, 302–4.

193. Lyons, 1971, p. 132; R. V. Comerford in Vaughan (ed.), 1996, pp 3–5; *Belfast News-Letter*, 5 Feb. 1874.

194. Kee, 1993, pp 181, 187–9.

195. Mitchell & Ó Snodaigh, 1989, pp 43, 46; Walker, 1989, p. 135.

196. Marlow, 1973, pp 148, 160, 189, 201.

197. Kee, 1993, p. 437; Abels, 1966, 217–18.

198. MacKnight, 1896, II, p. 116; Abels, 1966, pp 237, 242–3; Bardon, 1992, 376–7.

199. Loughlin, 1986, p. 146; Kee, 1993, pp 517–18; Moore, 1914, p. 62.

200. *Belfast News-Letter*, 10, 14 June 1886; Moore, 1914, pp 58–63; *Industries of Ireland, Part I: Belfast*, 1891, p. 40.

201. *Belfast Directory*, 1896; *Freeman's Journal*, 16 Jan. 1899.

202. Abels, 1966, pp 310, 321; Kee, 1993, pp 557–8, 584–6.

203. Kee, 1993, pp 587–8, 591; Kee, 1989, II, p. 117; *The Times, Northern Whig, Belfast News-Letter*, 18 June 1892.

204. Loughlin, 1986, p. 268; Buckland (ed.), 1973, p. 273; MacKnight, 1896, II, p. 329; Abels, 1966, p. 245.

205. David Fitzpatrick in Vaughan (ed.), 1996, pp 606, 624, 629, 635.

206. Deane (ed.), 1991, II, p. 104; H. D. Gribbon in Vaughan (ed.), 1996, pp 312– 14; Morrissey, 2001, pp 79–80; Gailey, 1987, p. 25.

207. Lyons, 1968, p. 182; Gailey, 1987, pp 165, 189–99; Jackson, 1989, p. 128; Mitchell & Ó Snodaigh, 1989, p. 82.

208. Taylor, 167, p. 91; Bell, 1988, pp 31–2, 55, 92, 103–5, 112, 202–3.

209. Mitchell & Ó Snodaigh, 1989, pp 81–6.

210. Lyons, 1968, pp 275, 288; Stewart, 1967, pp 48, 55, 58.

211. *Belfast News-Letter*, 30 Sept. 1912; Bardon, 1985, p. 22; Stewart, 1967, pp 65–6; *Irish News, Freeman's Journal, Manchester Guardian*, 30 Sept. 1912.

212. Curriculum Development Unit, Dublin, 1978, pp 70, 77, 81, 92–5; Larkin, 1968, pp 122–3.

213. Stewart, 1967, pp 59, 67, 107, 141, 150–51; Laffan, 1999, p. 31; F. X. Martin in Martin & Byrne (eds), 1973, p. 174; Kee, 1989, II, p. 183; Buckland (ed.), 1973, p. 249.

214. Buckland (ed.), 1973, p. 257; Buckland, 1973, p. 99; Stewart, 1967, pp 223, 227, 229; Bardon, 1982, p. 183.

215. Fitzgerald, 1966, pp 117–19 (poster illustrations); *Irish News*, 6, 10 Aug. 1914; Stewart, 1981, pp 94–5, 99; *Freeman's Journal*, 21 Sept. 1914.

216. Laffan, 1983, pp 46–7; Mitchell & Ó Snodaigh, 1989, p. 182; Foy & Barton, 1999, p. 40.

217. Foy & Barton, 1999, pp 45–6, 59; Edwards, 1979, pp 178, 245; Fitzgerald, 1966, p. 80.

218. O'Malley, 1961, p. 24; Foy & Barton, 1999, pp 79, 142.

219. Elizabeth O'Farrell in McHugh (ed.), 1996, p. 208; Caulfield, 1995, p. 288.

220. Jeffery, 2000, p. 61; Orr, 1987, p. 162; Private Beattie's letter transcribed for the author in 1969 by Kathleen Page; Denman, 1992, p. 177; Gregory & Pašeta, pp 8–25.

221. Laffan, 1999, pp 81–85, 96–103, 110; Fitzgerald, 1966, p. 126 (poster).

222. Buckland, 1973, p. 106; Buckland (ed.), 1973, p. 423; Kee, 1989, III, p. 45; Comerford, 1969, p. 109.

223. Kee, 1989, III, pp 58, 64, 73.

224. Kee, 1989, III, pp 113, 116, 119; Hart, 1998, pp 21–38.

225. de Paor, 1970, p. 101; Kee, 1989, III, p. 70; Lacy, 1990, p. 228; Barton, 1988, p. 28; Farrell, 1976, p. 28.

226. Laffan, 1983, pp 64–65; Bardon, 1992, p. 479.

227. Kee, 1989, III, pp 129, 143; Taylor, 1965, p. 155; Buckland (ed.), 1973, p. 143; Middlemas, 1971, p. 78.

228. Middlemas, 1971, pp 87, 151–83; Pakenham, 1962, pp 230, 236, 239–40; Dwyer, 1981, pp 97–8; Lyons, 1971, p. 437.

229. Dáil Éireann debates, Dec. 1921–Jan. 1922.

230. Dáil Éireann debates, Jan. 1922; Middlemas, 1971, pp 48, 187,190; Bardon, 1992, pp 474–6; 482–4.

231. Robert McElborough Memoirs, typescript edited by Andrew Boyd, Linen Hall Library, Belfast; Hopkinson, 1988, pp 67, 95, 97; Younger, 1968, p. 250; Lyons, 1971, p. 452.

232. Younger, 1968, p. 330; Holt, 1960, p. 63; McGarry, 2005, p. 109.

233. Bardon, 1982, p. 277; Bardon, 1992, p. 494; Middlemas, 1971, p. 186; Buckland, 1973, p. 146.

234. Farrell, 1976, pp 81–7; Laffan, 1983, 99–104; Farrell, 1983, 243–51.

235. Hymn parody recited to the author by Helen O'Donnell; Bardon, 1992, pp 525–9; 'Datsie-dotsie' skipping rhyme recited to the author by Helen O'Donnell; Bardon in Boal & Royle, 2006, pp 132–3 (PRONI, LA/7/3A/6 and LA/7/3A/20); Munck & Roulston, 1987, p. 31.

236. de Vere White, 1948, p. 83; Keogh, 1994, pp 39–49; Jackson, 1999, 282–8.

237. Ferriter, 2004, pp 296, 316; Keogh, 1994, pp 58–68; McGarry, 2005, p. 197.

238. Keogh, 1994, p. 80; McGarry, 2005, pp 216–18, 205 (on Blythe), 258 (Dillon on O'Duffy).

239. Children's rhyme recited to the author by Andrew Boyd; Kennedy, 1988, p. 165; Farrell, 1976, p. 90; Barton, 1988, pp 78–80, 98; Bardon, 1982, p. 228; skipping rhyme recited to the author by Helen O'Donnell.

240. Ferriter, 2004, pp 396, 447–8, 395 (*Irish Press* quotation); Munck & Roulston, 1987, pp 66, 70–75; Barton, 1989, p. 12; Bardon, 1992, pp 529–34.

241. Fisk, 1985, pp 104–13; O'Halpin, 1999, pp 151–71; Bew, 2007, pp 464–71, 473; Ferriter, 2004, pp 383–8; Keogh, 1994, pp 108–30.

242. Barton, 1989, pp 27, 40, 81, 107; Barton, 1988, pp 137, 149, Bowman, 1982, p. 180; Fisk, 1983, pp 495, 500; Barton, 1995, pp 94–101; Bardon, 1992, pp 577–86.

243. Keogh, 1994, pp 157, 185–94, 218; Carroll, 1975, p. 163; Patterson, 2002, pp 84–91.

244. Keogh, 1994, p. 197; Jones, 2001, pp 219–21; Whyte, 1971, pp 196–239; Patterson, 2002, pp 91–2.

245. *Belfast News-Letter*, 3 June 1941; Bardon, 1992, pp 589–98, 600, 614–16; Akenson, pp 16, 178, 184; *Belfast News-Letter*, 9 Nov. 1946.

246. Delaney, 2000, pp 143–99; Ferriter, 2004, pp 382, 473, 479; Keogh, 1994, pp 215–18.

247. Delaney, 2000, pp 143–97; Ferriter, 2004, pp 382–3, 463–79; Healy, 1968, pp 9, 22, 27, 52, 63, 71, 76, 88; Brody, 1973, pp 35, 86–93, 100, 180.

248. Whyte, 1971, pp 303–23; Keogh, 1994, pp 221, 238–9; Bardon, 1992, pp 604–7; Bell, 1972, pp 305–93; Kennedy, 1989, pp 6–13.

249. Bew, 2007, p. 477; Delaney, 2000, p. 227; Patterson, 2002, pp 191–2, 197, 372; Keogh, 1994, p. 246; Liam Kennedy in Hill (ed.), 2003, pp 472–6; Kennedy, 1989, pp 14–20.

250. O'Neill and Faulkner interviewed by the author in 1975 for 'O'Neill Meets Lemass', BBC Radio Ulster, 1976; correspondence between Douglas Carson and T. K. Whitaker lent to the author; Patterson, 2002, pp 191–2, 197, 372; Keogh, 1994, p. 246; Jackson, 1999, 319–23; Maloney & Pollock, 1986, pp 111, 119.

Epilogue. Max Hastings in *Sunday Times* (Culture section), 23 Mar. 2008; Diarmuid Doyle in *Sunday Tribune*, 22 July 2001; Patterson, 2002, pp 259–60, 275–86; Foster, 2007, pp 5–7, 14, 17–19, 31–4, 41–2, 57–60, 75–6, 81; Keogh, 1994, pp 329, 334, 375; Garret FitzGerald in *Irish Times*, 23 Feb., 1 Mar. 2008; Vincent Browne in *Irish Times*, 13 Feb. 2008.

BIBLIOGRAPHY

Abels, Jules, *The Parnell Tragedy*, London, 1966

Act of Union Virtual Library, Queen's University Belfast / New Opportunities Fund, 2001, www.actofunion.ac.uk

Adamson, Ian, *Bangor: Light of the World*, Bangor, 1979

Akenson, Donald Harman, *Education and Enmity: The Control of Schooling in Northern Ireland, 1920–50*, Newton Abbot & New York, 1973

Allingham, Hugh, *Translation of Captain Cuellar's Narrative of the Spanish Armada and his Adventures in Ireland, by Robert Crawford*, London, 1897

Armstrong, Olive, *Edward Bruce's Invasion of Ireland*, London, 1923

Bagwell, Richard, *Ireland under the Tudors*, 3 vols, London, 1885–90

—— *Ireland under the Stuarts and during the Interregnum*, 3 vols, London, 1909–16

Bardon, Jonathan, *A History of Ulster*, Belfast, 1992

—— *Belfast: An Illustrated History*, Belfast, 1982

—— *Belfast: 1000 Years*, Belfast, 1985

—— *A Guide to Local History Sources in the Public Record Office of Northern Ireland*, Belfast, 2000

—— *Dublin: One Thousand Years of Wood Quay*, Belfast, 1984

Bartlett, Thomas, and D. W. Hayton (eds), *Penal Era and Golden Age: Essays in Irish History, 1690–1800*, Belfast, 1979

Bartlett, Thomas, and Keith Jeffery (eds), *A Military History of Ireland*, Cambridge, 1996

Barton, Brian, *Brookeborough: The Making of a Prime Minister*, Belfast, 1988

—— *The Blitz: Belfast in the War Years*, Belfast, 1989

—— *Northern Ireland in the Second World War*, Belfast, 1995

Beaumont, Gustave de, *Ireland* (1839), ed. Tom Garvin and Andreas Hess, Cambridge, Mass. & London, 2006

Beckett, J. C., *The Making of Modern Ireland, 1603–1923*, London, 1966

Bell, J. Bowyer, *The Secret Army: A History of the IRA*, Dublin, 1970

Bell, Robert, *The Book of Ulster Surnames*, Belfast, 1988

Bew, Paul, *Ireland: The Politics of Enmity, 1789–2006*, Oxford, 2007

—— and Henry Patterson, *Seán Lemass and the making of modern Ireland, 1945–66*, Dublin, 1982

Boal, Frederick W., and Stephen A. Royle, *Enduring City: Belfast in the Twentieth Century*, Belfast, 2006

Board of Works, Distress. *Papers relating to Proceedings for the Relief of Distress and State of the Unions and Workhouses in Ireland*, 4th series, H.C. 1847–8

Bowman, John, *De Valera and the Ulster Question, 1917–1973*, Oxford, 1972

Boyce, D. George, *Nineteenth-Century Ireland: The Search for Stability*, Dublin, 1990

Brady, Ciaran, and Raymond Gillespie (eds), *Natives and Newcomers: Essays on the Making of Irish Colonial Society, 1534–1641*, Dublin, 1986

Brody, Hugh, *Inishkillane: Change and Decline in the West of Ireland*, London, 1973

Buckland, Patrick, *Irish Unionism 2: Ulster Unionism and the Origins of Northern Ireland, 1886–1922*, Dublin & New York, 1973

—— (ed.), *Irish Unionism, 1885–1923: A Documentary History*, Belfast, 1973

Byrne, F. J., *Irish Kings and High-Kings*, London, 1973

Cabot, David, *The New Naturalist: Ireland*, London, 1999

Canny, Nicholas, *The Elizabethan Conquest of Ireland: A Pattern Established, 1565–1576*, Hassocks, 1976

—— *Making Ireland British, 1580–1650*, Oxford, 2003

Carroll, Joseph T., *Ireland in the War Years, 1935–1945*, Newton Abbot, 1975

Carson, Douglas, 'The Battle of Garvagh', BBC Radio Ulster, 1976

Cary, M., and E. H. Warmington, *The Ancient Explorers*, London, 1929

Caulfield, Max, *The Easter Rebellion*, London, 1963 (references are to 1995 edition)

Chambers, Anne, *Granuaile: The Life and Times of Grace O'Malley, c. 1530–1603*, Dublin & Colorado, 1998

Clark, Samuel, and James S. Donnelly jr (eds), *Irish Peasants: Violence and Political Unrest, 1718–1914*, Manchester, 1983

Comerford, Máire, *The First Dáil*, Dublin, 1969

Connolly, Sean J., *Priests and People in Pre-Famine Ireland, 1780–1845*, Dublin, 1982

—— *Contested Island: Ireland, 1460–1630*, Oxford, 2007

Cosgrove, Art (ed.), *A New History of Ireland*, II: *Medieval Ireland, 1169–1534*, Oxford, 1987

Craig, Maurice, *Dublin, 1660–1860*, Dublin, 1980

Crawford, W. H., *Domestic Industry in Ireland: The Experience of the Linen Industry*, Dublin, 1972

—— and Brian Trainor (eds), *Aspects of Irish Social History 1750–1800*, Belfast, 1969

Curl, James S., *The Londonderry Plantation, 1609–1914*, Chichester, 1986

Curriculum Development Unit, Dublin (Gary Granville), *Divided City: Portrait of Dublin, 1913*, Dublin, 1978

Dasent, G. W., *The Story of Burnt Njal from the Icelandic of Njal's Saga*, London, 1911

Day, Angélique (ed.), *Letters from Georgian Ireland: The Correspondence of Mary Delany, 1731–68*, Belfast, 1991

—— and Patrick McWilliams (eds), *Ordnance Survey Memoirs of Ireland: Counties of South Ulster, 1834–8*, Belfast, 1998

Deane, Séamus (ed.), *The Field Day Anthology of Irish Writing*, Vols I–III, Derry, 1991

Delaney, Enda, *Demography, State and Society: Irish Migration to Britain, 1921–1971*, Liverpool, 2000

Denman, Terence, *Ireland's Unknown Soldiers: The 16th (Irish) Division in the Great War*, Dublin, 1992

de Paor, Liam, *Divided Ulster*, Harmondsworth, 1970

de Paor, Máire and Liam, *Early Christian Ireland*, London, 1958

de Vere White, Terence, *Kevin O'Higgins*, London, 1948

Dickson, Charles, *Revolt in the North: Antrim and Down in 1798*, Dublin, 1960

Dickson, David, *New Foundations: Ireland, 1660–1800*, Dublin, 1987

—— *Arctic Ireland: The Extraordinary Story of the Great Frost and Forgotten Famine of 1740–41*, Belfast, 1997

Dickson, R. J., *Ulster Emigration to Colonial America, 1718–1775*, London, 1966

Docwra, Henry, 'A Narration of the Services done by the Army ymployed to Lough-Foyle', *Miscellany of the Celtic Society*, ed. John O'Donovan, Dublin, 1849

Dunlevy, Mairéad, *Dress in Ireland*, London, 1989

Dwyer, T. Ryle, *Michael Collins and the Treaty: His Differences with de Valera*, Cork, 1981

Edwards, Ruth Dudley, *Patrick Pearse: The Triumph of Failure*, London 1977

Elliott, Marianne, *Partners in Revolution: The United Irishmen and France*, New Haven & London, 1982

—— *Theobald Wolfe Tone: Prophet of Irish Independence*, New Haven & London, 1989

—— *The Catholics of Ulster: A History*, London, 2000

Ellis, Peter Berresford, *Hell or Connaught! The Cromwellian Colonisation of Ireland, 1652–1660*, Belfast, 2000

—— *The Boyne Water: The Battle of the Boyne, 1690*, 1989, Belfast

Ellis, S. G., *Tudor Ireland: Crown, Community and the Conflict of Cultures, 1470–1603*, London & New York, 1985

English, Richard, *Irish Freedom: The History of Nationalism in Ireland*, London, 2006

Fallon, Niall, *The Armada in Ireland*, London, 1978

Falls, Cyril, *Elizabeth's Irish Wars*, London, 1950

Fanning, Ronan, *Independent Ireland*, Dublin, 1983

Farrell, Michael, *Northern Ireland: The Orange State*, London, 1976

—— *Arming the Protestants*, London & Dingle, 1983

Ferriter, Diarmaid, *The Transformation of Ireland, 1900–2000*, London, 2004

Fisk, Robert, *In Time of War: Ireland, Ulster and the Price of Neutrality, 1939–45*, London, 1985

FitzGerald, Garret, *All in a Life: An Autobiography*, Dublin, 1991

Fitzgerald, Redmond, *Cry Blood Cry Erin*, London, 1966

Foster, R. F., *Modern Ireland, 1600–1972*, London, 1988

—— *Luck and the Irish: A Brief History of Change, c. 1970–2000*, London, 2007

Foy, Michael, and Brian Barton, *The Easter Rising*, Stroud, 1999

Frame, Robin, 'The Bruces in Ireland, 1315–18', *Irish Historical Studies*, xix, no. 73 (Mar. 1974)

Freeman, A. Martin (ed.), *Annala Connacht: The Annals of Connacht* (AD 1224–1554), Dublin, 1983

Gailey, Andrew, *Ireland and the Death of Kindness: The Experience of Constructive Unionism, 1890–1905*, Cork, 1987

Gantz, Jeffrey, *Early Irish Myths and Sagas*, Harmondsworth, 1981

Garvin, Tom, *The Evolution of Irish Nationalist Politics*, Dublin, 1981

Geoghegan, Patrick M., *The Irish Act of Union: A Study in High Politics, 1798–1801*, Dublin, 1999

—— *Robert Emmet: A Life*, Dublin, 2002

Gilbert, J. T. (ed.), *A Contemporary History of Affairs in Ireland (1641–9)*, 3 vols, Dublin, 1879

Gillespie, Raymond, *Colonial Ulster: The Settlement of East Ulster*, Cork, 1985

Grattan, Henry, *Speeches*, ed. Daniel Owen Madden, Dublin, 1854

Gregory, Adrian, and Senia Pašeta (eds), *Ireland and the Great War: 'A War to Unite Us All'?*, Manchester, 2002

Haddick-Flynn, Kevin, *Sarsfield and the Jacobites*, Cork, 2003

Hand, Geoffrey J. (ed.), *The Report of the Irish Boundary Commission*, Dublin, 1969

Handley, James E., *The Irish in Modern Scotland*, Cork, 1947

Hanson, R. P. C., *Saint Patrick: His Origins and Career*, Oxford, 1968

Harbison, Peter, *Pre-Christian Ireland*, London, 1988

Haren, Michael, and Yolande de Pontfarcy (eds), *The Medieval Pilgrimage to St Patrick's Purgatory*, Enniskillen & Monaghan, 1988

Hart, Peter, *The I.R.A. and its Enemies: Violence and Community in Cork, 1916–1923*, Oxford, 1998

Hawthorne, James (ed.), *Two Centuries of Irish History*, London, 1966

Hayes-McCoy, G. A., *Scots Mercenary Forces in Ireland, 1565–1603*, Dublin, 1937

—— *Irish Battles: A Military History of Ireland*, London, 1969

—— (ed.), *The Irish at War*, Cork, 1964

Healy, John, *The Death of an Irish Town*, Cork, 1968

Hill, George (ed.), *The Montgomery Manuscripts*, Belfast, 1869

Hill, Lord George, *Facts from Gweedore*, London, 1845

Hill, J. R. (ed.), *A New History of Ireland*, VII: *1921–1984*, Oxford, 2003

Holt, Edgar, *Protest in Arms*, London, 1960

Hopkinson, Michael, *Green against Green: The Irish Civil War*, Dublin, 1988

The Industries of Ireland, London, 1891; repr. Belfast, 1986

Hoppen, K. Theodore, *Ireland since 1800: Conflict and Conformity*, London, 1999

Jackson, Alvin, *Ireland, 1798–1998*, Oxford, 1999

—— *The Ulster Party: Irish Unionists in the House of Commons, 1884–1911*, Oxford, 1989

—— *Home Rule: An Irish History, 1800–2000*, London, 2003

Jeffery, Keith, *Ireland and the Great War*, Cambridge, 2000

Johnston, Dorothy, 'Richard II and the Submissions of Gaelic Ireland', *Irish Historical Studies*, XXII, no. 85 (Mar. 1980)

Jones, Greta, *'Captain of All These Men of Death': The History of Tuberculosis in Nineteenth and Twentieth Century Ireland*, Amsterdam & New York, 2001

Jordan, Anthony J., *John A. Costello: Compromise Taoiseach*, Dublin, 2007

[Joy, Henry, jr], *Historical Collections relative to the Town of Belfast*, Belfast, 1817

Kee, Robert, *The Green Flag*, II: *The Bold Fenian Men*, London, 1989

—— *The Green Flag*, III: *Ourselves Alone*, London, 1989

—— *The Laurel and the Ivy: The Story of Charles Stewart Parnell and Irish Nationalism*, London, 1993

Kelly, Fergus, *Early Irish Farming*, Dublin, 1997

Kelly, Maria, *A History of the Black Death in Ireland*, Dublin, 2001

Kennedy, Dennis, *The Widening Gulf: Northern Attitudes to the Independent Irish State, 1919–49*, Belfast, 1988

Kennedy, Liam, *The Modern Industrialisation of Ireland, 1940–1988*, Dundalk, 1989

Keogh, Dermot, *Twentieth-Century Ireland: Nation and State*, Dublin, 1994

—— and Mervyn O'Driscoll (eds), *Ireland in World War Two: Neutrality and Survival*, Cork, 2004

Killen, John (ed.), *The Famine Decade: Contemporary Accounts, 1841–1851*, Belfast, 1995

Kinsella, Thomas, *The Tain*, Oxford, 1970

Lacy, Brian, *Siege City: The Story of Derry and Londonderry*, Belfast, 1990

Laffan, Michael, *The Partition of Ireland, 1911–1925*, Dundalk, 1983

—— *The Resurrection of Ireland: The Sinn Féin Party, 1916–1923*, Cambridge, 1999

Larkin, Emmet, *James Larkin: Irish Labour Leader, 1876–1947*, London, 1968

Latocnaye, Chevalier de, *A Frenchman's Walk through Ireland, 1796–7*, repr. with introduction by John Gamble, Belfast 1984

Lecky, W. E. H., *A History of Ireland in the Eighteenth Century*, 5 vols, London, 1892–6

Lee, J. J., *Ireland, 1912–1985: Politics and Society*, Cambridge, 1989

Lennon, Colm, *Sixteenth-Century Ireland: The Incomplete Conquest*, Dublin, 1994

Loughlin, James, *Gladstone: Home Rule and the Ulster Question, 1882–93*, Dublin, 1986

Lydon, James, 'Richard ii's Expeditions to Ireland', *Journal of the Royal Society of Antiquaries of Ireland*, xciii (1963)

—— (ed.), *England and Ireland in the Later Middle Ages*, Dublin, 1981

Lyons, F. S. L., *Ireland since the Famine*, London, 1971

—— *John Dillon*, London, 1968

McCavitt, John, *The Flight of the Earls*, Dublin, 2005

—— *Sir Arthur Chichester: Lord Deputy of Ireland, 1605–16*, Belfast, 1998

McCorristine, Laurence, *The Revolt of Silken Thomas: A Challenge to Henry viii*, Dublin, 1987

McCracken, Eileen, *Irish Woods since Tudor Times*, Newton Abbot, 1971

Mac Cuarta, Brian (ed.), *Ulster 1641: Aspects of the Rising*, Belfast, 1993

McCutcheon, W. A., *The Industrial Archaeology of Northern Ireland*, Belfast, 1980

MacDermot, Frank, *Theobald Wolfe Tone and his Times*, Tralee, 1969

MacDonagh, Oliver, *The Life of Daniel O'Connell, 1775–1847*, London, 1991

McGarry, Fearghal, *Eoin O'Duffy: A Self-Made Hero*, Oxford, 2005

MacKnight, Thomas, *Ulster As It Is*, 2 vols, London, 1896

MacLysaght, Edward, *Irish Life in the Seventeenth Century*, Cork, 1939, New York, 1969

McNally, Robert (ed.), *Old Ireland*, Dublin, 1965

McNeill, Mary, *The Life and Times of Mary Ann McCracken, 1770–1866*, Dublin, 1960; repr. Belfast, 1988

Mac Niocaill, Gearóid, *Ireland before the Vikings*, Dublin, 1972

Macrory, Patrick, *The Siege of Derry*, London, 1980

Mallory, J. P., and T. E. McNeill, *The Archaeology of Ulster*, Belfast, 1985

Maloney, Ed, and Andy Pollak, *Paisley*, Dublin, 1986

Marlow, Joyce, *Captain Boycott and the Irish*, London, 1973

Marsh, Arnold, *Saint Patrick and his Writings*, Dublin, 1966

Martin, F. X., and F. J. Byrne (eds), *The Scholar Revolutionary: Eoin MacNeill and the Making of the New Ireland*, Shannon, 1973

Maume, Patrick, *The Long Gestation: Irish Nationalist Life, 1891–1918*, Dublin, 1999

—— (ed.), *The Repealer Repulsed: William McComb*, Dublin, 2003

Maxwell, Constantia, *Irish History from Contemporary Sources (1509–1610)*, London, 1923

—— *Country and Town in Ireland under the Georges*, Dundalk, 1949

—— *Dublin under the Georges*, London, 1936

Maxwell, W. H., *History of the Irish Rebellion in 1798*, London, 1880

Middlemas, Keith (ed.), *Thomas Jones: Whitehall Diary*, III: *Ireland, 1918–1925*, Oxford, 1971

Miller, David W. (ed.), *Peep o' Day Boys and Defenders: Selected Documents on the County Armagh Disturbances*, Belfast, 1990

Mitchell, Arthur, and Pádraig Ó Snodaigh (eds), *Irish Political Documents, 1869–1916*, Dublin, 1989

Mitchell, Frank, *Reading the Irish Landscape*, Dublin, 1998

Moody, T. W., 'Redmond O'Hanlon', *Proceedings and Reports of the Belfast Natural History and Philosophical Society*, 2nd series, I (1937)

—— *The Londonderry Plantation, 1609–41*, Belfast, 1939

—— *Davitt and Irish Revolution, 1846–82*, Oxford, 1981

——, F. X. Martin and F. J. Byrne (eds), *A New History of Ireland*, III: *Early Modern Ireland, 1534–1691*, 2nd ed., Oxford, 1986

—— *A New History of Ireland*, IX: *Maps, Genealogies, Lists*, Oxford, 1984

Moore, F. Frankfort, *The Truth about Ulster*, London, 1914

Morgan, Hiram, *Tyrone's Rebellion*, Dublin, 1993

Morrissey, James, *On the Verge of Want: Ireland's Western Seaboard in the Late 19th Century*, Dublin, 2001

Moryson, Fynes, *An History of Ireland, from the year 1599 to 1603*, London, 1617; repr. Dublin, 1735

Munck, Ronnie, and Bill Roulston, *Belfast in the Thirties: An Oral History*, Belfast, 1987

Murray, Robert H. (ed.), *The Journal of John Stevens ... 1689–1691*, Oxford, 1912

Newsinger, John, *Fenianism in Mid-Victorian Britain*, London, 1994

Nicholls, Kenneth, *Gaelic and Gaelicised Ireland in the Middle Ages*, Dublin, 1972

O'Clery, Lughaidh, *The Life of Hugh Roe O'Donnell, Prince of Tirconnell (1586–1602)*, ed. Denis Murphy, Dublin, 1893

O'Connell, Maurice, *Irish Politics and Social Conflict in the Age of the American Revolution*, Philadelphia, 1965

O'Connor, Frank, *A Book of Ireland*, London & Glasgow, 1959

Ó Corráin, Donncha, *Ireland before the Normans*, Dublin, 1972

Ó Cróinín, Dáibhí (ed.), *A New History of Ireland*, I: *Prehistoric and Early Ireland*, Oxford, 2005

O'Donoghue, P., 'Causes of the Opposition to Tithes, 1830–38', *Studia Hibernica*, no. 5 (1965); 'Opposition to Tithe Payments in 1830–31', *Studia Hibernica*, no. 6 (1966); 'Opposition to Tithe Payment in 1832–3', *Studia Hibernica*, no. 12 (1972)

O'Donovan, John (ed.), *Annála Ríoghachta Éireann: Annals of the Kingdom of Ireland by the Four Masters, from the Earliest Period to the year 1616*, 2nd ed., Dublin, 1856

O'Farrell, Patrick, *Ireland's English Question: Anglo-Irish Relations, 1534–1970*, London, 1971

O'Flaherty, Roderic, *A Chorographical Description of West or H-Iar Connaught, written AD 1684*, ed. James Hardiman, Dublin, 1846

O'Halpin, Eunan, *Defending Ireland: The Irish State and its Enemies since 1922*, Oxford, 1999

O'Kelly, M. J., 'Excavations and Experiments in Ancient Irish Cooking-Places', *Journal of the Royal Society of Antiquaries of Ireland*, LXXXIV (1954)

O Lochlainn, Colm (ed.), *The Complete Irish Street Ballads*, London, 1984

O'Malley, Ernie, *On Another Man's Wound*, London, 1936 (references are to 1961 edition)

O'Meara, John J. (trans.), *The History and Topography of Ireland: Gerald of Wales*, Harmondsworth, 1982

Orpen, Goddard H., *Ireland under the Normans, 1169–1333*, 4 vols, Oxford, 1911–1920; Dublin, 1968

—— (ed.), *The Song of Dermot and the Earl: an old French poem about the coming of the Normans to Ireland, edited with a literal translation*, Felinfach, 1994

Orr, Philip, *The Road to the Somme: Men of the Ulster Division Tell their Story*, Belfast, 1987

Pakenham, Frank, *Peace by Ordeal: The Negotiation of the Anglo-Irish Treaty, 1921*, London, 1935 (references are to 1962 edition)

Patterson, Henry, *Ireland since 1939*, Oxford, 2002

Perceval-Maxwell, Michael, *The Scottish Migration to Ulster in the Reign of James I*, London & New York, 1973

Public Record Office of Northern Ireland, *The Act of Union*; *Eighteenth-Century Ulster*; *Emigration to North America*; *The Great Famine*; *The Penal Laws*; *The '98 Rebellion*; *The United Irishmen*; *The Volunteers, 1778–84*, all in the Education Facsimile Series, Belfast, n.d.

Quinn, D.B., *The Elizabethans and the Irish*, New York, 1966

Ranelagh, John, *Ireland: An Illustrated History*, London, 1981

Regan, John M., *The Irish Counter-Revolution, 1921–1936*, Dublin, 1999

Reid, J. S., *History of the Presbyterian Church in Ireland*, ed. W. D. Killen, 3 vols, Belfast, 1867

Roebuck, Peter (ed.), *Plantation to Partition: Essays in Ulster History in honour of J. L. McCracken*, Belfast, 1981

Robinson, Philip S., *The Plantation of Ulster: British Settlement in an Irish Landscape, 1600–1670*, Dublin & New York, 1984

Sayles, G. O., 'The Siege of Carrickfergus Castle, 1315–16', *Irish Historical Studies*, x, no. 37 (Mar. 1956)

Scott, A. B. and F. X. Martin (eds.), *Expugnatio Hibernica: The Conquest of Ireland by Giraldus Cambrensis, edited with translation and historical notes*, Dublin, 1978

Silke, John J., *Kinsale: The Spanish Intervention in Ireland at the End of the Elizabethan Wars*, Liverpool, 1970

Simms, Katharine, 'The Medieval Kingdom of Lough Erne', *Clogher Record*, IX (1977)

Smyth, William J., *Map-making, Landscapes and Memory: A Geography of Colonial and Early Modern Ireland, c. 1530–1750*, Cork, 2006

Somerville-Large, Peter, *Dublin*, London, 1981

Speed, P. F., *The Potato Famine and Irish Emigrants*, London, 1976

Sténuit, Robert, *Treasures of the Armada*, Newton Abbot, 1972

Stevenson, David, *Scottish Covenanters and Irish Confederates: Scottish–Irish Relations in the Mid-Seventeenth Century*, Belfast, 1981

Stewart, A. T. Q., *The Ulster Crisis*, London, 1967

—— *Edward Carson*, Dublin, 1981

—— *The Summer Soldiers: The 1798 Rebellion in Antrim and Down*, Belfast, 1995

Story, George, *A True and Impartial History of the Most Material Occurrences in the Kingdom of Ireland during the Two Last Years*, London, 1691

Sweetman, H. S., and G. F. Handcock (eds), *Calendar of Documents relating to Ireland, 1171 –1307*, 5 vols, London, 1886

Taylor, A. J. P., *English History, 1914–45*, Oxford, 1965

—— *The Habsburg Monarchy, 1809–1918*, Harmondsworth, 1967

Todd, James H. (ed.), *Cogadh Gaedhel re Gallaibh: The War of the Gaedhil with the Gaill*, London, 1867

Townsend, Horatio, *An Account of the Visit of Handel to Dublin*, Dublin, 1852

Vaughan, W. E. (ed.), *A New History of Ireland*, v: *Ireland under the Union*, I: *1801–70*, Oxford, 1989

—— (ed.), *A New History of Ireland*, vi: *Ireland Under the Union*, II: *1870–1921*, Oxford, 1996

Viney, Michael, *Ireland: A Smithsonian Natural History*, Belfast, 2003

Waddell, John, *The Prehistoric Archaeology of Ireland*, Bray, 2000

Walker, Brian, *Ulster Politics: The Formative Years, 1868–86*, Belfast, 1981

Walsh, Micheline Kerney, *Destruction by Peace: Hugh O'Neill after Kinsale*, Armagh, 1986

—— *An Exile of Ireland: Hugh O'Neill, Prince of Ulster*, Dublin, 1996

Watson, J. Steven, *The Reign of George III, 1760–1815*, Oxford, 1960

Whyte, J. H., *Church and State in Modern Ireland, 1923–1970*, Dublin, 1971

Woodham-Smith, Cecil, *The Great Hunger: Ireland, 1845–1849*, London, 1985

Woodman, P. C., 'A Mesolithic Camp in Ireland', *Scientific American*, CCXLV (Aug. 1981)

—— *Excavations at Mount Sandel, 1973–77, County Londonderry*, Belfast, 1985

Wright, Thomas, *A History of Ireland from the Earliest Period of the Irish Annals to the Present Time*, 2 vols, London & New York, 1870

Young, Arthur, *A Tour in Ireland, 1776–1779*, 2 vols, ed. A.W. Hutton, London, 1892

Younger, Calton, *Ireland's Civil War*, London, 1968

Zimmermann, Georges-Denis, *Songs of Irish Rebellion: Political Street Ballads and Rebel Songs, 1780–1900*, Dublin, 1967

INDEX